THE
WORLD'S
PROTECTED AREAS

STATUS, VALUES AND PROSPECTS IN THE 21ST CENTURY

**Published in association with UNEP-WCMC
by University of California Press**
University of California Press
Berkeley and Los Angeles, California
University of California Press, Ltd.
London, England

**© 2008 UNEP World Conservation
Monitoring Centre**
UNEP-WCMC
219 Huntingdon Road
Cambridge CB3 0DL, UK
Tel: +44 (0) 1223 277 314
Fax: +44 (0) 1223 277 136
E-mail: info@unep-wcmc.org
Website: www.unep-wcmc.org

The contents of this volume do not necessarily
reflect the views or policies of UNEP-WCMC,
contributory organizations, editors or publishers.
The designations employed and the presentations
do not imply the expression of any opinion
whatsoever on the part of UNEP-WCMC or
contributory organizations, editors or publishers
concerning the legal status of any country,
territory, city or area or its authority, or concerning
the delimitation of its frontiers or boundaries or the
designation of its name or allegiances.

Clothbound edition ISBN: 978-0-520-24660-7

Cataloging-in-Publication data is on file with the
Library of Congress

Citation: Chape S., Spalding M., Jenkins M.D.
(2008) *The World's Protected Areas*. Prepared by
the UNEP World Conservation Monitoring Centre.
University of California Press, Berkeley, USA.

University of California Press, one of the most
distinguished presses in the United States,
enriches lives around the world by advancing
scholarship in the humanities, social sciences, and
natural sciences. Its activities are supported by the
UC Press Foundation and by philanthropic
contributions from individuals and institutions.
For more information visit www.ucpress.edu.

Photograph, pages i and iii
Kinabalu Park World Heritage Site, Malaysia
© S. Chape

THE
WORLD'S
PROTECTED AREAS

STATUS, VALUES AND PROSPECTS IN THE 21ST CENTURY

Edited by STUART CHAPE, MARK SPALDING and MARTIN JENKINS

Foreword by Achim Steiner and Julia Marton-Lefèvre

UNIVERSITY OF CALIFORNIA PRESS
Berkeley Los Angeles London

The World's Protected Areas
Status, values and prospects in the 21st century

PREPARED AT

UNEP World Conservation Monitoring Centre (UNEP-WCMC)
219 Huntingdon Road
Cambridge CB3 0DL, UK
Website: www.unep-wcmc.org
Director Jon Hutton
Programme Director Tim Johnson

A **Banson** production
17f Sturton Street
Cambridge CB1 2QG, UK
banson@ourplanet.com

Production editors
Christine Hawkins
Angela Jameson-Potts
Lucia Leade
Brigid Barry
Karen Eng

Index
Jill Dormon

Printed and bound
Sirivatana Interprint Public Co. Ltd.,
Thailand

SUPPORTING ORGANIZATIONS

UNEP
PO Box 30552
Nairobi 00100, Kenya
Tel: +254 (0) 20 7621234
Fax: +254 (0) 20 7623927
Website: www.unep.org

IUCN
Rue Mauverney 28
1196 Gland, Switzerland
Tel: +41 22 999 0000
Fax: +41 22 999 0002
Website: www.iucn.org

Total Corporate Foundation
2, place de la Coupole,
La Défense 6,
92078 Paris La Défense Cedex, France
Tel: +33 (0) 1 44 47 44 24
Fax: +33 (0) 1 44 47 25 32
Website: www.total.com/fondation/en

Anglo American plc
20 Carlton House Terrace
London SW1Y 5AN, UK
tel: +44 (0)20 7968 8888
fax: +44 (0)20 7968 8500
Website: www.angloamerican.co.uk

The World Bank
1818 H Street, NW
Washington, DC 20433, USA
tel: +1 202 473 1000
fax: +1 202 477 6391
Website: www.worldbank.org

The Nature Conservancy
4245 North Fairfax Drive,
Suite 100, Arlington,
VA 22203-1606, USA
tel: +1 (703) 841 5300
fax: +1 (703) 812 1283
Website: www.nature.org

Acknowledgements

This publication has been made possible by the generous support and cooperation of a large number of organisations and individuals. In particular, the partnership between UNEP, IUCN and UNEP-WCMC on protected area and biodiversity issues has provided the impetus for the development and completion of this review of the world's protected areas. However, it would not have been possible to gather the wealth of information needed to cover the wide-ranging topics discussed in the book without the input of the more than 80 contributing authors whose work has been synthesised within these pages.

The editors thank contributors and their organisations for generously providing their time and technical expertise, and for their patience in waiting for the final product. We thank those who also took the time to review final drafts. Contributors are individually credited elsewhere. However, the editors wish to thank Graeme Worboys, Michael Lockwood and Oxford University Press for permission to use extracted material from *Protected Area Management: Principles and Practice* (2nd edition) for Chapters 4 and 5. NASA generously provided satellite imagery, and special thanks are due to the time and effort of Gary Geller and Mike Abrams at the Jet Propulsion Laboratory in California in dealing with our requests. The editors and UNEP-WCMC take responsibility for any licence taken, and errors arising, in order to produce an integrated coherent publication.

The protected areas data presented in the book is sourced from the World Database on Protected Areas (WDPA) held at UNEP-WCMC. Thanks are due to the many protected area agency staff around the world that provide national statistical updates for the WDPA as part of the periodic United Nations List of Protected Areas process. Since 2002 this process has been supplemented by the work of the WDPA

Consortium, a group of international conservation organisations that have agreed to cooperate to improve the quality of global protected areas data, and all Consortium members are thanked for their input. Thanks are due to Silvio Olivieri of Conservation International, who has chaired the Consortium during this period, and to Carola Borja, who ensured that regular updates were sent to the WDPA.

Lucy Fish, Simon Blyth and Corinna Ravilous at UNEP-WCMC worked long and hard on data input, analysis and preparation of the book's maps, and Igor Lysenko undertook the extensive work required for the habitat analyses in Chapter 2. Jerry Harrison provided valuable comments on the various drafts as well as specific contributions.

Mary Cordiner, the Centre's former librarian, helped with sourcing important reference material. Thanks are also due to Mark Collins, former Director of UNEP-WCMC, and Tim Johnson, Deputy Director, for fully supporting the project from its inception. Thanks are also due to The Nature Conservancy, which generously supported the continued work of Mark Spalding on the book from October 2004.

The project has been generously supported by David Sheppard, Pedro Rosabal and Peter Shadie of the IUCN Programme on Protected Areas. We would also like to thank Kenton Miller, Chair of the IUCN World Commission on Protected Areas during 2001-2004, for his interest in and support for effective global protected areas information and its application, and Nikita Lopoukhine, the current WCPA Chair, for his support.

Thanks are also due to Achim Steiner, Executive Director of UNEP, and his predecessor, Dr Klaus Töpfer; and to Svein Tveitdal, former Director UNEP DEC/DEPI, for their institutional and financial support of the project.

University of California Press gratefully acknowledges the generous contribution to this book provided by the Gordon and Betty Moore Fund in Environmental Studies.

Contributors

Editors
Stuart Chape
Mark Spalding
Martin Jenkins

Contributors
Octavio Aburto-Oropeza
Tom Allnutt
Rolando Fernández de Arcila
Mohamed Bakarr
Jim Barborak
Juan C. Barrera
Liz Bennett
Michelle Bennett
Michael Beresford
K. Berkmüller
Seema Bhatt
Andrew Bignell
Delmar Blasco
Grazia Borrini-Feyerabend
Timothy Boucher
Charlotte Boyd
Peter Bridgewater
Philip Bubb
Neil Burgess
Georgina Bustamante
Chris Carpenter
Eleanor Carter
Roberto B Cavalcanti
Pete Coppolillo
Roger Crofts
Natalia Danilina
Will Darwall
Paul K. Dayton
Philip Dearden
Ruth DeFries
Eric Dinerstein
Nigel Dudley
Bud Ehler
Reinaldo Estrada
Simon Ferrier
Monica T. da Fonseca
Gary N. Geller
Jose Luis Gerhartz

Ed Green
Larry Hamilton
Elery Hamilton-Smith
Jeremy Harrison
William Henwood
Enrique Hernández
Juan Antonio Hernández
Juan Carlos Godoy Herrera
Mark Hockings
Jonathan Hoekstra
Natarajan Ishwaran
Rodney Jackson
Jargal Jamsranjav
Jim Johnston
Sam Kanyamibwa
Val Kapos
Margaret Kinnaird
Rebecca Kormos
Ashish Kothari
Alessandra Vanzella Khouri
Carmen Lacambra
Fiona Leverington
Ken Lindeman
Estherine Lisinge
Ghislaine Llewellyn
Michael Lockwood
Colby Loucks
Igor Lysenko
Ricardo B. Machado
Andy Mack
John MacKinnon
Chris Magin
John Marsh
Elaine Marshall
Ed McManus
Kenton Miller
Les Molloy
John Morrison
Carolina Murcia
Tim O'Brien
Silvio Olivieri
Jeanne Pagnan
Michael Painter
Gustavo Paredes

Ivan Parra
Arthur Paterson
Antonio Perera
Adrian Phillips
Luiz Paulo de S. Pinto
George Powell
Bob Pressey
Allen Putney
Alan Rabinowitz
Madhu Rao
Carmen Revenga
Jane Robertson Vernhes
Ana Rodrigues
Pedro Ruiz
Anthony Rylands
Enric Sala
Elsa Sattout
Roger Sayre
Samuelu Sesega
Sue Stolton
Holly Strand
Mohammad S. A. Sulayem
Effendy A. Sumardja
Michelle Taylor
Russell Taylor
Michele Thieme
Jim Thorsell
Pragati Tuladhar
Tony Turner
Alan Tye
Carlos Castaño Uribe
Amy Vedder
D. Watling
Graeme Worboys
David Zeller
Shin Wan

Cartography
Lucy Fish
Simon Blyth
Igor Lysenko

Foreword

Achim Steiner
UN Under-Secretary-General
and Executive Director of the
United Nations Environment Programme

Julia Marton-Lefèvre
Director-General
International Union for
the Conservation of Nature

For centuries people all over the world have set aside places to which they ascribe special values. In many cases these values have been spiritual or cultural in nature, but many places have also been set aside for practical purposes – to conserve essential everyday resources such as fish, wildlife and non-timber forest products. Some have been set aside for the excusive use of an elite minority, in other cases for the benefit of many. Nonetheless, all have been set aside for one purpose – to protect something that humankind perceives as valuable.

Over the last 100 years or so the pace of establishment of such areas has increased, partly as a result of human population growth, but more particularly because of a greater appreciation of the natural world, changing patterns of resource use, broader understanding of the impacts of man on nature, and increasing globalization. Since the foundation of the original Yellowstone National Park in 1872, well over 100 000 sites have been established as parks, reserves and sanctuaries by all levels of government, by many types of organization and institution, and by civil society.

Over the same period of time, our impact on the Earth's natural systems, and on the biodiversity that comprises them, has grown exponentially. This has prompted a broadening of approaches to conservation and sustainable use of biodiversity, and has encouraged the development of clearer linkages between protected areas and human development goals. Protected areas are now being increasingly seen as one of the tools for supporting sustainable development, rather than as something set aside from the mainstream.

This brings with it major challenges for those involved in all aspects of the establishment and management of protected areas; from the governments setting national policy to practitioners on the ground. When protected area professionals met in 1962 at the first World Parks Congress the concerns and issues were very different from those on the agenda at the fifth World Parks Congress in 2003. And perhaps more significantly for many, thirty years ago there were few international agreements concerned with biodiversity conservation and the protection of the world's special places, and few international organizations working on the ground. Now there is a plethora of international activity and interest impacting on conservation on the ground.

Because of the nature of the changes affecting the world's protected areas it is essential that we periodically make the effort to review their status and to understand the challenges that these special places face. This is what *The World's Protected Areas* aims to do. It not only provides us with a status report of our progress in establishing protected areas, but also discusses their role in biodiversity conservation, the threats they face, and the complex issues of management. Importantly it delivers a frank assessment of our likely progress in achieving the goals that we have collectively set.

The World's Protected Areas challenges any complacency that we may have about our apparent success in establishing effective protected area systems around the world. There is much to be applauded, but also considerably more that needs to be done to ensure effective biodiversity conservation, to integrate protected areas into landscape planning and human development, and to make protected areas part of our mitigation strategy for climate change. These are some of the real challenges of our time.

In September 2003, more than 3 000 people interested in protected areas, from 157 countries, participated in the fifth World Parks Congress that took place in Durban, South Africa. They were concerned not only with reviewing progress and sharing experience, but also with planning for the future – identifying the actions necessary in the coming years to ensure effective networks of protected areas, conserving biodiversity and meeting human needs.

But, vital though it is, the goodwill and commitment of professionals in the field is not enough, and the understanding and commitment of governments is also essential. A year after the Durban Congress, the Parties to the Convention on Biological Diversity (CBD) adopted a Programme of Work on Protected Areas. In this, governments commit themselves to a range of activities and time-bound targets which, if they are all achieved, will do much to ensure biodiversity conservation and environmental sustainability.

So the pieces are in place. We have many experienced professionals working in protected areas and we have the commitment of governments.

We have a wide range of both national and international organizations working to achieve effective protected areas and protected area networks. We have both the private sector and civil society increasingly recognizing the value of protected areas. And we have an understanding of what we need to do.

There is now a compelling imperative to resolve our global environmental issues. *The World's Protected Areas* was being researched and written as the fifth World Parks Congress was taking place, and as the CBD Conference of Parties was adopting its Programme of Work on Protected Areas. It sets the scene, telling us where we are at the start of this period of renewed action for protected areas. A fundamental message of this book is that protected areas are a key part of our strategy to ensure biodiversity conservation and to secure a sustainable future for biodiversity.

Contents

Key to regional maps

National protected areas
▥ · IUCN cateroties Ia-VI
▥ · No category

International protected areas
▤ · Wetlands of International Importance (Ramsar)
▧ · World Heritage Sites
▨ · UNESCO Man and Biosphere Reserves (MAB)

Introduction

With the increasing recognition of the importance of protected areas, it is timely to review their global status, not only in terms of location and extent but also of the range of issues that are critical in understanding their values, threats, management, and future prospects. There are many thousands of publications on protected areas, ranging from site-specific assessments of design and management; through broader issues of species and ecosystem conservation, the involvement of local and indigenous peoples, and the design of protected areas networks; to global issues addressing extent, status, threats, and management effectiveness. The purpose of this book is to present, in one volume, a comprehensive overview of the world's protected areas in relation to these and many other issues, not only highlighting their importance to humanity but also examining the critical issues that will determine their relevance and long-term viability.

The World's Protected Areas is a review of the current state of knowledge, especially in relation to regional and global numbers and extent. The rapid growth in the number of conservation areas in the latter part of the 20th century, and the commitments made at the Vth World Parks Congress in 2003, suggests that governments and communities remain committed to establishing further protected areas. The critical issues and imperatives concerning the role of protected areas in conserving biodiversity, the effectiveness of their management, and their relationship to local-to-global development agendas will also intensify. This book therefore not only provides an overview of the current global protected areas situation but will also provide a benchmark for future evaluation of how well we have addressed these critical issues and imperatives. The book is made up of the following chapters:

❐ Chapter 1 provides an overview of the development of protected areas; it discusses current definitions; provides global statistics on the numbers, extent, and types of protected areas; considers the values of protected areas and describes the various international efforts that strengthen the global protected areas estate.

❐ Chapter 2 examines the critical role of protected areas in conserving global biodiversity, provides an analysis of the extent of protection provided to the world's terrestrial and marine habitats, and highlights the gaps in the global network of protected areas.

❐ Chapter 3 reviews the diverse range of threats confronting protected areas in virtually all areas of the world.

❐ Chapter 4 deals with the issues associated with establishing and managing protected areas and the importance of governance.

❐ Chapter 5 looks at management planning, the management of threats, and the evaluation of management effectiveness.

❐ Chapter 6 reviews the special management issues and opportunities relating to the marine environment, the realms in which most work needs to be done to develop a global marine protected areas network.

❐ Chapter 7 offers an assessment of what the future may hold for protected areas in the 21st century, examining the key issues of their roles and values, conservation effectiveness, resourcing, and the need for political commitment to ensure that protected areas achieve their goals.

❐ The Regional Analysis provides an assessment of the status of protected areas, and a review of major issues and prospects, by the regions of the world as defined by the IUCN World Commission on Protected Areas.

The World Database on Protected Areas (WDPA) is compiled from multiple sources and is the most comprehensive global dataset on marine and terrestrial protected areas available. It is a joint venture of UNEP and IUCN, produced by UNEP-WCMC and the IUCN World Commission on Protected Areas (IUCN-WCPA) working with governments and collaborating NGOs. The WDPA is continually updated. The regional protected areas maps and statistics have been produced using the 2004 and 2006 editions of the WDPA.

Dedication

This publication is dedicated to those whose commitment makes protected areas around the world a reality on the ground or in the seas. These are the field staff - the superintendents, field scientists and, above all, the rangers and wardens. Most protected areas around the world are under-resourced and under-staffed, and many lie in conflict zones, only surviving because of the devotion of field staff that protect the values of these special places against frequently overwhelming odds.

Every year field staff are killed or injured while protecting conservation areas that are now almost universally recognised as having a critical role in our survival, and the survival of the millions of species with which we share this planet. We recognize their dedication and commitment to ensuring that collectively we can achieve a truly effective global protected areas network in the 21st century.

Chapter 1

History, Definitions, Values and Global Perspective

Contributors: S. Chape; Values and benefits of protected areas: M. Spalding, M. Taylor and A. Putney; World Heritage Convention: N. Ishwaran, J. Thorsell, S. Chape; Ramsar Convention on Wetlands: D. Blasco; Biosphere reserves: J. Robertson Vernhes and P. Bridgewater; Transboundary protected areas, biological corridors and networks: J. Harrison; Antarctica: E. McManus.

The human desire to protect and revere special places is as old as our species, but it has become even more important as human impact on the planet continues its relentless change of natural ecosystems and destruction of biological diversity. The global population now exceeds 6 billion people and is predicted to rise to 9 billion by 2050. Not surprisingly, mapping of the 'human footprint' on the planet has concluded that more than 80 percent of the Earth's land surface is directly influenced by humans (Sanderson *et al.*, 2002) (see Figure 1.1). We already use an estimated 40 percent of the Earth's net primary productivity (Rojstaczer, Sterling, and Moore, 2001), 35 percent of oceanic shelf productivity (Pauly and Christensen, 1995), and 60 percent of freshwater runoff (Postel, Daily, and Ehrlich, 1996). As well as natural resource consumption, human-induced climate change is bringing changes to temperature, precipitation, sea levels, and the distribution and intensity of extreme events to all corners of the globe, and threatening much greater change in the coming decades.

As a result, remaining natural landscapes are rapidly being modified, and the Earth's biological diversity (biodiversity) continues to decline at an alarming rate. However, the factors driving this modification and change are complex, and not only related to the simple equation of increasing human numbers. Global poverty and inequitable development are fundamental drivers for negative environmental change and loss of natural landscapes, species, and the benefits that we derive from them. The economic, health, and educational disparities between wealthy and poor countries continue to grow, with increasing pressure on limited resources

and living space. The eminent American scientist E.O. Wilson has observed: 'for the entire world population to enjoy US consumption with existing technology, the present-day human population would have to spread itself over two more planet Earths' (Wilson, 2000). With such enormous pressure on the planet, what are our chances of conserving the natural world in which we have evolved?

Fortunately, recognition of the need to protect the world's remaining natural places is almost universal among the nations of the Earth. We now have thousands of nature reserves, national parks, protected landscapes, and other forms of designated conservation areas. There are now more than 1 000 such designations that we collectively refer to as 'protected areas.' Protected areas are not only the last strongholds of nature; they also have a vital role in providing humankind with a range of valuable ecological services. In the face of the human-induced global change that has occurred since the Industrial Revolution, governments, organizations, and community groups recognize that if concerted action is not taken, only scattered remnants of natural ecosystems will remain, and most of those will be in the most inhospitable and economically unproductive areas of the planet. This recognition has been reflected in a number of international and regional environmental and conservation agreements over the past two decades and, more importantly, by the decisions of governments to establish or expand national protected area systems. As well as formal intergovernmental and governmental responses, non-governmental organizations (NGOs) and community groups have become instigators of conservation action,

1

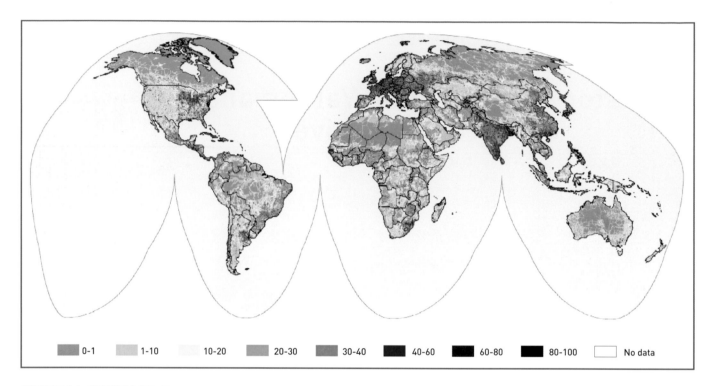

FIGURE 1.1: THE "HUMAN FOOTPRINT" AS A PERCENTAGE OF HUMAN INFLUENCE IN EVERY BIOME ON THE EARTH'S LAND SURFACE

Derived from "a quantitative evaluation of human influence on the land surface, based on geographic data describing human population density, land transformation, access, and electrical power infrastructure, and normalized to reflect the continuum of human influence across each terrestrial biome defined within biogeographic realms".   *Source: Sanderson et al., 2002*

including the establishment and management of protected areas.

In September 2003, more than 3 000 people from 157 countries gathered in Durban, South Africa, for the Fifth World Parks Congress. It was the largest and most diverse gathering in history of people concerned with conservation of the world's natural heritage through the establishment and management of protected areas. The Congress was a milestone in a process that has seen the development of the modern conservation movement, initiated by the establishment of the first national parks and reserves in the 19th century. At the time of the meeting the world's protected area network, which is still growing, had exceeded 100 000 sites, covering 12.5 percent of the Earth's land surface, although only a tiny fraction (0.5 percent) of the ocean surface (Chape *et al.*, 2003).

In terms of terrestrial area, protected areas are now one of the most important land-use

allocations on the planet. However, while this concrete commitment to global conservation is a remarkable achievement, we must also recognize that setting aside conservation areas is just the beginning – effective management action and provision of financial and technical resources are essential if conservation objectives are to be achieved. Moreover, we also need to ensure that the location and extent of protected areas effectively conserves the Earth's remaining biodiversity. The existing protected area system still falls short of this objective; a recent study (Rodrigues *et al.*, 2003) identified more than 700 threatened species believed not to occur in any protected area.

The Durban Congress adopted wide-ranging recommendations to improve the coverage and management of protected areas, and reinforced the need for a spectrum of different types of protected areas to effectively conserve natural and cultural values. The outcomes of Durban were supported in February 2004 by the Seventh Meeting of the Conference of the Parties (CoP7) to the Convention on Biological Diversity (CBD) (SCBD, 2004). The CBD CoP7 not only adopted a Programme of Work on Protected Areas to be implemented by the 188 Parties to the Convention, but also endorsed the key role of protected areas as indicators for measuring success in significantly reducing the loss of global biodiversity by 2010. This latter target is closely

S. Chape

Hin Namno National Protected Area, Lao PDR.

associated with two other intergovernmental initiatives: the Plan of Implementation of the World Summit on Sustainable Development and the Millennium Development Goals (MDGs). Thus, a critical link has been made at international policy level between development and protected areas.

WHAT IS A PROTECTED AREA?
An old but evolving concept

The concept and practice of setting aside natural and semi-natural areas for protection, special or restricted use have a long history (see Table 1.1). From 300 BC, the Mauryan kings of northern India established reserves to protect forests, elephants, fish, and wildlife (Grove, 1995; Dhammika, 1993), and the *Al Hema* form of land management, practiced for at least 2 000 years across the Middle East, set aside large tracts of rangeland to prevent overgrazing. Similarly in Oceania, placing permanent and seasonal restrictions on access to certain areas and/or resources, such as reefs, lagoons and certain marine species, was practiced extensively. Often these historic reservations and prohibitions, such as the hunting reserves of Europe and India, were for the benefit of a ruling elite. In some ways, this approach was replicated, in the 19th century, in the establishment of the large game reserves in southern and eastern Africa by European colonial powers; for example, Sabi Game Reserve in South Africa (later to become Kruger National Park) was established by President Kruger in 1892.

As the human population continues to grow, and our ecological impact on the planet's resources increases, our living space is reduced and natural resources are depleted. The phrase 'island Earth' is no longer a poetic metaphor – it describes the hard reality that faces humankind, as it did historically for many societies who had to manage their populations and natural resources within physically limiting conditions (for example, on atolls and in Arctic and desert environments). We should not be surprised, therefore, that there has been increasing awareness of the need to conserve nature. The first 'modern' protected areas were often inspired by the very clear ecological impacts of Western conquest and colonization on Africa, the Americas, Asia, Australia, and numerous oceanic islands (Grove, 1995). Parks were established to preserve permanent remnants of the local ecosystems that many of these colonists saw disappearing under cities, farms, and plantations.

Yellowstone National Park in the USA is recognized as the first of these new parks. Established in 1872, the area was 'reserved and withdrawn from settlement, occupancy or sale... and dedicated and set apart as a public park or pleasuring-ground for the benefit and enjoyment of the people' (from the establishing Act of Congress). Declaration of the Royal National Park in Australia followed in 1879, with other well-known parks established in the closing decades of the 19th century and the early ones of the 20th century. These include New Zealand's Tongariro National Park (1894), Canada's Banff National Park (1898), Yosemite National Park in the USA (1890, although the original federal grant was signed in 1864 by Abraham Lincoln), and the Gorilla Sanctuary in the then Belgian Congo (1925). Other protected areas were established in Asia and other parts of Africa.

In Europe early reserves included those in Laponia in Sweden (1909), the Swiss National Park (1914), and the Bialowieza Forest in Poland (1947). The dominant underlying philosophy in establishing protected areas until the second half of the 20th century, especially in the USA and other 'new world' countries, remained the preservation of "nature islands of solitude and repose [as] an indispensable ingredient of modern civilization" (Udall, 1964), while recognizing their potential economic values for tourism and for science. Unfortunately, in quite a few cases these early national parks were established in areas where indigenous peoples had been removed or were excluded.

In his keynote address to the First World Conference on National Parks held in Seattle, Washington, in 1962, Stewart Udall, Umited States Secretary of the Interior, advised: 'So great is the power of men and nations to enlarge the machine-dominated portion of the world that it is not an exaggeration to say that few opportunities for conservation projects of grand scope will remain by the year 2000 ...with few exceptions the places of superior scenic beauty, the unspoiled land-scapes, the spacious refuges for wildlife, the nature parks and nature reserves of significant size and grandeur that our generation saves will be all that is preserved. We are the architects who must design the remaining temples; those who follow will have the mundane tasks of management and housekeeping.' (Udall, 1964).

In 1962 there were almost 10 000 parks and reserves worldwide; 45 years later the World

Database on Protected Areas, maintained by the UNEP World Conservation Monitoring Centre, holds information on more than 100 000 protected sites. In addition, there are now almost 5 000 internationally designated areas, including World Heritage sites, biosphere reserves and Ramsar sites. In some ways Udall was correct in his assessment of the prospects for global conservation. Many of the large, high conservation value areas of the globe were protected by the early 1990s. Yet the number of designated areas has continued to grow and we know that there is still much more to conserve. The average size of protected areas has been decreasing as newer sites tend to be much smaller. However, even here there are exceptions with, for example, Brazil recently adding large areas of the Amazon to its protected area system. The coverage of protected areas also varies between different biomes, with some, such as marine and freshwater, being particularly poorly represented (see Chapter 2).

Of course the function of protected areas, and their role in wider society, has changed over time. As McNeely (1998) has noted: 'Protected areas are a cultural response to perceived threats to nature. Because society is constantly changing, so too are social perspectives on protected areas and the values that they are established to conserve.' The current concept of a protected area has evolved significantly from that originally proposed by 19th-century American and European visionaries.

What was not apparent even through the 1950s and 1960s was the evolution of the protected area concept and the 'repackaging' of conservation concerns under the umbrellas of sustainable development and biodiversity that would occur from the 1970s through to the 1990s. This was heavily influenced by a number of international events and agreements, including: the Stockholm Conference on Environment and the adoption of the World Heritage Convention in 1972; the 1980 World Conservation Strategy; the 1992 UN Conference on Environment and Development, and the adoption of the CBD that same year. Another critical factor has been the expansion of the World Commission on Protected Areas (WCPA) network (originally formed as the Commission on National Parks in 1958), and the technical and scientific outputs from World Parks Congresses held in 1972, 1982, 1992, and 2003. All of these factors have resulted in:

❐ the formulation of specific protected area management categories that recognize the scope and values of different approaches to conserving natural areas;

❐ 'mainstreaming' of conservation concerns into development agendas;

❐ rethinking the role of protected areas vis-à-vis conservation and sustainable human use;

❐ recognition of the importance of cultural values;

❐ recognition of the role of protected areas as key indicators for assessing achievement of global sustainable development objectives, and as contributing measures for combating desertification, climate change, and loss of genetic diversity.

In a sense, we have come full circle in recognizing

MJ Willett/UNEP

Yosemite National Park, USA – one of the world's first protected areas.

TABLE 1.1: HISTORIC MILESTONES IN THE DEVELOPMENT OF PROTECTED AREAS

10 000 BC	As agriculture began to transform the relationship between people and nature, local communities recognized specific sites as "sacred", and protected them from certain human uses. Applied differently in different places over the subsequent millennia, the concept was a widespread practical measure that people found beneficial in both material and spiritual ways.
252 BC	Emperor Asoka of India established protected areas for mammals, birds, fish, and forests, the earliest recorded areas where a government protected certain resources.
684 AD	First Indonesian nature reserve was established by order of the King of Srivijaya, on the island of Sumatra. Sumatra is now recognized as one of the world's centers of megadiversity, with numerous protected areas – the major sites comprising the recently declared 25 000 km² Tropical Rainforest of Sumatra World Heritage site.
1079	William the Conqueror claimed the New Forest (England) as a royal hunting reserve and protected it against illegal harvesting from rural people; poaching became a major law enforcement issue, but timber from the forest was essential to England's war efforts in the 17–19th centuries. Today the New Forest is still a valued protected area and became the UK's newest national park in 2005.
1865	Yosemite (California) was established by US Congress as effectively the first of a new national-level model of protected areas; Yellowstone (1872) was first to be called a national park.
1882	El Chico National Park established in Mexico, the first in Latin America.
1903	The Society for the Protection of the Wild Fauna of the Empire was established in the UK, the first non-governmental organization devoted to international conservation – now known as Fauna and Flora International (FFI). Hundreds of other civil society conservation organizations now support protected areas in all parts of the world.
1925	First "modern" national park was established in Asia (Angkor Wat, Cambodia).
1926	South Africa's Kruger National Park was established.
1934	Argentina's Iguazu National Park was established.
1948	IUCN – The World Conservation Union was founded (as the International Union for Protection of Nature) as a means of promoting conservation worldwide, but especially in the former colonies gaining independence in the post-war world, based on the prediction of significant habitat loss if nothing were done. The establishment of protected areas has always been seen as an important area of focus.
1961	WWF was set up (as the World Wildlife Fund) as a new international non-governmental organization to mobilize support for conservation, especially from the general public. This marked the beginning of an era of growing funding for international conservation.
1962	The First World Conference on National Parks, in Seattle, Washington, began a more formal worldwide movement in support of protected areas, called for a UN List of Protected Areas, and recommended a category system. Prior to this, each country kept its own records, so nobody knew the extent of the world's protected area system.
1963	College of African Wildlife Management at Mweka, Tanzania was established. By 2003, more than 4 200 Africans had graduated from Mweka.

the spectrum of values and benefits provided by lands and waters protected from unsustainable use and despoliation – not as isolated societies but as a global community, and recognizing the diversity of social values that are placed on protected areas. Phillips (2003) suggests that such concerns have been reflected in a 'new paradigm' of protected areas (see Table 1.2). But in view of the long history of resource protection over thousands of years, it is perhaps not so much a new paradigm as one rediscovered.

Definitions of protected areas

More generalized, internationally accepted, definitions of protected areas were first provided in some of the early international conventions relating to protected areas, notably the London Convention in 1933 and the Western Hemisphere Convention in 1940 (see Table 1.4). The first IUCN protected areas definition focused on national parks, adopted at the 10th General Assembly of

IUCN in New Delhi in 1969 and subsequently endorsed by the Second World Conference on National Parks in 1972. The definition placed emphasis on prevention or elimination of resource exploitation or occupation by people, and did not include privately owned land.

In more recent decades, an understanding of the importance and role of protected areas has broadened considerably. It is now acknowledged that there are many places where humans have a vital role in the landscape and are part of ecosystem processes, and that these places and systems are also in need of protection. This, in turn, has led to the understanding that nature protection needs to be part of a complex system of management allowing for different levels of human interaction. This realization led to the adoption of the present IUCN definition of a protected area at the IVth World Parks Congress in 1992, with its emphasis on protection of both natural and cultural assets:
"An area of land and/or sea especially dedicated to

Biodiversity of the seas more than matches that on land. Yet less than one per cent of marine environments are protected. Mamanuca Islands, Fiji.

S Chape

TABLE 1.1: (continued)

1968	UNESCO Man and the Biosphere Programme began, establishing biosphere reserves (529 reserves in 105 countries covering more than 5 million km^2 as of 2007).
1971	Ramsar Convention adopted; 1 708 sites covering more than 1.5 million km^2 and 157 contracting parties at the end of 2007.
1972	UN Conference on Environment and Development, Stockholm, Sweden endorsed new conventions affecting protected areas and led to the establishment of the United Nations Environment Programme (UNEP) based in Nairobi
	World Heritage Convention adopted. By 2006, 166 natural World Heritage sites and 25 mixed natural and cultural sites had been recognized, covering more than 1.8 million km^2.
	Second World Conference on National Parks, Yellowstone and Grand Teton, USA, promoted development assistance for protected areas in the tropics.
1977	Training program for protected area personnel established at CATIE, Turrialba, Costa Rica; continues until the present time and has provided trained staff for much of Central America.
1978	IUCN system of categories of protected areas published; set framework for worldwide assessment of protected area coverage. Latest revision in 1994, now being promoted for other management applications.
1980	World Conservation Strategy, published by IUCN, WWF, and UNEP, popularized the concept of sustainable development and a partnership between conservation and development.
1981	Protected Areas Data Unit established by IUCN and its Commission on National Parks and Protected Areas, at the IUCN Conservation Monitoring Centre, UK; this provided first worldwide database on protected areas.
1982	Third World National Parks Congress, Bali, Indonesia emphasized the importance of protected areas as a key element in national development plans; set 10 percent protected area coverage of each of the world's biomes as a target.
1987	*Our Common Future* (the Brundtland Report), the report of the UN Commission on Sustainable Development calls for 12 percent of the land to be given protected area status and advocated global action to conserve biodiversity.
1991	Global Environment Facility (GEF) created by World Bank, UNDP, and UNEP, providing a major new intergovernmental funding mechanism for protected areas, especially through the CBD then under negotiation.
1992	IVth World Congress on National Parks and Protected Areas, Caracas, Venezuela. Emphasized linkages between protected areas and other sectors of society.
1992	The Earth Summit, Rio de Janeiro, Brazil, produced Agenda 21 and approved the CBD and Framework Convention on Climate Change, both highly relevant to protected areas.
2000	UN General Assembly approves Millennium Development Goals, with Goal 7 calling for environmental sustainability.
2002	World Summit on Sustainable Development, Johannesburg, South Africa, called for loss of biodiversity to be reversed by 2010, and for a comprehensive system of marine protected areas to be established by 2012.
2003	Vth World Parks Congress held in Durban, South Africa. Focused on "benefits beyond boundaries," re-emphasizing the importance of protected areas for sustainable development.
2004	Seventh Meeting of the Conference of the Parties to the CBD adopts a comprehensive Programme of Work for Protected Areas to support implementation of the *in-situ* conservation components of the CBD.

Source: Adapted from McNeely, 2003.

the protection and maintenance of biological diversity, and of natural and associated cultural resources, and managed through legal or other effective means."

This definition, which is used throughout this publication, is now widely accepted at international, regional, and national levels, and provides the basis for the work of IUCN, the WCPA, and the inclusion of sites on the periodic UN List of Protected Areas. It is particularly significant as the starting point for the definitions and objectives included within the IUCN Protected Area Management Category system (Box 1.1), discussed in Chapter 4.

Although widely accepted, other definitions for protected areas have been developed, including those in legal frameworks for regional and global agreements, a number of which are listed in Box 1.2. Among them is the protected area definition of the CBD: 'A geographically defined area which is designated or regulated and managed to achieve specific conservation objectives.' The CBD has been adopted by 188 countries and this definition clearly carries considerable weight. It is, however, less precise than the IUCN definition and does not refer to cultural aspects of protected areas.

THE GLOBAL BALANCE SHEET: HOW MANY PROTECTED AREAS?

The value in measuring the numbers and extent of protected areas on a global basis was first formally recognized in 1959 by the 27th Session of the UN Economic and Social Council (ECOSOC), in a decision that called for compilation of a World List of National Parks and Equivalent Reserves (UN ECOSOC, 1959). It recommended the list be produced on a periodic basis through the collaboration of national and UN agencies and IUCN. The resolution was subsequently endorsed by the UN General Assembly in 1962 (UN General Assembly 1962), starting a process that produced 13 editions of the UN List of Protected Areas between 1962 and 2003 – probably the first and longest-running global environmental reporting mechanism. This early UN recognition, supported by IUCN, has also provided an important impetus for the establishment of new protected areas over the past 40 years.

The global reporting in the UN List has, from the outset, been undertaken by IUCN and the WCPA (and its precursors), and since 1981 the actual data collection and collation have been the responsibility of the UNEP-WCMC in partnership

S Chape

with IUCN and the WCPA. The information is managed in the World Database on Protected Areas (WDPA), maintained by UNEP-WCMC on behalf of the international community. In 2002, a WDPA Consortium of international non-governmental stakeholders involved with global protected area issues was formed to strengthen the quality and reliability of the data holdings. (Membership includes: IUCN, UNEP-WCMC, Conservation International, The Nature Conservancy, American Museum of Natural History, Fauna & Flora International, BirdLife International, WWF, and Wildlife Conservation Society.)

Despite the apparently straightforward nature of basic protected area data (latitude, longitude, area, name, etc.), obtaining accurate and up-to-date information remains a challenging task, highly dependent on the cooperation of national governments and their protected area agencies, private organizations, and the support of the WCPA network. Obtaining accurate boundary information is particularly problematic. Knowing the location and extent of existing protected areas is essential for undertaking gap analyses to ensure that important habitats and species are included in conservation areas, and to implement effective protected area system planning. At present the WDPA holds boundary data on about 40 percent of the protected areas held in the database, although this includes most of the largest and most important protected areas. Central geographic coordinates are known for the vast majority of sites.

The IUCN protected area definition includes both natural and cultural values. Uluru-Kata Tjuta National Park World Heritage Area, Australia.

TABLE 1.2: OLD AND NEW PARADIGMS OF PROTECTED AREAS

	As it was: protected areas were...	As it is becoming: protected areas are...
Objectives	Set aside for conservation Established mainly for spectacular wildlife and scenic protection Managed mainly for visitors and tourists Valued as wilderness About protection	Run also with social and economic objectives Often set up for scientific, economic, and cultural reasons Managed with local people more in mind Valued for the cultural importance of so-called "wilderness" Also about restoration and rehabilitation
Governance	Run by central government	Run by many partners
Local people	Planned and managed against people Managed without regard for local opinions	Run with, for, and in some cases by local people Managed to meet the needs of local people
Wider context	Developed separately Managed as "islands"	Planned as part of national, regional, and international systems Developed as "networks" (strictly protected areas, buffered and linked by green corridors)
Perceptions	Viewed primarily as a national asset Viewed only as a national concern	Viewed also as a community asset Viewed also as an international concern
Management techniques	Managed reactively within short timescale Managed in a technocratic way	Managed adaptively in long-term perspective Managed with political considerations
Finance	Paid for by taxpayer	Paid for from many sources
Management skills	Managed by scientists and natural resource experts Expert led	Managed by multiskilled individuals Drawing on local knowledge

Source: Phillips, 2003

FIGURE 1.2: GLOBAL GROWTH IN PROTECTED AREA, 1872–2005

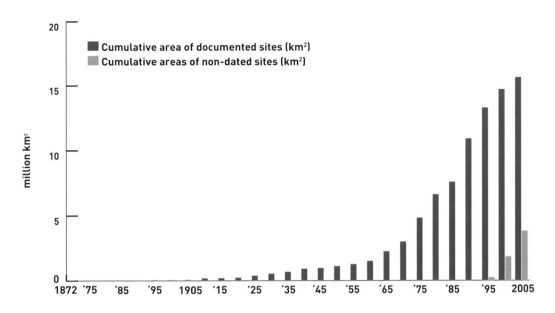

Improving information held in the WDPA is an ongoing process and, as the quality of data is refined, these improvements can lead to adjustments to the known global numbers and extent of protected areas. Sometimes these adjustments can result in a reduction of protected area numbers in specific localities as errors are removed, but the overall trends of cumulative growth are clear.

Figure 1.2 shows the growth in the global protected areas estate over time, while Table 1.3 provides a listing of some of the world's largest protected areas. By the end of 2005, the WDPA had recorded over 114 000 sites. These protected areas covered more than 19 million km², or 12.9 percent of the Earth's land surface. It is apparent that nature conservation has become one of the most important human endeavors on the planet, and the area under

FIGURE 1.3: GLOBAL GROWTH IN THE NUMBER OF PROTECTED AREAS, 1872–2005

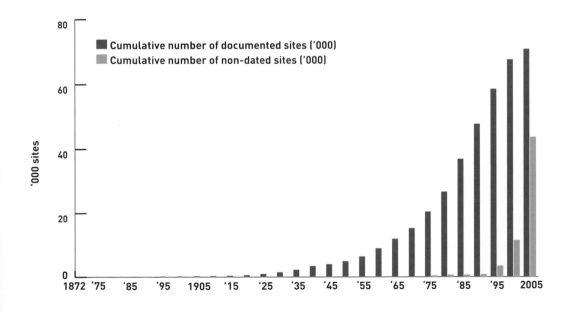

BOX 1.1: IUCN PROTECTED AREA MANAGEMENT CATEGORIES

CATEGORY Ia

Strict Nature Reserve: protected area managed mainly for science

Area of land and/or sea possessing some outstanding or representative ecosystems, geological or physiological features and/or species, available primarily for scientific research and/or environmental monitoring.

CATEGORY Ib

Wilderness Area: protected area managed mainly for wilderness protection

Large area of unmodified or slightly modified land, and/or sea, retaining its natural character and influence, without permanent or significant habitation, which is protected and managed so as to preserve its natural condition.

CATEGORY II

National Park: protected area managed mainly for ecosystem protection and recreation

Natural area of land and/or sea, designated to (a) protect the ecological integrity of one or more ecosystems for present and future generations, (b) exclude exploitation or occupation inimical to the purposes of designation of the area, and (c) provide a foundation for spiritual, scientific, educational, recreational and visitor opportunities, all of which must be environmentally and culturally compatible.

CATEGORY III

Natural Monument: protected area managed mainly for conservation of specific natural features

Area containing one, or more, specific natural or natural/cultural feature that is of outstanding or unique value because of its inherent rarity, representative or aesthetic qualities or cultural significance.

CATEGORY IV

Habitat/Species Management Area: protected area managed mainly for conservation through management intervention

Area of land and/or sea subject to active intervention for management purposes so as to ensure the maintenance of habitats and/or to meet the requirements of specific species.

CATEGORY V

Protected Landscape/Seascape: protected area managed mainly for landscape/seascape conservation and recreation

Area of land, with coast and sea as appropriate, where the interaction of people and nature over time has produced an area of distinct character with significant aesthetic, ecological and/or cultural value, and often with high biological diversity. Safeguarding the integrity of this traditional interaction is vital to the protection, maintenance and evolution of such an area.

CATEGORY VI

Managed Resource Protected Area: protected area managed mainly for the sustainable use of natural ecosystems

Area containing predominantly unmodified natural systems, managed to ensure long-term protection and maintenance of biological diversity, while providing at the same time a sustainable flow of natural products and services to meet community needs.

FIGURE 1.4: THE WORLD'S PROTECTED AREAS BY REGION, 2005

(see Chapter 7 for regional definitions)

Area	Ia	Ib	II	III	IV	V	VI	No Category	Total	% of land area protected
Antarctic										
Area ('000 km²)	68.14	-	0.16	0.01	0.47	0.01	0.00	1.53	70.32	0.50
No. sites	87	-	4	2	19	5	1	4	122	
Australia/New Zealand										
Area ('000 km²)	217.04	41.90	347.41	33.81	269.25	22.50	596.25	9.70	1 537.85	19.19
No. sites	2 136	38	701	3 946	1 657	217	489	411	9 595	
Brazil										
Area ('000 km²)	112.02	-	160.68	0.70	5.07	135.71	212.55	984.81	1 611.55	18.85
No. sites	182	-	179	5	259	115	70	476	1 286	
Caribbean										
Area ('000 km²)	0.18	0.09	26.97	0.50	11.20	3.57	22.22	3.47	68.20	29.05
No. sites	11	18	163	40	283	37	192	223	967	
Central America										
Area ('000 km²)	4.13	0.34	40.03	2.22	13.25	1.25	44.62	52.11	157.93	30.28
No. sites	18	3	104	48	225	5	100	280	783	
East Asia										
Area ('000 km²)	62.84	43.40	98.82	19.51	6.11	1 444.75	59.34	29.87	1 764.64	15.00
No. sites	43	34	79	34	121	2144	78	734	3 267	
Eastern and Southern Africa										
Area ('000 km²)	2.79	1.25	508.60	0.15	265.11	12.56	543.87	354.55	1 688.88	14.70
No. sites	17	7	220	24	497	30	219	3 053	4 067	
Europe										
Area ('000 km²)	85.84	39.95	108.57	4.46	70.59	348.59	22.01	194.48	874.47	16.72
No. sites	1 577	542	275	3 570	16 331	3 035	203	27 527	53 060	
North Africa and Middle East										
Area ('000 km²)	3.50	0.03	215.87	12.43	69.81	114.76	790.66	78.69	1 285.75	10.02
No. sites	28	2	71	50	269	162	30	712	1 324	
North America										
Area ('000 km²)	68.86	473.01	1 658.85	72.59	614.73	135.06	1 015.14	70.56	4 108.82	17.31
No. sites	841	702	1 349	591	1 334	2 083	1 425	5 229	13 554	
North Eurasia										
Area ('000 km²)	362.22	-	125.42	24.44	841.56	14.79	84.22	302.46	1 755.10	7.94
No. sites	195	-	66	11 321	5 256	407	54	398	17 697	
Pacific										
Area ('000 km²)	1.15	-	8.13	0.52	1.10	10.52	11.70	33.02	66.13	11.95
No. sites	29	-	38	23	86	16	59	160	411	
South America (excl. Brazil)										
Area ('000 km²)	12.48	14.75	505.12	74.35	185.55	126.20	586.30	593.69	2 098.44	22.55
No. sites	55	4	220	72	143	96	314	546	1 450	
South Asia										
Area ('000 km²)	2.49	0.83	67.34	-	160.88	1.39	26.13	51.23	310.28	6.91
No. sites	19	2	133	-	661	11	12	379	1 217	
South East Asia										
Area ('000 km²)	22.53	11.40	254.66	24.85	142.53	20.84	200.83	184.09	861.71	18.60
No. sites	292	12	329	83	206	129	985	859	2 895	
Western and Central Africa										
Area ('000 km²)	21.74	11.74	348.46	0.40	347.80	0.19	67.81	322.80	1 120.94	8.75
No. sites	19	7	91	4	119	3	45	2 313	2 601	
TOTAL										
Area ('000 km²)	1 048	639	4 475	271	3 005	2 393	4 284	3 267	19 381	12.90
No. sites	5 549	1 371	4 022	19 813	27 466	8 495	4 276	43 304	114 296	

FIGURE 1.5: GLOBAL PROTECTED AREAS BY
IUCN CATEGORY, 2005

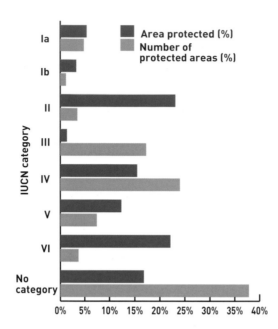

FIGURE 1.6: GLOBAL PROTECTED AREAS,
LEVEL OF PROTECTION, MANAGEMENT, AND
USE, 2005

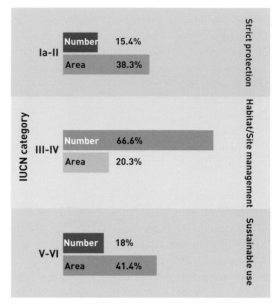

protection now exceeds the total area of permanent crops and arable land. What is also clear is the great disparity between terrestrial and marine conservation efforts, with only 0.5 percent of the world's marine area in protected areas. The global distribution of protected areas on the basis of the world's major habitats is discussed in Chapter 2, and detailed protected area statistics by region are presented in the regional overviews in Part 2.

Statistics about protected areas can tell us more than "how many and how much" at global, regional, and national levels. If protected area management categories (Box 1.1) are properly assigned on the basis of protected area management objectives, then statistical information about protected areas can reveal a great deal about how conservation objectives are being applied. If the categories are consistently and accurately applied by all countries we will have a clear understanding of why individual protected areas have been established and the type of conservation role that they fulfill. The history of the categories and their application are discussed in Chapter 4.

Currently about two thirds of the protected areas in the WDPA are assigned categories, covering just over 80 percent of the total area protected. Analyses of the data reveal some interesting global and regional trends (Figures 1.4, 1.5 and 1.6). There are relatively few strictly

protected areas (Ia and Ib), and they cover a small percentage of the Earth's surface. However, in the case of Category II (into which most of the "traditional" national parks fall), there is a stark difference between the relatively low numbers of these sites and the large global area that they cover – reflecting the fact that national parks tend to encompass large geographic areas. The reverse is true for Category III and to a lesser extent Category IV, which are characterized by numerous smaller sites. Of particular interest is the growth in Category VI, with its emphasis on sustainable use of natural resources, which was adopted by IUCN in 1994. This category is also characterized by a small number of larger sites, eight of which are among the current 20 largest protected areas in the world (Table 1.3). Figure 1.6 summarizes the three main groups of categories by their primary emphasis: strict protection, intensive management, and sustainable use.

VALUES AND BENEFITS OF PROTECTED AREAS

In addition to their specific contribution to global biodiversity conservation, protected areas have a number of wide-ranging values and benefits. As early as 1959, the UN ECOSOC noted that national parks and equivalent reserves were an important factor in the wise use of natural resources, and they "contribute to the inspiration, culture and welfare of mankind". IUCN (1994) defines the main purposes of protected areas as:

- scientific research;
- wilderness protection;
- preservation of species and genetic diversity;
- maintenance of environmental services;
- protection of specific natural and cultural features,
- tourism and recreation;
- education;
- sustainable use of resources from natural ecosystems;
- maintenance of cultural and traditional attributes.

Attempts to place a value on protected areas and the ecosystems they encompass invariably expand to consider many functions and activities essential for human existence, broadly defined as ecosystem goods and services. They provide us with food, water, and other resources, regulate our weather patterns, and provide us with precious medicines and crop varieties. Tourism, now one of the world's largest industries, is dependent in many areas on the attractions of protected areas, and sites generate income, foreign exchange earnings, and employment at local, regional, and national levels.

The quantitative values of protected areas

are increasingly being used as a tool to justify and support the development of protected area networks. Information on values to different user groups, and on the driving forces behind these values, is also important in enabling better management and in avoiding threats or conflicts. The most powerful arguments for establishment and retention of protected areas in many circles are economic. However, it is quite widely accepted that, at present, "ecosystem services are not fully 'captured' in commercial markets or adequately quantified in terms comparable with economic services and manufactured capital, they are often given too little weight in policy decisions" (Costanza et al., 1997). The concept of total economic value (TEV) has been widely used to attempt to convert all values and benefits into simple economic terms. Figure 1.7 shows the main categories of values and benefits that contribute to TEV. However, many values are notoriously difficult to evaluate in economic terms, and results remain somewhat subjective. (See, for example, Munasinghe and McNeely 1994; IUCN, 1998; Putney, 2000.) Although typically expressed in economic terms, it is important to consider other approaches to valuation. Differences in available wealth to particular communities and differences in overall wealth between countries, mean that the use of simple "dollar values" can be misleading. Protected areas may be the only source of employ-

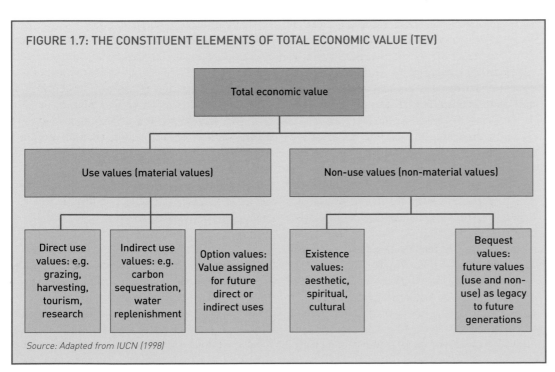

FIGURE 1.7: THE CONSTITUENT ELEMENTS OF TOTAL ECONOMIC VALUE (TEV)

Total economic value

Use values (material values)

Non-use values (non-material values)

Direct use values: e.g. grazing, harvesting, tourism, research

Indirect use values: e.g. carbon sequestration, water replenishment

Option values: Value assigned for future direct or indirect uses

Existence values: aesthetic, spiritual, cultural

Bequest values: future values (use and non-use) as legacy to future generations

Source: Adapted from IUCN (1998)

ment in some areas, or may provide a critical source of fuelwood, or of animal protein in local diets. Converted to dollar values on open markets, such measurements may appear trivial, but their loss could be devastating to many people.

Direct use values and benefits

Recreation/tourism: Sometimes simply expressed as the receipts in terms of park fees, it is important to include the combined economic impact of park-related tourism for regional economies, including travel and accommodation costs, and other expenditure. Such values can also be viewed in terms of employment of local populations.

Harvesting: Depending on its management objectives it is often feasible and desirable to allow sus-

tainable extraction of selected natural resources from protected areas. This, for example, is the case with IUCN Category V and VI protected areas. Activities may include grazing of livestock, fishing, hunting, the use of non-timber forest products, agriculture, water extraction, and extraction of genetic resources. An example of such renewable resource use is in the Danayiku Nature Park at Shan-Mei in Taiwan. Years of community cooperation and investment have changed a once depleted and unsustainably harvested stock of freshwater game fish, kooye minnow (*Varicorhinus barbatulus*), into a financially lucrative sport fishing and ecotourism venture (Tai, 2002).

Extraction of non-renewable resources: Certain

BOX 1.2: EXAMPLES OF CURRENT PROTECTED AREA DEFINITIONS

GLOBAL

❐ **IUCN**
"An area of land and/or sea especially dedicated to the protection and maintenance of biological diversity, and of natural and associated cultural resources, and managed through legal or other effective means."

❐ **Convention on Biological Diversity (CBD)**
"A geographically defined area which is designated or regulated and managed to achieve specific conservation objectives."

❐ **Ramsar Convention on Wetlands**
"For the purpose of this Convention wetlands are areas of marsh, fen, peatland or water, whether natural or artificial, permanent or temporary, with water that is static or flowing, fresh, brackish or salt, including areas of marine water the depth of which at low tide does not exceed six metres."

❐ **UNESCO Man and Biosphere Programme**
Biosphere reserves: "Areas of terrestrial and coastal-marine systems which are internationally recognized for promoting and demonstrating a balanced relationship between people and nature."

REGIONAL

❐ **Europe**
Ministerial Conference on the Protection of Forests in Europe: "Protected or protective forest" definition allows for non-permanent designation, although requires protection for at least 20 years.

Natura 2000 Common Database on Designated Areas: "Designated area" is based on IUCN definition but can be extended to cover, for example, complete distribution of certain habitats.

Helsinki Convention on Protection of the Marine Environment of the Baltic Sea Area: "Natural coastal areas where land and sea meet are in a constant dynamic relation to each other and are: systems of great biological richness, variety and productivity; form the habitats of highly specialized and often endangered species of wild fauna and flora as well as large populations of breeding and

---

extractive activities are non-sustainable, notably of petroleum products and minerals. In general, this appears to be contrary to the concept of "protection and maintenance" associated with the definition of protected areas. There may be a few cases where the extraction process has limited impacts and the material being extracted may not be essential to the objectives and functioning of the protected area. In such cases it may be argued that economic benefits (direct payments) for the extraction process may justify this activity. However, considerable debate on the issue of mineral and hydrocarbon extraction in protected areas continues (see Chapter 3).

Scientific research: Protected areas offer some of the best opportunities to understand and explain

One of the many values of protected areas is the provision of recreational experience, especially in an increasingly urban world. Linnansaari National Park, Finland.

migratory birds; landscapes of great natural beauty; highly important for public recreation; a natural resource which is becoming more and more scarce."

Bern Convention on the Conservation of European Wildlife and Natural Habitats: Areas of special conservation interest should: "*a.* [contribute] substantially to the survival of threatened species, endemic species, or any species listed in Appendices I and II of the convention; *b.* [support] significant numbers of species in an area of high species diversity or [support] important populations of one or more species; *c.* [contain] an important and/or representative sample of endangered habitat types; *d.* [contain] an outstanding example of a particular habitat type or a mosaic of different habitat types; *e.* [represent] an important area for one or more migratory species; *f.* otherwise [contribute] substantially to the achievement of the objectives of the convention."

❏ Southeast Asia

ASEAN Agreement on the Conservation of Nature and Natural Resources: National Parks: "natural areas that are sufficiently large to allow for ecological self-regulation of one or several ecosystems, and which have not been substantially altered by human occupation or exploitation." Reserves: "for the purpose of preserving a specific ecosystem, the critical habitat of certain species of fauna or flora, a water catchment area or for any other specific purpose relating to the conservation of natural resources or objects or areas of scientific, aesthetic, cultural, educational or recreational interest."

❏ South Pacific

Convention on Conservation of Nature in the South Pacific (Apia Convention): "*a)* 'Protected area' means national park or national reserve; *b)* 'National park' means an area established for the protection and conservation of ecosystems containing animal and plant species, geomorphological sites and habitats of special scientific, educative and recreational interest or a natural landscape of great beauty, which is under the control of the appropriate public authority and open to visits by the public; *c)* 'National reserve' means an area recognized and controlled by the appropriate public authority and established for protection and conservation of nature, and includes strict nature reserve, managed nature reserve, wilderness reserve, fauna or flora reserve, game reserve, bird sanctuary, geological or forest reserve, archaeological reserve and historical reserve, these being reserves affording various degrees of protection to the natural and cultural heritage according to the purposes for which they are established."

natural ecosystem processes. They also offer a natural baseline against which to measure changes in natural environmental systems – an issue of growing importance in this period of unprecedented global environmental change.

Indirect use benefits and option values

Climate influences: Many protected areas play a role in maintaining microclimatic or climatic stability, including rainfall patterns. Protected areas are also widely cited as playing a critical role in mitigating the impacts of climate change, acting as carbon reservoirs or sinks.

Water services and erosion control: In addition to climatic influences, protected areas play an important role in water catchment protection, guaranteeing the supply of water to adjacent populations and stabilizing steep slopes. The presence of natural vegetation, notably forests and wetlands, reduces extremes of water flow and plays a role in flood control. These services can help ensure water provision to the local vicinity. Without them, flooding in rainy seasons becomes more likely, as does drought in dry seasons. Canaima

Canopy walk, Bukit Lagong Forest Reserve, Malaysia.

S Chape

National Park and World Heritage site in Venezuela protects the Caroni River catchment. This, in turn, provides over 70 percent of the country's electricity needs through hydroelectricity production.

Coastal processes: Protected habitats such as salt marshes, mangroves, dune systems, and coral reefs are widely cited for their role in coastal protection. The retention of mangrove systems played a significant role in buffering the impact of the tsunami that devastated many parts of South and Southeast Asia in 2004.

Wider ecological influences: Protected areas can have positive benefits for adjoining land and seascapes. This is particularly the case in marine communities. The declining state of the oceans and the collapse of many fisheries create a critical need for more effective management of marine biodiversity, populations of exploited species, and the overall health of the oceans. There is now widespread international scientific consensus that the establishment of highly protected Marine Protected Areas (MPAs) can be essential in sustainable fisheries management through protection of sensitive habitats and species, the provision of reference sites, and assistance with stock management (Murray *et al.*, 1999; Halpern, 2003; Gell and Roberts, 2003). For example, a network of five small reserves within the Soufriere Marine Management Area in St Lucia increased adjacent artisanal fisheries by 49-90 percent over a wider area, depending on the fishing gear utilized (Roberts *et al.*, 2001).

In Tanzania, poaching and uncontrolled hunting of elephants to the southeast of Tarangire National Park led to an increase in woody plants within the park. This is believed to have caused an increase in tsetse flies and livestock losses for local people. Conservation of elephants may well have enhanced the productivity of the livestock industry (IUCN, 1998).

Genetic resources: Protected areas have a role as *in-situ* reservoirs of important genetic material, such as wild crop progenitors and pharmaceuticals. Although impossible to calculate in its entirety, the global protected areas estate is of great importance for the maintenance of food resources and supply of medicines. For example, by the early 1990s, 3 000 plants had been identified by the US National Cancer Institute as being active against cancer

TABLE 1.3: THE WORLD'S 20 LARGEST PROTECTED AREAS IN 2005

Country	Protected area	National designation	Size (km^2)	IUCN management category
Greenland	Northeast Greenland	National park	972 000	II
Saudi Arabia	Ar-Rub'al-Khali	Wildlife management area	640 000	VI
Australia	Great Barrier Reef	Marine park	344 360	VI
USA	Northwestern Hawaiian Islands	Coral reef ecosystem reserve*	341 362	VI
China	Qiangtang	Nature reserve	298 000	V
Australia	Macquarie Island	Marine park	162 060	IV
China	Sanjiangyuan	Nature reserve	152 300	V
Ecuador	Galapagos	Marine reserve	133 000	VI
Saudi Arabia	Northern Wildlife Management Zone	Wildlife management area	100 875	VI
Australia	Ngaanyatjarra Lands	Indigenous protected area	98 129	VI
Venezuela	Alto Orinoco-Casiquiare	Biosphere reserve	84 000	VI
Brazil	Vale do Javari	Indigenous area	83 380	No category
Chad	Ouadi Rimé-Ouadi Achim	Faunal reserve	80 000	IV
Brazil	Yanomami (AM-RO)	Indigenous park	77 519	No category
USA	Yukon Delta	National wildlife refuge	77 425	IV
USA	Arctic	National wildlife refuge	72 843	IV
Venezuela	Sur del Estado Bolívar	Protective zone	72 624	V
Algeria	Tassili N'Ajjer	National park	72 000	II
Angola	Coutada	Integral nature reserve	68 164	No category
USA	Tongass	National forest	67 404	VI

Note: These areas represent 0.02 percent of the total number of the world's protected areas, but comprise more than 4 million km² or 21 percent of the total area protected.

* Site designation changed to National Monument IUCN Category III in 2006.

cells; 70 percent of these plants came from rainforests, which are best conserved in protected areas (Bird, 1991).

Refugia: With growing concerns about climate change, together with more immediate and widely reported impacts such as pollution incidents, the potential importance of protected areas as refugia for future restoration and recovery of adjacent areas is being increasingly understood and realized.

INTANGIBLE VALUES OF PROTECTED AREAS

The WCPA has defined "intangible values" (Harmon and Putney, 2003) as those which enrich "the intellectual, psychological, emotional, spiritual, cultural and/or creative aspects of human existence and well being" (WCPA 2000).

Such values have been fundamental to the recognition and protection of special places by many cultures for millennia. Intangible values of protected areas include:

Recreational values: the intrinsic qualities of natural areas that interact with humans to restore, refresh, or create anew through stimulation and exercise of the mind and body.

Spiritual values: those qualities of protected areas that inspire humans to relate with reverence to the sacredness of nature.

Cultural values: qualities, both positive and negative, ascribed to sites by different social groups, traditions, beliefs, or value systems that fulfill humankind's need to understand and connect in

TABLE 1.4: INTERNATIONAL ENVIRONMENTAL CONVENTIONS, TREATIES, AND AGREEMENTS, AND ASSOCIATED PROTOCOLS WITH PROTECTED AREA PROVISIONS

Title (Short title)	Place of adoption	Adopted	Notes
European Landscape Convention (Council of Europe)	Florence	2000	1
Southern Africa Wildlife Protocol	Maputo	1999	2
Statutory Framework of the World Network of Biosphere Reserves	Seville	1995	2
Protocol Concerning Specially Protected Areas and Biological Diversity in the Mediterranean (SPA and Biodiversity Protocol)	Barcelona	1995	2
Agreement on the Conservation of African-Eurasian Migratory Waterbirds	The Hague	1995	1
Agreement on the Preparation of a Tripartite Environmental Management Programme for Lake Victoria	Dar-es-Salaam	1994	
Convention for the Conservation of the Biodiversity and the Protection of Wilderness Areas in Central America	Managua	1992	
Convention on Biological Diversity (CBD)	Nairobi	1992	1
Council Directive on the Conservation of natural habitats of wild fauna and flora (EU) (Habitats Directive)	Brussels	1992	2
Convention on the Protection of the Black Sea Against Pollution (Bucharest Convention)	Bucharest	1992	4
Convention for the Protection of the Marine Environment of the Northeast Atlantic – Oslo and Paris Conventions (OSPAR Convention)	Paris	1992	4
Convention on the Protection of the Marine Environment of the Baltic Sea Area (Helsinki Convention)	Helsinki	1992	4
Protocol to the Antarctic Treaty on Environmental Protection	Madrid	1991	3
Protocol Concerning Specially Protected Areas and Wildlife to the Convention for the Protection and Development of the Marine Environment of the Wider Caribbean Region (SPAW Protocol)	Kingston	1990	2
Protocol for the Conservation and Management of Protected Marine and Coastal Areas of the Southeast Pacific	Paipa (Colombia)	1989	2
Convention for the Protection of Natural Resources and Environment of the South Pacific Region (Nouméa or SPREP Convention)	Nouméa (New Caledonia)	1986	4
Convention for the Protection, Management and Development of the Marine and Coastal Environment of the Eastern African Region (Nairobi Convention)	Nairobi	1985	
Protocol Concerning Protected Areas and Wild Fauna and Flora in the Eastern African Region	Nairobi	1985	2

S Chape

The Mekong River and its ecosystems link China and a number of Southeast Asian countries.

meaningful ways to the environment of its origin and the rest of nature.

Identity values: natural sites that link people to their landscape through myth, legend, or history.

Existence values: the satisfaction, symbolic importance, and even willingness to pay, derived from knowing that both outstanding natural and cultural landscapes have been protected, and exist as physical and conceptual spaces where all forms of life and culture are valued and held sacred.

Artistic values: the qualities of nature that inspire human imagination in creative expression.

Aesthetic values: an appreciation of the harmony, beauty, and profound meaning found in nature.

Educational values: the qualities of nature that enlighten the careful observer with respect to the relationships of humans with the natural environment and, by extension, relationships of humans with one another, thereby creating respect and understanding.

Peace values: encompass the function of protected areas in fostering regional peace and stability through cooperative management across international land or sea boundaries (transfrontier or transboundary protected areas); as "intercultural spaces" for the development of understanding between traditional and modern societies, or between distinct cultures; and peace between society and nature. Transboundary protected areas

have played a role in the peaceful settlement of disputes among a number of countries in the last ten years. Recognizing the importance of transboundary protected areas for peace and cooperation, the WCPA has developed guidance based on the experiences of managers around the world.

Therapeutic values: the relationship between people and natural environments in protected areas that creates the potential for healing, and enhancing physical and psychological well-being.

INTERNATIONAL DIMENSIONS OF PROTECTED AREAS

Terrestrial, aquatic, and marine ecosystems and species are rarely confined within human political boundaries. Often, the success of conservation and sustainable resource management of these ecosystems and species depends on collaboration between countries, especially in the joint management of major ecosystem divides such as rivers, watersheds, and mountain ranges, for example the Mekong River Basin, the Amazon River system, the Andes, and the Himalayan Mountain range. Conservation of migratory species also requires international collaboration. At the same time, lessons learned by one country in managing particular species or ecological systems often have a value elsewhere and need to be shared.

In fact, such international collaboration has formed the basis of numerous environmental agreements going back many decades, including agreements that specifically address the need for protected areas (Table 1.4). The role of protected areas within a wider framework of global biodiversity

TABLE 1.4: (continued)

Title (Short title)	Place of adoption	Adopted	Notes
ASEAN Agreement on the Conservation of Nature and Natural Resources	Kuala Lumpur	1985	1
ASEAN Declaration on Heritage Parks and Reserves	Bangkok	1984	5
Convention for the Protection and Development of the Marine Environment of the Wider Caribbean Region (Cartagena Convention)	Cartagena de Indias (Colombia)	1983	
Protocol concerning Mediterranean Specially Protected Areas (SPA Protocol)	Geneva	1982	2
Benelux Convention on Nature Conservation and Landscape Protection	Brussels	1982	
United Nations Convention on the Law of the Sea (UNCLOS)	Montego Bay	1982	1
Regional Convention for the Conservation of the Red Sea and Gulf of Aden Environment (Jeddah Convention)	Jeddah	1982	4
Convention for Co-operation in the Protection and Development of the Marine and Coastal Environment of the West and Central African Region (Abidjan Convention)	Abidjan	1981	4
Convention for the Protection of the Marine Environment and Coastal Area of the Southeast Pacific (Lima Convention)	Lima	1981	4
Convention on the Conservation of Antarctic Marine Living Resources (CCAMLR)	Canberra	1980	1
European Outline Convention on Transfrontier Co-operation between Territorial Communities or Authorities	Madrid	1980	
Convention on the Conservation of European Wildlife and Natural Habitats (Bern Convention)	Bern	1979	1
Council Directive on the conservation of wild birds (EU) (Wild Birds Directive)		1979	2
Convention on the Conservation of Migratory Species of Wild Animals (Bonn Convention)	Bonn	1979	
International Convention for the Prevention of Pollution from Ships, 1973, as modified by the Protocol of 1978 relating thereto (MARPOL 73/78)		1978	3

conservation is implicit or explicit in all of these. More recently still, the role of protected areas within the framework of human well-being and development has been given clear prominence in the United Nations Millennium Development Goals (MDGs), agreed by all 191 Member States. Under MDG Goal 7, Member States are committed to ensuring environmental sustainability by 2015, and must "integrate the principles of sustainable development into country policies and programs and reverse the loss of environmental resources (Target 9)." One key measure for success (Indicator 26) is the "land area protected to maintain biological diversity."

International conservation agreements at global, regional, and bilateral levels, and almost 50 international environmental conventions, treaties,

TABLE 1.4: (continued)

Title (Short title)	Place of adoption	Adopted	Notes
Kuwait Regional Convention for Co-operation on the Protection of the Marine Environment from Pollution (Kuwait Convention)	Kuwait	1978	4
Convention for the Protection of the Mediterranean Sea Against Pollution (Barcelona Convention)	Barcelona	1976	
Convention on Conservation of Nature in the South Pacific (Apia Convention)	Apia	1976	1
European Network of Biogenetic Reserves: Resolutions of the Committee of Ministers Council of Europe*		1976	2
Convention for the Conservation of Antarctic Seals	London	1972	1
Convention Concerning the Protection of the World Cultural and Natural Heritage (World Heritage Convention)	Paris	1972	2
Convention on Wetlands of International Importance especially as Waterfowl Habitat (Ramsar Convention)	Ramsar	1971	2
Man and the Biosphere Programme* (MAB)		1970	2
African Convention on the Conservation of Nature and Natural Resources‡	Algiers	1968	1
European Diploma: Resolutions of the Committee of Ministers of the Council of Europe*		1965	2
Agreed Measures for the Conservation of Antarctic Fauna and Flora	Brussels	1964	3
The Antarctic Treaty	Washington	1959	3
International Convention for the Protection of Birds	Paris	1950	1
International Convention for the Regulation of Whaling	Washington	1946	3
Convention on Nature Protection and Wild Life Preservation in the Western Hemisphere (Western Hemisphere Convention)	Washington	1940	1
Convention Relative to the Preservation of Fauna and Flora in their Natural State (London Convention)	London	1933	1

Notes:
1: Text encourages states either directly or in equivalent language to establish protected areas.
2: Text establishes a defined form of protected area (specific to that convention or agreement).
3: Encourages protection of areas, but such areas not recognized by IUCN.
4: General text simply exhorts environmental protection, often linked to protocols or other measures that require designation of protected areas.
5: Text specifies a list of sites.
* Regarded as a "non-treaty agreement", or "soft law", not legally binding under the Vienna Convention on the Law of Treaties.
‡ Revision adopted Maputo 2003 - not yet in force

agreements, and associated protocols now exist, which encourage the protection of land or sea for nature conservation (see Table 1.4). A number of these include specific protected area definitions and provide a legal framework for the designation of sites. Here we consider four of the most important agreements in more detail, before considering the interactions between such agreements and then looking more closely at finer-scale agreements associated with transboundary protected areas, networks, and corridors.

Convention on Biological Diversity

The Convention on Biological Diversity (CBD) was signed by 150 government leaders at the United Nations Conference on Environment and Development (UNCED) in Rio de Janeiro, Brazil, in June 1992, and entered into force on 29 December 1993. The CBD was an attempt not just to raise the profile of environmental concerns at the global level but also to embrace a range of disparate perspectives on what aspects of the natural world were important and why. To this end it uses a very broad definition of biological diversity, namely: "the variability among living organisms from all sources including, inter alia, terrestrial, marine and other aquatic ecosystems and the ecological complexes of which they are part; this includes diversity within species, between species and of ecosystems." It emphasizes not just the intrinsic value of biological diversity, but also the goods and services that biological diversity supplies, stressing the need for these to be maintained for future generations. Reflecting this, it has established three parallel objectives, namely the conservation of biological diversity, the sustainable use of its components, and the fair and equitable sharing of the benefits arising out of the utilization of genetic resources.

As of 2006, the CBD had 188 Parties, including all but a handful of the world's countries (the exceptions are Andorra, Brunei Darussalam, Holy See, Iraq, Somalia and the USA). Eight ordinary meetings of the Conference of Parties and 11 meetings of the Subsidiary Body of Scientific, Technical and Technological Advice had been held.

Ecological linkages: improved conservation of elephants in Tanzanian protected areas has led to a reduction in tree cover to historic levels, decreasing populations of tsetse flies and thereby benefitting domestic livestock in adjacent areas.

J Bauvois/UNEP

The CBD is the broadest-ranging environmental agreement and second only to the United Nations Framework Convention on Climate Change in terms of membership. Consequently, the Convention has established a significant political momentum. While the CBD establishes no specific network of sites, it is one of the most important developments for protected areas in the last decade. The Convention implicitly acknowledges the importance of protected areas, and explicitly recognizes their fundamental role in the conservation of biological diversity, devoting a major part of Article 8, on *in-situ* conservation, to them. Under this Article, Parties to the Convention are called on to, among other things: establish a system of protected areas or areas where special measures need to be taken to conserve biological diversity; develop, where necessary, guidelines for the selection, establishment, and management of protected areas or areas where special measures need to be taken to conserve biological diversity; and promote the protection of ecosystems, natural habitats, and the maintenance of viable populations of species in natural surroundings.

In April 2002, the Sixth Meeting of the Conference of Parties (CoP6) to the CBD adopted a strategic plan for the Convention. Within the strategic plan, Parties commit themselves to "achieve by 2010 a significant reduction of the current rate of biodiversity loss at the global, regional and national levels as a contribution to poverty alleviation and to the benefit of all life on Earth." This target was endorsed by the World Summit on Sustainable Development in September 2002.

At the Seventh Meeting of the Conference of Parties (CoP7) to the CBD in February 2004, protected areas were one of the main themes for discussion. The Parties at the meeting adopted a Programme of Work on Protected Areas to implement the relevant articles of the Convention, including endorsement of the IUCN protected areas management category system and encouragement of countries to adopt these categories. They also endorsed protected area coverage as an indicator for "immediate testing" in relation to the globally adopted target of significantly reducing the loss of biodiversity by the year 2010.

International site-based conventions and programs

At the global level the principal site-based conservation area conventions and programs are:

S Chape

Jungfrau-Aletsch-
Bietschhorn World
Heritage Area in
Switzerland, designated
in 2001.

The World Heritage Convention

The Convention Concerning the Protection of the World Cultural and Natural Heritage (the World Heritage Convention) was adopted by the General Conference of UNESCO in 1972 and entered into force on 17 December 1975. By October 2006, 184 States were party to it, making it the most globally adopted international instrument for protecting the world's cultural and natural heritage. A study (Magin and Chape, 2004) noted that, while the total number of natural and mixed World Heritage sites – 172 at the time of the study – comprised only 0.17 percent of the total number of the world's protected areas, their combined area of 1.7 million km² was just over 9 percent of the total area protected.

The Convention is governed by the World Heritage Committee, which reviews and administers operational guidelines and assesses nominations for World Heritage Listing presented by States Parties at its annual meetings. The Committee is assisted in its evaluation of nominations by Advisory Bodies:

❑   for Natural World Heritage: IUCN – The World Conservation Union;

❑   for Cultural World Heritage: the International Council on Monuments and Sites (ICOMOS) and the International Centre for the Study of the Preservation and Restoration of Cultural Property (ICCROM).

For a site to be included on the World Heritage List, the World Heritage Committee must find that it has "outstanding universal value." The recently revised Convention Operational Guidelines define outstanding universal value as:

...cultural and/or natural significance which is so exceptional as to transcend national boundaries and to be of common importance for present and future generations of all humanity. As such, the permanent protection of this heritage is of the highest importance to the international community as a whole.

At the time of inscription of a property on the World Heritage List, the Committee will agree on a statement of outstanding universal value.

Sites can also be nominated and listed as mixed sites: those that have outstanding natural and cultural values. Since 1992, significant interactions between people and the natural environment have also been recognized as cultural landscapes. In 2007, the World Heritage List consisted of a total of 851 properties in 141 States Parties. Of these, 660 were inscribed as cultural properties, 166 as natural sites, and 25 as mixed properties.

It is on the basis of the overriding principle of outstanding universal value that the Committee has defined ten criteria for inclusion of cultural and natural properties on the World Heritage List. The Convention Operational Guidelines define

25

the following criteria for sites nominated for natural values:

(vii) Contain superlative natural phenomena or areas of exceptional natural beauty and aesthetic importance.

(viii) Be outstanding examples representing major stages of the Earth's history, including the record of life, significant ongoing geological processes in the development of landforms, or significant geomorphic or physiographic features.

(ix) Be outstanding examples representing significant ongoing ecological and biological processes in the evolution and development of terrestrial, freshwater, coastal, and marine ecosystems and communities of plants and animals.

(x) Contain the most important and significant natural habitats for *in-situ* conservation of biological diversity, including those containing threatened species of outstanding universal value from the point of view of science or conservation.

As well as fulfilling one or more of these criteria, the protection, management, and integrity of a site are also important considerations that are taken into account by the Committee when assessing nominations for listing. The World Heritage List represents the pinnacle of the world's natural and cultural heritage, hence the need for rigorous application of stringent criteria. The fundamental difference between Natural and Mixed World Heritage sites and other types of protected areas is the use of the framework of outstanding universal value and site integrity as a determinant for inscription. Figure 1.8 illustrates one conceptual view of the relationship of World Heritage sites to other types of national and international protected areas in terms of relative scale (global numbers) and the application of outstanding universal value as the key determinant for moving protected areas on to the World Heritage List. Below the outstanding universal value line, all protected areas are vital for ecosystem, landscape, and species conservation based on the principle of effective representivity. Of course, World Heritage sites also have a vital role in conserving landscapes and biodiversity.

Ramsar Convention on Wetlands

The Convention on Wetlands of International Importance, adopted in Ramsar, Iran, in 1971, is an intergovernmental treaty that provides the framework for national action and international cooper-

FIGURE 1.8: THE RELATIONSHIP OF WORLD HERITAGE SITES TO OTHER TYPES OF PROTECTED AREAS

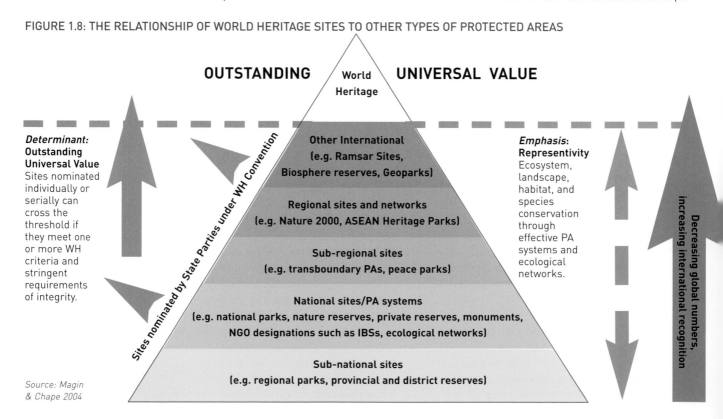

Source: Magin & Chape 2004

ation for the conservation and wise use of wetlands and their resources. Parties to the Convention have adopted a vision "to develop and maintain an international network of wetlands that are important for the conservation of global biological diversity and for sustaining human life through the ecological and hydrological functions they perform." In 2007, there were 157 Contracting Parties to the Convention, with 1 708 wetland sites covering 1.53 million km^2 included on the Ramsar List of Wetlands of International Importance. The target is to have 2.5 million km^2 by 2010.

The Convention requires that each member state designate suitable wetlands within its territory for inclusion in the List, which is maintained by the Convention Secretariat. The listed wetland sites range from one hectare of some of the world's largest and oldest mangroves, found on Australia's Christmas Island, to the 68 640 km^2 of the Okavango Delta Ramsar Site in Botswana.

The Ramsar definition of "wetland" is very broad: "areas of marsh, fen, peatland or water, whether natural or artificial, permanent or temporary, with water that is static or flowing, fresh, brackish or salt, including areas of marine water the depth of which at low tide does not exceed six metres." Thus, the Ramsar Convention applies to coastal zones as well as inland waters. The key determinant for inclusion on the Ramsar List is that sites should be selected on the basis of "their international significance in terms of ecology, botany, zoology, limnology or hydrology." This provision is implemented through the Ramsar Criteria for Identifying Wetlands of International Importance:

❏ **Group A – Sites containing representative, rare, or unique wetland types**
Criterion 1: A wetland should be considered internationally important if it contains a representative, rare, or unique example of a natural or near-natural wetland type found within the appropriate biogeographic region.

❏ **Group B – Sites of international importance for conserving biological diversity**
Criteria based on species and ecological communities
Criterion 2: [The wetland] supports vulnerable, endangered, or critically endangered species or threatened ecological communities.
Criterion 3: [The wetland] supports populations of plant and/or animal species important for maintaining the biological diver-

sity of a particular biogeographic region.
Criterion 4: [The wetland] supports plant and/or animal species at a critical stage in their life cycles, or provides refuge during adverse conditions.

❏ **Specific criteria based on waterbirds**
Criterion 5: [The wetland] regularly supports 20 000 or more waterbirds.
Criterion 6: [The wetland] regularly supports 1 percent of the individuals in a population of one species or subspecies of waterbird.

❏ **Specific criteria based on fish**
Criterion 7: [The wetland] supports a significant proportion of indigenous fish subspecies, species, or families, life-history stages, species interactions and/or populations that are representative of wetland benefits and/or values, and thereby contributes to global biological diversity.
Criterion 8: [The wetland] is an important source of food for fishes, spawning ground, nursery, and/or migration path on which fish stocks, either within the wetland or elsewhere, depend.

Almost 90 percent of the current Ramsar sites have

Winter in Dalälven-Färnebofjärden Ramsar Site in Sweden, designated in 2001.

G.Ziesler/Still Pictures

**Red-and-green macaws
(*Ara chloropterus*) in
Manú Biosphere Reserve,
Peru.**

other forms of protected area status (for example national parks, nature reserves, and wildlife sanctuaries). This leaves around 110 000 km² that do not have other forms of protection, other than their designation as Wetlands of International Importance. Ramsar site status reinforces other forms of protected area categories by adding an international dimension and creating additional commitments by national governments to the international community.

Biosphere reserves
Nominated by governments, biosphere reserves are areas of terrestrial, coastal, or marine ecosystems that are internationally recognized under UNESCO's Man and the Biosphere (MAB) Programme. By 2007, there were 529 reserves in 105 countries. The philosophy underlying biosphere reserves has evolved over more than 30 years since the first reserves were established. However, it has always sought to combine biodiversity conservation, rural development, and support for scientific research, training, and education. The original intention of the World Network of Biosphere Reserves in the 1970s was to promote a systematic approach to conservation, such that biosphere reserves would be

internationally designated "representative eco-logical areas" for each of the 193 biogeographical provinces of the Udvardy (1975) classification. The idea was also to set up an operational network of MAB sites for cooperative research in similar ecosystem types or in areas facing comparable ecological problems. To carry out the complementary activities of nature conservation and use of natural resources, biosphere reserves are organized into three interrelated zones, known as the core area, the buffer zone, and the transition area (see Figure 1.9).

In 1995, the conservation function of biosphere reserves evolved to embrace natural and cultural values. New emphasis was placed on the sustainable use of natural resources in buffer zones and on the role of the outer transition area for maintaining cultural values and for ecosystem rehabilitation or redevelopment. The biosphere reserve was defined as being "more than a protected area," with a new task of providing concrete testing grounds for regional approaches to sustainable development in the wake of UNCED in 1992. Biosphere reserves are also viewed as field laboratories for the implementation of the ecosystem approach advocated by the CBD. With this expanded definition of biosphere reserves, it is obvious that the criterion of "representativeness" and the degree of world "coverage" are less easy to evaluate.

With this background, it can be understood why there are numerous "old generation" biosphere reserves in the temperate broadleaf forests, evergreen forests, and mountain systems, corresponding to where the traditional types of protected areas and scientific research sites (IUCN Protected Area Management Categories I and II) were first established. As MAB is a voluntary, intergovernmental program, coverage of the World Network is also linked to the willingness of countries to participate, which has also evolved. The participation of a number of countries since 1992, including Brazil, the Dominican Republic, India, Morocco, South Africa and Vietnam, has improved geographic representation. The majority of countries have adopted a pragmatic, systematic approach at the national level to give more or less "representative" coverage of their main environmental and developmental features: examples of national networks can be found in Argentina, Canada, China, Cuba, France, Mexico, and the Russian Federation. However, while MAB is an

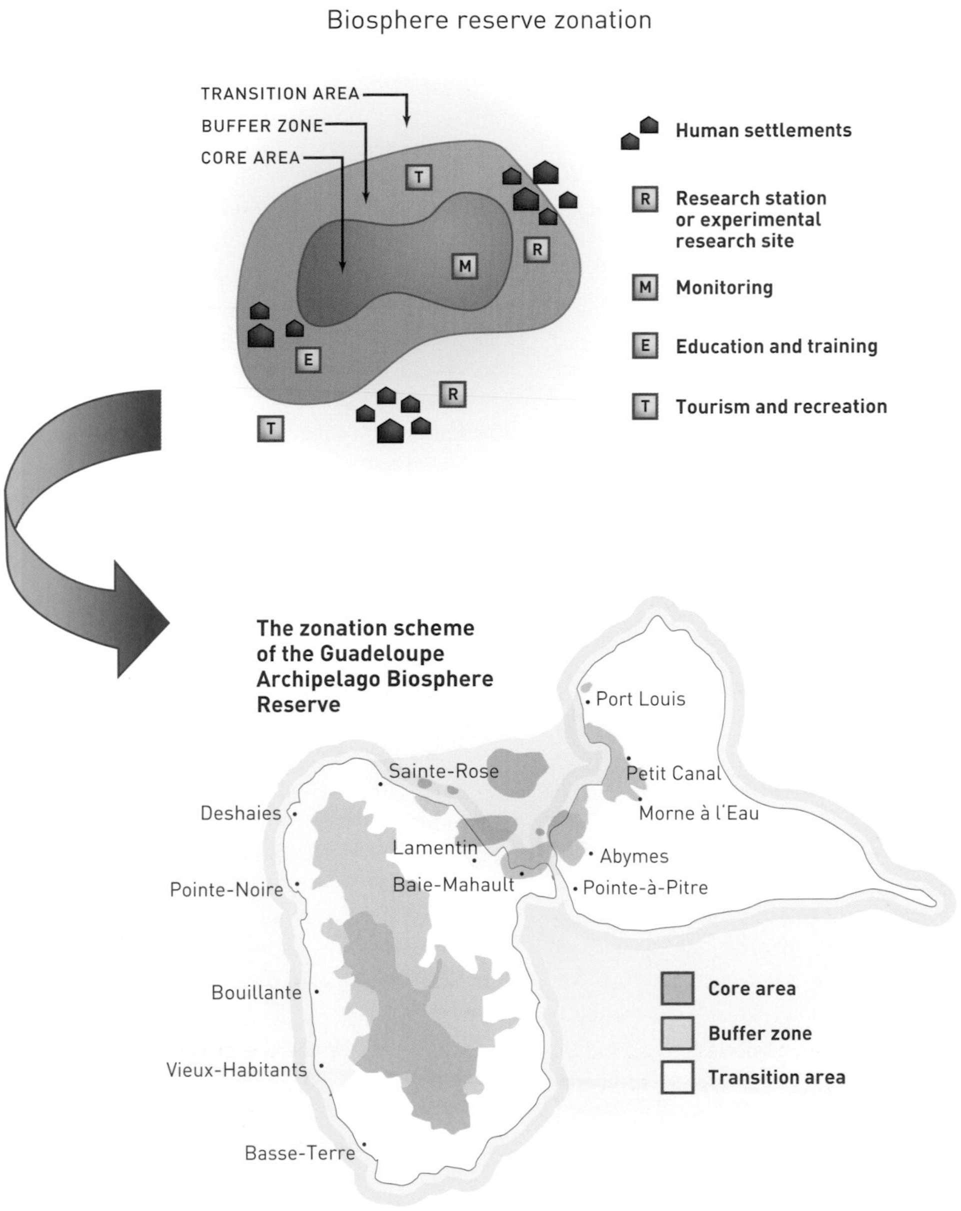

Biosphere reserve zonation

The zonation scheme
of the Guadeloupe
Archipelago Biosphere
Reserve

FIGURE 1.9: BIOSPHERE RESERVE ZONATION – CONCEPT AND PRACTICE

intergovernmental UN program and hence bio-sphere reserve nominations need to be made through national governments, increasingly the nomination process is initiated and led by local communities, seeking official international recognition of their efforts. More and more biosphere reserves contain a combination of protected area categories and cover large landscapes and seascapes, with an increasing number corresponding to Category V (protected landscapes). Many

are set up without reference to a pre-existing protected area.

In recent years, the MAB International Coordinating Council has called attention to the need to create biosphere reserves in areas under intense human pressure, such as wetlands, coastal systems and islands, and semi-arid and arid lands. In response, new biosphere reserves have been designated that include these features. Examples include the Ciénaga de Zapata

H O'Mahony/UNEP

Plains zebra (*Equua quagga*) in Serengeti National Park in Tanzania.

biosphere reserves has been implemented through the ten-year periodic review of the Statutory Framework for the World Network, the "soft" law governing the development of biosphere reserves. As a result, many older sites have been completely revised – expanding in size, involving new stakeholders, and adding new functions. In recent years, a number of countries have voluntarily withdrawn sites that did not and could not meet the up-to-date biosphere reserve criteria. Thus, the World Network of Biosphere Reserves is evolving in coverage and quality.

Strengthening cooperation between international site-based agreements

Although each international site-based convention, agreement, or program serves a different purpose, they clearly complement one another. Failure to coordinate approaches at national or international levels may lead to confusion and duplication of effort, while connecting the work associated with these conventions and their related site-based activities can produce considerable synergies.

The value of achieving joint implementation of international instruments providing for *in-situ* conservation has already been recognized by the secretariats of many of these agreements and pro-grams, and by their technical and scientific advisory committees. In many cases there is already bi-lateral cooperation, as for example between the Bern Convention and Natura 2000 in Europe, or between the World Heritage and Ramsar Con-ventions in their support to sites under threat. There is also synergy between these conventions and the MAB Programme. In 2004, 78 biosphere reserves included, wholly or partially, Ramsar wetlands, 75 included World Heritage sites, and 18 had both Ramsar and World Heritage sites.

There remains significant opportunity for developing this cooperation further, through:

❑ Seeking ways to integrate implementation of initiatives on the ground, or at least to increase cooperation in implementation at the national level.

❑ Identifying opportunities for sensible multiple designation, and for using one network to help bridge gaps in another.

❑ Building collaboration on review and defining mechanisms for deciding what are key sites.

❑ Ensuring close cooperation in the review of those sites under threat, and recommendation on actions to be taken.

Biosphere Reserve in Cuba, the Seaflower (San Andrés Archipelago) in Colombia, and the Hustai Nuruu Biosphere Reserve in Mongolia. More attention is paid to *in-situ* conservation of plants and animals of economic importance (for example the *Argania spinosa* woodlands of Morocco), as well as to traditional use areas of indigenous peoples (for example Bosawas, Nicaragua). There is a recent upsurge of interest in transboundary biosphere reserves as a flexible tool for coordinating the conservation and sustainable use of ecosystems that straddle national boundaries: the most recent is the 'W' Region Transboundary Biosphere Reserve of Benin, Burkina Faso, and Niger in West Africa.

Today, there are still noticeable gaps in global geographic coverage, for example in the eastern Mediterranean, the Arabian Gulf region, Southern Africa, and the Pacific Islands. Work at the national level to fill these gaps is spurred by regional MAB networks – AfriMAB, ArabMAB, East Asian Bio-sphere Reserve Network (EABRN), EuroMAB, the South and Central Asia MAB Network (SACAM), IberoMAB (Latin America plus Portugal and Spain), and the Southeast Asian Biosphere Reserve Network (SeaBRnet). Over the last few years, an average of 15–20 new biosphere reserves have been designated each year.

Since 1995, a quality control examination of

❏ Seeking ways to harmonize and streamline the nomination and reporting procedures.

❏ Ensuring the improved sharing of information, both on sites and key documents such as strategies, guidelines, and other publications.

❏ Building an improved understanding at the national level, in particular, on how the initiatives relate one to another.

❏ Improving the sharing of information between site managers, including the sharing of case studies and best practice.

Transboundary protected areas, biological corridors, and networks

In 1932, the Governments of Canada and the USA established the world's first "international peace park" by combining the Waterton and Glacier National Parks on the border of the two countries in the Rocky Mountains. Established to commemorate the long history of peace and cooperation between Canada and the USA, the initiative owed much to people who saw the value of the concept for cooperative management of humankind's natural heritage, and for advancing international understanding and goodwill.

Seven years earlier, the Governments of Poland and then Czechoslovakia had signed the Krakow Protocol, which set the framework for management of protected areas along their joint border. Although the first park was not fully established until after the Second World War (and one of the countries has since split into two), this is still one of the more active areas of cross-border collaboration in the protected areas of the Krkonose and Tatra Mountains, and in the East Carpathians.

Since then, protected areas along international borders have provided a focus for cooperation between countries (Sandwith et al., 2001). A recent global survey (Besançon and Savy, 2005) identified 188 internationally adjoining protected area complexes, composed of 818 protected areas in 112 countries. While not all of these have cooperative arrangements in place, this is an important development, and a key area for future action.

For example, in southern Africa, opportunities are being actively sought to use transboundary protected areas to promote cross-border cooperation, at the same time as promoting job creation and biodiversity conservation. In May 2000, the Presidents of Botswana and South Africa opened the Kgalagadi Transfrontier Park, 38 000 km² in the southern Kalahari Desert, with joint management and tourists moving freely from one country to another. In 2002, South Africa, Mozambique, and Zimbabwe established the Great Limpopo Transfrontier Park.

The simple concept of transboundary protected areas envisages a contiguous area of protection irrespective of political boundaries, with resultant much-expanded ecological space. Moving beyond this concept, there are an increasing number of efforts to expand such connectivity – and to further reduce the fragmentation of natural ecosystems – through the development of biological corridors and networks of connected protected areas. The ecological and design aspects of such approaches are considered in more detail in Chapter 4, but as such processes have become established within nations, many have also taken root in international collaborations.

A recent study analyzed 38 ecological networks around the world (Bennett and Wit, 2001). A good example is the Mesoamerican Biological Corridor, a cooperative initiative between the seven countries of Central America. While the basic concept is the development of a protected area network throughout the region to ensure conservation of its biodiversity, linked to this is a program of capacity building, improved site management, promoting sustainable human development, and increased regional cooperation. This program is attracting significant international attention and funding.

The concept of protected areas networks does not necessarily imply physical connections between sites, but rather a more holistic approach to designing systems of protected areas that ensure representation of the full range of biodiversity and functionality of ecosystems, with a clear vision of longer-term viability (which may, of course, require increased physical connections between particular sites or ecosystem components).

A number of international initiatives are specifically aimed at the systematic development of networks of sites for the protection of identified species and/or habitats, and ensuring the protection of key features. The Ramsar Convention on Wetlands of International Importance is an excellent example of this and has been discussed above. Two related initiatives within Europe, the European Union (EU) Birds and Habitats Directives and the Bern Convention, led to the identification of protected areas that conserve the species and habitats listed in annexes to the agreements. The resulting Emerald Network and Natura 2000 network are complementary to each other. Particularly significant is the fact that EU Directives are statutory measures, and if a Member State fails to meet its obligations in identifying and protecting sites, it can be taken to the European Court and fined.

While these initiatives are leading to identification of what are, in effect, core protected areas right across Europe, another initiative, the Pan-European Ecological Network, aims to promote their implementation within a network approach also incorporating buffer zones, corridors, and, where appropriate, re-created habitats. This concept, which builds on the Netherlands Nature Policy Plan adopted in 1990, has led to a substantial increase in the planning and implementation of a network approach to protected areas over the last ten years, particularly in Central and Eastern Europe. Other conservation networks have been established for rather narrower aims. For example, the prime aim of the East Asian-Australasian Shorebird Site Network is to conserve key sites for migratory shorebirds, and to enable those involved in their protection and management to obtain international recognition and support for their sites and conservation efforts.

Some networks of sites have been established for various research purposes, including the International Long-Term Ecological Research Network. The Terrestrial Ecosystem Monitoring Sites directory, managed by the Global Terrestrial Observing System, identifies a significant number of such sites and networks. While such networks have existed for many years, international collaboration has recently increased significantly.

One of the key issues in site networks that are concerned with long-term monitoring and integrated research is the exchange of information. The last decade has seen substantial discussion of mechanisms and protocols for information sharing and exchange, as well as the development of on-line tools for access to information from multiple sources. This is particularly important in the context of using protected areas as key indicators for global environmental assessment processes linked to achievement of biodiversity conservation targets.

ANTARCTICA – A SPECIAL CASE
The management regime for Antarctica is a unique example of international cooperation. The continent is a largely undisturbed wilderness region, almost entirely buried by snow and ice, and so cold and hostile that it has no permanent human population. Importantly, it has no internationally recognized sovereign states within its boundaries, although seven nations have claimed territory: Argentina, Australia, Chile, France, New Zealand, Norway, and the UK. These claims are legal insofar as they are incorporated into national law; some of them – such as those of Argentina, Chile, and the UK – overlap.

All human activities on and around the continent are governed by a system of international agreements known as the Antarctic Treaty System. This means that a unilateral decision-making process for the designation of protected areas, as seen elsewhere on the globe, does not occur here. The Antarctic Treaty System began with the signature in 1959 of the Antarctic Treaty itself, negotiated following an 18-month international study program organized by the International Council of Scientific Unions. The original signatories were Argentina, Australia, Belgium, Chile, France, Great Britain, Japan, New Zealand, Norway, South Africa, the USA, and the USSR. The treaty entered into force on 23 June 1961 and covers the entire area south of the latitude line 60°S.

The Antarctic Treaty is open to accession by any United Nations Member State or any other state invited to accede by the consent of all of the Antarctic Treaty Consultative Parties (ATCPs). The ATCPs comprise the original 12 Parties and a further 15 States that have subsequently acceded to the Treaty and demonstrated their interest in Antarctica by carrying out substantial scientific research. In recent years, the treaty system has become more publicly accessible, and non-governmental environmental organizations are now represented at most meetings through the Antarctic and Southern Ocean Coalition (ASOC). The Treaty remains in force indefinitely, and its objectives are simple yet unique in international relations:

❏ to demilitarize Antarctica, to establish it as a zone free of nuclear tests and the disposal of radioactive waste, and to ensure that it is used for peaceful purposes only;
❏ to promote international scientific cooperation in Antarctica;
❏ to set aside disputes over territorial sovereignty.

While the Antarctic Treaty itself does not contain any provisions for protection of the environment, it does allow for the Parties to develop agreements on such issues. More than 200 recommendations

E Duebendorfer/UNEP

**Emperor penguins
(*Aptenodytes forsteri*)
on Ross Island,
Antarctica.**

and five separate international agreements have been adopted. These, together with the original Treaty, are what constitute the Antarctic Treaty System, and provide the rules that govern activities in Antarctica. Three of the agreements relate specifically to protected areas:

1   Protocol on Environmental Protection to the Antarctic Treaty (Madrid Protocol): 1991

The Madrid Protocol, to which there are currently 29 Contracting Parties, was negotiated to provide for comprehensive protection of the Antarctic

environment. Its objectives are to:
❏   designate Antarctica as a "natural reserve, devoted to peace and science";
❏   establish environmental principles for the conduct of all activities;
❏   prohibit mining;
❏   subject all activities to prior assessment of their environmental impacts;
❏   provide for the establishment of a Committee for Environmental Protection (CEP) to advise the Antarctic Treaty Consultative Meeting (ATCM);

❏ require the development of contingency plans to respond to environmental emergencies;
❏ provide for the elaboration of rules relating to liability for environmental damage.

Annex V of the Protocol came into force in May 2002 and is intended to rationalize the system of protected areas into three categories: Antarctic Specially Protected Areas (ASPAs), of which 66 have so far been designated; Antarctic Specially Managed Areas, of which there is one; and Historic Sites and Monuments, of which there are 76. In total, these cover an area of about 3 000 km². ASPAs are designated according to the following criteria:
❏ outstanding wilderness;
❏ scientific or environmental values;
❏ important or unusual plant communities or habitats;
❏ unusual landforms;
❏ historic, aesthetic, or wilderness values.

A permit of entry is required to enter such an area, and all activities must be conducted in accordance with the area management plan. Antarctic Specially Managed Areas require the coordination of human activities in order to avoid the risk of mutual interference, and are regulated by a code of conduct set out in their management plans. Historic Sites and Monuments are designated in order to preserve and protect historic sites and monuments from damage.

Under the Antarctic Treaty System, a proposing party can nominate a site for protection by submitting a draft management plan to the CEP in accordance with established guidelines. The CEP has established a contact group to review the draft, which is chaired by the proponent and includes the Scientific Committee on Antarctic Research and, where marine areas are involved, the Convention for the Conservation of Antarctic Marine Living Resources. On the acceptance of the management plan (following a review process taking 12 months or more), the revised management plan becomes law under the Agreed Measures.

2   Convention for the Conservation of Antarctic Marine Living Resources (CCAMLR): 1980

CCAMLR aims to conserve Antarctic marine living resources, including their rational use. There are currently 31 Parties to the Convention, 24 of whom are members of the CCAMLR Commission. The Convention is concerned not only with the regulation of fishing but is a pioneer of the ecosystem approach, and considers the Antarctic ecosystem and the Southern Ocean as a suite of interlinked systems. The need for CCAMLR was identified following an increase in krill fishing in the early 1970s. Krill move beyond the 60°S line of latitude (the Antarctic Treaty Area) but within an area known as the Antarctic Convergence. The CCAMLR area therefore extends beyond that specified under the Antarctic Treaty and is applicable to the Antarctic Convergence. Two other important fisheries – for Patagonian toothfish and icefish – are managed within this region. Strict measures are in place to reduce bycatch and seabird mortality. Under the Convention, CCAMLR Ecosystem Monitoring Programme (CEMP) sites can be designated. Entry to CEMP sites is prohibited without a permit, and an appropriate authority can only issue permits for its own nationals. Each CEMP site has a management plan that must be complied with. Currently there are two such sites: Seal Islands, South Shetland Islands (90 hectares), and Cape Shirreff and Telmo Island, South Shetland Islands (347 hectares).

3   Convention for the Conservation of Antarctic Seals (CCAS): 1972

The aims of CCAS are to promote and achieve the protection, scientific study, and rational use of Antarctic seals, and to maintain a satisfactory balance within the ecological system of the Antarctic. The Convention has 17 Contracting Parties and has three sites covering some 215 000 km² under its jurisdiction. These areas, in which it is forbidden to kill or capture seals, are breeding sites or sites where long-term scientific research on seals is carried out.

A GLOBAL REVIEW

Although their lineage traces back at least two millennia, the final decades of the 20th century represented the coming of age of protected areas as a global category of land use and management. This period saw vast increases in the numbers of protected areas and a burgeoning of international efforts to support, encourage and harmonize site designation and management. A phenomenal growth has happened as a direct result of growing knowledge of the threats to the natural world, as well as increasing awareness of the considerable values that protected areas bring to humanity. The result is a vast estate, covering almost 13 percent of the Earth's land surface where, at least in

G Wiltsie/Still Pictures

Melchior Island, Antarctica.

principle, natural processes are allowed to continue unaltered or are managed in a sustainable manner. Collaboration between peoples, partners, organizations and countries enable us to see this once highly fragmented estate, for the first time, as a global network. In some places direct or close connections enable free movement of species and wider maintenance of ecological processes, but the networking extends beyond the ecological, to the collaboration in management, in support, and in the sharing of knowledge.

In the remainder of this work we examine the phenomenon of the global protected areas estate in more detail. Chapter 2 takes an ecological perspective, looking at species and the major biomes that make up the Earth's surface and considering both the particular challenges they face, and the efforts to date in developing protected areas to represent this biodiversity. Chapter 3 provides a framework for considering the broad array of human threats to biodiversity, and considers the particular changes that individual threats pose in protected areas design and management. Chapters 4 and 5 look at protected areas from the perspective of design and management, considering how systems can be designed to support a functioning ecology, and managed to support human needs, while rising to the challenges of the many and varied threats that impinge upon them. Chapter 6 focuses on the specific challenges facing the marine environment, currently massively under-represented, but receiving growing attention at national and international levels. Chapter 7 concludes the global review with an assessment of the prospects for effectively maintaining the world's protected areas. Following this global review, the book focuses on protected areas around the world provided by regional experts.

CHAPTER 2

Protected areas
and biodiversity

Contributors: M. Jenkins; Terrestrial species coverage by the global protected area network: A. Rodrigues et al.; How WWF is using large-scale biogeographic approaches: J. Morrison; Habitat coverage by the protected areas network (introduction): I. Lysenko and M. Spalding; Forests: M. Jenkins and V. Kapos; Non-forested habitats (introduction), grasslands and savannas, and deserts and semi deserts: Henwood et al.; Wetlands: W. Darwall and C. Revenga; Caves and karst: E. Hamilton-Smith; Mountain ecosystems: L. Hamilton et al.; Biodiversity conservation in the Himalayas: T.F. Allnut et al.; Marine and coastal ecosystems: M. Spalding.

An historical perspective

As the outline presented in Chapter 1 has made clear, the global protected area network has, with exceptions in a few countries, developed in an *ad hoc* rather than in a planned and systematic manner. From the very beginning, protected areas have been established for a range of different reasons and were, and continue to be, expected to serve different and sometimes conflicting functions.

Historically, two major impulses in the designation of protected areas can be identified. The first is essentially concerned with landscape and notions of the wild and untamed, but is in itself the product of different ideas and ideals. In the modern world this can be traced back to the growing alienation from nature associated with the Industrial Revolution and the rapid growth in urbanization during the 19th century. During the latter half of that century the need was increasingly felt both for the provision of open space that could be enjoyed for its own sake, particularly by urbanized working peoples, and for the protection from development of areas of outstanding natural beauty, particularly those with dramatic landscape features. Although these two roles were essentially seen as complementary, the emphasis in individual cases might differ – the Royal National Park in Australia is an early example of an area set aside primarily to provide open space for the inhabitants of a large conurbation (Sydney), while the Grand Canyon and the geysers of Yellowstone in the USA are early examples of landscapes protected in the public name, but primarily for their own sake.

During the 20th century, these two functions, particularly the latter, continued to be among the most important reasons for the designation of protected areas almost everywhere, as exemplified by many of the world's best known national parks, such as Torres del Paine in Chile (protected primarily for its mountain peaks and glaciers), Iguaçu/Iguazu on the Brazilian/Argentinean border (waterfalls), Gunung Mulu, Sarawak, Malaysia (limestone caves), and Uluru, Australia (the megalithic Ayres Rock). In colonial Africa the notion of national phenomena worth preserving on a large scale was extended to include dramatic wildlife concentrations, perhaps most famously in Serengeti National Park, Tanzania, and the associated Masai Mara Game Reserve, Kenya. By and large, however, the presence of populations or assemblages of particular species of animals, plants, or other organisms has played relatively little part in the choice of such areas.

The second main historical impulse in the setting aside of areas was to ensure control over some harvested living natural resource. On land the most important such resources are game and timber. It is not surprising, therefore, that many of the earliest accounts of protected areas are of what are essentially game reserves and forest reserves. In almost all cases for which we have evidence, the intention behind the setting aside of the former was not to manage game species for maximum productivity, that is as an important source of protein for society at large, but to maintain populations of them as quarry for hunting by elites.

S. Chape

Grand Canyon National Park World Heritage Site, USA, which started as a federal forest reserve in 1893.

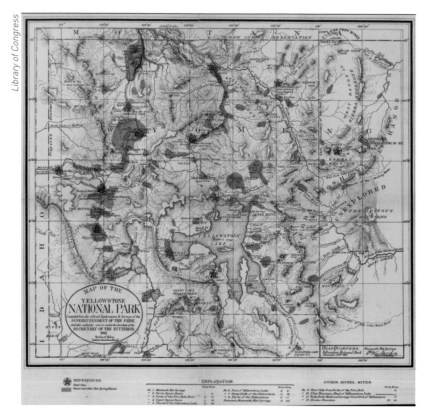

Yellowstone National Park, USA, 1881.

This concept was introduced widely in the European colonies in the 19th century and the first half of the 20th century, particularly in the French and British empires, so that many existing protected areas in the former colonies have their origins in hunting or game reserves (*Réserves de chasse* and *Réserves de faune*), and indeed often retain such designations. The focus for their establishment was usually the presence of substantial populations of large mammals, particularly ungulates, but also sometimes of game birds such as pheasants, grouse, bustards, and various kinds of waterfowl.

Governments everywhere have also had a long tradition of taking control of a nation's timber resources, with much of the forest estate in many countries considered government land (often regardless of any traditional tenure claims), and with timber production and processing either directly under government control or, more often, operated through a system of licensing concessionaires. Under many such systems, the forest estate was divided into a number of categories, for example areas designated for clear-felling or conversion to plantation forestry, areas identified for selective timber production, and forest reserves not intended for commercial timber extraction. The

last of these may have been set aside because the terrain was considered unsuitable for most kinds of logging, because the areas were perceived to be of importance for the protection of water catchments, or as samples of particular forest types, of interest in practical forestry studies. Typically, only small areas were set aside as samples of forest types.

As well as these two main motivations for the designation of protected areas, a third, historically less prominent, reason has been the setting aside of areas primarily for scientific interest. Such areas may contain representative samples of different habitats or ecosystems, or unusual and particularly interesting species or species assemblages, or geophysical phenomena. Sometimes the factors leading to their designation may be of wider interest – that is, they may also be considered important public attractions in the way described above – but often they may not.

Relatively early examples of this systematic, science-based approach can be found in the *zapovednik* system established in the former Soviet Union from 1919 onwards, and in the network of reserves set up in various parts of the world under the French colonial regime. In Madagascar, for example, a network of strict nature reserves (*Réserves naturelles intégrales*) was established, mainly in the 1930s, containing representative samples of the major vegetation types present on this extraordinarily diverse island. These were intended essentially as a resource for scientific research with access granted only under strictly controlled permit. In addition, a small number of special reserves (*Réserves spéciales*) were set up to protect features considered of particular interest, for example the *Réserve spéciale de Périnet*, established specifically to protect an accessible population of indri (*Indri indri*), the world's largest lemur species. These examples notwithstanding, until the second half of the 20th century, relatively few protected areas were established for what might be regarded as pure, science-based conservation ends, that is without other considerations being taken into account.

Moreover, the establishment of protected areas, for whatever reason, has always had to be made in the face of other competing interests. Allocation of land to this function has generally been accorded a low priority, particularly where that land is of potentially high value for other purposes, for example is agriculturally productive, rich in mineral resources, or well sited for residential or industrial development. This means that such areas are generally poorly represented in protected area networks. Conversely, networks tend to have heavy representation of areas that are not considered valuable for other uses, or at least were not considered so at the time they were gazetted. Such areas tend to be infertile, with difficult terrain, and often isolated. Where they are inhabited, the inhabitants are (or were) usually people with little political power.

Modern approaches

As we have seen in the previous chapter, the past few decades have seen great changes in the way that global environmental issues and the roles of protected areas are perceived, or at least articulated. Most importantly, discussions about nature and living natural resources are almost invariably cast in the rubric of biological diversity, or "biodiversity", a term whose meaning has become more diffuse as its political currency has grown. The major international expression of this has been the negotiation and entry into force in 1993 of the Convention on Biological Diversity (CBD), one of the three so-called Rio conventions that emerged from the 1992 United Nations Conference on Environment and Development (UNCED, or the Earth Summit).

In 2004, the Parties to the Convention decided on an extensive and ambitious work program on protected areas. In this they expanded the requirement for the development of national protected area systems as set out in Article 8 of the convention to a call to support the establishment and maintenance of a comprehensive, effectively managed, and ecologically representative global network of protected areas. In particular they recognized that such a network would play a vital contribution in meeting the target agreed by the Parties to the Convention and echoed at the 2002 World Summit on Sustainable Development of having mechanisms in place by 2010 to significantly reduce the rate of biodiversity loss at the global, regional, and national levels, and to establish an effective global marine protected area network by 2012. The program of action developed in 2003 as part of the Vth World Parks Congress similarly urged governments, non-governmental organizations, and local communities to maximize representation and persistence of biodiversity in comprehensive protected area networks.

These decisions, which reflect the current thinking of the world's governments and the protected areas community at large, have the effect of highlighting the role of protected areas in maintaining biodiversity, and have effectively brought the science-based approach, which was traditionally regarded as of minor importance, to the fore.

Central questions in assessing the role of protected areas in meeting the 2010 target, applicable at all levels from the local to the global, are:

❏   How well does any existing protected area network cover biodiversity?
❏   What are the major gaps in the network?

Because protected area networks were not usually designed to carry out this function of maintaining biodiversity, it is to be expected that there will generally be gaps. Identifying what these gaps are is not straightforward, chiefly because biodiversity is not a single entity. Rather, it is an expression of the extraordinary complexity and variability of living systems at all scales and at a range of hierarchical levels from the molecular through individuals, populations, and species to communities, habitats, and ecosystems, and ultimately the entire biosphere.

There are many ways to try to capture this variability and express it in a quantifiable way. Most generally, and as singled out by the CBD, three

The indri (*Indri indri*), endemic to Madagascar, is the world's largest lemur species.

different levels are considered important: genes, species, and ecosystems. Although genetic diversity is recognized as a fundamental underpinning of organismal diversity, it has to date proved very difficult to come up with useful measures for analysis. Most current approaches to assessing how well covered biodiversity is in protected areas therefore emphasize either species or habitats, communities, and ecosystems.

Ultimately, it is difficult to separate the two approaches: habitats and communities are often defined largely on the basis of their predominant species, while ecosystems can be considered as populations of species, the interactions between them, and the physical environment in which they exist. Nevertheless, these approaches do differ, and each has its advantages and disadvantages, as is discussed in further detail below.

Identifying and filling gaps

Any analysis of coverage should result in identifying major gaps – that is species, groups of species, habitats, communities, or ecosystems that are believed not to be represented or are inadequately represented in protected areas. Even given the various constraints outlined above, identifying gaps is, in theory at least, relatively straightforward. Determining how these gaps should be filled and, in particular, identifying priorities – that is singling out the most important areas to be protected – is a different matter entirely.

This is largely because it is difficult to reach agreement over which aspects or components of biodiversity are considered the most important. This applies both to judgments of the intrinsic value of the particular components being discussed and to the perceived urgency or intensity of the need to protect them. Different approaches may emphasize some or all of the following:

❏ areas of occurrence of individual species, particularly large, charismatic, and threatened ones;
❏ areas that are particularly rich in species;
❏ areas that have a significant number of local or endemic species;
❏ areas that contain unique communities, ecosystems, or landscape features;
❏ representative samples of identified communities, ecosystems, or landscapes.

There may also be debate as to whether it is more important or worthwhile to invest in vestigial or highly threatened systems or to concentrate efforts on maintaining still healthy and expansive systems or populations.

The plan of action developed in 2003 as part of the Vth World Parks Congress drew on a number of different approaches to set a series of species- and habitat-based targets:

1. All globally threatened species are effectively conserved *in situ* with the following immediate targets:
❏ All critically endangered and endangered species confined to single sites are effectively conserved *in situ* by 2006.
❏ All other critically endangered and endangered species are effectively conserved *in situ* by 2008.
❏ All other globally threatened species are effectively conserved *in situ* by 2010.
❏ Sites that support internationally important populations of congregatory and/or restricted-range species are adequately conserved by 2010.

2. Viable representations of every terrestrial, freshwater, and marine ecosystem are effectively conserved within protected areas, with the following immediate targets:
❏ A common global framework for classifying and assessing the status of ecosystems is established by 2006.
❏ Quantitative targets for each ecosystem type are identified by 2008.
❏ Viable representations of every threatened or underprotected ecosystem are conserved by 2010.

Whichever aspect, or combination of aspects, is chosen – it may be all the species in a particular plant family, or different vegetation communities in a particular region – information is needed on the spatial distribution of those components and on the distribution of existing protected areas in the district under analysis. On the basis of this, using more or less complicated algorithms, areas of high priority for protection can be identified.

A number of different approaches has been used, of which three of the most commonly applied are minimum-set analysis, richness, and irreplaceability. Minimum-set analysis attempts to identify the smallest set of areas, which together contain at least one example of each of the elements of biodiversity chosen; richness priorit-

D Cheeseman/Still Pictures

A cheetah (*Acinonyx jubatus*), Serengeti National Park, Tanzania.

izes sites on the basis of the number of unprotected elements that would be protected if that site were protected; irreplaceability prioritizes sites on the basis of the number of elements of biodiversity that would be lost within the planning region if that site were lost.

Each approach has advantages, but each also has limitations when applied in the real world. As noted above, it is rare for there to be complete information on even limited subsets of biodiversity in any given region. This is particularly the case in the tropics. Where detailed information is available, determining optimal solutions to protected area network design rapidly becomes computationally intractable unless scenarios are quite simple (i.e. a small number of elements and a small number of areas). There is also no single, unequivocal way of combining priorities established through analysis of different subsets of biodiversity: in a particular region, priorities determined through analysis of, say, the distribution of bird species will undoubtedly be different from those established using plant communities. Most importantly, it is often very difficult for such analyses to take into account real-life constraints on the availability of sites for protection, the costs of obtaining and maintaining such sites, and the fact that the landscape, in its broadest sense, is constantly changing, so that, for example, a site identified as high priority in a one-off analysis may no longer be of value once the opportunity arises for protecting it.

It is, nevertheless, clear that systematic planning in creating networks of protected areas is preferable to a completely opportunistic or *ad hoc* approach and, where certain conditions can be satisfied, these techniques can and have been successfully applied on the ground.

The following sections outline species-based, biogeographic, and habitat-based analyses of protected area coverage at the global level.

Species-based approaches

Species-based approaches have the advantage that species are in general the best characterized components of biodiversity, at least when it comes to groups such as animals and plants. In these cases, there is normally reasonable agreement on what constitutes a species and it is generally possible to distinguish one from another. It could theoretically be possible, therefore, to enumerate all the species in a given area and identify those that have populations included in protected areas and those that do not. However, in reality this is not possible because our knowledge of species and their distributions is incomplete.

To date, some 1.7 million species of all forms of life have been named and described scientifically. This is believed to include a high proportion of the true number of the world's larger terrestrial plants and animals, particularly the so-called higher vertebrates (birds, mammals, reptiles, and amphibians), but a far smaller percentage of other groups, especially invertebrates, fungi, and micro-organisms, which between them comprise the vast majority of living species. Estimates for the total number of species on Earth vary widely, but there may be between 10 and 20 million in total, the majority of these invertebrate animals. Even among the best known taxonomic groups (birds and mammals) new discoveries are still regularly being made. Detailed or complete information on distribution is available for only a very small proportion of described species – again mostly large and conspicuous ones – and there is reliable information on total population numbers for even fewer.

Knowledge of biodiversity is geographically, as well as taxonomically, biased. Most information is available for terrestrial temperate regions, with far less known about other parts of the world, particularly the tropics and aquatic regions. Even within temperate latitudes, there are extremely few areas, or sites, for which anything approaching complete species inventories exist, even if microorganisms are excluded. Moreover, such inventories as do exist for particular sites are often unpublished or hidden in the "gray literature" and may use different taxonomic systems. Collating, reconciling, and then analyzing this information is a major undertaking, although one that is becoming easier thanks to the spread of the internet.

Because of these limitations, analyses of coverage of species by protected areas invariably use surrogate measures for the whole of biodiversity, usually particular taxonomic groups that are well characterized in that area, often birds, sometimes other vertebrates (especially mammals), butterflies, and some groups of vascular plants. The assumption is that knowledge of these groups may give some indication of how well covered other taxonomic groups are. Empirical tests of this assumption, for example in the UK and South Africa, indicate that it often does not hold up very well – that is, for example, areas with a high diversity of butterflies do not necessarily have a high diversity of birds, and vice versa. However, other findings have been somewhat more encouraging – in Uganda, for example, it was found that protected areas that were rich in one group of species tended also to be rich in others.

Species-based analyses should, ideally, be based on actual records of species in protected areas. There is generally not enough information to do this, other than in a few intensively studied parts of the world. The alternative, much more approximate, approach is to map distributions of species using available information and then to overlay maps of protected areas on to these, in a way similar to that widely used for assessing habitat coverage. This approach allows first-order assessments of coverage, but in most cases is of limited accuracy. This is because, unless extremely detailed data are available, distributions of species are normally mapped as polygons showing the limits of their ranges. These ranges may be based entirely on field observations or may be extrapolated from them, generally using models of habitat suitability based on parameters such as climate, altitude, and soil type. Because species are virtually never ubiquitous within these limits, however the latter are derived, there is no guarantee that they will occur in any given protected area within or overlapping with the mapped range.

Areas with high diversity of butterflies do not necessarily indicate high diversity of birds.

W O'Byrne/UNEP

Terrestrial species coverage by the global protected areas network

Although global level data on species distributions are necessarily approximate, they can still yield valuable insights into the effectiveness of the existing protected area network in maintaining biodiversity, as in the global gap analysis carried out by Rodrigues *et al.* (2003). The analysis combined four very large datasets that are themselves the culmination of information-gathering efforts by thousands of individuals and dozens of institutions: the World Database on Protected Areas (WDPA); and global distribution maps for all mammals, amphibians, and globally threatened birds. The data on the world's globally threatened bird species were compiled by the BirdLife International partnership (BirdLife International, 2000).

Of the 1 183 globally threatened birds included in this analysis, 182 are critically endangered, 321 are endangered, and 680 are considered vulnerable species. Distribution maps for all mammal species were compiled as part of the IUCN Global Mammal Assessment (Boitani and Amori, unpublished; Sechrest, unpublished; Boitani et al., 1999; Patterson et al., 2003). All maps used were in draft form. In total, 4 734 mammal species were analyzed, including 131 critically endangered species, 229 endangered, and 618 vulnerable species. Distribution maps for amphibian species have been compiled by the ongoing Global Amphibian Assessment (IUCN-SSC and CI-CABS, 2003), with NatureServe providing the distribution maps for species in North America. Part of these correspond to reviewed data; others were still to be formally reviewed by experts. The analysis included 5 254 amphibians, including 291 critically endangered, 494 endangered, and 682 vulnerable species.

The analysis overlaid species distribution maps on to protected area maps using geographic information systems (GIS) to assess how well each species is represented in protected areas, and to identify gap species that are not covered in any part of their ranges.

The spatial units used in this analysis were of two types: protected and unprotected sites. Protected sites are individual or clusters of several protected areas, of variable area, while unprotected sites correspond to half-degree cells (~ 3 000 km² near the equator) from which protected sites were cut (i.e. there is no spatial overlap between protected and unprotected sites). Assessment of the highest priority areas for consolidation and expansion of the protected area network was based on information regarding irreplaceability and threat (Pressey, Johnson and Wilson, 1994; Margules and Pressey, 2000). Threat was calculated as the number of threatened species present at a site, weighting those with higher extinction risk. Sites of exceptional irreplaceability

and threat were identified as the most urgent conservation priorities (Pressey and Taffs, 2001). These include currently protected sites, which are clear priorities for strengthening the existing global network of protected areas, and unprotected sites which present priorities for the expansion of the global network.

The global gap analysis found on the basis of available data that at least 1 310 species (709 at risk of extinction) were not protected in any part of their ranges. In addition, a few thousand other bird, mammal, and amphibian species were represented only by marginal overlaps with existing protected areas. Amphibians overall were the group least covered by protected areas compared with birds or mammals. This is mainly due to their smaller ranges (higher levels of endemism), but also because they have received much less conservation attention than either birds or mammals.

Tropical forests, especially in regions of topographic complexity, and islands make up most of the areas highlighted as urgent priorities, both for strengthening and for the expansion of the global network of protected areas. Proportionally, Asia is a higher priority for the expansion of the global network, while the need for strengthening the existing network is mainly emphasized in Africa and South America.

Areas highlighted as urgent priorities for the expansion of the global protected area network (Figure 2.2) are mainly located in regions long recognized to be centers of endemism that are suffering high levels of habitat destruction. In the Americas, these include parts of Central America, the Caribbean, the Andes, and the Atlantic Forest region of Brazil. In Africa, identified important areas are mainly located in eastern Madagascar, the Cape Fynbos, the Succulent Karoo, Maputaland-Pondoland, the Eastern Arc, the Albertine Rift, the Ethiopian Highlands, the Cameroon Highlands, and the Kenyan Highlands. In Asia, highlighted areas include the Western Ghats and Sri Lanka, the eastern Himalayas, southwest, southeast, and central China, and continental and insular Southeast Asia. In Australia, urgent priority areas are mainly around coastal areas, particularly the Queensland Wet Tropics, the Kimberley tropical savanna, and the southeastern and southwestern regions.

These areas should be priorities for finer scale assessments, to investigate the feasibility and viability of expanding the existing protected area network while effectively protecting the species

Figure 2.1: Global distribution of protected sites of high urgency for consolidating the global network of protected areas in covering mammals, amphibians and threatened birds. These are protected sites (single or clusters of several protected areas) of high irreplaceability, for which it is fundamental to ensure that proper management is in place.

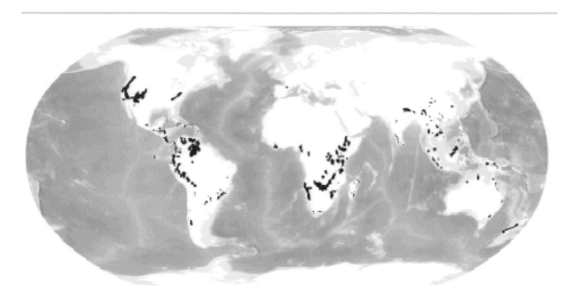

in each area that trigger their high values of irreplaceability and threat.

Protected sites identified as urgent for the consolidation of the global network (Figure 2.1) include some large complexes of protected areas in western North America, the Guyana Shield of South America, and areas in tropical and subtropical Africa. In addition, many smaller protected areas (not so visible at the global scale of Figure 2.1) are also highlighted as highly irreplaceable and threatened among the global network of protected areas, and these tend to be located in centers of endemism such as Southeast Asia, the Western Ghats (India), Madagascar, the Atlantic Forests of Brazil, the Andes, and Central America.

The results obtained in this analysis clearly demonstrate that the number of endemic species in a country is a powerful predictor of how much more protection is needed to ensure coverage of vertebrate species (Figure 2.2).

Habitat and ecosystem-based approaches

An alternative to the species-based approach is to use higher levels of biological organization: communities, habitats, and ecosystems. There are a number of advantages. In the first instance they may help to capture more of the ecological processes that contribute to the maintenance of ecosystem function (although this is still under debate). Secondly, they can in theory be mapped

Figure 2.2: Global distribution of unprotected sites (at half-degree resolution) of high urgency for the expansion of the global network of protected areas, in order to cover mammals, amphibians and threatened birds.

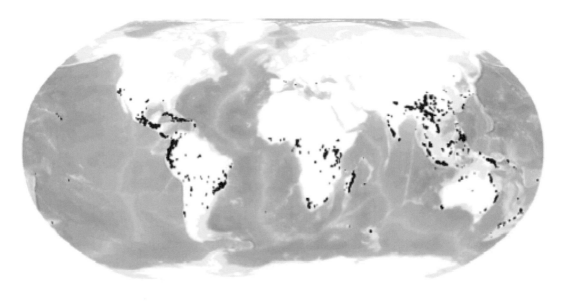

more easily over wide areas, particularly in light of the growing availability of remote-sensing data, and the growing sophistication of techniques for analyzing such data.

There are, however, persistent and non-trivial problems of definition and classification. Certainly, at global level, a universally accepted global habitat classification system has yet to be developed. This is not surprising – these systems are all essentially predicated on the assumption that the natural environment can be divided into a series of discrete, discontinuous units that can be given a label, either one that is highly simplified,for example forest or wetland, or a detailed and specific one, such as mixed alder-willow scrub.

In reality, the natural world is generally better represented as a highly variable natural continuum, where it is often virtually impossible to say where one habitat type begins and another ends. Even where simplified categories are used, it is extremely difficult to define and delimit them in a universally agreed way: for example, it is not possible to determine for how long, how regularly, and how intensively an area must be flooded before it can be classified as aquatic rather than as a terrestrial ecosystem. Similarly, the amount of tree cover present before an area is classified as a woodland rather than, say, a savanna or parkland, cannot be defined other than arbitrarily. Furthermore, almost all parts of the terrestrial world, at least, are to

---

BOX 2.1: WWF AND LARGE-SCALE BIOGEOGRAPHIC REGIONS

Comprehensive representation of existing habitats in protected area networks is one of the key goals of biodiversity conservation. Maps of biogeographic units at various scales can provide a useful framework for assessing such representation. They take into account the fact that the distributions of species and biological communities rarely coincide with political units and they approximate the dynamic arena within which ecological processes most strongly interact. This means that designing protected area networks within them is one of the best ways of ensuring the persistence of populations and ecological processes, although it does present significant challenges in working across administrative boundaries (Soulé and Terborgh, 1999; Groves *et al*, 2000; Margules and Pressey, 2000). Since the late 1990s, WWF has devoted a substantial proportion of its energies and resources to an effort now called Ecoregion Conservation, which uses what are essentially biogeographic regions for conservation planning. WWF has defined an ecoregion as a large area of land or water that contains a geographically distinct assemblage of natural communities that: share a large majority of their species and ecological dynamics; share similar environmental conditions; and interact ecologically in ways that are critical for their long-term persistence. Ecoregion Conservation aims to address the four goals of biodiversity conservation as espoused by Noss (1992): representation of all habitats in protected areas; maintenance of ecological and evolutionary processes; maintenance of viable populations of all species, and accounting for environmental change.

Believing that none of the existing global maps of biogeographic units provided the appropriate tractable spatial resolution necessary to plan protected area networks, WWF went about creating its own map of terrestrial ecoregions. For this it relied predominantly on a patchwork of existing regional classification systems used as a baseline for ecoregion boundaries, combined with other data and consultations from regional experts. Most existing systems required aggregating or dividing units, or modifying boundaries. It was acknowledged from the beginning that no single biogeographic framework would be optimal for all taxa – the WWF ecoregions reflect what the organization considered the best compromise for as many taxa as possible. It recognizes 825 terrestrial ecoregions around the globe, with a mean size of around 150 000 km^2 and a median size of just over 56 000 km^2. Working with The Nature Conservancy and other partners, comprehensive maps for freshwater and marine ecoregions have now also been developed.

WWF's Global 200 analysis (Olson and Dinerstein, 1998) relied heavily on the comprehensive terrestrial ecoregion framework. The Global 200 analysis scored the terrestrial ecoregions for species endemism, richness, and intact ecological phenomena. It also identified similarly outstanding freshwater and marine regions of the world. The resulting map of 238 ecoregions has become WWF's roadmap for the focus of its conservation activities, at least for the next decade or so.

some extent modified by human activity. Habitat classification systems have to decide whether to take this into account – describe actual conditions in any given place – or try to show potential conditions, that is the kind of habitat that might historically have been present or that might be expected in the absence of human influence.

Habitat or ecosystem analysis at the global level is also not easy to relate to other levels of biodiversity, particularly species. This is because similar habitats in different parts of the world may be formed by quite different assemblages of species. Because of this, what proportion of the world's tropical moist forests, for example, are protected gives relatively little information in itself on what proportion of the world's tropical moist forest species are protected.

Performing habitat or ecosystem analyses at continental, regional, or smaller scales helps to overcome this problem. In these cases, similar habitats are likely to share a significant proportion of their species, so that there is likely to be quite a good relationship between assessments of coverage of biodiversity at the habitat or ecosystem level and that at the species level. In addition, it is easier to produce consistent and widely acceptable habitat classification systems and associated maps at these scales. This regional, habitat-based approach was first used in the protected areas systems reviews undertaken in the 1980s by IUCN – The World Conservation Union.

Biogeographic approaches

Biogeographic approaches are essentially extensions of regional habitat- or ecosystem-based approaches. They are based on the observation that particular groups or associations of plants and animals are characteristic of particular regions and often confined to them. The protected area coverage in each of these regions is then measured, with the assumption that this will provide a measure of the degree of protection afforded to those groups or associations. Typically, such biogeographical approaches have a hierarchical character, and can be used to analyze coverage at a range of spatial scales.

For many years, the basis for such analyses when carried out for terrestrial ecosystems was that developed by Udvardy in 1975. Under this the land area of the world is divided into eight biogeographical realms, continent or subcontinent-sized areas, which are further subdivided into 193

provinces defined by significant differences in flora, fauna, or vegetation structure. The provinces range in size from a mere 11 km^2 in the case of South Trinidade Province in the Neotropical Realm to over 10 million km^2 in the case of Maudlandia Province, one of the two provinces in the Antarctic Realm. More recently, this concept has been modified and refined in the ecoregion approach developed principally by WWF, the global conservation organization (see Box 2.1).

HABITAT COVERAGE BY THE PROTECTED AREAS NETWORK

Assessing habitat coverage of protected areas at the global level requires, at the very least, a comprehensive and consistent habitat classification system that can be applied across the world, a reliable global map based on such a system, and a similarly reliable global map of protected areas. Each of these presents difficulties.

Once a single global habitat classification system is agreed upon, a reliable map needs to be created using such a system. Before the widespread availability of remote-sensing technologies this was quite problematic; although there were many excellent national or local land-cover or habitat maps, these had been produced using a whole range of different classification systems, with different methodologies and with different degrees of accuracy and resolution. Reconciling these to produce one consistent system applicable across national boundaries proved challenging.

Remote-sensing technologies have, in the last two decades, revolutionized our ability to observe the surface of the planet and to monitor changes. However, their use still depends on careful analysis and on the application of agreed classification systems. For the analysis used in this volume the Global Landcover 2000 (GLC2000) dataset was taken as a starting point for the land-based habitat information. This dataset was developed through the European Commission's Joint Research Centre and has been produced through a partnership of more than 30 institutions. It is based on SPOT 4 satellite imagery taken between November 1999 and December 2000. In order to establish a consistent base, all participants have agreed to work towards a globally consistent legend based on the Food and Agriculture Organization of the United Nations (FAO) Land Cover Classification System (FAO 2000). At the same time, the use of considerable regional expertise has ensured a

TABLE 2.1: MAJOR HABITAT TYPES, THEIR GLOBAL COVERAGE, AND THE AREAS PROTECTED
(in all sites including IUCN Categories I-VI and those with no category assigned)

Habitat	Total area (km^2)	Area protected (km^2)	IUCN categories I-IV (km^2)	% of total area protected	% of total in I-IV
Temperate and boreal needleleaf forest	10 749 000	1 539 000	1 263 000	14	12
Temperate broadleaf and mixed forest[1]	10 322 000	1 256 000	1 107 000	12	11
Tropical moist forest	12 104 000	2 798 000	1 579 000	23	13
Tropical dry forest	3 172 000	342 000	230 000	11	7
Open forests[2]	3 815 000	605 000	455 000	16	12
Savanna	13 010 000	1 653 000	1 178 000	13	9
Grassland (temperate)	7 551 000	1 175 000	1 094 000	16	14
Warm desert and semi-desert	22 269 000	2 242 000	2 123 000	10	10
Cold desert and semi-desert	7 285 000	606 000	550 000	8	8
Tundra	4 682 000	710 000	668 000	15	14
Shrubland	6 970 000	914 000	621 000	13	9
Inland waters[3]	5 078 000	628 000	545 000	12	11
Permanent snow and ice	15 404 000	1 130 000	1 118 000	7	7
Predominantly anthropogenic[4]	24 581 000	1 413 000	1 020 000	6	4
Ocean	362 630 000	1 639 000	1 578 000	0.5	0.4
Total	509 622 000	18 650 000	15 129 000	4	3

1   Includes some subtropical and tropical predominantly needleleaf forest.
2   Includes tropical savanna/tree-cover mosaic.
3   Includes non-marine water bodies, wetland, and mangroves.
4   Includes cropland and natural vegetation mosaic.
NB Figures for area protected, rounded to the nearest thousand km2, are based on the World Database on Protected Areas 2003.
Table excludes some 400 000 km2 for which no habitat data are available.

much greater degree of quality assurance than earlier land-cover assessments, while information from other sensors has been used to refine particular elements (Barolome *et al.*, 2002).

Although GLC2000 was a base, various alterations were made in this map in order to produce habitat classes that were more closely allied to the habitat classes used by the contributors to this chapter. There were also some gaps in the overall coverage provided by this map, most notably for the far northern parts of Eurasia and some of the island groups. It was possible to fill some of these gaps with data available at UNEP-WCMC from other sources. In addition to the basic habitat analysis, some additional analyses using non-GLC2000 data were undertaken. These included those of mountains and marine environments and

these are presented in the relevant sections of this chapter.

Like all datasets, the GLC2000 contains error. Probably the greatest source of error comes from problems of interpretation and, despite the considerable involvement of regional expertise in the development of habitat layers, ground-truthing on a project of this scale is limited. It is therefore quite likely that some areas have been mis-identified. The resolution of the image analysis further compounds such error. With findings being summarized by single square kilometer (km2) pixels, patchwork landscapes and transitional areas can create confusing spectral signatures, leading to misidentification. Fine-scale habitats, such as riparian and coastal habitats, are generally missed or underrepresented. Finally there may be errors of

Mangrove forests lining a tidal creek, Bowling Green Bay National Park, Queensland, Australia (left).

Mixed conifer-deciduous forest, Kolovesi National Park, Finland (right).

spatial location – particularly noticeable when any single layer is combined with another. In the present study the mismatch between the GLC2000 and the higher resolution ocean layer held at UNEP-WCMC led to the occurrence of a considerable area of "no data" along the coastline in many areas.

The data on protected areas used in the analysis were derived from the World Database on Protected Areas as it stood in 2003. Of the just over 100 000 sites in this database, boundary inform-ation is held in a GIS for some 40 000 sites. For a further 37 000 or so, information is available describing the geographic coordinates of the central point, and there is also information on the size of the site. With this information it was possible to create buffered points (circles of the correct size centered on the known central point). Combining these two data sources provided approximate spatial extent and location information for over 70 percent of the sites in the database. This includes most of the largest sites and hence it can be assumed that it represents a minimum estimate of the total protected area coverage assessed in this study. (Of the remaining sites a further 15 percent have a known area, but location is not known (beyond the country); 12 percent have a location, but the size of the site is unknown, and 2 percent have no known size or location.)

The sources of the information within the database are highly varied, and it must be assumed that the spatial accuracy of the information contains similar variation. Errors are likely to arise both from

inaccuracy (points are simply wrong, with errors potentially varying from tens of meters to tens of kilometers) and from issues of resolution (with effectively the same results – maps prepared for low-resolution use may show increasing levels of spatial misplacement associated with "pushing" them beyond their true resolution). At the present time it is not possible to provide an assessment of the level of these errors within the database.

Forests

Under natural conditions, about half of the Earth's land surface would be expected to be covered with forest and woodland. Under human influence this proportion has been reduced to around one quarter. Remaining forests provide habitat for more than half of the world's species, generate about half of the global terrestrial annual net primary production, and house about 50 percent of the world's terrestrial carbon stocks. As global loss and degradation of forests is continuing, establishment and effective management of protected areas will be key to ensuring the preservation of global biodiversity and main-tenance of forest ecosystem functions.

What and where are forests?

Despite their importance to people and the large amount of research focused on forest ecosystems, it has proved difficult to agree a precise definition of "forest". While the term clearly indicates an ecosystem in which trees are the predominant life form, the problem arises because of the broad range of systems in which trees occur. For example, tree species may dominate at high altitude, but be barely recognizable as trees because of their spreading prostrate forms; savannas may have a significant presence of trees, but it is problematic to define where trees are predominant.

Problems in defining forest make it difficult to carry out consistent analyses at global or regional scale of remaining forest cover or rates of loss. FAO, which has an international mandate to assess and monitor global forest resources, has defined forest as area with greater than 10 percent tree crown cover (FAO, 2001), but this definition includes sparse tree cover not considered as forest by many other organizations.

Forests and woodlands were originally distributed throughout the temperate and tropical latitudes of the Earth, except for areas of desert climate or extreme high altitude or latitude, as well as some areas of prairie and steppe. The factors determining their distribution are largely climatic: tree establishment and growth require a minimum number of days in the year with adequate climatic conditions for active growth. Substrate characteristics are also important: trees require access to enough soil for nutrient and water supply. Other non-anthropogenic factors limiting the distribution of forests include flooding, the incidence of wildfire, and the presence of toxic minerals in the substrate.

The forms and types of forest vary greatly throughout the world. A number of global classification systems have been suggested, but as yet none has gained universal acceptance. The UNESCO (United Nations Educational, Scientific and Cultural Organization) system proposed by Ellenberg and Mueller-Dombois (UNESCO, 1993) includes nearly 100 forest and woodland "subformations" and allows for yet finer subdivisions, but many of the characteristics that separate categories can only be determined in the field. Other classifications, such as the Earth Resources Observation and Science (EROS) Data Centre seasonal land-cover regions, with nearly a thousand classes, reflect more strongly the nature of land-cover data obtained from Earth-orbiting satellites and the processes involved in their classification (Loveland et al., 2000). The vast range of physiognomic, phenological, and other variation among forest types that these classifications identify within the very broad FAO definition of forest can be aggregated loosely into five wide

categories: temperate and boreal needleleaf forests; temperate broadleaf and mixed forests; tropical moist forests; tropical dry forests; and sparse trees and parklands. Each of these broad categories has a particular distribution and encompasses many different specific forest types that have some characteristics in common.

Threats to forests and their biodiversity and rates of loss

The principal pressures on forests and their biodiversity are conversion to other land uses, principally forms of agriculture, logging, and other types of natural resource extraction, such as hunting. These factors are of varying importance in different parts of the world and in different forest types. For example, conversion of forest to agriculture is the main cause of tropical moist forest loss, but is of negligible importance in boreal needleleaf forests. Timber extraction is an important pressure on biodiversity in both tropical and temperate forests. In 2000, global consumption of industrial roundwood was more than 1 500 million m^3 (FAO, 2003), and was projected to continue to rise.

Approaches to timber extraction vary among forest types, from clear-cutting in temperate needleleaf forests to selective logging in most tropical forest types. The impacts on logged ecosystems can be severe, though practices designed to reduce the negative effects are becoming more widely used. There is also strong evidence that logging can increase the probability of wildfire in temperate forests and even in tropical moist forests not usually subject to burning (Holdsworth and Uhl, 1997; Cochrane et al., 2002). Many tree species have suffered extensive population and genetic losses as a result of commercial exploitation. Furthermore, logging operations create access to forest areas that may otherwise have remained isolated. This improved access facilitates hunting and other activities that exert pressure on forest biodiversity, and may ultimately lead to colonization and conversion of the land to agricultural use.

In addition to loss of area, forest conversion and logging lead to changes in the condition or quality of the remaining forest. These can include fragmentation of large areas of continuous forest. Tropical forest fragments are distinct from continuous forests in both ecology and composition (Laurance and Bierregaard, 1997). There are physical and biotic gradients associated with fragment edges, and forest

I McAllister/UNEP

Old-growth coastal temperate rainforest, Koeye River, British Columbia, Canada.

structure undergoes radical change near edges as a result of the impacts of wind and increased tree mortality. Fragments are also more vulnerable to fire (Cochrane, 2001). Some animal species are "edge avoiders" and decline in abundance in forest fragments, while others become more abundant. Some non-forest and even non-native species of plants and animals successfully invade forest fragments but not continuous forest. In addition to affecting canopy composition directly, removal of large timber trees may also affect the availability of seed for regeneration and may affect animal species that depend on the timber species.

In many areas, wildfire is an important factor affecting the state and dynamics of forest eco-systems. It is particularly important in high-latitude coniferous forest, Mediterranean ecosystems, and in tropical dry forests. Logging activity and other forms of forest disturbance that alter the forest microenvironment increase the susceptibility to fire of many forest ecosystems and thus alter both the frequency and intensity of wildfire damage.

In countries with low forest cover, fuelwood collection combined with grazing is the principal cause of forest degradation (FAO, 2003). Globally, fuelwood and charcoal consumption more than doubled between 1961 and 1991, and was projected to rise by another 30 percent to 2 400 million m³ by 2010 (FAO, 2001).

Other factors that affect forests and their biodiversity include acid rain and global climate change. So far, most of the effects of acid precip-itation, which is caused by industrial air pollutants,

have been documented in temperate needleleaf forests and associated waterways of Europe and North America. Data on current trends in forest cover change reveal that the rates of deforestation continue to be high in the developing countries of the tropics, in both absolute and proportional terms. In contrast, temperate countries are losing forests at lower rates, or indeed showing a net increase in their forest area, principally due to active programs of plantation establishment, but also because of some natural afforestation in abandoned agricultural lands or areas logged during the 19th and early 20th centuries. FAO (2001) estimated the annual global loss of natural forest cover during the 1990s at 160 000 km², leading to a total loss over the decade of just over 4 percent of global natural forest cover. The bulk of this loss (c. 150 000 km²) was in the tropics, with 9 000 km² of natural forest lost outside the tropics. FAO suggests, therefore, that the rate of loss of natural forest has remained steady or declined slightly in comparison with the previous decade.

Forest protection status

Combining the most recent version of the World Database on Protected Areas with an approximate map of global forest cover derived from the Global Landcover database, it can be estimated that in the order of 11 to 12 percent of the world's current forest area falls within protected areas in IUCN Categories I–VI with an estimated additional 4 to 5 percent included in protected areas that have not been assigned to any one of the IUCN categories.

Based on the combined WDPA/GLC2000 analysis (using 2003 WDPA data), tropical moist forests are the forests that have the highest proportion of remaining cover protected, with around 13 percent of their extent recorded as included in protected areas belonging to IUCN Management Categories I–VI (Table 2.1). In addition, a further 10 percent is recorded by the analysis as occurring in protected areas for which no IUCN management category has been assigned. Globally, tropical dry forests are the least protected with only around 7 percent of their area apparently included in Categories I–VI and another 4 percent in areas with no category assigned. Temperate broadleaf and mixed forests, and temperate and boreal needleleaf forests, are intermediate, with around 11 to 12 percent protected in areas with Categories I–VI and a further 1 or 2 percent in areas with no category assigned.

Temperate and boreal needleleaf forests

Temperate and boreal needleleaf forests are estimated to cover around 11 million km², with a further 1.6 million km² or so of sparse forest. They mostly occupy the higher latitude regions of the northern hemisphere, as well as high-altitude zones and some warm temperate areas, especially on nutrient-poor or otherwise unfavorable soils. These forests are composed entirely, or nearly so, of coniferous species (Pinophyta). In the northern hemisphere, pines *Pinus*, spruces *Picea*, larches *Larix*, silver firs *Abies*, Douglas firs *Pseudotsuga*, and hemlocks *Tsuga* dominate the canopy, but other taxa are also important. In the southern hemisphere coniferous trees, including members of the Araucariaceae, Cupressaceae, and Podocarpaceae, often occur in mixtures with broadleaf species in systems that are classed as broadleaf and mixed forests.

Although tree species richness is low in most temperate and boreal needleleaf forests, old growth conifer stands, which may be many centuries old, represent an irreplaceable gene pool and an important habitat for many other organisms. Botanical species richness in these forests is commonly increased by a relatively high diversity of mosses and lichens, which grow both on the ground and on tree trunks and branches. For example, there are at least 100 species of moss growing in the coniferous forests between 1 300 and 2 000 m altitude on Baekdu Mountain, Democratic People's Republic of Korea (Hoang Ho-dzung, 1987). Vertebrate richness is generally lower in boreal needleleaf forests than in broadleaf temperate and tropical forests, and many species are wide-ranging generalists, often with a Holarctic distribution, for example, wolf *Canis lupus*, brown bear *Ursus arctos*.

Some of the conifer species within these forests, notably the giant redwood *Sequoiadendron giganteum*, are considered vulnerable to extinction (Farjon and Page, 1999), and a number of animals of conservation concern are dependent on temperate needleleaf forests. For example, the northern spotted owl *Strix occidentalis caurina* requires large expanses of old-growth coniferous forest in the northwest USA to provide nesting habitat and adequate food resources. Kirtland's warbler *Dendroica kirtlandii* needs young re-growing jack pine as a nesting habitat, and fire suppression programs have reduced the available habitat for this species to critical levels. While

TABLE 2.2: PROTECTION OF TEMPERATE AND BOREAL NEEDLELEAF FORESTS

Region	Ecosystem area (km²)	Protected area (km²)	% protected
Australia/New Zealand	8 000	400	5
East Asia	457 000	64 000	14
Europe	824 000	99 000	12
North Africa and Middle East	42 000	1 500	3
North America	3 660 000	835 000	23
North Eurasia	5 756 000	539 000	9

Analysis based on GLC2000 and WDPA 2003 data
Figures rounded to nearest thousand km²

there is relatively little information available on the conservation status of invertebrates, many common old-growth species are known to become much rarer in modern managed forests, often through the loss of essential microhabitats (Väisänen *et al.*, 1993).

Temperate needleleaf forests have lost about 30 percent of their potential area (UNEP-WCMC, 2002). The principal factors affecting them are clear-felling and fire. They are also susceptible to the impacts of acid rain and are believed likely to be particularly vulnerable to global climate change through both range restrictions and increasing fire frequency (IPCC, 2001).

Important protected areas for needleleaf forests include the Virgin Komi Forest complex, a World Heritage site in the northern Urals in Russia, which covers nearly 3 million hectares in total;

Beech forest, Rock Cities of the Bohemian Paradise Protected Landscape, Czech Republic.

S. Chape

TABLE 2.3: PROTECTION OF TEMPERATE BROADLEAF AND MIXED FORESTS

Region	Ecosystem area (km^2)	Protected area (km^2)	% protected
Australia/New Zealand	616 000	154 000	25
Caribbean	37 000	11 000	29
Central America	55 000	8 000	14
East Asia	1 836 000	192 000	10
Eastern and Southern Africa	95 000	7 000	7
Europe	985 000	112 000	11
North Africa and Middle East	61 000	2 000	4
North America	3 302 000	469 000	14
North Eurasia	2 926 000	239 000	8
South America	275 000	45 000	16
South Asia	129 000	13 000	10
Southeast Asia	5 000	4 000	82

Analysis based on GLC2000 and WDPA 2003 data
Figures rounded to nearest thousand km^2

Redwood National Park and World Heritage Site in California, USA, which includes important old-growth stands of redwood *Sequoia sempervirens*, including the world's tallest known living tree; and Wood Buffalo National Park and World Heritage Site in Canada, which also includes important wetland areas, including the only breeding site of the endangered whooping crane *Grus americana*.

Temperate broadleaf and mixed forests

Temperate broadleaf and mixed forests now cover about 10 million km^2 of the Earth's surface. They include such forest types as the mixed deciduous forests of the USA and their counterparts in China and Japan, including freshwater swamps and bottom-land forests throughout the temperate zone, the broadleaf evergreen rainforests of Chile, Japan, New Zealand, and Tasmania, and the sclerophyllous forests of Australia, California, USA, and the Mediterranean. Many of these forests have a significant presence of needleleaf and other coniferous species. Depending on the precise forest type, these forests tend to be structurally more complex than pure coniferous forests, having more layers in the canopy.

As might be expected from their structural diversity, temperate broadleaf and mixed forests are generally richer in species than coniferous forests. Southern mixed hardwood forests in the USA are commonly composed of as many as 20 canopy and subcanopy tree species and may include as many as 30 overstory species (Barnes, 1991). In comparison, European forests tend to be less species rich, while the deciduous forests of East Asia may be the richest of all (Ching, 1991; Schaefer, 1991). While many species in northern broadleaf forests are widespread in distribution, the more isolated temperate forests of southern South America, Australia, and New Zealand contain a significant number of restricted-range and endemic species.

About 60 percent of the potential cover of temperate broadleaf and mixed forests has disappeared, much of it having been converted to agriculture at various times during the Holocene. In parts of Europe and North America, however, the area of forest of this kind has stabilized or even increased in the past few decades.

A number of species from temperate broadleaf and mixed forests are of conservation concern. Japan alone has 43 threatened endemic tree species, which are mostly characteristic of its temperate broadleaf forests (Ohba, 1996), while most of the 140 globally threatened conifer taxa (Hilton-Taylor, 2000) occur in mixed forests, particularly those in the southern hemisphere. Threatened animal species of these forests include several New Zealand forest birds, such as the kakapo (*Strigops habroptilus*) and some kiwi species (*Apteryx* spp.); Leadbeater's possum (*Gymnobelideus leadbeateri*), an arboreal marsupial from southeastern Australia; the Amami rabbit *Pentalagus furnessi* of Amami Island (Japan); and several deer, including the South American southern huemul *Hippocamelus bisulcus* and southern pudu *Pudu puda*. Loss of habitat, hunting, and introduced predators are major threats to these and other animals of temperate broadleaf and mixed forests.

Notable protected areas include the complex of national parks and other areas that make up the 1.4 million hectare Tasmanian Wilderness World Heritage Area, with important stands of *Eucalyptus*-dominated temperate rainforest, the combined Belovezhskaya Puscha (Belarus) and Bialowieza Forest (Poland) National Parks, Biosphere Reserve and World Heritage Site, home of the European bison *Bison bonasus,* and Los Glaciares National Park and World Heritage Site in Argentina, which contains extensive areas of southern beech *Nothofagus* harboring a vestigial population of southern huemul.

Tropical moist forests

Tropical moist forests cover perhaps 12 million km² of the humid tropics and include many different forest types. The best known and most extensive are the lowland evergreen broadleaf rainforests including, for example, the seasonally inundated *várzea* and *igapó* forests and the *terra firme* forests of the Amazon Basin, the high forests of the Congo Basin, and the peat forests and moist dipterocarp forests of Southeast Asia. Together these make up more than half of the total remaining area of tropical moist forest, the great majority in two areas: the Amazon Basin in South America and the Congo Basin in Africa. Most mountain forests in the tropics are moist forests. These include cloud forest – the middle- to high-altitude forests that derive a significant part of their water supply from the clouds, and support a rich abundance of epiphytes. Mangrove forests and other swamp forests also fall within this broad category.

Many tropical moist forests have canopies 40 to 50 m tall, and some have emergent trees that rise above the main canopy to heights of 60 m or more. Such large-stature forests are characteristic of lowland forests and some lower montane forests on relatively nutrient-rich soils. Another characteristic of these forests is a relatively high frequency of woody lianas and, especially in the neotropics, palms (Gentry, 1988a). Moist tropical forests are also known for a high abundance and diversity of vascular epiphytes, which take advantage of the higher light availability found in the canopy and can survive because of abundant rainfall and high atmospheric moisture. On more nutrient-poor soils and at higher altitudes, forest stature decreases substantially; communities in upper montane environments (elfin forests) may be no more than a few meters tall.

In numerical terms, global terrestrial species diversity is concentrated in tropical rainforests. Generally speaking, the wet tropical forests of Africa have a lower tree species richness than those of Asia and America (Table 2.4), but there is great local variation. Within the Amazon Basin, for example, tree species richness ranges from 87 species per hectare in the east (Pires, 1957) to 285 species in central Amazonia (de Oliveira and Mori, 1999) and nearly 300 species in the west (Gentry, 1988b). The high diversity of epiphytes and lianas in lowland evergreen rainforests adds to the total botanical richness and parallels the pattern for trees, being much higher in neotropical forests than

in other regions (Benzing, 1989). Not all tropical moist forests are so rich in species. Mangrove ecosystems have low tree species diversity and generally low animal diversity despite their sometimes high productivity. Extremely nutrient-poor soils, such as white sands, lead to the development of low-diversity forests including *bana* and *campina* (Prance, 1989). As climate becomes more seasonal, tree species richness tends to decline (see dry forests, below); increasing altitude also tends to reduce species richness although isolated high-altitude areas tend to have a high proportion of endemic species (Jenkins, 1992).

Tropical moist forests are equally important for animal diversity. In Africa, the Guineo-Congolean forest block contains more than 80 percent of African primate species, and nearly 70 percent of African passerine birds and butterflies

TABLE 2.4: TREE SPECIES RICHNESS IN TROPICAL MOIST FORESTS
(after Phillips *et al.*, 1994)

Region	No. of tree species (>10 cm diameter at breast height) per hectare
Africa	56–92
Americas	56–285
Southeast Asia	108–240

TABLE 2.5: PROTECTION OF TROPICAL MOIST FOREST

Region	Ecosystem area (km²)	Protected area (km²)	% protected
Australia/New Zealand	160 000	29 000	18
Caribbean	12 000	3 000	25
Central America	246 000	83 000	34
East Asia	72 000	13 000	18
Eastern and Southern Africa	193 000	42 000	22
North America	204 000	15 000	7
Pacific	372 000	35 000	9
South America	6 846 000	1 924 000	28
South Asia	172 000	25 000	14
Southeast Asia	1 577 000	319 000	20
Western and Central Africa	2 250 000	310 304	14

Analysis based on GLC2000 and WDPA 2003 data
Figures rounded to nearest thousand km².

SChape

Lowland tropical forest, Tetepare Island community-conserved area, Solomon Islands.

(Jenkins, 1992). About half of the 1 100 South American reptile species are found in moist forests, with around 300 of these endemic to the habitat (Harcourt and Sayer, 1996).

Tropical moist forest cover is now about 45 percent of its potential extent (UNEP-WCMC, 2002). Conversion to agriculture is the major cause of tropical moist forest loss. This is due both to large-scale agricultural expansion and to expanding rural populations using shifting cultivation at an intensity that does not permit adequate fallow periods. Government resettlement programs that have moved large numbers of poor farmers have increased the rate of land colonization and clearance in parts of Southeast Asia and Latin America. In some areas, land has been converted to ranching principally as a means of gaining title in order to permit speculation in land values. Thus, population growth, poverty, and inequitable land tenure are among the causes underlying deforestation by conversion to agriculture.

In most regions, tropical forests at low altitude on fertile soils are those subject to major pressure as they are the prime targets for conversion to agricultural land. In many areas (e.g. Java and Sumatra in Indonesia, eastern Madagascar, West Africa, and southeastern Brazil) they have already been almost entirely cleared, leaving remnants in increasingly isolated protected areas. There are exceptions, however: in New Guinea the highest human population densities occur, and most forest conversion has taken place, at higher altitudes, with many lowland areas relatively undisturbed until recently, although these too are now under increasing pressure.

Because of the high rates of diversity in tropical moist forests and, often, high rates of local endemism, there are protected areas of global importance for biodiversity in every biogeographic region in which such forests occur. However, precisely because of this high diversity, and because of the difficulties of sampling and surveying species in tropical moist forests, the biota of such areas is almost invariably incompletely known. It is probably safe to say that there is, for example, no remotely comprehensive list of invertebrate species for any tropical moist forest protected area. For some areas that have been the focus of study and interest for many years there may be reasonably good inventories of some animal groups – usually birds, primates, and crodocilians; sometimes carnivores, ungulates, and chelonians; and occasionally butterflies (though rarely all Lepidoptera), amphibians, and lizards.

The situation is essentially similar for plants. For a tiny number of small, well-studied protected areas (usually associated with research stations, such as Barro Colorado Nature Monument, Panama) there are complete or nearly complete floristic inventories; for some other areas there may be reasonably good lists of tree species, often based on forest inventory work; here and elsewhere particular groups (e.g. cycads, palms, ferns, orchids) may be well known if they have been the focus of particular interest.

Despite this incomplete knowledge, it is possible to identify in each region protected areas that are certainly of particular importance for biodiversity, at least when measured in terms of species diversity. Some have been declared World Heritage sites, although this has not necessarily guaranteed effective protection, and in 2007 a significant number of these areas were on the World Heritage In Danger List, including all the sites in the Democratic Republic of the Congo.

On paper at least, a remarkably high proportion – nearly one quarter – of remaining tropical moist forest cover is included in some kind of protected area. However, caution must be exercised when interpreting this figure, and in particular in concluding that the overall conservation status of tropical moist forests is satisfactory, or at least better than that for other forest types. In the first instance, because (as with the statistics presented for other biomes) this figure is a proportion of existing forest cover protected, it does not indicate what percentage of original or potential forest is covered – indeed, if, as is evidently the case, forest continues to be cleared outside protected areas at a faster rate than forest inside protected areas, then the percentage of forest protected will continue to increase, even if the actual area protected remains static or even decreases (through deforestation within protected areas). If all forest outside protected areas were cleared, the proportion protected would rise to 100 percent with no additional forest having been protected.

Second, nearly half of protected forest is in areas for which no IUCN management category has been assigned. Much of this undoubtedly comprises forest reserves of various kinds – areas that are slated for timber production and other extractive uses. These do not have biodiversity conservation as their major aim, although they may still be important for many components of biodiversity.

Third, a global-level analysis of this kind does not differentiate between different categories of tropical moist forest. As noted above, lowland tropical moist forests are generally under much higher pressure than montane forests and, conversely, a much higher proportion of the latter is likely to be included in protected areas. In Southeast Asia, for example, montane areas overall are far more highly protected than non-montane areas (roughly 19 percent protected compared with 8 percent for non-montane).

Protected areas that are important for tropical moist forests include: Manu National Park, a biosphere reserve and World Heritage site in Peru, which covers some 1.8 million hectares in total, and is home to over 800 species of bird as well as globally threatened mammals such as the endangered giant otter *Pteronura brasiliensis*; the 1.3 million hectare Okapi Faunal Reserve and World Heritage Site in the Democratic Republic of the Congo, which covers around one fifth of the Ituri Forest in the Congo River basin, and has important populations of okapi *Okapia johnstoni* and chimpanzee *Pan troglodytes*, and was included in 1998 on the World Heritage In Danger List; and Ujong Kulon National Park and World Heritage Site in Indonesia, which is believed to be the last viable natural refuge of the critically endangered Javan rhinoceros *Rhinoceros sondaicus*.

Tropical dry forests

Tropical dry forests are those forests in the tropics that are subject to prolonged, usually seasonal drought. Such seasonal climates characterize much of the land between 10° and 30° latitude in all three major tropical regions, but only around 3 million km² of tropical dry forests remain. Throughout the tropics they have been converted for agriculture and pasture land. The principal zones of tropical dry forest in the Neotropics are along the Pacific coast of Central America and northern Colombia and Venezuela, in southeastern Bolivia, Paraguay, and northern Argentina, and in the northeast of Brazil. In Africa, the denser categories of miombo woodland are tropical dry forest as is some of the transitional forest at the edge of the Sahel. Large expanses of tropical dry forest were once characteristic of India and the seasonally dry areas of Southeast Asia, including northern Thailand and Cambodia. Dry forests occur in rain-shadow areas throughout the world, including some intermountain valleys, for example in the Andes, and the leeward sides of many tropical islands.

Though of lower species richness than tropical moist forests, tropical dry forests still have appreciably more tree species than most temperate forests. The richest neotropical dry forests are not the wettest ones, but those in western Mexico and in the Chaco of southeast Bolivia. These forests have around 90 woody species per 0.1 ha sample (Gentry, 1995) and have high rates of plant species endemism relative to wet forests in the tropics. Vertebrate species diversity is lower in dry forests than in moist forests, but many dry forests have high

TABLE 2.6: PROTECTION OF TROPICAL DRY FOREST

Region	Ecosystem area (km²)	Protected area (km²)	% protected
Central America	3 000	700	21
East Asia	8 000	3 000	34
Eastern and Southern Africa	620 000	155 000	25
North America	275 000	18 000	6
South America	875 000	72 000	8
South Asia	500 000	44 000	9
Southeast Asia	188 000	22 000	12
Western and Central Africa	632 000	22 000	3

Analysis based on GLC2000 and WDPA 2003 data
Figures rounded to nearest thousand km².

P Vaucoulon/Still Pictures

Dry forest, Bemahara National Park, Madagascar.

rates of endemism among mammals, especially among groups such as insectivores and rodents (Ceballos, 1995). Remaining areas of dry forest are often important refuges for once widespread species. The Gir Forest of Gujarat (India) contains the only population of Asiatic lion *Panthera leo persica*, which was once found throughout much of southern Asia and the Middle East; the dry forests of western Madagascar are inhabited by around 40 percent of the island's endemic lemurs. Invertebrate species richness in tropical dry forests tends to be poorly known, but in groups such as Lepidoptera (butterflies and moths) and Hymenoptera (ants, bees, and wasps), richness may be comparable to adjacent wet forest (Janzen, 1988).

Their seasonal climates and the resulting relatively slow rates of tree growth make tropical dry forests especially susceptible to degradation by

overgrazing and overcollection of fuelwood. Of the major types of closed forest, tropical dry forest is believed overall to have lost the greatest proportion of its potential area, nearly 70 percent (UNEP-WCMC, 2002). It is also the major forest type with the lowest remaining proportion included in protected areas.

Because of their high degree of endemism and because degradation and conversion of tropical dry forests has progressed further than in wet forests, their biota are often highly threatened. Threatened dry forest species include Spix's macaw *Cyanopsitta spixii* (now almost certainly extinct in the wild), the Chacoan peccary *Catagonus wagneri*, Verreaux's sifaka *Propithecus verreauxi*, and the Madagascar flat-tailed tortoise *Pyxis planicauda*, all of which are at risk from habitat destruction and hunting.

Notable protected areas with dry tropical forest include Guanacaste Conservation Area and World Heritage Site in Costa Rica, Ankarafantsika National Park in western Madagascar, with populations of at least seven lemur species, and the Gir Forest in India.

Open forests

Open forests with tree canopies of around 10–30 percent crown cover occur principally in areas of transition from forested to non-forested landscapes. The two major zones in which these ecosystems occur are the boreal region and the seasonally dry tropics.

At high latitudes, north of the main zone of boreal forest or taiga, growing conditions are not adequate to maintain a continuous closed forest cover, so tree cover is both sparse and discontinuous. This vegetation is variously called open taiga, open lichen woodland, and forest tundra (Tukhanen, 1999). It is species poor, has high bryophyte cover, and is frequently affected by fire. It is important for the livelihoods of a number of groups of indigenous people, including the Saami and some groups of Inuit. Current analysis indicates around 1.5 million km² of such forest, of which something over 200 000 km² is included in protected areas.

In the seasonally dry tropics, decreasing soil fertility and increasing fire frequency are related to the transition from closed dry forest through open woodland to savanna. The open woodland ecosystems include the more open *Brachystegia* and *Isoberlinia* miombo woodlands of dry tropical Africa and parts of both the *caatinga* and *cerrado* vegetations of Brazil (Menaut *et al.*, 1995). There is est-

TABLE 2.7: PROTECTION OF BOREAL AND SUB-BOREAL OPEN FORESTS

Region	Ecosystem area (km²)	Protected area (km²)	% protected
East Asia	29 000	3 000	10
Europe	5 000	1 000	20
North America	1 164 000	174 000	15
North Eurasia	377 000	40 000	11

Analysis based on GLC2000 and WDPA 2003 data
Figures rounded to nearest thousand km².

imated to be just over 2 million km² of this open tree cover, most of it in Eastern and Southern Africa.

Based on WDPA 2003 data, we can estimate that nearly 400 000 km² of tropical open forests are included in protected areas. Important areas include: Chapada dos Veadeiros and Emas National Parks in Brazil, which together constitute a single World Heritage site with significant populations of threatened *cerrado* species such as the giant armadillo *Priodontes maximus*, maned wolf *Chrysocyon brachiurus*, and giant anteater *Myrmecophaga tridactyla*; the Selous Game Reserve and World Heritage Site in Tanzania, the largest game reserve in Africa with enormous expanses of miombo woodland; and Kaziranga National Park and World Heritage Site in Assam, India, which is largely a mosaic of seasonally flooded grassland and open forest, and contains the world's largest population of Indian rhinoceros *Rhinoceros unicornis* as well as many other threatened species, including the endangered hispid hare *Caprolagus hispidus*.

Non-forest habitats

Around 75 percent of the world's land surface is not forested, either because it has been converted by humans for other purposes, or because conditions are not suitable for forest growth, usually because the climate is too arid or too cold, or both. Of the cold climate areas, some 15 million km² are currently permanent snow and ice cover (although the proportion may decrease as global climates warm). Some 60 million km² of the remainder, or just under half of the land surface, consists of a range of dryland biomes. These comprise natural or semi-natural, but in places often heavily disturbed and degraded, vegetation types. These biomes are present in approximately half the countries in the world and include almost 70 percent of Africa, 35 percent of Asia, 80 percent of Australia, 20 percent of the Americas, and 8 percent of Europe.

These systems have a wide spectrum of moisture availability. They are often broken down into hyperarid, arid, semi-arid, or dry subhumid regimes, with numerous different habitats recognized within them. The distinction between many of them and more open forest habitats is arbitrary. Using a modified version of the GLC2000 analysis we recognize the following: shrublands, savannas, and tropical grasslands (including savanna/tropical shrubland mosaic, but excluding savanna/tree cover mosaic, which is included under open forests),

TABLE 2.8: PROTECTION OF TROPICAL OPEN FORESTS			
Region	Ecosystem area (km²)	Protected area (km²)	% protected
Australia/New Zealand	323 000	29 000	9
East Asia	70 000	5 000	7
Eastern and Southern Africa	1 313 000	314 000	24
Pacific	34 000	2 000	5
South America	247 000	9 000	3
South Asia	28 000	2 000	6
Southeast Asia	220 000	26 000	12

Analysis based on GLC2000 and WDPA 2003 data
Figures rounded to nearest thousand km².

temperate grasslands, warm deserts and semi-deserts, cold deserts and semi-deserts, and tundra.

Protected areas in non-forested habitats
Analysis using the GLC2000 and the 2003 WDPA indicated that around 10 percent of the area of non-forested natural or semi-natural habitat was included in protected areas with IUCN Management Categories I to VI. This is slightly less than the 12 percent of forested habitats. Moreover, a much smaller additional area – some 1.2 million km² or two percent of the total area – is included in protected areas for which no management category has been assigned, giving an overall coverage of 12 percent for non-forested habitats as opposed to around 16 to 17 percent for forested habitats.

Blue wildebeest (*Connochaetes taurinus*) grazing on tropical grassland, Ngorongoro, Tanzania.

R Fogel/UNEP

TABLE 2.9: PROTECTION OF TROPICAL SAVANNAS

Region	Ecosystem area (km²)	Protected area (km²)	% protected
Australia/New Zealand	2 006 000	138 000	7
Caribbean	27 000	1 700	6
Central America	11 000	800	7
East Asia	194 000	21 000	11
Eastern and Southern Africa	3 743 000	667 000	18
North Africa and Middle East	109 000	3 000	2
North America	961 000	111 000	12
Pacific	10 000	700	8
South America	1 984 000	196 000	10
South Asia	581 000	66 000	11
Southeast Asia	205 000	17 000	8
Western and Central Africa	3 177 000	430 000	14

Analysis based on GLC2000 and WDPA 2003 data
Figures rounded to nearest thousand km².

Comparing different habitat types, the present data indicate that cold deserts and semi-deserts are the least well protected, with only around 8 percent of the total included in protected areas. Preliminary analysis of the size of protected areas over 100 km² indicates considerable variation. Current data show that the average size of such protected areas globally in all biomes is about 570 km². The average size for temperate grassland protected areas is much less, only around 180 km². In striking contrast, protected areas in the tropical grasslands and savannas biome, while fewer in number, are significantly larger with an average

TABLE 2.10: PROTECTION OF TEMPERATE GRASSLANDS

Region	Ecosystem area (km²)	Protected area (km²)	% protected
Australia/New Zealand	619 000	100 000	16
East Asia	2 477 000	742 000	30
Eastern and Southern Africa	460 000	19 000	4
Europe	396 000	49 000	12
North Africa and Middle East	679 000	15 000	2
North America	1 300 000	120 000	9
North Eurasia	1 277 000	76 000	6
South America	299 000	44 000	15
South Asia	43 000	9 000	21

Analysis based on GLC2000 and WDPA 2003 data
Figures rounded to nearest thousand km².

size of more than 3 000 km². Protected areas for deserts also tend be much larger than the norm, with the average size of protected areas in both warm and cold deserts being just under 2 000 km².

Grasslands and savannas

Grasslands are dominated by grasses and shrub vegetation, and are maintained by fire, low rainfall, freezing temperatures, and grazing by herbivores, acting in various combinations. They currently constitute perhaps 15 percent of the world's terrestrial cover and are one of the most extensive of all the terrestrial biomes. Natural temperate grasslands generally occur in the interior of the large continental land masses, and in the rainshadow of the world's main mountain ranges where the continental climate brings harsh winter conditions along with hot, dry summers. Examples include North America's prairies (or Great Plains), the pampas of Argentina and southern Uruguay, the vast steppe of eastern Europe and Asia, the grasslands of southeastern Australia, the tussock grasslands of New Zealand, and the veld in South Africa.

Temperate grasslands are currently estimated to cover around 7.5 million km², around half of this (3.75 million km²) in East Asia and North Eurasia, and some 1.3 million km² in North America. Tropical savannas and grasslands cover around twice the area of temperate grasslands, although some 2 million km² are classified as savanna/tree cover mosaic and treated here under open forests. The best known tropical grasslands are the African savannas; the llanos and *cerrados* of Brazil and northern Uruguay; the grasslands of inner India, home to the Asian tiger; and the hummock grasslands or spinifex of central and northern Australia.

Natural grasslands can be very rich in plant species. A square meter of meadow steppe in Russia may have 40–50 species. The tall grass prairie in North America has been known to contain up to 300 species in 3 hectares. However, over large areas, grasslands tend to be homogeneous; therefore diversity does not rise steeply with increasing area.

Most natural grasslands support or originally supported large and diverse populations of native grazing mammals. Historically, the temperate grasslands of North America's interior were home to tens of millions of bison *Bison bison*, pronghorn antelope *Antilocapra americana*, mule deer *Odocoileus hemionus*, and elk *Cervus elaphus*. The

Serengeti continues to sustain an impressive assemblage of ungulates and predators, with one and a half million blue wildebeest *Connochaetes taurinus* still making their extraordinary annual migration across the plains of Tanzania and Kenya. The saiga antelope *Saiga tatarica*, once numbering in the millions, were a common sight on the steppes of eastern Europe and western Asia. Hundreds of thousands of Mongolian gazelle *Procapra gutturosa* still roam the steppes of eastern Mongolia. Though lesser known, their annual migration is considered one of the last great wildlife spectacles on earth.

A high proportion of plant biomass in grasslands, in the form of roots and rhizomes, is located underground; there is a high turnover of those parts of the plant above ground. One important consequence of this is that grassland soils, especially in more humid environments, are often rich in organic matter and are therefore particularly prone to conversion to cropland. Where not converted, grasslands are almost invariably used, often heavily, for domestic livestock grazing. Little temperate grassland, in particular, is now in anything like its natural or undisturbed state.

The impact of livestock grazing and other human activities on grassland biodiversity is variable. Livestock have an impact on grassland ecosystems through trampling, removal of plant biomass, alteration of plant species composition through selective grazing, competition with native species, and spread of pathogens. In some areas where the native vegetation is well adapted, the impact on plant diversity may be relatively small; elsewhere, where the native vegetation has not evolved in the presence of hoofed herbivores, the impact has been great. Much anthropogenic grassland used for grazing consists of short-term monospecific sown pasture, with low diversity. However, other areas may support species-rich semi-natural grassland created over centuries by pastoralists in conjunction with livestock grazing.

As well as suffering impacts from habitat conversion and competition with livestock, large animal species in grasslands and savannas have been intensively hunted almost everywhere for their products (e.g. skins or meat), for sport, and as competitors with other predators of livestock.

Important grassland protected areas include the Serengeti National Park and World Heritage Site in Tanzania; the Eastern Mongolian Steppe Strictly Protected Area, which covers some 570 000 hectares and provides important habitat for migratory Mongolian gazelles; and the Tallgrass Prairie National Preserve, Kansas, USA, which covers only 4 400 hectares but protects one of the few unplowed remnants of North American tallgrass prairie left anywhere.

Deserts and semi-deserts

The world's hot, subtropical deserts and semi-deserts are distributed along the high pressure zone between 15° and 30° North and South latitudes. In the north along the Tropic of Cancer are the Sahara, the Arabian Peninsula, the Great Indian or Thar Desert, the Sonoran, Chihuahuan, and Mojave Deserts. South, along the Tropic of Capricorn, lie the Kalahari Desert in southern Africa and the interior deserts of Australia: the Great

---

TABLE 2.11: PROTECTION OF WARM DESERTS AND SEMI-DESERTS

Region	Ecosystem area (km²)	Protected area (km²)	% protected
Australia/New Zealand	2 862 000	267 333	9
East Asia	516 000	223 036	43
Eastern and Southern Africa	2 681 000	208 559	8
Europe	12 000	2 299	19
North Africa and Middle East	10 265 000	1 141 500	11
North America	236 000	41 696	18
North Eurasia	109 000	4 028	4
Pacific	9 000	1 267	14
South America	1 683 000	139 188	8
South Asia	389 000	20 225	5
Southeast Asia	58 000	4 603	8
Western and Central Africa	3 448 000	188 231	5

Analysis based on GLC2000 and WDPA 2003 data
Figures rounded to nearest thousand km².

TABLE 2.12: PROTECTION OF COLD DESERTS AND SEMI-DESERTS

Region	Ecosystem area (km²)	Protected area (km²)	% protected
Australia/New Zealand	9 000	6 000	67
East Asia	2 850 000	306 000	11
Europe	91 000	26 000	29
North America	339 000	89 000	26
North Eurasia	3 643 000	176 000	5
South America	353 000	3 000	1

Analysis based on GLC2000 and WDPA 2003 data
Figures rounded to nearest thousand km².

C Zockler

but occur at low population densities because of the low primary productivity of these areas.

The low productivity and inhospitable climate of true deserts means that, like tundra, they are less affected by conversion to alternative land uses than more productive ecosystems. Semi-desert areas are, however, susceptible to factors such as persistent overgrazing and may be slow to recover from adverse impacts. Many large vertebrates in arid lands are threatened with extinction through hunting; the openness of these areas means that animals such as antelopes and other ungulates are more conspicuous than forest species and thus more vulnerable. The nomadic peoples that often inhabit such areas usually have strong hunting traditions; when combined with modern weapons and all-terrain vehicles their impact can be catastrophic, as evidenced by the extinction or near extinction of species such as the scimitar-horned oryx *Oryx dammah*, addax *Addax nasomaculatus*, and dama gazelle *Gazella dama* in North Africa, the Arabian oryx *Oryx pseudoryx* in the Arabian Peninsula, and Przewalski's gazelle *Procapra przewalski* in the sub-desert steppes of China.

Notable desert and sub-desert protected areas include the Ouadi Rimé-Ouadi Achim Faunal Reserve in Chad, one of the largest protected areas in the world, and one which may still contain populations of the critically endangered addax and endangered dama gazelle, and the Great Gobi Strictly Protected Area in Mongolia, This has been designated as one of the world's largest biosphere reserves, and includes important populations of Argali sheep *Ovis ammon*, Saiga antelope *Saiga tatarica* and wild Bactrian camel *Camelus bactrianus*. A small human population lives traditional nomadic lifestyles within the boundaries.

Tundra lacks trees but contains woody species in dwarf or prostrate forms. Purinski Park, Western Taimyr Peninsula, Russian Federation.

Victoria, Gibson, Great Sandy, and the Simpson. Also found in this subtropical belt is a remarkable form of desert, the hyperarid coastal desert, which forms on the western margins of Africa and South America: the Namib Desert in Namibia and the Atacama Desert in Chile. Overall, warm deserts and semi-deserts cover more than 20 million km^2, 80 percent of this in Africa and the Middle East, and around half comprises the Sahara Desert and surrounding arid lands.

At higher latitudes, chiefly between 35° and 50° North and South of the equator, and in some high-altitude areas, are the cold deserts, which may be warm or hot in summer, but become frigidly cold in winter. These cover in total around 7 million km^2, or roughly one third of the area of warm deserts and semi-deserts. The largest of these cold deserts are located in Asia, and include the Taklamakan, Turkestan, Iranian Plateau, and the Gobi. In western North America, the Colorado Plateau and Great Basin Deserts lie in the rainshadow of the coastal mountain ranges. In South America, the Monte and Patagonian Deserts are formed in response to the moisture barrier of the Andes.

Biodiversity, assessed in terms of species numbers, tends to be moderate in semi-desert regions and to decline to low or very low levels as aridity increases. In contrast to this general rule, diversity in some groups, such as scorpions and other predatory arthropod invertebrates, tenebrionid beetles, ants, termites, snakes, and lizards, and annual plants, tends at first to increase as aridity increases. Desert animals are often wide ranging

Tundra

Tundra is the vegetation found at high latitudes beyond the low-temperature limits of forest growth; the same term is sometimes used for outwardly similar vegetation at high elevation at lower altitude. In both areas it grades into cold-desert formations as average annual temperature and rainfall decrease. GLC2000/UNEP-WCMC's analysis indicates some 4.7 million km^2 of tundra worldwide. Apart from a small amount in South America, tundra is essentially confined to the northern hemisphere, most (around 3.2 million km^2) in North America and virtually all the remainder in North Eurasia and northern Europe.

Tundra lacks trees but contains woody species (in the northern hemisphere chiefly birches *Betula*, willows *Salix*, and alders *Alnus*) growing in dwarf or prostrate forms, especially in locations with less extreme climates. As latitude or altitude increases, grasses, sedges, bryophytes, and lichens increase in importance while shrubs decrease. Many plants have tussock or cushion growth forms. Plants typically cover 80–100 percent of the ground, although the proportion decreases along the climatic gradient to desert conditions.

Compared with forest ecosystems, tundra is relatively species poor. A few groups, however, most notably shorebirds, can exploit the high biomass of invertebrates found in tundra soils during the brief summer months and can be both diverse and abundant at that time of year. In the wading bird family Scolopacidae (the sandpipers and their allies), 55 of the 87 species occur in the Arctic, and all 24 species of sandpiper are present, 17 breeding exclusively in the region. There are relatively few globally threatened species that are completely dependent on tundra. An exception is the once abundant Eskimo curlew *Numenius borealis*, which nests – or perhaps nested – exclusively in this habitat. There have been no confirmed sightings of the bird since the 1980s, so it may well now be extinct. Two other globally threatened birds, Steller's eider *Polysticta stelleri* and the spectacled eider *Somateria fischeri*, remain in the Arctic throughout the year and breed largely in tundra ecosystems.

Tundra ecosystems have a high biomass underground, and high soil carbon content. Thus, although such systems account for only around 2 percent of global net annual primary production, they make an important contribution to global carbon stocks, capable of storing more than 200 metric tons of carbon per hectare.

Because of its inhospitable climate, tundra is not widely subject to pressure for conversion to other land uses. However, there is a lack of ecological resilience, so that disturbances such as those associated with settlement or long-distance pipelines tend to have long-lasting effects. Global warming is also already having an impact, as such high-latitude areas are being subjected to the most rapid levels of climate change anywhere on Earth, causing melting of the permafrost, the loss of snow and ice cover (including access to adjacent marine resources via sea-ice), and replacement of habitat by non-tundra species.

TABLE 2.13: PROTECTION OF TUNDRA

Region	Ecosystem area (km²)	Protected area (km²)	% protected
East Asia	23 000	4 000	19
Europe	130 000	22 000	17
North America	3 228 000	525 000	16
North Eurasia	1 267 000	153 000	12
South America	33 000	6 000	18

Analysis based on GLC2000 and WDPA 2003 data
Figures rounded to nearest thousand km².

Important protected areas in the tundra zone include Wrangel Island Natural Reserve and World Heritage Site in the far eastern part of the Russian Federation, the core zone of which covers nearly one million hectares and which is the northernmost breeding site for over 100 migratory bird species.

Shrublands

Shrub communities, where woody plants, usually adapted to fire, form a continuous cover, occur in all parts of the world where annual rainfall lies in the range 200–1 000 mm. In more arid areas, including some semi-desert ecosystems, shrubs are the dominant life form, but cover is discontinuous. Areas dominated by shrubland systems may be found in boreal regions, where they form a transition between forests and tundra; in subtropical areas, particularly those with a Mediterranean-type climate; and in parts of the dry

Clanwilliam daisy (*Euryops speciosissimus*) in the Cedarberg Wilderness Area, South Africa.

S Sailer/A Sailer/Still Pictures

TABLE 2.14: PROTECTION OF SUBTROPICAL AND TROPICAL SHRUBLANDS

Region	Ecosystem area (km²)	Protected area (km²)	% protected
Australia/New Zealand	514 000	42 000	8
East Asia	249 000	18 000	7
Eastern and Southern Africa	99 000	7 000	7
Europe	119 000	8 000	7
North Africa and Middle East	118 000	1 000	1
North America	237 000	49 000	21
South America	364 000	15 000	4
Western and Central Africa	1 032 000	113 000	11

Analysis based on GLC2000 and WDPA 2003 data
Figures rounded to nearest thousand km².

TABLE 2.15: PROTECTION OF BOREAL SHRUBLANDS

Region	Ecosystem area (km²)	Protected area (km²)	% protected
Australia/New Zealand	22 000	1 000	5
East Asia	150 000	16 000	11
Europe	158 000	32 000	21
North America	2 061 000	430 000	21
North Eurasia	1 784 000	174 000	10
South America	59 000	7 000	12

Analysis based on GLC2000 and WDPA 2003 data
Figures rounded to nearest thousand km².

Chilean Matorral, and some parts of California. Mediterranean-type plants have attained extraordinary levels of both diversity and endemism. It has been estimated that as many as 20 percent of the Earth's plant species are residents of Mediterranean systems. The fynbos alone features 8 600 different plants, nearly 70 percent of which are endemic. The Mediterranean basin harbors about 25 000 species of vascular plants, of which 60 percent are endemic to the region. The arid Australian southwest has around 2 500 vascular plants that exist nowhere else in the world. More than 2 000 of just under 3 500 plant species native to California are endemic.

Because Mediterranean climates are so equable, areas with such climates are invariably heavily settled, with land under intense pressure for agriculture (particularly citrus fruit crops and wine) and building development. Protected areas in these regions are often small reserves or recreational parks. Nevertheless, because of the high diversity and endemism of the flora in particular, even small areas may be of great importance for the conservation of biodiversity. In South Africa the recently declared 16 000 hectare Cape Peninsula National Park is home to more than 2 000 vascular plant species, of which 90 occur nowhere else and more than 140 are considered threatened with extinction.

Caves and karst

The term karst refers to land systems that are predominantly formed by solution and these mostly occur in limestone or other carbonate rocks. Carbonic acid that forms in rainwater, largely from the solution of carbon dioxide, is critical to the solution process; however, sulfur-based acids formed from the oxidation of sulfides or by bacterial metabolism in the presence of sulfur are also commonly involved. Other solution processes are driven by rising hydrothermal waters, again often carrying acids formed from bacterial or volcanic action. The solution process often occurs underground, and caves are probably the best known of all karst features. However, a wide range of other features, including surface depressions, collapses into caves below, cliffs and gorges, pinnacles, hills or terraces of striking and distinctive shapes, and distinctive forms of rock pavements, can commonly be seen.

Karst scenery with its accompanying caves also occurs, though much less frequently, in some

tropics where a shrubland/savanna mosaic occurs. Under the GLC2000/UNEP-WCMC analysis used here, the last of these are included in savannas, discussed above. There are around 7 million km² of other shrubland in total, of which just over 4 million km² are in boreal regions and just under 3 million km² in the subtropics.

While boreal shrublands, like other cold or cold-temperate ecosystems, tend to have relatively low levels of biodiversity, subtropical shrublands, notably those in areas with a Mediterranean climate, have very high levels of biodiversity, being exceptionally rich in plant species.

Mediterranean-type drylands occur in only five regions in the world, characterized by cool, wet winters and warm, or hot, dry summers. These are: the Mediterranean basin itself, south-central and southwestern Australia, the Cape Floral Kingdom, or fynbos, of southern Africa, the

sandstones and quartzites, gypsum, and salt. Other caves are found in lava flows, or some other special contexts such as underneath talus, in cavities resulting from tectonic action, and in ice. The sea often carves out caves along coastal cliffs, while some caves are "constructed" in the course of coral deposition in the ocean. Other marine caves, including the "blue holes" found across the Caribbean, are probably terrestrial systems formed during sea-level lows and then flooded by the ocean. Karst is found on all continents and many oceanic islands, and there are few countries with no karst.

Quite apart from their outstanding geo-diversity, caves and karst house important biodiversity. Surface karst systems often have a rich flora and fauna, largely because of the extent to which solutional erosion has carved out a great number of microhabitats, each with its own distinctive microclimate and soil. Surface water, lakes, and rivers are often absent from karst areas and this in turn has driven specific adaptations. In cave systems, although biodiversity is low, there are extraordinary levels of endemism with a remarkable variety of specially adapted species living in total darkness in the caves and other fissures in the rock. Such adaptations often include loss or reduction of eyes, expanded appendages, improved olfactory organs, loss of pigmentation, and sometimes reduction in metabolic rate. Terrestrial cave species include harvestmen, spiders, and scavenging beetles. Aquatic cave fauna (stygofauna) includes fish and numerous crustaceans. Perhaps the most interesting are relict communities, typically of crustaceans, which have been found in karst groundwaters, whose origins date back to ancient oceans such as the Tethys Sea.

Karst biodiversity, and even the karst itself, suffers extensive impact through quarrying, cement manufacture, and flooding, and through exploitative land uses, including forestry and agriculture, which disturb the overlying soils and hence lead to sedimentation and changes in patterns of groundwater movement. In addition, the use of chemical fertilizers or pesticides further degrades groundwater quality and may lead to loss of biodiversity. Even misguided visitors can cause immense damage – while efforts are commonly made to protect stalactites and other spel-eothems, the floors, which are potentially the most important part of the cave from the scientific

perspective, are trampled, dug out to improve access, or otherwise damaged.

Despite these pressures, there is a relatively high level of protection for the more spect-acular cave and karst systems in many countries. Thousands of caves are now developed with paths and lighting for tourist visitors and a number of the most important and spectacular systems are listed as World Heritage sites. Overall, some 43 World Heritage sites are either karst or cave systems or have such systems within their boundaries (although in the latter case these systems would not necessarily have been the main reason for listing). This represented a significant proportion of the total number of natural (149) and mixed cultural and natural (23) sites inscribed on the list at mid-2004. Such representation is considerably higher than would be expected given the proportion of the land's surface covered by such systems, which is certainly far less than 25 percent.

Nine World Heritage sites were inscribed primarily because of caves and other karst features:
❏ Plitvice Lakes, Croatia – a series of terraced lakes;
❏ Mammoth Cave National Park, USA;
❏ Skocjanske Jame, Slovenia;
❏ Ha Long Bay, Vietnam – some 1 600 limestone pinnacle islands;
❏ Aggtelek-Domica Caves, which cross the border between Hungary and Slovakia;
❏ Carlsbad Caverns National Park, USA;
❏ St Paul's Cave (Puerto-Princesa Underground River), Philippines;
❏ Desembarco del Granma and the Cabo Cruz coastal terraces, Cuba;

Many cave species, such as this Georgia blind salamander, (*Haideotiton wallacei*), are restricted to very narrow ranges.

M Meadows/Still Pictures

BOX 2.2: BIODIVERSITY CONSERVATION IN THE HIMALAYAS AND TIBETAN PLATEAU

In many montane regions, as elsewhere, protected areas have generally been established where productivity and human use is low. The complex topography of mountains makes this an especially pertinent issue as protected areas will invariably include barren areas of rock and ice that are biologically depauperate. overrepresentation of barren habitats in protected areas can be detrimental to conservation efforts, placing an undue burden on conservation management and resources. It is also difficult to justify additional protected areas to address gaps when existing portfolios are inflated by the inclusion of barren habitats.

The protected area system of the Himalayan range and the Tibetan Plateau was assessed to determine whether the current configuration adequately represents the biologically important habitats, or if there is an overemphasis on rock, permanent snow, and ice.

Ecoregions were used as the ecological units for the analysis. A digital landcover map of 1 km resolution was used to identify areas classified as snow, permanent ice, barren, and sparse vegetation (hereafter "barren habitat") within the ecoregions. All protected area categories were considered (e.g. IUCN category) and types of protected areas equally.

Because of the complex topography in montane ecoregions, inclusion of barren habitat in protected areas is virtually inevitable, especially if the protected areas are large and representative of the ecoregion's landscape mosaic. We therefore created an index by dividing the percent of barren areas within the protected areas system of each ecoregion by the percent of barren ground within that ecoregion. A value of 1 indicates that the barren ground within the protected areas is in direct proportion to that within the ecoregion as a whole; values less than 1 indicate the protected areas include proportionately less barren ground than occurs in the ecoregion as a whole; and values greater than 1 indicate that barren areas are overrepresented in the protected areas system of that ecoregion.

The results showed that in ten of 18 ecoregions in the Himalayas and the Tibetan Plateau the protected areas systems overrepresent barren habitat (Table 2.16). In five of these the absolute extent of excess barren land within the protected areas systems was considerable, ranging from almost 1 000 km^2 to more than 4 000 km^2, areas far greater than many of Asia's protected areas.

With three exceptions, the ecoregions with overrepresentation of barren habitat were from the montane grasslands and shrublands biome. The other three comprised two subalpine conifer forest ecoregions and a temperate forest ecoregion, but the extent of overrepresentation in these three was marginal.

The analysis showed that several of the high-elevation ecoregions in the Himalayan range overrepresent barren habitat within the protected areas system.

Eventually, conservation success in the world's tallest mountain range will depend on the ability and the will to include its threatened biodiversity, rather than to protect extensive areas of barren habitat.

❏ Gunung Mulu, Malaysia, which includes both above-ground karst landscapes and caves, including the world's largest cavern, over 600 m across and 80 m in height, which is also extremely important for biodiversity.

There remain a number of countries where karst sites are not protected, or where protection is ineffectual. This is at least partly linked to a lack of understanding of the values of karst in many countries. In addition, traditional protection has focused on large and spectacular caves, with small caves often neglected even if they are of considerable importance scientifically or for conservation.

Mountain ecosystems

As with so many natural features, mountains are easy to recognize but hard to define for purposes of analysis. The definition of mountains used here is that developed by Kapos *et al.* (2000), which is based on height and slope, and includes all areas above 2 500 m, as well as lower altitudes if their average slopes are sufficiently great[1]. Using this definition, some 27 percent of the world's land surface (including Antarctica, almost all of which is mountainous) can be classified as mountains.

Mountain ecosystems are characterized by altitudinal belts of vegetation (and corresponding faunal components), largely determined by the changing climatic parameters associated with increasing elevation. Different aspects (compass directions) on a mountain add to climatic and ecological variation. Thus many different ecosystems can be represented on a single mountain or over relatively short distances. This high biodiversity is further enhanced by high levels of endemism, as many mountain habitats are isolated, even from adjacent mountains, by deeper valleys with different ecosystems, allowing for highly localized patterns of species divergence.

In the humid tropics the bases of mountains are dominated by **lower montane rainforest**, followed in ascending order by **montane rainforest** and then **upper montane rainforest**. This may merge into montane cloud forest, where there are persistent clouds. (These may be known as mossy, dwarf, or elfin forests, or a host of local names.) Here also can occur the bamboo forests of the tropics and subtropics. The treeline ecotone occurs at varying elevations depending on latitude, aspect, and exposure. In the Central Andes, *Polylepis* trees, the highest in the world, are found at up to 5 000 m.

Above treeline is the zone of alpine grasses, herbs, shrubs, and tall rosette plants. Here, in the tropical Andes, *Puya ramondi*, the world's tallest herb, grows reaching 9 m in height. Here too, the *paramo* (humid, cold grasslands) and *puna* (cold, arid areas with low vegetation) occur, roughly from

1: Lower altitude areas are included based on the following criteria: elevations between 1 500 and 2 500 m where the slope $\geq 2°$, elevations between 1 500 and 1 000 m where the slope $\geq 5°$ or the local elevation range (7 km radius) >300 m; elevations between 300 and 1 000 m where the local elevation range (7 km radius) >300 m; isolated inner basins <25 km^2 that are surrounded by mountains.

TABLE 2.16: BARREN HABITAT IN HIMALAYAN AND TIBETAN PLATEAU ECOREGIONS AND PROTECTED AREAS

The representation index indicates the proportion of barren habitat in the protected areas system, relative to the ecoregion. The excess (or deficit if negative) barren habitat represents the amount of barren habitat that is more (or less) than that expected under an equitable representation of amount found in the ecoregion.

Biome/Ecoregion	Ecoregion area (km^2)	Ecoregion in protected area (%)	Representation index (0-1)	Excess barren habitat in protected areas (km^2)
Deserts and xeric shrublands				
Qaidam Basin semi-desert	192 072	7	0.9	−778
Montane grasslands and shrublands				
Central Tibetan Plateau alpine steppe	653 994	8	0.7	−1 108
Eastern Himalayan alpine shrub and meadows	142 265	32	1.5	3 380
Karakoram-West Tibetan Plateau alpine steppe	172 265	19	1.3	4 192
North Tibetan Plateau-Kunlun Mountains alpine desert	385 851	52	0.7	−23 959
Northwestern Himalayan alpine shrub and meadows	52 271	9	1.5	717
Pamir alpine desert and tundra	125 999	6	1.6	1 912
Qilian Mountains subalpine meadow	73 232	11	2.2	1 483
Southeast Tibet shrublands and meadow	461 964	2	0.8	−20
Tibetan Plateau alpine shrublands and meadows	274 174	0	0.0	–
Western Himalayan alpine shrub and meadows	77 854	12	1.5	954
Yarlung Zambo arid steppe	59 427	8	4.5	112
Temperate coniferous forests				
Eastern Himalayan subalpine conifer forests	27 735	30	2.6	71
Northeastern Himalayan subalpine conifer forests	46 280	4	0.2	−32
Western Himalayan subalpine conifer forests	39 865	7	9.4	265
Temperate broadleaf and mixed forests				
Eastern Himalayan broadleaf forests	83 036	11		–
Northern Triangle temperate forests	10 730	3		–
Western Himalayan broadleaf forests	55 867	6	8.6	88

Protected area data based on WDPA 2003

3 000–3 500 m up to 4 800–5 000 m. These correspond to the Afroalpine vegetation belt above 5 000 m in Africa. Many alpine meadows are also important wetland habitats. At the highest elevations barren ground occurs, with scattered cushion, tuft, and rosette plants, and then permanent snow, ice, or bare rock. In addition, at different elevations are topographically dependent freshwater ecosystems, such as tarns, ponds, and lakes.

Mountains in the protected areas network
Mountains are well represented in the global protected area network. Excluding Antarctica,

which is almost entirely mountainous, according to the definitions used here, but not subject to a conventional protected areas regime, some 18 percent of the world's montane area is included in protected areas, compared with a global average for the world's terrestrial biomes of 12 percent. At a regional scale, of the mountain area of Eurasia and Africa only 10–15 percent is protected, compared with 23–32 percent in the other regions.

The fairly substantial extent of mountain protected area must not be grounds for complacency. Of the total, 970 000 km² are in the Greenland National Park, and many significant

TABLE 2.17: PROPORTION OF MOUNTAIN AREAS WITHIN PROTECTED AREAS

WCPA region	Mountain area (km²)	Protected mountain area (km²)	Mountain area protected (%)	Non-mountain area protected (%)
Australia/New Zealand	387 437	115 279	30	9
Caribbean	48 681	8 259	17	13
Central America	220 996	48 539	22	22
East Asia	6 158 088	1 375 130	22	9
Eastern and Southern Africa	2 667 385	396 477	15	15
Europe	1 564 138	239 889	15	9
North Africa and Middle East	3 121 156	180 817	6	11
North America	394 360	1 952 950	31	13
North Eurasia	5 461 429	510 826	9	7
Pacific	244 172	27 113	11	8
South America (incl. Brazil)	3 422 280	305 993	19	8
South Asia	1 170 684	123 333	11	6
Southeast Asia	1 583 691	305 993	19	8
Western and Central Africa	907 937	97 093	11	10
Total (excl. Antarctica)	33 352 434	5 996 075	18	12

Protected area data based on WDPA 2003
Lower altitude areas are included based on the following criteria: elevations between 1 500 and 2 500 m where the slope ≥2°, elevations between 1 500 and 1 000 m where the slope ≥5° or the local elevation range (7 km radius) >300 m; elevations between 300 and 1 000 m where the local elevation range (7 km radius) >300 m; isolated inner basins <25 km² that are surrounded by mountains.

mountain areas are either not represented or are poorly represented, for example the Atlas Mountains of North Africa, and montane regions of Papua New Guinea and the Middle East.

Wetlands

Inland water ecosystems incorporate highly productive habitats with a wide variety of physical and chemical characteristics, including lakes and rivers, wetlands and floodplains, small streams, ponds, springs, and underground aquifers. All in turn support a wide diversity of species that provide valuable goods and services to people.

Many information sources have used "inland waters" and "freshwaters" interchangeably, so in this review we define inland water ecosystems to include all inland aquatic systems extending to the upper limit of tidal reaches within river estuaries and including the world's inland saline lakes and lagoons such as Lake Magadi and the Caspian

TABLE 2.18: ESTIMATED DISTRIBUTION OF FRESHWATER RESOURCES BY CONTINENT

Resource	Africa	Europe	Asia	Australia	North America	South America
Large lakes	30 000	2 027	27 782	154	25 623	913
Rivers	195	80	565	25	250	1 000
Reservoirs	1 240	422	1 350	38	950	286
Groundwater	5 500 000	1 600 000	7 800 000	1 200 000	4 300 000	3 000 000
Wetlands[1]	341 000	925 000[2]		4 000	180 000	1 232 000

1 Wetlands are defined as including marshes, swamps, lagoons, bogs, floodplains, etc.
2 Eurasia.

Source: Groombridge and Jenkins, 1998. Data refer to volume in km³, except for wetlands which refer to area in km².

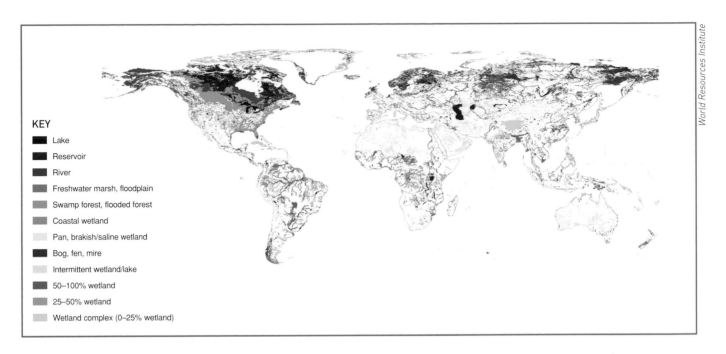

KEY
- ■ Lake
- ■ Reservoir
- ■ River
- ■ Freshwater marsh, floodplain
- ■ Swamp forest, flooded forest
- ■ Coastal wetland
- ■ Pan, brakish/saline wetland
- ■ Bog, fen, mire
- ■ Intermittent wetland/lake
- ■ 50–100% wetland
- ■ 25–50% wetland
- ■ Wetland complex (0–25% wetland)

World Resources Institute

Figure 2.3: Global distribution of wetlands

Source: Global lakes and wetlands database GWLD (Lehner and Döll, 2004)

Sea. Where "freshwater" is used, saline habitats and their associated taxa are excluded. The term "wetland", often used to define an aquatic system, is used here to describe a particular group of aquatic habitats representing a variety of shallow, vegetated systems such as bogs, marshes, swamps, floodplains, and coastal lagoons that are often transitional areas and can flood, seasonally or intermittently (Groombridge and Jenkins, 1998).

In spite of their clear economic value, many inland water ecosystems, especially wetlands, have long been considered a wasteful use of land and are rarely protected. Lack of recognition of the value of these systems has already led to the estimated loss of 50 percent of the world's shallow-water wetlands, and rates of species loss have, in some cases, been estimated at five times the rates seen in other ecosystems (e.g. Myers 1997; Ricciardi and Rasmussen, 1999).

Extent and distribution of inland water ecosystems
Freshwater makes up an estimated 3 percent of the Earth's total water volume, a large proportion of which is stored in the polar ice caps. The freshwater that is free to supply the world's lakes and rivers constitutes less than 0.01 percent of the total water volume. This small proportion supports all the world's freshwater ecosystems. Regional differences in the volume of precipitation, and the area and geomorphology of continental land surfaces have led to large regional differences in the distribution of these ecosystems (see Table 2.18).

Mapping and inventorying of wetland ecosystems, particularly seasonal wetlands, presents significant problems and it is very difficult to come up with consistent estimates of wetland extent at global and regional levels. The most comprehensive recent attempt is that of Lehner and Döll (2004), whose Global Lakes and Wetlands Database draws on a wide range of sources. They estimated that wetlands covered around 11–13 million km² globally, that is between 8 and 10 percent of global land surface area excluding Antarctica and glaciated Greenland. Of this, around 2.7 million km² was lakes and reservoirs and the remainder rivers, included flooded forests, floodplains, intermittent wetlands and wetland complexes (Figure 2.3). Their estimate of total wetland extent is around twice that produced by earlier analyses, including GLC2000. This is a reflection of different criteria and definitions used rather than major differences in the underlying data – the former analysis incorporates a range of wetland complexes including partially flooded and seasonally flooded areas that are not all labelled as wetlands under GLC2000. The latter, however, still provides a useful conservative estimate for wetland extent.

The biogeographic and ecological classification of inland water ecosystems is less well developed than that for terrestrial ecosystems and, although there are more than 50 classi-

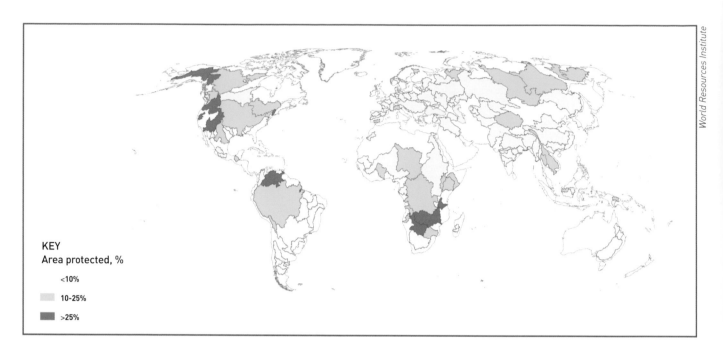

World Resources Institute

KEY
Area protected, %

<10%

10-25%

>25%

Figure 2.4:
Protected areas by
river basin, 2003

Note: This analysis does
not include all protected
areas. Protected areas
without polygon
(boundary) information
were excluded as it
was only possible to
determine the geographic
extent of the polygon data
in relation to the river
basins. This analysis
includes all nationally
and internationally
designated protected
areas with polygon
information. Australia's
most recent national
polygon data could not be
used for the analysis due
to licensing restrictions.

Source: Revenga et al.,
1998; UNEP-WCMC,
2002.

fications in use, there is no globally accepted hierarchical classification for this group of habitats.
Some of the better known wetland classification
schemes include the Canadian wetland classification system (Zoltai and Vitt, 1995), the Asian
wetland classification system (Finlayson *et al.*
2002a and 2002b), and the US national wetland
classification scheme (Cowardin *et al.* 1979,
Cowardin and Golet 1995).

Extent of existing protected areas

Because of the difficulty in defining and mapping
wetlands, it is not possible at present to come up
with a single agreed estimate of the global
percentage of inland water ecosystems under
protection. The WDPA (2003 figures) indicates that
roughly 12 percent of wetland area as recognized in
GLC2000 (including open water bodies and
mangroves) is under protection, almost all in
protected areas that have been assigned to IUCN
Management Categories I to VI. Preliminary
analysis using the the Global Lakes and Wetlands
Database (Lehner and Döll, 2004) and a slightly
though not significantly modified version of the
WDPA indicates a somewhat higher proportion
(around 20 percent) protected. A third approach,
extrapolating from the proportion of land area per
river basin that is under protection in a subset of the
world's larger river basins (Figure 2.4), indicates
global protection of around 13 percent, in line with
the GLC2000-based analysis.

At a regional level the three analyses show
good agreement on percentage of wetland area
protected in some regions, notably Australia, North
America and North Eurasia but considerable
variation elsewhere with, for example, estimates of
protection in North Africa and the Middle East
varying from 2 percent to 34 percent (Table 2.19). In
very general terms, all three analyses agree that
protection is relatively high (15 percent or more) in
Australia/New Zealand, the Caribbean, East Asia,
Eastern and Southern Africa, South America and
Southeast Asia. The analyses also agree that
protection is relatively low in North America and
North Eurasia (the two regions with the largest
areas of wetlands overall). Figures for the
remaining regions are either incomplete (Central
America) or confict (North Africa and Middle East,
Pacific, South Asia and Western and Central Africa).

As might be expected, the river basin analysis
shows that the rates of protection in different river
basins varies greatly both within and between
regions. Of the 115 basins analyzed, 73 (just over
60 percent) had less than 10 percent of their area
protected, 33 (30 percent) had between 10 and 25
percent of their area protected, and only nine basins
(8 percent) had more than 25 percent of their area
protected (Figure 2.5). In all, over 90 percent of the
basins analyzed had less than 25 percent of their
land area protected.

Although superficially it might appear
from GIS analysis that inland water ecosystems are

TABLE 2.19: PROTECTION OF WETLANDS

Region	Estimate Low ('000 km²)	Estimate High ('000 km²)	Estimated % of wetland included in protected areas Based on GLC2000	Estimated % of wetland included in protected areas Based on Global lakes and wetlands database	Estimated % of wetland included in protected areas Using river basin analysis
Australia/New Zealand	120	280	18	20	18
Caribbean	22	34	25	53	50
Central America	16	40	n/a	39	20
East Asia	200	1 000	27	49	26
Eastern and Southern Africa	260	600	19	27	17
Europe	160	200	15	28	10
North Africa and Middle East	110	450	2	18	34
North America	1 400	2 900	10	32	10
North Eurasia	1 800	2 200	9	13	11
Pacific	8	120	26	13	40
South America	625	1 700	15	35	17
South Asia	100	600	27	13	12
Southeast Asia	70	500	16	28	18
Western and Central Africa	150	900	10	20	7

Figures are rounded. Low estimate based on GLC2000. High estimates based on GLWD2006.

relatively well protected compared with some other major biomes, there are a number of important caveats. In the first instance, some areas that are extremely important for inland water biodiversity are very inadequately protected. Examples include species-rich basins such as the Paraná in South America, the Fly in Papua New Guinea, and the Mahakam and Salween Basins in Southeast Asia, all of which have less than 10 percent of their basin areas protected. More generally, inland water systems are rarely accorded priority in protected areas management plans; rivers, for example, often

Figure 2.5: Ramsar sites by river basin, 2003.

Source: Revenga, 1998; UNEP-WCMC, 2002.

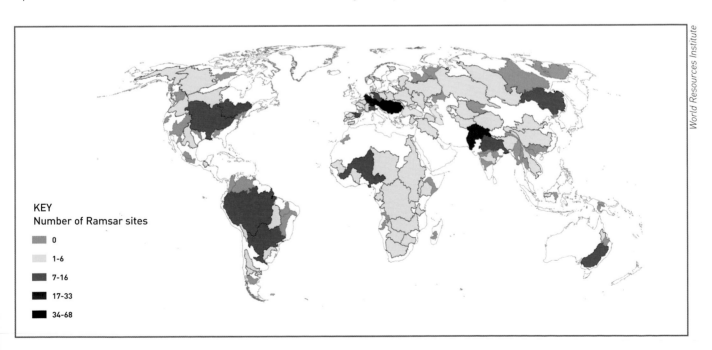

KEY
Number of Ramsar sites
- 0
- 1-6
- 7-16
- 17-33
- 34-68

World Resources Institute

TABLE 2.20: RAMSAR SITES OF DOMINANT WETLAND TYPES, 2006

Wetland types	Number of designated sites
Estuarine waters	106
Intertidal mud, sand, or salt flats, and/or intertidal marshes	178
Intertidal forested wetlands	76
Coastal brackish/saline lagoons	144
Coastal freshwater lagoons	26
Inland deltas	26
Permanent and/or seasonal rivers/streams/creeks	127
Permanent and/or seasonal freshwater lakes	346
Permanent and/or seasonal saline/brackish/ alkaline lakes and flats	123
Permanent and/or seasonal saline/brackish/ alkaline marshes/pools	43
Permanent and/or seasonal freshwater marshes/pools	185
Peatlands, non-forested and/or forested	200
Alpine wetlands	7
Tundra wetlands	16
Shrub-dominated wetlands	27
Freshwater, tree-dominated wetlands	72
Freshwater springs; oases	9
Geothermal wetlands	2
Subterranean karst and cave hydrological systems	21
Human made wetlands (all types)	125

There are 520 Ramsar sites with one or more coastal/marine wetland type dominant.
Source: Ramsar Secretariat 2006.

merely form the boundary of an area and are not themselves afforded any notable protection status. Furthermore, even in those cases where a relatively large proportion of the basin is included within protected areas, if associated habitats such as forests and river headwaters are not also protected, then the protected area may be largely ineffective. Indeed, inland water ecosystems perhaps more than any others call for an integrated approach to protection as they are almost invariably heavily influenced by factors beyond their boundaries.

Wetlands of International Importance (Ramsar sites)

Inland water bodies are well represented among Ramsar sites (Table 2.20). The total land area under Ramsar designation in 2005 covered approximately 8.5 percent of the estimated minimum total global wetland resources of around 1 300 million hectares (GroWI, 1999). Some sites include

adjacent areas (of both land and sea) that are not wetlands *per se*. The greatest number of sites (60 percent of the total) were in Europe, but many of these are small in size, such as Llyn Idwal (14 hectares), a small nutrient-poor mountain valley lake in Wales. Other regions may have fewer but larger sites, such as the Pacaya Samiria National Reserve in Peru (2 080 000 hectares), making the land area distribution of sites more evenly distributed at the global level.

Sites are designated using a flexible approach to scale and may range from individual springs or ponds of less than 1 hectare to wetlands such as the Okavango Delta and Brazilian Pantanal, more than 6 million and 3 million hectares, respectively.

The river basins with the greatest number of Ramsar sites include the Amur, Danube, Elbe, Niger, Murray-Daring, Paraguary sub-basin and Rhine-Maas, all of which have at least ten, with the Danube alone having more than 60. At the other extreme, many important river basins have no Ramsar sites at all (WRI *et al.*, 2003) (Figure 2.6).

Marine and coastal ecosystems

IUCN defines a marine protected area as:
"Any area of intertidal or subtidal terrain, together with its overlying water and associated flora, fauna, historical and cultural features, which has been reserved by law or other effective means to protect part or all of the enclosed environment."

This definition thus includes all sites, even largely terrestrial sites that include any intertidal element; they need not include any subtidal waters. This clearly differs from certain widespread perceptions of marine protected areas (MPAs) as sites with predominantly subtidal coverage. It remains a valuable definition, however, because coastal and intertidal areas include extensive and important habitats, including mangrove forests, rocky shores, and saltmarshes, which play a critical role in marine biodiversity functioning. Many protected areas have been designated to include these habitats, but would not be classified as "marine" if such a definition required the presence of subtidal waters. Here we consider marine and coastal areas to include all marine waters including semi-enclosed seas (but not the Caspian Sea) as well as intertidal habitats including estuarine waters.

BOX 2.3: MARINE ECOSYSTEMS

BENTHIC MARINE ECOSYSTEMS

Intertidal:

Unvegetated sediments	These include mud, sand, or salt flats, and beaches (sand and pebble).
Saltmarsh	Areas vegetated by herbs, grasses or low shrubs. Commonly developing in the upper tidal frame on finer sediments along protected coasts.
Mangrove	Area vegetated by woody plants (including *Nipa* palms and mangrove ferns), typically in upper tidal frame. Can form large forests.
Rocky shores	Large rock structures provide a secure base for a considerable diversity of species. Zoned across the tidal frame, further modified by patterns of exposure and the location of rock pools.

Subtidal:

Bare sediments, mud sand, or rubble	These represent the most widespread habitat on the surface of the globe. In all but the shallowest waters they dominate, without any cover of benthic algae.
Algal-dominated sediments	In places where sufficient light reaches the ocean floor. May include encrusting algae, cyanobacteria, and microalgae.
Seagrass beds	Shallow sediments with a cover of seagrass (subtidal vascular plants).
Rocky benthos, largely unvegetated	Quite rare in the open ocean, often associated with seamounts. Provides a holdfast for a great range of species including corals, bryozoans, worms, and mollusks.
Rocky benthos with macroalgae	Often referred to as kelp forests.
Coral reefs	Physical structures built from the carbonate skeletons of corals, often alongside other calcifying organisms, in shallow waters.
Chemoautotrophic communities	Associated with seismic activities including volcanic vents and cold seeps. Primary productivity utilizes chemical compounds rather than light as a source of energy.
Other biogenic structures	These include the deep-sea coral communities, but also structures built by worm and mollusk shells (vermitid reefs, oyster reefs).

PELAGIC ECOSYSTEMS

A range of classification schemes has been developed, with subdivisions based on oceanographic patterns of temperature, wind, or chlorophyll content in the waters. Longhurst (1998) has developed a global system based on sea-surface productivity information derived from satellites. This system divides the world into four major oceanic realms (Atlantic, Indian, Pacific, and Southern) and within each presents four primary biomes. Three, the Polar, Westerly Winds, and Trade Winds biomes, are approximately latitudinally divided, while a fourth recognizes the unique processes associated with coastal biomes.

These pelagic subdivisions can only be seen as generalized markers, partly because of the low resolution at which they have been prepared, but equally importantly because the boundaries are determined by fluid processes which change over timescales from days to decades. This latter point is of considerable importance when considering the designation of protected areas for pelagic ecosystems.

The marine and coastal realm

Around 71 percent of the Earth's surface is marine waters, with an average depth of 3 900 m. The vast majority (67 percent of the Earth's surface) lies off the continental shelf. From a political perspective about 37 percent of the ocean area lies within 200 nautical miles of a coastline and hence may fall under some level of national jurisdiction.

There is little agreement on a habitat classification scheme for the oceans, and even greater problems arise in the presentation of marine habitats on maps at the global level. Part of the problem stems from the very nature of the marine environment which, being three-dimensional, can be host to multiple different ecosystems through the water column. Such dimensions cannot be

TABLE 2.21: MARINE ECOREGIONS OF THE WORLD

The 12 Realms and 62 Provinces of the Marine Ecoregions of the World classification, which covers all coastal seas. Within these, some 232 ecoregions have been identified.

ARCTIC

1 Arctic

TEMPERATE NORTHERN ATLANTIC

2 Northern European Seas
3 Lusitanian
4 Mediterranean Sea
5 Cold Temperate Northwest Atlantic
6 Warm Temperate Northwest Atlantic
7 Black Sea

TEMPERATE NORTHERN PACIFIC

8 Cold Temperate Northwest Pacific
9 Warm Temperate Northwest Pacific
10 Cold Temperate Northeast Pacific
11 Warm Temperate Northeast Pacific

TROPICAL ATLANTIC

12 Tropical Northwestern Atlantic
13 North Brazil Shelf
14 Tropical Southwestern Atlantic
15 St. Helena and Ascension Islands
16 West African Transition
17 Gulf of Guinea

WESTERN INDO-PACIFIC

18 Red Sea and Gulf of Aden
19 Somali/Arabian
20 Western Indian Ocean
21 West and South Indian Shelf
22 Central Indian Ocean Islands
23 Bay of Bengal
24 Andaman

CENTRAL INDO-PACIFIC

25 South China Sea
26 Sunda Shelf
27 Java Transitional
28 South Kuroshio
29 Tropical Northwestern Pacific
30 Western Coral Triangle
31 Eastern Coral Triangle
32 Sahul Shelf
33 Northeast Australian Shelf
34 Northwest Australian Shelf
35 Tropical Southwestern Pacific
36 Lord Howe and Norfolk Islands

EASTERN INDO-PACIFIC

37 Hawaii
38 Marshall, Gilbert and Ellis Islands
39 Central Polynesia
40 Southeast Polynesia
41 Marquesas
42 Easter Island

TROPICAL EASTERN PACIFIC

43 Tropical East Pacific
44 Galapagos

TEMPERATE SOUTH AMERICA

45 Warm Temperate Southeastern Pacific
46 Juan Fernández and Desventuradas
47 Warm Temperate Southwestern Atlantic
48 Magellanic
49 Tristan Gough

TEMPERATE SOUTHERN AFRICA

50 Benguela
51 Agulhas
52 Amsterdam-St Paul

TEMPERATE AUSTRALASIA

53 Northern New Zealand
54 Southern New Zealand
55 East Central Australian Shelf
56 Southeast Australian Shelf
57 Southwest Australian Shelf
58 West Central Australian Shelf

SOUTHERN OCEAN

59 Subantarctic Islands
60 Scotia Sea
61 Continental High Antarctic
62 Subantarctic New Zealand

captured on a map's flat surface. In addition, the knowledge base for many of these ecosystems remains remarkably poor. The most widespread ecosystem on Earth is made up of deep-ocean muddy benthos and yet our knowledge of this is restricted to a minuscule area which has been trawled or cored with costly equipment. A further difficulty in the development of maps is the fact that biological boundaries in the fluid ocean environment shift constantly, season to season, year to year, and over longer timescales.

Most habitat classification schemes are based on a combination of physical and biological criteria. Although apparently simple, this system is both hierarchical and three-dimensional. We cannot map this from the air on a single sheet as there are multiple overlapping habitats. A protected area drawn on the water surface could incorporate these multiple systems, although in many cases protected areas may be targeted at only a single system, such as coral reefs, and fail to protect other systems such as overlying pelagic ecosystems.

S. Chape

Fringing coral reefs in Ningaloo Marine Park, Western Australia.

The vast majority of MPAs lie in near-coastal waters within the shallow photic zone or in the intertidal zone. Here more detailed habitat definitions have been developed. A simple schema derived from a number of these, including the Ramsar wetlands classification scheme, is presented in Box 2.3, together with brief notes about their definitions, biodiversity importance, and available knowledge of their distribution and status.

Another approach for classifying the marine environment, which avoids the challenges of detailed habitat mapping, looks at taxonomic or evolutionary patterns and describes areas of homogeneity across a range of habitats. This is the approach used in the Marine Ecoregions of the World classification, developed by a consortium of NGO scientists and academics (Spalding *et al.*, 2007). This classification divides coast and shelf waters into a tiered system of 12 realms, 62 provinces and 232 ecoregions (Table 2.21). The system has good synergies with other classifications, such as the Large Marine Ecosystems, while the finest-scale ecoregions have already been widely used in a number of regions (Australia, North and South America, East Africa) for conservation planning and for monitoring conservation progress.

To a very large degree, coastal and continental shelf waters are of greatest importance for biodiversity, and to human interest. The intertidal zone is a region of high productivity and biodiversity. Mangrove forests and saltmarshes are among the most productive ecosystems in the marine realm. Adjacent waters are generally nutrient rich and suffused with light, enabling high levels of productivity and supporting, in many areas, a vast array of life forms. Pelagic ecosystems can also be highly productive, particularly in areas of regular upwelling such as the western continental shelves of South Africa and South America.

Until the 1960s it was generally believed that deep-ocean silaceous muds were largely devoid of species. This was because of the sampling methods used, in which filters allowed most species to escape sampling. It is now suggested that there could be 10 million species living in these communities, almost entirely undescribed by scientists. The first hydrothermal vents were discovered in 1977 – these, together with cold seeps, are now known to be widespread, the only ecosystems on the planet that are totally independent of light and based rather on chemosynthesis. Also, in offshore waters, are large numbers of seamounts that rise great distances from the sea floor. These structures often include rocky benthos and play host to numerous species still little known to science.

Human impacts on the seas are pervasive and rapidly increasing. Overfishing is perhaps the most obvious case. FAO (2007) estimates that in 2005 "around one quarter of the stock groups monitored by FAO were underexploited or moderately exploited and could perhaps produce more, whereas about

TABLE 2.22: BREAKDOWN OF MARINE PROTECTED AREAS BY WCPA REGION, 2004

WCPA region	Number of sites	Protected marine area (km²)	Marine area in WCPA region (km² approx.)[1]	Marine area protected (%)
Antarctic	59	65 093	–	–
Australia/New Zealand	437	423 350	12 398 000	3.4
Brazil	83	14 190	3 661 000	0.4
Caribbean	357	42 037	3 976 000	1.1
Central America	104	16 018	1 501 000	1.1
East Asia	283	31 389	5 523 000	0.6
Eastern and Southern Africa	139	5 317	8 339 000	0.1
Europe	848	67 490	9 548 000	0.7
North Africa and Middle East	134	23 542	3 459 000	0.7
North America	695	212 125	17 740 000	1.2
North Eurasia	82	217 839	7 719 000	2.8
Pacific	168	357 203	32 372 000	1.1
South America	115	72 209	8 432 000	0.9
South Asia	184	5 160	4 692 000	0.1
Southeast Asia	387	75 934	8 652 000	0.9
Western and Central Africa	41	10 169	3 606 000	0.3

1: These estimates are based on preliminary and unverified estimates of marine waters within 200 nautical miles of the coastlines using unofficial EEZ boundaries. These are crude approximations only.

half of the stocks were fully exploited and therefore producing catches that were at, or close to, their maximum sustainable limits, with no room for further expansion. The remaining stocks were either overexploited, depleted or recovering from depletion and thus were yielding less than their maximum potential" owing to excess fishing pressure. Other studies have suggested that the situation may, in fact, be far worse. Recent studies on larger predatory fishes (including tuna and cod) have suggested that almost all stocks worldwide have declined by 90 percent from their pre-industrial levels. Nearshore fisheries have probably undergone similar collapses in many areas, although reporting is more difficult.

Some fishing techniques, particularly bottom trawling, may have serious collateral impact through habitat loss and degradation. In a recent study of trawling in 24 countries it was estimated that 57 percent of the continental shelf area was within trawling grounds. A separate study estimated that the total area actually damaged by these trawls was some 14.8 million km² (one and a half times the area of the USA) each year. In many ecosytems the use of trawls is highly destructive, destroying benthic species such as corals, sponges,

and seagrasses. Such impacts were until recently largely confined to inshore and continental shelf habitats, but are now extending into deeper waters (up to 1 500 m or more) on continental slopes and around seamounts. In such waters, recovery from these impacts could take centuries.

Habitat destruction is also widely reported in intertidal areas. Although there are no accurate global estimates it has been suggested that 30–50 percent of the world's mangrove forests have been lost. Although there have been various suggestions that between 10 and 30 percent of the world's coral reefs have also been lost, these are not based on any rigorous calculations. Many areas of mangrove, saltmarsh, and other habitat have been lost to land reclamation and/or the building of aquaculture ponds or salt-pans. Coastal construction and sand mining in wide areas has led to erosion and beach loss. A further cause for concern in inshore waters and semi-enclosed seas such as the Mediterranean and Black Sea is the rapidly increasing introduction of alien species, often in ships' ballast waters. The impact of the comb jelly *Mnemiopsis leidyi* on the Black Sea is a well-known case.

Human impacts on pelagic systems are more difficult to discern or to quantify. Habitat loss is no longer a relevant term in this environment; however, degradation is widespread, perhaps ubiquitous. The collapse of many pelagic fish stocks is one such indicator. Another is the presence of pollutants. Many coastal areas are afflicted by nutrient and chemical pollution arising from untreated sewage, industrial waste, and agricultural run-off. Certain highly persistent organic pollutants (POPs) can now be detected in all oceans, and there are particular concerns where these are building up in polar regions.

Marine protected areas

Major updates on marine protected areas in WDPA are underway, but unfortunately were not available for this work and so the information presented in Table 2.22 represents information from 2003. At this time there were just over 4 000 MPAs covering an estimated 1 600 000 km², or rather less than 0.5 percent of the world's ocean surface.

Regionally, there is considerable variation in the application of MPAs, with Australia/New Zealand currently the most highly protected region in terms of aerial coverage. The total marine area protected amounts to more than 3 percent of the exclusive economic zone (EEZ) of this region. Although this is heavily weighted by the influence of the Great Barrier Reef, there remains a large number of other sites, some quite big, throughout this region. While Europe has the highest number of sites, the average marine area covered by these sites remains small. In fact, caution is also necessary here, as many of these sites are essentially terrestrial, with only minor intertidal or subtidal areas, while few have any meaningful restrictions. The UK, for example, is listed as having 242 MPAs, and yet the vast majority have no restrictions on fishing or anchoring activities and must be considered to be of little value in offering direct protection to marine biodiversity.

North Eurasia also shows considerable protection in terms of area coverage. This is dominated by a few very large sites along the Russian Arctic. The Caribbean and Central America, being some of the smallest regions in geographic extent, show better protection than many other areas, both with about 1.1 percent of their EEZ areas protected, but this protection is broadly dispersed with sites across each region. The Indian Ocean represents perhaps the least protected region in the world, with the Eastern and Southern Africa and the South Asia regions protecting only 0.1 percent of their EEZ areas.

Many of the statistics relating to MPAs are skewed by the influence of a few very large sites, notably the Great Barrier Reef Marine Park and the Northwestern Hawaiian Islands National Monument. These two sites make up more than 680 000 km², or 41 percent of the entire MPA estate (0.2 percent of the global ocean surface). In reality most MPAs are relatively small – even the median size of sites assessed here (29 km²) is clearly inflated as most of the 1 000 sites of unknown area in this dataset lie at the smaller end of the spectrum.

Gaps and priorities: The existing global "network" of protected areas is, to date, very small indeed, and woefully inadequate in its coverage of marine ecosystems. Perhaps the most immediate gap is the lack of sites in the open sea. Few of the existing MPAs fall outside the 3–12-nautical-mile territorial waters that are claimed by most countries. Under the United Nations Convention on the Law of the Sea (UNCLOS), nations are allowed to manage waters up to 200 nautical miles. They have exclusive jurisdictional rights over living resources within this zone, and these rights are further weighted by obligations to conserve those resources. Despite this, only a few MPAs extend into the EEZ, and typically these are the largest sites, such as the Great Barrier Reef, the Northwestern Hawaiian Islands, the Heard Island and McDonald Islands Marine Reserve, and the Galápagos Marine Resource Reserve. The application of international conventions has been similarly limited outside territorial waters; there are precedents, however, including the Seaflower Biosphere Reserve in Colombia and the Pracel Manoel Luís Ramsar Site in Brazil.

There are, however, signs of change (see Chapter 6) – new and larger sites, and more comprehensive networks of MPAs are now being established. This may partly be in response to the commitments made at the World Summit for Sustainable Development to establish representative networks of MPAs by 2012. There are also growing moves to establish a legal and administrative framework for protection in the high seas.

CHAPTER 3

Threats to
protected areas

Contributors: S. Stolton and N. Dudley; Wildlife: E.L. Bennett; Alien species: J. Jamsranjav and M. Spalding; Impacts from beyond the boundaries: N. Dudley, B. Pressey, S. Stolton; Climate change: M. Spalding and S. Chape; Forest conversion, Lao PDR: K. Berkmüller; Resource extraction: Liz Bennett; World Heritage in Danger: N.Ishwaran

As we have seen in the preceding chapter, protected areas have been established, among other reasons, for the purpose of conserving natural heritage. For this conservation role to be fulfilled, essential natural and evolutionary processes and biodiversity composition (species and habitats) must be retained. A variety of factors can act on protected areas and the biodiversity they contain to compromise their functional integrity. This chapter reviews the most important threats and suggests ways in which some of these can be addressed.

This chapter gives an overview of some of the threats and pressures facing protected areas but does not attempt to discuss their underlying causes or to apportion blame. While we can be justifiably angry if a large company flagrantly degrades a protected area for profit, the relationship between many local communities and protected areas is far more complex. In some countries, people have lost land and resources during the creation of protected areas, often with little or no compensation; often the poorest members of society bear the brunt of such changes. Their continued "illegal" use of such resources is sometimes hard to criticise. We highlight here the real and serious threats to protected areas but recognise that these have many and varied causes, some of which are outside the control of the people actually involved in carrying out the degradation. Responding to pressures requires a wide range of different strategies that extend well beyond simple punitive actions.

HUMAN SETTLEMENT AND INCURSION
Protected areas are often the home or resource base for thousands of people. These populations

may be an integral part of a protected area and may contribute to the successful functioning of the site, but elsewhere the close proximity of humans and protected areas can be the source a broad suite of problems. Research suggests that 80 percent of Latin America's protected areas are inhabited (Amend & Amend, 1992), and the agricultural frontier has moved into many protected areas in Central America (Rojas & Cruz, 1998). Most African national parks contain human communities, some of whom may be oblivious to the aims of protection (Sournia, 1998). There is also extensive settlement within many protected areas in Asia and the Pacific. Research in India found human populations in 56 percent of national parks and 72 percent of sanctuaries, often at higher population densities than the average for the country (Singh, 2000). Even when protected areas remain un-settled, clearance of land up to the borders is common, leaving them as "islands" in a sea of altered landscape and undermining the concept of buffer zones or a protected area network.

In some areas humans are an integral part of the ecosystem, and indeed their presence may be vital for ecosystem function to be maintained, but human settlement can also act detrimentally on protected areas. Adverse impacts can arise through:

❑ Expansion of numbers or influence of existing settlements within or around protected areas, either through illegal activities, such as hunting, or because agreed activities increase in scope and impact;

❑ Increase in permanent settlement within protected areas because of land shortages in

S.Chape

Clearing on edge of Dong Hua Sao National Protected Area, Lao PDR.

TABLE 3.1: TYPES OF THREATS TO PROTECTED AREAS

Threat type	Examples of threats
Physical	Fire (arson), severe storm events, geological incidents.
Biological	Introduced plants, introduced animals and organisms.
Direct human threats	Habitat fragmentation, mining, poaching, hunting, and disturbance to fauna, fishing, collecting, grazing, and harvesting of flora, trampling, structure development, access development, utility corridors, communications structures, urbanization, pollution, collecting, managerial damage, vandalism, emergency response damage, arson, squatting, drug cultivation and trafficking, terrorism, and damage from violent conflict
Indirect human threats	Adjoining community and land-use encroachments, impacts to climate, catchments, air and water quality, and poor land-use planning
Legal status threats	Absent or inadequate legal protection, lack of clarity of ownership, inadequate legislation
On-ground	Absence of on-ground management, absence of law enforcement, difficulty of monitoring management threats illegal activities
On-ground social threats	Conflict of cultural beliefs and practices with protected area objectives, presence of bribery and corruption, pressures placed on managers to exploit protected area resources, difficulty of recruitment and retention of employees
Socio-political-economic threats	Lack of political support, inadequate funding, inadequate staffing, inadequate resources, absent or unclear policies, and community opposition
Design threats	Inadequate geographic size, shape, location, connectivity, or replication of an individual protected area and/or a system of protected areas to achieve effective conservation of biodiversity and other heritage
Managerial threats	Absence of strategic planning, human resource and budget systems, plans of management, effective operations, and effectiveness evaluation systems

Sources: Hockings, Stolton & Dudley 2000, Ervin 2003, Worboys 2004.

surrounding areas or because protected areas offer particular benefits;

❏ Sudden, temporary incursions of human populations for a particular purpose, such as transhumance and search for good pasture, or seeking particular economic goals such as mining;

❏ Temporary settlements around protected areas, including, for example, of war refugees or refugees following disasters such as flooding, hurricanes, or the impacts of drought.

Agriculture in its various forms consistently emerges as the number-one "threat" to biodiversity and natural ecosystems in terrestrial habitats, with agricultural pollution also a significant damaging factor in many aquatic ecosystems. Although an increase in agricultural activity is often assumed to be the result of human population growth – causing an apparently simple tension to arise between food and wildlife – most of the impacts, particularly on protected areas, are more complex. Agriculture can influence protected areas in a number of ways.

❏ Incursion and settlement by farmers or landless migrants is a critical problem in those areas where land is scarce either as a result of total population size or because land ownership is concentrated in the hands of just a few people. For example, the need for more agricultural production to meet the increasing demand of buffer-zone communities in Pakistan has resulted in felling of forest patches within protected areas (Ahmad Khan, 1997).

❏ Incursion by nomadic people and grazing animals can conflict with wild animal populations and have an impact on grasslands. Nomadic people use virtually all the protected areas in West Africa, and this is a particular pressure on wildlife in Niger, Togo, and Benin (Sournia, 1998).

❏ Increases in the intensity of agricultural pressure can affect protected areas where traditional agriculture is still allowed.

Research in India found that the average density of livestock inside national parks in India is higher than outside (Singh, 1999).

❏ Illegal cultivation, for example of narcotics and other high value crops [See Box 3.1], can take place in protected areas. Drug production has been identified as a problem in at least 16 of Colombia's protected areas (Castaño Uribe, 1992).

❏ Illegal land clearance to establish agricultural operations can affect protected areas. The majority of the important forest fires that occurred in Brazil, Indonesia, and other countries at the end of the 1990s were created to establish plantations or cattle ranches; some of these spread to protected areas (Dudley, 1997).

❏ Drainage for agriculture can be a threat, particularly to wetlands where small changes in the water table can be disastrous. An extensive system of drainage channels established in the Neusiedler See region between 1900 and 1970 has led to a marked drop in groundwater levels. This poses a serious long-term threat for the shared Austrian and Hungarian Seewinkel/Fertö-Hanság Transboundary National Park's soda lakes, seasonally flooded alkaline steppes, calcareous fens, and wet meadows (Dick et al., 1994).

❏ Water extraction for irrigation can have serious impacts in some areas, either through the rapid exhaustion of groundwater resources or because irrigation has led to changes such as salinization, abandonment of land, and eventual desertification. The Sunderbans Wildlife Sanctuary in Bangladesh is threatened by changes to water flow and salinity as a result of abstraction and use in the Ganges Basin (Rashid & Kabir, 1998).

❏ Agricultural pollution runs off into freshwater and eventually also marine systems, and affects protected areas through eutrophication, pesticide pollution, and deposition of heavy metals. Intensive agriculture is suspected of causing a dramatic decline in amphibians in Point Pelee National Park in Canada, with 6 out of 11 species having disappeared (Parks Canada, 1998).

❏ In some areas, particularly in Europe, the abandonment of agriculture in protected areas is resulting in a reduction in biodiversity in areas where traditional cultural practices have become an established part of the ecosystem (Stolton, Geier & McNeely, 2000).

CHANGES IN FIRE REGIMES

The frequency of natural fires depends on climate, geography, and ecology. Under natural conditions some ecosystems almost never catch fire, whilst in others fire plays an important role, for instance by facilitating germination and release of seeds, or opening the canopy to allow in light and stimulate growth. Changing fire regimes can have a major impact on ecosystems. Changes are often associated with increased human creation of fire – for land clearance, through vandalism, or simply by accident – or may be because of more subtle changes in fire ecology resulting from particular management practices, agricultural systems, or as a result of climate change. Reduction of frequency and concomittant increase in intensity of fires can have particularly adverse effects on fire-adapted ecosystems.

INFRASTRUCTURE DEVELOPMENT

Badly planned roads or other routes into protected areas can increase damage, through tourist pressure or by increased incursion, illegal use, and settlement. A European Development Fund project to upgrade a road in southern Cameroon led to increased logging and poaching, with 27 poaching camps observed within the Dja World Heritage Site (Rice & Counsell, 1998). Problems are worse when people have no proper land tenure rights, suggesting that disenfranchised and resentful communities on the edge of protected areas are likely to use roads to remove salable resources. Research by the University of Florida, for example, found that subsistence farmers holding title to land along the Transamazon Highway in Brazil are more likely to maintain valuable wood and undertake reforestation activities, and are less likely to participate in the timber markets (Resources, 1999).

In Australia, the entire local population (estimated at 19 individuals) of the eastern quoll (*Dasyurus viverrinus*) in a part of Cradle Mountain National Park, Tasmania, was extirpated within 17 months of upgrading three kilometers of road in the protected area, apparently as a direct result of greatly increased road mortality. Introduction of remedial measures led to the species reestablishing itself within six months (Jones, 2000).

TABLE 3.2: Threats to Protected Areas from Tourism and Recreation

Element	Examples of threat from tourism and recreation activities
Ecosystems	The construction of accommodation, visitor centers, infrastructure, fences, access roads, walking tracks, and other services has a direct effect on the environment, by vegetation removal, animal disturbance, elimination of habitats, and changes to drainage patterns. Wildlife habitat may be significantly changed (travel routes, feeding areas, breeding areas, etc) by tourist development and use. Tourism and recreational activities including boating, off-road vehicle use, mountain-bike riding, horse riding, caving, mountaineering, hiking and camping, and loud noise affect natural values. Weeds (garden flowers and non-native grasses) and pest animals (cats and dogs) can be introduced by residents accommodated within protected areas.
Soils	Trampling and soil compaction can occur in certain well-used areas. Soil contamination can occur with fertilizers, pesticides, and pollution from vehicles. Soil removal and soil erosion also occur, and may continue after the disturbance is gone.
Geology	Damage to cave formations and mineral sites can occur from illegal fossil collecting. Sand dunes and reefs are also susceptible to damage.
Vegetation	Concentrated use around facilities has a negative effect on vegetation. Transportation may have direct negative effects on the environment (vegetation removal, weed introduction, animal disturbance). Fire frequency may change due to tourists and park tourism management.
Water	Visitation increases demands for fresh water. Disposal of sewage causes environmental effects even if it is within license limits. Visitation can also lead to solid waste dumped in waterways, erosion of stream banks, and increased turbidity.
Air	Motorized transportation may cause pollution from emissions; smoke from lodge fires can cause pollution in mountain valleys. Visitor use can increase energy consumption and cause greenhouse gas emissions.
Wildlife	Major issues include handfeeding, spotlighting, disturbance to nesting birds, disruption of foraging, and loss of energy reserves and local habitat disturbance. Fishing may change population dynamics of native species. Fishers may demand the introduction of foreign species, and increase populations of target animals. Impacts occur on insects and small invertebrates from effects of transportation and introduced species. Disturbance by visitors can occur for all species, including those that are not attracting visitors. Disturbance can be of several kinds: noise, visual, or harassing behavior. Habituation to humans can cause changed wildlife behavior, such as approaching people for food. Vehicle traffic gives rise to wildlife road kills.
Cultural impacts	Theft, vandalism, and overuse can adversely affect cultural sites, while culturally insensitive or inappropriate behavior can undermine cultural traditions and rules.

Sources: Buckley & Pannell, 1990; Gee, Makens & Choy, 1997; Green & Higginbottom, 2001; Eagles & McCool, 2002; Eagles, McCool & Haynes, 2002; Newsome, Moore & Dowling, 2002; Buckley, Pickering & Weaver, 2003; Christ *et al.*, 2003.

TOURISM AND RECREATION

While tourism and recreation bring much-needed recognition and considerable financial benefits to protected areas and local economies in most parts of the world, they are not without drawbacks. Without effective management and responsible action, growth in tourism can lead to the destruction of environments and destinations and may provide few benefits to local communities (Haroon, 2002; UNEP, 2002). The tourism industry, like many other industries, uses resources such as water and energy, contributes to greenhouse gas emissions, and produces solid wastes. International and national tourists use the equivalent of 80 percent of Japan's yearly primary energy supply (5 000 million kWh/year), produce the same amount of solid waste as France (35 million tons per year), and consume three times the amount of fresh water as is contained in Lake Superior, between Canada and the USA, in a year (10 million cubic meters) (Christ *et al.*, 2003). Major threats arising from tourism and recreation are examined in Table 3.2.

RESOURCE EXTRACTION
Resource extraction includes extraction by local people or park dwellers, and by outsiders. Local people tend to impact through hunting, fishing, fodder and fuelwood collection, water extraction, and in forests also by logging – all of these, however, can also have a commercial aspect. Resource extraction can have a wide range of impacts on both target and non-target resources.

Fuelwood
Fuelwood is the primary energy source for almost half the world's population. It is often collected from protected areas, either legally through agreements or illegally. Low-level collection for domestic use by surrounding communities probably has little long-term impact, except if particular types of wood are targeted over time (for example, if all dead wood is collected thus removing an important microhabitat). However, fuelwood collection can become problematic when demand becomes unsustainable. After the Rwandan war, refugee camps set up next to protected areas created major fuelwood demands (Kanyamibwa, 1998). Similarly, conditions of economic crisis can increase reliance on fuelwood: for example, many people in Romania turned to protected forests for fuel supplies as a result of an abrupt downturn in the economy (Radu, 1995). In Vietnam, the commercialization of fuelwood collection was reported to be putting stress on the forests in parts of the Ba Vi National Park (Poffenberger, 1998).

Timber
The wide-ranging threats to the Earth's forest ecosystems were discussed in Chapter 2. These threats remain significant in many parts of the world even when forests are placed within protected areas. Illegal or semi-legal felling of timber – for local use, local sale, or for export in the international timber trade – threatens many natural forests in conservation areas. Most illegal logging targets a few valuable species, although larger operations sometimes take place in protected areas where management is very poorly implemented or where the reserve is weakly protected by law. In Cambodia, civil war resulted in massive illegal logging during the 1990s (Global Witness, 1995; 1996; 1998), including within protected areas established by Royal Decree in 1993. A recent report (ICEM, 2003) concluded that "the past five years has seen a steady eating away at the quality of natural systems within protected areas and the surrounding environment, by major government and private development interests and local communities". In some countries, governments allow logging in protected areas, resulting in many "protected areas" not actually attaining the kind of old-growth characteristics that are essential for some species. In Gabon, logging activities are allowed within all protected areas and logging activities have affected sites in varying proportions (Brugière, 1999). A combination of logging and agricultural incursion often results in devastating impacts on tropical forest ecosystems as in Sumatra, Indonesia.

Wildlife
The presence of an intact-looking protected area on a map, or even in a satellite photo, is not necessarily indicative of conservation objectives being achieved. Across the tropical world, hunting is draining wildlife at ever-increasing rates, due to a synergetic linkage of many recent changes, including growing

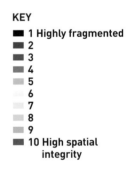

Forest fragmentation in Sumatra, Indonesia between 1982 and 2001.

KEY
- ■ 1 Highly fragmented
- ■ 2
- ■ 3
- ■ 4
- ■ 5
- 6
- 7
- ■ 8
- ■ 9
- ■ 10 High spatial integrity

Source: UNEP-WCMC

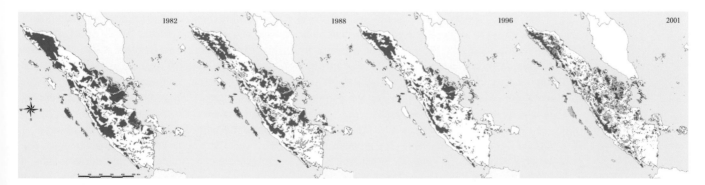

BOX 3.1: FOREST CONVERSION TO COFFEE IN DONG HUA SAO PROTECTED AREA , LAO PDR

The Lao People's Democratic Republic, or Laos, has 20 National Protected Areas or NPAs declared in 1993, 1995 and 1996. Dong Hua Sao (DHS) NPA was among the first 18 sites designated in October 1993, with an area of 1100 km². The area contains two rare habitats: lowland dry-evergreen forest interspersed with wetlands and the upland evergreen forest of the Boloven Plateau. Even at that time, only around 500 km² of the upland forest remained on the 3,800 km² plateau in large and contiguous tracts, having been subject to shifting cultivation for centuries. Approximately 100 km² of the upland forest was within DHS. Over the past decade this area has continued to decline as a result of incursions and clearance for commercial small-holder coffee plantations.

The problem and its causes

By the time DHS came under management in mid-1995, it already faced a major problem of upland deforestation. Aerial photographs from 1995 indicated that about 50 km² of upland forest inside the reserve area had been partly converted to coffee plantations. Protected area staff continued to locate new clearings but were unable to keep up with the pace of deforestation. It was evident that encroachment of prime upland forest posed a real threat to the conservation values of DHS, and at a scale far beyond that which the protected area staff could effectively deal with.

DHS is located on fertile volcanic soils. Despite the fact that the area of such soils with the protected area is much smaller than that outside, most of the expansion in coffee cultivation in Paksong, the major coffee growing district, between 1995 and 1999 was at the expense of the protected area. By 1997 a land and forest allocation drive by the government had formalized the boundaries for all villages adjacent to or near DHS. This campaign also marked the beginning of formal land-use planning and control by government through province, district and village organizations. However, the allocation failed to assign privileges and responsibilities for sections of the protected area to individual villages. It thus left DHS without even the protection of village custodianship and protected area staff were unable to fill the vacuum. Anyone in search of land with a minimum of fuss and expense turned to the protected area.

The risk associated with encroachment was taken as slight compared to the inconvenience of negotiating with villages or the cost of buying land. Land in the protected area also offered the option of clearing prime forest. Coffee planting becomes profitable more rapdly on cleared mature forest than on secondary forest, with a break-even point of just 3 to 4 years, as opposed to 5 or 6. For the smallholder without capital to tide them over, the clearing of secondary forest is not an attractive proposition.

The management response

The beginning of management in DHS coincided with a government drive against illegal clearing and logging in the uplands. While central government supported the expansion of cash crop agriculture it also clearly asserted that protected areas and prime natural forest were not the place to do it. In March 1996 more than 300 persons were found guilty of the illegal clearing of 216 ha of forest and fined the

human populations, protected areas increasingly becoming accessible fragments of natural habitat, the use of modern hunting technologies such as firearms and wire snares, and all of these compounded by vastly increased commercialization of hunting for pets, meat, skins, pelts, parts for traditional medicines, and anything else that will fetch a price (Robinson & Bennett, 2000a). Political instability and warfare can be further elements driving up hunting rates (Hart, 2002).

The problem is especially acute in tropical forests because of their very low productivity for large vertebrates. A tropical forest sustainably produces about 150 kg/km² of vertebrate biomass per year (Robinson & Bennett, 2000b), yet annual hunting rates in many tropical forest reserves are much higher than this: about 200 kg/km² in parts of the Okapi Wildlife Reserve, the Democratic Republic of Congo (Hart, 2000), 349 kg/km² in Arabuko-Sokoke Forest Reserve, Kenya (FitzGibbon et al., 2000), and 701 kg/km² in Menembonembo Nature Reserve, Sulawesi, Indonesia. This is leading to population declines (Robinson & Bennett, 2000a), and local (Peres, 2000; Maisels et al., 2001) and even global (Oates et al., 2000) extinctions.

This has a wider impact on the ecology of the protected areas. Animals hunted preferentially in such forests are the large vertebrates, which

G. Geller, JPL, NASA

equivalent of about US$ 64,000.

A land claims registration was initiated by the DHS management in 1996 to provide the basis of a problem-solving strategy, which was submitted to province and district level decision-makers in 1997. The fact that a considerable proportion of coffee plots and other types of cultivation predated the protected area, massive vested interest; a commitment to participatory management and the lack of enforcement capacity precluded a purely law and order approach.

Under the strategy, agriculture in the protected area would be legalized on the majority of established plots while a minority of plot owners would have to vacate theirs. Plot abandonment was advocated only when it fell inside a proposed core zone. Elsewhere, cultivation could continue on a permit system at present levels and, in the longer term, be phased out or regularized through excision from the protected area. It was also proposed that permit holders contribute to a fund to implement and enforce the permit system. This approach reduced the area slated for abandonment to manageable proportions and promised to generate funds for implementation.

The abandonment of plots and the issue of permits in priority sectors was a work plan target from mid-1998 onwards. While seemingly inching closer to action, by the end of 1999 not a single plot had been abandoned nor had a single cultivation permit been issued. It had become clear that management was probing the very limits of district and province capacity to control land use and/or that vested interests were simply too strong. Management was reduced to documenting the situation on the ground and outlining options for maximum conservation benefits from inevitable boundary adjustments.

A boundary adjustment for the area of Dong Hua Sao from 1100 km^2 to to 910 km^2 was recommended in the Protected Area Status Report of 1995 based on SPOT satellite images dated 1990 or earlier. In mid 1999, another boundary revision proposal was made, based on observations by field patrols, aerial inspection, and 1995 aerial photos of the upland sections. The information on which boundary recommendations were made had always been dated and incomplete until February 2000 when high resolution IKONOS satellite data were obtained. Using GIS software, these data were reanalysed, recent clearings identified and the area of all clrearings calculated. The results suggested that further excisions to 816 km^2 may be unavoidable, further eroding the conservation values of the area.

typically play vital roles as browsers, pollinators, and dispersers (Redford, 1992); 75 percent of the plant species in African rain forests depend on animals for seed dispersal (White, 2001). Loss of wildlife is also detrimental to people who live in or near protected areas who depend on hunting for their subsistence, either from hunting inside the reserve, or in the "sinks" surrounding the protected "source". Those who suffer most when the resource goes are the marginalized forest peoples who have few or no alternatives (Robinson & Bennett, 2002). Efforts to alleviate the problem can back-fire and exacerbate the problem if they result in increased access to the reserve and increased human populations around it, e.g. through badly planned integrated conservation and development projects (ICDPs) (Oates, 1995; 1999), or inappropriate ecotourism developments (Wildlife Conservation Society & Sarawak Forest Department, 1996). Given the low management capacity in protected areas across much of the tropics, often the only protection for wildlife lies in the inaccessibility of these areas.

The problems and issues are complex, so solutions must be multifaceted, and individually tailored to take account of the unique local biological, cultural, socioeconomic, and political conditions (van Schaik et al., 2002). Core elements

S Baker/UNEP

Mining often poses the first threat to natural ecosystems and can be responsible for major changes to ecology.

include education, enforcement, and, as necessary, development of sustainable sources of income and nutrition for local communities. Education must be at many levels, from senior land planners to local communities. Enforcement can be by a government agency (Karanth, 2002), non-governmental agencies, the private sector (van Schaik *et al.*, 2002), or local communities empowered or working with partners to exclude outsiders (Bodmer & Puertas, 2000). Buffer zones that control hunters going into reserves and wildlife products coming out can also be highly effective (e.g. Elkan, 2000).

Overfishing

A large proportion of marine and inland water protected areas are affected by overfishing. Remarkably few have extensive fishing regulations, and strict "no-take" protection is provided in only a small fraction of sites. Overfishing may thus be perfectly legal within many sites. Fishing regulations, where they do exist, can be hard to enforce. Illegal fishing may take place in remote areas, where enforcement is difficult and expensive, while at smaller scales reluctance by local communities to accept regulations can create problems.

Aside from the direct impacts of the excessive removal of aquatic species, many fishing methods are destructive and wasteful to the wider environment. Benthic trawling has destroyed vast areas of continental shelf habitat. Coral reef areas have been plagued by blast-fishing where the use of explosives destroys years of coral growth for a one-off catch of all species in an area. Poison-fishing has similar indiscriminate impacts in other areas. Bycatch (which may be of no commercial value) makes up a substantial proportion of many fisheries, and because it is not directly targeted, may also not be covered by legal regimes of fishing in protected areas: turtles, sharks, seabirds and other species are regularly killed in nets and on longlines. Lost fishing gear continues to snag and catch species, perhaps for many years, and can drift into protected areas.

Minerals

Non-renewable mineral deposits and hydrocarbon reserves are found in all of the world's terrestrial and marine biomes. Mining often poses the first threat to natural ecosystems and can be responsible for major changes to ecology through its direct impacts, pollution, and its role in promoting unplanned and uncontrolled development (Finger, 1999; Brandon, Redford & Sanderson, 1998). The search for new resources has continued to expand into increasingly remote regions, including many sensitive environments rich in biodiversity or harboring threatened species. It has been suggested, for example, that by 2007 more than 80 percent of new oilfield development will take place in the tropics, where most of the world's biodiversity is concentrated (Conservation International, 1997).

There are environmental and social impacts at each stage of the mining process. The trends toward open-pit mining and low-grade ores has increased tailings or waste products, including crushed rock, cyanide (in gold and silver mines), radioactive waste (in uranium mines), sulfuric acid, and heavy metals. Similarly, the wide-ranging methods of extraction of fossil fuels, on land and underwater, and the high risks of pollution during transport, use, and disposal mean that a very wide range of impacts is possible.

Many of the proposed locations for new or expanded natural resource extraction are in, or adjacent to, protected areas. Conflicts clearly arise between extractive activities and the need to maintain biodiversity values. As the demand for mineral resources continues to rise, and as existing reserves become exhausted, it seems unlikely that natural resource extraction can be kept out of all protected areas. Increasingly, however, there have been moves to engage with extractive industry, to develop a dialogue and establish agreements and protocols to restrict activities, mitigate damage, and restore exploited areas. While conflicts will doubtless continue in some areas, the extractive industry is increasingly being treated as a key stakeholder with interests in protected areas.

To date it has been impossible to fully gauge the true scale of these impacts on the world's thousands of individual protected areas. However, at an international level, the impacts on World Heritage sites have been well documented (Philips, 2001). Those affected by mining in recent years include: Kakadu National Park (Australia), Mt Nimba (Guinea/Côte d'Ivoire), Kamchatka National Park (Russian Federation), and Lorentz National Park (Indonesia) (Rössler, 2000; Philips, 2000). These sites are among the most highly valued protected areas in the world in terms of their universal biodiversity value. If these most

prized of sites suffer pressures from extractive industry activities it must be assumed that the problems of mining relative to other national and international protected areas (such as Wetlands of International Importance (Ramsar sites) and/or UNESCO Man and Biosphere reserves (MAB reserves) occur widely.

IUCN Amman Recommendation – "go and no-go areas"

Frequently, national legislation determines whether natural resource extraction activities are permitted within protected areas or their buffer zones. Mining may be prohibited within many protected areas in some countries but acceptable in others. Concern about mining within protected areas persuaded IUCN members to propose a recommendation at the 2000 World Conservation Congress in Amman that, among other things, governments ban mining in Category I-IV protected areas (Dudley & Stolton, 2002). Significant efforts by IUCN over the previous four years or so led to the adoption of the Amman Recommendation in 2000. Resolution 2.82, on the protection and conservation of biological diversity of protected areas from the negative impacts of mining and exploration, identifies that mining should not take place in IUCN Categories I-IV protected areas and only under strict conditions in Categories V and VI. This Declaration and the work

Volunteers at Cotwall End Local Nature Reserve, Dudley, clearing Japanese Knotweed (*Fallopia japonica*), an invasive alien species in the United Kingdom.

P Glendell/Still Pictures

BOX 3.2: WORLD HERITAGE IN DANGER

One of the tools available to the World Heritage Committee to support States Parties to the World Heritage Convention (see Chapter 1) is the "List of World Heritage in Danger". Frequently dubbed as the "Danger List", it is a "list of the property appearing in the World Heritage List for the conservation of which major operations are necessary and for which assistance has been requested under the Convention" (Article 11, paragraph 4 of the Convention).

In early 2006 there were 13 natural sites in the "Danger List" in 9 countries, including one transboundary site (Mount Nimba in Côte d'Ivoire and Guinea). Four of the these countries, incorporating nine sites, were affected by armed conflicts. The remainder were threatened by a range of factors, including water diversion, poaching, illegal settlements, unsustainable tourism and invasive species. A number of sites have recently been removed from the list, including Djoudj Bird Sanctuary in Senegal and Ichkeul National Park in Tunisia, as a result of improved management.

The why and how of the Committee's decisions to place sites on the "Danger List" have been subjects of heated debate in recent years. States Parties to the Convention and other stakeholders in World Heritage conservation have often taken diametrically opposite views on whether or not the Committee has the legal authority to declare a site to be "in Danger" when the State Party does not agree, or when it explicitly opposes the Committee's decision on the matter. A precedent was set as early as in 1992, when the Committee placed several sites on the "Danger List" without the explicit agreement of the States Parties concerned. Since 1999 the Committee undertook a complete revision of the Operational Guidelines for the Implementation of the World Heritage Convention.

While this presented an opportunity, and provoked considerable debate, the clauses pertaining to this issue were left unchanged in the Guidelines and the Committee's option to place a site any time in the "Danger List" remains open.

In October 1996, when a World Heritage workshop was convened at IUCN's First World Conservation Congress in Montreal, Canada, the Committee was deliberating on the need to declare Ecuador's Galapagos National Park, a flagship World Heritage site, as a "Danger site". At that workshop a site-representative insisted that Galapagos is like any other protected area in a less developed country facing a range of threats: immigration due to economic opportunities offered by a booming tourist industry, introduction of alien species, illegal and unsustainable fisheries etc. But his management's commitment to mitigate those threats was quite deliberate and hence he maintained that Galapagos did not deserve to be declared as a site In Danger.

Questions regarding the merits and justifiability of the inclusion of a site in the List of World Heritage in Danger have been raised in many other cases such as: Yellowstone (USA); Simen (Ethiopia); Kakadu (Australia) and El Viscaíno (Mexico). The Committee, in response to specific actions taken by the respective States Parties, decided against including Galapagos, Kakadu and El Viscaíno in the "Danger List". Yellowstone was included in the List with the consent of the State Party. In the case of Simen, Ethiopia, the Amhara Regional authorities, who assumed responsibility for its management following decentralization of administration from Addis Ababa in 1996, objected to the Committee's decision although authorities in Addis Ababa did not take a strong view on the matter. However, difference of

proceeding from it has shaped the development of many of the initiatives described, their proposed aims, and delivered outputs.

Following the Amman Recommendation, no single perspective on conservation and extractive industry impacts was agreed (Philips, 2001). However a broad consensus has started to emerge and protected areas are beginning to be recog-nized by the extractive industry as "sensitive areas". A number of extractive industry multi-nationals are starting to identify and screen where

their existing operations are in relation to current protected areas and identify where proposed extractive industry operations may impact protected areas (BP, 2003). Some companies are making firm commitments not to undertake operations in international protected areas such as World Heritage sites or IUCN Management Category I-IV protected areas.

In addition, a number of companies have begun to formulate biodiversity policies and intro-duce innovative operating management strategies

opinion between the Committee's position on the site's "in Danger" status and that of Regional authorities closest to the site slowed communications between the World Heritage Centre and site-management on conservation problems and mitigation actions needed to restore the outstanding universal values of Simen.

In October 2000, the role of the World Heritage in Danger Listing in promoting international co-operation for the conservation of World Natural Heritage became the subject of another workshop at IUCN's Second World Conservation Congress in Amman, Jordan. There a representative from the Amhara Region of Ethiopia re-iterated his displeasure on the lack of consultation and inadequate verification of information provided by consultant missions that seem to have led to the Committee's declaration of Simen as a site "in Danger". Discussions during that workshop however, convinced the Amhara auth-orities, as well as representatives of other natural World Heritage in Danger, that the intentions of the Committee in declaring sites to be "in Danger" was to call for international action to conserve the site and remove prevailing threats to their integrity. Soon after the workshop a World Heritage Centre/IUCN mission was able to visit Simen and establish a rehabilitation program including benchmarks and indicators for measuring progress and determining the time in the future for removing Simen from the List of World Heritage in Danger.

Participants at the Amman workshop invited States Parties, World Heritage Centre and IUCN to reflect on the conditions under which threats to out-standing universal values of sites could rise to levels that may justify the declaration of a site as World Heritage in Danger. A monitoring regime for con-tinuous threats-analysis and threats-status assess-ment, including triggers that signify changes in threat-levels meriting the declaration of the site as World Heritage in Danger, needs to be part of the management of any area nominated for World Heritage designation. They also felt that the Committee must promote steps to make systematic monitoring regimes an integral part of World Heritage area management practice and invited the Committee to describe in sufficient detail, at the time when it decides to include a site in the List of World Heritage in Danger, the reasons for the listing along with practical actions to be taken, guidelines for implementing the actions and benchmarks for measuring progress.

International debates surrounding the possible "Danger Listing" of Galapagos, El Viscaíno, Yellowstone and other sites have improved responses of the global conservation community and donors to support actions to conserve sites "in Danger". In 1999, the UN Foundation (UNF) targeted World Heritage sites containing biodiversity values of global significance as priorities for grant-aid. Since then several World Natural Heritage sites included at one time or another in the "Danger List" have received financial support

There is still an urgent need to communicate the meaning and the value of "Danger Listing" to key partners, i.e. governments, NGOs, site-staff, local communities, private sector, donors and foundations etc. Special emphasis in any such campaign should be placed on removing the perception that the Committee's interest in monitoring the state of conservation of World Heritage sites is an attempt to police the heritage conservation performance of less developed countries but rather to foster international co-operation to protect and effectively conserve World Heritage.

and design principles and criteria. These are often in addition to existing company efforts in bio-diversity research and conservation relative to their operations. Whilst encouraging, such actions as these still remain restricted to a small selection of major multinationals.

The issue of "no-go" for oil, gas, and mineral mining activities in protected areas will remain a key area of debate between extractive industry and conservation stakeholders. Indeed, it was keenly discussed at the World Parks Congress, Durban, South Africa, in 2003. Areas of divergence remain within and between industry and conservation groups. However, several proposals on how to move forward continue to be presented. The development and availability of decision-making frameworks and mechanisms, "best practice" guidelines, and metrics that consider protected areas may well assist with the more effective consideration of the relative costs and benefits of extraction at the planning stage. There remains a need for their continued development, as well as

Tui de Roy

In the Galapagos National Park goats, pigs, dogs, cats, rats, and many other species have altered ecosystem characteristics and contributed to the extinction of numerous endemic species.

an improved understanding and more widely available mechanisms of interpreting and applying IUCN Protected Area Management Categories.

ALIEN SPECIES

In the last few hundred years humans have greatly accelerated the rates and patterns of movements of a wide range of species. Dramatic increases in human migration, travel, and trade have begun to mix flora and fauna at the global level, across natural geographical barriers such as mountains, oceans, deserts, and rivers. In some cases, the barriers themselves have been removed with the building of canals or bridges. Although many introductions have been accidental, bringing so-called "silent invaders", there are also many cases of deliberate introductions of species, "purposeful invaders", including crops and livestock, but also wild species, to support new settlements or to "enhance" natural environments. In recent decades the constant trickle of species from one place to another has become a flood, following the boom in international trade and travel. It is estimated that at any given moment some 10 000 different species are being transported between biogeographic regions in ballast water tanks alone (Carlton, 1999).

Only a proportion of species that are

translocated from their natural habitats become established elsewhere – so-called alien species, and only a proportion of alien species become sufficiently abundant to have a major impact on the ecosystems in which they find themselves. Those that do, however, can be extremely damaging, to the extent that invasive alien species are now recognized to be one of the major threats to global biological diversity as well as a driving force behind declining quality of human life in many places. While larger species often receive attention, smaller or more hidden species, particularly various kinds of pathogen, can be equally or more destructive.

Islands have often been particularly susceptible to the impacts of alien and invasive species. Remote islands are often home to endemic species. Many are also used by seabirds as nesting colonies. Without natural predators, characteristics such as flightlessness have developed among birds, and species have not developed adequate defense responses to cope with an invasion of predators, grazers, or other competitors. In the Galapagos National Park goats, pigs, dogs, cats, rats, and other species have altered ecosystem characteristics and driven endemic species, including several endemic tortoise species, to extinction

(Schofield, 1989; Mauchamp, 1997). Feral pigs also threaten endemic species by eating the eggs of ground-nesting birds, giant tortoises, and sea turtles. In the 1970s, it was observed that a single pair of pigs destroyed 23 tortoise nests on Santa Cruz Island over a one-month period.

In the Seychelles, endemic birds and reptiles were once widespread across the islands. The impact of rats, mice, and cats have decimated the bird populations. Today the five remaining rat-free islands of the Seychelles are all protected areas, and provide a critical resource for the survival of several species. Similarly, nesting seabirds have proved highly susceptible, and rat-free islands remain some of the only major breeding grounds for petrels, terns, and boobies in all oceans. The 11 small rat-free islands of the British Indian Ocean Territory have all recently been declared protected areas and are used by up to 200 000 pairs of breeding seabirds, whereas, by contrast, the remaining rat-infested islands are largely devoid of nesting birds. The fire tree or fayatree *Myrica faya* has increased within Hawaii Volcanoes National Park from one tree in 1967 to cover 15 900 hectares, reducing the available space for the many endemic species that once thrived in this environment (Camrath *et al.*, 2001). The number of naturalized exotic plants species (2 071) in New Zealand now exceeds the number of native vascular plants (2 055) (Williams & West, 2000).

Four major management options are available for the prevention or control of alien species:

Prevention – legal measures, combined with intensive policing, may help to prevent many introductions. The the International Maritime Organization (IMO) has developed the International Convention for the Control and Management of Ships' Ballast Water and Sediments to minimize the transfer of harmful aquatic organisms and pathogens. Many countries and sub-national jurisdictions had unilaterally developed or are developing national or local legislation. These include Australia, Canada, Chile, Israel, New Zealand, the USA, various individual states within the USA, and various individual ports around the world, such as Buenos Aires in Argentina, Scapa Flow in Scotland, and Vancouver in Canada (Global Ballast Water Management Programme, 2005). The International Convention for the Control and Management of Ships' Ballast Water and Sediments will both harmonize and improve controls at a global level.

In order to prevent future invasion of alien species into protected areas, public education is critical. Tourists and visitors are frequently unaware of laws and regulations to prevent introductions of alien species, or of the serious biological harm such species can create. In the last decade, successful public awareness campaigns on native biodiversity have been conducted in New Zealand.

Accurate information to support identifying and highlighting problem species can be very valuable. Databases of invasive alien species with information on distribution, pathways, and management options are proving helpful for prevention: the global database produced by the Global Invasive Species Programme is one such instrument.

Early detection – can be a critical tool leading to action. When the marine algae *Caulerpa taxifolia* was first observed in the Mediterranean, close to the marine aquarium in Monaco, in 1984, it covered only a single square meter. Unfortunately nothing was done, and there are now well over 100 separate colonies in six different Mediterranean countries, and the species is causing local devastation to native species as well as to fisheries and the diving industry. Identifying alien species in the early stages of establishment is the most economically efficient method to prevent potential threats.

Eradication – is an option in certain circumstances, notably before an invasion has become too large, or on small islands. Eradication is the removal of invasive species from the invaded place or a reduction of their density below sustainable levels. New Zealand, in particular, has led the world in developing techniques for the successful removal from small islands of alien species such as the house mouse *Mus musculus*, black rat *Rattus rattus*, Norway rat *Rattus norvegicus*, and European rabbit *Oryctolagus cuniculus*. In mid-1997 the pig eradication program on Santiago island in the Galapagos National Park, Ecuador, was given priority status. In May 2002 Santiago Island was declared pig free – the first time in at least 127 years, and the largest ever island from which an established pig population was successfully eradicated (Galapagos Conservation Trust, 2005).

In Australia, rapid detection (within six months), isolation, and intensive chemical treatment led to the successful control of an outbreak of black striped mussel in Darwin in 1999. In California, a sabellid worm *Terebrasabella heterouncinata*, which encrusts native gastropod mollusks, reducing their growth rates and weakening their shells, was introduced in the 1980s. Manual removal of infested shells and of other susceptible individuals was undertaken by large numbers of volunteers (some 1.6 million mollusks were removed from the waters around the infestation). It is believed that the large reduction in density of available hosts led to the demise of the invader. Following the demise, the area was relatively rapidly repopulated by gastropod mollusks from adjacent areas (Myers *et al.*, 2000).

Control – is the only remaining option for many invasive species. If numbers can be kept sufficiently low and certain areas can be kept clear, then native species and ecosystems can continue to function.

Efforts to eradicate or control invasive alien species include mechanical removal (tree felling, hunting, and trapping), the use of chemical controls (poisons, herbicides, etc.), and the use of biological controls. There are problems and risks, particularly associated with the use of chemical and biological controls. The release, for example, of cats to control rats has invariably led to a wider suite of problems from two invasive aliens rather than one. In the Pacific, the deliberate introduction of the predatory snail *Euglandina rosea*, often known as the rosy wolf snail, to control feral populations of the giant African land snail *Achatina fulica* had little impact on the latter, but led to the extinction of many endemic partulid snails (*Partula* and *Samoana* spp.), particularly in French Polynesia (Civeyrel & Simberloff, 1996; Murray *et al.*, 1988). Chemical controls can have considerable success (eg. the use of the poison 1080 to control populations of Red foxes *Vulpes vulpes* and other species in Western Australia), but unless carefully used may have undesirable impacts on non-target species.

Growing awareness of the problems of invasive aliens has led to the establishment of a number of groups, including the IUCN Invasive Species Specialist Group and the Global Invasive Species Programme (GISP), coordinated by the Scientific Committee on Problems of the Environment (SCOPE), in collaboration with IUCN, and Commonwealth Agricultural Bureaux International (CAB International). The problems of invasive alien species are also highlighted within the Convention on Biological Diversity (1992) and the United Nations Convention on the Law of the Sea (Montego Bay, 1982). In addition, GISP's Global Strategy on Invasive Alien Species (2001) lists a further 42 international conventions, resolutions, and agreements which address or mention alien invasive species.

IMPACTS FROM BEYOND THE BOUNDARIES

Many of the most fundamental threats come from outside protected area boundaries, and cannot be tackled effectively by management choices made within the protected area or its buffer zones. These can range from relatively local issues, such as changes to the hydrology of a watershed, through to national or global issues such as water and air pollution, and climate change.

Management of such problems inevitably relies on often-distant political decisions, and protected area managers have, until recently, done little more than add their voices to those calling for better pollution control or rational watershed management. However, as the reality of issues such as climate change becomes increasingly accepted, managers are recognizing that they must consider potential impacts in the design and management of protected areas.

Dams and drainage

Freshwater protected areas are particularly vulnerable to impacts originating elsewhere in the catchment, sometimes far distant from the area itself and quite possibly in a different country. For example, the environmental and social impacts of large-scale hydroelectric schemes have received increasing attention, with critics arguing that their costs outweigh the potential benefits. Large dams are identified as causing major social upheaval through displacement of human communities, environmental damage by diverting rivers and flooding land, and more generally, impacts to the hydrological cycle and to local climate patterns (World Commission on Dams, 2000). Over half of the world's large river systems are affected by dams, including the eight most biogeographically diverse (Nilsson et al 2005) and dams have affected a number of important protected areas (Gujja & Perrin, 1999).

Because they affect protected areas or potential protected areas downstream, sometimes creating dramatic changes in ecology, dams are seen as a significant threat. Although the large reservoirs associated with dams can themselves create important habitats for waterfowl and fish, the constantly fluctuating levels make it difficult for shoreline species to survive, simplifying and

S.Chape

Dam construction, either outside or within protected areas, can have significant short and long term impacts on protected areas.

limiting biodiversity. By flooding existing wetlands, dams can dramatically reduce the environmental richness of a particular area. In India, Keoladeo National Park and World Heritage Site, although once a flood-prone area, now faces drought following the construction of the Panchna Dam in the catchment (Brar, 1996). However, in some instances, dams can support the establishment and long-term maintenance of protected areas that form their catchments, as is the case with Canaima National Park and World Heritage Site in Venezuela, Blue Mountains National Park and World Heritage Site in Australia and Nakai-Nam Theun National Protected Area in Lao PDR.

Marine and freshwater pollution

Marine and freshwater protected areas are also susceptible to water-borne pollution arising from beyond their boundaries. This includes both occasional pollution events that destroy large numbers of plants and animals in a short time and chronic pollution that gradually degrades and impoverishes the biodiversity. A number of important pollutants include concentrated nutrients, pesticides, and trace metals and other toxic chemicals.

Concentrated nutrients cause excessive algal growth and, when the algae die and decay,

shortages of oxygen: a process known as eutrophication. Key pollutants are sewage, soluble fertilizers, and pulp mill effluent. For example, the discharge of wastewater from paper mills and sugar plants into East Dongting Lake has seriously polluted the ecosystem in Dongdongtinghu Nature Reserve in China (Chen & Yan, 1996).

Pesticides and other biocides that have leached or drifted from their point of application – typically agricultural land, but also as a result of urban pest controls and even aquaculture – can cause pollution in protected areas far away. Persistent pesticides such as those based on organochlorines are particularly dangerous. The latter are now found in high concentrations in the body fat of marine mammals thousands of kilo-meters from where they were used (Johnston & McRea, 1992). Some freshwater species are extremely sensitive to pesticides (Manson, 1996). The Wadden Sea Trilateral Conservation Area, which straddles Denmark, Germany, and the Netherlands, is currently being polluted by tributyltin (TBT) and pesticides. There now is increasing evidence that some pesticides are hampering the grazing ability of zooplankton, and herbicides are interfering with the photosynthesis of phytoplankton (Enemark, Wesemüller & Gerdiken, 1998).

H Saesemann/UNEP/Still Pictures

Climate change is believed to be affecting food supplies for polar bears (*Ursus maritimus*) in the Arctic.

Trace metals and other persistent toxic chemicals enter water systems from mining operations, factories, domestic waste, or from shipping and boat maintenance. In Lake Nakuru National Park in Kenya, settlement and development of industry around the lake has increased levels of organic and chemical pollutants, especially oil and heavy metals, plus increased sewage discharges (Stolton, Dudley & Rowell, 1997). In April 1998, a tailings dam burst at the Los Frailes mine in Spain, spilling 5 million m³ of toxic waste into rivers near the Doñana National Park and World Heritage Site. The resulting floods affected 5 000–7 000 hectares of farmland and marsh, destroyed bird habitats, and killed large numbers of fish (Carey, Dudley & Stolton, 2000).

Atmospheric pollution

Atmospheric pollution is an important threat to both terrestrial and marine protected areas, particularly in the more developed countries, including industrialized parts of Europe, North America, and Asia. One of the most detailed surveys to date assessed the impacts on wildlife through a literature survey, which identified effects on 1 300 species, including 11 mammals, 29 birds, 10 amphibians, 398 higher plants, 305 fungi, 238 lichens, and 65 invertebrates. The results showed that among plants alone more than 100 species

have been extirpated, sometimes from quite large areas, due to air pollution in the UK (Tickle, 1996). Protected areas have tended to be established on land that is less suitable for agriculture or other commercial uses and thus often on acidic or base-poor soils, where the effects of acidification are generally more acute.

Connected ecosystems

Many mobile animal species spend a part of their lives outside protected areas. These include migratory species, but also others which depend on different areas at different phases in their life history, such as pelagic fish species, that come into coastal channels or into mangrove forests to breed. In some cases the daily movements of species may take them in and out of protected areas. In all these cases, the adjacent protected area becomes irrelevant, and legitimate activities such as hunting and fishing, or the destruction of a critical habitat, can severely reduce the numbers of a species able to return to, or to utilize, a protected area. This in turn may undermine the entire *raison d'être* of a site, and even undermine its ecological functioning. The solution to such problems can only be derived from the design of more holistic measures, such as the establishment of protected area networks and migratory corridors (often international), or other legal protection regimes such as seasonal or species-based hunting restrictions outside of protected areas.

CLIMATE CHANGE

During the course of the 20th century, the average surface temperature (combining surface air temperature over land and sea) across the planet increased by 0.6°C. The rate of change is accelerating: ten of the eleven warmest years since accurate records began in 850 have been since 1995 with 1998 almost certainly the single warmest year in the past millennium. The two second warmest years on record have both been since then (2003 and 2005). Since the 1960s there has been an estimated 10 percent decrease in the extent of snow cover and a two-week decrease in the average duration of snow and ice cover (northern hemisphere). The extent of Arctic sea ice has declined by 10–15 percent since the 1950s, with a 40 percent decline in sea ice thickness during the late summer/early autumn. Sea levels have risen during this period. Changes around the UK, when adjusted for isostatic rebound, vary from 0.3 mm/year to 1.8 mm/year.

Such changes have already occurred, and have been accurately measured. There is little doubt about their veracity. They tally closely with expected changes predicted from the observations of atmospheric change. Most notable has been a 31 percent increase in atmospheric CO_2 since the start of the industrial revolution (1750). This is largely linked to the burning of fossil fuels, with a further 25 percent coming mainly from land-use change and specially from deforestation. Other greenhouse gases , including methane and nitrous oxide, have also increased dramatically. There is good evidence that these gases have not existed in these concentrations in the global atmosphere for at least 420 000 years, and probably not for 20 million years. With these atmospheric changes there are also the beginnings of changes in ocean chemistry – a higher partial pressure of CO_2 has already led to a 0.1 unit reduction in the pH of ocean surface waters.

Models have been built to simulate future change in atmospheric conditions, taking into account anthropogenic and natural forcing. The best available models predict temperature rises in the range 1.4 to 5.8°C between 1990 and 2100. Such figures are global averages. They will be considerably higher over larger land areas than over the ocean. They will also be more extreme at higher latitudes in the northern hemisphere. Over the same period sea levels are projected to rise between 9 and 88 centimeters. Other changes are predicted, but with lower reliability. These include higher precipitation in northern latitudes and the Antarctic over the winter, but more variable changes at lower latitudes, with greater inter-annual variation. Changes in the extent, strength, and distribution of extreme events such as droughts, forest fires, floods, and tropical storms are difficult to predict. Similarly, although some models predict changes to some of the main ocean circulation patterns (with potentially massive regional climatic impacts), most predict gradual shifts rather than rapid cessation or reversal.

Impacts on biodiversity and protected areas

Some impacts of climate change have already been widely observed. In Europe, studies showed an increase in the growing season of some 11 days between 1959 and 1996. Of a sample of 35 butterfly species in Europe, about two thirds were found to have shifted their ranges northwards by distances of 35–340 kilometers during the 20th century.

Changes in the incidences of pests and diseases have also been observed. The likely impacts of global climate change on forests are still being debated, but there seems to be general consensus that the boreal coniferous forests are particularly vulnerable to both range restrictions and increasing fire frequency. Another forest type that is especially vulnerable to climate change is tropical montane cloud forest, which depends upon clouds to supply it with atmospheric moisture. Research has shown that the mean cloud base is moving upwards on tropical mountains as a result of climatic shifts. The forest species are not able to migrate at a comparable rate and, in any case, range shifts will be limited by the land area existing at higher elevations. Local extinctions in cloud forest amphibians, including the Costa Rican golden toad *Bufo periglenes*, not recorded since 1989, have been attributed to climatic fluctuations that may be linked to long-term global climate change (Pounds *et al.*, 1999).

Future ecosystem changes are likely to be far more extreme, and also more complex, as climate change accelerates. In many cases there are likely to be synergistic responses where the impacts of multifaceted change may be different from any apparent "sum of the parts".

Protected areas represent static surfaces that are increasingly hemmed in by human land uses, like islands. Quite aside from the problems of small or isolated populations, such islands are, to varying degrees, closed off from the sorts of dynamic responses that may be required for ecosystem survival in the face of changing climates. Small fragments also lack the resilience that comes from the genetic diversity and broad spatial extent of unimpacted ecosystems.

In a recent analysis, WWF (2003) categorized the types of climate change impacts on protected areas as:

Disappearance of Habitats and Ecosystems
This is clearly the most drastic of impacts for protected areas, and one which is anticipated to affect low-lying, coastal and marine areas, principally coral reefs, mangroves and saltmarshes. Indeed, these kinds of impacts are already being recorded at a number of sites as a result of sea-level rise, unseasonable flooding and increased sea temperature. Examples include the Sundarbans National Park and World Heritage Site, where an estimated 75 km² of mangroves has been lost to

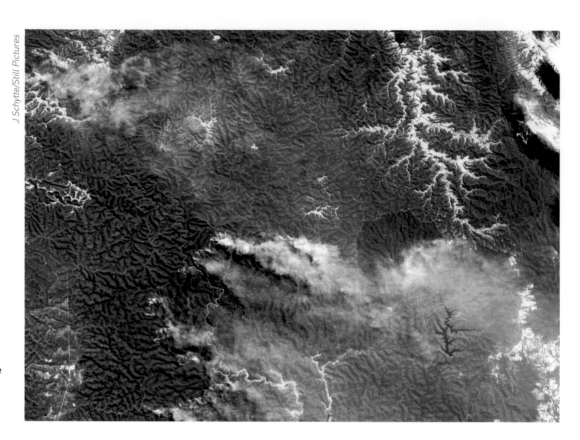

J Schytte/Still Pictures

Fires viewed from space in the Blue Mountains National Park, Australia.

sea-level rise (although aggravated by deltaic subsidence). In a worst-case scenario the Intergovernmental Panel on Climate Change (IPCC) pre-dicts that 75 percent of the mangroves will disappear as a result of sea-level rise. As well as the loss of biodiversity and natural heritage values, it has been estimated that it would cost almost $300 million to construct 2 200 km of cyclone/ flood embankments. A further annual cost of $6 million would be required for maintenance to mitigate the impacts of tropical storms (Dudley and Stolton, 2003). We have already seen, in December 2004, the value of natural coastal ecosystems, especially mangroves, in mitigating the impacts of the Asian tsunami. Although the cause of tsunamis is geological, the predicted increase in the frequency and intensity of cyclonic storms and resulting sea surge arising from climate change is likely to have similar impacts on low-lying ecosystems and human communities.

Catastrophic Long-Term Changes to Ecosystems
Even where ecosystems are not completely eliminated, there are a range of impacts that may cause major and irreversible damage. One of the most alarming predictions is the complete loss of

summer ice in the Arctic within 50 years, with potentially catastrophic impact on polar bears, seals, and other species, as well as on indigenous communities. Similarly, break-up of the Antarctic ice sheet will impact on penguin populations. In 1998 it was reported that the Adelie Penguin population had declined by 33 percent in the last 25 years as a result of reduced winter sea ice habitat. More recently, we have seen satellite images of major ice fractures in the Antarctic.

Coral bleaching events are now recorded with increased frequency, but notably in 1998 when tropical sea surface temperatures were the highest on record. Climate change is postulated to be the primary cause of steadily rising marine temp-eratures, in concert with more frequent El Niño and La Niña-type events. The death of coral reefs would have a severe impact on the world's most valuable protected coral reef ecosystems, such as the Great Barrier Reef in Australia and the Aldabra Atoll in the Seychelles. It would also affect the innumerable reefs that provide subsistence and livelihoods for island and coastal communities in the tropical regions of the world.

A rise in water levels in estuaries and shallow coastal areas will reduce the size and connectivity of small islands and protected areas (Lal, Harasawa & Murdiyarso, 2001). A study in the USA concluded that over 11 000 linear km of protected coastline, including 80 coastal protected areas, are at risk from sea-level rise (Beavers, 2001).

Catastrophic Temporary Changes to Ecosystems
This includes the impacts of more frequent long-term drought events on ecosystems and species, especially wetlands, but also a wide range of other ecosystems that already have a fine balance of ecosystem dynamics and seasonal aridity. The consequences of sustained droughts can result not only in impacts associated with water deficits but also the frequency of catastrophic fires that can potentially change even fire-adapted ecosystems. This occurred in Eastern Australia where wildfires caused by lightning strikes following sustained drought resulted in severe damage to alpine vegetation in Kosciusko National Park where such vegetation was already located at the edge of an ecological range and susceptible to climate change. The Blue Mountains National Park World Heritage Site also suffered major damage from forest fires, and water levels in the catchments protected within the national park, which provide water to Sydney's 4 million people, fell drastically.

The impacts on ecosystems that are less fire-adapted are likely to be long lasting. The IPCC predicts that the frequency of forest fires is likely to increase in the coniferous forests of boreal Asia. We have already seen the catastrophic impacts of anthropogenic fires on the tropical forests of Southeast Asia and the subsequent regional smoke haze, causing major environmental and health problems costing millions of dollars. Further deforestation in the Amazon region is predicted to result in less evapotranspiration and less rainfall in dry periods, estimated to decrease average rainfall by 32 percent (Lean *et al.*, 1996). These examples highlight the circular nature of climate change, as humans continue to reinforce and worsen the root causes of climate change through large-scale forest clearance and burning.

It is predicted that changes in fire regimes in Africa will impact on forest plant communities that form centres of endemism, many of which contain protected areas. More than 90 percent of world antelope and gazelle species are concentrated in Africa and it is predicted that climate change-induced habitat alteration will alter the distribution range of many of these (Desanker & Madadza,

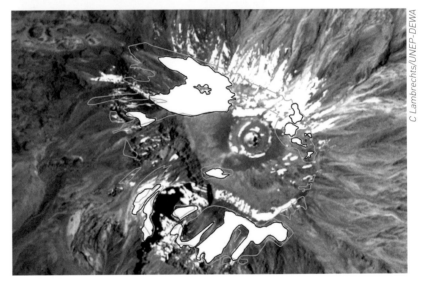

C Lambrechts/UNEP-DEWA

2001). Considering that wild biodiversity forms an important resource for African people, both consumptive and non-consumptive, major changes in the distribution and availability of key species could further impact negatively on the economy and livelihoods of societies in Africa.

Dramatic Changes to Habitats and Ecosystems
These changes cover issues such as melting montane ice caps and glaciers, and species shifts to cooler latitudes and altitudes. There are now stark examples of retreating glaciers, and disappearing ice and snow cover on the mountains of the world. For example, the snow and ice cap on Mount Kilimanjaro has been in retreat for several decades and is predicted to completely disappear

The southeastern side of Kibo, the highest peak of Kilimanjaro (top), and (below) Kilimanjaro's icecap in 1962 (yellow), and 2000 (black outline).

95

B O'Connor/Still Pictures

The golden toad (*Bufo periglenes*) in the Monteverde cloud forest, Costa Rica. It has not been recorded since 1989.

by 2020; it formed more than 11 000 years ago, but has decreased by 82 percent over the past century (Thompson *et al.*, 2002). Thus, some of the most iconic protected natural heritage places in the world are likely to undergo major transformation. In many protected areas the values for which they were established will alter or diminish as species that are able to shift their range outside the boundaries of established protected areas. The extent of such shifts has been measured in some areas. For example, in the European Alps global warming is believed to be the cause for the up-ward altitudinal movement of some plant species by 1–4 meters per decade and the loss of some taxa restricted to high elevations, threatening the values in areas such as the Swiss National Park (WWF, 2003).

Responses

Efforts to slow and halt climate change are being addressed by the UN Framework Convention on Climate Change and its protocols.

At the same time, there is an urgent need to consider more practical responses to the ongoing problem. Climate change will not cease even when greenhouse gas emissions are halted. The impacts of climate change will be great, and protected areas will suffer particularly from these impacts. A number of responses are being considered to reduce the impacts. These can be considered under three broad headings.

Avoidance

Certain aspects of climate change may be prevented through direct physical intervention. Examples of this include the building of barriers to prevent flooding of adjacent sites by sea-level rise; riverine management, including diversion or irrigation to maintain stable conditions in wetland areas. Other forms of impact avoidance might include the removal of species that migrate into sites, the control of pests that benefit from benign climatic conditions, or the building of fire management systems in the face of increasing threats from fire.

Another means of avoiding impacts is to prevent or remove the synergistic threats that might be enhanced through a changing climate. By minimizing other disturbances, such as alien invasive species introductions or unnatural sources of fire, the impacts of climate change may be avoided, or at least delayed.

Alleviation

In other cases change may be unavoidable, but direct measures may allow for the amelioration of impacts, often taking action at a systematic level rather than responding at individual sites. By 2050 many species are predicted to have changed their ranges by tens of kilometers, or by hundreds of meters in altitude. This may take them beyond the natural boundaries of existing protected areas, or into the boundaries of others.

One of the most important measures to deal with such changes, which is now being addressed by a number of protected area systems plans, is the concept of biological corridors (discussed further in Chapter 4). By ensuring connectivity between protected areas, the natural migration of species and even entire ecosystems may be supported. Even if a species is threatened by change in one site, changing conditions may favor its survival at another, while migration corridors will support its movement to that new location over years or perhaps decades.

Such knowledge should also be used in the planning of individual new protected areas. Where there is some idea of direction in climate change trends, and hence in potential changes in species range, it is logical to try to encompass a broad part of key species ranges, over latitudinal, altitudinal, or other gradients. It may also be reasonable to look for edge-of-range areas if these areas are likely to become increasingly hospitable to key species, or even to produce potential future range maps to help in system design.

There is quite good evidence that certain species, notably long-lived sedentary species such as trees, may not be able to migrate as fast as the changing climatic conditions. Under certain circumstances it may be considered necessary to enhance natural migration to accommodate this, by transporting tree species to new locations where climatic conditions permit. (Although this may sound like unacceptable interference, there is good evidence that "natural" migration patterns have often followed such rare "long jumps", but that these same processes are today thwarted by habitat fragmentation).

It is only a small step from this to consider the creation of new habitats where natural migration might not occur sufficiently quickly (e.g. islands). Conservationists are also becoming engaged in the current dialogues relating to carbon sequestration. There are a number of schemes that are proposing to create or to restore forest ecosystems as a means of offsetting CO_2 production. With proper planning, such new habitats could provide a critical benefit for biodiversity conservation.

Adjustment
Perhaps linked to the processes of alleviation are the processes of adapting to change. It may be necessary to "let go" of some key species or habitats from protected areas under changing conditions, allowing for drying out, flooding, and emigration or immigration processes, and changing management regimes appropriately. With sea-level rise, it may be appropriate to allow flooding of coastal habitats, but where possible efforts should be made to support migration rather than a squeezing of the coastal habitat zonation. It may

also be relevant to designate, or even to create, areas of new habitat, and new protected areas, as new patterns of climatic conditions evolve.

As with all aspects of protected areas management, it is critical to monitor change, including climatic parameters, the ecological responses, and the impacts of management interventions in as many sites as possible. The transfer of knowledge and information, including planning tools and successes and failures in management response, between sites will greatly improve management efficiency in the face of changing climates, and will reduce costs. The wider application of models to develop predictive surfaces and support management planning or network design will enable an increase in pre-emptive management responses.

These responses to climate change may appear drastic. In many cases they will not be needed for years or decades, while our own systems for avoiding, alleviating, or adjusting may have become far more sophisticated. It will be necessary, in all cases, to proceed carefully – interference with natural processes can lead to greater problems.

Climate change is bringing into focus some of the key problems of reliance on protected areas as the main tool for *in situ* biodiversity conservation, most notably those associated with trying to maintain small isolated populations in a "wilderness" of agricultural, degraded, or urban landscapes. Discussions about avoiding or mitigating the impacts, or even of adapting, are somewhat belittled by the sheer magnitude of the problems, but there is little choice. Climate change will doubtless claim many victims in the efforts to preserve natural landscapes. It will be essential to keep up the pressure to halt greenhouse gas emissions, but immediate action may also need to be considered in many sites.

CHAPTER 4

Protected areas in the wider context

Contributors: M. Lockwood and G. Worboys; Kaa-Iya del Gran Chaco National Park: M. Painter; Species conservation and traditional resource ownership, Yadua Taba: D. Watling; Private protected areas: M. Spalding and E. Carter; International trends in protected area governance: P. Dearden, M. Bennett, and J. Johnston; Corridors: C. Boyd; Community Conserved Areas: A. Kothari et al.; IUCN PA Management Categories: S. Chape; Participatory planning and management – the mixed experience of the Galapagos Marine Reserve: G. Borrini-Feyerabend and A. Tye.

The progress made in setting up protected areas was celebrated at the IUCN Vth World Parks Congress (WPC), in Durban, South Africa in 2003. The 3 000 people present also recognized the many values of protected areas and their role in bringing "benefits beyond boundaries" to millions of people. But, as we have seen in Chapter 3, protected areas are under threat as never before. They are exposed to pollution and climate change, irresponsible tourism, insensitive infrastructure, and ever-increasing demands for land, water, and other resources. Many protected areas lack political support and are short of financial and other resources. There are still too many gaps in the global protected areas system, management is often poor, and too often local communities are alienated from, rather than linked to, protected areas.

The Parties to the Convention on Biological Diversity recognized this when they agreed their Programme of Work on Protected Areas at Kuala Lumpur in 2004. One of the program's goals was "to substantially improve site-based protected area planning and management". An ambitious target was adopted, namely: all protected areas to have effective management in existence by 2012, using participatory and science-based site planning processes that incorporate clear biodiversity objectives, targets, management strategies, and monitoring programs, drawing upon existing methodologies and a long-term management plan with active stakeholder involvement. This chapter presents the wider context, both ecological and social, in which protected areas need to operate, while Chapter 5 provides a brief overview of protected area management and the challenges faced by management agencies.

SOCIAL CONTEXT AND CHANGING PARADIGMS

Protected area policy and management is strongly influenced by prevailing social and economic circumstances, as well as cultural and ethical norms. Managing protected areas is essentially a social process. The meanings, purposes, and management of protected areas are not static, but develop in conjunction with wider social, economic, and cultural influences. There is a plurality of views about how we should relate to the natural world, why we should protect natural environments, and how we should manage and use them. Protected area managers must take account of politics, the legal system, the internal dynamics of institutions, and broad social and political structures and trends.

In many parts of the world, the declining power of nation states has been associated with an expansion of market capitalism. Major forces affecting all areas of society include the internationalization of capital and markets through the development of an international financial sector; the expansion of free trade agreements; the emergence of dominant transnational corporations; and the development of power blocs based on economic association, such as the European Union (EU) and the Asia-Pacific Economic Cooperation (APEC). These forces have fostered such changes as a reduction in the size of government, corporatization of public agencies, and the redefinition of the role of the public sector. A key policy debate throughout the world is, and has been for many years, about a desirable balance between the public sector and private sector. How much power should the public and private sectors have? How should they relate to each other? The debate is crucially important to

S.Chape

Village in Nam Et National Protected Area, Houaphan Province, Lao PDR.

S Pathirana/UNEP

Protected areas are now seen as part of a mosaic of land and natural resource uses that are interdependent with communities and economies.

protected area managers. It influences, among other things: who is given the responsibility for managing protected areas; what resources are allocated for managing protected areas; who pays for these resources; who has the power to make decisions and how those decisions are made.

The traditional view of protected areas as isolated repositories for natural and cultural heritage protection and conservation ignores the interactions between protected areas and regional and local communities. Protected areas are now conceived as a long-term societal endeavor that goes well beyond the original "Yellowstone" vision of what a national park should be. As noted in Chapter 1, this shift has been summarized by Phillips (2003), who characterizes the old and new paradigms according to factors such as the objectives of protected areas, their governance, attitudes towards local people, and management. In the context of conserving natural and cultural heritage, important elements of the shift encompass building a wide constituency that supports protected areas, locating protected areas within the wider agenda of sustainable development, and responding to calls from indigenous

peoples and local communities for more recognition of their rights, needs, and cultures.

In all, these constitute a "paradigm shift" in thinking about protected areas. Protected areas, with their conservation emphasis, are now seen as part of a mosaic of land and natural resource uses that are interdependent with communities and economies. Increasing recognition is being given to the importance of protected areas in furthering regional development. Protected area managers have a responsibility to explain the local and regional benefits that protected areas provide, as well as engaging more fully with local communities to minimize costs and maximize the flow of these benefits. Managers must recognize and meet responsibilities concerning regional communities and indigenous peoples. The fact that many protected areas are being managed by indigenous and local communities is also gaining recognition.

There is a two-way relationship between regional communities and protected areas. For the values of a protected area to be maintained, it must function as part of its community. Protected areas cannot be divorced from local and regional land uses. Most exist in a matrix of multiple-use public lands and private lands devoted to agriculture, private forestry, urban development, and other uses. Protected areas typically require transportation routes, energy grids, water supply, and waste disposal systems. They can create employment, housing needs, and business opportunities, particularly those related to the supply of goods and services needed to support visitor activities. These needs and opportunities in turn trigger development requirements within a region for infrastructure, waste disposal, and natural resources, such as water (Machlis and Field, 2000a).

Management issues ranging from fire protection and prevention to the spread of introduced species can arise from such development activity. This implies that management policies for protected areas should be integrated into the broader context of community sustainability. Strategic planning is required to integrate those concerns within the boundaries of the protected area network (biodiversity conservation, visitor service provision, environmental protection) with wider environmental, economic, and social sustainability. Machlis and Field (2000b) advocate that protected area managers should:

❑ take responsibility to influence development in rural areas and aggressively seek to maintain the viability of communities that surround protected areas;

❏ promote a sense of local identity that allows people to determine their own destinies;

❏ create allies among local citizens, especially local leaders, to develop a management capability at a landscape scale;

❏ emphasize the local and regional benefits of protected areas;

❏ adopt a collaborative approach to planning, with citizen participation understood as being crucial to the development of leadership and capacity for sustainable development;

❏ contribute to preserving the overall character and lifestyle adjacent to protected areas while maintaining opportunities for planned growth;

❏ give technical assistance to rural and gateway regions, train staff in rural development and collaboration skills, and assess progress in achieving sustainable rural development.

ESTABLISHING PROTECTED AREAS

Chapter 2 discussed the need for systematic planning of protected area networks with respect to the coverage of biodiversity, particularly in relation to the targets under the protected areas work program adopted by the Parties to the Convention on Biological Diversity in 2004 and the action plan developed in 2003 as part of the Vth World Parks Congress. However, as well as identifying gaps in the existing network, a variety of other factors need to be taken into consideration when planning a comprehensive system of protected areas at the national level. These include:

❏ defining the priority of protected areas as a worthwhile national concern – but often linked to international concerns and obligations;

❏ defining the relationships between various categories of protected area;

❏ defining the relationships between protected areas and other land-use and tenure categories;

❏ habitat requirements of rare or other species and their minimum viable population sizes;

❏ connectivity between units (corridors) to permit wildlife migration;

❏ perimeter/area relationships;

❏ natural system linkages and boundaries;

❏ traditional use, occupancy, and sustainability;

❏ cost of achieving protected area status (Davey, 1998).

In general, most protected areas have been established through political processes: that is, government agencies and/or interest groups have

S Chape

The meaning, purpose, and management of protected areas develop within wider social, economic, and cultural influences. Bukit Timah Nature Reserve, Singapore, at 164 ha, may be small but it fulfills important conservation and social objectives in one of the world's smaller countries.

BOX 4.1: PRIVATE PROTECTED AREAS

In 2003 the World Parks Congress defined a private protected area (PPA) as "a land parcel of any size that is 1) predominantly managed for biodiversity conservation; 2) protected with or without formal government recognition; and 3) is owned or otherwise secured by individuals, communities, corporations or non-government organizations" (WPC, 2003). Carter et al. (in press) further consider the governance regime of PPAs and introduce the term "private sector conservation enterprise (PSCE)" for the diverse array of "non-state actors or organizations that might be involved in either the management and/or ownership of PPAs; from corporate institutions and limited companies, through to private individuals and trusts".

PPAs have the potential to supplement government initiatives to protect natural ecosystems, particularly in areas where remaining natural lands are already held in private ownership. Although not new (the first land trust in the USA dates back to 1891, while the National Trust established the first nature reserve in the United Kingdom in 1899), PPAs have become widespread in recent decades and in many countries they now represent a significant proportion of the total protected areas estate.

In North America and a number of European countries, many such reserves are owned and managed by membership organizations. In the United Kingdom some 2 250 private local nature reserves are owned or managed by a group of 47 local wildlife trusts while hundreds more are managed by other national conservation NGOs – the National Trust, with over 3 million members, owns some 2,480km².

Although many such sites are smaller than national protected areas, they may be critically important for certain species, or for the role they may play in a wider network, or for public education.

In the United States, a system of more than 1 600 private, non-profit organisations known as "land trusts" hold large areas in PPAs and have transferred ownership of even larger areas to public authorities (see Regional Analysis, North America). The Nature Conservancy (TNC) has successfully exported many of its PPA approaches, working with partners, to other countries. TNC is also undertaking important work on private sector approaches in marine environments, including the purchase of fisheries leases around shellfish beds, kelp communities and offshore trawling grounds.

In Southern and Eastern Africa private reserves make up a significant area of the total protected areas network – in Tanzania PPAs cover and estimated 126 000 km² – 13.3 percent of all terrestrial land (Carter et al., in press). Several large private reserves in South Africa lie adjacent to the Kruger National Park allowing free movement of game and adding 1 800 km² to the total area protected. Worldwide, the largest sites of all include the Pumalin Park in Chile (3 000 km²); the NamiRand Nature Reserve in Namibia (1 800 km²); and the Diamond A Ranch in New Mexico USA (1 300 km²).

Funds for purchase and management of PPAs comes from a range of sources. Many are purchased or supported by grants from the private and/or the public sector, and from membership fees of the

---

supported the reservation of an area, and this support has ultimately been manifested in declaration of the area under appropriate legislation or alternative governance arrangements. Such political approaches to selecting protected areas are often ad hoc or opportunistic, heavily influenced by threat and availability, and primarily determined by economic and cultural factors (Margules, 1989; Pressey, Bedward, and Keith, 1994). While many important natural areas have been protected in this manner, regional conservation of biodiversity and consideration of other significant conservation values are not guaranteed. In many countries, protected area systems reflect bias towards some types of landscapes and ecosystems rather than

others. Many large parks are in mountainous or relatively inaccessible areas or in areas of low productivity for other uses.

Formal selection procedures, while not a substitute for the political process, can allow for more informed land-use decisions based on key biological and social criteria. A procedure for the selection of protected areas should be explicit, systematic, and straightforward, and should consider the extent to which the options for reservation are lost if a particular site is not preserved, while also recognizing the values of efficiency and flexibility (Pressey, Johnson, and Wilson, 1994). Systematic approaches to protected area selection are characterized as being:

supporting NGOs. In some countries a major drive for PPA establishment has been the economic value of nature-based tourism, wildlife-based photo tourism and recreational hunting (Christiansen *et al.*, 2005). Nearly half of the reserves in Southern Africa and South America surveyed by Langholz (1996) received 90 percent of their revenues from tourism and many sites are considered more profitable than, for example, agriculture.

Approaches to visitor access are highly varied. Those relying on tourism may charge high entry fees and may limit visitor densities: in Kenya 84 percent of PPAs exhibited a high level of control over 'access' to the area (Carter *et al.*, in press). Others are open access and may see such access as a critical means of strengthening local support for conservation or for encouraging membership or donations.

Although sometimes controversial, hunting is an important driver behind PPA establishment in many countries. Properly managed, hunting can be entirely sustainable, and in some cases may actually contribute to maintaining ecosystem processes, for example the removal of invasive mammals, or the maintenance of stable large-herbivore numbers in the absence of a natural predator population. In Tanzania some hunting companies provide dividend flows to local community projects, as well as providing employment in the region.

Concern is sometimes expressed at the possibility that private protected areas may be less secure than public sites over the long-term, particularly in the case of individual private landholders, who may decide to sell the land, or change its use. In many countries such change of use

may be prevented by the granting, or imposition, of legal status on to such lands, incorporating them into the national protected areas system, while allowing certain private property rights to be maintained. An increasingly popular system in North America is that of the conservation "easement" whereby certain rights typically associated with private property are relinquished in a manner that is binding on all subsequent landowners, in perpetuity. Such agreements vary on a case-by-case basis, but often restrict the right to building, mining, timber extraction or agricultural use. In some cases these are given voluntarily by the land owners, but recognizing the cost in terms of loss of resale value, and the potentially great conservation benefits, such easements are often paid for by state and federal agencies, or by conservation groups .

Given the complex range of governance regimes and management mechanisms exhibited in PPAs, categorizing them and gathering concrete information on their scale and scope is challenging. Carter *et al.* (in press) have developed an outline typology for PPAs that differentiates the various approaches observed in East Africa, ranging from "Individual Private Protected Areas" through to "Community Conservation Concessions". However, considerable work is needed to understand the scale and scope of PPA growth internationally and the efficacy of PPAs in meeting biodiversity imperatives and the associated social impacts of such initiatives. To date a very large number of PPAs remain unreported within the WDPA and remain unrepresented in the global statistics presented in this volume.

❏ data-driven, using features such as species, vegetation types, reserve size, or connectivity; and selection units that are divisions of the landscape that are to be evaluated for their contribution to satisfying some objectives;
❏ objective-led, based on a set of criteria that have quantitative targets for each feature;
❏ efficient, in that they attempt to achieve the goals at a minimum cost in terms of other potential land uses;
❏ transparent, in that reasons behind selection of each reserve are explicit;
❏ flexible, because features and targets can be varied to explore how changing these parameters influences the configuration and

extent of the selected reserve network (Pressey, 1998).

Formal criteria are used to assess whether each unit should be included in the reserve network. Biophysical criteria include factors such as: rarity of species; representativeness of ecosystems; diversity of habitat, and naturalness. Social criteria include: threat of human interference; community appeal; aesthetics; education value; and recreation and tourism. Planning criteria include: adherence to catchment principles; bioregional boundaries; natural boundaries; fire control; and availability of the land. Reserve design criteria are concerned with the spatial placement and characteristics of protected area networks and individual units, including their size, boundaries, shape, connectivity, and geographic relationship to other units. The use of these criteria reflects the importance of considering the relationship of individual units to a network as a whole and to the landscape or seascape in which each protected area sits. From the perspective of biodiversity, one useful conceptual approach is that of biological and conservation corridors.

Biological corridors

As habitat conversion and alteration outside protected areas (and often within them) continues, protected areas themselves can increasingly be seen as isolated islands of habitats. This affects their ability to maintain biodiversity as even the largest protected areas may be too small to support important ecosystem processes and viable populations of some species in the long term.

Small isolated populations of species are vulnerable to extinction due to inbreeding depression and random demographic and environmental variation – analysis carried out by population biologists indicate that anywhere from 50 to 5 000 individuals may be the minimum population size for the long-term survival of a species in any area, depend on the biology of the species concerned and prevailing environmental conditions. However, populations can persist below this level where there is sufficient movement between areas to allow regular replenishment or recolonization. Linked fragments are therefore expected to support greater numbers of species in the long-term than isolated fragments of the same size.

Wide-ranging or migratory animal species face a particular challenge. Such species typically move periodically or seasonally from one core habitat area to another. These areas may be widely separated from each other – by thousands of kilometers in the case of some migratory species. Effective connectivity between core areas is determined by the relative ease with which individuals or populations can move from one to another through the intervening areas. Where such movement is made difficult or impossible, the survival of the population may be threatened even if the core areas remain intact.

From a biodiversity perspective, the ideal response to such problems would be the expansion of existing protected areas, but often this is not feasible, particularly in the case of wide-ranging migratory species. One alternative approach has been to focus on biological corridors or movement pathways between core areas. These may be continuous or a series of "stepping stones" (for example, the Western Hemisphere Shorebirds Network in North America provides stepping stones of protected habitat along a continental flyway).

Design of biological corridors aimed at conserving particular species may be based on direct studies or simulations of their migration or dispersal pathways. Designing biological corridors is more challenging when the goal is wider biodiversity conservation. This is particularly the case in marine environments – some species are active dispersers, others passive, and species disperse at different times and for different periods, interacting with seasonally variable currents. In this context, one option is to clearly identify priority species, such as globally threatened, keystone or umbrella species. Another is to look at core areas and biological corridors in the wider landscape or seascape – the so-called conservation corridor approach, discussed below.

There has been significant controversy about the concept of biological corridors. The value of connectivity is not in question as much as whether

Blue wildebeest (*Connochaetes taurinus*) in the Serengeti, Kenya.

UNEP

corridors actually provide connectivity and, from an economic perspective, whether investing in corridors makes the best use of scarce conservation resources. The problem of demonstrating connectivity in part reflects the difficulty of designing rigorous studies of corridor use by target species in real landscapes, and the poor design of many studies. It is also difficult to generalize from existing studies, because the results are both species and landscape-specific. Further concerns have been raised about the potential dangers of corridors – they may stimulate an influx of invasive species; expose animals to poachers; or encourage dispersal to sink habitats (those in which mortality rates exceed reproduction rates). The stepping stone approach may perpetuate habitat fragmentation.

Conservation corridors

Some of these concerns can be addressed by careful design of corridors within a protective matrix of compatible land and resource uses: the conservation corridor approach. Delineation of the boundaries of conservation corridors is most effectively undertaken with a rigorous scientific base, including the assessment of the habitat requirements of minimum viable populations of target species, the ecological processes required and disturbance patterns. Mapping the overlapping habitat and connectivity needs of a number of different target species may lead to the identification of large-scale biodiversity conservation corridors whose boundaries will often correspond to biogeographical frontiers. Biogeographical frontiers may therefore offer a useful first-cut at corridor boundaries while further information is being compiled.

The key components of a conservation corridor are core areas, biological corridors or linkages, and compatible land or resource use areas. In planning corridors, ideally such areas should be identified for all target species and key ecological processes, although identifying priority ecological processes and locating them in the landscape or seascape for the purposes of spatial planning has been a real challenge for conservationists. Analyses should include an assessment of the area required to enable species and ecosystems to recover from expected disturbance patterns, whether natural or anthropogenic. Of particular importance is the need to try to build in the capacity to respond to global climate change, discussed in detail in Chapter 3.

BOX 4.2: THE BAJA TO BERING MARINE CONSERVATION INITIATIVE

The Baja to Bering Marine Conservation Initiative (B2B) aims to support the creation of a fully representative network of marine protected areas (MPAs) (including core no-take areas and connecting corridors) and the protection of fully functioning marine ecosystems, including the full range of species, by strengthening existing MPAs, fostering the creation of new areas and linking these with related marine conservation initiatives in Canada, the United States and Mexico. As scientific underpinning, the Marine Biology Conservation Institute has compiled data on blue whale and sea turtle migration patterns, deep sea corals, major current patterns, biogeographic regions and other biological, biophysical and socio-economic variables. Research has focused on identifying areas that are important for migratory species over many years, despite variable conditions. This research is combined with information on threats and opportunities to identify priority conservation areas.

Orca (*Orcinus orca*) off Vancouver Island, Canada.

H S Hystek/UNEP

The identification and definition of compatible land or resource uses has also often proved something of a challenge. Considerable research may be required to provide a comprehensive picture as different species groups are likely to have very different needs. Canopy bird species, for example, may be satisfied with intermittent patches of natural or semi-natural canopy in an agroforestry landscape, whereas ground-dwelling species may need more or less continuous natural or semi-natural groundcover.

The design process for conservation corridors depends on the local context. It is often iterative, with boundaries and areas refined as more information becomes available. In many regions of high biodiversity importance, there are a number of competing pressures on land and resources, and poverty elimination and development goals are priorities. In these contexts, large-scale conservation plans are only likely to be realized if they are compatible and even contribute to these objectives. Fortunately, the large scale of conservation corridors provides greater flexibility to identify areas where conservation may generate both conservation and development benefits, for example, through ecosystem services such as the protection of water catchments or fisheries stock recovery. They also allow for targeting of development activities at areas with minimum negative impacts.

Conservation corridor design in context

Within conservation corridors, all efforts should be made to ensure that core areas are legally protected with biodiversity conservation as the primary goal. Corridors and linkages also need legal protection with biodiversity conservation as a recognized goal to protect them from incursions that erode their contribution to connectivity. The selection of implementation mechanisms for compatible land and resource use areas needs to be based on a systematic threats-and-opportunities analysis, which traces direct threats to underlying causes and pinpoints the most effective entry point. Compatible land or resource uses may be promoted through incentives or regulation and through spatially targeted approaches or higher-level policy initiatives. For example, Conservation International has targeted its Conservation Coffee Program at farmers in high biodiversity areas, such as those in Mexico's El Triunfo Biosphere Reserve. In return for reducing agrochemicals, diversifying the shade canopy with native tree species, conserving on-farm forest, and respecting the rules and regulations of the adjacent protected area, farmers receive access to higher and more stable prices. Where the policy framework allows, planning restrictions or special planning requirements, such as those on certain types of development and more rigorous requirements for environmental impact assessments or more stringent environmental quality standards, can help secure compatible land/resource uses. Usually, spatially specific strategies will be strengthened by policy action at a higher level, such as addressing "perverse" incentives or subsidies that encourage non-sustainable resource use.

IUCN PROTECTED AREA MANAGEMENT CATEGORIES

The plurality of roles for protected areas is reflected in the IUCN Protected Areas Management Category system, which identifies a range of protected areas based on management objectives. The category system has been incorporated into national legislation and policy of a number of countries and accommodates a range of levels of human intervention. Thus, we have protected areas that include highly protected nature reserves, modified landscapes, manipulated ecosystems and resident peoples.

Despite the growth in global agreements on nature conservation and establishment of protected areas, protected area designations are not necessarily directly comparable across countries because legislative regimes may differ. More than 1 000 different terms are used around the world to designate protected areas. These terms are often defined within national legislation with respect to objectives and legal protection for the area in question. Sometimes there may be only marginal differences between countries for essentially the same type of protected area. For example, there are managed nature reserves in the Bahamas, strict nature reserves in Bhutan, nature reserves in Ontario, Canada, national nature reserves in the Czech Republic, nature reserves and marine nature reserves in Indonesia, nature conservation areas in Japan, and strict natural reserves in Sri Lanka, which are all strictly protected and accessible primarily for scientific research (Green and Paine, 1997). However, in many cases the same terms have very different management objectives. The classic example is the term "national park" which is used for protected areas such as the large, predominantly natural areas in Africa, Asia, Australia, Canada, and the USA, but also for areas in Europe where intensively managed and transformed landscapes have been created through continuous modification by people for thousands of years.

The need for internationally standardized protected area nomenclature and definition was raised at the First World Conference on National Parks in 1962 (Brockman and Curry-Lindahl, 1964). The conference recommended that the then International Commission on National Parks (today's World Commission on Protected Areas (WCPA)) "establish a clarification of terms concerning national parks and equivalent reserves". A debate on the issue then ensued for the next 30 years. Initially, in 1978, IUCN adopted a classification system based on ten categories. Following a review process that ran from 1984 to 1990, a proposal was made to reduce the number of categories to five. The present system of six categories, as follows, was finally adopted in 1994:

Category Ia: Strict nature reserve
Category Ib: Wilderness area
Category II: National park
Category III: Natural monument
Category IV: Habitat/species management area
Category V: Protected landscape/seascape
Category VI: Managed resource protected area (see Chapter 1 for details).

These categories also serve a range of secondary management objectives as illustrated in Table 4.1.

IUCN management categories serve a critical role in regional and global analyses. They provide a common language and enable the comparison and summary of management objectives for the conservation estate. They also enable the interpretation of national protected area definitions and introduce an element of compatibility within them. The IUCN WCPA has provided long-term international guidance on the categorization of protected areas to:

❏ alert governments to the importance of protected areas;

❏ encourage governments to develop systems of protected areas with management aims tailored to national and local circumstances;

❏ reduce the confusion that has arisen from the adoption of many different terms to describe different kinds of protected area;

❏ provide international standards to help global and regional accounting and comparisons between countries; and

❏ provide a framework for the collection, handling and dissemination of data about protected areas; and generally to improve communication and understanding between all those engaged in conservation' (IUCN, 1994).

In any overarching categorization system, the application of the basic principles to the real world is not straightforward, for example the application of multiple classifications. Many protected areas, especially larger sites, include a range of values and management objectives that are often reflected in use and management zonation schemes within the park. Thus, a single protected area can legitimately be subdivided into a number of IUCN management categories that reflected the range of management objectives applied to substantial components of its total area. The 1994 IUCN guidelines noted that this is "entirely consistent with the application of the system, providing such areas are identified separately for accounting and reporting purposes".

Taveuni Forest Reserve, Fiji - an uncategorised protected area with high biodiversity conservation values.

S,Chape

TABLE 4.1: MATRIX OF PROTECTED AREA MANAGEMENT OBJECTIVES AND IUCN CATEGORIES

Management objective	Ia	Ib	II	III	IV	V	VI
Scientific research	1	3	2	2	2	2	3
Wilderness protection	2	1	2	3	3	-	2
Preservation of species and genetic diversity	1	2	1	1	1	2	1
Maintenance of environmental services	2	1	1	na	1	2	1
Protection of specific natural and cultural features	na	na	2	1	3	1	3
Tourism and recreation	na	2	1	1	3	1	3
Education	na	na	2	2	2	2	3
Sustainable use of resources from natural ecosystems	na	3	3	na	2	2	1
Maintenance of cultural and traditional attributes	na	na	na	na	na	1	2

Key: 1 = Primary objective, 2 = Secondary objective, 3 = Potentially applicable, na = Not applicable
Source: IUCN 1994.

In 2001, WCPA agreed that a multiple categorization approach could be applied to MPAs.

A number of countries have formally adopted the IUCN management categories as the basis for planning and managing their national protected area systems. In July 2003, the international credibility of the categories was further strengthened by the formal adoption of the system for African protected areas in the revised African Convention on the Conservation of Nature and Natural Resources approved by the Assembly of the African Union. The importance of the IUCN categories was also highlighted by Recommendation 2.82 of the Amman World Conservation Congress held in 2000, which called on IUCN state members to prohibit exploration and extraction of mineral resources in areas with IUCN Protected Areas Management Categories I to IV and recommended that they restrict such activities in those with Categories V and VI.

Category assignment does not equate to management effectiveness (Section 17). The 1994 IUCN guidelines noted that they are "two separate judgements: what an area is intended to be; and how it is run". However, they are interrelated, because if a protected area is not managed to achieve its defined objectives – the basis of the category system – and its values are degraded or otherwise significantly changed, then the validity of the original category assignment in real terms is questionable. Clearly, to be an effective international system, IUCN's management categories need to be applied consistently to protected areas that are managed effectively to achieve their stated objectives.

IUCN and the WCPA membership continue to review and refine the protected area category system to ensure that it is relevant and able to be implemented effectively. Since the 2003 World Parks Congress there have been numerous meetings and debates on the categories, culminating in a global "summit" in Spain in May 2007, attended by over a hundred experts from around the world. As a result of this process revised guidelines will be released in 2008.

PROTECTED AREA MANAGEMENT AS GOVERNANCE

Good governance has emerged as a key issue in protected area management over the last decade. Attaining protected area objectives, such as biodiversity protection and support for and by local communities, is strongly influenced by governance. Many of the challenges related to ecosystem-based management of protected areas also hinge upon improving governance. Protected area management is more than just an activity of the state. Governance modes range from the traditional exercise of government authority, through to a wide variety of partnership, co-management, and informal arrangements involving multiple agencies, interest groups, and individuals (Ostrom, 1990; Reeve, Marshall, and Musgrave, 2004). Graham, Amos, and Plumptre (2003) defined governance as:

"the interactions among structures, processes and traditions that determine how power and responsibilities are exercised, how decisions are taken, and how citizens or other stakeholders have their say. Fundamentally, it is about power, relationships and accountability: who has influence, who decides, and how decision-makers are held accountable."

Government management is the traditional mode of protected area governance, and remains the dominant mode in many developed countries. Government agencies can be established within national, provincial or local tiers of government. Governments can also delegate their authority to another government agency, statutory authority, or non-governmental organization.

Co-managed protected areas are where authority, responsibility, and accountability are shared among two or more parties, which may include government agencies, indigenous people, non-governmental organizations, and private interests. There are two types of co-management. With **collaborative management**, authority is held by one party (often a governmental agency), but this party is required to collaborate with other parties. **Joint management** involves true sharing of authority among two or more parties, with none of these parties having ultimate authority in its own right.

Private management can be done voluntarily by individuals, not-for-profit organizations, or commercial enterprises (see Box 4.1). Generally, the authority of these parties to identify and manage land arises from the private property rights they hold over an area of land or water. Protected area designation can be formalized through mechanisms such as a covenant on the title of the property. In some cases, government agencies provide management and financial support to the private owners.

Community managed protected areas (also called community conserved areas) are managed voluntarily by indigenous or local communities. Management regimes may be established through customary laws and institutions using traditional knowledge, or through partnership agreements among consortia of local people.

Examples of protected areas managed under various governance modes are given in Table 4.2.

WORKING WITH THE COMMUNITY

The Millennium Development Goals highlight the importance of addressing social issues in order to achieve sustainability. The goals include eradicating poverty and hunger, and improving access to health services. These goals are now a major focus of most international programs and protected area organizations have a role in their implementation.

TABLE 4.2: MODES OF PROTECTED AREA GOVERNANCE

Mode	Type	Example
Government	National	Taman Negara National Park, Malaysia
	State or province	Big Basin Redwoods State Park, California, USA
	Local	Waipa, New Zealand
	Delegated (to another government agency)	Heard Island and McDonald Islands Marine Reserve, Australia
	Delegated (to statutory authority)	Peak District National Park, UK
	Delegated (to local government or community group)	Parc Naturel Régional Normandie-Maine, France
Co-management	Collaborative	Bwindi Impenetrable National Park, Uganda
	Joint	Annapurna Conservation Area, Nepal
Private	Individual	Winlaton Grassland, Northern Victoria, Australia
	Not-for-profit organization	Big Courtin Island, Prince Edward Island, Canada
	Commercial organization	Chumbe Island Coral Park Ltd, Zanzibar, Tanzania
Community	Indigenous	Reserva Etnica Forestal Awá, Ecuador
	Local	Shimshal Community Conservation Area, Pakistan

BOX 4.3: SPECIES CONSERVATION AND TRADITIONAL RESOURCE OWNERSHIP IN THE PACIFIC ISLANDS: THE CASE OF THE CRESTED IGUANA ON YADUA TABA ISLAND, FIJI

Land is a sacred inheritance to most Pacific Islanders and is treasured for its social, cultural, historical and development values. Many of these values do not sit comfortably with modern norms of land management, and use and/or ownership change whether permanent or temporary. These problems are often compounded by factors such as rapidly increasing populations, development and/or cash income requirements, which challenge ill-equipped traditional management structures. Most Pacific Island governments are loud in their rhetoric for conservation and environmental protection, but provide minimal technical and financial resources to effect it.

It is not surprising therefore that, in general, protected area management in the Pacific Islands has travelled, and continues to travel, on a bumpy road with no clear direction or destination.

In Fiji, the colonial response was to declare Nature Reserves under forestry legislation, and six of these persist to this day, but not one of them has a management plan and not one of them is under any form of active management. In the modern era, there has been a welcome shift to community-managed protected areas, but in many cases the switch has been total and without much thought. The success remains limited, in large part due to the lack of benefits accrued by the landowners. So often well-meaning conservationists try to convince landowners that official protection of a particular area will bring extra benefits over and above those that the landowners already enjoy from the area. In many cases landowners are asked to reduce extractive uses of land or sea areas with only fuzzy indications of future benefits. Until such time as Pacific land or marine owners can receive immediate and tangible benefits, community-managed protected areas are unlikely to be any more successful than traditional western approaches.

What is clear is that a lot more innovation is required in enabling land and marine owners to be tangible and immediate beneficiaries of protected area initiatives, than has hitherto been the case.

Conservation of Fiji's crested iguana (*Brachylophus vitiensis*) on Yadua Taba island illustrates some of the typical challenges which all Pacific island countries are facing. Yadua Taba is a 70 ha island that supports the world's last viable population of crested iguana , which number some 7 000–8 000. The island also contains a fine stand of dry littoral forest, a habitat that has been almost completely lost elsewhere in Fiji. When the iguana population was first "discovered" in 1979, it received worldwide attention and the Fiji government moved quickly to establish a sanctuary through a traditional approach to the Buli Raviravi (the title of the landowning chief of the island). Thereafter, management was delegated to the National Trust for Fiji but minimal, or no resources were provided other than a payment of approximately US$ 1 500 annually to the Buli Raviravi.

The problem here was that the landowners receiving the rental lived on the mainland of Vanua Levu some 60 km away while the inhabitants of the immediately neighboring Yadua Island who maintained usufruct rights on the island received nothing. They were even asked to remove their goats from the island. This they eventually did in 1989, but only after receiving payment from the Worldwide Fund for Nature. The National Trust appointed a warden from the community, but he received no regular pay and,

---

At the 2003 Vth WPC there was a focus on social issues and encouraging community participation in protected area management. Some of the topics included recognition and integration of indigenous conservation practices and the concept of community conserved areas.

As the population continues to grow, involving the community in protected area management and the creation of protected areas becomes increasingly important. The demands of an ever-increasing population, for infrastructure and services, place pressure on natural and cultural spaces. Protected area managers and community groups need to work together if the values of such spaces are to be maintained.

The success or failure of protected areas as a land use will be dependent on public support. Although protected areas bring a rich array of benefits, experience shows that the task of engaging support among some communities is not easy. Investment in communicating and involving the community in the benefits of parks, their management, and activities is an ongoing priority for agencies. The needs and desires of people must

although the Trust managed to attract some small-scale grants from a variety of international donors and agencies, little or none of this saw its way to either the landowning or neighboring communities. Meanwhile, relations between the Yadua villagers and the landowners deteriorated as a result of the annual payment, which was believed to be much greater than it actually was.

In 1992, WWF funded a management plan for the island, which officially recognized for the first time that a lease of the island from the landowners was desirable if not essential. This at a time when "community management" was the universal answer, and western approaches of land alienation considered totally inappropriate. But for Yadua Taba it was essential to ensure that the rightful landowners, although "absent", were benefited through the receipt of lease rentals, thus enabling all attention to be paid to engaging the neighboring community in management and tourism initiatives on the island. It took over ten years for the National Trust to effect a lease, but in the meantime they entered into a five-year association with Greenforce, an NGO supplying volunteers for conservation action. The Greenforce Camp was on Yadua Island and they were ostensibly tasked with baseline data collection and monitoring of the marine environment around Yadua Taba, such that a combined island-marine protected area could be considered for World Heritage listing. The association proved an effective initiative, not so much for the biological data collected as for the diverse benefits it brought to the community, which were associated with Yadua Taba's status as a protected area.

Currently Yadua Taba is leased to the National Trust for Fiji, with the landowners enjoying an annual rental with clauses allowing a share of any commercial take from the island. A full-time ranger is

S.Chape

employed from the local community and there are management, restoration, and research initiatives on the island using community labor. The leasing arrangement has brought some stability and purpose to the conservation of the island and has attracted an NGO to assist in long-term iguana research and dry forest restoration activities.

Yadua Taba provides several interesting lessons, including:

❏ even a situation with the very highest conservation priority and urgency is unlikely to gain active management support from a Pacific Island nation with limited resources;

❏ each site needs a conservation arrangement tailored to its needs, and this may be traditional or a western-oriented approach or a combination of both;

❏ money, in even small amounts, can easily disrupt traditional relationships;

❏ legal distinctions between landowners and usufruct rights holders are of little significance in effecting conservation outcomes; and,

❏ indirect conservation benefits to communities can be as important as direct ones.

be considered from the outset and throughout the management process. Agencies, in working with the community to achieve conservation outcomes, must understand the community and be part of it. To communicate effectively, agencies need to understand the community's needs, attitudes, values, and behavior.

Constituency-building is a global trend that involves establishing broadly based coalitions and partnerships directed towards sustainable environmental management, including conservation through various forms of protected area. Long-term

conservation at the landscape scale requires genuine support and commitment from a wide range of constituencies. Protected area managers must secure widespread community support, both to legitimize their work and to gain approval for them to expand and strengthen their activities. It is acknowledged that achieving satisfactory conservation outcomes will require considerable expenditure of funds – funds that will only be raised if there is community understanding of, and support for, protected area management objectives. But no matter how much funding is available, protected

BOX 4.4: KAA-IYA DEL GRAN CHACO NATIONAL PARK AND INTEGRATED MANAGEMENT AREA

The Wildlife Conservation Society (WCS) and the *Capitanía de Alto y Bajo Izozog* (CABI) have been collaborating in the design and implementation of a major community-based wildlife management program in Bolivia's Chaco region. WCS is an international conservation organization recognized for research on wildlife populations and ecology, and site-based approaches to the conservation of wild areas. CABI is the indigenous organization that represents some 9 000 Izoceño-Guaraní people living in 23 communities along the Parapetí River, south of the Bañados de Izozog wetlands.

A key accomplishment was the establishment of Kaa-Iya del Gran Chaco National Park and Integrated Management Area (KINP), in 1995. With technical support from WCS, CABI successfully proposed the establishment of the park to the Bolivian government. Subsequently, CABI was named KINP co-administrator, under an agreement with the government. At 3.4 million hectares, KINP is the largest protected area in Bolivia, and contains the largest area of dry tropical forest under protection in the world. Establishing the KINP was part of a broader CABI land management strategy. In early 1997, under the terms of Bolivia's agrarian reform law, CABI claimed for a 1.9 million hectare indigenous territory. In contrast to other cases in Bolivia, where parks and indigenous territorial claims overlap and are a source of conflicts, CABI's approach created the opportunity to manage 5.3 million hectares of the Bolivian Chaco based on principles of conservation and sustainable use of wildlife and other natural resources.

Moving beyond the political success of having created this vast area, the major focus of continuing CABI-WCS collaboration has been to assume the technical and administrative challenges of effectively managing it. At the local level, this effort has focused on: strengthening CABI's technical and administrative capacities; participatory wildlife population and ecology research and defining wildlife management practices; environmental planning and monitoring; and environmental education. Since 1995, USAID/Bolivia has provided critical financial support in each of these areas.

However, these local efforts needed to occur in the context of addressing larger regional issues affecting land use, specifically the rapid expansion of natural gas exploitation and export, deeply rooted land conflicts, and weak government capacity to maintain basic funding levels for national parks. With support from WCS, CABI led indigenous organizations affected by the Bolivia-Brazil Gas Pipeline in negotiating a landmark agreement with pipeline sponsors, which, among other things, created a private trust fund with an initial capital of US$ 1 million to provide a permanent revenue source for the park, and established a US$ 1.5 million fund for the titling of indigenous lands. CABI and WCS worked with Bolivia's National Agrarian Reform Institute to design an approach for land titling that reduced the cost from an official estimate of US$ 3 per hectare to US$ 0.36 per hectare. CABI and WCS also pioneered a participatory land use zoning approach, which allowed CABI to reach agreements with almost all the ranchers and farmers in the area, creating a basis for broad participation in the management of the KINP, and settling conflicts that obstructed titling its territorial claim.

In 2001, these efforts led to the International Association of Impact Assessment recognizing the Bolivia-Brazil Gas Pipeline for excellence in addressing environmental and social impacts associated with a major infrastructure project. In 2002, CABI received the XI Annual Bartolomé de las Casas prize from the Government of Spain, for extraordinary contributions to environmental conservation and the defense of indigenous cultures.

area management will not be successful in the long term unless it is recognized as a core part of a wider social, cultural, economic, and political agenda. Protected areas are already widely supported, yet they need to become more internalized in popular consciousness and acceptance, so that they are recognized as a key element in people's quality of life, linked to their personal identity and aspirations.

For protected area managers to work in isolation from the community is neither practical, desirable, nor usual. Apart from legal processes that prescribe formal consultation procedures, managers are interacting with the community every day on what are regarded as routine matters. Five important questions are:

❑ Who are the stakeholder groups and what is there about the ways they perceive and behave that may affect the protected area?

□ What community or environmental issues and attitudes may affect the relationship?

□ How are decisions made and power shared in the community?

□ Which media can best reach all potential stakeholder groups?

□ What impacts will management plans have on the local and wider community?

Interpretation is also an aspect of communication that has long been at the heart of managing protected areas. Interpretation is a means of communicating to the community the exceptional heritage values of protected areas. It thereby facilitates conservation outcomes by helping to develop a keener awareness, and greater understanding and appreciation, of protected areas, as well as enriching the visitor's experience. Interpretation helps orientate visitors, allowing them to find the recreation they prefer, and to do so safely and with enjoyment. It can persuade visitors to treat sites respectfully, without the need for regulations and policing. It can be used to subtly direct most visitors' attention towards less fragile sites.

INDIGENOUS PEOPLE AND PROTECTED AREAS

Indigenous or "first peoples" are "the original or oldest surviving inhabitants of an area, who have usually lived in a traditional homeland for many centuries" (Stevens, 1997). Their subsistence practices (now or until relatively recently at least) rely on the use of local resources and ecosystems. The actual number of indigenous people surviving today is a matter of definition (Kempf, 1993). In 1997, it was estimated that between 200 and 600 million of the 5.5 billion people living on Earth were indigenous (Stevens, 1997). Constituting only 5 to 10 percent of the world's population, indigenous groups contribute as much as 90 to 95 percent of the world's cultural diversity (Stevens, 1997). They inhabit more than 70 countries, in habitats ranging from the Arctic to the Amazon, claiming as traditional homelands 20 to 30 percent of the Earth's surface: four to six times more territory than is encompassed within the entire global protected area system. Many of these environments are fragile or under threat from development and are characterized by high levels of biodiversity; they are therefore significant to global conservation. Typically, indigenous groups have suffered from the colonization of their land by others, with their populations decimated by violence and disease

(Kempf, 1993; Furze, de Lacy, and Birckhead, 1996).

Recognition is increasingly being given to the special situation of indigenous people in relation to land and sea management. Indigenous involvement in conservation and protected area management has emerged as a much lauded, but highly charged, domain of policy and practice (Birckhead *et al.*, 2000). There is growing international and national recognition of the rights of indigenous peoples, and the realization that the conservation of biodiversity is unlikely to succeed without the support of local and indigenous communities, and that denying their resource rights eliminates incentives to conserve these resources (Ghimire and Pimbert, 1997).

Although indigenous rights are far from secure, indigenous people are increasingly active on the world stage, fighting for rights to land and self-determination, and the preservation of the environment (Burger, 1990).

For some time the issues of rights and responsibilities in natural resource management, as well as issues of rights to information and participation in decision-making, have been addressed internationally. The United Nations Declaration on Government and Development, Principle 2.2 states:

"Indigenous people and their communities, and other local communities, have a vital role in environmental management and development because of their knowledge and traditional practices. States should recognize and duly support their identity, culture and interests and enable their effective participation in the achievement of sustainable development."

The rights of indigenous people are also addressed in the work of the UN Working Group on Indigenous Peoples and its Permanent Forum as well as under

Involving the local community has become an important component in protected area planning.

N. Dickenson/UNEP

Stuart Chape

Ecotourists in the Kinabatangan Wildlife Sanctuary, Sabah, Malaysia.

ducting environmental research and in interpreting cultural and natural history information (Cordell, 1993). For indigenous owners, co-management arrangements may include funding for community projects, income from tourism, control of cultural sites, and support for the continuity of traditional resource management practices. Jointly managed protected areas have achieved, and can continue to achieve, much for both indigenous peoples and for conservation. Success requires people with goodwill, flexibility, and much dedication. In Australia, for example, three of the six federal national parks – Kakadu, Uluru-Kata Tjuta, and Booderee – are jointly managed by the Department of Environment and Heritage and traditional Aboriginal owners.

the United Nations Charter, Resolution 169 of the International Labour Organisation, the Arhus Convention and the Convention on Biological Diversity, in the last of these specifically in Article 8(j), which states that:

"Each Contracting Party shall [...] Subject to its national legislation, respect, preserve and maintain knowledge, innovations and practices of indigenous and local communities embodying traditional lifestyles relevant for the conservation and sustainable use of biological diversity and promote their wider application with the approval and involvement of the holders of such knowledge, innovations and practices and encourage the equitable sharing of the benefits arising from the utilization of such knowledge, innovations and practices."

Traditional knowledge and wisdom of indigenous peoples can help us to develop more sustainable relationships between people and resources. It can also help us to understand that cultural diversity itself serves as a form of insurance, which can expand the capacity of our species to change (McNeely, 1995).

As already noted, indigenous communities are significant managers of protected areas. When they do not have ultimate governance responsibilities, recognition must be given to their special situation, rights, and interests. Co-management of protected areas has proved to be one effective means of respecting the rights of indigenous people as well as achieving conservation outcomes. For non-indigenous protected area managers, co-management translates into greater access to traditional management knowledge, and assistance in con-

COMMUNITY CONSERVED AREAS

Community Conserved Areas can be broadly defined as "natural and modified ecosystems including significant biodiversity, ecological services and cultural values voluntarily conserved by concerned indigenous and local communities through customary laws or other effective means". These initiatives vary widely in their origin, purpose, and form but there are three essential characteristics defining them:

❑ Relevant indigenous and local communities are concerned about the given ecosystem — it usually being culturally significant or important for livelihoods;

❑ Voluntary management decisions and efforts by communities are effective in conserving habitats, species, ecological services, and associated cultural values — although the stated objective of the management practice may be unrelated to conservation;

❑ Indigenous and local communities are the major players (hold power) in decision making and implementation of decisions on the management of the ecosystem at stake (some form of community authority exists and is capable of enforcing regulations).

Examples of Community Conserved Areas include: sacred sites, for example the kaya forests of coastal East Africa; communally managed rangelands and forests, found in many parts of the world; community fisheries areas, such as the communally managed reef fisheries prevalent in much of the South Pacific; and community run green spaces in urban areas, such as City Gardens in the USA.

Community Conserved Areas can serve many important functions, as repositories of important components of biodiversity in their own right, as parts of conservation corridors linking formal protected areas and as sites of great cultural and economic importance for local peoples. They can offer valuable lessons in participatory governance of official PAs, providing examples of multilayered legal systems of conservation, which integrate customary laws with statutory laws and are often built on sophisticated ecological knowledge systems, elements of which have wider potential application.

They do, however, face several critical challenges to their continued existence and growth. Despite a long history, in many parts of the world Community Conserved Areas are fast eroding, as inappropriate "development" and "education" inputs are sweeping aside the knowledge systems that helped manage them. This is exacerbated by the tendency of colonial or centralized political systems to undermine traditional institutions by taking over many of the customary functions and powers of communities. A lack of official recognition often hampers community efforts to maintain such areas and, where incentive programs are in place, they are typically underresourced. Rapid social change can mean that communities themselves attach less value than before to such areas, and may prefer to convert them into some commercial use. Social changes often also lead to increased stratification and growing inequities within communities, making sustained management of Community Conserved Areas even more difficult.

INTERNATIONAL TRENDS IN PROTECTED AREA GOVERNANCE

Governance was a major theme of the 2003 World Parks Congress. The Congress endorsed the acceptance of a range of governance types as a means of expanding the global protected area network and increasing its legitimacy. In preparation for the WPC, a survey of international protected area agencies was undertaken to assess the main changes in protected area governance around the world during the previous decade (1992–2002), highlight the main trends in protected area governance, and identify whether these trends were leading to more effective decision making and management. Because of the variability in management responses to some IUCN categories, the survey concentrated on Categories I–III.

Forty-eight protected area agencies – just under half of those approached – responded, split almost equally between highly developed nations

---

BOX 4.5: ALTO FRAGUA-INDIWASI – THE GOVERNMENT OF COLOMBIA RECOGNIZES A COMMUNITY CONSERVED AREA AS A NATIONAL PARK
(adapted from Oviedo, 2003)

The Alto Fragua-Indiwasi National Park was created in February 2002, after negotiations involving the Colombian government, the Association of Indigenous Ingano Councils and the Amazon Conservation Team, an environmental non-governmental organization focusing on projects to assist the Ingano Indians and other indigenous groups in the Amazon basin. The Park is located in the Colombian Amazon Piedmont on the headwaters of the Fragua River. The park is part of a region that has the highest biodiversity in the country and is also one of the top global biodiversity hotspots. The site will protect various ecosystems of the tropical Andes including highly endangered humid sub-Andean forests, endemic species such as the spectacled bear (*Tremarctos ornatus*), and sacred sites of cultural value.

Under the terms of the decree that created the park, the Ingano will be the principal actors in the design and management of the park. The area, whose name means "House of the Sun" in the Ingano language, is a sacred place for the indigenous communities. This is one of the reasons why traditional authorities have insisted that the area's management should be entrusted to them. Although several protected areas of Colombia share management responsibilities with indigenous and local communities, this is the first one where the indigenous people are fully in charge.

The creation of Indiwasi National Park has been a long-time aspiration of the Ingano communities of the Amazon Piedmont, for whom it is a natural part of their Life Plan (*Plan de Vida*); that is, a broader, long-term vision for the entirety of their territory and the region. In addition, the creation of the Park represents an historic precedent for the indigenous people of Colombia, as for the first time an indigenous community, in this case the Ingano Indians, is the principal actor in the design and management of an official protected area that is fully recognized by the state.

BOX 4.6: PARTICIPATORY PLANNING AND MANAGEMENT: THE MIXED EXPERIENCE OF THE GALAPAGOS MARINE RESERVE

Located approximately 1 000 km from mainland Ecuador, the volcanic Galapagos Islands contain remarkable terrestrial and marine ecosystems inscribed as a World Heritage site in 1978 and extended in 2001. Some years ago the islands became the focus of complex and violent stakeholder conflicts. Rapid demographic and economic change, unregulated fishing, the appearance of high-value fisheries for Asian markets, state-imposed policies and regulations and general non-compliance with the management plan of the Marine Reserve were all factors fuelling those conflicts.

Response

In 1998, in response to national and international concern about the threats facing Galapagos, Ecuador passed innovative legislation through a Special Law that, amongst other measures, introduced the control of migration to the islands, created one of the largest marine reserves in the world of about 130 000 km², prohibited industrial fishing and established institutions for participatory management of the Marine Reserve. The creation of the Galapagos Marine Reserve was the result of a local participatory planning process, which took two years, 74 meetings of a multi-stakeholder planning group, two fisheries summit meetings and three community workshops, and produced a consensus management plan (Heylings and Bravo, 2001).

Implementation

Its implementation, through a legally based participatory management regime, has been in progress since then, but with mixed results. Conflicts still remain, although the management regime in theory provides a better forum for trying to resolve these. The Galapagos co-management institution consists of a tripartite arrangement uniting a local Participatory Management Board (PMB), an Inter-institutional Management Authority (IMA) and the Galapagos National Park (GNP). The PMB is made up of the primary local stakeholders, while the IMA comprises representatives of ministries and local stakeholders. In the PMB, the members present specific management proposals, for example regulations of fisheries and tourism,

which are analyzed, negotiated and eventually agreed upon by consensus. In principle, proposals are channeled for approval to the IMA and then for implementation and control to the GNP. Proposals that have reached a consensus in the PMB carry important weight at the IMA level. However, if no consensus is reached in the PMB, the different stakeholder positions are submitted to the IMA, where the decision is left in the hands of a majority of mainland ministerial officials. The consensus-based co-management setting is intended to create a strong incentive for local stakeholders to develop and agree on viable proposals in the PMB.

However, despite the establishment of participatory management 10 years ago, fishery and tourism interests still manage to force through their own requirements either, in the case of fisheries, by the threat or actual use of violence and non-compliance or, for tourism, by political manipulation. Unfortunately, every fishery that is being monitored in Galapagos has shown continuing decline since the establishment of participatory management, while tourism in the marine reserve is still largely unregulated and continues to expand. One of the key issues when initially establishing the participatory approach was the mis-identification of the fisher group as wholly artisanal whereas it includes a large proportion of economic opportunists (mainly recent migrants to the islands).

Presidential Decree

In April 2007 the government issued a Presidential Decree declaring the conservation and environmental management of the Galapagos ecosystem in a state of risk and a national priority, and outlined an agenda to systematically address the various factors affecting the state of conservation of the area. UNESCO also sent a mission that confirmed the threats to the outstanding value and physical integrity of the World Heritage site, including increasing human immigration, uncontrolled development of tourism, and the failure of various institutions and agencies to deal with these threats. The World Heritage Committee subsequently placed Galapagos on the List of World Heritage in Danger in 2007 (Watkins and Cruz 2007).

and others, with no discernible pattern of response. Some of the largest, oldest, and most active protected area agencies did not respond, while some of the smallest and most resource-challenged agencies did. However, overall the results were a good representation of the current perception of global protected area governance.

Protected area agency structure and decision making

Park agencies vary greatly in organizational structure and range of responsibilities. Just over 80 percent are part of a larger government ministry. Significant changes have occurred since 1992, with 65 percent of countries having experienced changes in structure over the decade to 2002, and almost three quarters having enacted new legislation or altered existing legislation.

Central government agencies have the greatest overall responsibility for protected area systems. Over 1992–2002, many countries encouraged greater attention to regional differences through the decentralization of protected area agencies, and more than one third of the survey respondents suggested that their agency structure was currently less centralized than it was in 1992. As a result, decision-making power has been increasingly delegated to various levels of government and other stakeholder groups, allowing for the differences between individual protected areas within a country to be taken into consideration in management.

Protected area management has also engaged a wider range of stakeholders in decision making. The amount and strength of stakeholder involvement have dramatically increased over the past ten years, and participatory management is now legally required in more than half the protected area agencies surveyed. The survey also highlighted a general trend towards increased private sector involvement, specially in the development of (eco)tourism opportunities. Services such as park maintenance are also increasingly contracted out to the private sector.

Many protected area governance issues revolve around the balance of responsibility for management between protected area agencies and other interests. A continuum exists, ranging from full control by the official state agency to full control by other interests. During 1992–2002 there was a shift towards greater involvement of other interests in decision making. Some 42 percent of agencies in 1992 reported that the government was the sole decision-making authority, compared with only 12 percent a decade later. Furthermore, 2002 saw an increase to 30 percent of agencies involved with cooperative decision making, against 12 percent in 1992, and some agencies (15 percent) indicated they now had a joint decision-making regime, whereas none had had one a decade earlier.

Overall, the results suggest that managers recognize that community support is a requirement of "good governance", and more effort is being directed at involving various stakeholder groups. The general perception is that increased participation has resulted in more effective decision making and management overall.

Accountability mechanisms

An important aspect of effective protected area governance is the accountability of decision makers to the public they represent. The purpose of accountability mechanisms is to ensure that tasks and objectives are completed on time and that funds are spent appropriately. During the last decade, a trend towards the increased use of such mechanisms is evident. Accountability measures designed to involve the local community, improve communication between protected area managers and the public, and make the process more inclusive for stakeholders have become increasingly popular. Currently, approaches such as State of the Parks reports, annual reports, external

Wildlife rangers in Zimbabwe.

UNEP

UNEP

There has been a sharp increase in the involvement of a range of stakeholders in protected area planning and management over the last decade.

audits, national advisory committees, stakeholder roundtables, and parliamentary debates are more commonly used than they were a decade ago. More than two thirds of the survey respondents perceived that these changes in accountability measures had helped to achieve more effective protected area management overall.

Protected area management plans (see Chapter 5) play an important role in effective governance by holding decision makers accoun - table to the public. More than two thirds of respondents indicated that both the formation and implementation of management plans were now required by law, with these requirements having changed over the last decade for about a third of the agencies. However, public participation in the creation of these plans is required by law by fewer than half of the agencies, even though, for over a third, this has changed over the last decade.

Influence

A variety of "players" are involved in the decision-making process for protected area systems. Since decision making ultimately drives management, a variety of sources exert influence on the manage - ment of protected areas. Survey respondents were asked to estimate the influence of various forces on decision making in 1992 and 2002. The results

indicate that the sphere of influence surrounding the management of protected areas has increased. In 1992, more than one third of respondents perceived that global forces, local communities, the private sector, and various stakeholders had no influence on protected area decision making in their country. By 2002, these proportions had decreased, often dramatically. For example, while in 1992, 41 percent of local communities had no influence, by 2002 this proportion had dropped to 2 percent.

Governance capacity building

Almost three quarters of protected area agencies have programs in place to improve the capacity of their staff, including workshops, seminars, and collaboration with scientific organizations. Capacity-building programs are also increasingly common among stakeholder groups and within other government agencies closely related to the management of protected areas.

Nonetheless managers recognize significant gaps in training opportunities. The results suggest a variety of training needs for protected area agencies including: environmental education; community involvement; park planning and administration; enforcement and conflict management; and detailed training in of remote sensing and geographical information systems (GIS).

Funding

Funding is a critical component of effective governance, as adequate funding allows managers to fulfill protected area objectives by meeting their operating, research, and staff salary requirements. Thus, the degree and strength of financial support that a protected area agency receives strongly influence, and are strongly influenced by, governance. The survey highlighted several trends relating to the funding of protected area systems during 1992–2002. The proportion of total funds provided by both government agencies and private donors decreased during this period, while non-governmental organizations and user fees provided an increased amount of funding.

Significant changes in the overall budgets of protected area agencies also occurred between 1992 and 2002. Twenty-six percent of survey respondents indicated that the protected area budget decreased during the period, 14 percent suggested it had remained the same, while 60 percent saw budget increases. Despite these increases, respondents indicated that the number, size, and complexity of protected areas had increased during the period; the use of the protected areas had increased; and the responsibilities of the protected area agencies had increased as well. Almost two thirds of respondents suggested that, as a result, the budget for their protected area did not keep pace with the growth and additional use of the system, and stressed that additional funding is required to ensure the maintenance of protected area values.

Current and future challenges

In addition to highlighting the main trends in protected area governance, it is important to assess whether such changes have led to more effective decision making and management overall. More than 90 percent of respondents felt that the governance of their protected area system was more effective in 2002 than in 1992. Respondents were also asked about the main challenges to protected area governance and to identify the strategies that may be required to address these challenges. The main challenges

over the next decade included (in descending order of frequency of mention):

❑ the involvement of, and cooperation with, stakeholder groups;
❑ obtaining adequate funding;
❑ achieving institutional transformation within protected area agencies and improving relationships between government bodies;
❑ ensuring adequate and effective training of park management and personnel (capacity building);
❑ enforcement of protected area rules, policies, regulations, and mandates.

The main strategies required to address these challenges included:

❑ securing funds on an ongoing basis;
❑ increasing capacity-building and training opportunities for park staff and managers at all levels;
❑ increasing the involvement of local communities and providing adequate education opportunities for stakeholder groups;
❑ promoting collaborative efforts between protected area agencies and various government agencies related to protected areas;
❑ improving accountability and providing transparent decision making for protected areas.

Overall the survey has helped confirm many of the suspected trends in governance with a greater degree of stakeholder involvement in all aspects of protected area management, greater use of accountability mechanisms, growing influence of global forces, and the need for more capacity building and funding. The last decade has been a period of rapid change, with many agencies experiencing changes in legislation and policy direction. Managers indicate that, overall, these changes have led to more effective management. In all likelihood the next decade will see a slowing down and consolidation of these changes. There is a need not only for change, but also for a degree of stability, to allow managers opportunity to learn from these changes and adopt the most effective governance tools for the challenges they face.

CHAPTER 5

The functions and processes of protected area management

Contributors: M. Lockwood and G. Worboys; The role of rangers: D. Zeller; Developing capacity: J. Marsh; Evaluating management effectiveness: M. Hockings, F. Leverington, S. Stolton, and N. Dudley.

To manage protected areas effectively requires organizations, individuals, or communities that operate under a recognized set of policies, powers, and/or traditions. A variety of protected area management organizations exist for this purpose. International coordinating bodies also exist to promote conventions and other means of establishing protected areas. They develop and disseminate effective management standards, strategies, and skills.

An understanding of management processes is fundamental to successful management, particularly with respect to government, co-managed, and private protected areas. Management is about people. It is a process through which goals are achieved. It involves coordinating all human and technical resources to accomplish specific results.

The establishment of a protected area is just the start of the process for achieving the objectives for which it was reserved. Active management is required. There is a multiplicity of threats and other actions that need to be dealt with to maintain the purpose and integrity of protected areas (MacKinnon *et al.*, 1986; Brandon, Redford, and Sanderson, 1998; Van Schaik *et al.*, 2002; Du Toit, Rogers, and Biggs, 2003). The phenomenon of "paper parks" – where protected areas are designated but never managed – is recognized as a serious issue (Dudley, Hockings, and Stolton, 1999). Simply designating protected areas does not ensure their survival, nor guarantee that social and economic benefits are derived from them.

It is therefore worthwhile to consider the general process of management, as well as how management concepts can be applied specifically to protected areas. The four basic management functions are planning, organizing, leading, and controlling (Bartol *et al.*, 1998; Robbins *et al.*, 2003).

Planning

Planning is commonly undertaken at three levels of detail within an organization. An organization cannot achieve its primary goal unless each level of management carries out the appropriate level of planning. Theorists of management often prescribe a top-down system whereby senior executives turn the organization's goals into a series of high-level "strategic" plans. These plans, as they pass down the hierarchy, are translated first into a series of "tactical" and then "operational" plans, which finally become the instructions to the frontline staff (Bartol *et al.*, 1998). Such a system can only work if each level in the agency clearly understands its role and is provided with the freedom to manage.

Organizing

As a management function, organizing is concerned with how managers allocate and arrange human and other resources to enable plans to be implemented (Bartol *et al.*, 1998). It involves managers determining the range of tasks to be performed and allocating the available resources to obtain the best results most efficiently. Organizing never stops. In a fast-changing world, managers and staff are constantly refining how their organizations work towards required goals.

Demands on protected area agencies are somewhat different from those facing most organizations. There is a need to ensure other public and private sector organizations are aware of these differences, and that standard organizational

S.Chape

Te Wahipounamu, South West New Zealand World Heritage Area, South Island, New Zealand.

models are not inappropriately applied to undertake protected area management. Some of the special characteristics are listed here:

❏ Protected area lands and waters are dynamic, living systems, and the dynamics of natural events are superimposed on the routine bureaucratic timetable of events.

❏ Protected areas are often rugged and remote, requiring special management needs related to organizational time and resource allocation, as well as staff competencies and capacities.

❏ Protected areas are 24-hours-a-day, seven-days-a-week operations, and operational matters that arise on protected area lands or waters often need a rapid response.

❏ Terrestrial protected areas are usually surrounded by neighbors, and, again, a round-the-clock response capability is usually required.

❏ Protected areas are used by a wide range of recreational and other users, with peak use periods often clashing with peak incident periods.

❏ Unplanned incidents, such as fires, are normal occurrences, and they may cut across bureaucratic process timetable events.

❏ The practical and experiential knowledge accumulated by protected area staff is crucial for wise decision making.

❏ Protected areas need planning and management investments that are continuous and long term – much longer than election and budget cycles, for example.

Leading

Leading involves influencing others' work behavior towards achieving organizational goals (Bartol *et al.*, 1998). In the process of leading, effective managers become catalysts in encouraging innovation. Leaders kindle the dynamic spirit needed for success. How well an organization performs depends on the motivation and commitment of staff.

Controlling

Controlling is concerned with monitoring the performance of an organization against management benchmarks. Managers need to set performance measures and the criteria for how they will be evaluated. Controls help managers and staff cope with uncertainty, detect irregularities, identify opportunities, handle complex situations, and de-

centralize authority (Bartol *et al.*, 1998; Robbins *et al.*, 2003). The basic process involves establishing standards, measuring performance, and comparing performance to those standards. It also involves responding with corrective actions.

OBTAINING AND MANAGING INFORMATION

Obtaining and managing data is essential for most protected area management. Knowledge is synthesized from information derived from data analysis. Data on visitor numbers, behavior, and attitudes, for example, are collected and stored. These data provide information about comparative visitor use of resources and responses to management actions and this can be used to help managers prioritize investment decisions in relation to the provision of infrastructure and services for visitors. Vital to this process is an information management system that provides a framework for collecting and analyzing data of importance to protected area management. This is not a simple process and often considerable resources and expert knowledge need to be invested in information management systems.

Where there are already sufficient reliable and relevant data, managers need to know how to find and organize them, otherwise they need to arrange or commission research to produce the data. Managers need data management skills to identify the facts relevant to a given decision. They must be able to spot the gaps where more research is needed and to interpret data, especially where there are no "black or white" conclusions. Managers should be familiar with different types of data, the different ways they may be accessed or organized, and the different places where they may be collected and stored.

A range of information is required for managing protected areas, from detailed scientific knowledge of flora and fauna to visitation figures and financial records. Information requirements include physical inventory, biological inventory, environmental condition, cultural inventory, social and land-use history, visitor use, non-recreational uses, socio-economic costs and benefits, and infrastructure and facilities.

Accurate and comprehensive data are crucial as is the capacity to store and retrieve them quickly and simply. This is true at local, state, national, and international levels. Local systems are just as important as the more sophisticated information systems that cover national and international areas. Research collections, even in the simplest form, are valuable aids for managers. The larger systems are used more for setting priorities and close comarative analysis. By contrast, local data are used directly by local managers as a basis for the actions they take. The development of a local information system and establishing databases on which they depend, is of vital importance.

Electronic systems for storing and retrieving data range from the simple to the sophisticated. Information can be stored using a range of computer programs and hardware, and there are as many ways of retrieving information, especially with the use of the internet and electronic library and journal catalogues. Researchers have developed a range of systems for accessing this information.

Ideally, individual protected area managers should also have a well-developed information management system. For example, German Technical Cooperation, in conjunction with the Uganda Wildlife Authority (UWA), has developed a management information system, termed MIST, to provide managers and planners at all levels with timely and up-to-date information for planning, decision-making, and evaluation (see Figure 5.1). All users have easy access to a central database through the local area network, or by using digital data transfer or zip-disks. The system integrates information on the ecological, social, and economic dimensions of wildlife conservation as well as tourism data, and literature and address databases. MIST includes data collected by frontline staff, air surveillance, communities, and researchers. Practical data sheets have been generated for use by ranger law-enforcement patrols and by communities. Outputs from MIST include monthly/quarterly/annual reports, and routine or specific requests for information. MIST improves management and measures management effectiveness by providing baseline data for planning and information for decision making, as well as monitoring and evaluation of annual operations and management plans, and creating a culture of information exchange. MIST has also been adapted for use in two national parks in Cambodia (Schmitt and Sallee, 2002).

In general, obtaining and managing information for protected area management should be based on the following principles.

❑ Effective stewardship requires the best available information on all aspects of protected areas and their surrounding environments, including natural heritage, cultural heritage, economics, and social aspects such as visitor values, attitudes, and behavior. It is critical to understand the limitations of the data.

❑ Access to and the ability to use the most relevant, recent, and cutting-edge information is vital in achieving management objectives.

❑ A systematic approach to collecting, organizing, storing, accessing, and analyzing data is fundamental to delivering useful information. Recent advances, such as GIS and electronic databases, are important tools.

❑ Research is a core function of protected area management and should be facilitated by protected area organizations. Research priorities should be clearly documented. Research partnerships should be developed with universities, science organizations, and other research providers.

❑ Monitoring (including the appropriate selection of indicators) provides critical information for evaluating progress, understanding the consequences of management actions, and establishing the basis for adaptive management.

❑ Processes should be in place to ensure that information is easily accessible to all interested parties. It needs to be recognized that those accessing the data have different levels of skill and access, and hence the information needs to be provided in different formats.

❑ Agencies should ensure that staff have the capability to access, understand, interpret, and apply information made available from research, monitoring, and other sources.

MANAGEMENT PLANNING

In essence, planning is concerned with the future, and, in particular, future courses of action. Planning is a process for determining "what should be" (usually defined by a series of objectives), and for selecting actions that can help achieve objectives. Planning can occur at various geographic scales and for different planning goals.

Land use planning is the process of deciding in a broad sense which areas of land will be used for what purpose, including the designation of protected areas. This may be undertaken at a national, state, or regional scale.

Area management planning is concerned with how to manage these areas once their land-use

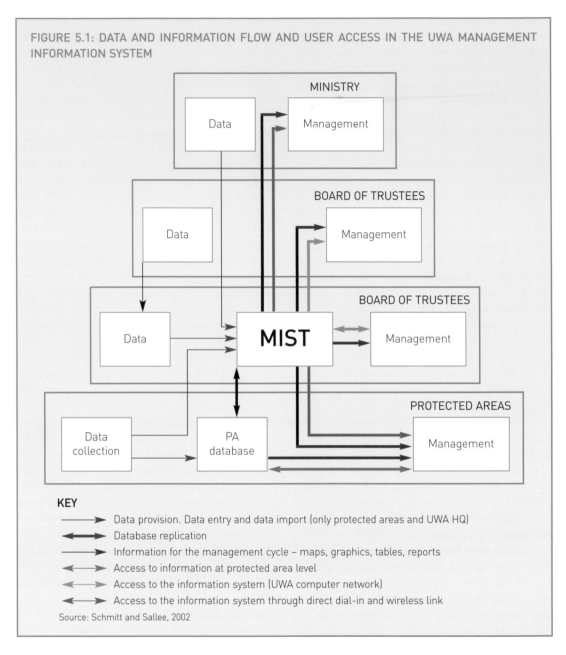

FIGURE 5.1: DATA AND INFORMATION FLOW AND USER ACCESS IN THE UWA MANAGEMENT INFORMATION SYSTEM

KEY

→ Data provision. Data entry and data import (only protected areas and UWA HQ)

◄► Database replication

→ Information for the management cycle – maps, graphics, tables, reports

◄► Access to information at protected area level

◄► Access to the information system (UWA computer network)

◄► Access to the information system through direct dial-in and wireless link

Source: Schmitt and Sallee, 2002

designation has been determined. A park management plan for a national park is an example of an area management plan. Both land-use and area management planning typically deal with a wide range of management issues.

Site planning deals with design details associated with, for example, the development of a visitor facility. A park management plan might recommend the establishment of a camping area of a certain standard in a particular location to provide for a specified number of people. A separate and subsidiary site plan will specify the location and design of access, barriers, campsites, toilets, and so on within the camping area.

Functional planning focuses on a particular issue, for example, fire management or conserving a significant species.

Organizational planning is concerned with the purpose, structure, and procedures of a management agency. Within an organization responsible for managing natural areas there may be several levels and types of management planning documents and activities. If the organization is working well, all these activities and documents should be coordinated and integrated. For example, the objectives of a plan for an individual park should relate to, and be consistent with, a plan at a higher level such as a regional, tactical, or corporate plan. A corporate plan identifies an organization's collective goals, objectives, policies, and activities, and provides a context and guidelines for area management and functional plans.

There are many other types of planning and related activities associated with establishing and managing protected areas. Examples include impact assessment, economic planning, financial planning, business planning, species recovery planning, and incident planning. Here we will focus on area management planning.

There are several reasons why it is necessary to plan for the management of protected areas. In general, planning can help conserve a resource while providing for its appropriate use. More specific reasons for embarking on a planning project include:

❏ meeting global responsibilities under such agreements as the Convention on Biological Diversity;
❏ meeting statutory obligations;
❏ directing management towards achieving the goals established in legislation or elsewhere;
❏ refining broad goals into specific, achievable objectives;
❏ facilitating the making of sound decisions;
❏ facilitating the resolution of conflicts over resource management;
❏ aiding communication between different levels within a hierarchical organization, eg. between top-level staff and front-line staff such as rangers who are often responsible for on-ground implementation of actions;
❏ providing continuity of management despite staff changes;
❏ making explicit decisions and the means by which they were arrived at – important components of management that might otherwise remain hidden;
❏ giving the community, interested groups, and individuals an opportunity to take part in decisions;
❏ providing for public accountability.

Protected area management planning has gone through several phases. Plans in the 1970s and early 1980s tended to be dominated by extensive inventories of natural and cultural resources. They were developed with little community participation and the data collection effort tended to be at the expense of strategic considerations and substantive management decisions. From the mid-1980s until the early 1990s, plans were more focused on specific management objectives and actions, often framed by a zoning scheme. Community participation also became an important component of planning processes. While these plans provided more management guidance than the earlier plans, they often quickly became out of date, and were generally written with little regard for available management resources. They tended to be "wish lists" rather than realistic management prescriptions. Such rigidity and implementation difficulties meant that they often "sat on the shelf" and so did little to guide day-to-day management.

As a reaction to these failings, and under the influence of wider trends, such as the increasing popularity of strategic planning derived from business management, plans from the mid-1990s were typically much leaner documents. They articulated a strategic direction, but often did not detail specific outcomes or management decisions. Such plans were politically expedient in that, in the absence of any performance measures, agencies could not be held to account. Their lack of specificity meant that they were also of little use in guiding management. Of course specific decisions were still needed – these tended to be made in within-agency operational planning processes that took place out of the public gaze.

We are now entering an era where plans are attempting to address these various limitations. State-of-the-art planning now seeks to produce relatively short strategic documents that nonetheless contain a realistic set of objectives to enable performance evaluation, as well as actions that, in the immediate future, are considered the best options to meet the objectives. Ideally, the plans are also flexible enough to allow modification of actions on the basis of experience and new information, as well as some adjustment of objectives and performance measures.

Important influences on the approaches that are adopted include agency traditions, the prevailing mode of public policy development, institutional structures, and the intellectual traditions most influencing the people directing the planning process. There are four major approaches to a planning project: rational comprehensive; incremental; adaptive; and participatory (Briassoulis, 1989). These are rarely used in their pure form – in general, planning projects can be described as of mixtures of them them all. The approach or mixture of approaches adopted will determine the particular stages undertaken in the planning process, as well as the relative importance given to each stage.

Planning is often connected with the word "process". This means that planning is not simply an event or an outcome. Planning is best seen as an interrelated sequence of stages. These stages are linked in a dynamic fashion – the interactions between them may occur in one or more directions and change over time. In addition, while there may be a clearly defined starting point, it is often difficult to define an end point. Indeed, many planning practitioners emphasize the adaptive nature of planning, with the need to regularly review the success and relevance of both a particular plan and even the planning process itself. An illustration of a typical planning process is given in Figure 5.2.

There is no consensus on the best approaches and processes – there is also no single best way to undertake a planning project. Nonetheless, there are some basic principles of good practice.

1. Planners should consciously adopt a suitable mix of planning approaches that are:
   - ❏ participatory at a level that matches the interests and concerns of stakeholders;
   - ❏ cognizant of the multi-value, multicultural context of protected area management;
   - ❏ rational and participatory in the collection and identification of information to inform management;
   - ❏ rational in the application of formal procedures to assess any changes in land use or major investment issues;
   - ❏ rational and participatory in the assessment of options and selection of preferred actions;
   - ❏ adaptive in the implementation, assessment, refinement, and modifications of objectives and actions;
   - ❏ incremental in addressing urgent or minor management requirements that, given information, organizational, or resource constraints, cannot be dealt with in any other way.

2. Effective linkages should be established across planning levels such that:
   - ❏ strategic planning occurs at the organizational and regional levels, including specification of goals and guidelines;
   - ❏ specific planning occurs at the local level, including development of measurable and realistic objectives that are framed in the context of strategic goals and have clear performance indicators;
   - ❏ explicit linkages are present between objectives and actions and outcomes;
   - ❏ actions are consistent with strategic guidelines, and at a level of detail that allows for consistent interpretation and application.

3. Effective implementation of actions arises from:
   - ❏ availability of suitably trained staff to guide the planning process and implement the plan;
   - ❏ links between actions, resources, the budget process, and performance evaluation;
   - ❏ definitions of roles and lines of responsibility in the managing agency regarding implementation of particular actions;
   - ❏ works programs that are linked with the plan, contain dates for completion of actions, and are fed back into the performance evaluation.

4. Formal evaluation of success or otherwise is an essential part of a successful planning process and involves:
   - ❏ lines of responsibility in the managing agency regarding evaluating performance against objectives;
   - ❏ mechanisms for formal recognition (and removal from the plan) of objectives that have been met and completed;
   - ❏ mechanisms for addressing unmet objectives and/or actions, including, where appropriate, their modification;
   - ❏ clear guidelines for reviewing plans, objectives, and actions, including participants, responsibilities, and periodicity of revisions.

FINANCE AND ECONOMICS

Although the number of community conserved, co-managed and private protected areas are increasing most protected areas are still managed by government agencies. As such, they rely heavily on government funds - although these are often limited in many developing countries. In general, this situation should continue. Governments must fund protected areas because of the public good benefits that they provide and to maintain the intrinsic values of natural areas. Funding to

FIGURE 5.2: A TYPICAL PLANNING PROCESS

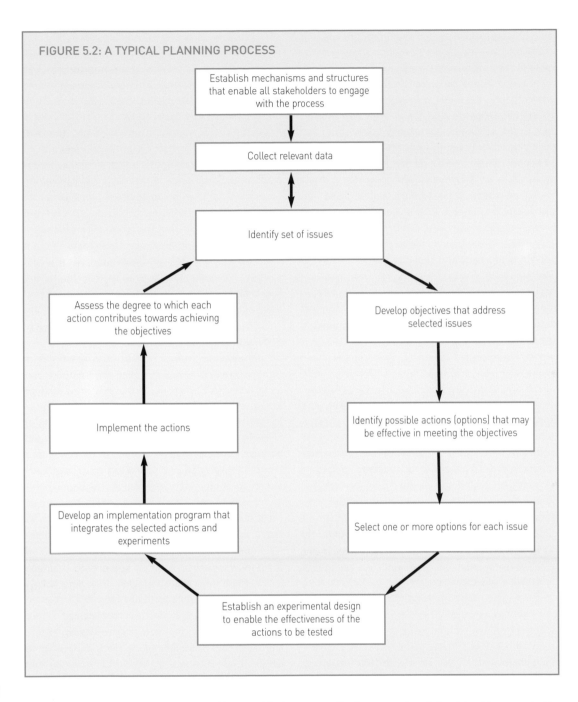

government departments is typically provided through annual appropriations from a provincial or national treasury. When available, these appropriations are usually divided into recurrent and capital expenditure components. Agencies responsible for protected area management may also be able to attract support funding through various grant and donor programs, especially in developing countries.

The private sector (see Box 4.1), while making a contribution, cannot and should not be expected to meet many of the costs associated with protected area management. Non-use values of natural areas, for example, are pure public goods. They reflect the value people place on the existence of such an area, regardless of the importance of other values related to consumption, either of products (such as timber) or experiences (such as recreation). Such values would be undersupplied by private nature reserves.

However, political and fiscal realities mean it is unlikely that the funding needed to satisfactorily meet all protected areas acquisition and management requirements will ever be made available by governments. Financial resources often constrain effective management of protected areas and fall well short of needs. Increasing taxes is always politically difficult, even with community support for additional conservation expenditure, and there are always many other calls on government from health, education, social welfare, and so on. In fact, the proportion of public funding going into protected areas is in decline in many countries (IUCN, 2000).

There are opportunities to expand on this public funding base and generate further revenue to meet agency needs. Funding sources include national environmental funds, multilateral banks, Global Environment Facility, debt swaps, bilateral development cooperation agencies, philanthropic foundations, non-governmental organizations, grants from private foundations, corporate donations, and individual donations (IUCN, 2000). Both public and private revenue need to be optimized, with public revenue linked to public goods and private revenues to private goods. While governments will continue to have a primary role in ensuring the supply of pure public goods, the private sector is becoming increasingly important for providing visitor services and facilities, and for contributing to resource management and the restoration of sites. The provision of public incentives to support conservation activities on private property is also crucial. Further opportunities exist for protected area management agencies to develop constructive partnerships with the private sector.

Business plans are used to guide business development activities. They are being more widely adopted by conservation agencies. Business plans must be developed in the context of a wider management plan that has clearly defined goals and objectives (see above). This ensures that generating revenue is a means toward the end of more effective management, and does not become an end in itself. A key component of a typical business plan is a financial plan. The financial plan determines the amount and timing of funding required to achieve management objectives, and identifies income sources to meet these needs. Financial planning differs from budgeting in that it is more focused on forecasting-required funding, as well as the best potential sources to meet short, medium, and long-term needs.

Different sources of funding have different characteristics: some are more reliable; some sources are easier to raise; and some can be used freely according to management priorities, while others come with strings attached, such as inability to pay for recurrent costs. The short term (3-5 years in most cases) nature of most donor funding, including the GEF, often limits its effectiveness in producing sustainable protected area management outcomes. Some funding mechanisms take a long time and a lot of effort to establish; they therefore do not provide a short-term return, but over the longer term they offer the possibility of steady, reliable financing to meet recurrent costs. A good financial plan identifies these characteristics, and builds a revenue stream that matches both the short- and long-term requirements of the protected area, or protected area system (IUCN, 2000).

Pricing services and facilities

Conservation of natural and cultural resources is rightly regarded as a community service obligation for government agencies, and a user-pays system is not applicable to secure the continued supply of these values (QPWS, 2000). However, the costs of providing appropriate infrastructure, facilities, and services, repairing environmental damage, and limiting congestion are generated by private consumption of protected area values. The beneficiary- and polluter-pays principles suggest that these costs should not be borne by the taxpayer, but by users who either gain benefits from the infrastructure, facilities, and services (beneficiaries pay) or impose environmental or congestion costs on others (polluter pays).

Resource managers are under increasing pressure to adopt user-pays approaches and, where possible, to recover the costs of providing recreation and other services. Managers should be able to justify their pricing of recreation goods and services, so that decisions are neither arbitrary nor inequitable (Loomis and Walsh, 1997). Some agencies charge a fixed fee for all parks, some charge for only certain parks, and some have fees for particular uses or value-added services.

Demand for the recreation opportunities afforded by protected areas is likely to continue to rise. This growth is promoted by, among other things, enhanced information availability about the attractions of protected areas and improved access and transport connections, together with a growing consumer preference for "quality-of-life experiences", including outdoor recreation. Increased visitor numbers will impose additional costs on protected area management agencies. Services and facilities (car parks, walking tracks, toilets, visitor centers, and so on) will require upgrading and expansion. Environmental damage, and therefore the need to expend resources on rehabilitation, will increase. Costs may also be imposed on visitors in areas of high use, as congestion diminishes the quality of recreational experiences.

These increased costs make the problem of who should pay for them particularly pressing. Non-users effectively subsidize users when fees are not charged. Subsidies may be justified to enable low-income earners to visit natural areas. However, at sites primarily visited by high-income earners, the poor may be worse off as they subsidize the free entry of rich visitors through their taxes. A related issue arises when sites have a significant number of foreign visitors who are wealthier than the local people – an issue when visitors from developed countries visit developing ones (Lindberg, 1998).

Recreation activities are not the only uses that impose environmental costs. Some protected areas are subject to honey production, fishing, cattle grazing, and other extractive uses. Again, the user-pays principle has potential application here. However, while local communities may benefit from such uses, they often also have to forgo potential benefits to ensure biodiversity and other public-good values are maintained. Equity and strategic considerations make it generally inappropriate to impose additional costs on locals.

As noted in Chapter 1, protected areas provide a range of ecosystem services that benefit people some distance away. For example, the quality of water supply is often partly due to the catchment protection afforded by national parks and other reserves some distance from the city. In this case, applying the beneficiary-pays principle is not easy, but there are examples where a mechanism has been developed. In 1998, Inversiones La Manguera Sociedad Anonima (INMAN), a Costa Rican hydro-electric company, signed a contract with the Monteverde Conservation League (MCL) to pay for ecological services provided by the Bosque Eterno de los Niños (Children's Eternal Rain Forest), a 22 000-hectare private reserve managed by MCL. Approximately 3 000 hectares of the protected forest is part of a watershed that is used by INMAN for generating electric power. Recognizing the ben-

efits they receive from protection of this watershed, INMAN entered into an agreement with MCL to pay for the protection of the ecological services provided by Bosque Eterno de los Niños (IUCN, 1998).

The level of charges in a user-pays system should be determined by a clear set of objectives. An agency's choice of revenue objectives can vary according to the type of value and the beneficiary. Objectives for developing a user-fees policy may include:

❑ equitable allocation of costs;
❑ cost recovery;
❑ economic efficiency through identification of a market rate;
❑ generation of revenue in excess of costs so that other activities such as biodiversity conservation can be financed;
❑ improving facilities and management;
❑ generation of foreign exchange and/or tax revenues from tourist purchases;
❑ demand management – that is, using fees to limit or redistribute the number of visitors, in order to reduce environmental damage, congestion, or user conflicts (Lindberg, 1998; QPWS, 2000).

The cost of collecting user fees is an important factor in establishing a pricing policy. Costs associated with the implementation and administration of a user-pays system are called transaction costs. There is no point charging user fees if the transaction costs are such that they substantially offset the revenue collected. For a park with many entrances, the transaction costs associated with establishing numerous fee collection stations would be high. For a park with

Differential pricing for access and use can help spread the use of and impact on protected areas.

J Kostrzewa/UNEP

T Natiano/UNEP

Protected areas provide a range of ecosystem services that benefit people some distance away, for example, the quality of water supply.

low annual use, the revenue generated would be low. In both cases, transactions costs are likely to be a high proportion of total costs. Full recovery of these costs is difficult to justify, relative to the value of the damage being caused and/or the services being provided. Of course, transaction costs are also dependent on the collection method employed and, with changing technology, opportunities may arise to significantly reduce transaction costs.

If demand management is the objective, peak-load pricing can be used to control visitor numbers or redistribute them over different time periods. Peak-load pricing refers to the practice of charging different prices at different times for the same service. The cost of having excess capacity during off-peak periods can be covered by increasing the amount charged to peak users. Charging higher fees for prime camping sites can help to spread use more evenly. Higher peak-period prices can also be used to perform a rationing function.

Another common practice is price discrimination – that is, charging different prices for the same goods or services where the price differences are not proportional to differences in costs. There

are a number of reasons why price discrimination may be used. For equity reasons, certain individuals may be charged low prices, or given goods or services free of charge. Such equity-based price discrimination may apply to the very old or very young, local residents, or low-income earners.

ADMINISTRATION

Administration lies at the heart of a protected area organization's capacity to operate. As is the case with much in this chapter, this section is primarily written with a government or major non-governmental organization in mind.

People are needed to implement an organization's primary mission. Staff (and contractors) often need to be hired and paid. They need a base from which to operate. Hence offices and workshops must be either purchased, constructed, or leased. People need to be mobile and to have access to equipment and materials. This requires the hire or purchase of vehicles, plant, and other equipment. Staff also need a supportive operating framework, which ranges from employment contracts to skills training.

All of this requires well-designed administration systems. Budgets need to be secured and managed. Bills need to be paid. Staff need to be treated fairly. Workplaces need to be safe. Systems need to be in place to evaluate and monitor staff performance so that professional standards remain high. Numerous routine administrative tasks and systems are needed to support the conservation of a protected area. Organizations need to operate fairly and equitably, and to be accountable.

For long-term success, an organization must invest in capacity building and development of its staff. Staff across an organization need to be up to date with advances in computer software, legislation, project management techniques, accounting systems, and other organizational aspects. Training helps create an internal culture focused on constant improvement. It can also be used to give staff background information on the history of the organization. Training is usually administered through the organization's human resources section. Capacity building for a protected area organization needs to be strategic and long term. It should be a systems approach linked to organizational needs and the demography of the workforce.

Local area managers may also run their own training programs, for example to train new staff in basic operational skills such as using a chainsaw, operating a four-wheel drive, or conducting customer service. Training needs of staff should be recognized in performance development agreements or other similar arrangements with their supervisors. Most organizations foster such an environment of continuous learning, and they reward or explicitly recognize their staff's vocational training. Staff may also benefit from time-release schemes that allow them to be seconded to other organizations or undertake specialist study or project work.

Asset management should be part of an integrated management system. Assets are items of value that an organization owns or controls. Assets include constructed items such as roads, sewer lines, bridges, buildings, trails, and various cultural heritage structures, as well as tools, vehicles, or even intellectual property. Most organizations have a range of assets to manage, and typically these are inventoried. Asset management systems allow managers to predict when assets will need to be refurbished or replaced (maintenance cycles). They can allow for these expenses in their annual budget. They can also keep track of the total value of assets, which is important in accrual accounting.

SUSTAINABLE MANAGEMENT

The major objectives of protected area managers are to ensure biodiversity and cultural heritage conservation. At the same time, sustainable management principles need to be adhered to, as the very process of conservation management consumes energy and natural resources and produces wastes, thus impacting upon the global environment. Sustainable protected area management considers these impacts and focuses on reducing greenhouse gas emissions, water and energy consumption, minimizing waste production, and ensuring maximum benefits to local communities. Protected area managers operate within the wider context of environmental management and, as such, there are a number of international environmental policies that govern their operations.

Protected area organizations should be leaders in the field of sustainable management practice. Sustainable environmental management needs to be part of the daily operations of protected area management. Managers have a responsibility to address environmental issues, provide leadership, and be accountable to the community. Reduction in the use of fossil-based energy

S.Chape

decreases the amount of greenhouse gases generated; consuming less water will assist in maintaining the health of catchment and river systems; and creating less waste helps preserve our ecosystems. Protected area managers are accountable for the resources that they utilize and they have a responsibility to limit the environmental impacts of their activities.

Strategies to reduce greenhouse gases and ensure sustainability outcomes need to be developed and implemented for park management operations. An important component of this is environmental performance assessment and monitoring. Energy, water, and other resource use, waste production, and greenhouse gas emissions need to be assessed for operations. These can then be benchmarked and continual improvement systems implemented. Such sustainability assessment should be an integral part of park management planning and operations.

Sustainable development criteria need to be part of the planning, design, and construction of new facilities. Issues considered include design for natural lighting, ventilation, and heating; the use of

Haleakala National Park, Hawaii.

131

renewable energy sources; the use of recycled materials; water minimization, recycling, and retention systems; and life cycle assessments of building products to reduce the ecological footprint of a development and its continued operation.

Environmental performance reporting on a regular basis will ensure that management continues to operate at the highest sustainability standards and that protected areas assist in educating the community on sustainability principles and practices. Such performance achievements should be made publicly available.

OPERATIONS MANAGEMENT

Operations are essential activities and tasks that underpin the conservation management of protected areas. Managed correctly, operations directly help in achieving conservation outcomes. They are the major difference between so-called "paper parks" (legally reserved areas with no active management) and parks that are effectively managed and contributing to conservation outcomes.

Operations management is defined as the management of the productive processes that convert inputs into goods, services, and activities (Slack, Chambers, and Johnston, 2001). It is considered to be part of the "controlling" function of management, because much of the emphasis is on regulating the productive processes that are critical to reaching organizational goals (Bartol *et al.*, 1998). Protected area management operations are those inputs, processes, and systems that directly contribute to the achievement of conservation outcomes. Such operations should recognize the following principles.

❏ Effective protected area management operations are an essential and integral part of the conservation of natural and cultural heritage. Protected areas require active, effective, and continuous management if the purposes for which they were reserved are to be retained.

❏ Operational standards, best-practice systems, staff competencies, operational procedures, on-site leadership, and operations team discipline are all integral and essential parts of effective protected area operational management.

❏ Leadership, inclusiveness, and attention to operational detail are essential parts of successful operational management.

❏ Research, operational performance monit-

oring, and adaptive management are essential parts of successful operational management.

❏ Local knowledge and local community involvement is a fundamental part of an operation.

MANAGING THREATS

The wide range of threats facing protected areas was reviewed in Chapter 3. A number of these threats are generated well beyond the boundaries of individual protected areas, and their ultimate resolution needs to be dealt with in the context of national- and regional-level planning, and global collaboration (such as threats from climate change and pollution). However, the impact of threats often needs to be dealt with and managed at the individual protected area level, as well as within the context of regional land-use planning and development.

Management responses for dealing with threats and unwanted change to maintain conservation values may involve some or all of the following (ACIUCN, 2002).

❏ **Regeneration**, which involves the recovery of natural integrity following disturbance or degradation, with minimal human intervention.

❏ **Restoration**, which requires returning existing habitats to a known past state or to an approximation of the natural condition by repairing degradation, by removing introduced species, or by reinstatement.

❏ **Reinstatement**, which means reintroduction to a place of one or more species or elements of habitat or geodiversity that are known to have existed there naturally at a previous time, but that can no longer be found at that place.

❏ **Enhancement**, which involves introduction to a place of additional individuals of one or more organisms, species, or elements of habitat or geodiversity that naturally exist there.

❏ **Preservation**, which means maintaining the biodiversity and/or an ecosystem of a place at the existing stage of succession, or maintaining existing geodiversity.

❏ **Modification**, which involves altering a place to suit proposed uses that are compatible with the natural significance of the place.

❏ **Protection**, which requires taking care of a place by maintenance and by managing impacts to ensure that natural significance is retained.

❏ **Maintenance**, which involves continuous protective care of the biological diversity and geodiversity of a place.

CULTURAL HERITAGE MANAGEMENT

As well as maintaining natural heritage, protected areas are important for the perpetuation, representation, and conservation of cultural heritage values. Cultural heritage values refer to qualities and attributes possessed by places or items that have aesthetic, historic, scientific, or social value for past, present, and future generations. These values may be seen in places and physical features, but can also be associated with intangible qualities such as people's associations with or feelings for a place or item, or in other elements such as cultural practices, knowledge, songs, and stories. When natural elements of the landscape acquire meaning for a particular group, they may become cultural heritage. These may include land forms, flora, fauna, and minerals (Sullivan, 2005).

Cultural heritage resources need active management because they are essentially non-renewable, and often perishable. They are manifestations of past events, and only a limited number of them were created. Their material fabric also suffers with time, incidents, and disasters. If destroyed, they may be copied or reconstructed, but we cannot renew the spiritual, social, and historical moments in which they were created. Each site may be a unique physical manifestation of the activities, ideologies, technologies, and social practices of a particular place and time.

In most areas, natural and cultural heritage are inextricably entwined. They form a continuum rather than being separate entities. The interaction between the natural and cultural heritage values of a protected area add richness and depth to the story of the place (Sullivan and Lennon, 2003).

Successful conservation of cultural heritage requires:
❏ an objective assessment of all the elements of significance, both natural and cultural, of the protected area;
❏ development of policies and priorities, which protect both the natural and cultural heritage and strike a balance in cases of conflict;
❏ close consultation with, and involvement of, the people whose cultural heritage is represented in the protected area;
❏ development among park staff of specialized

N.Dudley

skills, or access to specialized advice, to effectively protect cultural heritage;
❏ familiarity, on the part of the manager, with best-practice methodology for cultural heritage identification and conservation.

TOURISM AND RECREATION

Tourism is travel away from home for recreation or associated activities, and industries and services that aim to satisfy the needs of tourists. Growth in global tourism has been one of the great phenomena of the late 20th and early 21st centuries. In 2002, there were 715 million international arrivals worldwide – 22 million more than in 2001 and 690 million more than in 1950 (Commonwealth of Australia, 2003). The World Travel and Tourism Council (WTTC) has forecast that the number of international arrivals will increase to nearly 1.6 billion by 2020, despite a potential scarcity of petroleum by this time (Commonwealth of Australia, 2003; Mason 2003). Many tourist destinations are protected areas.

In an era of (relatively) cheap petroleum-based fuel, transport systems have delivered visitors

The demand for the recreational opportunities afforded by protected areas is forecast to rise rapidly. Kaziranga National Park World Heritage Area, India.

BOX 5.1: THE ROLE OF RANGERS IN PROTECTED AREA MANAGEMENT

Sustaining the integrity of protected areas is a key function of any robust management regime and differentiates between so-called "paper parks" and those parks that truly make a contribution to world conservation. Active management requires negotiation and persuasion, and sometimes coercion and enforcement. It needs to bring together disparate and often conflicting aims and aspirations for the good of the protected area and its linkages to the wider landscape and adjacent communities. When dealing with people, it also needs a human face. At the grass roots level that human face is usually the ranger.*

The primary responsibility of the ranger is to maintain the integrity of the protected area where they work. In this context, ranger corps often form the "Thin Green Line", preserving such areas from destruction by outside forces. Many of the different titles by which they are known throughout the world, such as guardeparques, used throughout Spanish-speaking Latin America, reflect their guardian or custodian role.

Over time, however, the focus of the ranger's role has expanded, reflecting a much greater critical interface with both local and broader communities. At any given time a ranger may be: an environmental interpreter, community liaison officer, field naturalist, facilitator, and, when called for, rescuer or enforcer. The ranger acts as a day-to-day bridge in community liaison programs, developing key partnerships and engendering a sense of ownership for those living, visiting, and working within protected areas. A central part of their role includes the development and delivery of environmental education, both in terms of the protected area and wider conservation principles. The ability of rangers to be seen as "authoritative" and not "authoritarian" reflects this increasingly complex role. It engenders a feeling of approachability yet retains respect for

themselves and the area they are there to protect. Rangers are also uniquely positioned and qualified to implement, evaluate and advise on the effectiveness of management and sustainable development, and to monitor the health of the area.

Many rangers have, through the course of their careers, risen through the ranks to become directors and executives of protected area administrations, but for the most part the dedication and invaluable work of rangers carries on unrecognized, reflecting the vocational nature of the job.

Lives on the Line

As guardians of often highly valuable natural or cultural resources, rangers are all too frequently faced with combating illegal commercial and non-sustainable exploitation of these resources, frequently at great personal risk. Regional conflict, civil wars, and political upheaval have a profound impact on protected areas, but even under these circumstances rangers will be found at their posts. In Mozambique, rangers stayed at their posts throughout the civil war without getting paid. Similar stories can be found elsewhere, not just in Africa, where dedicated rangers have remained resolutely in their parks throughout internal strife and conflict, and all too often have paid for their dedication with their lives.

In addition to human threats, rangers often have to battle the elements and unforgiving terrain at inopportune times, especially when involved in activities such as search and rescue, wild fire control or wildlife capture operations. Particularly in the developing world, rangers often live and work in remote and isolated areas, with minimal logistical and institutional support. Far too often they carry out their work without even the most rudimentary equipment or uniform, and often go without pay for months at a time.

quickly and efficiently to visitor destinations around the world. Such tourism is important to the economies of many nations, and brings many benefits to local communities. Managed responsibly, tourism can provide many sustainable benefits to protected areas, including opportunities for both education

and the appreciation of nature and cultural heritage, as well as fostering a conservation constituency (Eagles and McCool, 2002).

However, as noted in Chapter 3, tourism has also led to conflicts and environmental impacts. The tourism industry's global bodies, the World Tourism

S Chape

Patrolling Ta Phraya National Park in the Dong Phayayen-Khao Yai Forest Complex World Heritage Area, Thailand, on the border with Cambodia. Rangers have to contend with armed poachers and illegal loggers and are at risk from land mines left over from the Cambodian conflict.

International Ranger Federation

Rangers need training, mentoring and knowledge to support their efforts. Inadequate resources, including limited financial resources and a shortage of skilled personnel, undermine an area's integrity and management effectiveness. Threats to biodiversity from climate change, natural disasters, alien invasive species, and a wide array of human activities and impacts also pose distinct challenges.

The International Ranger Federation (IRF), a world-wide Federation of National Ranger Associations in over 53 countries, has been instrumental in the development of key competencies that define the areas of knowledge a ranger must have, with the flexibility to be applied at different levels to reflect differing geopolitical contexts. The IRF is now actively engaged in the dissemination of best practice and the raising of professional standards, and using key competencies as a benchmark for training and mentoring programs in a number of areas around the world. The strength of the Federation lies in the fact that its member associations also reflect regional differences, for example, allowing South American rangers of one country to offer mentoring to rangers working in other South American countries. It also means that the IRF can develop locally based prescriptions for generic terminologies such as "area integrity". Since its inception in 1992, the IRF has been successful in a number of initiatives designed to reflect and raise the standards of professionalism of rangers. It has also been actively involved in the area of youth development; for example, jointly hosting a Young Conservationist Award with the IUCN World Commission on Protected Areas.

* The IRF defines a ranger as "the person involved in the practical protection and preservation of all aspects of wild areas, historical, and cultural sites. Rangers provide recreational opportunities and interpretation of sites while providing links between local communities, protected areas, and area administration."

Organization (WTO) and WTTC, have responded to the substantial environmental problems and are aware that growth in tourism is dependent, among other considerations, on the sustainability of destinations. The WTO has contributed to international declarations on the environment, environmental codes of ethics, guidelines, and policies that promote sustainable tourism. The strategic document, Blueprint for New Tourism, was launched by the WTTC in 2003 (WTTC, 2003). The strategy sets balancing economics with environment, people, and cultures as a key goal,

---

BOX 5.2: DEVELOPING CAPACITY AND TRAINING FOR PROTECTED AREAS

The importance of developing capacity for protected areas, at individual and institutional levels and in the wider enabling environment, has long been recognized. At individual-level training – the enhancement of knowledge, skills and competencies among individuals involved in the running of protected areas – is fundamental to developing capacity. There are a number of initiatives at national, regional, and global levels to provide training.

At national level a number of protected area agencies, most but not all in developed countries, offer ongoing training, mainly aimed at their own staff. Examples include agencies in Australia, Canada, Kenya, New Zealand, and the US. Training in developing countries may be supported through capacity-building projects funded by bilateral or multilateral agencies such as the Global Environment Facility. In addition, a number of universities and colleges offer training in subjects relevant to the design and management of protected areas, often tailored to conditions in their own countries.

Internationally, apart from the International Ranger Federation, there is no agency primarily responsible for overseeing training and to produce a comprehensive international training strategy for protected areas. However, various initiatives have been undertaken, chiefly by IUCN – the World Conservation Union, UNEP and UNESCO. In 1996, the Global Task Force on Training was established under the World Commission on Protected Areas, but this has never had the resources to be effective. In 2001, the UNESCO World Heritage Centre prepared a Global Training Strategy for World Heritage, and in 2003, a strategic process for capacity building.

Some institutions offer courses aimed at an international audience, such as the International Short Course for Senior Park Managers, run since 1998 by the Glynwood Centre in New York State, USA, in cooperation with the US National Parks Service. There are also a number of regional training centres, some with a long history, such as the Centro Agronómico Tropical de Investigación y Enseñaza (CATIE) in Costa Rica (established in 1973), the College of African Wildlife Management at Mweka in Tanzania (1963), the Garoua Wildlife College, Cameroon (1970) and the Southern African Wildlife College in Northern Province, South Africa (1997). In addition there are several international exchange programs for protected area staff intended to facilitate training. One of the most successful of these has been the Latin American Technical Cooperation Network on National Parks, other Protected Areas and Wildlife, which, since its inception in 1983, has held over 40 workshops, trained scores of technical staff and produced a large number of training documents and manuals.

Despite these various initiatives, a number of pervasive problems still need to be solved. These include:

❑ inadequate school or tertiary-level training or education relevant to protected areas;
❑ lack of a "training culture" in many protected area agencies;
❑ lack of resources;
❑ ineffective training because of inappropriateness to local conditions or lack of effective targeting at recipients;
❑ barriers to the application of what has been learned in training;
❑ unclear, unspecified and continuously changing skill set required to manage protected areas;
❑ once trained, people often leave protected area agencies, especially in developing countries.

---

and indicated that "new tourism" should look beyond short-term considerations to focus "on benefits not only for people who travel, but also for people in the communities they visit, and for their respective natural, social and cultural environments".

In 1983, Mexican architect and environmentalist Hector Ceballos-Lascurain coined the word "ecotourism". Ecotourism is now a major segment of the tourism industry and a major growth area. As often happens with an emerging phenomenon, it has several similar names: nature tourism, green tourism, adventure tourism, sustainable tourism, appropriate tourism. In describing its evolution, Honey (1999) noted that: "broadly stated, the concept of ecotourism can be traced to four sources: (1) scientific, conservation, and non-governmental organization circles; (2) multilateral aid institutions; (3) developing countries; and (4) the travel industry and traveling public."

The term ecotourism implied a genuine attempt to respect nature and to manage for the future. It linked the tourism industry with the community's concern for the environment, and so was popular with both environmentalists and managers. Common sense dictated that it was simply not sustainable for the tourism industry to degrade its own destinations. Around the world, ecotourism has been hailed as a panacea: a way to fund conservation and scientific research, protect fragile and pristine ecosystems, benefit rural communities, promote development in poor countries, enhance ecological and cultural sensitivity, instill environmental awareness and a social conscience in the travel industry, satisfy and educate the discriminating tourist, and, some claim, build world peace. Although green travel is being marketed as a win–win solution for developing countries, the environment, the tourist, and the travel industry, close examination shows a much more complex reality.

For Ceballos-Lascuráin (1996), if an activity is to be considered as ecotourism:

It should promote positive environmental ethics and foster "preferred" behavior in its participants.

It should not degrade the resource (that is, the natural environment).

Facilities and services may support the tourist's encounter with the "intrinsic resource", but should never become attractions in their own right.

Ecotourists should accept the environment as it is, not expecting it to change or be modified for their convenience.

Ecotourism must benefit the wildlife and environment, contributing to their sustainability and ecological integrity (this may be through the effects on the local community or economy).

It should provide a first-hand encounter with nature. Visitor centers and on-site interpretive slide-shows may be part of an ecotourism activity only if they direct people to a first-hand experience.

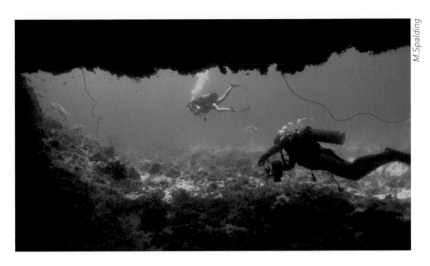

M.Spalding

It should actively involve and benefit local communities, thus encouraging them to value their natural resources.

It should offer gratification through education and/or appreciation rather than through thrill-seeking or physical achievement.

It should involve considerable preparation, and demand in-depth knowledge on the part of leaders and participants.

Recreation, an aspect of park tourism, is also an important part of the human experience of protected areas (Pigram and Jenkins, 1999). Visitors undertake an extraordinary diversity of recreation activities within protected areas. Most activities have a constituency that lobbies in support of its continuation or expansion within the protected area estate. Staff are often required to be involved with facilities supporting bushwalking, skiing, boating, canoeing, caving, four-wheel driving, and a range of other activities. Adventure recreation activities, such as canyoning, white-water rafting, cross-country skiing, abseiling, ice climbing, and rock climbing, may need management attention for safety reasons (response to emergencies in bad weather) and for potential environmental impacts.

The tourism and recreation values of protected areas are influenced by a number of geographical, social, managerial, and biophysical factors, including proximity and accessibility to markets, cultural links, availability of services, affordability, peace and stability, positive market image, pro-tourism policies, and availability of attractions (Weaver and Opperman, 2000). Visitor attractions in protected areas may be natural

Diving tourism in Jardines de la Reina National Park, Cuba. Low intensity, low impact tourism can bring considerable benefits to local communities, often in turn leading to greater efforts to protect the environment.

Tan Yik Yee/UNEP

The demands of an ever increasing population for commodities, infrastructure and services place pressure on species and natural and cultural spaces. Orangutans (*Pongo* spp.) are now highly endangered in the wild.

features or destinations with more developed facilities and services such as visitor centers, boardwalks, and limestone "show caves". Artificial attractions or high-impact, derived activities that may diminish the natural or cultural heritage values of protected areas are inconsistent with the concept and purpose of most protected areas.

The value of protected areas for tourism and recreation use can be described in terms of opportunity settings found within them. These can be defined as the combination of physical (such as scenery), biological (such as native plants and animals), social (such as family, friends and/or other visitors), and managerial (such as the facilities and regulations imposed at a setting) conditions that give value to a place (Clarke and Stankey, 1979). Managing for tourism and recreation opportunity settings is typically achieved through the management planning process and the use of zoning and recreation planning tools. Protected area managers, in cooperation with other land managers, should ensure that a spectrum of recreation settings is available within a region. The setting of planning limits for visitor destinations is also an essential tool in sustainable visitor-use management.

EVALUATING MANAGEMENT EFFECTIVENESS

Management effectiveness evaluation measures the degree to which a protected area is protecting its values and achieving its goals and objectives. Agreed methods of evaluating management effectiveness will be crucial in the attempt to assess whether the world's nations have been successful in their CBD target of ensuring that all protected areas have effective management in place by 2012. More importantly, such methods should actually enable managers to improve conservation and management of protected areas on the ground. They should enable managers to allocate resources efficiently and plan for potential threats and opportunities. Because evaluation involves judging management, some people see it as negative or threatening. However, management effectiveness evaluation should be a positive process that allows us to learn from our mistakes and build on success.

Protected area declaration alone does not guarantee the conservation of values. Globally, substantial investments of money, land, and human effort are being put into protected area acquisition and management, and into specific intervention projects. It is a remarkable achievement for the world's governments and conservation organizations that more than 12 percent of the world's land surface is in some form of protected area. However, in most cases we have little idea of whether management of individual protected areas, or of whole systems, is effective.

Managers and authorities, landowners and communities, academics, and the general public are beginning to ask some serious questions. Are the values for which the area is declared being protected? Are the current and future impacts on the area's values overwhelming it, resulting in loss of species and degradation, ecosystems, or cultural values? How could management be improved to better conserve the values in the face of growing social expectations, often scarce resourcing, and sometimes significant biophysical change? Are interventions and projects, which are often very expensive, achieving their objectives?

To answer these critical questions, an increasing number of people have been developing ways to monitor and evaluate the effectiveness of protected areas and apply the findings. This is leading to a growing awareness that evaluation of management effectiveness is at the core of resilient, adaptive, and anticipatory protected area management. Four broad purposes for undertaking evaluation of management effectiveness can be identified.

Promoting better protected area management
This includes a more reflective and adaptive approach to management. By comparing evaluations over time, emerging threats may be noticed, as well as the impacts of changes to management. For example, an individual park evaluation may indicate that the condition of visitor facilities and visitor satisfaction at a particular national park is declining. Sometimes, a significant outcome of evaluation is to demonstrate effective management practices and to provide justification for their continued support.

Guiding project planning, resource allocation, and priority setting
Some conservation organizations are developing models to set priorities and allocate resources. Evaluation plays a key role in these models, which generally establish a minimum acceptable standard for different criteria and then assess protected areas against these standards. The conservation importance of protected areas, their suitability for particular uses (such as tourism), and their current threats are usually taken into account. Findings of evaluation can also influence resource allocation by indicating which programs are most effective in achieving objectives. Management effectiveness evaluation provides a mechanism for adaptive management – feeding the results of research and monitoring into management on the ground and giving a basis for decision making.

Providing accountability and transparency
Evaluation can provide reliable information to the public, donors, and other stakeholders about how resources are being used and how well an area is being managed. For example, the public often want concrete evidence that funding is benefiting conservation or that a particular project is achieving its goals. Where protected areas are managed by more than one party, through joint management arrangements, regular and impartial evaluations provide a basis for ensuring that obligations are met.

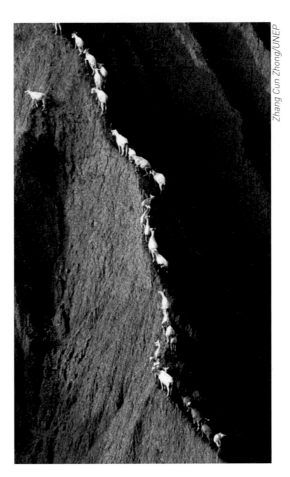
Zhang Cun Zhong/UNEP

Protected area status alone does not necessarily guarantee the conservation of values.

Increasing community awareness, involvement, and support
Since chronic resource shortage is a common feature of protected area systems, public support – sometimes serious public concern – is needed to convince governments to provide better resourcing. Evaluation processes can alert the community to threats and can demonstrate the need for improved support for protected areas. Results, especially from independent evaluators, can spur public action on park management issues.

Essentially, evaluation enables practitioners to reflect on experience, to understand what is happening here and now, and to assess potential threats and opportunities. Evaluation of management effectiveness can play an important role in providing transparency and accountability, and in identifying mistakes and dead-end approaches. However, it is an essentially positive process, and is best viewed as a critical part of an improving management cycle. Indeed, an increasing number of scientists now believe that the application of knowledge from multiple sources into management

TABLE 5.1: THE WCPA MANAGEMENT EFFECTIVENESS FRAMEWORK

Elements of evaluation	Context	Planning	Inputs	Processes	Outputs	Outcomes
Explanation	Where are we now? Assessment of importance, threats, and policy environment	Where do we want to be? Assessment of protected area design and planning	What do we need? Assessment of resources needed	How do we go about it? Assessment of the way management is conducted	What were the results? Assessment of implementation of management programs and actions; delivery of products and services	What did we achieve? Assessment of outcomes and the extent to which they achieved objectives
Criteria assessed	Significance Threats Vulnerability National context	Protected area legislation and policy System design Reserve design Management planning	Resourcing of agency Resourcing of site Partners	Suitability of management processes	Results of management actions Services and products	Impacts: effects of management in relation to objectives
Focus of evaluation	Status	Appropriateness	Resources	Efficiency Appropriateness	Effectiveness	Effectiveness Appropriateness

Source: Hockings, Stolton & Dudley, 2000.

should be the most critical focus, and that "the priority for ecosystem management is evolving improvements through reflection on experience that follows decision and action" (Brunner and Clarke, 1997). A system of evaluating management effectiveness can help to integrate a variety of information sources, such as traditional and community knowledge, scientific findings, and the perceptions and experience of managers and stakeholders. Evaluation focuses on relevant management-oriented knowledge, and on group learning about how this should be practically applied to meet future challenges.

Evolution of management effectiveness evaluation
The need to develop tools and guidelines to "evaluate the ecological and managerial quality of existing protected areas" was recognized in the Bali Action Plan adopted at the end of the IIIrd

WPC (Bali) in 1982. Following the Bali Congress, the issue of management effectiveness of protected areas began to appear in international literature and particularly within the work and deliberations of the WCPA.

The IVth WPC (Caracas) in 1992 identified effective management as one of the four major protected area issues of global concern and called for IUCN to further develop a system for monitoring management effectiveness of protected areas. In 1996, a Task Force was formed within the Commission and in 2000, it published the WCPA Management Effectiveness Framework (Table 5.1) and guidelines for assessing the management of protected areas (Hockings, Stolton, and Dudley, 2000) which have been subsequently revised (Hockings *et al.*, 2006).

The Task Force has now been replaced by a thematic program within WCPA, which is continuing

TABLE 5.2: METHODS OF DATA COLLECTION, PARTICIPANTS INVOLVED AND WCPA FRAMEWORK ELEMENTS COVERED IN 21 CASE STUDIES OF MANAGEMENT EFFECTIVENESS EVALUATION

Methods of data collection	%	Participants	%	WCPA Framework elements	%
Workshop	62	Site managers	100	Outcomes	81
Interviews	52	Off-site managers/agency staff	90	Inputs	71
Questionnaires	52	Local NGO	57	Process	67
Field monitoring	24	International NGO	57	Context	57
MIS	19	Scientists/researchers	57	Outputs	57
Map analysis	19	Local communities and institutions	52	Planning	52
		Consultants	38	All	38
		Government bodies	33		
		Management advisory committee	10		
		Indigenous communities	5		

work on the issue. At the same time as the Task Force was preparing these guidelines, a number of other groups and individuals around the world were addressing the same issue by developing a range of methodologies for assessing management effectiveness. A suite of methodologies now exist, some developed using the WCPA Management Effectiveness Framework and others derived independently (Hockings, 2003). Experience in application of these various methodologies is now increasing. Some examples of this application are summarized in Table 5.3, based on information drawn from case studies prepared for an international workshop on management effectiveness evaluation held in the lead up to the Vth WPC (Durban) in 2003 (Leverington and Hockings, 2004).

These methodologies vary considerably in their overall approach, including in the type of information used in the assessment process, in how the information is collected, and in who is involved in the assessment process (Table 5.2). These differences, in part, reflect the purpose and context of the evaluation and the resources available for the work. Indeed, a variety of approaches that can be adapted for use in different biomes and regions, and applied with different levels of resources, is one of the fundamental ideas behind the development of the WCPA Management Effectiveness Framework, as opposed to the development of one global system for assessing management effectiveness.

The majority of the case studies reviewed in the development of approaches to management effectiveness evaluation relied principally on existing data and perceptions of participants in the evaluation process with less than a quarter of the case studies using techniques such as field monitoring, use of management information systems, or analysis of mapped data to inform the assessment. This may reflect the relative youth of management effectiveness evaluation, with many case studies having been undertaken as one-off or initial assessments. Hopefully, more widespread and regular application of evaluation systems will see a rise in the availability and use of monitoring data in the assessment process.

All the case studies involved site managers in the assessment process; local and international non-governmental organizations and scientists were the next most common participants. Only half the studies involved participation by local communities and institutions, and only one provided explicitly for indigenous communities – although indigenous representatives may have been included within the local community group in others. Wider involvement of communities and stakeholders in evaluation processes should be encouraged.

Management effectiveness of protected areas has been selected by the CBD as one of the indicators that will be used to assess achievement of the UN 2010 biodiversity target. The impetus provided by this decision is leading many countries to undertake assessments of management of their protected areas. Over the next few years we should have a much clearer picture of the state of the world's parks based on the results of this work.

TABLE 5.3: CASE STUDIES OF MANAGEMENT EFFECTIVENESS EVALUATION COLLATED AS PART OF A PREPARATORY WORKSHOP FOR THE VTH WORLD PARKS CONGRESS

Case study	Background information	Reasons for evaluating management	
Bwindi Impenetrable National Park, Uganda (BINP) evaluation of management effectiveness	World Heritage listed BINP is managed primarily to protect the park's montane forests and their diverse wildlife – especially nearly half the world's remaining mountain gorillas. It is one of the pilot sites in Enhancing Our Heritage: monitoring and managing for success in Natural World Heritage sites.	To improve on existing management strategies and reduce resource wastage.	
Evaluation of management of Protected Areas (PAs) of Catalonia, Spain	Catalonia is a region covering 32 000sq km in the north east of Spain. Most protected areas are managed by the Catalonian Govt, who, since 1992 have attempted to base conservation planning on ecological criteria instead of social preferences.	European Pilot Study; Increase information; Assess condition of PA system and propose changes.	
Evaluating the management effectiveness of PAs in India	A World Bank-funded project by the Govt of India to assess the management effectiveness of PAs in India.	Reassess results of 1984–1987 evaluation by applying same methodology. Recommend areas for attention as well as legal and policy changes.	
IUCN WCPA-Marine/WWF MPA Management Effectiveness Initiative	IUCN WCPA and WWF initiative to improve management of Marine Protected Areas (MPAs).	To enhance overall capacity of adaptive management of MPAs by focusing on indicators specific to MPAs and their surrounds.	
Conservation International's Pilot Evaluation of Management Effectiveness of Protected Areas in Peru and Ecuador	Peru and Ecuador manage PAs with some of the most biologically diverse ecosystems on earth. Some areas of the Amazon have little human activity, while parts of the Andes and coastal forests have major human impacts. This results in very different management contexts across the countries.	To improve understanding and management of issues relating to social context, physical context and budget on PAs.	
Evaluation of Management Effectiveness of the Sian Ka'an Biosphere Reserve (SKBR)	WH-listed SKBR covers over 600 000ha on Mexican Caribbean Coast and protects diverse marine, freshwater and terrestrial ecosystems. It is threatened by urban growth and tourism.	Prepare and monitor a Sustainable Development Plan – to limit external threats to the park.	
Forest Innovations Project: Developing a Protected Area Effectiveness Methodology for Africa	It was recognized that little work had been done on management effectiveness evaluation (MEE) in Africa. A methodology was developed by the IUCN/WWF/GTZ Forest Innovations Project and tested on a number of African Reserves.	Develop and field test WCPA methodology and promote MEE of African PAs.	
Evaluation of World Heritage Management program for the Tasmanian Wilderness World Heritage Area	The Tasmanian Wilderness World Heritage Area is one of the largest conservation reserves in Australia protecting temperate wilderness and cultural heritage. It is managed according to a ten-year Statutory Plan, which details policies and actions needed to be implemented to achieve the plan's objectives.	Provide reliable feedback to managers and stakeholders about achievement of management objectives. Enable ongoing management to be more effective and accountable.	
Assessment of Federal Protected Areas in Brazil	Brazil has 91 Federal Protected Areas. All 86 PAs created more than six years ago were part of this assessment. Six years was considered the requisite timeframe to allow for minimum implementation of park management measures.	Support a WWF-Brazil campaign to positively highlight PAs before a Protected Area Bill in Congress was voted on.	

Data collection: W = workshops; I = interviews; MIS = management information system; M = field monitoring; Q = questionnaires/surveys; MA = Map Analysis; MP = Existing Management Plan. Participants: SM = site managers/field staff; MA = Management agency staff (off-site); NGO(L) – local NGO; NGO(I) – international NGO;

Methodology	Data collection	Participants in evaluation process	WCPA Framework elements	Identifiable results from evaluation process
Enhancing Our Heritage project methodology based on WCPA Framework.	W, I, MIS	SM, MA, S, NGO(L), NGO(I), LC	C, PL, I, PR, OP, OC	Led to increase in staffing, development of training plans, infrastructure and equipment acquisition, plans for boundary changes to reserve. Refocus on gorilla research and monitoring.
Indicator system based on the WCPA Framework.	I, W	SM, MA, S, G, NGO(L), LC	C, PL, I, PR, OP, OC	Too early in process to determine, although managers considered issues not previously thought about.
Survey of PA managers and experts.	Q, I,	SM, MA, NGO(I), NGO(L), LC, G, S	C, PL, I, PR, OP, OC	1984–1987 study led to increased resourcing, amendments to law and policy, acceptance of ecodevelopment near PAs.
Based on WCPA Framework proposing indicators for biophysical, socio-economic and governance objectives.	Q, I, W	NGO(I), NGO(L), C, SM, MA, LC, S	Mostly OP and OC	Too early in process to determine.
Based on WCPA Framework	MA, I	NGO(I), NGO(L), SM, MA,	C, PL, I, OC	Results of the evaluation are being finalized. Organization and dissemination of background information to allow more informed management decisions.
WWF/CATIE (2000) methodology	W	SM, MA, C	All – although mostly PR	Action plan to be incorporated into Management Plan
Based on WCPA Framework. Used participatory and rapid rural appraisal techniques concentrating on social aspects	W, I, Q	C, NGO(I), G, NGO(L), SM, MA, LC	C, PL, I, PR, OP, OC	Too early in process to determine.
Primarily outcomes-based evaluation focused on objectives in the management plan for the site.	MP, M, Q	SM, MA, C, G, WH, IC, S	Focuses on OC with some consideration of OP, I	Evaluation results are guiding development of next management plan. Results are expected to influence budgeting and allow stakeholders to be more involved with management performance.
Questionnaire developed for this study.	W, Q	NGO(I), MA, SM, G, S	C, PL, I, PR, OP, OC	Follow-up evaluation has not been done. The evaluation was used to determine the status of PAs not to directly influence management. Results contributed to successful campaign in support of legislation.

G = Govt bodies; LC = Local community; C =Consultants; S = Scientists/Researcher institution; IC = Indigenous communities; AC= Independent Management Advisory Committee. WCPA Framework elements: C = Context; PL = Planning; I = Inputs; PR = Process; OP = Outputs; OC = Outcomes

TABLE 5.3: (continued)

Case study	Background information	Reasons for evaluating management	
Rapid Assessment and Prioritization of Protected Areas Management (RAPPAM) Methodology	WWF-International has developed a tool for assessing the management effectiveness of protected area systems. It is intended to: (1) identify strengths and weaknesses; (2) analyze threats and pressures; (3) identify areas of high ecological and social importance and vulnerability; (4) indicate the urgency and conservation priority for individual PAs; and (5) help to improve management effectiveness.	Depended on each area, but included assessing management effectiveness of entire PA systems, prioritizing support for critically threatened PAs; establishing baseline data and identify areas for improving management.	
Queensland Parks and Wildlife Service rapid assessment and ecological integrity statements	Queensland Parks and Wildlife Service is responsible for managing most of the state's natural areas. Two systems of management effectiveness evaluation have been piloted across the state: evaluation of natural and cultural integrity and rapid assessment of management processes.	To develop an efficient and replicable system to encourage – better reporting; adaptive management, and monitoring for extension and community involvement.	
Learning about The Effectiveness of Specific Conservation Tools across Protected Areas: Lessons on Sustainable Agriculture in Central America and Mexico	This study was a three-year field test in two biosphere reserves in Guatemala and Mexico. The NGOs responsible for managing these PAs conducted the evaluations as part of an adaptive management process. They were also learning about the application of sustainable agriculture as a conservation tool in these areas.	It was facilitated by the Biodiversity Support Program (BSP) to field test a framework for conducting adaptive management at site and cross-site levels.	
Application of the Nature Conservancy's conservation audit process at Cosumnes River Project, California, USA.	For 15 years, the Nature Conservancy and partners have managed the Cosumnes River area of California's Central Valley Lowlands. This evaluation was done as part of a Conservation Audit Process being used by the Nature Conservancy to assess conservation success.	Primarily to assess the threat status and viability status of the focal conservation targets of the Cosumnes River Area.	
The Enhancing our Heritage Project	Enhancing our Heritage: monitoring and managing for success in Natural World Heritage sites is a four-year project of IUCN and UNESCO working in ten pilot sites in Asia Africa and Latin America.	Project aims to demonstrate the use of the WCPA Framework to develop monitoring and assessment systems to improve management and reporting in World Heritage sites.	
Evaluation of Management Effectiveness in the Oulanka National Park, Finland	Oulanka National Park in the Arctic Circle supports spruce forest, peatlands and diverse lake and river habitats. Some 150 000 visitors a year enjoy outdoor activities and provide substantial tourist income to the local community.	Obtain PAN Parks certification for Oulanka. Balance tourism and conservation and improve overall management effectiveness.	
Evaluating Management Effectiveness of the Fraser Island World Heritage Area	WH-listed Fraser Island is managed by Queensland Parks and Wildlife Service. The case study aimed to develop a methodology of assessing management effectiveness in PAs by building in a process for evaluation and review of the extent to which management plan was being implemented and its objectives were being achieved.	Provide information to managers and stakeholders on effectiveness of management as a basis for informed decision making, improved management practices, reporting and accountability.	
Regional Project on Evaluation of Management of Protected Areas in Central America	Central America comprises seven countries over half a million km² as a land bridge between North and South America. The region's diverse topography and climate supports a range of ecosystems. A model was developed for evaluation of management of protected areas as part of a regional project.	National Park authorities requested that the model be tested on various pilot sites.	

Data collection: W = workshops; I = interviews; MIS = management information system; M = field monitoring; Q = questionnaires/surveys; MA = Map Analysis; MP = Existing Management Plan. Participants: SM = site managers/field staff; MA = Management agency staff (off-site); NGO(L) – local NGO; NGO(I) – international NGO;

Methodology	Data collection	Participants in evaluation process	WCPA Framework elements	Identifiable results from evaluation process
Rapid Assessment and Prioritization of Protected Area Management (RAPPAM) Methodology	W, Q	SM, MA, C, NGO(I), NGO(L), LC, G, S	C, PL, I, PR, OP, OC	Although only recently completed, initial management changes for various areas include: plans to undertake annual management effectiveness assessments; using results to set priorities for park support; using results to set annual budgets.
Rapid assessment questionnaire developed using the WCPA Framework	Q, I	SM, MA	I, C, OC	Too soon to assess, although awareness of management issues has been increased and managers are thinking about better ways to use resources and improve management.
BSP "Measures of Success" framework for conducting adaptive management at site and cross-site levels.	W, I, Q, M	C, NGO(I), NGO(L), LC, SM	None specifically but Measures of Success is similar to the WCPA framework.	Adaptive Management principles were integrated into routine management. Partners were able to compare results using common terminology. Able to generate concrete guiding principles for using sustainable agriculture under varying conditions. Able to see why sustainable agriculture did or did not work at different sites.
Conservation Audit process built around the Nature Conservancy's Five-S Framework for Site Conservation.	W, MA	C, SM, MA, NGO(I)	Mostly C and OC with consideration of other Framework elements	Helped to focus on indirect threats to biodiversity. Also helped to focus on conservation needs not relating to increasing the size of the protected area.
The Enhancing our Heritage Toolkit draws on different methodologies designed around application of the WCPA Framework.	W, I, MIS, M, MA, MP	S, LC, MA, SM, NGO(L), NGO(I)	C, PL, I, PR, OP, OC	Too early to assess, although suggestions for change from the initial assessments will soon be implemented at project sites.
PAN Parks Certification model based on specified criteria and indicators	Q, MIS, I	C, MA, SM, S, LC	C, PL, I, PR, OC	Better cooperation between the national park and tourism organizations, leading to more sustainable tourism.
Field-monitoring programs designed to assess achievement of objectives, monitoring of management inputs and outputs, assessment of management processes.	M, W, MP	SM, S, MA, WH	I, PR, OP, OC	Used in camping, fire and dingo management decisions. Some research programs initiated in response to findings. Information used in review of management plan and in review of World Heritage Values of the site.
Questionnaire based around five broad management aspects. Performance in relation to indicators within each aspect assessed on a five-point scale.	W, MA, MP	SM, MA, LC, NGO(L), IC	Mostly I, PR with some consideration of OC	A new perception by managers of what could be achieved with the same resources. The monitoring model is mandatory for protected areas in five countries. National annual reports on the state of these protected areas draws largely on this monitoring.

G = Govt bodies; LC = Local community; C =Consultants; S = Scientists/Researcher institution; IC = Indigenous communities; AC= Independent Management Advisory Committee. WCPA Framework elements: C = Context; PL = Planning; I = Inputs; PR = Process; OP = Outputs; OC = Outcomes

CHAPTER 6

Managing the marine environment

Contributors: M. Spalding and E. McManus

In terms of resource use and management, two factors distinguish the marine from the terrestrial environment. Firstly, as a liquid medium, connectivity is continuous and near absolute. Few actions or processes in the oceans are spatially restricted in the same way as they may be on land – impacts in one part are likely to affect those elsewhere. Secondly, marine areas and marine resources are typically of open access to all. They rarely fall under any form of ownership or property regime below that of the state, while 64 percent of the world's ocean surface lies in "international waters", beyond any form of national sovereignty.

As pressures on such "common" resources rise, there is an inevitable drive towards over-exploitation. Individuals who break the rule of sustainability make an individual gain while the costs of their actions are buffered by a communal loss. This "tragedy of the commons" was noted for the sea as it was for land in 1968 by Garrett Hardin:

> "Maritime nations still respond automatically to the shibboleth of the 'freedom of the seas'. Professing to believe in 'inexhaustible resources of the oceans', they bring species after species of fish and whales closer to extinction." (Hardin 1968:1244).

The problems facing the ocean environment are immense. In 2006, the United Nations Food and Agriculture Organization (FAO) estimated that about 75 percent of the world's fish stocks were being exploited beyond sustainable limits. Pollutants including persistent organic pollutants and solid wastes are now found in all of the world's oceans. Invasive species have decimated natural eco-systems and devastated economies.

MANAGEMENT INTERVENTIONS

As on land, numerous management interventions have been applied to control resource use and human impacts in the marine environment. These include direct conservation measures, but also an array of measures whose primary aim may not be biodiversity conservation but which, nevertheless, have positive "side-effects" for biodiversity – fisheries controls; regulations on mineral extraction; controls on pollution and the dumping of solid waste; to name just a few.

Many of these management interventions have developed in an ad hoc manner, and their success is highly variable. Marine protected areas (MPAs) may be the most important management tool for marine biodiversity conservation, but as has already been noted, their global coverage remains minimal – a mere 0.5 percent of the global ocean surface. Even within this small estate, few sites are adequately protected from the many threats that arise *ex situ* from adjacent marine or terrestrial areas. Even fewer sites have developed integrated management to incorporate the concerns and wishes of the broad array of stakeholders, or are placed within a wider framework of coastal zone management. Without such efforts the positive benefits of one intervention can be quickly undone by conflicting actions elsewhere.

MARINE MANAGEMENT AREAS – A BROAD ARRAY

Strictly speaking, MPAs are defined as areas set aside for environmental protection (Chapter 2), however the differences between such a definition and areas set aside for fisheries protection can be subtle. In a few cases a broader suite of regulations and management structures may protect more extensive areas through forms of integrated coastal

M.Spalding

Bluestriped snapper and goatfish.

BOX 6.1: The International Framework

The United Nations Convention on the Law of the Sea (UNCLOS) provides a critical legal framework for establishing legal controls on activities in the marine environment. Under this convention, most states have now declared territorial seas and exclusive economic zones, within which all existing marine protected areas have been declared.

The territorial sea is a belt of water not exceeding 12 nautical miles in width measured from the territorial sea baseline. Generally the baseline is the low-water line along the coast, although provisions are included for extending the baseline out across narrow embayments, fringing and atoll reefs, and between islands of archipelagic states.

This area lies under full sovereignty of the adjacent state, covering the sea, airspace, benthos and sub-benthos (subsoil).

The exclusive economic zone is an area beyond and adjacent to the territorial sea, extending out up to 200 nautical miles from the baseline. Nations maintain sovereign rights over the natural resources within this region and have jurisdiction, among other things, for the protection and preservation of the marine environment.

Currently the majority of marine protected areas are concentrated in the territorial sea of nations, but a growing number have been extended out into the exclusive economic zone.

---

management (ICM), which again do not conform to the definition of an MPA. The term marine management area (MMA) is sometimes used to cover this broader suite of spatially confined management interventions which have some positive impact on the natural marine environment. Here we briefly consider some of the different classes of MMAs before going on to consider the key issues that arise in the establishment and management of such areas.

Marine Protected Areas

As in terrestrial protected areas, a spectrum of levels of protection exists in MPAs. Many sites focus on fishing as one of the few, relatively easy and direct impacts that can be controlled. This may consist of partial protection such as protecting particular species or size classes, reducing or banning access to particular user groups (commercial, recreational, or local) or to particular fishing practices (spearfishing, trawling, use of nets or lines), or it may consist of full closure of all or part of a site to any extractive activity. Sites also regularly restrict other damaging activities, notably anchoring, waste disposal, and sand extraction. The use of zoning systems within MPAs is widespread, and can create a challenge in assignation of IUCN management categories, though probably no more than in zoned terrestrial sites.

One group of MPAs that has received particular attention in recent years are no-take marine reserves (variously referred to as fully protected marine reserves, no-take zones, or sometimes simply marine reserves). These are areas where no natural resource extraction is permitted and they typically equate to IUCN Categories IA or II. Many of these are small, but they have a profound impact on natural resources, particularly in heavily exploited regions, typically leading to burgeoning fish populations and spillover effects to surrounding waters.

Fisheries Management Areas

In many cultures, fisheries controls of different sorts go back millennia. Such measures have included limiting access (who may fish); controlling the size of the catch; the removal of subsidies; and buy-back schemes to take fishers out of the market. A further suite of fisheries control measures tackle the actual fishing techniques, setting limits on how, where, or when fish may be caught.

A fisheries management area (FMA) is a geographically defined area where the fishing sector (e.g. industrial/artisanal), gear, target or bycatch species, effort, and/or seasonality are restricted. This term clearly includes many MPAs, but may also include sites designated by the fisheries sector without any specific reference to environmental protection. As with MPAs, there is a spectrum of interventions, from restrictions on some gears at some times through to a completely closed area protected from any anthropogenic impact (a no-take marine reserve). The term also includes areas that are under national zoning schemes.

At a national level, FMAs can reduce the conflict between different fishery sectors (e.g. the coastal zone in Costa Rica is restricted for the use of artisanal fisheries only), and between fishers and other users (e.g. divers). At a local/smaller level, fishery management interventions are often linked to MPAs, but seasonal and temporary closures, or monospecific interventions such as the UK cod boxes are rarely included in the MPA statistics.

Integrated Coastal Management

Concept papers developed prior to the United Nations Conference on Environment and Development (UNCED) in 1992, recognized that the coastal zone was too complex to be managed effectively at the sectoral level. The term "integrated coastal management" (ICM), was coined to describe a more comprehensive approach, to coastal management, which incorporated all sectors influenced by the coastal zone, as well as integrating economic, social, and ecological concerns.

Conceptually very simple, ICM has yet to be widely embraced in formal legal or administrative structures. Most examples are sub-national. They vary considerably in approach and in the degree of integration they provide, but most cases bear witness to the considerable social and economic benefits to be had from integrating the interests of different sectors and concerns. Some offer only very limited additional protection to natural resource protection, but others embrace this as a primary objective, and many incorporate MPAs within their overall planning framework.

M.Spalding

Fishing in the Jardines de la Reina National Park, Cuba.

ESTABLISHMENT AND MANAGEMENT ISSUES
Building stakeholder and community support

First and foremost in any MMA establishment and management process is the involvement and integration of key stakeholders. A broad array of stakeholders, often dispersed over wide areas, may be linked to any marine area. Direct stakeholders include fishers, recreational users (for swimming,

---

BOX 6.2: Fisheries Benefits and Limitations

There is now considerable evidence that marine protected areas do benefit the fish populations that exist within them. Halpern (2003) has reviewed 76 studies of protected areas, which were protected from at least one type of fishing. On average, he found that the abundance of fish doubled, the average body size increased by fully one third (which can equal increased egg production of 240 percent), the biomass doubled, and numbers of species increased by 33 percent.

Strict no-take areas have particularly dramatic effects on resident fish stocks, and there is growing evidence that these effects can lead to considerable social and economic benefits to fishers in adjacent areas. Benefits may occur through two processes, larval export and spillover. Larval export occurs when

the propagules are produced in the marine protected area and are then distributed to settlement areas; to date it has been hard to prove, but seems very likely. Spillover occurs when mature individuals move from the MPA. It seems that in areas under heavy fishing pressure, yields will continue to grow, despite the reduction in total fishing area, up until some 30 percent of the area is set aside in this way (Roberts and Hawkins, 2000; Roberts, Bohnsack *et al.*, 2001).

It is evident that marine protected areas cannot readily guarantee the protection of highly migratory species, for example tunas or whales. For these and many other species, marine protected areas need to be seen as tools to be used in combination with other management interventions, for example, effort reduction schemes.

M.Spalding

Aldabra World Heritage Site, Seychelles.

Problems of overexploitation can be far better handled if the user community is small and subject to socio-cultural as well as legal controls – limits to use can be set by the adjacent community and these can be adequately enforced. In some cases this may lead to a sort of *de facto* MPA, with the levels of control arising from ownership providing important and unprecedented levels of protection. The owners of such areas may also choose to establish protected areas within their TURF area, giving partial or complete protection. Such approaches are widely found in traditional societies (see below), but are increasingly being established in formal legal regimes.

Raising awareness
Many "stakeholders" are unaware of their reliance on, or use of, particular aspects of the marine environment, such as fresh fish or clean beaches, before these become degraded or lost. Education can be a critical tool in empowering such stakeholders to take control and support management efforts, particularly where previously a single dominant stakeholder group is driving environmental degradation to the detriment of others.

Education and outreach must be focused towards the individual needs of target groups. A growing number of marine management areas are using fishers themselves as communicators. Efforts to establish new no-take zones in Fiji were greatly advanced when a spokesperson from a successful project in a village on Viti Levu was taken to talk to chiefs on the island of Kadavu. His words were probably far more persuasive than those of outside experts in generating interest in establishing no-take zones on this island.

Some of the most enduring MPAs are those in which local people are able to benefit. Programs such as the Club Mer initiative in Rodrigues in the Indian Ocean, in which schoolchildren are trained to swim and then to snorkel, should guarantee support for MPAs into the next generation.

Of course, growing recreational interest can bring further challenges, but impacts can be greatly reduced through education and interpretation programs. Diver impacts on coral reefs have been greatly reduced through simple instruction by dive-schools. Well-designed notification, especially where the rules and regulations are placed in a positive context of ecological benefits and general information about ecology, are powerful tools. A number of sites, including the Cerbère-Banyuls

diving, boating, fishing, or scenic values), industry (maritime transport and non-living resource extraction), and those with direct interests in biodiversity. Indirect stakeholders are those who impact the ocean as well as those who rely on the ocean or its ecosystems for services such as food (consumers), water purification, climatic controls, or protection from storm damage (coastal communities living near coral reefs, mangroves, seagrasses). There are often conflicts of interest between these stakeholders, associated with both access and exploitation. Dealing with conflict and establishing collaboration between stakeholders is a key challenge in the development of equitable and sustainable management systems.

Resource ownership
Private ownership (and the establishment of private reserves) in the marine realm is rare. However, partial ownership or recognition of stewardship is not unusual. From a fisheries perspective this ownership can take the form of resource ownership, for example in the form of individual transferable quotas (ITQs), which effectively give ownership to a certain amount of a particular fishery stock. Such ITQs may then be fished, or the quota traded.

From a protected area perspective, the establishment of territorial use rights in fisheries (TURFs), or other forms of direct ownership are particularly interesting and often very effective.

Marine Nature Reserve in France, have developed underwater trails for snorkelers.

Operation and enforcement in the marine environment

While community involvement and education may reduce levels of infringement, further efforts are required to ensure full compliance. Marine areas are beset with challenges when it comes to field-based management. Access to marine areas is costly, requiring boats, engines, navigational equipment, and other resources. Impacts on the benthos and in the water column are not immediately detectable. Boundaries cannot be easily marked.

At the same time, because of the considerable benefits to resource users, including many fishers, it is possible, more than in many terrestrial parks, to engender considerable community support for marine management areas. The same community can often be used to regulate the area, or to pass on information regarding infringements. Other approaches to ensuring compliance often take advantage of existing authority patrols such as coastguards. The Strict Nature Reserves in the British Indian Ocean Territory have no staff. However, their boundaries are known to the Fisheries Protection Vessel that operates in these waters, and which also occasionally takes members of the British army, acting as police, customs, immigration, and biodiversity protection officers, to these areas.

Approaches to enforcement may be very site specific. In some cases it may be valuable to take a soft approach to first offenders as a means of maintaining community support. Elsewhere, strict and rapid enforcement at an early stage can be invaluable in establishing a clear baseline. If it is relevant, the designation or use of customary leaders and procedures in enforcement processes can be of considerable value.

Boundary demarcation is often possible through the use of buoys, while having a clear boundary definition greatly eases policing and reduces opportunities for disagreement and infringement. For larger sites, this may involve the use of lines between named geographic coordinates, while in some cases the use of clear and visible landmarks on land serves the same purpose.

Many MPAs are designed to permit multiple sustainable uses within their boundaries, and the development of zoning systems provides a cost-effective means of managing different uses. Zoning systems permit selective control of activities at different areas within a site, including both strict protection and various levels of use. These may include core conservation areas (e.g. spawning sites) as sanctuaries where all disturbing or extractive activities are prohibited, or where damaged areas are left undisturbed to enable recovery. Zoning systems can also be used to separate incompatible recreational activities (such as waterskiing and snorkeling).

A considerable number of marine parks now charge user fees, particularly to the generally high-value tourist visitors associated with sailing and diving activities. The diving industry has led the way in many areas and a number of sites, such as the Bonaire Marine Park in the Netherlands Antilles, levy a user fee on all divers which is paid via the dive operators. Many countries have fixed fees for yachts and, in those parks with some permitted fishing, this may also be license driven. In many cases such fees provide a substantial part of the running costs for protected areas. A hidden, but also valuable function of the fees is to raise levels of expectation, which in many cases also leads to increased vigilance against non-payers and rule breakers within protected areas.

The use of new technology is likely to increase in coming years, particularly for more remote sites. Ship-borne satellite transponders already play a critical role in some pelagic fisheries, and it is entirely plausible, at very broad scales, to require such technology within the licensing system for fishing or recreational vessels, which can enable immediate detection of vessels that stray beyond particular boundaries.

Monitoring and response

Information is critical for any management program. A baseline description of a protected area provides a foundation for considering change, while monitoring provides repeated quantitative assessment of parameters likely to highlight change. It is useful to consider two broad arenas of monitoring: ecological and socio-economic.

Typically, detailed ecological information about the marine realm is scarce and often anecdotal. Improving such information is often highly costly. Remotely sensed technology is increasingly providing the means to map shallow-water resources in areas of clear water even at quite high resolutions, although it remains expensive. Without such technology simple base maps, particularly of smaller sites, can be prepared from anecdotal information and direct observation. Baseline descriptions should cover both physical and ecological parameters, and it is important to realize that certain parameters may not be detected through a single mapping exercise. Habitat maps provide no information at all about spatially restricted species, or any of the mobile fauna or planktonic species. Certain species, activities, and even entire communities may exhibit seasonal patterns and be missed entirely on single surveys.

Quite often, anecdotal and local knowledge provide a further critical basis for planning and for establishing monitoring techniques. Following development of baseline knowledge, monitoring approaches must be tailored towards specific points of interest or concern, but may include: repeat habitat mapping; assessment of numbers or biomass of key species; assessment of juveniles; spawning aggregations; migratory species; invasive species or pathogens. Physical parameters may include water-quality indicators, temperature, currents, nutrients, dissolved oxygen, and key pollutants.

Socio-economic monitoring is necessary to understand the uses and potential pressures on protected areas and particularly to observe trends which may, over time, lead to problems. Some of this may take place outside of the protected area, in the adjacent communities and fishing ports, but it is also important to find geospatial variation in uses and impacts within a site. Typical data may include: local population size and demographic trends; fishing methods, locations, and catch details; tourist activities and numbers; economic parameters associated with fishing, tourism, and other activities; perceptions of protected areas; and willingness to pay for access and/or resources (Wilkinson *et al.*, 2003).

The science of reactive management in response to environmental change for marine protected areas is still in its infancy. In developing management responses the linkage between socio-economic and ecological parameters must often be established. If rising fishing levels can be clearly linked to declines in stocks, there is a clear and powerful argument for intervention. Similarly, if the benefits to fishers of no-take zones can be numerically and economically quantified, support for these measures will increase. It is very important, as with all monitoring and response measures, to place the findings for a particular site

into a broader context. Other MPAs are highly likely to have exhibited similar impacts or changes; many may have developed appropriate management responses. In ecological surveys, cyclical or stochastic factors of change may cause considerable concern, but comparison with longer-term datasets from other sites may help in understanding such change.

The question of who does the monitoring often requires careful consideration. Particularly in coral reef protected areas there are a large number of individuals and organizations offering volunteer services to undertake monitoring. These provide a basic minimum, but many monitoring techniques require high levels of accuracy and consistency. The danger of relying on basic, volunteer-based, monitoring is that this offers only a crude tool, since there is often limited capacity and time input for noticing subtle change and impacts.

Managing *ex-situ* threats

Some of the greatest concerns of MPA management are from threats beyond the boundaries. Understanding the distribution of such threats, and monitoring changes in them, needs to be incorporated into the wider monitoring process already discussed. There are, however, significant difficulties in dealing with such threats.

Some *ex-situ* threats may be reduced through protected area design or through development of protected area networks. For example, the incorporation or expansion of boundaries to include entire adjacent watersheds or small islands within sites may greatly reduce the threat of new activities creating problems of pollution and sedimentation. With more specific ecological knowledge it may also be possible to design sites to include elements of interconnected habitats. For example, many coral reef species utilize adjacent seagrass and mangrove ecosystems as a spawning or larval habitat, so inclusion of these within the boundary of an MPA can help recruitment of new individuals to the ecological community. On a broader scale, some countries are now developing networks of protected areas. Given the high levels of connectivity in the marine environment, the incorporation of multiple sites provides a level of resilience to the system. Should a pollution event or even a natural disaster such as a hurricane have an impact on a site, recovery may be much more rapid if natural restocking can occur from other well-protected and unimpacted sites within a system of MPAs.

Biós/C.Brandon/Still Pictures

Belize barrier reef, a World Heritage site since 1996.

Looking beyond the protected areas themselves, a clear priority must be to place existing sites in a wider framework of coastal management. The development of integrated coastal management (ICM) can be a critical tool. ICM is ideally a broadly inclusive and iterative process that uses the informed participation and cooperation of all stakeholders to define goals and to balance environmental, economic, social, cultural, and recreational objectives. It is intended to reduce the inefficiencies and damage arising from conflicting uses of the coastal zone by harmonizing policy, administration, and management in all sectors

Despite the importance of ICM, and the clear societal benefits that it can produce, there are few working examples. Belize offers one national-level working example. A large number of marine protected areas have been declared in this country and in 1996 these were collectively incorporated into the Belize Barrier-Reef Reserve System, a World Heritage site. In 1998 a Coastal Zone Management Act was adopted and a Coastal Zone Management Authority established. Although still somewhat centralized, some degree of integration between government agencies has been achieved, and public consultation has been undertaken.

This region is also advancing a new degree of international cooperation in the coastal zone through the Mesoamerican Barrier Reef Project, in collaboration with Guatemala, Honduras, and Mexico. In Xiamen, China, the Partnership in Environmental Management for the Seas of East Asia (PEMSEA) has assisted the city government to implement integrated coastal zone management (ICZM), resulting in an integrated zoning scheme for the use of both land and coastal resources.

In many other cases the actual development of ICM is an organic process in which the role for the individual protected area may provide a critical catalyst. The Great Barrier Reef Marine Park, the Portland Bight Protected Area in Jamaica, the Soufriere Marine Management Area in St Lucia, and the Ras Mohammed protected areas complex in Egypt all provide examples of protected areas that are developing and encouraging levels of integrated management and full community involvement that provide a basis for what can clearly be seen as ICM.

Approaches to managing MPAs and other marine conservation areas
Traditional approaches
In the Asia-Pacific region, traditional marine management systems were once widespread and many still offer an important model. In Palau in the Pacific Ocean two such systems are prevalent in the fisheries sector (Yoshi 2003):

Traditional marine tenure systems. The geographical boundaries in a fishing area are defined by marine or geographical landmarks using the fishers' notion of property and ownership of the area. Those boundaries are historically constructed and enforced by the fishing community as a whole.

Community control on traditional techniques for fishing within defined areas. Particular fishing techniques are considered to be the property of certain groups (e.g. clans or families). Thus fishers can use these techniques only with the permission of those groups in specific sites. This restriction is extended even to the authority to "speak about" these techniques and thus represents a traditional copyright for transmitting knowledge.

Systems like these are also still widely respected in countries such as the Solomon Islands and the Cook Islands. Elsewhere, recognition of their effectiveness has led to similar systems being revitalized. In both Fiji and Vanuatu such customary tenure of marine resources is now being upheld through the modern legal system, as it is believed that traditional owners will provide better protection for their natural resources than more centralized ownership with open access to all (Spalding, Ravilious & Green 2001).

The same concepts, those of devolving ownership and management of marine resources to local communities, are now also being tried in other countries with some success. These approaches in the Philippines, for example, have led to a rapid increase in locally designated fisheries restricted areas.

Modern approaches
Single objective sites: Leigh Marine Reserve, New Zealand

Frequently, MPAs are designated for a single reason, e.g. resource conservation, ecotourism, extraction, or water-quality protection. One of the world's first no-take fishing reserves was the Leigh Marine Reserve in New Zealand, established in 1975 adjacent to the Leigh Marine Laboratory. The campaign to establish the site lasted ten years, and was undertaken because of concerns of over-extraction and the degradation of natural resources. Following establishment, the densities and average sizes of fish and invertebrate target species greatly increased within the site. Many fishers now choose to fish right on the reserve boundaries, and because of the increases in their catches in these places the fishers have now joined the wider community in actively supporting the park. Many fishers even report incidents of poaching. Dive tourism to the site is a major contributor to the local economy (Gell & Roberts 2002).

Multiple objective sites: Sian Ka'an, Mexico

There is much pressure on aquatic systems in the Mexican coastal zone from a number of stakeholders. In many areas the stakeholder base is also growing with rapid economic development, further increasing the potential for resource conflict.

In the Sian Ka´an Biosphere Reserve the community has developed a co-management system that includes a wide variety of stakeholders in both decision-making and management activities. Stakeholders include: the government; fishers' groups; research agencies; the recreational dive industry; the tour industry; developers; and land owners. One example of how different stakeholders are cooperating in the reserve is the agreement between the tourism and fishers' organizations. This defines a closed period for the lobster fishery (between March and June), during which the fishers stop fishing for lobster and tourists are allowed to participate in recreational catch-and-release fly fishing. These activities do not interfere with other species that are important to the local community. This arrangement greatly reduces the potential for conflict between the fishers and the tourism sector.

M.Spalding

Cinque Terre National Park, Italy, a cultural World Heritage Site, also provides protection for the adjacent Cinque Terre Marine Natural Protected Area.

Zoning systems: The Great Barrier Reef Marine Park

The Great Barrier Reef Marine Park operates a zonation scheme originally established under the Great Barrier Reef Marine Park Act 1975. The zoning has recently been completely revised and this has led, among other things, to a major increase in the total area of no-take "green zones" within the park, from less than 5 percent to about 30 percent. The new zoning includes:

❏ **General Use Zone:** The least restrictive of the zones, this provides for all reasonable uses including shipping and trawling. Prohibited activities are mining, oil drilling, commercial spearfishing, and spearfishing with underwater breathing apparatus.

❏ **Habitat Protection Zones:** These provide for reasonable use, including most commercial and recreational activities. Trawling and general shipping are prohibited as well as those activities not allowed in the General Use Zone.

❏ **Conservation Park Zone:** Prevents most commercial fishing, but allows recreational fishing with lines.

❏ **Buffer Zone:** All extractive activity is forbidden, other than trawling from a moving boat for pelagic "game" fish. All recreational visits, diving, and snorkeling are permitted.

❏ **Scientific Research Zones:** Set aside close to research locations. Most are open to public access and are equivalent to Marine National Park Zones.

❏ **Marine National Park Zones:** All extractive activity is forbidden, but non-extractive recreational use and passage are permitted

❏ **Preservation Zones:** All entry is prohibited with the exception of scientific research that could not be conducted elsewhere.

These zones can be mapped on to the IUCN Protected Areas Management Categories as shown in Table 5.1.

The High Seas

The high seas are defined as the area of ocean beyond national jurisdiction (WWF/IUCN/IUCN WCPA 2001). Approximately 64 percent of the oceans are beyond the 200-nautical-mile limit of the EEZs of coastal states. These high-seas areas are open-access areas and so there are few measures available to control extractive or other activities. In

TABLE 6.1: IUCN Protected Areas Management Categories in the Great Barrier Reef Marine Park

Equivalent IUCN category	GBRMP zone type		Area km² (%)	
1a	Preservation zone		710	
	Scientific research zone		155	
		Total	865	(0.3)
II	Marine national park zone		114 530	(33.3)
IV	Buffer zone		9 880	
	Conservation park zone		5 160	
		Total	15 040	(4.3)
VI	Habitat protection zone		97 250	
	General use zone		116 530	
	Commonwealth islands		185	
		Total	213 965	(62.1)
	Total all zones		**344 400**	

Source: Great Barrier Reef Marine Park Authority.

recent years human activities on the high seas have intensified and a number of direct and indirect human activities now present significant threats, including disposal of wastes (obsolete structures, radioactive wastes, and munitions), deep-sea fishing, oil and gas extraction, mining of marine minerals, and climate change.

A number of geographic features, habitats, and biological communities in the high seas are regularly identified for their scientific, societal, or economic interest and are currently thought to be at threat from anthropogenic pressures. They are: hydrothermal vents; deep-sea trenches; poly-metallic nodules; gas hydrates; seabirds; trans-boundary and other migratory marine species fish stocks; seamounts; deep-sea "coral reefs"; cold seeps and pockmarks; submarine canyons; and cetaceans (WWF, IUCN & WCPA 2001).

At present there is no clear legal framework under which protected areas could be designated in the high seas receiving considerable attention from the UN and from various member states (UNEP, 2006). A number of conventions provide a general background, notably the United Nations Convention on the Law of the Sea and its Fish Stocks Agreement, which includes requirements for parties to protect biodiversity and implement "conservation and management measures" (Fish Stocks Agreement Art. I [b]). Similar general support is provided under the Convention on Biological Diversity, which calls upon parties to cooperate in areas beyond national jurisdiction

NOAA/MBARI

Crinoid (*Florometra serratissima*) and brisingid seastar on black coral, Davidson Seamount in the Monterey Bay National Marine Sanctuary, USA.

(Art.5) and to "establish a system of protected areas ... including both marine and terrestrial areas". Great impetus to these requirements has been provided by the World Summit for Sustainable Development commitment to the "establishment of a representative network of MPAs by 2012; and (ii) restoration of fisheries to maximum sustainable yields by 2015" (WSSD Plan of Implementation, para. 31c). Proposals under consideration include the development of a new implementing agreement to UNCLOS to ensure existing commitments are realized and to strengthen existing bodies; or simple to work with, and possibly add to, some of the existing regional bodies (UNEP, 2006).

Two types of regional agreements can be singled out as of particular importance for high seas management: the Regional Seas Conventions and the regional fisheries agreements. A number of the Regional Seas Conventions make provision for the establishment of protected areas within the waters of member states, but the recently declared Pelagos Sanctuary or International Sanctuary for Mediterranean Marine Mammals as a Specially Protected Area of Mediterranean Interest (Barcelona Convention) provides an important precedent. As many of the Mediterranean states have not formally claimed EEZ areas, this site can be said to lie in the high seas. Apart from representing an important level of

international collaboration, the site, although still only providing protection for a small group of species, includes regulations on all activities that might impinge on these species, even going beyond the boundaries of the site itself (Anon. 2003).

Regional fisheries agreements provide another model. A number of existing agreements allow, among other things, for the definition of high-seas sanctuaries and management areas for various marine species. These include:

❏ The Northwest Atlantic Fisheries Organization (NAFO), which has regulatory responsibility for all fish resources (with the exception of cetaceans and sedentary species) outside of national jurisdiction in a defined area of the North Atlantic.

❏ The International Commission for the Conservation of Atlantic Tunas (ICCAT), whose convention applies to all water of the Atlantic Ocean and adajacent seas, including the Mediterranean Sea. The species covered in this agreement are the tuna and tuna-like species, and species exploited in tuna fishing but not under investigation by any other international organization.

At the global level the only body to have overseen the establishment of areas of protection has been the International Whaling Commission (IWC), established in 1946. The IWC established the Indian Ocean Sanctuary in 1979, extending south to 55°S latitude, as an area where commercial whaling was prohibited. This Sanctuary was initially established for ten years and its duration has since been extended twice. At the 46th (1994) Annual Meeting the IWC adopted the Southern Ocean Sanctuary as another area in which commercial whaling is prohibited. One of the arguments in favor of the Southern Ocean Sanctuary was to protect the Indian Ocean's whales when they migrated south to feed in the waters around the Antarctic. Efforts to add new whale sanctuaries for the South Atlantic and the South Pacific, as well as opposing efforts calling for the removal of the Southern Ocean Sanctuary, have all failed in recent years, as such decisions require a clear 75 per cent majority.

These sanctuaries provide cetaceans with protection in their foraging and breeding areas and there are proposals to greatly increase the sanctuary areas to include a large part of the southern hemisphere. Given their highly focused protection for only one species group, it is not clear if these areas should be considered as protected areas in the sense defined by IUCN. Furthermore, despite the broad agreement for the establishment of these sanctuaries, their strength has been undermined by the unilateral decision of one member state, Japan, to continue killing hundreds of whales each year using the justification of scientific research, mainly in the Southern Ocean. This points to a much wider problem of potential failings with international agreements.

Managing the high seas: what is stopping us?
There is a growing acceptance that political divisions across the ocean surface are poor tools for natural resource management. Oceanographic boundaries, and hence the movement of species such as the yellowfin tuna, rarely follow such divisions. For marine resources it will be far more valuable to utilize oceanographic properties representing ecosystems, or even to use activity ranges of species themselves, to define areas for management.

As technology develops, humankind's ability to gather meaningful information for the management of the marine environment increases. Radio-tracking and acoustic survey techniques allow scientists to know where and how much of different species exist. Remote satellite imagery allows for detailed analysis of habitat distribution and health (coral and seagrasses, etc.), the primary productivity of specific areas, and the location and activities of fishing vessels. Other telemetry and sensing equipment can predict the presence or absence of large pelagics (e.g. tuna species) through the collation of information on sea-surface temperatures and current information. All of this technology is already being used by the larger fishing vessels and fleets to target their quarries with ever-increasing accuracy; it could equally be used to manage the activities of the fishing fleets as well as other marine activities.

The question for the international community is "What are the limiting factors that hinder the management of the marine environment on the high seas?" The technologies exist, but the international frameworks to harness the information and manage the marine environment beyond national jurisdictions are currently not in place. The priority must now be to develop and implement equitable, sustainable, and effective ecosystem-based agreements that respect the marine environment as interrelated ecosystems.

CHAPTER 7

Prospects for protected areas in the 21st century

Contributor: S. Chape

ASSESSING THE GLOBAL ENVIRONMENT: THE CHALLENGES OF CHANGE

Enormous strides have been made in the last few decades in the creation of a global protected area network – governments, communities, and organizations now protect more than 12 percent of the Earth's land surface, making protected areas one of the planet's dominant land-use allocations. If effectively managed, this network will play a crucial role in the conservation of the world's biodiversity, providing a service of incalculable value to future generations. However, challenges remain. The world has changed dramatically in the past century – certainly more than during any other stage in human history. More changes, some predictable, some less so, can be expected in the forthcoming century. These changes will not only place more pressure on the world's protected areas but also bring their role into sharper focus.

Where are we now, and where are we going?

Chapter 1 presented a map of the human footprint on the world. The study that produced that assessment is one of a number of analyses over the past decade that have attempted to measure human impact on the Earth's ecosystems and resources. We live in an age when such impacts, and the pace of global environmental change, have generated international concern. The most recent and comprehensive global assessment to be completed is the Millennium Ecosystem Assessment (MA), requested by the UN Secretary-General in 2000 and initiated in 2001. The results published in 2005 make somber reading and have direct implications for the values and prospects of protected areas in the 21st century. A principal finding of the MA (MA 2005a) is that:

"over the past 50 years, humans have changed ecosystems more rapidly and extensively than in any comparable period of time in human history, largely to meet rapidly growing demands for food, fresh water, timber, fiber, and fuel. This has resulted in a substantial and largely irreversible loss in the diversity of life on Earth."

The MA report *Ecosystems and Human Well-being: Biodiversity Synthesis* (MA, 2005b) notes that over half of the world's biomes have already undergone 20–50 percent conversion to human use, and such conversion is likely to continue (Figure 7.1). During the past few hundred years human-induced species extinction rates have increased by up to 1 000 times background rates occurring throughout Earth's history (Figure 7.2), and 10–50 percent of mammals, birds, amphibians, conifers, and cycads are currently threatened with extinction. How much biodiversity will remain by the end of the century depends on how much society values biodiversity and understands the ecological services that it delivers, and what action it takes to ensure conservation. Unfortunately, all the scenarios examined by the MA "project continuing rapid conversion of ecosystems in the first half of the 21st century" (MA, 2005b:5).

Over the next half century, barring unforeseen catastrophe, the world's human population can be expected to increase by half as much again, to around 9 billion people. This is a much slower rate of increase than seen in the previous century, but still represents an enormous additional pressure on the world's resources, with an extra 3 billion people to be fed, clothed, and housed.

An increase in the food supply is likely to be achieved through a combination of agricultural

S.Chape

In the 21st century the role and values of protected areas will become increasingly important, including intangible values.
Dong Phayayen-Khao Yai Forest Complex World Heritage Area, Thailand.

FIGURE 7.1: RELATIVE LOSS OF BIODIVERSITY OF VASCULAR PLANTS BETWEEN 1970 AND 2050

Extinctions will continue after 2050, as natural populations reach equilibrium with remaining habitat. Note that the biomes in this figure are from the IMAGE model and are significantly different from the biomes mentioned elsewhere in this report.

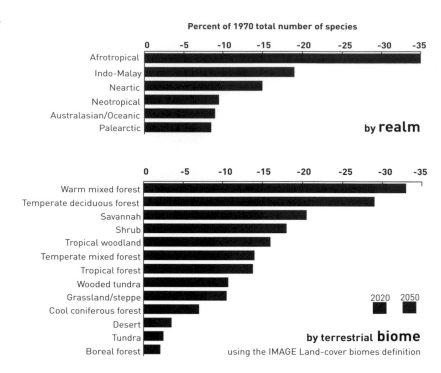

Percent of 1970 total number of species

by **realm**

by terrestrial **biome**
using the IMAGE Land-cover biomes definition

Source: Millennium Ecosystem Assessment

FIGURE 7.2: SPECIES EXTINCTION RATES

"Distant past" refers to average extinction rates as calculated from the fossil record. "Recent past" refers to extinction rates calculated from known extinctions of species (lower estimate) or known extinctions plus "possibly extinct" species (upper bound). A species is considered to be "possibly extinct" if it is believed to be extinct by experts but extensive surveys have not yet been undertaken to confirm its disappearance. "Future" extinctions are model-derived estimates using a variety of techniques, including species-area models, rates at which species are shifting to increasingly more threatened categories, extinction probabilities associated with the IUCN categories of threat, impacts of project habitat loss, and correlation of species loss with energy consumption. The time frame and species groups involved differ among the "future" estimates, but in general refer to either future loss of species based on the level of threat that exists today or current and future loss of species as a result of habitat changes taking place roughly from 1970 to 2050. Estimates based on the fossil record are low certainty. The lower-bound estimates for known extinctions are high certainty, while the upper-bound estimates are medium certainty; lower-bound estimates for modelled extinctions are low certainty, and upper-bound estimates are speculative.

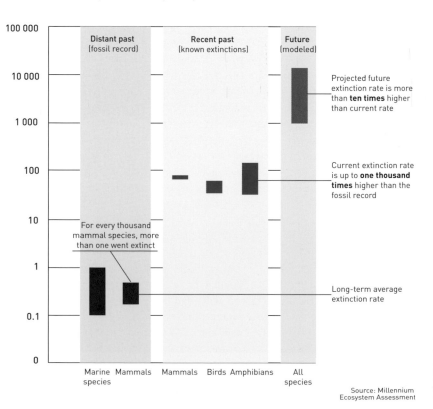

Extinctions per thousand species per millennium

Source: Millennium Ecosystem Assessment

intensification and the bringing of new areas into production. Most of the latter will almost certainly take place in the low-lying areas of the humid tropics, particularly Amazonia and, if political stability permits, Central Africa, these being still two of the world's most biodiverse areas with, currently, large expanses of forest cover. Most of this production is likely to be on an industrial scale, designed to meet international markets. In many areas, exhaustion of existing agricultural land through overuse and unsustainable management practices means that extensive areas of land will be largely abandoned and may begin to revert to some, usually degraded, semi-natural state. This phenomenon has already occurred extensively in temperate parts of the world, particularly North America and Europe. This abandonment is accompanied by growing urbanization (or, in the developed world, suburbanization) with, in most countries, cities growing at a far faster rate than rural populations through rural-to-urban migration. In the developed world, and in some middle-income countries, this has reduced the overall pressure for conversion of land to agriculture as marginal lands are no longer considered economic (although perverse incentives, for example in the form of agricultural subsidies, continue to have a distorting effect on this). However, in countries with substantial rural populations living in poverty, land degradation has increased pressure on marginal lands as those people remaining in rural areas are forced to try and eke out what living they can.

Growing demand for food production may lead to pressure to de-gazette protected areas on highly productive lands. Increasing abstraction of freshwater for agriculture will almost certainly lead to degradation of wetlands in protected areas. In areas with marginalized rural communities, protected areas often already represent some of the few undegraded areas left. Unless other options can be implemented, such as restoration of productivity of existing used lands, the pressure to exploit the land in protected areas will intensify. Similarly, growing demand for wild products (e.g. timber, medicinal plants, and wild or bush meat) and depletion of such resources outside protected areas will lead to increasing exploitation of resources within protected areas. Although in many protected areas such exploitation is a management objective, it is very often not undertaken on a sustainable basis.

While high levels of rural poverty will continue to have a direct effect on land use, increasing wealth

S.Chape

in other sectors of society will also exacerbate pressures on wild lands. In particular, burgeoning economic expansion in the two most populous nations on Earth, China and India, is likely to increase the demand for resources both within those countries and elsewhere.

In the seas, pressure on fishery resources can be expected to intensify. There has been little manifest success to date in sustainable management of marine fisheries on a large scale. As stocks become further depleted, it is likely that competition to squeeze the last few benefits from them will increase rather than decrease. Some 50 percent of commercial fisheries are already fully exploited and 25 percent overexploited.

As an overarching issue, global climate change is predicted to have growing impacts both on natural ecosystems and areas of agricultural production. One major manifestation of this is likely to be the shifting of bioclimatic zones so that areas suitable or optimal for particular species and species assemblages will move from their present positions. In the most extreme cases there may be no overlap between existing suitable areas and future ones. The MA has concluded that by the end of the 21st century, climate change and associated impacts "may be the dominant direct driver of biodiversity loss and changes in ecosystem services globally" (MA 2005b:10). Climate change will mean that the climatic conditions in many protected areas may cease to be optimal or even adequate for some proportion of the biota they currently contain. Those

The Israeli–Palestinian conflict has had a major impact on environmental quality and protected areas. In Gaza the Wadi Gaza Nature Reserve, an important stopover point for birds on the Africa-Eurasia migratory route, has become an open sewer.

for which conditions may cease to be suitable are likely to include a disproportionately high number of restricted range or threatened species, as these are more likely to have more precise requirements than widespread and abundant species, and may well include those whose preservation was a major motivation for the establishment of the area in the first place.

Current analyses suggest that major changes in global energy supply are extremely likely to take place in the next few decades, with global oil production peaking some time between the present and 2030 and following a continuing decline thereafter. (Some analysts believe that the peak has already passed.) The implications for human society and the impact of humans on the biosphere are unclear, and vigorously debated, but are bound to be far-reaching. With the increasing demand and a decreasing supply, hydrocarbon fuel costs are almost certain to increase sharply and have wide-ranging repercussions on all aspects of human endeavor, including development economics and the management of protected areas. At the very least, a growing scarcity of available oil combined with growing demand is extremely likely to lead to increased pressure to open up to production any remaining areas with hydrocarbon reserves. This will certainly increase pressure to allow extraction from existing protected areas, even where this is currently not allowed. This has already manifested itself in a decision by the US Government in March 2005 to permit the opening up of the Arctic National Wildlife Refuge in northeast Alaska for oil exploration. Efforts to reverse this decision are ongoing, but meanwhile the oil companies are lining up to begin offshore drilling in the nearby shallow shelf areas of the Beaufort Sea despite concerns of native peoples and the large potential threats posed by the impacts of spills in such a sensitive region. Oil reserves in the Refuge itself are unlikely to make a major contribution to that country's massive levels of consumption, raising the issue of the benefits of very short-term alleviation of the US energy problem against the likely costs of long-term damage to one of the world's most important remaining natural areas, with ecosystems that are also highly susceptible to the impacts of climate change.

Apart from the impact of exploitation of remaining oil reserves, a major concern for biodiversity conservation is the growing shift to biofuels. As the cost of fuel rises, large-scale production of biodiesel and ethanol-producing crops becomes more economical, and indeed the process has already started on a large scale in the US, China and India. There will be increasing pressure to continue to clear natural areas, especially in the tropics, to produce a range of crops for fuel, such as oil palm, soybean, coconut and sugar cane. Brown (2006:36) notes: "in the absence of government constraints, the rising price of oil could quickly become the leading threat to biodiversity, ensuring that the wave of extinctions currently underway does indeed become the sixth great extinction."

Other factors that directly impinge on the current and future capacity to manage protected areas include civil unrest with, in some areas, growing threats to the safety and welfare of protected areas staff. War and civil conflict have had severe impacts on protected areas and ecosystems outside protected areas in Central and West Africa, Iraq, and the Occupied Palestinian Territories. The Vth World Parks Congress also identified the HIV/AIDS pandemic as a growing threat to the capacity to manage protected areas in many developing countries through its impact on staff numbers.

Meeting global biodiversity targets: pursuit of the unattainable?

The international community has commendably set targets for achieving global biodiversity objectives, as well as those for broader human development that have implications for biodiversity conservation. Thus we have the 2010 target under the Convention on Biological Diversity (CBD) for significantly reducing the "current rate of biodiversity loss at the global, regional and national level as a contribution to poverty alleviation and to the benefit of all life on Earth" (CBD Decision VI/26); the 2015 Millennium Development Goals (MDGs); and a series of specific goals and targets agreed at the 2002 World Summit on Sustainable Development, including, for example, the target to establish an effective global marine protected area (MPA) network by 2012.

With the possible exception of this last target, which is at least theoretically attainable through action by national governments, other targets and goals are unlikely to be achieved in the next three to eight years. In fact, the MA has concluded that without "unprecedented international efforts" the biodiversity targets will not be achieved. The assessment observed that "the magnitude of the challenge of slowing the rate of biodiversity loss is demonstrated by the fact that most of the direct drivers... are projected to either remain constant or to increase in the near future. Moreover, inertia in natural and human institutional systems [often] results in time lags – of years, decades, or even centuries – between actions being taken and their impact on biodiversity and ecosystems becoming apparent" (MA, 2005b:14). Furthermore, there are inherent tensions between the development goals and the biodiversity targets, since some of the actions needed to reduce poverty in the short to medium term – such as the expansion of agriculture and the creation of road networks and other infrastructure – are likely to accelerate or at least continue rates of biodiversity loss. Avoiding

such problems will require hitherto unachieved levels of integrated conservation and development planning and action.

Implications for protected areas

Paradoxically, the current rate of global change and continuing loss of biodiversity presents both threat and opportunity for protected areas. On the one hand, the predicted continuing loss of biodiversity and other impacts threaten the viability of protected areas as core elements of national, regional, and global conservation strategies. On the other, the values and importance of protected areas are increasingly recognized, and the constituency of

NASA Jet Propulsion Laboratory

Parque Nacional Pacaas Novos

Terra Indigena Rio Branco

There are obvious tensions between development goals and biodiversity targets. Some of the actions needed to reduce poverty in the short to medium term, including the expansion of agriculture, are likely to at least continue rates of biodiversity loss. Forest incursion in Rondonia, Brazil.

Laurie Wein

Tetepare Island, in the Solomon Islands, is an outstanding example of a community-conserved area, protecting 120 km of mainly primary rainforest – a significant area in the insular Pacific – and other features, and addressing Outcomes 5 (rights of indigenous people) and 8 (improved governance) of the Durban Action Plan.

support for their establishment has broadened considerably, particularly as governments and communities become more aware of the ecological and economic services provided by these areas, notwithstanding significant shortcomings, particularly with regard to MPA networks. Of course, if integrated conservation and development approaches can be successfully implemented, there is considerable scope for synergies between protected areas, conservation objectives, and achievement of the MDGs – even if the time horizon must be made more realistic.

The importance of protected areas is reflected in their use as indicators for both the CBD 2010 biodiversity targets and the MDGs, and the Millennium Ecosystem Assessment has also emphasized the need to strengthen the global protected area system. However, both the 2010 targets and the MDGs have emphasized changes in the number and extent of protected areas as the principal indicators to be used to assess progress towards targets. Unfortunately, measurements of the number and extent of protected areas are likely to provide only a superficial indication of political commitment to conserving biodiversity (Chape, 2005) as they do not assess how effectively

they are conserving biodiversity, or even if they are adequately covering priority habitats and species (Rodrigues *et al.*, 2003). A comprehensive suite of indicators is required that includes conservation and management effectiveness in addition to numerical and spatial data.

GLOBAL "BLUEPRINTS" FOR PROTECTED AREAS
The worldwide interest in protected areas and their growth into one of the most important land-use allocations on the planet culminated in 2003 and 2004 in agreement on two important global frameworks for guiding future directions for protected areas. Critically, the first framework, the Durban Action Plan, informed the second, the CBD Programme of Work on Protected Areas. This was an important step in the integration of global civil society views on the future direction of protected areas into formal intergovernmental decision-making processes.

Outcomes of the Vth World Parks Congress
The Vth World Parks Congress (WPC) held in Durban, South Africa, in September 2003, was attended by 3 000 people with direct and indirect interests in protected areas. These included resource managers, scientists, politicians, ministers, civil servants, and industry leaders from 144 countries. However, as a non-intergovernmental meeting, any recommendations and agreements by participants of the Congress, held every ten years, have no international legal status. Nevertheless, previous congresses have played an important part in guiding the scientific and professional development of protected area philosophies and methodologies for over 40 years. The opportunity for the 2003 Congress was the linkage of its outputs and recommendations to debates at the CBD (COP7) in February 2004 on the proposed Programme of Work on Protected Areas to be implemented under the Convention. The 2003 Congress produced two major outputs:

Durban Accord
The Accord was a broad statement of commitment from the 3 000 participants to the rest of the world and, recognizing rapid global change, proposed a new paradigm for protected areas:

"In this changing world, we need a fresh and innovative approach to protected areas and their role in broader conservation and development agendas. This approach dem-

ands the maintenance and enhancement of our core conservation goals, equitably integrating them with the interests of all affected people. In this way, the synergy between conservation, the maintenance of life-support systems and sustainable development is forged. We see protected areas as a vital means to achieve this synergy efficiently and cost-effectively. We see protected areas as providers of benefits beyond boundaries –

beyond their boundaries on a map, beyond the boundaries of nation states, across societies, genders and generations."

Durban Action Plan
The Action Plan adopted at the Congress set an international agenda for improving the status of protected areas over the next decade, when the outcomes will be assessed at the next World Parks Congress, to be held in 2013. The Action Plan

BOX 7.1: THE DURBAN ACTION PLAN OUTCOMES AND KEY TARGETS

Outcomes	Key Targets
1: Protected areas fulfil their full role in biodiversity conservation	1: A significantly strengthened role for protected areas in implementing the Convention on Biological Diversity. 2: All sites whose biodiversity values are of outstanding universal value are inscribed on the World Heritage List.
2: Protected areas make a full contribution to sustainable development	3: The management of all protected areas is reviewed so that they help alleviate poverty, and do not exacerbate it.
3: A global system of protected areas, with links to surrounding landscapes and seascapes, is in place	4: A system of protected areas representing all the world's ecosystems is in place. 5: All protected areas are linked into wider ecological/environmental systems of resource management and protection on land and at sea.
4: Protected areas are effectively managed, with reliable reporting on their management	6: All protected areas have effective management systems in place. 7: All protected areas have effective management capacity.
5: The rights of indigenous peoples, including mobile indigenous, and local communities are secured in relation to natural resources and biodiversity conservation	8: All existing and future protected areas are established and managed in full compliance with the rights of indigenous peoples, including mobile indigenous peoples, and local communities. 9: The management of all relevant protected areas involves representatives chosen by indigenous peoples, including mobile indigenous peoples, and local communities proportionate to their rights and interests. 10: All participatory mechanisms for the restitution of indigenous peoples' traditional lands and territories that were incorporated in protected areas without their free and informed consent are established and implemented.
6: Younger generations are empowered in relation to protected areas	11: There is a significantly greater participation of younger people in the governance and management of protected areas.
7: Significantly greater support is secured for protected areas from other constituencies	12: Programs of support for protected areas are achieved among all major stakeholder constituencies.
8: Improved forms of governance are in place	13: Effective systems of governance are implemented by all countries.
9: Greatly increased financial resources are secured for protected areas	14: Sufficient resources are secured to identify, establish and meet the recurrent operating costs of a globally representative system of protected areas.
10: Better communication and education are achieved on the role and benefits of protected areas	15: All national systems of protected areas are supported by communication and education strategies.

BOX 7.2: CBD PROGRAMME OF WORK ON PROTECTED AREAS: ELEMENTS AND GOALS

Program Elements	Goals
1: Direct actions for planning, selecting, establishing, strengthening, and managing protected area systems and sites	Goal 1.1 To establish and strengthen national and regional systems of protected areas integrated into a global network as a contribution to globally agreed goals. Goal 1.2 To integrate protected areas into broader land- and seascapes and sectors so as to maintain ecological structure and function. Goal 1.3 To establish and strengthen regional networks, transboundary protected areas (TBPAs) and collaboration between neighboring protected areas across national boundaries. Goal 1.4 To substantially improve site-based protected area planning and management. Goal 1.5 To prevent and mitigate the negative impacts of key threats to protected areas.
2: Governance, participation, equity, and benefit sharing	Goal 2.1 To promote equity and benefit-sharing. Goal 2.2 To enhance and secure involvement of indigenous and local communities and relevant stakeholders.
3: Enabling activities	Goal 3.1 To provide an enabling policy, institutional and socio-economic environment for protected areas. Goal 3.2 To build capacity for the planning, establishment and management of protected areas. Goal 3.3 To develop, apply and transfer appropriate technologies for protected areas. Goal 3.4 To ensure financial sustainability of protected areas and national and regional systems of protected areas. Goal 3.5 To strengthen communication, education, and public awareness
4: Standards, assessment, and monitoring	Goal 4.1 To develop and adopt minimum standards and best practices for national and regional protected area systems. Goal 4.2 To evaluate and improve the effectiveness of protected areas management. Goal 4.3 To assess and monitor protected area status and trends. Goal 4.4 To ensure that scientific knowledge contributes to the establishment and effectiveness of protected areas and protected area systems.

identifies ten outcomes and 15 key targets to be achieved by that date. See Box 7.1.

To support these outcomes there are a range of recommended actions at global, regional, and national levels. As well as the Accord and Action Plan, the Congress endorsed 32 comprehensive recommendations tabled by participants, covering subjects as diverse as the cultural and spiritual value of protected areas, mining and energy, evaluating management effectiveness, and private sector funding. In addition, a number of supporting targets were adopted for ecosystems and species:

Ecosystem-related supporting targets
❏ Develop a common global framework for classifying and assessing the status of ecosystems by 2006.

❏ Identify quantitative targets for each ecosystem type by 2008.

❏ Ensure that, by 2006, protected area systems adequately cover all large, intact ecosystems that hold globally significant assemblages of species and/or provide ecosystem services and processes.

❏ Ensure that viable representations of every threatened or underprotected ecosystem are conserved by 2010.

❏ Ensure an increase in the coverage of freshwater ecosystems by protected areas (as proposed by CBD Recommendation VIII/2) by 2012.

❏ Secure a representative network of marine protected areas by 2012, as called for in the WSSD Plan of Implementation.

Species-related supporting targets

❏ Ensure all Critically Endangered and Endangered species globally confined to single sites are effectively conserved *in situ* by 2006.

❏ Ensure all other globally Critically Endangered and Endangered species are effectively conserved *in situ* by 2008.

❏ Ensure all other globally threatened species are effectively conserved *in situ* by 2010.

❏ Ensure that sites that support internationally important populations of species that congregate and/or have restricted-range species are effectively conserved by 2010.

The main elements of the Action Plan and adopted recommendations were reflected in a formal message from the Congress to the CBD Cop7.

CBD Programme of Work on Protected Areas

A Programme of Work on Protected Areas was adopted at the CBD Cop7 in Kuala Lumpur in February 2004, and largely reflected the recommendations of the 2003 World Parks Congress. The adoption by Contracting Parties to the CBD is an important step in further formalizing at the intergovernmental level the values and roles of protected areas in global conservation, and their linkage to conservation and development agendas:

> "The overall purpose of the programme of work on protected areas is to support the establishment and maintenance by 2010 for terrestrial and by 2012 for marine, areas of comprehensive, effectively managed, and ecologically representative national and regional systems of protected areas that collectively, inter alia through a global network, contribute to achieving the three objectives of the Convention and the 2010 target to significantly reduce the current rate of biodiversity loss at the global, regional, national and sub-national levels and contribute to poverty reduction and the pursuit of sustainable development, thereby supporting the objectives of the Strategic Plan of the Convention, the World Summit on Sustainable Development Plan of Implementation and the Millennium Development Goals." (SCBD, 2004b)

The work program comprises the elements and goals outlined in Box 7.2, each of which has a series of time-bound targets (Box 7.3).

CAN THE "BLUEPRINT" BE IMPLEMENTED?

There is sufficient correlation and synergy between the outcomes and recommendations of the 2003 World Parks Congress and the Programme of Work on Protected Areas agreed by the Parties to the CBD that the Programme can be considered as a defining framework or "blueprint" for protected areas for the next decade. The Programme of Work has the benefit of intergovernmental endorsement as part of an international agreement and, as such, theoretically brings responsibilities to the Parties of the CBD and is subject to the Convention's reporting processes. If all elements, goals, and targets of the Programme of Work are implemented by 2015, an effective and resilient global protected area network could well be in place for the remainder of the 21st century.

The problem with time-bound targets

A difficulty with the Programme of Work lies in the ambitious time-scale of its targets. While it is important in any endeavor to set timelines for achieving targets, both as an incentive for achievement and so that progress can be measured, they must be realistic. Most of the Programme of Work, to be achieved between 2006 and 2015, is interlinked and sequential, with both national- and regional-level objectives. A number are theoretically achievable by the designated target year, such as gap analyses and capacity assessments at national levels. Others are more problematic – for example, it is unlikely that national-level reviews of existing and potential forms of conservation and types of governance were undertaken "with full and effective participation of indigenous and local communities" by 2006. Many of the targets will require technical and financial support to developing countries, which will need allocation and mobilization of considerable resources and, in the case of many supporting bilateral donor agencies, a refocus on funding priorities for conservation activities in their assistance programs. The inescapable conclusion is that the Programme of Work will only be implemented in part within currently designated time frames.

The role of protected areas: stretching the limits?

In Chapter 1 we discussed the "new paradigm" for protected areas – the increasing recognition over the past few decades of the full range of values provided by protected areas that include many social, cultural, and economic benefits. This has

BOX 7.3: CBD PROGRAMME OF WORK ON PROTECTED AREAS TIME-BOUND TARGETS

2006	❏ Establish time-bound and measurable national- and regional-level protected area targets and indicators.
	❏ Establish or expand protected areas in any large, intact, or relatively unfragmented or highly irreplaceable natural areas, areas under threat, with threatened species, and taking into account migratory species.
	❏ Conduct, with full and effective participation of indigenous and local communities, national-level reviews of existing and potential forms of conservation and types of governance.
	❏ Address under-representation of inland water ecosystems in national and regional protected area systems.
	❏ Complete protected area system gap analyses at national and regional levels.
	❏ Evaluate national and sub-national experiences and lessons learned on specific efforts to integrate protected areas into wider land/seascapes.
	❏ Identify legislative and institutional gaps and barriers that impede effective establishment and management of protected areas.
	❏ Complete national protected area capacity needs assessments, and establish capacity-building programmes.
	❏ Develop and adopt appropriate methods, standards, criteria, and indicators for evaluating protected-area management effectiveness and governance, and set up a database.
2008	❏ Address under-representation of marine ecosystems in national and regional protected-area systems.
	❏ Identify and implement practical steps for improving integration of protected areas into wider land/seascapes, including policy, legal, planning, and other measures.
	❏ Effective mechanisms for identifying and preventing, and/or mitigating, negative impacts of key threats to protected areas are in place.
	❏ Mechanisms established for equitable sharing of costs and benefits of establishment and management of protected areas.
	❏ Full and effective participation of indigenous and local communities in the management of existing protected areas, and in the establishment of new protected areas.
	❏ Review and revise policies, including social and economic valuation and incentives, to provide a supporting enabling environment for more effective establishment and management of protected areas.
	❏ Establish and begin to implement country-level sustainable financing plans that support national protected-area systems, including necessary regulatory,

been reflected in the rapid growth in the designation of IUCN Management Category VI – Managed Resource Area protected areas with their emphasis on sustainable use. Globally, Category VI protected areas now exceed the area of Category II – National Parks, and together Category V – Protected Landscape/Seascape and category VI protected areas account for almost 43 percent of the total area protected. While the broadening of the role of protected areas – which is also reflected in new (or reinstated) approaches to governance – is to be applauded, there needs to be a careful approach to the promotion of the benefits that can be delivered by such areas.

	legislative, policy, institutional, and other measures.
	❑ Sufficient financial, technical, and other resources to effectively implement and manage national and regional protected-area systems are secured.
	❑ Public awareness, understanding, and appreciation of the importance and benefits of protected areas significantly increased.
	❑ Standards, criteria, and best practices for planning, selecting, establishing, managing, and governance of national and regional protected-area systems developed and adopted.
2009	❑ Designate protected areas identified through gap analyses.
	❑ Effectively address legislative and institutional gaps and barriers that impede effective establishment and management of protected areas.
2010	❑ Global network of comprehensive, representative and effectively managed national and regional terrestrial protected areas established.
	❑ Establish and strengthen transboundary terrestrial protected areas and other forms of collaboration.
	❑ Develop or update management plans for protected areas.
	❑ Comprehensive capacity-building programs and initiatives implemented.
	❑ Development, validation, and transfer of appropriate technologies and innovative approaches for effective management of protected areas is substantially improved.
	❑ Frameworks for monitoring, evaluating, and reporting protected-area management effectiveness adopted and implemented by Parties.
	❑ Management effectiveness evaluations implemented for at least 30 percent of each Party's protected areas and ecological networks.
	❑ National and regional systems established to enable effective monitoring of protected-area coverage, status, and trends at national, regional, and global scales, and to assist in monitoring global biodiversity targets.
2012	❑ Global network of comprehensive, representative, and effectively managed national and regional marine protected areas established.
	❑ Establish and strengthen transboundary marine protected areas and other forms of collaboration.
	❑ All protected areas effectively managed using participatory and science-based planning processes that incorporate clear biodiversity targets.
2015	❑ All protected areas and protected-area systems integrated into wider land/seascapes.

A major objective of the CBD Programme of Work on Protected Areas is to "contribute to poverty reduction and the pursuit of sustainable development" in support of the World Summit on Sustainable Development Plan of Implementation and the MDGs. Indeed, the 2003 World Parks Congress was also framed within the concept of "benefit beyond boundaries", including the role of protected areas in ameliorating poverty. A two-page flyer released by the Congress and sponsored by the IUCN Commission on Ecosystem Management, Ramsar, and the UNESCO Man and Biosphere Program listed ten target action areas for strengthening protected areas over the next decade.

S.Chape

There needs to be a better understanding of the opportunities and limitations of linking protected areas to development outcomes and poverty reduction.

Target 1 was poverty alleviation, with specific reference to National Poverty Reduction Strategies, while ecological targets were ranked at fifth (marine) and sixth places.

It is fundamental that we have a holistic and integrated approach to resolving the problems of poverty, resource access inequities, and global environmental change if we are to be successful in conserving the world's remaining and rapidly diminishing biodiversity. Such an approach must include the roles and values of protected areas, and the environmental services that many such areas provide. Too few protected areas are linked into development planning, land use, and other resource management decision-making systems beyond their boundaries. Many protected areas thus function as isolated units, and the ecological linkages that they ultimately depend on often have no legal protection.

However, it is essential that we do not demand too much. Protected areas cannot be a panacea for the world's development problems, even if they can significantly contribute to the solutions. Even at the local level, delivery of benefits from protected areas is problematic. One of the major problems to be overcome in developing countries is the inequitable distribution of the costs and benefits of maintaining protected areas. Most notably, people living in the vicinity of a protected area may bear significant costs from the presence of that area, chiefly through foregoing the often short-term benefits that would otherwise accrue if they were allowed to exploit its

natural resources in an unrestrained way. Solving this in an equitable fashion that is sustainable (socially, ecologically, and financially) in the long term and acceptable to all interest groups has proved highly intractable. Sustainable use of wild resources, through direct harvesting or tourism, has often been promoted as a means by which local people and national agencies can derive income to offset the immediate and future opportunity costs of maintaining protected areas. However, as Hutton and Leader-Williams (2003) noted: "Notwithstanding the potential financial benefits that often flow from the use of living wild resources, such use has not often realized its full potential as an incentive to support habitat and species conservation objectives, or to benefit the rural poor." In some countries, such as Costa Rica, successful partnerships have been built with local private businesses, resulting in regular income for local people and national management agencies. However, as McClanahan (2004:4) has noted: "Ecological and economic benefits of protected areas are often indirect and most relevant at the national and international level, making it difficult for conservation to pay for itself at the local level."

Recent reviews of the integrated development and conservation experience (Wells *et al.*, 2004; MacKinnon, 2002) have concluded that there is little evidence that developmental improvements for local people near protected areas results in more effective biodiversity conservation, based on the many integrated conservation and development programs implemented in the 1980s to 1990s. We have to define more achievable goals and have a more realistic understanding of the opportunities and limitations of linking protected areas to development outcomes and not set the criterion for success of protected areas based on their alleviation of poverty alone. The fundamental challenges facing protected areas over the next century, and against which most are likely to be assessed by future generations, are successfully conserving biological diversity and providing sustainable environmental services.

CLIMATE CHANGE AND ECOLOGICAL NETWORKS

As well as the issues relating to the problematic interface between protected areas and development, over the coming century a major global challenge facing protected areas and the biodiversity that they conserve is adapting to climate change. This is, of course, a predicament that affects all aspects of human endeavor, not only protected areas, and is dependent upon the resolution of wide-ranging issues at the highest political levels and across all strata of society. Nevertheless, protected areas need to be a central strategy in the amelioration of climate change impacts on ecosystems.

Climate change provides a critical argument for, and underscores the urgency of, not only ensuring the protection and management of our existing conservation areas, but also expanding present national systems into an effective global network. Even though protected areas are wide-ranging across the Earth's biomes, they are highly vulnerable to the impacts of climate change and tend to already exist as remnants in modified landscapes. Adaptation to climate change at the species and ecosystem levels, where adaptation is feasible, will include the ability of species to shift latitudinally and altitudinally. One of our greatest challenges, therefore, is to strengthen the capacity of protected areas to provide for these potential lateral and vertical shifts. This will require enhanced levels of cooperation within and between countries to develop effective ecological networks and corridors that work across intranational and international geopolitical boundaries, and to engage in landscape-scale ecological restoration.

In recent years, the concept of ecological networks has gained increasing support as a mechanism for enhancing connectivity between protected areas, and protecting remaining bio-diversity not contained within declared conservation sites. While many existing networks are based on contiguous landscape connectivity, others help to conserve migratory species by protecting breeding and stopover sites scattered across the globe; for example, migratory waterbird agreements such as the East Asian-Australasian Shorebird Site Network and the Bonn Convention Agreement on the Conservation of African-Eurasian Migratory Waterbirds (Bennett and Wit, 2001).

Almost 50 percent of the total number of the world's protected areas are in Europe, although most are very small and collectively they constitute only 4 percent of the total global area protected. The ecological network approach has therefore gained considerable momentum in Europe with the development of the Pan-European Ecological Network (PEEN) (see Figure 7.3) to enhance ecological connectivity in the region, and in Central America, with the establishment of the Meso-American Biological Corridor. These examples provide an indication of what can be achieved, and it is this type of large-scale cooperative ecological planning that must occur across all continents if we are to build adaptability into protected area networks to meet the challenges of climate change and existing issues associated with habitat fragmentation.

In addition to developing and implementing

As a result of global climate change, the ecological viability of small protected areas will likely be dependent on effective connectivity through ecological networks – Mt Egmont National Park, New Zealand.

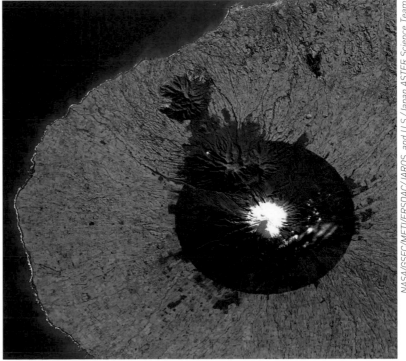

NASA/GSFC/METI/ERSDAC/JAROS, and U.S./Japan ASTER Science Team

FIGURE 7.3:
PAN-EUROPEAN
ECOLOGICAL
NETWORK

**The Pan-European
Ecological Network
is an example of
the transnational
cooperative ecological
planning that must
occur if we are to
build adaptability into
protected-area
networks to meet the
challenges of climate
change and habitat
fragmentation.**

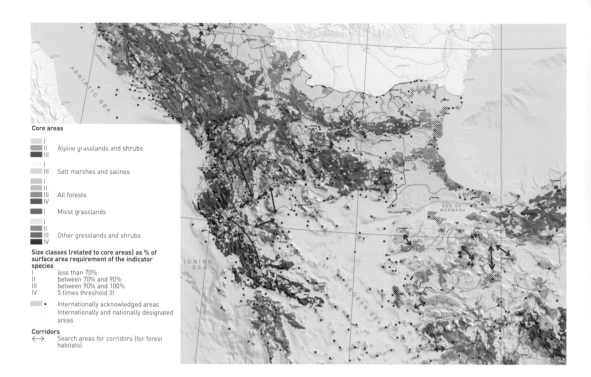

strategies for improving connectivity of protected areas and providing for the movement of species, protected areas have value in mitigating some of the broader impacts of climate change. Almost all are fundamental for human development and survival, through, for example:

❏ retention of vegetated catchments, especially forests, to protect water supplies;

❏ retention of large forest and wetland eco-systems to reduce levels of emissions (from deforestation or breakdown of below-ground carbon reserves); assist in absorption of increasing levels of atmospheric CO_2; and ameliorate changes in regional rainfall patterns;

❏ protection of upland forests and other vegetation to reduce the impact of storms on soil and slope stability;

❏ protection of inland areas from the impacts of cyclonic waves and storm surge by mangroves and other coastal systems. Allowance for natural (managed) retreat of these systems as sea levels rise will continue this role into the future;

❏ protection of fish breeding and migration areas, and associated habitats, allowing greater resilience of important fish-stocks against changes in water temperature and current patterns;

❏ provision of livelihood buffers of managed

natural resources – including non-timber forest products, wild foods, and water supplies – for local rural communities in times of food crop deficits arising from droughts and depredation by pests;

❏ retention of genetic diversity for restoring degraded ecosystems; and

❏ the potential for better control of disease vectors (predicted to extend their ranges as a result of climate change) by natural predators in protected areas.

In the coming decades there will be increased availability of monitoring technology to protected-area managers especially in developing countries, such as interactive satellite imagery (see Box 7.4). This will greatly assist monitoring and modelling of ecosystem changes in protected areas to enable better management responses to deal with environmental change issues.

RESOURCING THE FUTURE

Support for effective management and protection of conservation areas still requires a permanent, widespread solution. Participants at the Vth World Parks Congress concluded that there was almost universal underinvestment by governments in protected areas, with the result that they often lack effective protection and management and therefore fail to meet their conservation and social objectives. This situation undoubtedly stems in large measure from the fact that protected areas often lack broad public support. Indeed, specific groups, from local peoples to multinational corporations, often see protected areas as actual barriers to their activities and aspirations. It is scarcely surprising, therefore, that protected areas are generally accorded low investment priority by governments. Not only is there acknowledged to be inadequate direct investment, but a range of subsidies and other financial instruments and institutional arrangements often act perversely and have a negative impact on protected areas and more generally biodiversity.

Participants at the Vth World Parks Congress estimated that an annual sum in the region of US$ 20–30 billion would be required over the next 30 years to establish and maintain a comprehensive protected-areas system including terrestrial, wetland, and marine ecosystems. This is of a similar order of magnitude for, but somewhat lower than, an estimate of some US$ 45 billion made by Balmford *et al.* in 2002. They estimated that US$ 6.5

billion was actually spent annually on the existing protected area network. Not only is this considerably less than the amount needed, it is also highly inequitably distributed, with half spent in the USA alone.

The sum required might seem large, but it pales into insignificance when set against the economically and ecologically perverse subsidies, estimated globally at US$ 950–1 950 billion annually, that continue to drive habitat loss. For example, the MA (2005b) reports that agricultural sector subsidies paid to the OECD countries alone between 2001 and 2003 averaged over US$ 324 billion annually, with a significant proportion leading to overproduction, reducing the profitability of agriculture in developing countries and thus helping to perpetuate rural poverty that leads to much of the pressure on protected areas in those countries. The amount required to better conserve the world's natural heritage is also insignificant compared to global expenditure on the most destructive human activity: war and conflict, estimated at US$ 1 035 billion in 2004 (SIPRI 2005).

The problem of chronic under-resourcing and

The Vth World Parks Congress estimated that an annual sum in the region of US$ 20–30 billion would be required over the next 30 years to establish and maintain a comprehensive protected-areas system, including terrestrial, wetland, and marine ecosystems. Los Glaciares National Park and World Heritage Area, Argentina.

Chris Magin

BOX 7.4: THE ROLE OF REMOTE SENSING IN PROTECTED AREAS MANAGEMENT IN THE 21st CENTURY

Gary N. Geller, Protected Areas Conservation Liaison, Jet Propulsion Laboratory, NASA

Observations of Earth from space or aircraft are playing an increasingly significant role in protected areas management. The main uses include a range of sophistication levels, from simply looking at color images to detailed quantitative analysis and computer modeling. Extracting the full value from these observations, however, requires making the data and tools more user-friendly so they are accessible to users whose expertise is in conservation management.

Perspective and context. An image facilitates understanding of a site and its context. For example, it puts the size of a protected area, which may seem large from the ground, into perspective, and helps the viewer to recognize the significance of finite boundaries. Because features within a protected area are often obvious from space, an image may help provide an understanding of problems or potential problems that may otherwise be missed, such as the extent of agricultural encroachment around and within a protected area.

Communication. Satellite images can be a powerful communication aid because they can convey certain problems much better than words can. For example, an image showing agricultural encroachment into a protected area can be immediately understood, and have more impact than words. Such an image can also be very difficult to argue with, making images a useful advocacy tool.

Historical value. For conservation management, an image should be considered as a biophysical dataset captured at a particular point in time. An image archive can thus be extremely valuable in understanding how an area has changed over time, or for establishing a "baseline" condition to be used as a reference for historical and future comparisons.

Maps and measurements. Satellite images can be used for a variety of maps and measurements. One of the most significant is the classified vegetation or land-use map, where each pixel in an image is assigned a particular "class" representing its vegetation type or land use. However, generating such maps typically requires fairly intensive groundwork to achieve sufficient accuracy. This is due to the limitations of the available and affordable technology, primarily spatial and spectral resolution, though also image processing and analysis tools. But there are many simpler uses for images, including generating maps of roads or management units, measuring area and distance, assessing encroachment, or as an aid to fieldwork. Also, images make an excellent "base map" upon which other kinds of data – such as management units, poaching incidents, fire history, census, poverty, or any type of spatially referenced dataset – can be overlaid. Bringing these datasets together with a satellite image can be very revealing.

Modeling and ecological forecasting. One active area that is likely to change much over the next decade is the use of remote sensing data in predictive models that will help protected-areas managers assess the consequences of alternate scenarios. For example, past trends in deforestation, as determined from a series of satellite images, can be used to predict future forest extent in and around

lack of political commitment is most clearly seen in (but not limited to) developing countries, which hold much of the world's threatened biodiversity and most important protected areas, and many of which are faced with rapidly growing populations often in rural areas, high levels of poverty and unemployment, and low levels of health, education, and basic infrastructure. The stability of governance in a number of these countries, at national, provincial, and community levels, is further strained by conflict, epidemic diseases, and/or endemic institutional corruption. As a result, the resources available for effective management of conservation areas are usually minimal – despite the best intentions at the national policy level in initially establishing protected areas.

Currently the viability of protected areas is often maintained through the efforts of dedicated

2001   2005

Source: NASA/GSFC/ METI/ERSDAC/JAROS, and US/Japan ASTER Science Team

a park. Somewhat more sophisticated is the potential to use models in assessing the impact of climate change. For example, a variety of satellite-derived environmental parameters can be used to determine the relationship between environmental variables and species habitat; then, using climate models, the range of an important species under various climatic regimes can be predicted. Such environmental measurements can also be used to predict a variety of parameters that may be of use to protected areas managers, such as water availability for wildlife, or fire risk (for example, seeecocast.arc. nasa.gov). As new models become available, existing models improve, and all become easier to use, more and more model-based tools will become available for protected areas management.

Monitoring. Another active area is the use of remote sensing for monitoring protected areas. Monitoring can be done in two ways. The simplest, which could be called "watchful eye" monitoring, is to manually review images for problems and changes (good and bad) in and around a protected area. A step up in sophistication is to automate this process, which is just getting underway, with, for example, the use of an automated fire detection and reporting system (see http://maps.geog. umd.edu). Monitoring may also be more formalized and extract specific,

quantitative indicators such as deforestation or reforestation, fragmentation and connectivity, and threats such as density of road networks or agricultural expansion. Indicator development using Earth observation data is an area of much research activity with a range of sophistication levels. For satellite-aided monitoring to become widespread among the 100 000-plus protected areas, however, the data and tools to use it will need to become more accessible. An excellent reference on satellite-aided biodiversity monitoring is available at http://biodiv. org/doc/ publications/cbd-ts-32.pdf.

Addressing the access problem. For remote sensing to become a widespread technology among protected areas managers it will need to be made easier to use. Currently, most of the tools for finding and using satellite images are for experienced users, and while training is gradually increasing the capacity of the conservation community, the tools need to become both simpler and friendlier. One recent approach to addressing this problem is called TerraLook. TerraLook combines collections of images on a particular theme (such as the protected areas of a particular country or region) with simple tools to find and use them. It is designed for users who have no experience using satellite images. TerraLook is available at http://terralook.cr.usgs.gov.

Ichkeul National Park World Heritage Site in Tunisia badly deteriorated as the result of the construction of three dams on rivers supplying it and its marshes. The dams cut off almost all inflow of fresh water, causing a destructive increase in the salinity of the lake and marshes. Reed beds, sedges and other freshwater plant species have been replaced with salt-loving plants, with a consequent sharp reduction in the migratory bird populations dependent on the habitat the lake formerly provided. The Tunisian Government plans to undertake various measures to retain freshwater in the lake on a year-round basis and reduce the salinity of the lake. The two ASTER 3-2-1 RGB composites depict vegetation in shades of red. In 2005, the water level is higher than 2001, but a large part of the lake appears red due to the presence of aquatic plants.

staff in head offices in capital cities and in the field, and in many developing countries supported by bilateral or multilateral donors. Often the problem with donor support is its short-term nature, often tied to three-to-five-year funding cycles, the political agendas of the donor countries themselves, loan conditions (in the case of the multilateral banks), and the frequent inability of donor funds to meet recurrent management costs.

In 1999, James *et al.* estimated that donor funding only supported about 20 percent of total expenditure on nature reserves in developing countries. In some countries, official development assistance is supplemented or even replaced by direct financial and technical assistance from privately funded international conservation organizations. Although the Global Environment Facility (GEF) has provided millions of dollars for conservation activities,

Balmford and Whitten (2003) noted that in the case of tropical conservation, there is little evidence that the level of donor support has increased significantly since the first commitments in the early 1990s. They also suggested that the recent broadening of the scope of GEF funding to cover land degradation and persistent organic pollutants will dilute the funds available for conservation.

The ecological benefits of protected areas are global and their value will increase as pressures intensify on unprotected natural resources and as global environmental change continues. There is a need for equity in the disbursement of the real costs of developing countries maintaining protected areas for the global good – the high level of global benefits accruing from protected natural ecosystems needs to be reflected in the way we support protected areas. Balmford *et al.* (2002) calculated that a "hypothetical global reserve network" costing some US$ 20–45 billion per year would ensure the delivery of goods and services with an annual value (net of benefits from conversion) of between about US$ 4 400 billion and US$ 5 200 billion, depending on the level of resource use permitted within protected areas – a cost benefit ratio of around 100:1.

FUTURE PROSPECTS

As a species, we are faced with enormous challenges to manage the Earth sustainably and equitably in the coming century and beyond. Increasing realization of the scale of our problem has prompted considerable international agreement on what needs to be done, including establishment and effective management of protected areas as a key mechanism for conserving what remains of our dwindling biodiversity – with hopes that such action will also have wider "benefits beyond boundaries".

International discussion now focuses on the role of protected areas as part of global conservation strategies and ecological networks, and the extensive growth of the conservation estate has reflected increasing political commitment at national levels. But, as always, political commitment needs to be followed by action – simply adding more areas to comply with the statistical objectives of global agreements will not do. This means action at all levels of protected area planning and management, as well as effective integration of site-based conservation into wider development planning and broader response strategies to fundamental issues such as climate change, poverty reduction, energy, and cessation of armed conflict – and not as a competing or lower priority. Most importantly, the values and importance of protected areas must be reflected in the provision of sufficient resources, and the recognition of and support for diverse governance models. In short, we need to apply the adopted principles and goals of the CBD Programme of Work on Protected Areas, but within realistic and manageable time frames.

If these issues are addressed, building on the obvious synergies with all elements of environmental and development agendas, protected areas will succeed over the long term as key global, national, and local conservation mechanisms .

Certainly there is cause for optimism in the recent actions of some governments, such as the 2006 announcement by Pará State in Brazil to conserve almost 150 000 km in Amazonia and the 2005 decision by Micronesian countries in the Pacific to conserve 30 percent of near shore marine areas and 20 percent of forests by 2015. Equally, at the community level more and more communities are conserving areas and placing them under sustainable use regimes, such as the locally managed marine areas in Fiji and other countries. What we are seeing, and what needs to be fostered and strengthened at all levels of society, are crucial cultural, political, and scientific responses to the interrelated threats to nature and human survival as we deal with the enormous environmental and social challenges of the 21st century.

Regional analysis

This chapter assesses the extent of the world's protected area coverage, and planning and management issues, on a regional basis. There are a number of different schemes used by international organizations to divide the world into regional units, but most of these are very broad scale. For its purposes, the IUCN World Commission on Pro tected Areas (WCPA) has divided the world (excluding Antarctica, see Chapter 1) into 15 regions on the basis of geographical, geopolitical, and/or linguistic factors:

> North America
> Caribbean
> Central America
> Brazil
> South America
> Europe
> West and Central Africa
> Eastern and Southern Africa
> North Africa and Middle East
> Northern Eurasia
> South Asia
> East Asia
> Southeast Asia
> Australia and New Zealand
> Pacific

Overall these divisions are a useful way of reviewing the global status of protected areas.

However, for the purposes of presenting coherent geographic analyses, they are not without difficulties when the basis for defining a region includes a linguistic criterion. For example, the West and Central Africa region includes the francophone island states of the Indian Ocean, which from a geographic perspective are more efficiently dealt with in the context of Eastern and Southern Africa. Similarly, Brazil is an artificially separated region within the South American continent. In the case of West and Central Africa adjustments have been made in this chapter to improve geographic coherence.

The regional analyses follow a standard format covering regional description, historical perspective, extent of national and international protected areas, and an assessment of future directions. These analyses have been undertaken by regional experts, including WCPA regional vice chairs.

The protected area data used here for each region are derived from analyses undertaken in 2007 using 2005 information held in the World Database on Protected Areas (WDPA). It should be noted that revision and updating of the database, using national agency and other sources, is an ongoing process and statistical information currently held in the WDPA for individual countries and for regions may vary from the information presented in these analyses.

North America

CANADA, GREENLAND (DENMARK), MEXICO, ST PIERRE AND MIQUELON (FRANCE), UNITED STATES OF AMERICA

Contributor: A. Turner

REGIONAL DESCRIPTION

North America has a combined population of more than 425 million people and is primarily governed by three federal, 82 state, 10 provincial, and three territorial governments with responsibilities for protected areas. Greenland, although closely tied to Denmark, has self rule, with a population of 57 000 in three regions. St Pierre and Miquelon is a tiny 'territorial collective' of France with a population of some 7 000. (The US state of Hawaii is considered in the statistics to be part of the Pacific region.)

North America is distinguished from other continents by the diversity of its ecosystems, ranging from tundra to tropical. Many terrestrial, freshwater, and marine ecosystem types are shared among the countries, in addition to the pathways of migratory species, ranging from songbirds and butterflies to waterfowl and whales.

Permanent snow and ice cover more than 80 percent of Greenland, and are also widespread on some of the Arctic islands of northern Canada. The Arctic tundra and taiga north of the treeline gives way to boreal forests throughout the lower two thirds of Canada. Temperate forest ecosystems stretch from the Great Lakes region to cover much of the eastern third of the USA, and extend southward through the western mountains into Mexico.

Mountain ranges form a spine dividing the western quarter of the continent, giving rise to complex ecosystems such as the Cordillera and Sierras. Mountains also strongly influence the climate of the northwest temperate rainforests as well as the intermontane desert ecosystems and Great Plains that stretch down the continent from Canada to Mexico.

Tropical dry forest ecosystems begin near the Mexican-USA border in the foothills of western Mexico's mountains, spreading southwards to Central America. Tropical humid forest ecosystems are found primarily along the Gulf of Mexico coast and the Yucatán Peninsula.

North American marine ecosystems are equally diverse – Arctic waters, under permanent to semi-permanent sea ice, give way to productive open water that supports large populations of marine mammals. The western Atlantic, with an extensive continental shelf, and warm Gulf Stream Current and cold Labrador Current, has produced a highly productive marine environment and, as a result, a centuries-old fisheries industry, now heavily depleted.

The eastern Pacific's cold temperate to tropical waters are influenced by the North Pacific Current, Alaska Gyre, and Davidson and California currents. Many species such as gray whales and sea otters range along the entire western coast. Upwellings within the Alaska Gyre have created one of the world's most productive areas for marine invertebrates.

Coastal areas of the Gulf of Mexico feature biologically diverse estuarine ecosystems, mangroves, saltmarshes, and tidal marshes, while the Caribbean Sea contains extensive coral reef and seagrass bed habitat.

In terms of identifying and prioritizing areas for conservation importance, there are some 50 centers of plant diversity located right across the

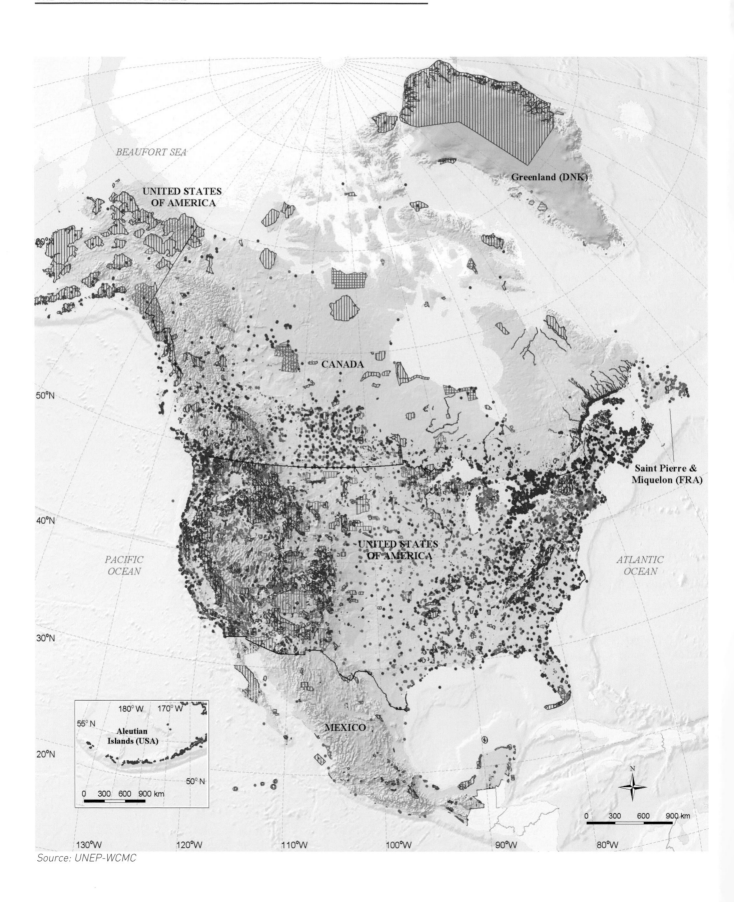

Greenland (DNK)

BEAUFORT SEA

UNITED STATES
OF AMERICA

CANADA

50°N

40°N

PACIFIC
OCEAN

UNITED STATES
OF AMERICA

ATLANTIC
OCEAN

Saint Pierre &
Miquelon (FRA)

30°N

180° W   170° W
55° N
Aleutian
Islands (USA)

20°N

50° N

0 300 600 900 km

MEXICO

N

0 300 600 900 km

130°W   120°W   110°W   100°W   90°W   80°W

Source: UNEP-WCMC

region. By contrast, endemic bird areas are largely restricted to Mexico, with only two in the US mainland and none elsewhere. At a broader level some 31 priority ecoregions (WWF Global 200) have been recognized, covering wide areas of Mexico, the western seaboard and mountains of the USA, the Appalachian region, and wide areas of Arctic biomes.

HISTORICAL PERSPECTIVE

Prior to European settlement in North America, indigenous peoples recognized and respected special areas such as productive wild game areas and sacred sites. European settlement brought temporary protection of selected areas in response to advancing settlement and resource harvesting. Formal long-term protection began about 140 years ago when areas were set aside for their outstanding scenery, and economic and recreational benefits. In 1864 the natural landscape of the Yosemite Valley and the giant sequoias of Mariposa Grove in California were first protected. The first national parks (Yellowstone (1872), Banff (1885), and Desietro de Los Leones (1917) were all protected natural landscapes around springs.

Other sites were soon established for the protection of wild species. Last Mountain Lake (1887) in Saskatchewan protected critical habitat for migratory waterfowl, while Pelican Island in Florida was established as a federal bird reservation in 1903. Isla Guadalupe (1928) protected the unique biodiversity of the island and surroundings, including three varieties of seal.

The protection of forest and freshwater resources were also seen as important criteria for setting up protected areas. Examples include many Cordilleran mountain parks and the Algonquin Provincial Park in Ontario. Areas protected for their intrinsic ecological or wilderness values began with Gila Wilderness in New Mexico in 1924.

Protecting marine ecosystems dates back to the earliest coastal wildlife refuges (Pelican Island, 1903) and bird sanctuaries that protected the inter-tidal habitat of migratory and other species, although the first sites to offer protection to subtidal resources came later. Today there are marine protected areas across the regions, including parks, marine ecological areas, no-take reserves, and multiple-use zones.

THE PROTECTED AREAS NETWORK

In the past 30 years the number of sites (IUCN Protected Area Management Categories I-VI) across North America has almost tripled to 13 554, and the area protected has increased to more than 4.10 million km², to include about 17.3 percent of the total land area. Protected areas that prohibit extractive activities (primarily IUCN Categories I-III) account for just under half of this area.

Protected area statistics for the region are heavily influenced by one site, the Greenland National Park, which is the largest protected area in

North America: Growth of protected areas network, 1872-2005

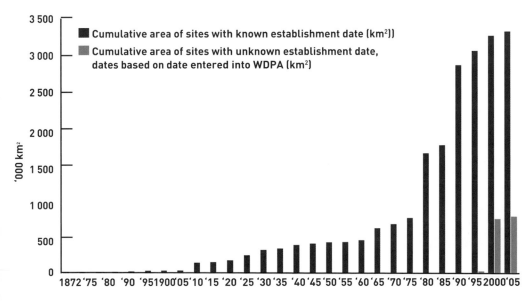

S. Chape

Yosemite National Park, USA, a World Heritage Site.

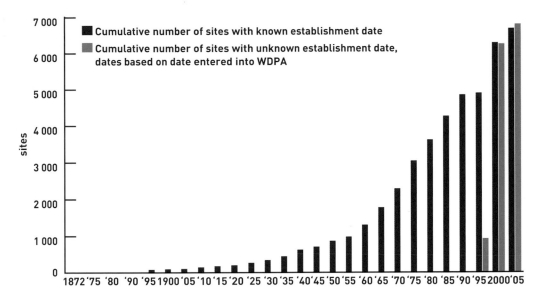

Cumulative number of sites with known establishment date

Cumulative number of sites with unknown establishment date, dates based on date entered into WDPA

North America: Growth in the number of protected areas, 1872-2005

the world at 972 000 km². If Greenland is left out, the proportion of the land surface of the region protected comes closer to 15 percent. In addition to this, designated in 1974, several other large protected areas in the vast northern areas of Canada and Alaska have been declared since the 1980s.

None of the countries can yet claim full representation of ecological regions within their protected area systems, although boreal habitats are generally well represented at the regional level. Only about 1.2 percent of the region's very extensive marine areas (out to 200 nautical miles) are protected in 754 marine protected areas covering 218 000 km² (not including Hawaii).

In Canada the federal agency Parks Canada has responsibility for some 300 000 km² of IUCN Category II protected areas. Along with many of its provincial and territorial counterparts, it has adopted park establishment strategies based on the representation of various ecosystem types. Parks Canada also has a newly legislated National Marine Conservation Areas program, also based on ensuring ecosystem representation. The Canadian

Wildlife Service manages a network of national wildlife areas and migratory bird sanctuaries. The Department of Fisheries and Oceans has recently begun establishing a network of marine protected areas (MPAs). The Canadian Wildlife Service, Parks Canada, British Columbia, and Newfoundland have all designated MPAs, but the total still represents only a very small fraction of Canada's enormous (5.6 million km²) exclusive economic zone (EEZ). Almost all provinces and territories have ecological or wilderness area programs (IUCN I) and wildlife areas (IUCN IV).

The most comprehensive protection in the USA is found within the national park network administered by the US National Parks Service. However, very large tracts of the landscape (IUCN Categories V and VI) are managed through other federal agencies such as the Bureau of Land Management, the US Forest Service, and the Fish and Wildlife Service. Except for national parks, only a small fraction of the total area is managed as wilderness, although many areas contain substantial biodiversity conservation value. The Depart-

Areas of North America protected (by country), 2005

Country/territories	Land area (km²)	Total protected area (km²)	Total number of sites
Canada	9 970 610	861 300	5 455
Greenland	2 175 600	980 099	7
Mexico	1 958 200	195 950	193
St Pierre and Miquelon	240	127	6
USA	9 612 453	2 063 337	7 833

Agreements and policies (by country)

Convention, legislation, agreement, or policy	Coverage	Key role re protected areas (PAs)
North American Agreement on Environmental Cooperation (side agreement to NAFTA)	North America	Commission on Environmental Cooperation facilitates continental cooperation on land and marine PA systems and biodiversity protection
Western Hemisphere Shorebird Network	North America	Links PAs within hemispheric migratory routes
UN Convention on Biological Diversity	Canada/Mexico	Agree to complete PA systems to protect biodiversity
Cartagena Convention	Mexico/USA	Protocol on specially protected areas & wildlife
Canada National Parks Act	Canada	Protects ecological integrity in national parks
Canada Oceans Act	Canada	Enables establishment of marine protected areas
Species at Risk Act	Canada	Identifies critical habitat requiring protection
National Park Service Organic Act	USA	Balances protection of nature and visitor use
Land and Water Conservation Fund	USA	Protects land and recreational activities
MPA Executive Order 13158	USA	Strengthens and expands a national MPA system
General Law of Ecological Equilibrium and Environment Protection (Ley General del Equilibrio Ecológico y la Protección al Ambiente – LGEEPA)	Mexico	Directs a multi-stakeholder approach to PA management
Federal Fisheries Law (Ley Federal de Pesca)	Mexico	Uses reserves and fishing bans to repopulate and preserve fisheries

ments of Commerce and the Interior through other agencies, especially the National Oceanic and Atmospheric Administration (NOAA) and the Fish and Wildlife Service, are strengthening and expanding a national system of MPAs by working closely with state, territorial, local, tribal, and other stakeholders. When complete, such a system will include most existing terrestrial-based designations as well as fishery management zones, marine sanctuaries, critical habitats, research and no-take reserves.

Mexico's protected areas network comprises six federal categories – biosphere reserves, national parks, flora and fauna protection areas, sanctuaries, natural monuments, and natural resource protection areas – making up a national system of protected areas (SINAP). Of these categories, the first four have been applied in the marine environment. The Comisión Nacional de Areas Naturales Protegidas (CONANP) is the main agency establishing Mexico's protected areas,

including MPAs. A total of 193 sites are listed in the World Database on Protected Areas, and although these probably include most or all of the federal sites, and the largest sites, it is estimated that there may be more than 500 protected areas if all state, municipal, and private protected areas are included.

Significant gaps in protection remain to be addressed. These include tallgrass and shortgrass prairie, Sonoran desert, freshwater areas such as the Mississippi watershed, temperate forests, tropical dry forests, coastal estuaries, and marine ecosystems.

The past decade has seen a number of important political and legislative changes that are influencing protected areas at the continental, regional, and national levels. Some major examples are outlined in the table.

There are also a growing number of players involved in the establishment and management of protected areas, including local and indigenous peoples, non-governmental organizations (NGOs) such as land trusts, and an increasing number of stakeholders who are practicing land and sea stewardship. New agencies, such as CONANP in Mexico, have been created to oversee diverse protected area activities. Securing protected areas has thus become an increasingly complex business; however cooperation has greatly improved, at scales from local to Americas-wide.

Other forms of protection

Innovative protected area strategies involving NGOs, landowners, coastal communities, local agencies, and indigenous communities are an increasingly important complement to government efforts. Private protected areas, particularly those established and run by NGOs, are widespread across the region. Information on many of these is held in the WDPA, but the work remains incomplete. There is a lack of coordination within and between NGOs, and at the present time the gathering of such information requires approaching (and getting responses from) hundreds of separate sources.

In Canada private non-government work is most active and effective in southern Canada. Organizations such as Ducks Unlimited, numerous nature trusts, and private conservancies are obtaining protection through mechanisms ranging from land purchases to landowner agreements. Initiatives such as the North American Waterfowl Management Plan (NAWMP) provide funding to facilitate such agreements. Changes to federal tax laws have attracted the donation of private, ecologically valuable land to registered conservation agencies. The total land area secured through private means is unknown but reaches many tens of thousands of square kilometers.

Government agencies are now routinely collaborating with stakeholders, including indigenous and local communities, in the establishment of national parks and MPAs, and there are growing numbers of examples of co-management. Multistakeholder partnerships have become an important means of reconciling diverse interests on working landscapes and seascapes.

In the USA there is a long history of including private sector ownership within protected areas. The Nature Conservancy (TNC) has established more than 1 500 preserves in the USA with nearly 39 000 km² protected. Other private land conservation programs include the Conservation Fund,

North America: Protected areas network by IUCN category, 2005

IUCN category	Total sites	Total area (km²)
Ia	839	66 384
Ib	700	472 435
II	1 345	1 657 785
III	590	72 589
IV	1 334	611 315
V	2 075	134 971
VI	1 425	1 015 141
No category	5 206	70 193
Total	13 554	4 100 813

North America: Protected areas network by IUCN category (percentage of total area protected), 2005

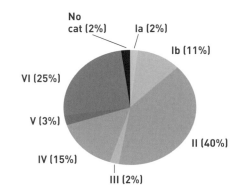

North America: Protected areas by IUCN category (percentage of protected areas), 2005

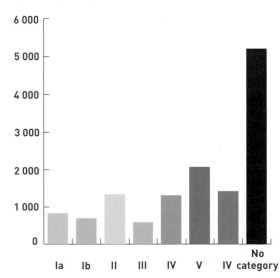

Ducks Unlimited, and Trout Unlimited. The Land Trust Alliance, a national collective, controls development on some 20 000 km² secured through landowner agreements. Operation Stronghold, an alliance of 800 to 900 private landholders who have undertaken conservation measures, protects an estimated further 20– 25 000 km² of private land. Some marine protection is now being gained through leasing arrangements.

Community protected areas within the Mexican communal landholding system (Ejidos and Comunidades) are rapidly gaining importance in states with large indigenous populations such as Oaxaca. Private conservation mechanisms are also now increasingly being adopted in Mexico, mainly through TNC's in-country partners, including conservation easements (legally binding agreements where landowners can permanently limit the type and amount of development on their property in perpetuity), transfer of development rights, and direct acquisitions. An innovative compensation mechanism has been established to protect the core zone of the Monarch Butterfly Biosphere Reserve, in which landowners are compensated for not harvesting timber with winter habitat value.

International sites

Large tracts of the region have been designated under one or more of the three major international conventions, totaling some 1.85 million km², although this statistic is once again dominated by Greenland and the 972 000 km² Greenland Biosphere Reserve. Most of this area is also legally protected through in-country designations.

Collectively there are 73 biosphere reserves across the region, the first dating back to 1976. The continental USA has 43; Mexico has 16; Canada 13; and Greenland one. Mexico has implemented a national Biosphere Reserve program, consisting of 26 sites, that is modeled on the UNESCO program.

The Ramsar Convention on Wetlands of International Importance has designated 134 sites across North America, with sites dating back to the 1980s. Most recent sites have been in Mexico, which designated 34 new sites in 2004, including some very large coastal and marine sites such as Laguna Madre, Archipiélago de Revillagigedo, and Laguna de Términos. Canada's 37 sites under Ramsar have remained stable since 1996. The largest Ramsar site is Queen Maud Gulf

North America: Internationally protected areas, 2005

Country	No. of sites	Protected area (km²)
Biosphere reserves		
Canada	13	48 529
Greenland	1	972 000
Mexico	16	71 697
USA[1]	43	312 250
TOTAL	73	1 404 476
Ramsar sites		
Canada	37	130 666
Greenland	11	13 423
Mexico	65	52 639
USA[2]	21	13 031
TOTAL	134	209 759
World Heritage sites		
Canada[3]	8	106 635
Greenland	1	4 024
Mexico	3	27 370
United States[3, 4]	11	100 407
TOTAL	23	238 436

1 Four further biosphere reserves are found in the US Virgin Islands, Puerto Rico, and Hawaii and are not included here.
2 One further Ramsar site is found in Hawaii and is not included here
3 There are two transboundary World Heritage sites between the USA and Canada – Kluane/Wrangell-St Elias/Glacier Bay/Tatshenshini-Alsek; and Waterton Glacier International Peace Park – and hence the total figure for numbers of sites is lower than the sum of all country totals.
4 One further World Heritage site is found in Hawaii and is not included here.

in Canada's Northwest Territories which extends over 62 000 km².

UNESCO's World Heritage program has designated 23 sites for their natural heritage values. The largest of these is Kluane/Wrangell-St Elias/Glacier Bay/Tatshenshini-Alsek, with 86 000 km², straddling parts of British Columbia, Yukon, and Alaska. One of the most recent, the Ilulissat Icefjord in Greenland inscribed in 2004, is one of the world's most active glaciers – moving at 19 meters per day.

In addition to the three major global protected area agreements, other global and regional conventions and treaties include provisions to safeguard species and ecosystems, thereby influencing protected area efforts. Examples include the Migratory Birds Convention (Canada, USA), the Cartagena Convention (Caribbean, Mexico, USA), the North American Plant Protection Agreement, and the UN Convention on Biological Diversity (Canada, Mexico).

An increasing number of species and ecosystem conservation agreements exist between the countries, including the North American Waterfowl Management Plan and the Western Hemisphere Shorebird Initiative. The countries are also linked through economic, social, and cultural interaction. The Commission for Environmental Cooperation (CEC) was created under the North American Free Trade Agreement (NAFTA) to facilitate this cooperation with respect to the conservation, protection, and enhancement of the North American environment.

FUTURE DIRECTIONS

The extent and complexity of North America's natural diversity demands an ecosystem approach to selecting new areas and to managing all

S.Chape

Hoh Rainforest, Olympic National Park World Heritage Site, Washington State, USA.

areas. Managing for ecological integrity while including socioeconomic interests will be a significant challenge.

The need for an ecosystem approach is heightened by a significant increase in the level of threat to the species and ecosystems that protected areas are designed to protect. These threats include land and marine uses surrounding and within protected areas, visitor impacts, resource harvesting practices, invasive species, pathogens, pollution, and climate change. Impacts from these threats include habitat degradation and fragmentation, species losses, and reduced ecological integrity. Assessing and managing the combined impact of all threats is an ongoing challenge to ecologists and managers.

Key continental directions are discussed below.

Connecting nature

Large-scale programs are linking protected areas and the landscapes or seascapes in-between. The Yellowstone to Yukon Conservation Initiative has provided a large-scale vision of both protection and sustainable use. The North American MPA Network and the Baja to Bering initiatives seek to protect ecologically critical ecosystems and promote integrated management for the marine and coastal waters of North America and the eastern Pacific, respectively. Mexico is involved in the Mesoamerican Biological Corridor and the Mesoamerican Caribbean Coral Reef Systems Initiative as well as having its national biosphere reserve program. The North American Bird Conservation Initiative (NABCI), the Western Hemisphere Shorebird Network, and other migratory species initiatives create functionally connected networks of protected areas across North America. Initiatives that connect nature and people, and land and ocean connections, are maturing and become proving grounds for putting ecosystem management principles into practice.

Systematic planning

Common terrestrial and marine ecoregional frameworks, which now exist for North America, are instrumental in protected area systems planning and connecting nature on a larger scale. Completing federal, state, provincial, and territorial protected area networks throughout North America requires a well-planned systematic approach. The NOAA's National Marine Sanctuaries Program is

striving for a systems approach that could influence other agencies throughout North America. Mexico, through the National Commission for the Conservation and Sustainable Use of Biodiversity (CONABIO) and other priority conservation exercises, has identified a large number of candidate sites waiting for the appropriate social or political opportunity to secure them.

Establishment criteria based on other factors such as ecological importance and uniqueness will complement systematic approaches. CEC's trinational focus on species of common conservation concern for grasslands, NABCI's priority-setting exercise, and the Marine Species of Common Conservation Concern program are examples. Systematic planning for networks of marine protected areas, such as through the North American MPA Network initiative, and urban protected areas are two growth areas.

Partnerships

The 100 or so major government agencies that manage protected areas are developing closer ties with scores of non-governmental agencies, special interest groups, aboriginal peoples, and an increasing number of individual stakeholders committed to stewardship. Cooperation in conservation appears to be the key operating principle associated with marine protected areas' identification, designation, and management.

Examples of agencies and programs whose success relies on partnerships include NAWMP, NABCI, Mexico's National Council of Nature Protected Areas, the Neotropical Migrants Management Plan, the US National Parks and Conservation Association, the Wilderness Society, and Defenders of Wildlife, the Nature Conservancy of Canada, the Canadian Prairie Conservation Action Plan, and the Mexican Biosphere Reserve model. For marine areas, the North American MPA Network enables the collaboration of more than 200 stakeholders concerned with conserving marine biodiversity.

Science, information, communication, and education

Protected area experts must demonstrate through good science and creative communication methods that protected areas contribute to emerging issues such as protecting endangered species, conserving biodiversity, improving the knowledge of climate change impacts, in addition to contributing to a healthy economy. Developing effective information management technology and procedures at multiple scales requires increased sophistication to support the underlying science and the development of ecological indicators. Increasing use of state of environment, state of parks, state of forests, and other reports helps to assess and convey key messages about protected areas. These and other means are aiding the communication of science to the public and decision makers, and support shifting societal attitudes towards sustainability.

Financing

The rapid growth of North American protected areas has generally been matched by decreasing resources available to manage these areas. Finding innovative financing mechanisms is critical to all future work on protected areas. Harnessing public support, lobbying, and education will help convince government decision makers of the need for more financing. A hopeful sign in Mexico has been a 1 500 percent growth of the federal budget assigned for protected areas during the last decade, an endowment fund to establish up to 22 areas, and entrance fees earmarked for management needs, resulting in improved management capacity for 61 protected areas. Other creative approaches such as the generation of green revenue from protected areas, providing more tax incentives for conservation, and engaging the non-profit sector will help ensure protected areas are fulfilling their intended purposes into the future.

The Caribbean

ANGUILLA (UK), ANTIGUA AND BARBUDA, ARUBA (NETHERLANDS), BAHAMAS, BARBADOS, BERMUDA (UK), BRITISH VIRGIN ISLANDS (UK), CAYMAN ISLANDS (UK), CUBA, DOMINICA, DOMINICAN REPUBLIC, GRENADA, GUADELOUPE (FRANCE), HAITI, JAMAICA, MARTINIQUE (FRANCE), MONTSERRAT (UK), NETHERLANDS ANTILLES (NETHERLANDS), PUERTO RICO (USA), ST KITTS AND NEVIS, ST LUCIA, ST VINCENT AND THE GRENADINES, TRINIDAD AND TOBAGO, TURKS AND CAICOS ISLANDS (UK), UNITED STATES VIRGIN ISLANDS (USA)

Contributors: R. Estrada, J. l. Gerhartz, E. Hernández, R. Fernández de Arcila, J. A. Hernández, P. Ruiz, A. Perera, G. Bustamante, K. Lindeman, A. Vanzella Khouri

REGIONAL DESCRIPTION

The Caribbean region, as defined by the World Commission on Protected Areas (WCPA), incorporates the two major island chains that border the north and the east of the Caribbean Sea, the Greater and Lesser Antilles, and also the island territories of the western Atlantic: the Bahamas, the Turks and Caicos Islands, and Bermuda.

Plate tectonics have created many of the present-day landforms. The Greater Antilles were largely formed by the strike-slip motion of the Caribbean Tectonic Plate against the North American Plate. By contrast the Lesser Antilles were formed by a more active subduction process, and contain a number of active volcanoes, including Morne Trois Pitons in Dominica, Soufriere in St Lucia, Mont Peleé in Martinique, Soufriere in Montserrat (which has been undergoing continuous

Rainforest at El Yunque, Puerto Rico.

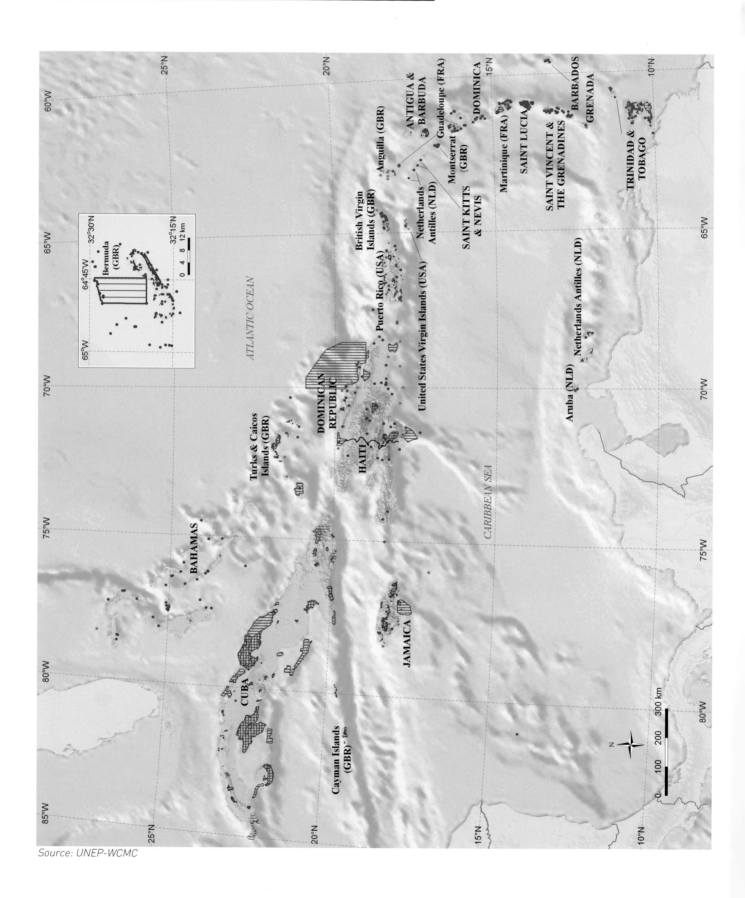

Source: UNEP-WCMC

destructive activity since 1995), and the underwater volcano 'Kick 'em Jenny,' near Grenada.

Limestone deposition has also shaped this region. The Bahamas archipelago is built over a series of shallow carbonate banks formed from both coral deposits and the chemical precipitation of limestone particles (oolites). These limestone deposits have also been modified into a wide variety of karst landforms, including the marine terraces at Maisi and Cabo Cruz, Cuba; the cavern systems in Cuba, Dominican Republic, Puerto Rico, and the Bahamas; and the more complex landforms of hills and caves found in Viñales (Cuba), Los Haitises (Dominican Republic), Pepino Hills (Puerto Rico), and Cockpit Country (Jamaica). Collapsed sink-holes or dolines which have since been filled by the sea have also formed the famous blue holes which are found across the Bahamas.

The region includes more than 5 000 islands and cays, with some 700 being more than 1 km², which constitute 25 island nations or overseas territories. Biogeographically the region traverses the Tropic of Cancer, and encompasses a unique and diverse array of landscapes, ranging from ocean basins and deep troughs, coral reefs, seagrass ecosystems, mangroves, and extensive beaches, to mountains, forests, and semi-deserts. Located between two continents the region has been both a bridge and a barrier for species movements, and a center of evolutionary processes.

Although occupying only about 0.1 percent of the Earth's terrestrial surface, it is home to 2 to 3 percent of all known vertebrates and plant species. The region includes five of the 237 ecoregions (the Global 200) classified by WWF as areas of conservation priority (Greater Antillean Marine, Greater Antillean Freshwaters, Greater Antillean Moist Forests, Greater Antillean Pine Forests, Southern Caribbean Sea), while the entire region is described by Conservation International as a hotspot. About 58 percent of the 12 000 plant species and about 51 percent of the 1 500 terrestrial vertebrates are endemic. Cuba is particularly important in terms of endemic species, and about half of the region's 6 550 single-island endemic plants are from Cuba. Taking the relation between endemism and area, the insular Caribbean has one of the highest endemism indices in the world (Mittermeier, Meyers & Mittermeier, 1999). Many species, including lizards and birds such as trogons, todies, and parrots, are endemic to single islands, or island groups. Almost all of the region has been incorporated into a series of six endemic bird areas by Birdlife International, and many species of bird are restricted to single islands. For plants a slightly different pattern has been recognized, with 12 centers of plant diversity.

Prior to European 'discovery' there had already been several waves of human settlement, with the first arrivals in Cuba dating back to 5 000-6 000 BC. Three major groups were present before the European arrival – the Ciboney people, restricted to parts of Cuba; the Arawak (Taino or Lucayan) people across the Greater Antilles and the

Caribbean: Growth of protected areas network, 1910-2005

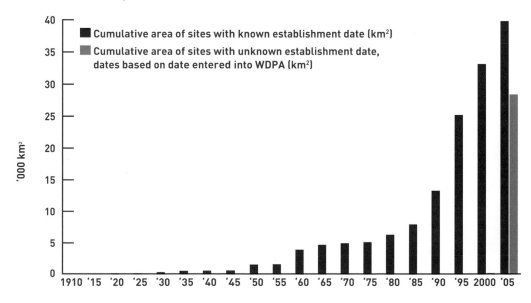

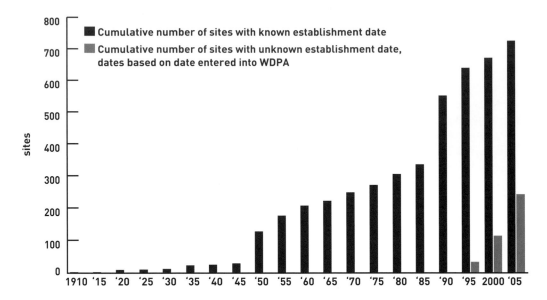

Caribbean: Growth in the number of protected areas, 1910-2005

Bahamas; and the Carib people in the Lesser Antilles. European settlement wrought massive changes, with the disappearance of these peoples from most islands within one or two generations. A few remain, but today the islands have developed a complex mosaic of cultures and ethnic groups combining indigenous American, Hispanic, African, Anglo-Saxon, French, and Asian cultures.

Human influences on the natural environment have been widespread, and most particularly over the last three decades. There is evidence of localized overfishing in a few islands even before the arrival of Europeans, but since this time the changes have been profound. Wide tracts of land were cleared for plantation agriculture, while population growth has driven agricultural clearances high up on mountain slopes. Today less than 10 percent of the original vegetation remains, and overfishing is reported everywhere.

The driving forces behind these problems include local issues such as poverty, economic inequality, or uncontrolled development, but international issues also impinge heavily on this region, due to the small size and high degree of connection between countries. Some issues, such as fisheries, require attention at regional level. Others, such as climate changes, the depletion of the ozone layer, globalization, and the creation of socioeconomic blocks and trade barriers, are problems facing most parts of the world. There remain, however, great opportunities for the region including ongoing efforts for regional integration, sustainable tourism, and the existing and enhanced protection of unique and highly valuable natural resources.

HISTORICAL PERSPECTIVE

With the widescale loss of traditions and cultures from the original inhabitants of the Caribbean, there is little information regarding any efforts they may have made at natural resource management, such as the closure or protection of wild areas. The history of protected areas in the Caribbean thus dates back to the colonial era, and to the first protected area established in 1765. This site, the Main Ridge Reserve of Tobago, was established as 'woodlands for the protection of the rain' (Cross 1991). In 1791, the Kings Hill Reserve was established in St Vincent for 'the purpose of attracting the clouds and rain... for the benefit and advantage of the owners and possessors of lands in the neighborhood thereof' (Birdsey, Weaver & Nicholls, 1986).

The earliest marine protected area in the western hemisphere were the Sea Gardens which lay between Hog and Athol Islands in the Bahamas, established in 1892 (although no longer regarded as a protected area, these waters are still very popular with tourists). Other protected areas were established in Jamaica in 1907 (the Morant and Pedro Cays, still nominally protected), Puerto Rico (the Caribbean or Luquillo National Forest, 1907),

Grenada (Grand Etang Forest Reserve, 1910), and Cuba (Sierra Cristal National Park, 1930).

Despite these relatively early origins, the widescale declaration of protected areas was relatively slow in the Caribbean region – even by the mid-1980s fewer than 400 sites had been declared in the 25 territories. The momentum for their establishment has increased tremendously over the last 20 years, however, particularly since the Earth Summit held in 1992 at Rio de Janeiro. This interest has been enhanced in some cases by increasing evidence of the economic and social value of protected areas in supporting valuable ecotourism, and in improving fisheries.

THE PROTECTED AREAS NETWORK

The World Database on Protected Areas (WDPA) lists some 967 protected areas in the region, covering 68 196 km². Over half of this area is marine; however, the total land area protected is still more than 36 000 km², or almost 15.5 percent of the region's terrestrial surface.

Notably, protected areas are concentrated in IUCN Management Categories II, IV, and VI, and indeed the stricter levels of protection (I-III) make up less than one third of the total number of sites.

The breakdown of sites by country shows that there is considerable variation in the total area protected. Figures appear relatively high in relation to land areas, but it should be remembered that many sites are marine and coastal ones, and a number of countries and territories, including the Bahamas, Cuba, the Cayman Islands, Netherlands Antilles, Turks and Caicos Islands, and Bermuda, include extensive marine areas in their boundaries.

There are an estimated 370 marine and coastal sites in total, and they play a very important role in the conservation of coastal biodiversity resources for human use both locally and regionally. The number of strictly protected areas (no-take zones) is estimated to be more than 25 in this region. These include a number of sites, such as the Soufriere Marine Management Area in St Lucia, which have been highlighted for their positive contribution to both conservation and to improved livelihoods for fishers, by breaking the cycle of overfishing. Among other sites there is considerable variability in management effectiveness (Appeldoorn & Lindeman, 2003).

Despite the progress, networks of protected areas have developed unevenly and are incomplete in many parts of the insular Caribbean (WCPA,

Caribbean: Protected areas network by IUCN category, 2005

IUCN category	Total sites	Total area (km²)
Ia	11	183
Ib	18	92
II	163	26 972
III	40	497
IV	283	11 195
V	37	3 567
VI	192	22 222
No category	223	3 467
Total	967	68 196

Caribbean: Protected areas network by IUCN category (percentage of total area), 2005

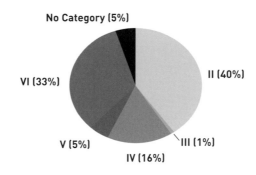

Caribbean: Number of protected areas by IUCN category, 2005

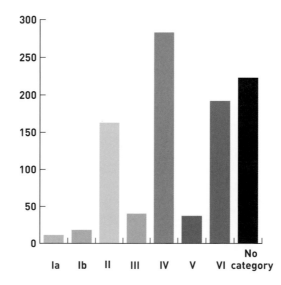

M .Spalding

SPAW PROTOCOL

The Convention for the Protection and Development of the Marine Environment in the Wider Caribbean Region (Cartagena Convention, 1983) is one of the only region-wide environmental treaties that protects critical marine and coastal ecosystems, while promoting regional cooperation and sustainable development.

In April 1990, Parties to the Cartagena Convention adopted 'the Protocol Concerning Specially Protected Areas and Wildlife (SPAW Protocol),' a regional agreement for biodiversity management and conservation. This Protocol became international law in June 2000.

The governments of the Caribbean recognize SPAW as a significant vehicle to assist with implementation of the Convention on Biological Diversity (CBD), and an important complementary tool to implement the protected area national plans. Cooperative agreements exist with other global initiatives related to and collaborating with SPAW including the Ramsar Convention and the Intergovernmental Oceanographic Commission (IOC). Further collaboration exists with the Convention on International Trade in Endangered Species (CITES), the Convention on the Conservation of Migratory Species of Wild Animals (Bonn Convention), the International Coral Reef Initiative (ICRI), and ICRI's Global Coral Reef Monitoring Network. The main objectives of SPAW are as follows:

❑ Safeguard sensitive habitats. Protect, preserve, and sustainably manage critical ecosystems such as coral reefs and mangroves, and promote their value to ecological health and economic well-being.

❑ Protect endangered and critical species. Undertake conservation measures to protect threatened and endangered species of plants and animals, as well as measures to prevent species from becoming threatened or endangered, and to ensure recovery and restoration.

❑ Provide support to the Caribbean Environmental Programme (CEP) member governments in the following areas:

promotion of best practices and training for sustainable tourism within the public and private sectors;

monitoring and management of coral reef ecosystems;

establishing a regional network of marine protected areas and an accompanying database to assist these areas with information sharing and problem solving;

strengthening of protected areas through technical assistance, training, capacity building, and revenue generation;

developing guidelines and recovery plans for species conservation;

linking to other protocols of the Cartagena Convention;

education and public awareness on species and ecosystems conservation and sustainable management.

(Modified from SPAW Brochure)

Areas of the Caribbean protected (by country), 2005

Country/territories	Land area (km²)	Total protected area (km²)	Total number of sites
Anguilla	90	<1	8
Antigua and Barbuda	440	66	13
Aruba	190	3	4
Bahamas	13 880	2 832	45
Barbados	430	3	7
Bermuda	50	154	132
Cayman Islands	260	241	48
Cuba	110 860	35 192	70
Dominica	750	204	7
Dominican Republic	48 730	20 451	62
Grenada	340	7	2
Guadeloupe	1 710	456	22
Haiti	27 750	74	9
Jamaica	10 990	3 909	168
Martinique	1 100	774	25
Montserrat	100	11	18
Netherlands Antilles	800	144	15
Puerto Rico	8 950	2 187	58
Saint Kitts and Nevis	270	26	2
Saint Lucia	620	104	52
Saint Vincent and the Grenadines	390	83	28
Trinidad and Tobago	5 130	322	86
Turks and Caicos Islands	430	717	34
Virgin Islands (British)	150	52	35
Virgin Islands (US)	340	183	17

2003). Only 30 percent of the marine protected areas in the region are considered to be adequately managed (PNUMA, 2000). Ongoing assessments of biodiversity and its protection are producing a more detailed vision of the creation and efficient management of protected areas, individually or as national systems, as tools to preserve the interrelated suite of biodiversity values in the region. However, national and regional strategies developed to date for protected areas have not been entirely successful (WCPA, 2003).

International efforts

Certain of the region's characteristics, such as its consisting of small nations with high connectivity, mean that the Caribbean requires the joint cooperation of all its nations, territories, and other regional jurisdictions to achieve integrated biodiversity management. Despite this, participation in some of the major global agreements for the establishment of protected areas has been relatively poor across the Caribbean. The larger countries, notably Cuba, and also several of the smaller territories of France, the UK, the Netherlands, and the USA, are more actively involved, but many of the smaller independent nations are not. This may reflect some of the difficulties and costs of working at the global level for small, low-income countries rather than pointing to any lack of interest. For this reason regional cooperation may be more important in the Caribbean than for many other regions.

In 1990 the Caribbean states adopted the Specially Protected Areas and Wildlife (SPAW) Protocol as one important measure for collaborative biodiversity protection (see box). This protocol has become the main cooperation mechanism for many aspects of conservation in the region, with a key leadership role.

Other regional groupings include a number of intergovernmental organizations such as the Association of Caribbean States (ACS), the Caribbean Community (CARICOM), the Caribbean Forum (CARIFORUM), and the Organization of Eastern Caribbean States (OECS). There are a number of important regional non-governmental

Caribbean: Internationally protected areas, 2005

Country/territories	No. of sites	Protected area (km²)
Biosphere reserves		
Cuba	6	13 837
Dominican Republic	1	4 767
Guadeloupe	1	697
Puerto Rico	2	41
US Virgin Islands	1	61
TOTAL	11	19 539
Ramsar sites		
Antigua and Barbuda	1	36
Aruba	1	1
Bahamas	1	326
Barbados	1	0
Bermuda	7	0
Cayman Islands	1	1
Cuba	6	11 884
Dominican Republic	1	200
Jamaica	2	132
Netherlands Antilles	5	19
St Lucia	2	1
Trinidad and Tobago	3	159
Turks and Caicos Islands	1	586
TOTAL	32	13 346
World Heritage sites		
Cuba	2	1 038
Dominica	1	69
St Lucia	1	29
TOTAL	4	1 136

organizations including the Caribbean Conservation Association (CCA), the Island Resources Foundation (IRF), and the Caribbean Natural Resources Institute (CANARI). External international conservation organizations are also increasingly active in the Caribbean, including The Nature Conservancy (TNC), the Ocean Conservancy, WWF, Conservation International (CI), and Environmental Defense (ED).

One important regional project is the Caribbean Regional Environment Programme (CREP) being implemented by CARIFORUM. A major component of this project are the amenity areas demonstration activities, which focus on existing or proposed protected areas that provide benefits to local communities. CREP is undertaking ten demonstration activities in ten insular Caribbean countries during a 30-month period which started in July 2003.

UNEP-CEP, the Caribbean Environment Programme, is jointly operated as a UNEP Regional Seas Programme and the implementing mechanism for the Cartagena Convention. The SPAW program is coordinated by a Regional Co-ordinating Unit (RCU) in Jamaica.

FUTURE DIRECTIONS

In October 2002 a WCPA Caribbean Regional Planning in Nassau, Bahamas, considered how it might take protected area issues forward in the region, providing tangible benefits for members, and enhancing the development of protected areas. Critical among the conclusions were the development of a strategic program which would link regional protected areas in general and marine protected areas in particular. It was seen as especially critical to:

- ❑ work toward the development of a comprehensive network of protected areas with full ecological representation;
- ❑ use existing policy targets as well as existing regional alliances (such as, but not limited to, the World Summit on Sustainable Development, SPAW, and CARICOM);
- ❑ elevate the Caribbean region in global conservation policy decision making;
- ❑ build short-term deliverables for early success on which expanded, long-term work could then be founded.

J Tyndale-Bisae/UNEP

Blue Mountains, Jamaica

Central America

BELIZE, COSTA RICA, EL SALVADOR, GUATEMALA, HONDURAS, NICARAGUA, PANAMA

Contributor: J. C. Godoy Herrera

REGIONAL DESCRIPTION

The seven countries of Central America make up one of the smaller World Commission on Protected Areas (WCPA) regions, covering a combined territorial area of 521 600 km². Within this area they are home to 8 percent of the world's known plant species and an extraordinary diversity of landscapes and habitats. This region forms the land bridge connecting the Americas, but also stands as a barrier between the Caribbean Sea and the Pacific Ocean.

The land area has largely been formed by the subduction of the Cocos and Nazca tectonic plates beneath the Caribbean Plate. This process has thrown up extensive areas of highlands close to the Pacific coast, including a conspicuous volcanic chain rising to more than 4 000 meters. The mountain slopes are home to extensive areas of rainforest with cloud forests on the higher areas. There are typically narrow, dry lowlands along the Pacific coast and the more extensive and humid lowlands of the Caribbean. Mean precipitation ranges are between 500 and 7 500 millimeters per year. There are mangrove areas (more than 500 000 hectares) along both coasts and coral reefs in the offshore waters. The latter are extensive in the Caribbean waters, and the region includes large numbers of coral islands, particularly off Belize, Honduras, Nicaragua, and Panama. There are few islands close to the Pacific coast, but the volcanic Isla del Coco National Park and World Heritage site is an important exception.

Almost the entire region has been included in the Conservation International Mesoamerican hot-spot, which also extends far into Mexico. There are an estimated 15 000–17 000 plant species (others estimate 20 000) and rates of endemism have been estimated at about 19 percent. Eight separate centers of plant endemism have been described. Six important ecoregions have been singled out in Central America (WWF Global 200 ecoregions), including the Mesoamerican pine-oak forests, Talamancan-Isthmian Pacific forests, and the Chocó-Darién moist forests extending from eastern Panama into Colombia. The marine waters include parts of the Southern Caribbean ecoregion, the Mesoamerican reef, and the Panama Bight.

Central America also possesses a rich array of animal species, with elements from North and South America as well as many endemics. Birdlife International has identified some eight endemic bird areas in the region. Guatemala has some 250 mammal species, and 929 bird species have been described from Panama.

The region is one that is exposed to considerable natural threats – hurricanes, earthquakes, volcanic eruptions, flooding, and even localized drought have all ravaged parts of the region in recent times. Human pressures come on top of these natural problems, and often greatly exacerbate their impact.

The combined population of 38 million is heavily centered in the central volcanic chain and along the Pacific coast. Population growth rates are high, and industrial development is growing in the areas of highest population density, and along coasts. More than 70 percent of the region's sewage remains untreated, while solid waste is a problem in many areas. Agriculture is critical to the region, including the production of export crops such as

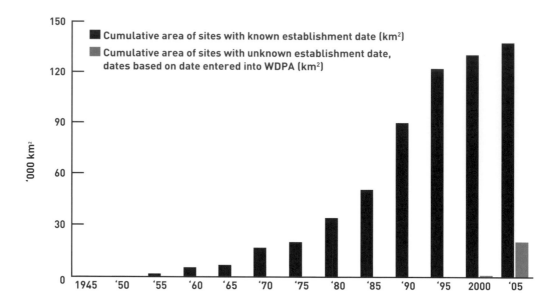

Central America: Growth of protected areas network, 1945-2005

coffee, cocoa, sugar, and bananas. Unfortunately, this agriculture, particularly for export markets, is linked to high levels of agrichemical use, further adding to pollution problems.

HISTORICAL DEVELOPMENT

The date of the first human arrivals in Central America is still disputed, although it seems likely that populations were widespread by 8 000-9 000 BC. Unlike the Caribbean islands, many indigenous

peoples of Central America still remain, and some continue to practice traditional lifestyles, with simple agriculture, hunting, and fishing. Such life-styles for the most part remain highly sustainable, and territorial ownership and rights have been given back to these people. These lands are often listed as part of the protected areas coverage.

Protected areas came to Central America very slowly. The oldest site is Barro Colorado Island in Panama which was first established as a biological

Central America: Growth in the number of protected areas, 1945-2005

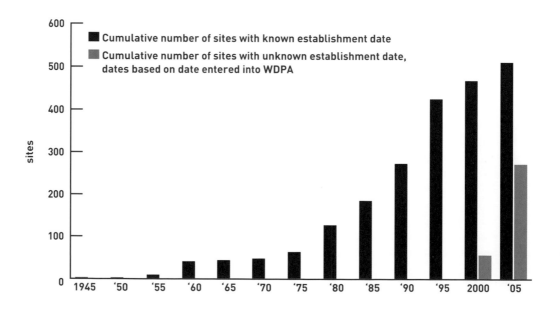

Bo L Christiensen/UNEP

Cloud forest, Costa Rica.

Source: UNEP-WCMC

reserve in 1923. Belize established a more systematic approach of Crown reserves and forest reserves, beginning with the declaration of Half Moon Cay Crown Reserve in 1928. Panama gave recognition and partial autonomy to the Kuna people and their land (the Kuna Yala Indigenous Commarc) in 1938. In 1955 Guatemala declared ten national parks and the protected area systems in most countries began after this date. In 1964 there were still fewer than 100 protected areas in Central America but, despite this late start, the region has become one of the most extensively protected in the world.

Forest clearance for timber or agricultural development has been very high since the 1960s and 1970s, although rates of loss are a little lower today (2 500-3 000 km^2 per year for the region). In many areas the only natural forests remaining are those within protected areas, but the protected areas themselves are also subject to considerable pressures. These include problems of poor site demarcation and disputes over land ownership. Pressures for development within protected areas come from sectors ranging from tourism to mineral extraction. Illegal forestry, clearance, and settlement by small-scale farmers, drug cultivation, and illegal hunting and fishing are all problems, and, as the intervening land areas are converted to other uses, habitat fragmentation is a growing problem.

THE PROTECTED AREAS NETWORK

In total there are some 783 protected areas across Central America, covering a total of 157 933 km^2; 103 of these sites are marine or coastal. Terrestrial sites, however, predominate, and cover in total more than 30 percent of the land area, making this the most extensive terrestrial protected areas network of any WCPA region.

Less than one third of sites fall into the stricter IUCN Protected Area Management Categories (I-III),

with the remainder having some degree of multiple use. A very large proportion of sites are of unassigned IUCN management category, and these include a number of sites which may have relatively low levels of protection such as biological corridors and buffer zones.

Looking at individual countries, El Salvador stands out for its low levels of protection, although there are a large number of sites in this country which are currently being considered for protection. Costa Rica has the largest number of protected areas, although for its size Belize has better protection. The high figures for Belize include a number of sizable marine protected areas.

In terms of ecosystem cover, well represented ecoregions include Belize Wetlands (Belize); Panama Humid Forests (Costa Rica, Panama); the Central American Pacific dry forest (Nicaragua, Costa Rica); the pine forests of La Mosquita (Honduras, Nicaragua); the mangroves of Golfo de Fonseca (El Salvador, Honduras, Nicaragua) and the Yucatán (Belize, Guatemala); and the Southern Reefs (Costa Rica, Panama). Less well represented ecoregions include: the Sierra Madre Humid Forest (Guatemala and El Salvador); the high forests of Central America (Guatemala, El Salvador, Honduras, Nicaragua); the Nicoya Seasonal Humid Forest (Costa Rica); the Nenton dry mountain (Guatemala); the Panama dry forest (Panama); the pine forest Islas de la Bahia (Honduras); the Peten savannas (Guatemala); the Cuchumatanes Paramo (Guatemala); and the Valley of Motagua (Guatemala).

Administrative regimes vary considerably between the countries. In Belize protected areas fall under three different ministries: the Forestry Department in the Ministry of Natural Resources and Environment; the Fisheries Department in the Ministry of Fishing, Agriculture and Co-operatives; and the Archaeology Department in the Ministry of Tourism. Each one maintains its financial and

Areas of Central America protected (by country), 2005

Country	Land area (km^2)	Total protected area (km^2)	Total number of sites
Belize	22 960	11 320	106
Costa Rica	51 100	17 724	183
El Salvador	21 040	280	77
Guatemala	108 890	35 941	163
Honduras	112 090	29 762	99
Nicaragua	130 000	29 406	93
Panama	75 520	33 501	62

Central America: Protected areas network by IUCN category, 2005

IUCN category	Total sites	Total area (km²)
Ia	18	4 125
Ib	3	342
II	104	40 028
III	48	2 222
IV	225	13 247
V	5	1 248
VI	100	44 615
No category	280	52 106
Total	783	157 933

Central America: Protected areas network by IUCN category (percentage of total area), 2005

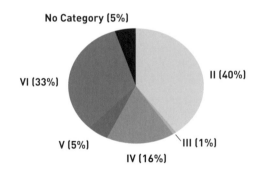

Central America: Number of protected areas by IUCN category, 2005

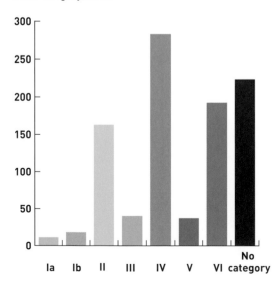

administrative independence and defines its own policies. By contrast, in Costa Rica, El Salvador, Nicaragua, and Panama protected areas all fall under the remit of a single ministry.

In both Guatemala and Honduras there is some coordination of effort between the various responsible agencies. Guatemala has a Protected Areas National Council (CONAP), which is made up of government and academic representatives, including the ministries responsible for protected areas. In Honduras the Environment Natural Resources Secretariat (SERNA) coordinates and assesses policies related to the environment, although implementation of protected areas falls under both agriculture and forestry sectors.

A number of countries have also declared protected areas at the subnational level, including El Salvador, Guatemala, and Honduras. It is not clear how well these have been recorded within the WCPA; however their total contribution to protected area statistics across the region is probably still relatively small.

Other forms of protection
Private reserves have now been established in a number of countries. In Costa Rica there are more than 90 private reserves covering about 650 km², some 22 percent of which have some level of state recognition. In Guatemala private reserves have been recognized by protected areas legislation since 1989: by 2003 more than 50 reserves were recognized, covering 207 km².

Non-governmental organizations (NGOs) are important in coordinating and supporting the development of protected areas, including the Voluntary Reserve Net in Costa Rica and the Private Reserve Association in Guatemala. In Belize there is only one private reserve, although this site covers some 926 km².

International approaches
Considering the relatively small size of the region, a large number of sites have been designated under international agreements. The largest are two biosphere reserves, the 22 000 km² Bosawas Biosphere Reserve in northern Nicaragua, dominated by lowland forests, and the 21 000 km² Maya Biosphere Reserve in Guatemala. The latter site includes the Tikal National Park, a mixed World Heritage site, and the Natural Park Laguna del Tigre, a Ramsar site.

In addition to these global efforts, there is

considerable coordination of protected area activities within the region, particularly since the establishment of the Convention for the Conservation of the Biodiversity and the Protection of Wilderness Areas in Central America (Managua, 1992).

This convention requires, *inter alia*, that:

❑ Each country should develop conservation strategies... that should include, as a priority, the creation and management of protected areas (Article 14).

❑ Efforts should be made to ensure representative samples of the regional ecosystems are protected (Article17).

❑ Particular areas are singled out for attention, including: Reserva de la Biosfera Maya; Reserva de la Biosfera Fraternidad o Trifinio; Golfo de Honduras; Golfo de Fonseca; Reserva Rio Coco o Solidaridad; Cayos Miskitos; Sistema Internacional de Areas Protegidas para la Paz; Reserva Bahia Salinas; Reserva de la Biosfera La Amistad; Reserva del Sixaola; Region del Darien (Article18).

❑ The Central American Commission on Environment and Development (CCAD) is responsible for ensuring the development and implementation of the Action Plan 1989-2000 for the creation and strengthening of a Central American Protected Areas System (SICAP) (Article 20).

❑ Associated to the CCAD it establishes a Central American Council of Protected Areas (CCPA), to work with the WCPA, to help coordinate regional efforts and ensure that SICAP becomes an effective Mesoamerican Biological Corridor (Article 21).

In 1997, during the Presidents' Summit in Panama, a conceptual plan for the Mesoamerican Biological Corridor (CBM) was adopted. This provides "A system for territorial planning, made up of natural areas...nucleus areas, buffer zones, multiple use areas and connecting areas that together provide environmental goods and services to the Central American society and the wider world." The CBM thus offers a strategic program to support a better balance between local socioeconomic needs, development, and the maintenance of natural resources.

Transboundary initiatives have also grown considerably since 1974, notably with the Trifinio or La Fraternidad Biosphere Reserve between

Central America: Internationally protected areas, 2005

Country	No. of sites	Protected area (km²)
Biosphere reserves		
Costa Rica	2	7 290
Guatemala	2	23 496
Honduras	1	8 000
Nicaragua	2	35 744
Panama	2	15 149
TOTAL	9	89 678
Ramsar sites		
Belize	1	167
Costa Rica	11	5 053
El Salvador	1	16
Guatemala	4	5 027
Honduras	5	1 797
Nicaragua	8	4 055
Panama	4	1 599
TOTAL	34	17 714
World Heritage sites		
Belize	1	963
Costa Rica[1]	3	8 433
Guatemala	1	576
Honduras	1	5 000
Panama[1]	2	8 040
TOTAL	7	23 012

1 The Talamanca Range-La Amistad Reserves/La Amistad National Park is a transboundary World Heritage site between Costa Rica and Panama and hence the total figure for number of sites is lower than the sum of all country totals.

Guatemala, Honduras, and El Salvador; La Amistad Reserve between Costa Rica and Panama; and the Protected Areas System for Peace (SIAPAZ), between Nicaragua and Costa Rica. Other transboundary areas being considered for more active development include Rio Coco/Bosawas/Río Plátano/Tawanka, between Honduras and Nicaragua; the Area Chiquibul/Montañas Mayas between Guatemala and Belize; and the initiative to create a Protected Areas System in Gran Peten (SIAP), between Mexico, Guatemala, and Belize (Calakmul, Mirador/Río Azul, y Río Bravo/Lamanai).

Another form of international collaboration comes from the support provided by international agencies. During the 1990s it was estimated that at least 33 international organizations (notably

SGR Warner/UNEP

Rio Chagres, Panama

from Germany, the EU, Canada, the USA, Spain, the Netherlands, and the Scandinavian countries) contributed technical and financial assistance to approximately 70 projects that benefited roughly 145 protected areas. Such support has encouraged national, binational, and multinational projects through the region.

FUTURE DIRECTIONS

Despite the large extent of protected areas, a number of important or unique ecosystems are not adequately covered. Priorities for improved protection include Los Morrales de Pasaquina in Chalatenango, El Salvador; the Morazan region in the semi-arid zone and Los Cuchumatanes cold high plateau in Guatemala; the pine forests in Guanaja Island in Honduras; the Maya Mountains in the south of Belize; and the Volcanic Cordillera of Guanacaste or Tilaran in Costa Rica. Coastal wetlands are another priority for protection.

In the most densely populated areas, typically along the Pacific coast and the medium-to-high plains, protected areas are often small and are also more threatened by various human pressures. In these areas there is an urgent need to protect remaining vegetation relicts, create corridors, and restore degraded areas.

Many sites are still not clearly demarcated in the field and there may still be disputes over land ownership and registration. Only about one third of sites have even a minimal institutional or staffing presence on the ground and, even among these, management may be poor. There are a growing number of initiatives to promote co-administration and management as a means of bringing in further support and utilizing the growing interest of civil society in protected areas. Many ground staff are already paid by NGOs or other partners rather than by central governmental sources.

Priorities for the future

Protected areas conservation in Central America has improved considerably during the last decade. Critical issues facing the future of protected areas management are those of funding, sustainable management, local and stakeholder involvement, and international cooperation.

From a management perspective the states can no longer afford sole responsibility for protected areas. At the same time adjacent communities are increasingly interested in becoming involved. For both of these reasons it will be important to broaden stakeholder participation and encourage co-management. While states may need to remain the final arbiters of protected areas issues, decentralization of technical and administrative tasks to local stakeholders (including indigenous peoples) and local governments should reduce costs and improve efficiency. There may also be calls to hand over management of certain sites to private non-profit initiatives, which may be able to offer independent funding and other resources to ensure good management.

There is a considerable need to improve the capacity for management on the ground. This should include better pay and living conditions for staff, including training programs and even exchanges with other protected areas to encourage the transfer of ideas. Linked to such improvements will be the development of greater professionalism within the workforce, which is currently dominated by young, temporary personnel, no doubt in part due to poor funding and a lack of secure or tenured management positions. Many sites also need transport and telecommunications equipment to improve administration efficiency.

Park boundaries and legal systems also need improvement. Clearer demarcation of boundaries is required, and in many cases funds and administrative support are needed to buy, or compensate, individuals whose land falls within sites. Communication between administrative agencies must be improved, and the level of penalties must be raised to reduce levels of infringement within protected areas. Greater support at the levels of highest political authority is needed to ensure the stability and security of protected areas management.

A broad array of efforts will be needed to improve funding. Large-scale international support may be required for land purchase and the development of large new sites. International partners may also help in more general management costs. It will be important to support conservation in private lands, including the possibility of subsidies, tax breaks, or payment for environmental services on these lands. Protected areas balance sheets must be moved away from simply paying salaries (currently 90-97 percent of states' budgets) to a more balanced spending on other resources, outreach, and training. More innovative funding, including entrance fees, tourism, or other concessions, permitted sustainable uses, and handicrafts need to be developed.

Additionally, technical studies which provide proper economic valuations of goods and services provided by protected areas, including water production, carbon fixation, and recreational values, will help to convince national agencies of the need for adequate funding for protected areas. As tourism grows across the region such activities must be developed in harmony with the environment, while mechanisms must be found to ensure that a share of the benefits accrued from tourism is returned to offset protected areas management costs.

It is necessary to build capacity for monitoring and assessing status and change in protected areas, in order to direct management. Linked to this is a need for biological inventories for each protected area. There is also a need to be able to further adjust and refine the national systems of protected areas. In particular it may be necessary to ensure full ecosystem representation and support projects that build connectivity between sites, perhaps establishing minimum targets of protection for all ecoregions and supporting the development of biological corridors.

Outreach and education to the wider society will help build support for protected areas, and increase the benefits these areas provide, while engendering greater environmental responsibility. Visitor facilities should be constructed in the more accessible areas, and environmental education in civil society should be broadened.

Regional collaboration is already good in Central America, and should continue – there are considerable economies of scale from such collaboration, enabling the sharing of planning, training, management, and technical assistance. The region would benefit from information exchange as a form of capacity building between sites and countries.

Global climate change is likely to affect many Central American protected areas, although changes may not be evident for some years. The region must be aware of these threats, particularly in mountain and cloud-forest ecosystems, and in coastal ecosystems (river deltas, brackish waters, or small islands, coral reefs). Possible management interventions must be considered.

Brazil

Contributors: A. B. Rylands, M. T. da Fonseca, R. B. Machado, L. P. de S. Pinto, R. B. Cavalcanti

REGIONAL DESCRIPTION

Brazil is the fifth largest country in the world, occupying more than half of South America, with a land area of 8 547 400 km². The Amazon Basin, bounded by the ancient crystalline shields of Guyana (in the north) and Brazil (in the south), and the Andes to the west, occupies slightly more than half the country. The tropical forests there, along with the Atlantic coast forests (including *Araucaria* pine forests), and further forest areas inland in the south and southeast, cover some 3.6 million km².

The natural vegetation of the central plateau of Brazil is sclerophytic savanna and savanna forest (the Cerrado), and to the west, on the borders with Bolivia and Paraguay, is the enormous floodplain of the Rio Paraguay, the so-called Pantanal. The northeast of Brazil is characterized by tropical xerophytic vegetation and deciduous thorn scrub (the Caatinga), much of it being secondary vege-tation, formed over former humid and dry forest areas that existed in pre-Columbian times. Both the Atlantic forest and the Cerrado rank as biodiversity hotspots: both have extraordinary levels of diversity and endemism, and both have been devastated by human activities. The Atlantic forest is today reduced to about 7 percent of its original extent of 1.2 to 1.6 million km². Subtropical grasslands (the Campos Sulinos) predominate in the far south.

The Brazilian coastline extends for 7 491 km, characterized by *restinga* (scrub and forest on sandy soils) and globally significant estuaries, mudflats, and mangroves. Cliffs and rocky shores are found, especially in the south, associated with the southern hills, the Serra do Mar. Oceanic islands include the Archipelago of Fernando de Noronha and the Island of Trindade; important reef complexes of the western Atlantic include those of the Atol das Rocas and Abrolhos.

Mountain ranges are found in the northern Amazon on the frontiers of Venezuela and Guyana (Serras Pacaraima and Parima), which include sandstone tepuis such as Monte Roraima and Pico da Neblina, and the Serra Tumucumaque on the border with the Guyanas. Further mountains are widespread in southeast Brazil – the Serra do Espinhaço, Serra do Mar, Serra da Mantiqueira, and Serra Geral. The major freshwater ecosystems are rivers, with extraordinary diversity in terms of their structure, chemistry, and biodiversity. These include the gigantic black-water, white-water, and clear-water rivers of the Amazon Basin, and the Rios São Francisco, Paraguay, Paraná, and Doce in the south.

HISTORICAL PERSPECTIVE

The legal basis for national parks was established under the 1934 Forest Code, and the first site was established in Itatiaia in 1937. Two more were established in 1939, a further three in 1959, and eight in 1961, although detailed regulations for this protected area category were published only in 1979. The category of biological reserve was created in the 1965 revision of the Forest Code, but the first site, Poço das Antas in Rio de Janeiro, was created only in 1974. National parks and biological reserves were the responsibility of the Forest Service of the Ministry of Agriculture until 1967, when this became the charge of the Department of National Parks and Equivalent Reserves of the Brazilian Forestry Development Institute (IBDF).

In the late 1960s and early 1970s, national and international attention was drawn to the Brazilian Amazon with the construction of the Trans-amazônica highway, and the creation of the "Altamira Polygon": 60 000 km² were placed under the jurisdiction of the National Institute for Colonization and Agrarian Reform (INCRA), while key components of the National Integration Programme (PIN) were established by decree in 1970. Plans for the widespread development of the Amazon were based on "development poles," the "Polamazônia" program (under the Superint-endency for the Development of Amazonia – SUDAM, established in 1974). The Amazônia National Park was created in 1974 within the Tapajós Agricultural Pole, but the IBDF's response

Ocelot (*Leopardus pardalis*), Brazil.

Source: UNEP-WCMC

was to draw up a similarly ambitious proposal in 1976 for a system of protected areas using biogeographic principles: representation of phytogeographic regions and vegetation types; and focusing on Pleistocene refuges – forests identified by high endemism believed to have resulted from their persistence through drier climates during the last major ice age around 18 000 years ago. Until 1979, there were only two protected areas in the Brazilian Amazon, but a further seven national parks (69 734 km2) and six biological reserves (22 398 km2) were decreed for the region in the following ten years. Nine of these fell within nine of the 25 Brazilian Amazonian priority areas of IBDF's 1976 proposal.

Ten forest reserves were created in the Amazon by the Ministry of Agriculture in 1911 and 1961, but this category was not given legitimacy in the 1965 Forest Code, which instead recognized the national forest and equivalent categories at the state level. The original forest reserves have been abandoned, settled, or converted into biological reserves or indigenous reserves. The first national forest was Araripe-Apodi, Ceará, created in 1946. Caxiuanã, Pará, was decreed in 1961 and a further 61 national forests have been created since then. In 1981, the National Environment Policy created the category of environmental protection area, roughly equivalent to a biosphere reserve, while the category of "area of particular ecological interest" was created in 1984.

In 1973, the government created the Special Environmental Secretariat (SEMA) within the Ministry of the Interior. In 1981, SEMA set up a program for ecological stations to protect representative samples of Brazilian ecosystems, while promoting ecological research and environmental education. Twenty-five ecological stations and reserves (7 579 km2) were created from 1981 to 1989. In 1989, IBDF and SEMA were combined to form the Brazilian Institute for the Environment and Renewable Natural Resources (IBAMA), now within the Ministry of the Environment.

Provision for private reserves was first established in the 1965 Forest Code through the little-used category of the private fauna and flora reserve. The concept and regulations were revised by IBAMA in 1990 and it was replaced by the private natural heritage reserve (RPPN), a more robust legal mechanism for a landowner to protect, in perpetuity, forests, watersheds, and areas of natural beauty, with the additional incentive of exemption from land tax.

Extractive reserves were first established in 1987, not as protected areas, but as an instrument for agrarian reform, attending particularly to the needs of rubber tapper communities suffering encroachment and the destruction of their forests by cattle ranchers in the southwest Amazon. In 1989, extractive reserves were included in the National Environment Programme (PNMA) and placed under the responsibility of IBAMA, and

Brazil: Growth of protected areas network, 1900-2005

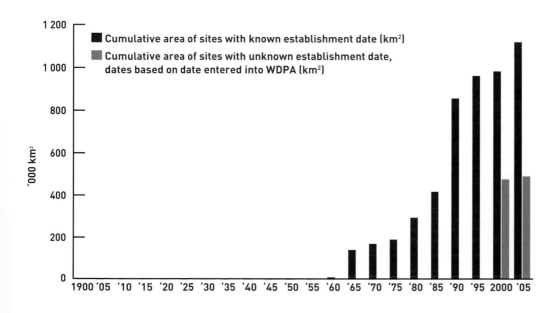

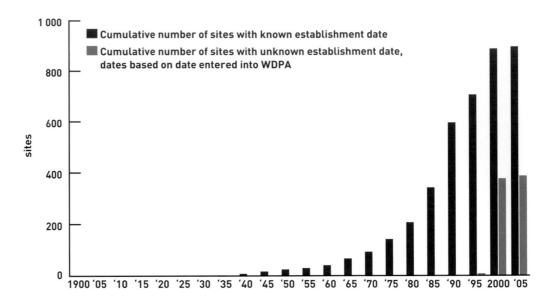

Brazil: Growth in the number of protected areas, 1900-2005

were regulated as part of the protected areas system in 1990.

A revision of the protected areas system was proposed as part of the National Environment Programme, begun in 1987 in collaboration with the United Nations Environment Programme (UNEP). In 1988, the Brasília-based non-governmental organization (NGO), Fundação Pró-Natureza (Funatura) was given the task of drawing up a consolidated national protected areas system for Brazil (Sistema Nacional de Unidades de Conservação da Natureza – SNUC), and after more than ten years of discussion and deliberations it was officially established in July 2000. The system included the private RPPN category as an official protected area. A subsequent decree (2001) determined that IBAMA should adjust the categories of protected areas which do not comply with the definitions and determinations of the new system.

THE PROTECTED AREAS NETWORK

The World Database on Protected Areas (WDPA) contains information on 1 286 protected areas across Brazil, covering a total area of 1 611 547 km^2. Only 88 sites have marine or coastal elements, and the total marine area protected is less than 16 000 km^2. The protection of terrestrial areas amounts to 15.3 percent of the total country, a little higher than the global average, but actually the lowest proportion of any of the American World Commission on Protected Areas (WCPA) regions.

In terms of the levels of protection provided, less than 17 percent falls into strict IUCN Protected Area Management Categories (I-III). Over 61 percent of the total protected areas have not been given an IUCN category.

National parks (52, covering 166 324 km^2) are the largest strictly protected areas, allowing for education, recreation, and scientific research. Their equivalent at the state level is the state park (130, totaling 56 959 km^2). Biological reserves and ecological stations (58 federal areas covering 70 970 km^2, and 120 state areas covering 6 353 km^2) protect representative and threatened ecosystems, and sometimes target particular species (for example, the Mico-Leão Preto Ecological Station was created specifically to protect the black lion tamarin). National forests and state forests are generally large reserves for silviculture, sustainable logging, protection of watersheds, research, and recreation. Thirty-six of the 63 national forests are in Amazonia, accounting for 172 820 km^2 or 99 percent of the area given over to this category.

Extractive reserves focus on protecting areas for sustainable resource use, both terrestrial and marine (for example, Brazil nuts, copaiba oil, latex, and palm fruits), under joint administration of government and local communities. currently, there are 30; 23 in Amazonia (96 percent of their total area). A further eight sites of various denominations have been declared with similar objectives at the state level (all in Amazonia, covering 43 567 km^2).

Environmental protection areas (EPAs) restrict human activities to allow the conservation of natural resources and environmental quality for local communities, using management plans and zoning, including areas of strict protection for wildlife. This mechanism has been widely adopted in Brazil, increasingly as a buffer for parks and reserves. Areas of particular ecological interest (ARIEs) are small (50 km² or less) and provide protective measures for notable natural phenomena, or wildlife populations and habitats in areas where human populations are minimal (while still allowing public use). Private natural heritage reserves (more than 500, state and federal, covering about 4 500 km²) are important instruments to protect forest fragments, which now predominate in the once continuous Atlantic forest. The majority of still unprotected forest in this area is now in private hands.

The national protected areas system (SNUC), established in 2000, is administered by three government institutions. The National Council for the Environment (CONAMA) (a consultative and deliberative organ of the National Environment System – SISNAMA, linked directly to the Presidency) monitors its implementation, which is coordinated by the Ministry of the Environment (MMA). Within the MMA, the Directorate of Ecosystems of IBAMA is responsible for the creation and management of the federal protected areas. Analogous secretariats and forestry institutes are responsible for the equivalent areas at the state and municipal levels.

Indigenous reserves, historically not listed among protected areas, have been included in the present analysis. The majority, in both area and number, are located in Amazonia, and administered by the National Indian Foundation (FUNAI). Some 441 indigenous reserves, areas, and territories total 989 546 km² (11.8 percent of Brazil's land surface). Of these 361 cover about 20 percent of the Brazilian Amazon, and some are playing a significant role in protecting the forest from ongoing destruction and development, particularly those in northern Mato Grosso and southern Pará. A remarkable example is the 100 000 km² Kayapó Indigenous Reserve, intact but now isolated – entirely surrounded by roads, cattle ranches, and farms. A further 139 indigenous areas are currently under evaluation.

The major threat to public protected areas is unresolved ownership by the state of the lands they

Brazil: Protected areas network by IUCN category, 2005

IUCN category	Total sites	Total area (km²)
Ia	182	112 033
Ib	-	-
II	179	160 677
III	5	704
IV	259	5 070
V	115	135 707
VI	70	212 548
No category	476	9 848 809
Total	1 286	1 611 547

Brazil: Protected areas network by IUCN category (percentage of total area), 2005

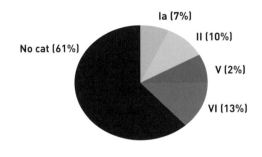

Brazil: Number of protected areas by IUCN category, 2005

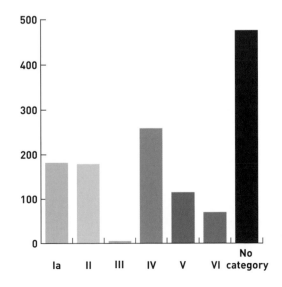

D Cavalher/UNEP

Firewood gathering in degraded former Atlantic forest, Brazil.

encompass. Five national parks, two biological reserves, the Iquê Ecological Station, and 16 national forests in Amazonia overlap partly or entirely with indigenous land claims (totaling close to 110 000 km²). Problems of land title, lack of infrastructure, management, guards, hunting, squatters, indigenous claims (three covering more than 50 percent of the park), gold mining (erosion and mercury pollution), highways, military occupation, and immense mineral deposits are all threats to the Pico da Neblina National Park.

Most of the Amazonian protected areas are subject to diverse combinations of these threats. The Gurupí Biological Reserve has lost more than half of its forest due to logging. In the rest of Brazil, well-established parks still have substantial portions under private ownership owing to the state not having paid the indemnities required for stewardship. Examples include the Chapada dos Veadeiros, Serra da Canastra, and Serra da Bocaina national parks, and Una Biological Reserve. Other medium- to long-term threats include efforts to fragment or reduce the extent of the parks, for instance the operation of the 'Colono' road in Iguaçu National Park, presently closed by court order. Other systemic threats are fire and invasive species.

Other forms of protection

Numerous conservation areas are maintained and administered by a broad range of groups and institutions. Examples include:

❑ Scientific and agricultural research institutions – for example the Adolfo Ducke and Walter Egler Forest Reserves administered by the National Institute for Amazon Research (INPA), Manaus; the Ecological Reserve of the Brazilian Institute for Geography and Statistics (IBGE) in Brasília; and the Santa Lucia Biological Station of the Museu de Biologia Mello Leitão in Espírito Santo.

❑ Universities – the Tapacurá Ecological Station of the Federal Rural University of Pernambuco.

❑ NGOs – examples include the Mata do Sossego Biological Station of the Fundação Biodiversitas, Belo Horizonte; the Fazenda Rio Negro (Pantanal) of Conservation International do Brasil; and a network of wildlife refuges maintained by Funatura, Brasília.

Industries with governance over large areas of land, such as those in the energy and mining sectors, and pulp and paper with large timber plantations, also maintain reserves where wildlife and the maintenance of ecosystem functions are given priority. Examples are the Linhares Forest Reserve of the Companhia Vale do Rio Doce, and a number of small reserves of the Aracruz Cellulose Company, both in Espírito Santo.

The 1965 Forest Code defined areas of permanent preservation to protect particularly sensitive or important natural areas, such as vegetation along rivers; lakes and areas of spring water; steep slopes and the edges of raised plateaus; coastal shrub (restinga) for the stabilization of dunes; mangrove ecosystems; and forests above 1 800 meters. The National Environment Policy of 1981 determined that these areas, and localities used by migratory birds protected by international conventions, be turned into ecological reserves and areas of particular ecological interest.

Another important legal instrument is that of the 'legal reserve' (Law 7.803, July 18 1989) which determines the preservation of the natural vegetation of 80 percent of any rural property in Amazonia, 35 percent in the Cerrado, and 20 percent in the Atlantic forest. A Provisional Measure of the Presidency (May 2000) defined the functions of this legal reserve as essentially for the sustainable use of natural resources and biodiversity conservation, and allowed for a compensatory mechanism of creating a protected area of similar ecological relevance and in the same hydrographic basin, when all or part of the legal reserve of a property has been, or needs to be, destroyed.

International sites

The Ramsar Convention was ratified by Brazil in 1993. Currently there are eight Ramsar sites, totaling 64 341 km². The largest of these sites, the 27 000 km² Reentrâncias Maranhenses, is coastal, protecting mudflats, islands, and mangroves. Others cover a broad range of habitats including the alluvial floodplains of the Pantanal Matogrossense; the 18 000 km² Baixada Maranhense Ramsar site protecting flooded grassland, lagoons, mangroves, and babassu palm forest; and the 11 000 km² Mamirauá Ramsar Site protecting a significant area of várzea (white-water flooded forest). One site, the coral reefs of the Parcel Manuel Luís off the coast of Maranhão, is one of the only Ramsar sites to lie in open ocean, with no intertidal waters or dry land.

Seven natural World Heritage sites are listed, but a further 10 have been declared under cultural criteria. As is often the case, sites designated under

Brazil: Internationally protected areas, 2005

Agreement	No. of sites	Protected area (km²)
Biosphere reserves	6	1 280 419
Ramsar sites	8	64 341
World Heritage sites	7	85 957

cultural criteria only may still hold important natural resources, such as the Serra da Capivara National Park, designated a cultural site in 1991 due to its archaeological significance, but which is also an important natural site in the Caatinga.

Brazil is also host to five of the 10 largest biosphere reserves in the world, which have been established for all the major terrestrial biomes. They cover about 1.25 million km², or nearly 15 percent of the land surface of the country. These are the 295 000 km² Reserva da Biósfera da Mata Atlântica; the 297 000 km² Cerrado (with varied savanna and forest ecosystems); the 252 000 km² Pantanal; the 199 000 km² Caatinga (deciduous forest and desert scrub in the northeast of Brazil); and the Central Amazon Corridor (a range of contiguous protected areas in the Amazon basin).

FUTURE DIRECTIONS

Brazil is the megadiversity country of the world, with global responsibility for three major wilderness areas: the large majority of the Amazon (about 20 percent lost to date), the world's largest wetland – the Pantanal of Mato Grosso, and the Caatinga of the northeast. It also contains two biodiversity hotspots: the remains of the decimated Atlantic forest, and the richest tropical savanna in the world in terms of plant diversity and endemism – the Cerrado. Protected areas are the key to conserving what remains of these hotspots, and to counterbalancing huge, ambitious infrastructure development schemes such as the Avança Brasil program (2000-07) for Amazonia, which envisions doubling the extent of paved roads in the region, the construction of dams, waterways, ports, and railways to advance its occupation and development over enormous areas.Deforestation in Amazonia proceeds apace, with an average annual rate of loss of 18 051 km² since 1977. The Brazil Ministry of Science and Technology has estimated that 23 750 km² were deforested in 2002–2003 alone.

Key challenges include expanding the protected areas system, essentially through securing additional baseline information on the

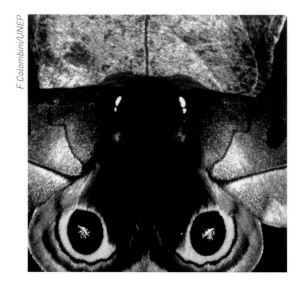

F Colombini/UNEP

F Colombini/UNEP

JL Gasparini/UNEP

The Amazon is home to more than more than 100 000 invertebrate species (top) and perhaps as many as 30 million. (Center) Male black caimans (*Melanosuchus niger*) can grow to 6 m. Frequent rain and high humidity have enabled many frog species (bottom) to live and breed in the trees.

country's biodiversity, besides refining policies and guidelines and improving the capacity of the governmental institutions for their management and protection. The future and integrity of many of the protected areas are threatened. Improving connectivity between protected areas, the chief aim of the Corridors project (see below), will also be vital for the viability and success of these areas over the long term.

Five workshops, compiling data on biodiversity, socioeconomic variables, and land use, were held during 1998–2000 to identify and prioritize conservation areas in the major biomes in Brazil (Brazil, MMA, 2002). Nine hundred areas were identified as of priority for the conservation of the country's biodiversity: 385 in the Brazilian Amazon; 182 in the Atlantic forest and Campos Sulinos; 164 in the coastal and marine zones; 87 in the Cerrado and Pantanal; and 82 in the Caatinga. The creation of protected areas was the most frequent recommendation for conservation measures for these areas in all the regions, except Amazonia where it came second after 'sustainable resource use'. By 2002, 55 protected areas had been created as a result of these workshops, and the priority areas will be targets for new areas over the coming years.

Two other major initiatives underway are the Biological Corridors Project of the Pilot Programme for the Protection of Brazilian Tropical Forests PP-G7 (IBAMA, Sociedade Civil Mamirauá, and Conservation International do Brasil) and the Amazon Region Protected Areas (ARPA) Programme (MMA and WWF Brazil). Both began in 1997 and are supported by the World Bank, and the latter also by the Global Environment Facility. The Corridors project idealized seven major corridors (very large stretches of contiguous protected areas of diverse categories): five in the Amazon and two in the Atlantic forest. The rationale was to avoid the creation of 'island' protected areas, doomed to lose their species over the long term. The corridors were placed strategically to maximize representation of the biodiversity of the Atlantic forest and Amazonia. Their initial design has been modified as a result of the workshops mentioned above, and the project has already resulted in some major advances in consolidating the protected areas system.

The ARPA program was officially launched at the World Summit on Sustainable Development in Johannesburg (2002), and aims to increase the area of the Amazon rainforest under federal protection to

500 000 km² (12 percent), based on the representation of 23 Amazonian ecoregions identified by WWF, besides support for the development of management plans and protective measures for some existing areas, such as the Serra da Cutia and the Mountains of Tumucumaque National Parks, and the Cautário Extractive Reserve.

As can be seen from this brief report, over the last 30 years Brazil has considerably expanded its parks system, with some of the largest tropical forest protected areas in the world, including, for example, the national parks of Pico da Neblina (22 000 km²), Jaú (22 720 km²), the Mountains of Tumucumaque (38 670 km²), and the Mamirauá (11 240 km²) and Amanã (23 500 km²) State Sustainable Development Reserves. The PP-G7 Corridors Project and ARPA are underpinning the last chance to protect Brazil's natural biodiversity. Over the next 20 years, it will be the parks and reserves which will draw the map of the natural areas that will remain.

South America

ARGENTINA, BOLIVIA, CHILE, COLOMBIA, ECUADOR, FRENCH GUIANA (FRANCE), GUYANA, PARAGUAY, PERU, SURINAME, URUGUAY, VENEZUELA

Contributors: C. Castaño Uribe, C. Lacambra

REGIONAL DESCRIPTION

South America, as defined by the World Commission on Protected Areas (WCPA), includes all of the countries of continental South America except Brazil. Although this definition is used here, a number of issues deal with the entire continent, including Brazil.

The continent of South America can be divided into two quite distinct geological parts. The large eastern areas consist of a series of ancient (pre-Cambrian) shield formations with higher ground, separated by wide alluvial basins. The largest of these is the Amazon Shield (in Brazil), with the Guyana Shield to the north and the Plata Shield to the south. The western part of the region is much smaller, but dominated by the Andes Cordillera, a vast mountain range that emerged 230 million years ago as the result of the subduction of the Pacific Plate beneath the South American Plate. The Andes extend for 7 240 km from the sub-Antarctic lands of southern Chile through seven countries to Colombia and Venezuela (where the chain turns eastwards). They range from 200 to 400 km wide; many peaks are above 5 000 meters and the highest, at 6 960 meters, is Aconcagua in Argentina. Between the mountains are areas of high plateaus (Altiplano). The average altitude is 3 660 meters. There are numerous volcanoes and the region is regularly impacted by earthquakes.

Many of the important rivers that run across the subcontinent have their headwaters in the Andes. The rivers running down the western slopes into the Pacific Ocean tend to be more turbulent and short. Rivers running eastwards traverse the continent, feeding or receiving waters from other rivers before they arrive at the Atlantic. Among these are the Amazon, Rio Negro, Magdalena, and some of the tributaries of the Paraná.

The continent is bounded by the Pacific and Atlantic Oceans and by the Caribbean Sea to the north. The Pacific coastline is dominated by the cold Humboldt Current, and by upwelling water close to the coastline. Typically, these are nutrient-rich and highly productive waters, but during the irregularly timed El Niño years these upwellings are reduced or absent; warmer waters predominate and weather patterns across much of the region are significantly altered.

The continent has a remarkably diverse and complex mosaic of fauna and flora. Among the very important and unique ecosystems found in the region are the Peruvian, Ecuadorian, Colombian, and Venezuelan Páramo (wetlands and wet grasslands with distinctive species such as frailejones, *Espeletia* sp.) 3 000 meters above sea level; and the snow chains along the subcontinent from Argentina to the Colombian Caribbean at Sierra Nevada de Santa Marta. The tropical Andes make up one of the most diverse ecosystems in the world, ranging from forested foothills and humid cloud forests to cold páramos, punas (cold, arid areas above the treeline with low plant formations), and glaciers sometimes within a very short distance. Other important habitats include the Colombian and Venezuelan plains and savannas; the tepuis or rocky formations in the Formacion Roraima on the Guyana Shield; the Brazilian, Uruguayan, and Paraguayan Pantanal (probably the

J Flores/UNEP

Patagonia, Argentina.

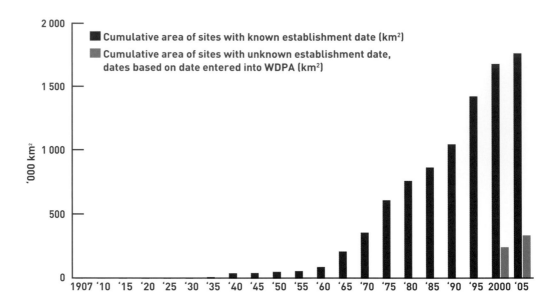

South America: Growth of protected areas network, 1907–2005

world's largest wetland), and the vast dry Chaco region with thorn forests and savanna, shared by Bolivia, Paraguay, and Argentina. The Amazonian forest comprises 5.5 million km² shared by Brazil, Venezuela, Guyana, Suriname, French Guiana, Colombia, Ecuador, Peru, and Bolivia. Due to its vast area and productivity, this region plays an important role in regulating the world's climate.

The South American coastline covers a broad range of habitats. There are coral reefs, principally in the Caribbean Sea, but also in scattered communities in Pacific waters. Mangroves are widespread, both in the tropical and subtropical Atlantic waters and in the Pacific as far south as northern Peru. Chilean and Peruvian waters provide one of the most important fisheries worldwide. Some of the most productive estuaries in the world are also found in the region: La Plata River estuary in the Atlantic and in the gulfs of Guayaquil and Fonseca in the Pacific, among others. In addition to many

South America: Growth in the number of protected areas, 1907–2005

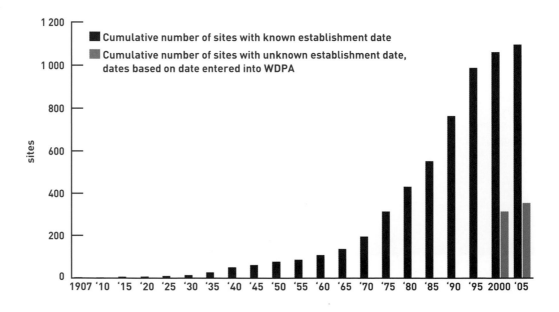

coastal islands, notably in southern Chile and Argentina, oceanic islands are found, including Juan Fernandez and Easter Island/Isla de Pascua (both Chile), Galapágos (Ecuador), as well as the San Andres and Providencia Archipelago (Colombia) in the Caribbean Sea.

Biological diversity in this region is almost unparalleled. Colombia, Ecuador, Venezuela, and Peru are all considered megadiverse countries, with among the highest levels of both diversity and endemism of any nations. Most of the land surface, and the adjacent waters, fall within priority ecoregions as identified by WWF (the Global 200). There are some 37 endemic bird areas, many of which overlap some 36 centers of plant diversity. These centers are particularly concentrated along the Pacific coast and the Andes, where the mountains have created a great array of isolated and unique habitats and communities.

The human population of South America is a mix of the indigenous peoples who were present when the European explorers first arrived, along with peoples of European (mainly Spanish, except for Brazil) and African descent. As a consequence of Spanish colonization, the main language in South America is Spanish, while in Guyana, Suriname, and French Guiana it is English, Dutch, and French respectively. The indigenous peoples are still a major part of the population, particularly in Peru (45 percent), Bolivia (over 50 percent), and Ecuador (25 percent), and many still live traditional lifestyles, often highly sustainable. Most countries achieved independence during the 19th century – periods of instability, totalitarian regimes, and civil disruption have now largely given way to relative stability and democracy across the region.

The value of some of these lands with reliable water sources and fertile soils led to anthropogenic pressures on some ecosystems even before European colonization. In the last 50 years, the human population has tripled to 181 million (2002 estimate, excluding Brazil). Population density is not homogeneous – there are extensive territories with low populations, and some large cities such as Santiago de Chile, Bogotá, Buenos Aires, and Lima. Most of the population is concentrated in the Andean region or in coastal areas, adding particular pressures to natural ecosystems in these places.

HISTORICAL PERSPECTIVE

It is very likely that indigenous peoples in many parts of South America had developed a variety of

A Gellweiler/UNEP

systems to ensure natural resource protection, which in some places may have included protection of specific areas.

The first modern protected areas were established in Argentina and Chile. In 1903, a public natural park was created in Argentinian Patagonia (renamed Parque del Sur in 1922 and now part of the Nahuel Huapi National Park). In Chile the Malleco Forest Reserve (now a national reserve) was established in 1907. Many of the first national parks were established in the 1920s and 1930s, including the Vicente Pérez Rosales National Park in Argentina (1926), the Kaiteur National Park in

Blue-footed booby (*Sula nebouxii*), Galapagos Islands National Park, Ecuador.

221

South America: Protected areas network by IUCN category, 2005

IUCN category	Total sites	Total area (km²)
Ia	55	12 478
Ib	4	14 754
II	220	505 116
III	72	74 349
IV	143	185 554
V	96	126 204
VI	314	586 300
No category	546	593 690
Total	1 450	2 098 445

South America: Protected areas network by IUCN category (percentage of total area), 2005

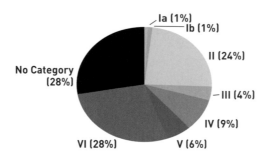

South America: Number of protected areas by IUCN category, 2005

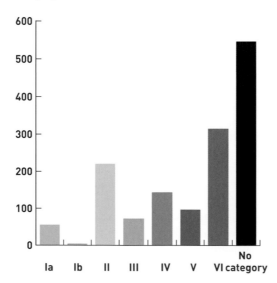

Guyana (1929), the Galápagos National Park in Ecuador (1936), and the Sajama National Park in Bolivia (1939). Many more protected areas, such as the Sierra de la Macarena (originally a biological reserve, now a national park) in Colombia, were created after the Washington Convention in 1940, which also led to an assessment and rearrangement of management processes in the existing protected areas.

Rapid increases in the protected area systems in almost all countries began in the 1960s, and from this period onwards the declaration of protected areas became a more systematic process. Most countries now have technical and scientific criteria and guidelines for protection that have evolved over time. Most also have national-level organizations with technical expertise that monitor and administer national parks and other protected areas.

THE PROTECTED AREAS NETWORK

South America has the second highest proportion of its land area under protection of any WCPA region. There are 1 450 protected areas, which extend over 2 million square kilometers, covering almost 23 percent of the land area. Despite this, being such a diverse region, there are several ecosystems that remain poorly protected or not even included in this network.

Thirty-seven percent of protected areas in the South America region in the World Database on Protected Areas (WDPA) have no assigned management category. These include a broad range of types of protection, including lands of indigenous peoples, forest reserves, and buffer zones around other protected areas. The region also includes a large number of Category VI protected areas, where a broad suite of sustainable-use practices may be undertaken, particularly where there are local communities, such as indigenous groups, living within, or adjacent to, sites. As a general rule, certain non-extractive activities are permitted even in Category I–III sites, although these may be restricted to research, restoration, education, recreation, eco-tourism, or craftwork.

Marine areas are still very poorly protected across the region. There are 114 marine protected areas, covering a total of over 161 000 km². However, this latter figure is considerably skewed by the Galapagos Marine Reserve, which makes up 133 000 km².

Areas of South America protected (by country), 2005

Country/territory	Land area (km²)	Total protected area (km²)	Total number of sites
Argentina	2 780 400	182 052	328
Bolivia	1 098 580	230 509	50
Chile	756 630	143 565	103
Colombia	1 138 910	439 666	414
Ecuador	283 560	209 497	140
French Guiana	90 000	5 306	34
Guyana	214 970	4 860	3
Paraguay	406 750	23 664	37
Peru	1 285 220	179 257	61
Suriname	163 270	19 812	15
Uruguay	176 220	725	29
Venezuela	912 050	659 530	236

Other forms of protection

In addition to protected areas declared at the national level, almost all countries have other systems of regional, non-governmental organization (NGO), and private protected areas. For the most part, these sites are included in the statistics provided above.

In Colombia there are 32 regional autonomous corporations administering 122 natural protected areas, while municipalities add a further 79. There are also 89 private reserves that cover 245 km². The provincial system of natural protected areas in Argentina is very significant, covering some 120 000 km². In Chile, the Private Protected Areas Network (RAPP), an NGO, coordinated by the National Committee for the Defense of Fauna and Flora (CODEFF), protects 3 222 km², including many sites that do not have any official recognition. In Peru the Natural Protected Area Law promotes the existence of complementary systems through regional conservation areas and municipal conservation areas. This law also recognizes private reserves, although none is recorded.

International sites

All countries except Guyana have declared protected areas under one or more of the major international protected areas agreements.

The 37 biosphere reserves make up the largest area of any of the international categories. However, the figure is dominated entirely by the two largest sites. The Galapagos Islands in Ecuador (148 000 km²) and the Seaflower Biosphere Reserve in Colombia (300 000 km²) are predominantly marine areas with only a small portion of land.

The 71 Ramsar sites are spread across the region, and include a number of coastal and marine sites. The largest Ramsar sites are the Complejo de Humedales del Abanico del Río Pastaza in Peru (more than 38 000 km²) and the 32 000 km² Pantanal Boliviano in Bolivia.

Apart from the global agreements, there are a number of treaties, conventions, commissions, and regional and international programs that have active participation from Latin American countries. One highly important regional development has been that of the Latin American Network for Technical Cooperation on National Parks, other Protected Areas, Wild Fauna and Flora. This network, created in 1983 as an initiative from the FAO Regional Office and the UNEP Office for Latin America and Caribbean, is made up of more than 1 000 public and private specialist institutions relating to biodiversity conservation and protected areas management. The network has been working officially since 1985 as a way of complementing traditional technical assistance by supporting technical cooperation among developing nations. It has had a number of important impacts: supporting an increase in technical cooperation between countries; the establishment of joint projects and the exchange of knowledge and experience between national specialists and institutions; and in strengthening and modernizing national technical capacities and training opportunities.

Further mechanisms under development include the Iberoamerican Network (which incorporates Spain and Portugal as additional countries for international cooperation); and the National Parks and Other Protected Areas Foundation (FUPANAP). The latter has established links between former senior executives from

South America: Internationally protected areas, 2005

Country/territory	No. of sites	Protected area (km²)
Biosphere reserves		
Argentina	11	41 770
Bolivia	3	7 350
Chile	8	73 792
Colombia	5	333 323
Ecuador	3	173 751
Paraguay	2	77 723
Peru	3	32 684
Uruguay	1	2 000
Venezuela	1	82 662
TOTAL	37	825 055
Ramsar sites		
Argentina	14	35 829
Bolivia	8	65 181
Chile	9	1 592
Colombia	3	4 479
Ecuador	11	1 585
French Guiana	2	1 960
Paraguay	6	7 860
Peru	10	67 774
Suriname	1	120
Uruguay	2	4 249
Venezuela	5	2 636
TOTAL	71	193 265
World Heritage sites		
Argentina	4	11 362
Bolivia	1	15 230
Colombia	1	540
Ecuador	2	145 384
Peru	4	21 799
Suriname	1	16 000
Venezuela	1	30 000
TOTAL	14	240 315

national protected area systems to channel their experiences in support of South American and Central American protected areas.

Another important development has been the Amazonian Protected Areas Sub-Network (SURAPA). In a process developed between 1989 and 1998, this was one of the first regionally coordinated activities supported by the Amazonian Environment Special Commission (CEMMA) under the Amazonian Cooperation Treaty (TCA) signed by Bolivia, Brazil, Colombia, Ecuador, Guyana, Peru, Suriname, and Venezuela. The project encouraged development of regional criteria, parity, and standardization for the establishment and management of protected areas. It further supported capacity building and training; the formation of areas of excellence; publication of technical support documentation; exchange of staff and provision of scholarships between countries, and the expansion of protected areas cover and representativeness.

The region includes parts of three regional seas, two of which have legally binding conventions: the Convention for the Protection of the Marine Environment and Coastal Zone of the South-East Pacific (Lima Convention) and the Convention for the Protection and Development of the Marine Environment of the Wider Caribbean Region (Cartagena Convention). Both conventions have been signed by the relevant South American nations adjoining the region and both provide a broad range of provisions for coastal protection. Importantly, both have specific protocols dealing with the establishment of protected areas.

FUTURE DIRECTIONS

In a region where the spatial area of protection is already high, many of the key requirements for the future are aimed towards strengthening management. Under a proposed action plan for the World Parks Congress in 2003, ten key points were outlined to give orientation and assistance to all those institutions working on protected areas in the region for the next ten years.

1: Construction of protected area systems

❑ Design and implement national systems of protected areas across a range of management categories, or enforce the existing ones; these should include sites that allow sustainable use of resources and those that restrict resource extraction. Management objectives and selection criteria should be clearly defined. Private areas should receive special attention to ensure their long-term future.

❑ Analyze the possibility of including community conservation areas as a natural protected area category of each country.

❑ Obtain financial, scientific, and technical support to assess the biogeographic, ecosystem, and biome coverage in protected area systems.

2: Assessment of management effectiveness

❏ Design and implement systems to assess the management effectiveness of natural protected areas orientated to improve management of such areas.

❏ Share experiences, prepare guidelines and principles, and apply rapid and efficient methodologies to assess natural protected areas.

3: Institutional strengthening

❏ Consolidate a political framework for protected area systems.

❏ Strengthen protected area institutions and the technical, operative, and administrative capabilities of employees.

❏ Develop and publish concepts, tools, and methods for designing and implementing protected areas management plans.

❏ Establish strategic alliances between global, regional, and national training and research centers, and provide advice on protected areas management.

❏ Promote the establishment of regional centers for protected areas personnel.

❏ Address the needs of protected areas staff in relation to their health and safety, quality of life, salaries, accommodation, and opportunities for professional development.

❏ Encourage technical exchange between countries to support training and the exchange of ideas and techniques for protected area management.

4: Encourage local participation in planning and management

❏ Enhance the decentralization of public entities in charge of protected areas administration and strengthen local organizations to encourage their involvement.

❏ Promote strategic alliances among protected areas management agencies, local communities, NGOs, government institutions, the private sector, and corporate bodies.

❏ Study the experiences of protected areas co-management in the region, and establish a database accessible to all stakeholders.

5: Ensure financial sustainability for protected areas

❏ Produce and assess financial sustainability experiences in the region's protected areas.

Establish strategic, solid, and permanent alliances among protected areas, governmental institutions, and the private sector.

❏ Design and establish economic instruments to enhance conservation and consolidation of protected area systems. Design regional strategies for sustainably financing protected areas at the level of shared ecosystems or pilot areas shared by a group of countries, using international funding sources and bilateral cooperation agencies.

6: Increase marine and coastal protected areas

❏ Propose, design, and adopt an ecological classification system for South American coastal and marine environments.

❏ Develop and broadly disseminate concepts, guidelines, and tools for the establishment of marine and coastal protected areas at national and regional levels.

❏ Establish representative national systems of marine protected areas and develop regional approaches that multiply benefits in terms of biodiversity conservation and resource productivity.

❏ Create a regional specialist group on coastal and marine protected areas, to produce guidelines and orientation on the subject.

❏ Revise existing legislation or develop a new law that includes recommendations for management categories, establishment mechanisms, zoning and management plans, community participation, research regulations, financial arrangements, allowed and forbidden activities, sanctions and incentives, conservation awareness and education.

7: Establish or strengthen national and regional information systems

❏ Strengthen technical cooperation networks in financial, operative, institutional, and functional terms.

❏ Promote and develop a regional information system on declared areas, that also provides a forum for sharing information on priority setting, professional contacts, new declared areas, events, etc.

❏ Design, develop, and implement national information systems that allow the rapid dissemination of information in useful formats. National and international institutions should coordinate this data sharing.

Henri Pittier National Park, Venezuela.

8: Strengthen legislation and effective implementation

❏ Assess existing legislation in relation to protected areas, seeking opportunities for improvements and additions, or to use existing measures more broadly, to address international agreements, and to address global change.

❏ Revise internal legislation to ensure effectiveness and efficiency, and to facilitate access and utilization of economic resources, and establish connections between protected areas and financial plans at local and national levels.

9: Develop economic and ecological valuation methods for environmental goods and services

❏ Design and implement, as a planning and management tool, a regional system for the economic valuation of protected areas' goods and services.

10: Support control and vigilance in protected areas

❏ Organize, train, and empower teams specialized in control and vigilance issues on illegal settlement, hunting, logging, archeological theft, pollution, illegal fisheries, etc. Provide the means for education and environmental interpretation at local levels.

❏ Promote the involvement of local communities, governmental organizations, and different social sectors in natural resources protection, including training for preventative action, ensuring awareness of existing legislation.

❏ Provide adequate mechanisms to supervise and follow up permits, licenses, or authorizations granted to users of protected areas.

❏ Supply protected areas with the infrastructure and technological resources needed for the development of control and protection activities within their boundaries.

Europe

ALBANIA, ANDORRA, AUSTRIA, BELGIUM, BOSNIA AND HERZEGOVINA, BULGARIA, CROATIA, CZECH REPUBLIC, DENMARK, ESTONIA, FAROE ISLANDS (DENMARK), FINLAND, FRANCE, GERMANY, GIBRALTAR (UNITED KINGDOM), GREECE, HUNGARY, ICELAND, IRELAND, ITALY, LATVIA, LIECHTENSTEIN, LITHUANIA, LUXEMBOURG, THE FORMER YUGOSLAV REPUBLIC OF MACEDONIA, MALTA, MONACO, MONTENEGRO, NETHERLANDS, NORWAY, POLAND, ROMANIA, SAN MARINO, SERBIA, SLOVAKIA, SLOVENIA, SPAIN, SVALBARD AND JAN MAYEN ISLANDS (NORWAY), SWEDEN, SWITZERLAND, UNITED KINGDOM, VATICAN CITY STATE

Contributor: R. Crofts

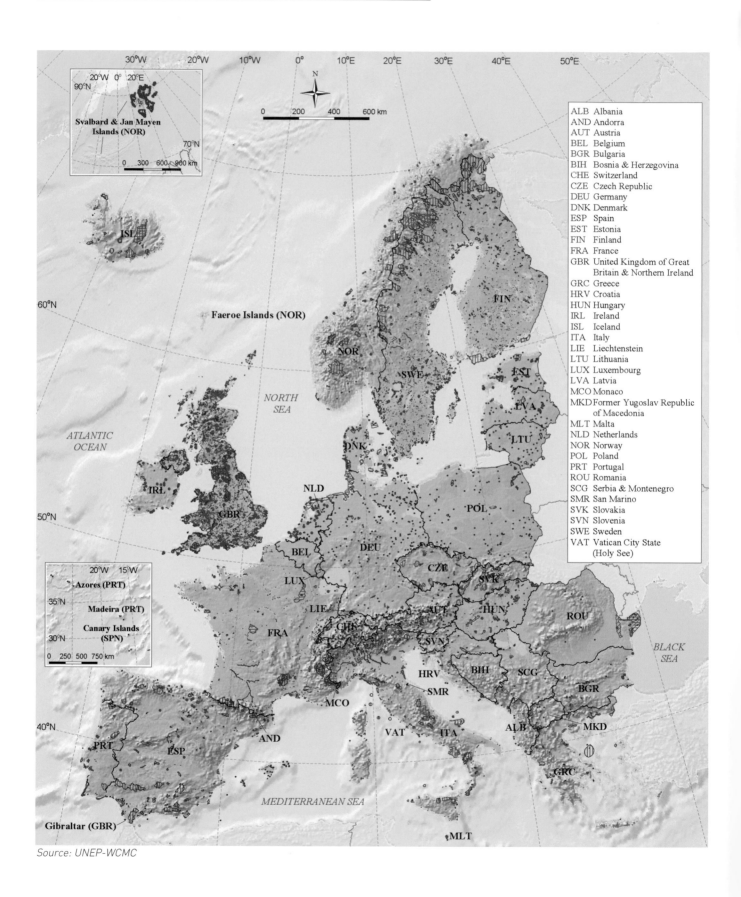

Source: UNEP-WCMC

REGIONAL DESCRIPTION

The World Commission on Protected Areas (WCPA) European region comprises 35 countries stretching from the Arctic to the Mediterranean, and from the northeast Atlantic to the Black Sea. Although generally classified as temperate, the region extends from dry scrubland to Arctic tundra. Marine areas include the northern and central waters of the Mediterranean Sea, the Baltic Sea, and the complex of seas around the northeast Atlantic including the Irish Sea, North Sea, Norwegian Sea, and Barents Sea. Oceanic islands include Iceland, the Faroe Islands (Denmark), and Svalbard and Jan Mayen Islands (Norway) in the North Atlantic, as well as the Azores and Madeira (Portugal), and the Canary Islands (Spain). The last lie in subtropical waters just off the coast of southern Morocco.

Geologically the region divides into an ancient (pre-Cambrian) shield in the north; Fennoscandia, a wide, relatively simple plain of sedimentary strata dominating the central and eastern areas; and a topographically complex region in the western and southern areas. The last includes a number of mountain ranges, notably the Alps, Carpathians, Balkans, and Pyrenees, all formed by tectonic activities dating back to the Tertiary.

The Europe region is biogeographically diverse as a result primarily of its geological history and rock strata, and the degree of oceanic or continental, and Arctic or Alpine, influences on its climate. Various classifications of the major biogeographic regions exist. These can be used as a basis for selecting protected areas and ensuring that there is adequate coverage in each of the regions. The standard regions for Europe are: boreal, humid mid-latitude, and Mediterranean. These are rather too broad for identifying protected areas, particularly as they ignore the Alpine and extreme oceanic components. The European Union (EU) has used a sixfold approach as the basis for the implementation of the Natura 2000 protected area network: boreal, continental, Atlantic, Alpine, Macaronesia, and Mediterranean. A detailed natural vegetation map has been compiled which can be used to define habitats. Individual countries have developed more detailed divisions to represent the subtleties of biogeography, e.g. Norway and Scotland. Overall, there is no systematic application of a biogeographical framework for the selection of protected areas, with the exception of the Natura network, as each country has developed its own approaches over a long period of time.

Despite millennia of human interactions with the natural environment, there remain high levels of biodiversity, particularly around the Mediterranean basin. Some 12 500 vascular plants have been described, about 28 percent of which are endemic. Centers of diversity and endemism are particularly concentrated in the mountain ranges and around the Mediterranean coast – 25 centers of plant diversity have been recognized, and nine important ecoregions (WWF Global 200). Vertebrate endemism tends to be much lower, however, and only one endemic bird area has been recognized, around Madeira and the Canary Islands.

With a long history of human settlement, including 10 000 years of agriculture, there has been continuous modification of natural habitats. Many of the original habitats of Europe have been lost or highly modified, and very little of the land surface remains in a purely natural state. Species have proved to be adaptable to changing habitats, even developing niches in entirely man-made habitats, and today many human-modified cultural landscapes have a critical role in the maintenance of Europe's biodiversity.

Despite this history, profound changes have affected natural habitats, species, and cultural landscapes in recent decades. Most significant have been the growth of coastal resort complexes, particularly along the shores of the Mediterranean Sea; the rapid intensification of agriculture supported by financial incentives provided for food production; the development of transport infrastructures to speed public and private transit over long distances; the continuing high exploitation of marine fish stocks; and the effect of armed conflict in certain parts of the region.

Keswick, Lake District National Park, United Kingdom.

S. Chape

The single most significant change in the distribution of population is the growth of major urban areas through infilling within the urban space, expansion on the periphery, and amalgamation of settlements. The space for green areas has been reduced with consequent diminution in landscape quality and species niches.

Politically, the independence achieved by many countries in eastern Europe and the desire of many of them to join the European Union (now including 25 out of 35 countries in the region) will have long-term significance for protected areas. Under the EU Directives on the Protection of Wild Birds (1979) and on the Conservation of Natural Habitats and Wild Fauna and Flora (1992), a coherent European ecological network is being established, known as Natura 2000. Its implementation requires countries to update and strengthen their nature conservation laws and implement monitoring of scheduled species and habitats.

There remains concern among the conservation community, led particularly by the large international charities such as Birdlife International and WWF, that the distribution of protected areas inadequately represents key habitats and species, and that the gaps in the system should be filled. These organizations have been instrumental in pressing for the implementation of already agreed systems, such as the Natura network. In addition to these concerns, there are still many protected areas that, in effect, exist only on paper, and measures to make them effective for biological and landscape diversity conservation are not being taken.

Perhaps of even greater significance is the continuation of land uses which degrade the natural environment and undermine its natural functioning. Foremost amongst these pressures is the continuation of intensive agriculture with very substantial public funding under the EU Common Agricultural Policy. It is too early to tell whether the reform package agreed in mid-2003 will have the beneficial effects on species, habitats, and landscapes which have been claimed. In addition, commercial pressures are resulting in a reduction in the remaining remnants of natural forests.

Political will to ensure that areas are protected from development has strengthened in a number of countries with the tightening of existing law or the implementation of new law. The implementation of the European Union birds and habitats directives resulting in the Natura 2000 network, with strong challenges on the inadequacy of some countries'

proposals, has been an important driver in a largely positive direction. However, other EU policies and financial support, especially for agriculture, for roads and other infrastructure, for economic development, and for fisheries, have resulted in a reduction in biological and landscape diversity and the fragmentation of habitats. There are clear dangers of this pattern occurring in the countries newly joined or about to join the EU.

HISTORICAL PERSPECTIVE

During most of the last millennium, national rulers established protected areas to safeguard their hunting grounds; particularly significant were the deer and other hunting forests in, for example, Germany, Poland, and England (the New Forest was first established as a royal hunting reserve in 1079 and has been protected ever since).

Modern protected areas took a long time to become established compared with other continents – in some parts these delays may have been linked to the near-complete ownership and use of the landscape going back for many centuries. Some of the first sites were small nature reserves, mostly established under private ownership. The first national parks were established early in the 20th century (seven were established in Sweden in 1909, one in Switzerland in 1914, and one in Italy in 1922), while Poland had established 39 small nature reserves by 1918. Many other countries did not begin to establish protected area networks until the 1940s or later.

THE PROTECTED AREAS NETWORK

There are many different types of protected area networks in Europe arising from international, regional, national, and local initiatives developed for a variety of reasons to safeguard species, habitats, and landscapes. For example, many countries have national parks comprising large areas representing the most significant habitats and landscapes of the country; nature reserves representing small areas devoted primarily to nature protection; natural monuments to protect special features, often presenting key stages in the Earth's history and the representative landforms; and regional or nature parks, and landscape parks or protected landscape areas, combining landscape conservation, recreation, and other economic activity.

With more than 53 000 protected areas, Europe has one of the most complex systems of protected areas in the world. At the same time the

S. Chape

Hikers in Kolovesi National Park, Finland.

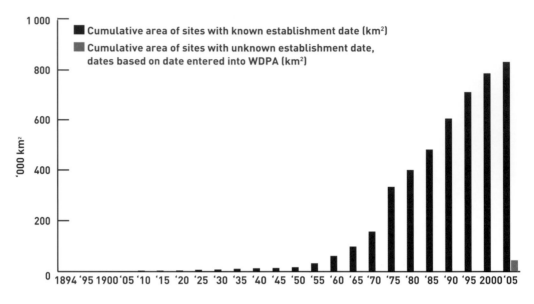

Europe: Growth of protected areas network, 1894-2005

total area covered by these sites, 874 473 km², only represents about 17 percent of the land area, close to the global average, and the average size of sites in Europe is much smaller than in any other region.

Almost 52 percent of the sites do not have IUCN management categories. For many this may indicate a lack of information; these also include a large number of sites, such as the sites of special scientific interest in the UK, for which legal protection is quite limited, and hence they do not easily fit into the IUCN scheme. The stricter categories of protection (I-III) make up about 11 percent of the total area. Category V, although making up only 6 percent of sites, covers 40 percent of the total protected area – these large protected landscapes reflect the importance of cultural landscapes and semi-natural habitats across this region. By contrast with the global position, Category II sites constitute only 12 percent of the total area, reflecting the relative weakness of protection of many national parks and landscape protection areas.

Europe: Growth in the number of protected areas, 1894-2005

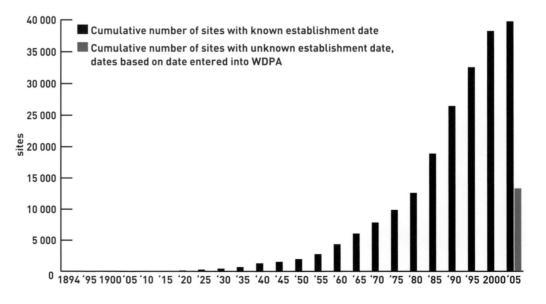

Some 829 sites are classed as coastal and marine, and these are distributed through all of the regional seas – Mediterranean, Baltic, North, Irish – and around the coasts of most countries. There remain significant gaps in the systems for the coastal and marine environment, however, and a large number of these sites are only coastal and do not include significant marine areas. The total marine surface area protected is some 66 000 km².

Most protected areas in Europe are on land owned by national or regional governments and state organizations. There is now a greater diversity of ownership types as a result of the expansion of the protected areas to implement the Natura 2000 network, for example on private land in Finland; the growth of charitable environmental organizations in countries such as the UK that own and manage land; and the privatization of land following the changes of government in central and eastern Europe. A good deal of cooperation exists between the protected areas authorities and the owners and managers of sites.

With the development of devolved decision making, particularly in Austria, Germany, Italy, and Spain, and more recently in the UK, protected area jurisdiction has passed to the provincial level of government. However, national responsibility remains due to international obligations.

The Natura 2000 network has been largely established across 15 countries and preparations are well advanced for implementation in a further ten. Some 236 000 km² have been classified as sites under the birds directive; this represents between 5 and 24 percent of the national territory in the 15 countries. Under the habitats directive some 458 000 km² have been classified, representing 7–24 percent of the territory in the 15 countries.

A number of lessons can be learned from the implementation process. EU Member States have had to implement the new measures but have done so at a variable pace. Consultation with stakeholders was not a formal part of the process and, as many sites in some countries were on private land, there was a great deal of resentment and also many legal challenges. From a slow initial pace, the implementing authorities were forced to quicken the process under threat of legal challenge either from non-governmental organizations or from the European Commission. A number of cases were subject to proceedings at the European Court and

Europe: Protected areas network by IUCN category, 2005

IUCN category	Total sites	Total area (km²)
Ia	1 577	85 835
Ib	542	39 945
II	275	108 569
III	3 570	4 455
IV	16 331	70 586
V	3 035	348 593
VI	203	22 010
No category	27 527	194 479
Total	53 060	874 473

Europe: Protected areas network by IUCN category (percentage of total area), 2005

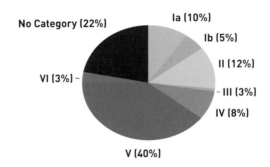

Europe: Number of protected areas by IUCN category, 2005

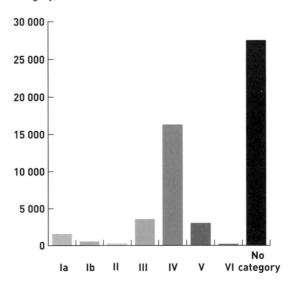

Areas of Europe protected (by country), 2005

Country/territories	Land area (km²)	Total protected area (km²)	Total number of sites
Albania	28 750	1 029	52
Andorra	450	33	2
Austria	83 860	23 475	1 087
Belgium	30 510	1 052	618
Bosnia and Herzegovina	51 130	271	31
Bulgaria	110 910	11 184	754
Croatia	56 540	5 721	200
Czech Republic	78 870	12 451	1 768
Denmark	43 090	7 156	357
Estonia	45 100	21 473	11 242
Finland	338 150	30 698	3 466
France	551 500	75 277	1 334
Germany	357 030	114 914	7 261
Gibraltar	10	<1	1
Greece	131 960	6 884	147
Hungary	93 030	8 300	236
Iceland	103 000	9 807	79
Ireland	70 270	810	91
Italy	301 340	59 886	780
Latvia	64 600	10 583	542
Liechtenstein	160	64	10
Lithuania	65 200	7 170	297
Luxembourg	2 590	441	63
Macedonia FYR	25 710	1 833	83
Malta	320	59	93
Monaco	2	1	3
Montenegro, Rep.	n/a	1 034	38
Netherlands	41 530	7 844	1 596
Norway	323 880	20 703	1 795
Poland	323 250	90 712	1 822
Portugal	91 980	7 639	69
Romania	238 390	12 277	181
San Marino	60	0	0
Serbia, Rep.	n/a	2 837	140
Slovakia	49 010	12 347	1 176
Slovenia	20 250	1 496	48
Spain	505 990	54 400	621
Svalbard and Jan Mayen Islands	62 010	116 076	29
Sweden	449 960	49 137	5 032
Switzerland	41 290	11 852	2 190
United Kingdom	242 910	75 546	7 7263

these helped to clarify the terms of the directives in favor of species and habitat protection and against commercial pressures. The definition of habitats varies from the very detailed to the broad brush, and some major inshore habitats are missing. The sites have been identified without complementary measures to adjust policies and land uses which impact unfavorably on them, such as financial support for agriculture. The financial resources and associated instruments for implementing the network have only just been investigated, many years after the start of the process of designation, and there is no guarantee that the substantial costs can be met.

Europe: Biosphere reserves, 2005

Country	No. of sites	Protected area (km²)
Austria	6	528
Bulgaria	16	378
Croatia	1	2 000
Czech Republic[1]	6	4 505
Estonia	1	15 600
Finland	2	7 700
France[2]	7	7 619
Germany[2]	14	17 716
Greece	2	89
Hungary	5	1 289
Ireland	2	111
Italy	8	5 659
Latvia	1	4 744
Montenegro, Rep.	2	2 367
Netherlands	1	2 600
Poland[1,3,4]	9	3 980
Portugal	1	6
Romania	3	6 620
Serbia, Rep.	2	2 367
Slovakia[3,4]	4	2 413
Slovenia	2	1 957
Spain	33	22 717
Sweden	2	1 965
Switzerland	2	2 121
United Kingdom	9	435
TOTAL[5]	138	117 486

1 Krkonose/Karkonosze Biosphere Reserve is transboundary between Czech Republic and Poland.
2 Vosges du Nord/Pfälzerwald Biosphere Reserve is transboundary between France and Germany
3 East Carpathian Biosphere Reserve is transboundary between Poland, Slovakia, and the Ukraine.
4 Tatra Biosphere Reserve is transboundary between Poland and Slovakia.
5 Because of the transboundary sites, the total figure for number of sites is lower than the sum of the country totals.
Overseas territories, departments, and dependencies (notably of France, the Netherlands, and the UK) are only included in this table if they lie within the geographic boundaries of Europe; otherwise they are included in the relevant WCPA region.

International sites

More than any other region, Europe has embraced the concept of working internationally and collaboratively in the designation of protected areas. It has a greater number of World Heritage and Ramsar sites and biosphere reserves than any other region, although, mirroring the national protected areas, these are generally not very large and so the total area they occupy is much lower than for many other regions. A number of these sites

Europe: World Heritage sites, 2005

Country	No. of sites	Protected area (km²)
Bulgaria	2	410
Croatia	1	295
France[1]	2	231
Germany	1	1
Greece	2	7
Hungary[2]	1	<1
Italy	1	<1
Macedonia FYR	1	380
Montenegro, Rep.	1	320
Norway	1	1 227
Poland[3]	1	55
Portugal	1	150
Romania	1	6 792
Serbia	1	320
Slovakia[2]	1	<1
Slovenia	1	4
Spain[1]	4	869
Sweden	2	12 769
Switzerland	2	561
United Kingdom	3	189
TOTAL[4]	29	24 580

1 Pyrénées-Mont Perdu World Heritage Site is transboundary between France and Spain.
2 Caves of Aggtelek Karst and Slovak Karst World Heritage Site is transboundary between Hungary and Slovakia and comprises a small area of the cave system.
3 Belovezhskaya Pushcha/Bialowieza Forest World Heritage Site is transboundary with Belarus.
4 Because of the transboundary sites, the total figure for number of sites is lower than the sum of the country totals.
Overseas territories, departments, and dependencies (notably of France, the Netherlands, and the UK) are only included in this table if they lie within the geographic boundaries of Europe; otherwise they are included in the relevant WCPA region.

have been developed on the borders with neighboring countries, and many are managed as transboundary sites.

In addition to the major international conventions, most countries have additional requirements for establishing protected areas under various European obligations. These include Natura 2000, the Convention on the Conservation of European Wildlife and Natural Habitats (Bern Convention), and the establishment of the Emerald network (within EU countries this network is, in effect, established under the Natura 2000 network). The importance of cultural landscapes in Europe is recognized through the European Landscape Convention, signed in 2000 but not yet ratified to bring it into operation.

Europe: Ramsar sites, 2005

Country/territories	No. of sites	Protected area (km²)
Albania	2	335
Austria	19	1 382
Belgium	9	429
Bosnia and Herzegovina	1	74
Bulgaria	10	203
Croatia	4	805
Czech Republic	11	434
Denmark	27	7 365
Estonia	11	2 183
Finland	49	8 022
France	20	6 203
Germany	32	8 400
Greece	10	1 635
Hungary	23	1 772
Iceland	3	590
Ireland	45	670
Italy	46	571
Latvia	6	1 492
Liechtenstein	1	1
Lithuania	5	505
Luxembourg	2	172
Macedonia FYR	1	189
Malta	2	<1
Monaco	1	<1
Montenegro, Rep.	5	408
Netherlands	43	8 169
Norway	32	1 159
Poland	13	1 258
Portugal	17	738
Romania	2	6 646
Serbia, Rep.	5	408
Slovakia	13	389
Slovenia	2	10
Spain	49	1 731
Svalbard and Jan Mayen Islands	5	6
Sweden	51	5 145
Switzerland	11	87
United Kingdom	150	7 790
TOTAL	738	77 374

Overseas territories, departments, and dependencies (notably of France, the Netherlands, and the UK) are only included in this table if they lie within the geographic boundaries of Europe; otherwise they are included in the relevant WCPA region.

Other international agreements operate in parts of the region. The cohesion mechanisms in the Mediterranean under the Barcelona Convention have resulted in the development of Special Protected Areas of Mediterranean Importance. Marine and coastal areas of the Baltic are covered under the Helsinki Convention. The Alpine Network of Protected Areas has been established under the Alpine Convention. The Carpathian Convention, signed in 2003, will result in the establishment of a Carpathian National Park Convention.

All of these initiatives have reinforced the role of national governments and authorities in protected area identification and management, and can bring about tensions between the different levels of legal jurisdiction in each country.

FUTURE DIRECTIONS

The protection of the marine environment will be a major priority for the future. New approaches are required rather than transferring the terrestrial approach. Marine systems are more dynamic and unpredictable in space and time, and reflect major global climatic and ocean circulation changes. The ownership of the water column, the sea bed, and marine natural resources add further challenges. Third party access is a critical issue, especially with respect to navigation and fishing rights. Scientific information on the key marine features and their management needs is required. With this, development of mechanisms for safeguarding biomass and recruitment, including no-take zones and zoning for different levels of sustainable exploitation, should form the basis for the new approaches. Completion of the designation of protected areas within territorial limits alongside the implementation of protection within the exclusive economic zones and on the high seas will be necessary. Effective engagement with key interests, especially the various fishing and aquaculture interests, will be essential.

For terrestrial protected areas the emphasis must change from the identification and designation of sites to improving their management to achieve conservation and wider environmental goals. It will be essential to ensure that natural processes and functions are maintained, and restored where they have become degraded (notably those Natura 2000 sites designated for their restoration potential), species reinstated, and some translocated to take into account climate changes. This will require changes in those land uses and financial incentives which impact natural resources and processes in and adjacent to protected areas. Such changes are essential in the operation of agriculture policies to stimulate environmental

M. Spalding

**Adamello Brenta
Natural Park, Italy.**

management. Management improvement will need to embrace all components of protected areas: fund raising, economic activity, business planning and management, stakeholder engagement. It will be necessary to ensure that the skills needed are available among protected area staff and cooperative training programs established throughout the region.

Terrestrial protected areas are too often seen in isolation from each other in space. Therefore the further implementation of connectivity measures, such as the Pan-European Ecological Network, and where appropriate the physical development of corridors connecting protected areas, will be necessary. Also, protected areas should be seen increasingly as part of whole environmental systems; it will be prudent to develop and implement strategies and plans for biogeographical regions rather than the slavish adherence to administrative boundaries which often have no relevance in nature. National and regional efforts will also be required to identify any gaps in the systems of protected areas. A biogeographical framework should be adopted for this work. None of these improvements can be achieved without a substantial increase in financial resources from all sources: public, private, and charitable.

There are many different structures for the governance of protected areas in Europe. Future challenges will be to ensure a greater degree of meaningful involvement by local and other stakeholders. This will require a change from the present governance structures in many protected areas to those which are representative and inclusive of all relevant interests. Increasing the engagement of other stakeholders, especially local communities, and improving their capacity to contribute to management, will be vital.

Action is likely to be taken at different scales. Within the expanding European Union, the Natura 2000 network will be implemented, and monitoring regimes established, with the focus of attention on management effectiveness in relation to the species and habitats of significance. Informal approaches through corridors and networks are likely to continue, for instance for the major river systems such as the Danube, and in the regional seas such as the Mediterranean, which cross many national boundaries. Attention should also be paid to the further possibilities of "peace parks" as part of the environmental and societal reconstruction in the Balkans, and cooperation on transboundary protected areas where the management is out of step between the adjacent authorities.

West and Central Africa

ANGOLA, BENIN, BURKINA FASO, BURUNDI,

CAMEROON, CAPE VERDE,

CENTRAL AFRICAN REPUBLIC, CHAD, CONGO,

CÔTE D'IVOIRE, DEMOCRATIC REPUBLIC OF THE CONGO,

EQUATORIAL GUINEA, GABON, GAMBIA, GHANA,

GUINEA, GUINEA-BISSAU, LIBERIA, MALI, MAURITANIA,

NIGER, NIGERIA, RWANDA, SAÕ TOMÉ AND PRÍNCIPE,

SENEGAL, SIERRA LEONE, TOGO

Contributors: M. Bakarr, R. Kormos, and E. Lisinge

REGIONAL DESCRIPTION

In total, this WCPA (World Commission on Protected Areas) region includes 31 countries, including the francophone African countries of Djibouti on the east coast, and the Indian Ocean island nations of Madagascar, Comoros, and Mauritius, based on an administrative decision by IUCN. In this study, these countries have been included in the Eastern and Southern Africa region analysis for reasons of geographic logic.

West Africa stretches from the Cape Verde islands and Mauritania in the west to Niger and Nigeria in the east; while Central Africa extends from Cameroon and Chad in the north to Rwanda and Burundi in the east, and Angola in the south, including the island nation of Saõ Tomé and Príncipe. West and Central Africa are endowed with a rich biological heritage, with representation of most of the world's major tropical biomes, including deserts, mountains, forests, lakes, rivers, and coastal marine ecosystems.

The ecology of West and Central Africa's biomes is primarily determined by rainfall gradients. In West Africa, the climate is wettest in the southwest and becomes progressively drier to the north and east, transitioning from lowland rainforest in the southwest into savanna woodlands further north. In Central Africa, the climate becomes drier to the north. The rainforests in Africa are drier than those on other continents, receiving on average between 1 600 and 2 000 millimeters of rain per year. Most areas experience two peak rainfalls and a dry season of three months.

The Congo Basin contains the second largest continuous tropical rainforest in the world, where dense forest covers more than 1.9 million km². The southern fringes of the Sahara Desert and savanna woodlands of the Sudano-Sahelian region also

Orphaned western lowland gorilla (*Gorilla gorilla gorilla*).

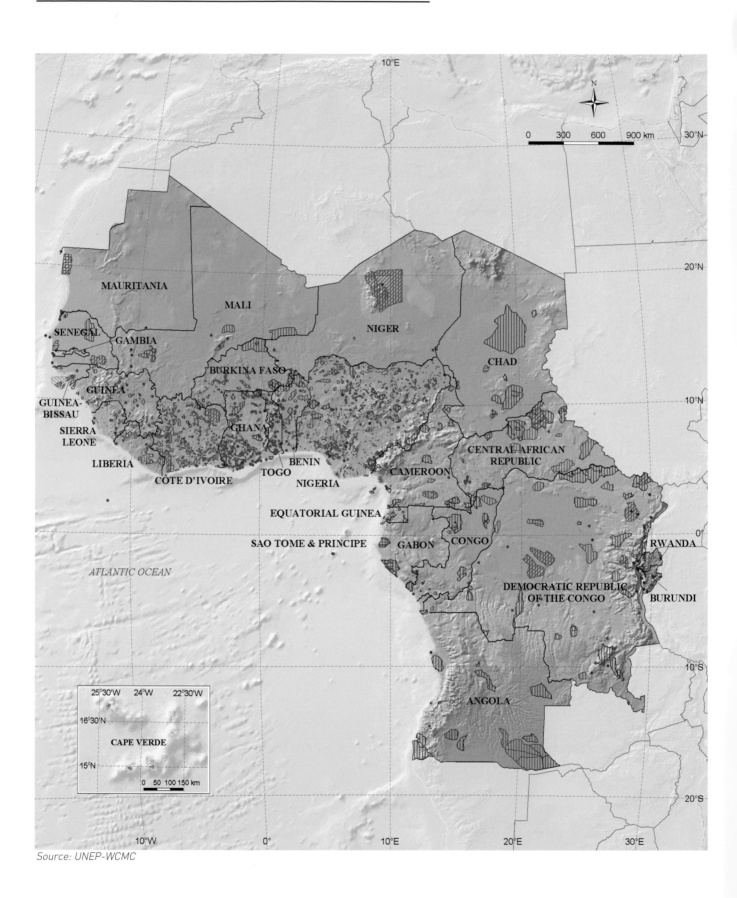

Source: UNEP-WCMC

support large populations of wildlife, including a diverse array of megaherbivores such as elephants, antelopes, and hippopotamus. The region is drained by dozens of major rivers, including the Gambia, Niger, and Congo. Further north the region grades into the dry deserts of the southern and central Sahara, including the Tibesti Mountains rising to over 3 400 meters in northern Chad, with a slightly more reliable water supply and an important array of desert species, including several rare antelopes.

The Guinea-Congolian lowland rainforests are one of Earth's biologically richest ecosystems. They form a belt along the Gulf of Guinea coast and into the vast Congo Basin wilderness, within which several distinct vegetation units have been defined (White 1983, Sayer, Harcourt & Collins 1992). The lowland rainforests occur in two major blocks: the Upper Guinea forest to the west; and the Nigeria-Cameroon coastal forests from western Nigeria through southwestern Cameroon. These are separated by the 'Dahomey Gap,' an area of savanna and degraded dry forest in Togo and Benin.

The Central Africa or 'Congolian' forests are relatively more extensive and constitute several distinct units: the Cameroonian highlands (along the Nigeria-Cameroon border, and including the offshore island of Bioko), the Albertine Rift highlands (eastern Democratic Republic of the Congo (DRC), Rwanda, Burundi, and western Uganda), forests of the Angolan Escarpment (northwestern Angola), and lowland Congolian forests. The lowland forests are further subdivided into the western equatorial forest, the eastern lowland forest, and the so-called 'Cuvette Centrale' (low-lying area within the curve of the Congo River).

The freshwater systems are extremely rich. At the heart of Africa, the Guinea-Congolian forested rivers are some of the richest waters on the continent, with species adapted to life in rapids, swamp forests, large and small rivers, and lateral lakes. More than 700 fish are recorded from the Congo Basin alone, about 500 of which are endemic. Other important systems include the floodplains of the Inner Niger Delta (Mali), the crater lakes of the Cameroonian highlands, the forested rivers of Upper Guinea, and the swamp forests of the Niger Delta. In the drier areas beyond the forests, water is a more precious resource, but there remain some important wetland areas, notably the large riverine, lacustrine, and flooded grassland ecosystems around the Inner Niger Delta and Lake Chad.

This region is also endowed with rich coastal and marine communities. There are extensive mangrove habitats in most countries. Offshore waters are highly productive, centered around the Canary Current, Guinea Current, and Benguela Current large marine ecosystems. Despite their tropical location, both the Canary and Benguela Current systems are dominated by temperate waters, and by powerful upwellings creating nutrient-rich waters with valuable, although already overexploited, fisheries. The Guinea Current ecosystem is tropical, with considerable terrestrial inputs of both freshwater and nutrients, but also seasonal upwellings of cooler, nutrient-rich waters. No large coral reefs are found here, but there are important and unique coral communities around some rocky shores and the offshore islands. Sites such as Bijagos Archipelago Biosphere Reserve and Banc D'Arguin World Heritage Site provide a critical staging post and overwintering site for migrating birds and are home to many wetland species.

In attempting to quantify and map the diversity of the region, almost all surveys have drawn particular attention to the areas of rainforest. Some 41 centers of plant diversity and 21 priority ecoregions (from the WWF Global 200) have been mapped. There is important regional endemism, but smaller scale pockets of local endemism are not so common, and only ten endemic bird areas have been identified, including the oceanic offshore islands of Cape Verde, Saõ Tomé and Príncipe, and Annobón (Equatorial Guinea).

Topi (*Damaliscus lunatus*), Akagera National Park, Rwanda.

H Thomashoff/Still Pictures

241

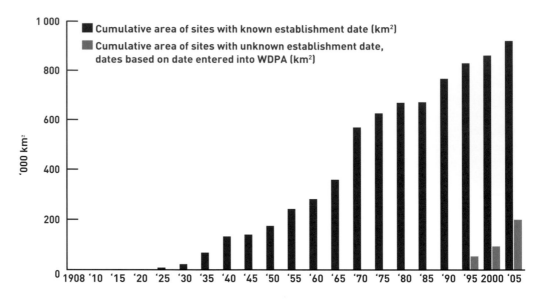

West and Central Africa: Growth of protected areas network, 1908-2005

The biological richness in West and Central Africa is rivaled by the region's cultural heritage. More than 352 million people are found in the two regions combined (a little over half of the sub-Saharan population). Use of traditional resources is widespread in many ethnic groups, from the Tuaregs of the Sahel to Pygmies in the Congo Basin, including hunting for bushmeat, fishing, collection of medicinal plants, and harvesting of products for food and shelter. In addition, habitat clearance for growing crops is also widely practiced, particularly in the West African forest region where slash-and-burn farming is the dominant form of land use. Though the exploitation of resources by people has been sustainable in the past, current patterns suggest that the rich natural heritage is facing increasing degradation. The lowland rainforests constitute one of the world's most threatened ecoregions (Myers *et al.*, 2000).

HISTORICAL PERSPECTIVE

Conservation efforts in West and Central Africa date back to the colonial era. Early protection was established to regulate the use of, or prevent

West and Central Africa: Growth in the number of protected areas, 1908-2005

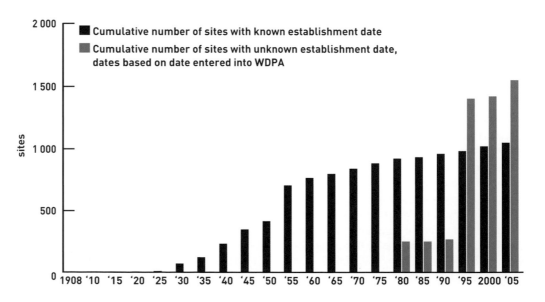

depletion of, natural resources. Elephant reserves were established in what is now the Democratic Republic of the Congo in the late 19th century, while a series of game reserves was established in Ghana in 1909. Timber protection was also an early priority and the first forest reserve systems were established in Nigeria at the turn of the 19th century and in Sierra Leone in 1910. Gambia established a water catchment area in 1916, in what was to become the Abuko Nature Reserve. These trends continued through the 1920s and 1930s, but this period also saw the declaration of some of the first national parks.

Today's Virunga National Park in DRC and Rwanda's Volcans National Park were founded as one in 1925 as Albert National Park, Africa's first, followed by Odzala National Park in Congo in 1935. Burkina Faso established five *parcs de refuge* in 1926, one of which now forms part of the 'W' National Park, while Niger's portion of the same transboundary park dates back to 1937. Many of these sites were located in remote areas and often accessible only to isolated human settlements.

These protected areas, established under colonial rule, were often bounded by arbitrary and artificial boundaries, with only limited understanding of local political and cultural sensitivities. In most countries, the colonial governments created centralized Forest Departments, usually combining wildlife management and protected areas under Water and Forestry as part of the Ministry of Agriculture. Wildlife was generally claimed as Crown property and local hunting was often banned. In many places little has changed since colonial times; the management of protected areas remains centralized in most countries and there is very uneven division of resources, with little local ownership or involvement in protected areas.

As in other parts of Africa, protected area creation increased during the post-colonial period in West and Central Africa, and indeed many countries continue to add new areas as opportunities emerge. However, protected areas are facing increasing management challenges associated with the expansion of human populations and agricultural systems, often right up to protected area boundaries. Subsistence activities, such as the hunting of bushmeat, have become increasingly commercialized, resulting in uncontrolled overexploitation of biological resources. This in turn has fueled poverty and threatens the subsistence livelihoods of millions of people. More recently, civil

unrest has greatly impacted the protected area systems of this region. Protected areas in Liberia, Sierra Leone, and the DRC, for example, have faced increased pressure as displaced people try to eke out a living under the most difficult circumstances.

It is against this backdrop – of a rich natural heritage facing overexploitation, ecosystem degradation, and civil crisis – that conservation in West and Central Africa must now take place. Innovation is needed in the institutions, the policies, and the management strategies to integrate conservation with mainstream initiatives in other sectors. The growing challenge of addressing human livelihood needs (often couched as 'poverty alleviation' by the development community) implies that protected area management must accommodate the priorities and interests of local people living across the broader landscape. Governments, development agencies, and local communities need to understand the significance of protected areas not just for preserving the unique natural heritage, but also for maintaining ecosystem processes that are vital to local, national, and regional economies.

THE PROTECTED AREAS NETWORK

The World Database on Protected Areas (WDPA) holds information on some 2 601 protected areas in West and Central Africa, which cover a total of 1.1 million km^2. This represents almost 9 percent of the total land area – a lower proportion than most other regions, which is exacerbated by the large number of sites in which effective, strict protection is absent.

The majority of sites (89 percent) have no assigned IUCN management category, and represent 29 percent of the total area protected. These sites are dominated by around 2 000 forest reserves where levels of protection are probably very low. IUCN Management Categories II and IV are well represented. All countries have designated some proportion of their territory as protected areas with the exception of Saõ Tomé and Príncipe. However, only a few have very extensive protected area systems, with Benin, Burkina Faso, Central African Republic, Congo, Côte d'Ivoire, Equatorial Guinea, and Ghana all exceeding 15 percent of their total territory protected.

There are only 43 marine and coastal protected areas, covering a marine area estimated at only 9 600 km^2 – these are among the lowest figures of any region. The few sites which cover open ocean areas are almost entirely restricted to countries affected by the Sahelian upwelling,

Areas of West and Central Africa protected (by country), 2005

Country	Land area (km²)	Total protected area (km²)	Total number of sites
Angola	1 246 700	154 580	16
Benin	112 620	26 428	59
Burkina Faso	274 000	42 082	83
Burundi	27 830	1 548	15
Cameroon	475 440	43 816	37
Cape Verde	4 030	14	51
Central African Republic	622 980	97 769	69
Chad	1 284 000	119 773	32
Congo	342 000	48 740	22
Côte d'Ivoire	322 460	54 854	325
DR Congo	2 344 860	191 406	83
Equatorial Guinea	28 050	5 860	13
Gabon	267 670	41 464	22
Gambia	11 300	565	72
Ghana	238 540	36 872	321
Guinea	245 860	17 075	153
Guinea-Bissau	36 120	4 040	10
Liberia	111 370	15 785	16
Mali	1 240 190	26 333	13
Mauritania	1 025 520	17 730	9
Niger	1 267 000	84 141	6
Nigeria	923 770	55 891	1 007
Rwanda	26 340	2 008	5
Senegal	196 720	22 422	14
Sierra Leone	71 740	3 244	55
Togo	56 790	6 501	93

where fisheries conservation priorities have helped raise awareness for increased protection. Parc National du Banc d'Arguin (1 200 km²) in Mauritania and the Bolama Bijagos Archipelago Biosphere Reserve (1 046 km²) in Guinea-Bissau are among the most important marine protected areas in the region.

As noted in other regions, there have been some recent developments in several countries where the protected area systems are being expanded to enhance coverage and representation of existing biodiversity. In West Africa, the government of Ghana has launched a major initiative to designate 12 of its forest reserves as globally significant biodiversity areas (GSBAs) that will be managed exclusively for protection of biodiversity. In Central Africa, the government of Cameroon recently added two new protected areas to its existing system – Campo-Ma'an (2 700 km²) and Mbam et Djerem (4 165 km²) national parks. In the Congo, the Odzala National Park was significantly expanded fivefold to

13 600 km² in 2000, making it one of the largest tropical forest parks in Africa. In Gabon, the government announced in 2002 the creation of 13 new protected areas totaling 40 000 km², enlarging the system to cover 10 percent of the country.

Other forms of protection

Throughout West and Central Africa, many countries have historically maintained a system of habitat reserves that are designated primarily to regulate exploitation of resources. For example, most forest countries in the regions have forest reserves or *forêt classées* (classified forests) that are often protected from exploitation and encroachment until assigned to a concessionaire. There are some 2 000 such reserves in West and Central Africa, and, although these areas seldom have any form of management in place, their existence has been crucial for maintaining forests that would otherwise be converted to other uses. In addition to the national system, the people of West and Central Africa are also known for protecting natural habitats as 'sacred groves' that are either revered for spiritual reasons or used for ceremonial purposes. The crucial importance of these non-conventional protection strategies is gaining momentum throughout the region as countries face increasing challenges with management of conventional protected areas.

In the last five years, at least two regional-scale conservation priority-setting processes for West Africa's Upper Guinea region and the Central African forests, respectively, have helped promote the value of forest reserves for biodiversity protection (Bakarr *et al.*, 2001, Kamdem-Toham *et al.*, 2003). Also, a meeting on the Niger River Basin inspired the need for freshwater protection across much of the Sahelian region of West Africa (Issa Sylla, 2002). Because these processes are largely driven by expert opinion and analysis of biodiversity distribution data, they are facilitating the creation of new protected areas that maximize the coverage and representation of both species and habitats.

International sites

Most of the countries in West and Central Africa are party to several major international treaties, including the Convention on Biological Diversity, the World Heritage Convention, and the Wetlands (Ramsar) Convention. In an effort to meet the commitments associated with these conventions, many countries have made progress in expanding and strengthening their protected area networks. There are 16 natural and mixed World Heritage sites covering more than 211 000 km² (some 70 percent of the total land area for World Heritage sites in sub-Saharan Africa). In addition, there are a total of 73 Ramsar sites and 31 biosphere reserves.

FUTURE DIRECTIONS

The challenges for protected areas in West and Central Africa are similar to other regions, yet the opportunities for meeting them remain limited as a result of major civil conflicts across the region. Nevertheless, important progress has been made through the regional initiatives that have been underway during the last decade. These include large-scale conservation planning processes such as the Upper Guinea, Niger River Basin, and Congo Basin priority-setting workshops; regional initiatives such as the Central Africa Regional Program for the Environment (CARPE); and the IUCN-coordinated Regional Marine Conservation Program in West Africa. To build upon the momentum

West and Central Africa: Protected areas network by IUCN category, 2005

IUCN category	Total sites	Total area (km²)
Ia	19	21 742
Ib	7	11 740
II	91	348 462
III	4	398
IV	119	347 801
V	3	185
VI	45	67 806
No category	2 313	322 805
Total	2 601	1 120 942

West and Central Africa: Protected areas network by IUCN category (percentage of total area), 2005

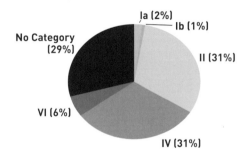

West and Central Africa: Number of protected areas by IUCN category, 2005

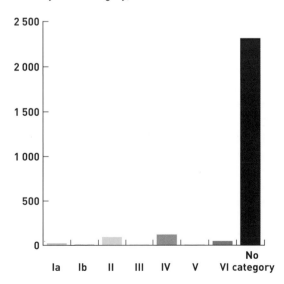

West and Central Africa: Biosphere reserves, 2005

Country	No. of sites	Protected area (km²)
Benin[1]	2	29 283
Burkina Faso[1]	2	5 320
Cameroon	3	8 760
Central African Republic	2	16 402
Congo	2	2 460
Côte d'Ivoire	2	17 700
DR Congo	3	2 827
Gabon	1	150
Ghana	1	78
Guinea	4	11 927
Guinea Bissau	1	1 012
Mali	1	25 000
Mauritania	1	<1
Niger[1]	2	251 281
Nigeria	1	1 306
Rwanda	1	125
Senegal	4	10 938
TOTAL	31	384 568

1 Region "W" is a transboundary site shared between Benin, Burkina Faso and Niger

West and Central Africa: World Heritage sites, 2005

Country	No. of sites	Protected area (km²)
Cameroon	1	5,260
Central African Republic	1	17 400
Côte d'Ivoire[1]	3	14 843
DR Congo	5	68 546
Guinea[1]	1	130
Mali	1	4 000
Mauritania	1	12 000
Niger	2	79 560
Senegal	2	9 290
TOTAL	17	211 029

1 Mount Nimba Strict Nature Reserve is a transboundary World Heritage site and hence the total number of sites in the region is less than the sum of the national sites.

West and Central Africa: Ramsar sites, 2005

Country	No. of sites	Protected area (km²)
Benin	2	1 391
Burkina Faso	3	2 992
Burundi	1	10
Central African Rep.	1	1013
Chad	4	49 571
Congo	1	4 390
Côte d'Ivoire	6	1 273
DR Congo	2	8 660
Equatorial Guinea	3	1 360
Gabon	3	10 800
Gambia	1	200
Ghana	6	1 784
Guinea	14	55 879
Guinea-Bissau	1	391
Liberia	1	761
Mali	1	41 195
Mauritania	3	12 311
Niger	12	4 3179
Nigeria	1	581
Senegal	4	997
Sierra Leone	1	2 950
Togo	2	1 944
TOTAL	73	243 631

generated by these regional initiatives, an integrated strategy for developing a comprehensive protected area systems is needed to maximize biodiversity and ecosystem representation across the region.

A crucial step in this regard will be to mobilize government agencies, donors, conservation organizations, and research institutions to jointly identify and refine targets based on an adequate understanding of biodiversity patterns, ecosystem processes, and socioeconomic realities. The extinction risks facing many large mammals in West and Central Africa suggest that biodiversity-driven targets will need to become a primary focus of any comprehensive protected area strategy. Such an effort will also help establish baseline information and strengthen local institutional capabilities for effective long-term management and monitoring. Regional-scale ecosystem assessments have already shown the need to increase the proportion of lowland rainforests in the existing network because of their crucial role in protecting watersheds and providing a range of ecological services.

In West Africa's Upper Guinea region, options for forest protection are already very limited due to the highly fragmented nature of the ecosystem, and one critical response will be to target forest reserves for biodiversity conservation. The GSBA approach in Ghana provides a valuable model, as this has enabled forest reserves to be quickly upgraded and managed without major infusions of external funding. Although deforestation trends are still relatively slow in Central Africa (0.02-0.45

M. Spalding

The future of protected areas in West and Central Africa will increasingly depend on the commitment of civil society toward understanding and appreciating their value to livelihoods, environmental stability, and rural development.

percent per year) compared with most West African countries, the potential for rapid clearance exists due to rising populations in the region.

Other key targets include coastal marine habitats (primarily mangroves) along the entire Gulf of Guinea, freshwater habitats (e.g. floodplains, lateral lakes, swamp forests), and the montane ecoregions (notably the Fouta Djallon highlands in Guinea and Mount Cameroon, and adjacent highlands in the Nigeria-Cameroon cross-border area).

The potential for transboundary conservation also needs further development (van der Linde et al. 2001). In addition to improving management across borders, transboundary protected areas tend to foster integrated landscape approaches, and help secure large areas for wide-ranging species such as elephants. Efforts are already under way in the West Africa region between Benin, Burkina Faso, and Niger (Park 'W'), Guinea and Senegal (Niokolo-Badiar); and in Central Africa between Cameroon,

Central African Republic, and Congo (Sangha River Trinational Area). Transboundary conservation will obviously present new challenges, particularly in respect to governance and institutional issues. And while decentralization of power is becoming more common in other parts of Africa, it is still relatively nascent in West and Central Africa. There will be a need to reconcile roles of wildlife and forestry departments to help improve the management of protected areas in a landscape context.

Finally, the future of protected areas in West and Central Africa will increasingly depend on the commitment of civil society toward understanding and appreciating the value of such areas to livelihoods, environmental stability, and rural development. Because of the potential to mainstream protected areas in national development, government investment in protected area agencies will likely improve considerably when the interest of civil society is enhanced.

Eastern and Southern Africa

BOTSWANA, COMOROS, DJIBOUTI, ERITREA, ETHIOPIA, KENYA, LESOTHO, MADAGASCAR, MALAWI, MAURITIUS, MAYOTTE (FRANCE), MOZAMBIQUE, NAMIBIA, RÉUNION (FRANCE), SEYCHELLES, SOMALIA, SOUTH AFRICA, SUDAN, SWAZILAND, TANZANIA, UGANDA, ZAMBIA, ZIMBABWE

Contributors: N. Burgess, S. Kanyamibwa, G. Llewellyn, M. Thieme, R. Taylor

REGIONAL DESCRIPTION

The WCPA administrative region covers 19 territories. However, for the purpose of better geographic coherence for this study, four countries from the West and Central Africa region have also been included: Comoros, Djibouti, Madagascar, and Mauritius. On the African mainland, countries in the region range from Sudan in the north through the countries of the Horn of Africa, eastern Africa, and into southern Africa to the Cape of Good Hope. Away from the coastal plains, most of the region is found at altitudes over 1 000 meters, in particular across the vast Central Plateau of southern Africa.

The vegetation of mainland Eastern and Southern African is dominated by the Somali-Masai and Zambezian biomes – large arid to seasonally arid regions supporting savanna woodland habitats with high plant endemism distributed across a dynamic landscape mosaic. Moving south, the Zambezian vegetation types are replaced by those of the Karoo-Namib regional center of endemism, with low shrubs and grasses; the grassland-dominated Kalahari-Highveld regional transition zone; and finally by the Cape Floral Kingdom (White, 1983). This region, in particular, contains an amazing diversity of short shrubby vegetation types supporting globally exceptional levels of plant and invertebrate endemism. Lowland rainforests are restricted to the Lake Victoria region and along the coastal strip of eastern Africa (Sayer, Harcourt, and Collins, 1992).

In the midst of a predominantly dry region there are a number of moist mountain ranges, which, because of their isolation, have formed archipelago-like centers of endemism (White, 1983). The most important of these, biologically, are the Eastern Arc (Tanzania and Kenya), the Albertine Rift (Uganda, Rwanda, Burundi, western Tanzania, and eastern Democratic Republic of the Congo), and the Ethiopian highlands. These areas all possess high rates of species endemism; the Eastern Arc and Albertine Rift are globally exceptional in this regard (Burgess *et al.*, 2004).

The Indian Ocean islands are highly distinct

M Spalding

An Aldabra Sacred Ibis (*Threskiornis bernieri abbotti*), Aldabra Atoll World Heritage Site, Seychelles.

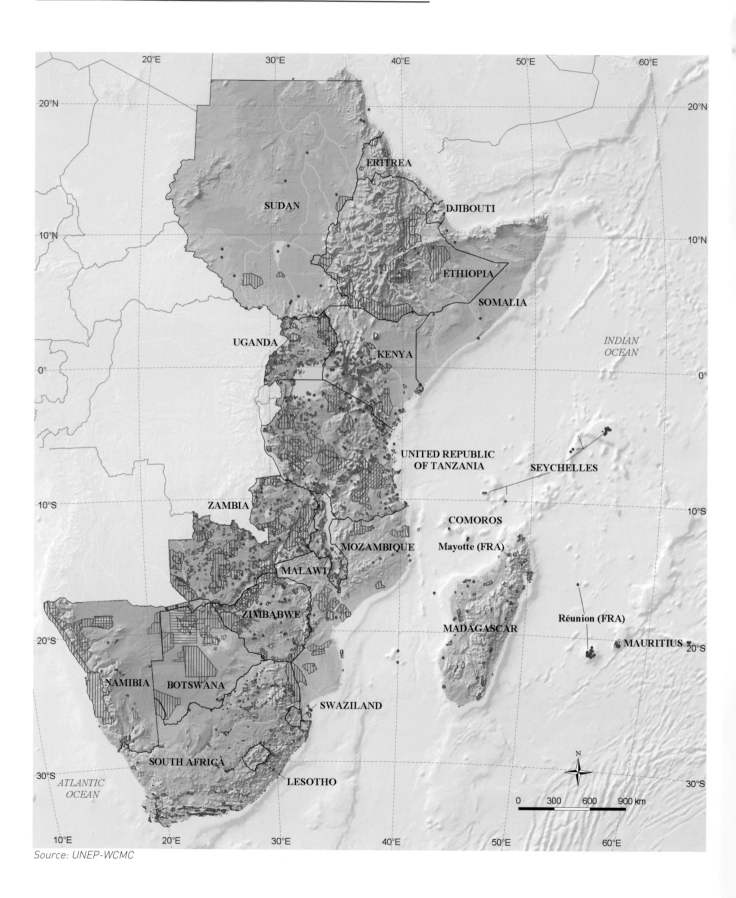

Source: UNEP-WCMC

from the African mainland, and have over 70 percent of all their species as strict endemics. These endemic species are often found within endemic genera and families, including those with ancient lineages within families, such as the lemurs of Madagascar, that have been extinct on the mainland for millions of years (Mittermeier *et al.*, 1999). The offshore islands have witnessed high rates of recent extinction, especially the smaller islands of Seychelles, Mascarenes, and Comoros (Burgess *et al.*, 2004).

Within the freshwater realm, Eastern and Southern Africa contains the large Rift Valley lakes and an extensive network of rivers and streams with associated wetlands and swamps. The Great Lakes of eastern Africa (Lakes Victoria, Tanganyika, and Malawi) are the most important in the world in terms of their concentrations of endemic fish, with Lake Malawi alone possessing upwards of 700 endemic cichlids (Turner *et al.* 2001). Further north in the highlands of Ethiopia, Lake Tana hosts the only intact cyprinid species flock in the world.

Extensive wetlands are found in Kilombero Valley, Moyowosi/Malagarasi system, and the Ugalla River, the Okavango Delta, the Sudd, Lake Chilwa, the Barotse Floodplain, the Kafue Flats, Busanga and Lukanga swamps, and Lakes Mweru and Bangweulu and associated swamps. These contain large congregations of wetland birds and other wildlife. In addition to large freshwater wetlands, saline water bodies such as Etosha,

Natron, and Makgadikgadi provide specialized habitats for most of the world's flamingos. Madagascar's rivers and lakes are also home to a distinctive freshwater fauna – including endemic taxa of crayfish, aquatic insects, amphibians, and fish. Endemic fish and frog species also survive in the Mediterranean climate of the Cape region at the southern tip of the continent.

The marine and coastal habitats of the region are part of a western Indian Ocean center of biodiversity. Subcenters of marine endemism occur around the border between South Africa and Mozambique, and the Mascarene Islands (Roberts *et al.*, 2002). The South Equatorial Current hits the eastern African coast at Cabo Delgado in Mozambique, and then splits to flow north and south. There is considerable coral reef development, primarily of the fringing reef type, concentrated around the islands and along portions of the coasts of Kenya, Tanzania, and Mozambique. Seagrass beds are also extensive in shallow marine areas. Southern Mozambique is dominated by muddy waters and coastal dune fields, caused by localized upwellings, combined with nutrient input from major rivers such as the Zambezi.

The eastern African region is also the cradle of humanity with the oldest fossils of hominids extending back over five million years. Over the millions of years that hominids and humans have inhabited this region, they developed the use of fire to facilitate hunting and farming, which may have

Eastern and Southern Africa: Growth of protected areas network, 1895–2005

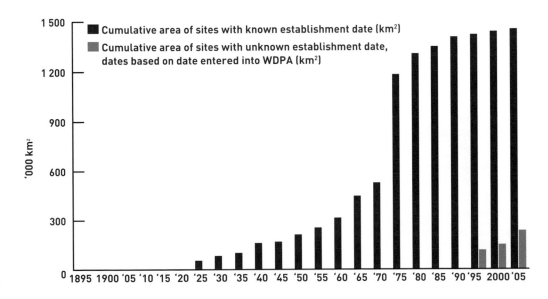

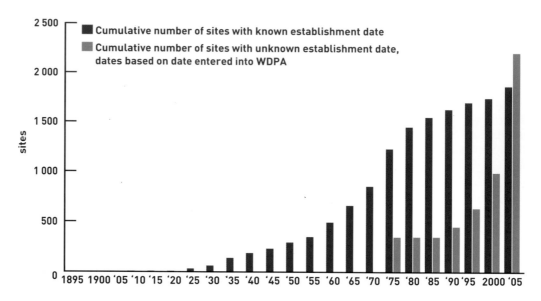

Eastern and Southern Africa: Growth in the number of protected areas, 1896–2005

changed the appearance of the landscape. Due to this ancient interaction between humans and their environment, the habitats and species composition of this region may be far more anthropogenically altered than is currently accepted.

HISTORICAL PERSPECTIVE

Traditional African societies used a variety of systems to protect habitats and species. For example, most (perhaps all) villages maintained small patches of habitat as burial areas or for traditional religious purposes. Many habitat management systems are still operational, for example those of the Masai of eastern Africa and the San Bushmen of southern Africa. However, strictly protected areas were generally small in traditional societies, and these approaches to conservation are gradually being lost over many parts of the region.

With European colonization, the creation of government-designated protected areas began. The first protected area in Africa, the Greater St Lucia Wetland Park, was declared in 1895. During the early 20th century, large protected area systems were developed in colonial African countries. The primary motivation of the colonial governments was the preservation of 'wilderness' to provide opportunities for hunting big game animals (Neumann, 1998), and to a lesser extent for the protection of water supply (e.g. Rodgers, 1993). Most reserves dating from this period are located in areas unsuitable for farming or commercial forestry, but

suitable for large game mammals – principally the savanna woodland habitats that extend over large parts of the region. For example, the Selous Game Reserve (44 000 km²) and the Kruger National Park (19 000 km²) both date from this period. At the end of the colonial period in the early 1960s, Eastern and Southern Africa possessed over 500 parks and reserves spanning more than 400 000 km² of land.

The newly independent African nations have continued to create government-controlled protected areas. At the same time there has been an increasing effort to develop community-managed reserves to support both human development and achieve conservation goals. The majority of these community-managed areas are found in southern Africa, but they are increasing in number in eastern Africa as well. Even more recently, companies and individuals have started to create private reserves, especially in southern Africa.

THE PROTECTED AREAS NETWORK

In total, there are more than 4 000 protected areas in a well-developed network across Eastern and Southern Africa. More than 200 of these are IUCN Category II national parks covering very large tracts of land with high levels of protection. More than 3 000 sites lack IUCN management categories and these include many forest reserves, wildlife management areas, hunting areas, and private reserves. In total, these different protected lands cover 14.7 percent of the region.

In the marine realm, the declaration of· reserves has lagged behind that of terrestrial habitats, with the first known marine protected area (MPA) being the Tsitsikama National Park in South Africa, first designated in 1964. However, over the past decade there has been a dramatic increase in the number and size of MPAs in the region. The World Database on Protected Areas currently lists 139 MPAs, covering some 12 000 km² of coastal and oceanic water. This figure represents some 0.15 percent of the exclusive economic zone areas claimed by the region's countries, and the majority are focused in coastal waters and around high-profile ecosystems such as coral reefs (more than 2 000 km², or 14 percent of all coral reefs, are protected). In several cases (e.g. St Lucia in South Africa, Sadaani in Tanzania, and Maputo Elephant in Mozambique), marine components are in the process of being added to existing terrestrial parks.

Eastern African protected areas are not randomly distributed; they are clumped geographically and disproportionately cover certain habitat types. For example, the protected area networks of Tanzania and Kenya cover much larger percentages of those countries than the corresponding areas in Sudan or Somalia – due mainly to political instability in the latter countries. In terms of habitat coverage, reserves cover disproportionate areas of savanna woodland habitat with large mammals. In recent decades, governments have worked to address this situation and have increased the coverage of less-represented habitats within their protected area systems. New reserves have been established to cover montane forest (e.g. Udzungwa Mountains National Park in Tanzania) and Mediterranean habitats in South Africa (e.g. the Knersvlakte and Groenefontein Provincial Nature Reserves). Countries emerging from war are also enhancing their protected area networks. For example, Mozambique declared its new Quirimbas National Park in 2002; it covers about 7 500 km² of miombo woodland, eastern African coastal forest, mangrove, and marine habitats.

Despite these advances, recent analyses indicate that the current protected area network does not fully cover the distribution of biodiversity in the region. Using data from all mammals, amphibians, and threatened birds, significant gaps in the protected area network are found in the montane habitats of the region (the Eastern Arc, the Albertine Rift, the Ethiopian highlands, and the Kenyan highlands), the eastern African

Eastern and Southern Africa: Protected areas network by IUCN category, 2005

IUCN category	Total sites	Total area (km²)
Ia	17	2 787
Ib	7	1 251
II	220	508 603
III	24	150
IV	497	265 115
V	30	12 560
VI	219	543 869
No category	3 053	354545
Total	4 067	1 688 879

Eastern and Southern Africa: Protected areas network by IUCN category (percentage of total area), 2005

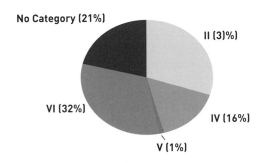

Eastern and Southern Africa: Number of protected areas by IUCN category, 2005

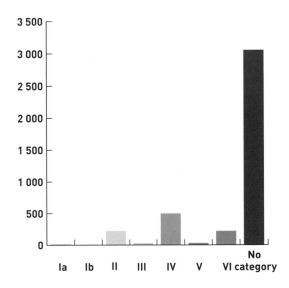

Areas of Eastern and Southern Africa protected (by country), 2005

Country/territories	Land area (km²)	Total protected area (km²)	Total number of sites
Botswana	581 730	175 650	71
Comoros	2 230	404	1
Djibouti	23 200	13	3
Eritrea	117 600	5 006	3
Ethiopia	1 104 300	186 198	40
Kenya	580 370	75 221	348
Lesotho	30 350	68	1
Madagascar	587 040	18 458	60
Malawi	118 480	19 405	130
Mauritius	2 040	162	26
Mayotte	370	64	8
Mozambique	801 590	65 260	42
Namibia	824 290	123 563	173
Réunion	2 510	246	40
Seychelles	450	453	20
Somalia	637 660	5 246	16
South Africa	1 221 040	81606	562
Sudan	2 505 810	1 198 424	26
Swaziland	17 360	601	8
Tanzania, United Republic of	945 090	378 520	811
Uganda	241 040	63 368	747
Zambia	752 610	312 002	683
Zimbabwe	390 760	57 525	249

lowland coastal forests and Maputaland-Pondoland, and in the Cape Fynbos and Succulent Karoo of South Africa (Rodrigues *et al.*, 2003; see also Chapter 10).

Ambitious conservation plans already exist and are being implemented for the Cape Fynbos and Succulent Karoo of South Africa (e.g. Cowling *et al.*, 2003). Similar planning and implementation processes are underway in the eastern African marine ecoregion, the eastern African coastal forests, the Albertine Rift Mountains, and the Eastern Arc Mountains. In all of these plans the creation of new reserves and the upgrading of some types of reserves (e.g. forest reserves) to higher levels of conservation are being advocated.

Another problem is that that many protected areas are 'paper parks' with almost no operational budget, few or no staff, and often with problems of encroachment and poaching of large mammals. In some countries there is pressure to reduce the area of protected land. For example, the Kenyan government tried to degazette sections of several forest reserves for allocation to local farmers. Although Kenyan public outcry prevented most of this, it could have resulted in significant loss of forest, biodiversity, and watershed protection. Similar issues have been seen in Uganda, Tanzania, and Zimbabwe.

Other forms of protection

Many countries in Eastern and Southern Africa possess large numbers of legally gazetted forest reserves managed by Forestry Departments. Outside of South Africa these reserves are not assigned an IUCN protected area management category (I–VI), and hence are often overlooked in assessments of government protected area networks. Throughout eastern Africa there are more than 3 300 forest reserves (the majority of which are included in the WDPA statistics) that cover approximately 340 000 km² of moist forest and savanna woodlands. In some parts of the region, forest reserves are the main type of habitat protection. For example, in the globally distinctive Eastern Arc Mountains of Tanzania and Kenya there are few IUCN I–IV protected areas. Nonetheless, more than 3 300 km², or 14 percent, of the mountain range is contained within forest reserves, and these reserves include up to 90 percent of the remaining forest. These reserves may contain as much biodiversity as the network of IUCN I-VI coded wildlife reserves.

A less well quantified form of protection that is particularly widespread in this region is that provided by private protected areas. Although some of these are included in the statistics from the WDPA, not all are held in this database.

Another important form of protection, which is becoming more popular, is the wildlife management area. In these areas land under local control is established as a community-managed area with conservation objectives, but management remains at the local level and benefits are derived directly by the communities themselves. In some parts of the region, especially in southern Africa, this mechanism represents the most promising way to augment the well-developed government protected area network.

International sites

Within the region only Djibouti and Somalia are not party to the World Heritage Convention, with 10 countries having natural or mixed World Heritage sites (43.5 percent of the countries). A total of 22 natural or mixed World Heritage sites are located in the region, including Ngorongoro, Kilimanjaro, Selous, and Serengeti in Tanzania, Greater St Lucia Wetland Park in South Africa, and Aldabra Atoll in the Seychelles.

Sixteen countries are also signatories of the Ramsar Convention, with a total of 49 sites designated in 2005, 17 in South Africa. There is an ongoing effort to expand the number of sites, particularly in new signatory countries such as Tanzania. Wetlands under this convention include Lake Natron, and the Kilombero Valley and Malagarasi-Moyowosi wetlands in Tanzania; Lakes Naivasha, Baringo, Bogoria, and Nakuru in Kenya; Etosha Pan in Namibia, the St Lucia System in South Africa, and the Okavango Delta in Botswana.

Eight countries in the region also have biosphere reserves under the UNESCO Man and the Biosphere Programme. These sites cover both terrestrial and marine areas, and include the 28 000 km² Lake Manyara in Tanzania.

Apart from the major international agreements, there is growing cooperation at the regional level, notably through the designation of transboundary parks. A number of ambitious transboundary parks and conservation areas are being promoted in southern Africa, including seven very large areas covering more than 200 000 km². These

Eastern and Southern Africa: Internationally protected areas, 2005

Country	No. of sites	Protected area (km²)
Biosphere reserves		
Kenya	6	15 434
Madagascar	3	4 938
Malawi	1	451
Mauritius	1	36
South Africa	4	33 711
Sudan	2	12 509
Tanzania, United Republic of	3	52 281
Uganda	2	2 465
TOTAL	22	121 825
Ramsar sites		
Botswana	1	68 640
Comoros	1	<1
Djibouti	1	30
Kenya	5	1 018
Lesotho	1	4
Madagascar	5	7 856
Malawi	1	2 248
Mauritius	1	<1
Mozambique	1	13 000
Namibia	4	6 296
Seychelles	1	<1
South Africa	17	4 987
Sudan	1	10 846
Tanzania, United Republic of	4	48 684
Uganda	2	370
Zambia	3	5 930
TOTAL	49	169 911
World Heritage sites		
Ethiopia	1	136
Kenya	2	3 050
Madagascar	1	1 520
Malawi	1	94
Seychelles	2	350
South Africa	7	10 655
Tanzania, United Republic of	4	68 605
Uganda	2	1 317
Zambia[1]	1	38
Zimbabwe[1]	2	6 797
TOTAL	22	92 562

1 Mosi-oa-Tunya/Victoria Falls is a transboundary World Heritage site between Zambia and Zimbabwe and hence the total of World Heritage sites is less than the sum of the individual countries.

are the Ai-Ais/Richtersveld Transfrontier Conservation Park between South Africa and Namibia

S Chape

**uKhahlamba/
Drakensberg Park
World Heritage Site,
South Africa.**

(5 921 km²); the Great Limpopo Transfrontier Park between South Africa, Mozambique, and Zimbabwe (35 000 km²); the Kgalagadi Transfrontier Park between Botswana and South Africa (37 991 km²); the Limpopo/ Shashe Transfrontier Conservation Area between Botswana, South Africa, and Zimbabwe (4 872 km²); the Lubombo Transfrontier Conservation Area between South Africa, Swaziland, and Mozambique (4 195 km²); the Maloti-Drakensberg Transfrontier Conservation and Development Area between South Africa and Lesotho (13 000 km²); and an area from Lake Malawi/Nyasa to the Indian Ocean through southern Tanzania and northern Mozambique (100 000 km²).

FUTURE DIRECTIONS
Filling reservation gaps

Despite the impressive protected area network of this region, gaps in the coverage of biodiversity remain. These gaps are most serious in the mountain areas where there are many species of narrow distribution range and few protected areas. Most existing protection in mountains is in forest reserves, and altering the status of some of these to nature reserve or national park would raise the level of protection and help to fill one of the key gaps in the region's protected area system. The same is generally true for the eastern African coastal forest mosaic habitats; here, too, there are many species with small distribution ranges, and once again most important habitat is either found within forest reserves or is unprotected.

Several countries announced the designation of new protected areas at the September 2003 Vth World Parks Congress, which will help to fill some of the gaps in protection. For example, the president of Madagascar stated that his country would triple its protected area coverage. In addition, Mozambique announced the creation of new MPAs to fill key gaps in protection along its coastline, and Tanzania said that it would increase its coverage of marine habitats to 10 percent by 2010 and 20 percent by 2025. In addition, South Africa will be expanding the existing St Lucia reserve northwards to the border with Mozambique.

Improving management effectiveness

Improving the management of paper parks in the region is a serious challenge, given the high demand for natural resources and extensive poverty. Government budgets are inadequate to the task such that other sources of funding are needed. Innovative market mechanisms, such as water payments, biodiversity markets, carbon sequestration, tourism, and revenue-sharing approaches are being tested. Other novel financing systems, including combining private business partnerships with conservation trust funds, must also be investigated and used when appropriate.

Transboundary protected areas

Many border regions across Africa have been areas of conflict. These are also areas that have been politically and economically neglected, have low population densities, and have relatively undamaged ecosystems. A number of transboundary parks have already been designated and others are being considered. Such sites represent opportunities for enhancing peace and cooperation between nations , as well as conserving the natural environment.

Private reserves and land purchase

In Africa, land purchase for conservation is relatively common in the savanna-woodland habitats of southern Africa, and in South Africa, for example, there are many private nature reserves. In eastern Africa land has traditionally been either communally owned or vested with the state; however, changes in the land laws of many eastern African nations are now making land purchase possible. Carefully targeted land purchase might achieve much for conservation in eastern Africa. For example, an Italian non-governmental organization purchased the Mkwaja Ranch in coastal Tanzania and donated it to the Tanzanian government as an

extension to the Sadaani Game Reserve, which was declared a national park in 2003.

Hunting concessions

Hunting concessions occur within government-managed game and hunting reserves in all southern African nations and in Tanzania. Companies or private individuals buy concessions and then sell the hunting rights to tourists. Local communities and private landowners, especially in southern Africa, are developing a similar approach to conservation. The financial benefits are clear, and these are giving an easily measured value to wild habitat and species. However, there remain challenges to ensuring sustainability, and preventing changes to the ecosystem from activities such as re-stocking, changes in natural fauna, or even vegetation clearance to encourage target species.

Community conservation

There has been a paradigm shift to community-based conservation in this region. Strictly protected areas remain a core component of conservation efforts, but more socially just and participatory approaches are increasingly practiced, with a number of emerging consequences. Incentive and utilization-based approaches to conservation are now common within communities and also among large private landowners. The economic importance of wildlife, fisheries, and watershed protection are also driving land restoration and purchases for conservation. Southern Africa is a world leader in community-based conservation, in which both communities and wildlife benefit, and similar community conservation areas are also common in Namibia, Botswana, and Zimbabwe. Changes in the laws of a number of eastern African countries are also providing communities with a greater role in establishing and managing their own protected areas. Both village forest reserves and community-based wildlife management areas are now being promoted as conservation areas in eastern African countries. These wildlife management areas can provide both wild meat and tourist viewing opportunities, and hence bring income to rural populations.

North Africa and the Middle East

AFGHANISTAN, ALGERIA, BAHRAIN, CYPRUS, EGYPT,

IRAN, IRAQ, ISRAEL, JORDAN, KUWAIT, LEBANON,

LIBYAN ARAB JAMAHIRIYA, MOROCCO, OMAN,

OCCUPIED PALESTINIAN TERRITORIES, QATAR,

SAUDI ARABIA, SYRIAN ARAB REPUBLIC, TUNISIA,

TURKEY, UNITED ARAB EMIRATES,

WESTERN SAHARA, YEMEN

Contributors: E. Sattout, M. S. A. Sulayem, M. Spalding

REGIONAL DESCRIPTION

Stretching across five time zones, the 23 countries and territories of the North Africa and Middle East region span a considerable portion of the continents of Africa and Asia, but are united by common strands of geology, climate, and ecology, as well as culture, history, and traditions.

Geologically the region covers parts of the African and Eurasian Tectonic Plates, as well as the entire Arabian Plate. The region encompasses a long coastline with the Atlantic, the entire southern and eastern shores of the Mediterranean Sea, the southern shores of the Black and Caspian Seas, and the seas surrounding the Arabian Peninsula – the Red Sea, the Gulf of Aden, part of the Arabian Sea, the Gulf of Oman, and the Arabian Gulf. Most of the region consists of drylands and deserts, including a large part of the Sahara Desert across North Africa, and the largest unbroken sand desert in the world, the Rub al Khali in southern Arabia. Mountains are also widespread, including the Atlas Mountains across Morocco, Algeria, and Tunisia (reaching to

4 165 meters), the Hejaz and Asir Mountains in southwestern Arabia (3 760 meters), the Zagros Mountains and Elburz Mountains of Iran (5 681 meters), and the various mountain ranges of Afghanistan reaching into the Karakoram Mountains (6 504 meters). The lowest land surface on Earth is also found in the region – the shores of the Dead Sea are some 400 meters below sea level.

Although dominated by arid and semi-arid conditions, the region does include more humid areas, and there are forests in some of the mountain areas, notably across Turkey, and important wetlands, such as the marshes and deltas of Mesopotamia (mostly in southern Iraq).

Lying between Europe, Africa, and Asia the region has a great range of biogeographical influences, reflected in the diversity of plants and animals from each of these regions. Other species are unique, having evolved, or having survived, as relicts from earlier times. During the last Ice Age this region was cooler and wetter, with more widespread savanna and woodland, and isolated

M.Spalding

Wadi Rum National Park, Jordan.

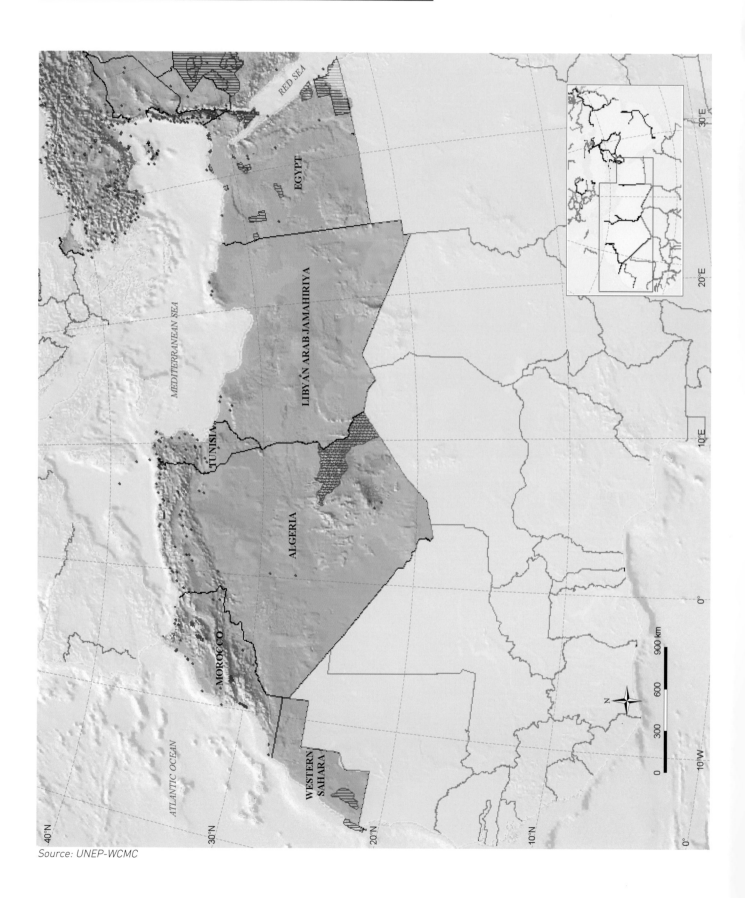

RED SEA

EGYPT

LIBYAN ARAB JAMAHIRIYA

MEDITERRANEAN SEA

TUNISIA

ALGERIA

MOROCCO

ATLANTIC OCEAN

WESTERN SAHARA

40°N

30°N

30°N

20°N

10°N

0°

0°

10°W

10°E

20°E

30°E

0

300

600

900 km

N

Source: UNEP-WCMC

pockets of more amenable climate still remain. The region has also given rise to many important crop species, including wheat, barley, certain legumes, olives, figs, pomegranate, and almonds. Significant genetic diversity in these species remains, both as wild progenitors of these crops, and as varieties still grown in traditional agricultural systems across the region. The Mediterranean Basin forms an important center of biodiversity, while other key ecoregions include the temperate forests and freshwaters of Anatolia (Turkey), the Mesopotamian wetlands and deltas, the highlands of southern Arabia, and the small island of Socotra (Yemen) with its highly distinct flora.

The marine ecosystems also encompass considerable diversity. The Atlantic coast is dominated by the south-flowing Canary Current which brings relatively cool waters and produces nutrient-rich upwellings that support highly productive ecosystems. The region's Mediterranean coast has suffered less from extensive coastal development than the European shores, and supports important shallow-water Mediterranean ecosystems. Coral reefs, mangroves, and seagrasses are found on all the shores around the Arabian Peninsula. The greatest marine biodiversity is found in the Red Sea with ideal conditions for coral growth and a rich fauna that includes a large number of endemic species. Cooler, nutrient-rich upwellings mean highly productive waters off the southern shores of the Arabian Peninsula, and onshore there are highly unusual algal-dominated communities alongside the coral reefs. These marine ecosystems support important fisheries, and are also home to a large number of charismatic species, including many cetacean species, marine turtles, dugongs, and the last remaining Mediterranean monk seals. The Arabian Sea, Red Sea, Mediterranean, and Canary Current areas are all listed as important marine ecoregions by WWF.

Humans have shaped the landscape of this region over many millennia. The earliest known human settlements, such as Jericho, are found here. As well as the cultivation of the first crop plants, it was in the region known as the Fertile Crescent, stretching from the Mediterranean to the Arabian Gulf, following the Tigris, Euphrates, and Jordan Rivers, that the first known domestication of livestock (including sheep, goats, cattle, and donkeys) occurred.

The degree of human usage and influence on the landscapes is highly varied; even in the human-dominated landscapes, biodiversity remains important, while away from regular water supplies, pastureland replaces arable farming, and in drier areas temporary grazing is undertaken with mobile or nomadic herders. There are still wide areas of wilderness in the driest areas, and on the high mountain peaks.

Unfortunately dramatic changes have taken place on many of these landscapes in recent decades. Massive alterations to water supplies, including dam building and drainage, have led to the loss of vast areas of wetlands. The annual Nile flooding, which built the vast Nile Delta and revitalized soils over the Nile valley, has ceased, affecting not only the immediate areas but the coastline and the Mediterranean offshore waters. The vast wetlands of southern Iraq have been heavily drained, destroying the landscape and culture of the people who once lived there, and even today these areas are contracting due to upstream dams and water extraction. Patchwork landscapes have been converted to industrial agriculture in wide areas of North Africa, the Levant, and Turkey.

Coastal areas have undergone rapid development in a few areas – tourism is a major driving force in Turkey, the Sinai Peninsula, and parts of North Africa. Around the Arabian Peninsula wide areas of coastal land have been altered by urban and industrial growth, as well as by the extensive development of the petroleum industry.

HISTORICAL PERSPECTIVE

Efforts to protect the landscape go back to ancient history – there are records from Pliny the Elder of efforts to administer forests, including programs of wardens, tree planting, and the setting aside of areas for wildlife. The Roman Emperor Hadrian (AD 117-138) was reported to have demanded protection for some of the remaining cedar forests on Mount Lebanon (though only a few remnants remain today).

One traditional form of land management, known as al hema (hima, hurah, or ahmia), has been used for more than 2 000 years, and was given a clearer legal standing by the Prophet Mohammed. This involves the setting aside of large tracts of rangeland and restricting their use to prevent overgrazing. In 1969, it was estimated that there were more than 3 000 hema in Saudi Arabia. A later survey in 1984, conducted in the mountain areas west of the country (where most of the hema

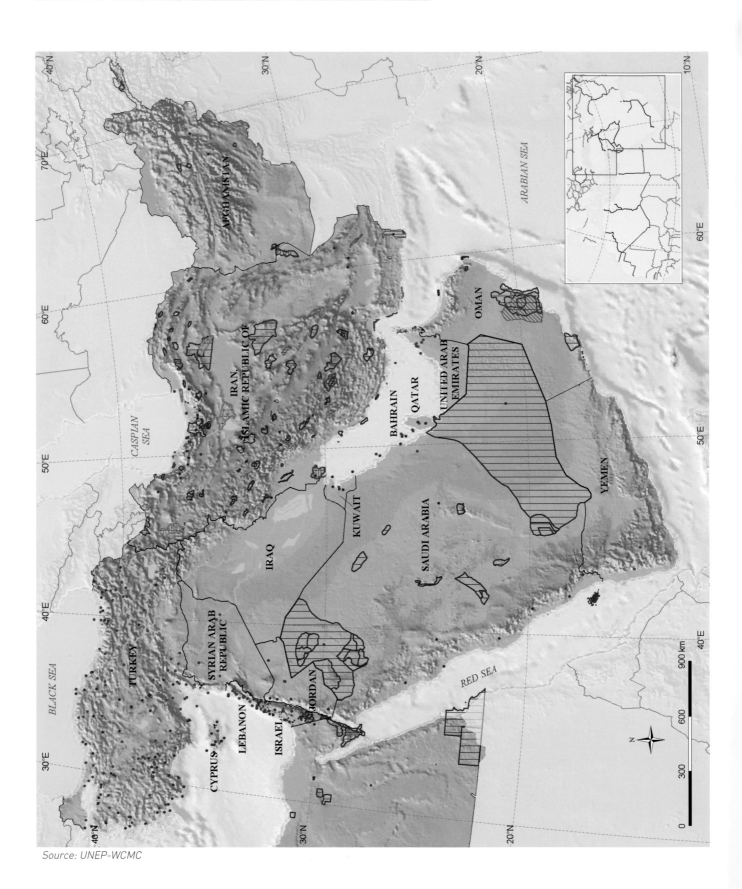

Source: UNEP-WCMC

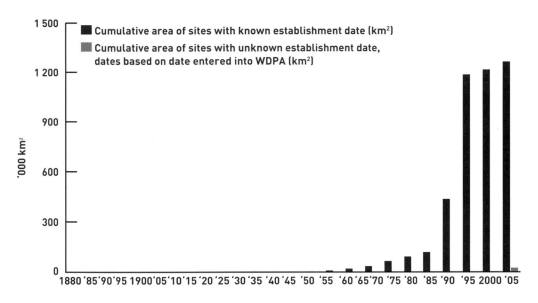

North Africa and the Middle East: Growth of protected areas network, 1880-2005

existed), found only 71 *hema*, under varying degrees of protection. Many of these have been now been formally recognized, however, and are included in the statistics below. Islam, which is the predominant religion across the region, preaches respect for creation, and in a few places this has been used to support conservation efforts. Hunting reserves dating back to 1240 were established at Lake Ichkeul in Tunisia.

Many more forest reserves and hunting reserves were declared in the 18th and 19th centuries when wide parts of this region fell under the Ottoman Empire. Protected areas focused more on biodiversity, however, have been slow to catch on. Some were established under French colonial rule in North Africa in the 1920s and 1930s, but the legislation behind these has largely been repealed post-independence.

Historically, and in present times, war and civil unrest have affected large parts of the region, and ongoing occupation and unrest in countries such as Western Sahara, Northern Cyprus, Palestine, Iraq, and Afghanistan are preventing the establishment and secure management of protected areas.

North Africa and the Middle East: Growth in the number of protected areas, 1880-2005

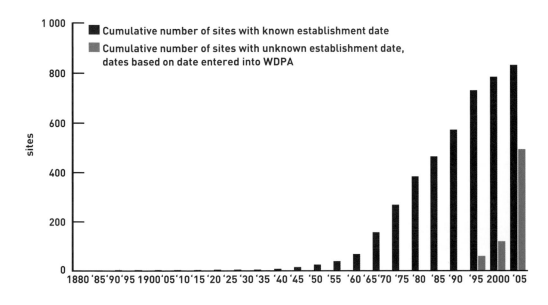

Areas of North Africa and the Middle East protected (by country), 2005

Country/territories	Land area (km^2)	Total protected area (km^2)	Total number of sites
Afghanistan	652 090	2 186	7
Algeria	2 381 740	119 726	26
Bahrain	690	60	4
Cyprus	9 250	920	19
Egypt	1 001 450	103 939	48
Iran, Islamic Republic of	1 633 190	112 878	142
Iraq	438 320	5	8
Israel[1]	21 060	4 145	288
Jordan	89 210	9 734	36
Kuwait	17 820	597	7
Lebanon	10 400	78	24
Libyan Arab Jamahiriya	1 759 540	2 209	12
Morocco	446 550	6 107	35
Oman	212 460	29 828	6
Qatar	11 000	137	13
Saudi Arabia	2 149 690	826 432	81
Syrian Arab Republic	185 180	3 583	28
Tunisia	163 610	2 579	42
Turkey	774 820	3 3532	474
United Arab Emirates	83 600	4559	19
Western Sahara	266 000	18 889	1
Yemen	527 970	527 970	4

1 Under the current, volatile, political situation, the Palestinian territories have only limited autonomy and protected areas largely fall under the control of Israel, where they are listed in this table.

THE PROTECTED AREAS NETWORK

Most protected areas have been established since the 1970s and 1980s. Today there are 1 324 protected areas in the region which cover an estimated 10 percent of the land area. The protection statistics, however, are heavily dominated by a small number of very large sites. If the two largest sites (both Category VI Wildlife Management Areas in Saudi Arabia) are excluded, the proportion of the region which is protected drops to around 4 percent, making it one of the most poorly protected regions in the world.

The large number of sites with no IUCN category represent a broad mix, including sites which probably offer only low levels of protection (recreation zones, game reserves, wetland zones, hunting reserves, and forest reserves), but also including a considerable number of sites which are in all likelihood well protected. These include nature reserves, marine reserves, and national parks in countries for which information on IUCN management categories is not available.

It is readily apparent from the national-level statistics that the total area protected in different countries is highly varied. While a few countries (Egypt, Israel, Jordan, Oman, and Saudi Arabia) have extensive protected areas, often in well-developed networks, a much greater number of countries have only a few small sites. Afghanistan, Iraq, Kuwait, Lebanon, Libyan Arab Jamahiriya, Morocco, Qatar, Syrian Arab Republic, Tunisia, the United Arab Emirates, and the Yemen all have less than 2 percent of their land area within protected areas. Even where there are protected areas there remain problems of management and enforcement.

Land ownership is a far more complex issue in this region than in many parts of the world. Large numbers of mobile peoples live across the region and their lifestyles of shifting pastoralism require open access, at least to the drier parts of the region. Most protected areas recognize this, and allow for continued access – there are fewer sites in IUCN Categories I-II in this region, and even some of the well-known Category II sites such as the Arabian Oryx Sanctuary in Oman and the Tassili N'Ajjer National Park in Algeria have resident human populations. Some level of continued human use is entirely compatible within most of these areas, but levels of protection may not allow for sufficient control of problems such as overgrazing and unsustainable hunting.

Other forms of protection

One of the best known forms of protection, the *al hema* system described above, is still important in some areas, and indeed has been given legal recognition in places. Even without such explicit protection, the nomadic or mobile peoples who are widespread across the region often practice a variety of measures to ensure environmental and livelihood sustainability. In many cases these peoples and their traditional activities have created or modified the particular biodiversity and landscape values of these areas over centuries. While changes to traditional societies may be reducing the effectiveness of such lifestyles in maintaining landscapes and biodiversity, there is an increasing number of examples of mobile peoples becoming more actively involved in conservation.

One example of this is that of the Kuhi sub-tribe of Qashqai nomadic pastoralists in southern Iran which has developed more effective internal organization and is now requesting government support for the continued traditional use and maintenance of its tribal lands, including an important wetland, as a community-conserved area. In another example, however, the Harasis tribal peoples in Oman took a leading role in the reintroduction and protection of the Arabian oryx in the Arabian Oryx Sanctuary. Their efforts have not been successful however, oryx numbers have declined dramatically since 1996, due to poaching and habitat degradation, while 90% of the site is about to loose its protected status, with opportunies for hydrocarbon prospecting in the site adding a further level of threat.

Another form of protection is the *de facto* protection provided by the landscape itself. Harsh environments, where human activities are scarce, such as dry desert and mountain landscapes, dominate a large part of this region. Such areas have been spared many of the impacts faced in more humid and productive parts of the world.

International sites

Only about half of the countries in the region are actively involved in any of the major international protected areas agreements and programs. In terms of the total number of sites, the Ramsar

North Africa and the Middle East: Protected areas network by IUCN category, 2005

IUCN category	Total sites	Total area (km²)
Ia	28	3 496
Ib	2	31
II	71	215 874
III	50	12 432
IV	269	69 806
V	162	114 762
VI	30	790 662
No category	712	78 687
Total	1 324	1 285 749

North Africa and the Middle East: Protected areas network by IUCN category (percentage of total area), 2005

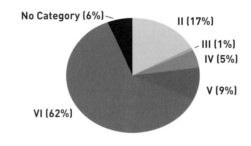

North Africa and the Middle East: Number of protected areas by IUCN category, 2005

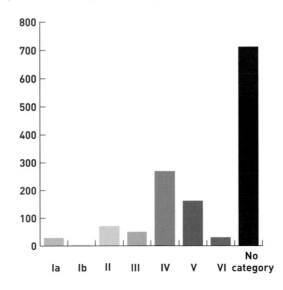

North Africa and the Middle East: Internationally protected areas, 2005

Country	No. of sites	Protected area (km²)
Biosphere reserves		
Algeria	6	73 547
Egypt	2	24 558
Iran, Islamic Republic of	9	27 534
Israel	1	266
Jordan	1	308
Lebanon	1	523
Morocco	2	97 542
Tunisia	4	756
Turkey	1	272
Yemen	1	26 816
TOTAL	28	252 121

Country	No. of sites	Protected area (km²)
Ramsar sites		
Algeria	42	29 596
Bahrain	2	68
Cyprus	2	38
Egypt	2	1 057
Iran, Islamic Republic of	22	14 811
Israel	2	4
Jordan	1	74
Lebanon	4	11
Libyan Arab Jamahiriya	2	1
Morocco	24	2 720
Syrian Arab Republic	1	100
Tunisia	1	126
Turkey	12	1 796
TOTAL	117	50401

Country	No. of sites	Protected area (km²)
World Heritage sites		
Algeria	1	80 000
Egypt	1	259
Oman[1]	1	27 500
Tunisia	1	126
Turkey	2	96
TOTAL	6	107 981

1 In August 2007, in the first case of its kind in the history of the World Heritage Convention, the Arabian Oryx Sanctuary was removed from the World Heritage List, based on collapsing oryx numbers, increasing threats and a decision to degazette 90%. This change has not been incorporated into the statistics in this volume.

Convention is clearly very important – indeed the convention was first agreed in Ramsar, Iran, in 1971. Both Iran and Algeria have been heavily involved in designating sites under this convention.

Only six natural and mixed World Heritage sites have been declared to date. The largest, the Tassili N'Ajjer National Park in Algeria, also incorporates a biosphere reserve and Ramsar site. It is somewhat representative of the tight inter-linkage between people and environment in the region. The site includes some of the most extensive and best-preserved prehistoric cave art in the world, spanning a period from 8 000 to 1 500 years ago. It also includes relict flora and fauna in an "island" of relatively high diversity in the central Sahara Desert.

The marine waters of the region are almost entirely incorporated into three UNEP Regional Seas Programmes with associated conventions: Mediterranean (Barcelona Convention); the Red Sea and Gulf of Aden (Jeddah Convention); and the Arabian Gulf and Arabian Sea (ROPME Sea Area, Kuwait Convention). While all of these are supportive of conservation measures, only one is actively promoting the development of protected areas: the Mediterranean Action Plan has a specific protocol calling on states to designate Mediterranean Specially Protected Areas.

FUTURE DIRECTIONS

The WCPA Regional Action Plan for the region identifies the following priorities for improving the planning and management of protected areas within the region.

Training and capacity to manage

Lack of skilled staff is a major constraint on the effective establishment and management of protected areas. The management of many protected areas falls below acceptable international standards. Such disciplines as protected area planning and management, wildlife management, and environmental sociology are not yet widely recognized by the region's academic institutions. One training center has recently been established in the region, but there are almost no university courses or degree programs in the subjects most closely related to protected area management.

Skills are particularly needed in the following areas: involvement of local stakeholders; conflict resolution; planning and management of protected areas including marine protected areas; application of information arising from research and monitoring programs; and development of environmental awareness and education programs. The development of skills must embrace legal and socio-economic as well as the ecological aspects of protected area management.

The primary focus of training must be on those directly involved in the management of protected areas, such as upper-level managers and administrators, middle-level managers, researchers, rangers, and tourist guides. However, there are other important target groups. These should include decision makers and legislators who work in other agencies but whose decisions may influence the establishment and management of protected areas. They should also include local stakeholders, educators, women, and youth.

Legislation

The legislative basis for protected areas is still weak in the region. Even though most countries have some protected area legislation, others do not have enough provisions to make creative use of the region's rich heritage of traditional institutions and indigenous conservation practices. There are also few provisions to involve local citizens as participants in the establishment and management of protected areas, or to ensure that any benefits generated from the use of protected areas be equitably shared with the local people. In many instances, implementation and enforcement are given insufficient attention.

Pilot protected areas

There is an acute need to expand the protected area systems to represent those ecosystems where there is no protection, and to conserve endangered endemic and relict species of plants and animals, as well as species of special ecological, economic, or cultural value. Especially important is the need to conserve key sites of biological productivity – wetlands, mountains, and woodlands, and coastal sites – that constitute the habitats of the majority of the region's flora and fauna.

Equally great is the need to manage protected areas, or suitable parts of them, in a manner that brings sustainable and tangible benefits to the local people who have in many cases been disadvantaged by their establishment. Such benefits will give these people incentives to become partners in conservation.

Broad agreement and commitment to these objectives exist among conservation agencies within the region. Nonetheless there is a need for highly successful pilot or "model" protected areas that are effective in conserving the region's biological diversity and at the same time demonstrate how community participation in the

M.Spalding

Natural and cultural landscapes throughout the Middle East remain poorly covered by the protected areas network.

management of protected areas can bring tangible sustainable benefits.

Ecotourism

One of the most promising ways for protected areas to generate tangible and sustainable benefits is from nature-based tourism. Ecotourism can provide a meaningful incentive and economic justification for conservation, as it depends on the maintenance of unspoiled nature and thriving communities of wild plants and animals. In addition, it can generate an influential and articulate clientele who can serve as advocates for the conservation of protected areas. If it is not managed very carefully, however, nature-based tourism tends to degrade the very resources upon which it depends, and this has been happening in the region.

According to the World Tourism Organization (WTO), one of five major tourism trends will be an important growth in adventure tourism and in ecotourism. The same organization also forecasts solid growth in cultural tourism, and North Africa and the Middle East are among the regions where this is expected to happen in the near future.

It is, therefore, critical that tourism be carefully planned to ensure that such developments and activities do not compromise the natural and cultural values for which protected areas were established in the first place. This can only be ensured through effective management of these areas. Emphasis also needs to be placed on the development of strong partnerships between protected area agencies and tourism agencies, including commercial operators.

Northern Eurasia

ARMENIA, AZERBAIJAN, BELARUS, GEORGIA, KAZAKHSTAN, KYRGYZSTAN, MOLDOVA, RUSSIAN FEDERATION, TAJIKISTAN, TURKMENISTAN, UKRAINE, UZBEKISTAN

Contributor: N. Danilina

REGIONAL DESCRIPTION

The Northern Eurasia region is located from 20 to 190°E, and from 48 to 90°N, extending from the Barents, Baltic, and Black Seas in the west to the Pacific Ocean in the east, and from the Arctic Ocean in the north to the Caucasus and Pamir Mountains in the south. It is one of the largest WCPA regions, with a total land area of over 22 million km^2.

The region encompasses all of the landscape/climatic zones of the temperate and Arctic regions of the northern hemisphere: Arctic tundra, coniferous, mixed, and broadleaf forest, steppe, semi-desert, desert, and subtropics. These zones exist in tracts that are larger and less disturbed than in most other regions, and the northern Arctic regions are home to some of the largest stretches of wilderness in the world.

The region has an extremely varied relief, marked by vast plains covering much of Siberia and the Turanian Plain (around the Aral Sea). Elevation ranges from 132 meters below sea level to 7 495 meters above sea level, and mountain ranges include part of the Carpathian Mountains and the Urals in the west, the Caucasus between the Black and Caspian Seas, the Tian Shan to the south, and other ranges in southern and eastern Siberia. Near the southern borders of the region these mountains encompass a broad variety of ecosystems: glacial-nival, alpine, subalpine, mountain forest, meadow, steppe, and desert. There are a number of active volcanoes in the far east along the Kamchatka Peninsula, marking the edge of the Eurasian Plate.

There is an extensive coast along the Arctic Ocean, and offshore some large island systems – much of this coast is ice-bound for large parts of the year. There is also a long Pacific coastline, facing the Bering Sea and with the complex formation of the Kamchatka Peninsula, Sakhalin Island, and the Kuril Islands almost entirely enclosing the Sea of Okhotsk. In the southwest of the region are found the northern coasts of the Black Sea and most of the coastline of the Caspian Sea. Inland water bodies include a great number of rivers and lakes, some of them the world's largest by length and by water volume, as well as vast wetlands.

With such a rich array of ecosystems, the

Peschanaya Bay, Lake Baikal, Pribaikal National Park, Russia.

P Arnold/Still Pictures

F Bruemmer/Still Pictures

Introduced Przewalski horses (*Equus freus przewalskii*) on the steppe of Askania Nova Biosphere Reserve, Ukraine.

Source: UNEP-WCMC

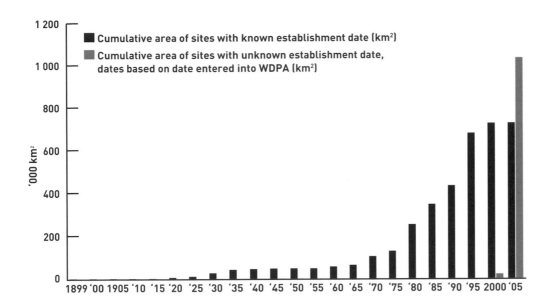

■ Cumulative area of sites with known establishment date (km²)
■ Cumulative area of sites with unknown establishment date, dates based on date entered into WDPA (km²)

North Eurasia: Growth of protected areas network, 1899–2005

region holds a great wealth of biodiversity. However, the vast size of many of these landscapes means that relatively few have been registered in investigations of concentrations of biodiversity. There are nine centers of plant diversity and only one endemic bird area (the Caucasus). Large tracts of the region have been singled out for wider ecological importance within 19 key ecoregions (the WWF Global 200). The region is also exceptionally valuable as a regulator of biosphere processes that maintain ecological stability on a global scale, notably as a major carbon sink.

HISTORICAL BACKGROUND

The modern history of conservation practice in the countries of Northern Eurasia is believed to have started in 1886, when Count V. Dzhedushitskii dedicated a portion of his estate (now in the Ukraine) for the preservation of an old-growth forest and the nesting sites of the white-tailed sea

North Eurasia: Growth in the number of protected areas, 1899–2005

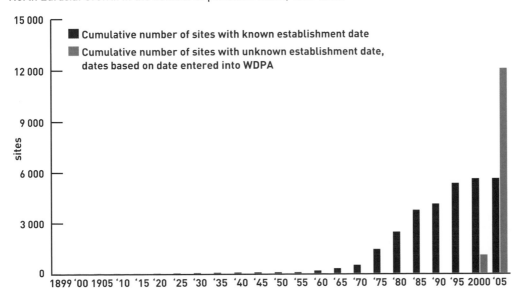

■ Cumulative number of sites with known establishment date
■ Cumulative number of sites with unknown establishment date, dates based on date entered into WDPA

eagle. In 1898, Baron Friedrich Falz-Fein fenced off 500 hectares of virgin steppe on his estate Askania Nova in the vicinity of Kherson, Ukraine.

In 1909, the zoologist Grigorii Kozhevnikov outlined the ecological principles of protected area establishment, emphasizing their importance as baseline areas. Some of the first large nature reserves (*zapovedniks*) were established around Lake Baikal in 1916, just before the Russian Revolution.

In 1917, the geographer Veniamin Semenov-Tian-Shanskii proposed the first long-term plan for the development of a network of *zapovedniks* representing all the biodiversity of Russian nature (see Shtilmark 2003). Further plans for a nationwide network of protected areas were developed over time, most recently in 1989 (Zabelina, Isaeva-Petrova and Karaseva, 1989), but these were typically summaries, while most of the network planning was undertaken at the level of the individual republics. Some of these proposals survived the collapse of the USSR and were eventually put into practice in the newly independent states.

Beginning in the 1920s, the Soviet *zapovedniks* started implementing a unified program of long-term scientific research and monitoring. Today, some of them can boast of having conducted regular ecological observations (known as the 'chronicles of nature') for more than 60 years.

In the 1970s, the USSR witnessed the establishment of its first national parks: in Estonia, Latvia, Lithuania, and Armenia. However, the development of national park systems became most active in the years following the dissolution of the USSR. *Zapovedniks* and national parks are established to protect the most valuable ecosystems. Most are federal or national entities, with state-employed staff, including rangers, scientists, educators, as well as administrative personnel.

Another traditional type of protected area in northern Eurasia is the *zakaznik* (nature refuge)[1]. Traditionally these were established as hunting refuges, dedicated to the propagation of particular game animals. However, this evolved into a more inclusive vision. Today, nature refuges may focus on particular zoological, botanical, hydrological, geological, or other features, or be designated to protect entire landscapes. Even more numerous in these countries, and encompassing an even greater variety of objects, are nature monuments.

Beginning in the 1970s, efforts began to integrate individual protected areas into a unified network. Under a system of centralized planning it was possible to develop tiered systems of protection for large territories and to place these within the wider planning schemes for different administrative units. With the drive towards decentralized planning, the implementation of such integrated systems has now become more difficult. The majority of *zapovedniks* has also been subject to standardized ecological monitoring, dating back more than 60 years. Most have scientific staff, while state inspectors (rangers) carry out protection of *zapovedniks* and national parks.

Today, the protected area networks in all the former Soviet republics suffer from limited state funding, directly linked to the difficult economic circumstances now prevalent in the region. In many countries the rate of designation of new protected areas has decreased or even stopped since 1990. Numerous conservation non-governmental organizations have emerged, and are now assisting state institutions in supporting the existing protected areas and developing protected area networks in various ways, including by generating funds from both domestic and international sources.

THE PROTECTED AREAS NETWORK

Northern Eurasia has the second largest land area of any WCPA region and, although there are 17 697 sites in the WDPA, covering almost 1.76 million km², protected areas represent less than 8 percent of the land area. Throughout the former Soviet Union, the term specially protected natural area (SPNA) has been applied to the range of protected areas developed in each state. Most of the old Soviet categories of protected area still remain and, in general, there are strong similarities in the protected area nomenclature between countries:

- ❑ state *zapovedniks* (nature reserves) (IUCN Category I);
- ❑ national parks (IUCN Category II);
- ❑ state nature refuges (*zakaznik*[1]) (IUCN Category IV);
- ❑ nature monuments (III).

Most of the countries have other categories of protected area, for example nature parks (IUCN Category II), nature sanctuaries, and refuges (e.g. forest, botanical, zoological, complex – Category IV).

The administrative systems for protected areas are also similar in many countries. For the most part the national parks and *zapovedniks* are managed by state agencies, typically environment ministries, but also agriculture, forestry, or hunting

1 The term *zakaznik* is derived from the Russian word *zakaz*, which can be translated into English as 'prohibition'.

departments. Several countries also have a smaller number of sites administered by scientific institutions, such as the Russian Academy of Sciences. In most cases, nature monuments, nature refuges, and other small sites are administered at subnational or local levels.

The very large number of sites in three countries – Belarus, Russia, and the Ukraine – are dominated by locally or nationally designated nature monuments and nature refuges. Typically the former represent very small sites (mostly Category III), and so the area statistics show quite a different pattern, with Category III sites making up only 1 percent of the area, and Category IV sites dominating the statistics. Northern Eurasia also has the largest area of strict nature reserves (Ia) of any region – these are largely the *zapovednik*, a protected area category somewhat emblematic of the region – inviolable nature reserves dedicated to the permanent protection of the native biota within their boundaries.

In Armenia there has been little growth of the protected areas network since 1990. The Armenian Ministry of Nature Protection (MNP) is the governmental agency responsible for the management and coordinated development of the national network of protected areas, but a small number of sites is administered by the Ministry of Agriculture, and one by the National Academy of Sciences. Azerbaijan has also shown a very slow growth of protected areas since 1990. The State Committee on Ecology and Nature Management Supervision of Azerbaijan administers the protected areas, and most sites are staffed.

Belarus has a considerable number of protected areas, and has continued to add to the network to the present day. There is an active ongoing program of scientific research in national parks and *zapovedniks*. In Kazakhstan the general supervision of *zapovedniks*, refuges, national parks, nature monuments, and genetic reserves is carried out by the State Committee on Forestry, Fisheries and Hunting of the Ministry of Agriculture, although their daily management is assigned to the regional authorities. The protection of the state nature refuges is carried out by the Forest Watch service, and by members of the Association on Hunting and Fishing, while national nature monuments are managed by their landholders.

Several governmental agencies are involved in protected area management in Kyrgyzstan, including the Ministry of Environmental Protection (nature

North Eurasia: Protected areas network by IUCN category, 2005

IUCN category	Total sites	Total area (km²)
Ia	195	362 219
Ib	–	–
II	66	125 416
III	11 321	24 440
IV	5 256	841 562
V	407	14 785
VI	54	84 216
No category	398	302 460
Total	17 697	1 755 098

North Eurasia: Protected areas network by IUCN category (percentage of total area), 2005

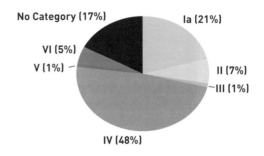

North Eurasia: Number of protected areas by IUCN category, 2005

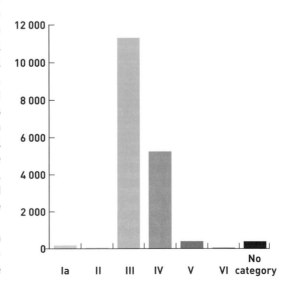

Areas of North Eurasia protected (by country), 2005

Country	Land area (km²)	Total protected area (km²)	Total number of sites
Armenia	29 800	2 991	28
Azerbaijan	86 600	6 328	42
Belarus	207 600	13 153	904
Georgia	69 700	3 040	36
Kazakhstan	2 724 900	76 275	76
Kyrgyzstan	199 900	7 152	93
Moldova, Republic of	33 850	473	63
Russian Federation	17 075 400	1 556 904	11 181
Tajikistan	143 100	26 029	23
Turkmenistan	488 100	19 782	29
Ukraine	603 700	22 468	5 198
Uzbekistan	447 400	20 503	24

Note: While the overall figures are accurate, it appears that there is some under-reporting of smaller sites, with several hundred nature monuments and nature refuges missing from countries such as Belarus, Tajikistan, and Ukraine.

reserves), the State Forestry Agency (Kyrgyz Ata National Park, nature parks, forest and some botanical refuges), the Recreation Department (Alaarcha Nature Park), the Main Department on Management and Regulation of Hunting Resources, and the Hunters and Fishermen Union (hunting refuges). Other nature refuges and nature monuments are administered by municipalities.

In Moldova the Department of Environmental Protection is responsible for the supervision of the national protected areas network, although the State Forest Service and the Ministry of Natural Resources and Ecological Control manage some sites, while others are administered by the local authorities and funded from local budgets.

A few hundred sites in Russia fall under federal control, mostly of the Ministry of Natural Resources of the Federation. These include almost all *zapovedniks* and national parks. In contrast, the majority of nature refuges and nature monuments are administered at regional and local levels.

Tajikistan has relatively few protected areas, although there are an additional 162 nature monuments that are not recorded in the WDPA. All large lakes in Tajikistan are included in *zapovedniks* or refuges. Nature reserves and nature refuges are administered by the State Forestry Enterprise, and national parks by the Ministry of Nature Protection. Law enforcement was weak during the civil war of 1992–93, and a lack of international support, political instability, as well as serious levels of pollution in the Takob River from the Takobskii mining plant, are threatening protected areas in the country.

Ukrainian protected areas are administered by a range of different bodies including: the Ministry of Environment and Natural Resources; State Committee on Forestry; National Academy of Sciences; Agrarian Academy of Sciences of Ukraine; Taras Shevchenko National University; and the Ministry of Education. In Uzbekistan, most sites are administered by the State Committee on Nature Protection, while the Ministry of Agriculture and Water Management administers six nature reserves and two national parks. Overall supervision of regime enforcement in SPNA is exercised by the State Committee on Nature Protection.

International sites

All Commonwealth of Independent States (CIS) countries have ratified the Convention on Biological Diversity, the Ramsar Convention, and other international agreements. The Ramsar Convention has been widely adopted by countries across the region, and in several countries new sites have regularly been added since 2000, including all five sites in Tajikistan, which were designated in 2001.

The biosphere reserves across the region include some very large sites, in particular the 53 000 km² Tzentralnosibirskii Biosphere Reserve in Russia, and the 43 000 km² Issyk Kul (also a Ramsar site) in Kyrgyzstan, designated in 2001.

World Heritage sites are confined to two countries, but cover a broad geographic range. The Russian sites include large areas of the central and eastern parts of the region, such as Lake Baikal – the world's oldest and deepest freshwater lake; the Volcanoes of Kamchatka; the Golden Mountains of

Altai; and the Central Sikhote-Alin mountains on the coast of the Sea of Japan. In the west of the region a number of nationally designated protected areas have also been awarded European Diplomas (Type A) by the Council of Europe, including Berezinskiy Zapovednik and Belarus' Belovezhskaya Pushcha National Park; four *zapovedniks* in Russia, and the Carpathian *zapovedniks* in the Ukraine.

There are also many important transboundary protected areas within this region and extending into neighboring regions. These include the Druzhba (Friendship) Nature Reserve, between Russia and Finland; the Dauria Nature Reserve between Russia, Mongolia, and China; Khanka Lake between Russia and China; the Bolshekhekhtsirsky Nature Reserve (Russia) with the Three Parallel Rivers Nature Reserve in China; and the Pasvik Nature Reserve between Russia, Finland, and Norway. Agreements have been elaborated between Georgia and Russia, and between Georgia and Azerbaijan, to facilitate coordinated management of a number of East Caucasian protected areas. Two Ukrainian protected areas form part of the tri-nation East Carpathian Biosphere Reserve with sites in Poland and Slovakia. The Danube Delta has also received particular attention and there is a biosphere reserve between Ukraine and Romania, while in 2000 Ukraine, Bulgaria, Romania, and Moldova adopted a declaration on cooperation for the establishment of the Lower Danube Green Corridor.

Another ongoing project is the Global Environment Facility (GEF) Central Asian transboundary project 'Establishment of protected areas network for biodiversity conservation in the Western Tien Shan'. The project plans the creation of a transboundary protected area to include Kazakhstan's Aksu-Djabagly Nature Reserve, Sary-Chelek and Besh-Aral Nature Reserves in Kyrgyzstan, and Chatkal Nature Reserve and Ugam-Chatkal National Park in Uzbekistan. It is supported by bilateral agreements between the national governments and the World Bank.

FUTURE DIRECTIONS

The regional program for WCPA has identified a number of key issues, which in many ways highlight the future needs for protected areas in the region. Its main objectives include:

❑ Increasing the participation of protected area managers in decision making at local, regional, national, and global levels;

North Eurasia: Internationally protected areas, 2005

Country	No. of sites	Protected area (km^2)
Biosphere reserves		
Belarus[1]	3	3 533
Kyrgyzstan	2	43 355
Russian Federation	37	252 857
Turkmenistan	1	346
Ukraine[1]	6	3 324
Uzbekistan	1	574
TOTAL	50	303 989
Ramsar sites		
Armenia	2	4 922
Azerbaijan	3	2 321
Belarus	8	2 831
Georgia	2	342
Kazakhstan	2	6 085
Kyrgyzstan	2	6 397
Moldova, Republic of	3	947
Russian Federation	35	103 238
Tajikistan	5	946
Turkmenistan	1	1 887
Ukraine	33	7 447
Uzbekistan	1	313
TOTAL	97	137 676
World Heritage sites		
Belarus[2]	1	50
Russian Federation[3]	8	209 970
TOTAL	9	210 020

1 Three biosphere reserves in the Ukraine and one in Belarus are transboundary sites with countries in the WCPA Europe region.
2 The Belovezhskaya Pushcha/Bialowieza Forest World Heritage Site is transboundary with Poland (WCPA Europe).
3 The Uvs Nuur Basin World Heritage Site is transboundary with Mongolia (WCPA East Asia).

❑ Creation of a favorable image of protected areas and raising the involvement of the wider public in the work of protected areas;

❑ Increasing cooperation and the exchange of information and experiences between protected areas in Northern Eurasia and elsewhere;

❑ Strengthening the role of protected areas in conserving biodiversity and maintaining the region's ecological stability. Establishing an ecologically representative network of protected areas for the region;

❑ Enhancing the role of protected areas in

F Bruemmer/Still Pictures

**Mount Kazbak,
Caucasus, Georgia.**

environmental education and awareness;

❏ Improving the economic basis of protected area activities;

❏ Improving the institutional and legal framework for protected area activities;

While it is clearly necessary to increase the total area of protected areas (as a percentage of national territory, but also ensuring representativeness),

many other strategies must be employed. Critical among these will be: improving existing legislation; raising the level of involvement and cooperation between government agencies, NGOs, and international bodies; improving environmental education and outreach; developing links with the private sector, industry, and particularly ecotourism; and the establishment of stronger economic bases, including the creation of trust funds.

South Asia

Bangladesh, Bhutan, British Indian Ocean Territory (UK), India, Maldives, Nepal, Pakistan, Sri Lanka

Contributors: S. Bhatt, A. Kothari, P. Tuladhar

REGIONAL DESCRIPTION

The South Asia region includes the countries of the Indian subcontinent, together with the remote island archipelagos of the central Indian Ocean. To the north the region is bounded by mountains, while to the west it borders the Arabian Sea and the Laccadive Sea, with the Bay of Bengal to the east.

The mountain borders stretch from the Makran Range in Pakistan to the great sweep of the Himalayas running from northern Pakistan along the borders of northern India and dominating the landscapes of Nepal and Bhutan. The Himalayas have been formed by the collision of two gigantic land masses, the Indian subcontinent and the Asian continent, which began about 70 million years ago. In geological terms, they are still relatively young and still growing, and the region is prone to earthquakes. The main range, or Great Himalayas, includes many of the world's highest peaks (including Sagarmatha or Mount Everest, 8 848 meters). There is also a number of other ranges, many with distinctive geological and ecological features. Vegetation is highly varied through these mountain ranges, influenced by both altitude and rainfall. The natural vegetation is subtropical in the lower foothills, but dominated in most areas by moist temperate forests with both broadleaf evergreen and coniferous trees. There are extensive areas of such forests, particularly in Bhutan. Higher still, the forests give way to alpine species and scrub before the bare slopes and permanent snow and ice. North of the Himalaya, are the vast cold desert areas of Ladakh and Spiti, bordering Tibet.

To the south of these mountain ranges are vast level plains, collectively described as the Indo-Gangetic Plain, bordering the Indus River in Pakistan, and in the center and east including the great plain of the Ganges, which flows for more than 2 800 km out to the Bay of Bengal. These lands were once forested, but for millennia have been cleared for human agriculture.

The Thar Desert dominates in northwest India and eastern Pakistan, with shifting sands, salt flats, rocky deserts, and sparse shrubs. Most of central and southern India is made up of the Deccan Plateau – a wide undulating terrain built largely of ancient rock, but also with more recent volcanic intrusions. Hilly or low mountain ranges fringe both the western and eastern edges of the subcontinent (the Eastern and Western Ghats). Forests are again the native vegetation, but less

Tigers (*Panthera tigris*), India.

Chaudhuri/UNEP

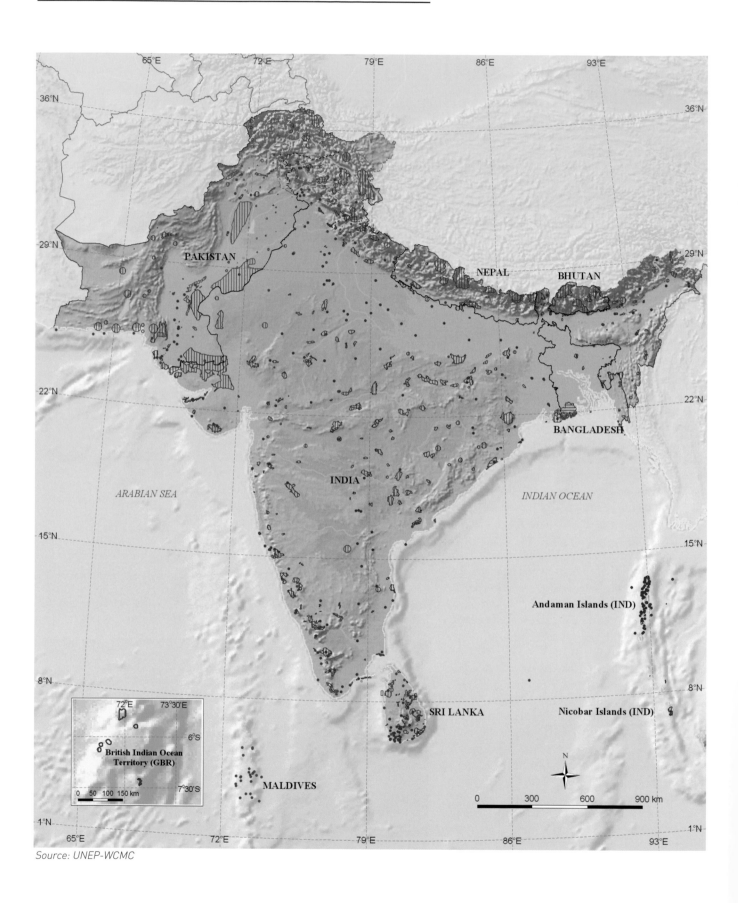

Source: UNEP-WCMC

than 10 percent of the subcontinent as a whole is now covered by forest. Sri Lanka has vegetation very similar to the Deccan Plateau and the Western Ghats.

The coastal and offshore waters of the Arabian Sea are highly productive, although overfishing is a problem, particularly close to the coasts. The dominant feature in the offshore waters is the Chagos Laccadive Ridge, a near-continuous string of coral atolls and associated islands, and shallow platforms. The Bay of Bengal is another highly productive sea, with substantial freshwater input, rich in nutrients, particularly in the north. Mangrove forests are widespread along these coasts, and include the Sundarbans, probably the most extensive mangrove forest in the world. In the far south-east of the region, India's Andaman and Nicobar Islands are home to a remarkable diversity of forest and marine ecosystems. Although remote, the islands are undergoing rapid immigration and population pressure on natural ecosystems is high.

The species composition of the region is influenced by both the Indo-Malayan Realm and, over a smaller area towards the north, by the Palearctic Realm. Some of the most important centers for biodiversity or endemism are the various mountain ranges, and especially the western Himalayas, the flooded grasslands of the Rann of Kutch, and the Western Ghats, which house some of the only tropical rainforest in the region. In many areas the total numbers of species remain poorly known: for example, estimates of the number of endemic plant species in the Himalayas range from 2 500 to 4 000. Marine biodiversity is also high, particularly in coral reef areas, although rates of endemism tend to be relatively low.

The region is one of the world's most densely populated, with a total population of over 1.37 billion, including the world's second most populous country, India. Furthermore, population growth rates are still high. A very large proportion of the population remains rural, and agriculture and pastoralism have transformed most of the landscapes away from the steepest mountain terrains. Ethnically and culturally the region is highly diverse, with numerous religions, and with lifestyles varying from wealthy urban societies to traditional agricultural, and to tribal groups whose lifestyles have remained largely unchanged for centuries.

DEP Kumar/UNEP

Nanda Devi and Valley of Flowers National Parks World Heritage Area, India.

HISTORICAL PERSPECTIVE

Human settlement and organized society have a long history across the region, and local communities have been practicing forms of natural resource conservation and management for at least three millennia. The first known recommendations for protected areas are laid down in the Arthashastra written by Kautilya at the end of the fourth century BC, while the first known government decree for the protection of wildlife and forests was set out by the Emperor Ashoka in the year 252 BC in central India. Not long after this, in Sri Lanka, King Devanampiyatissa also set up wildlife sanctuaries. Religious beliefs, linked to each of the main faiths in the region, have often supported conservation and the protection of features such as forests, or sacred groves, and mountains – even today many sacred groves remain. Maharajas and Mogul emperors established many hunting reserves across the region, and in the colonial era, further hunting and forest reserves were established – many of these now form the basis for the modern system of protected areas.

Many of Sri Lanka's current forest reserves date back to the end of the 19th century, such as

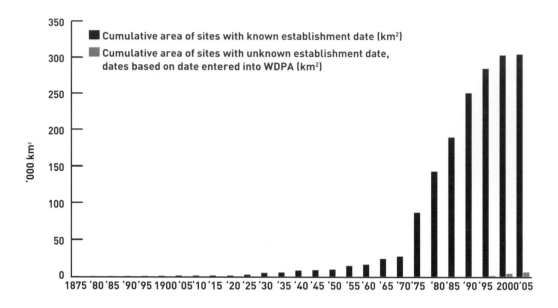

South Asia: Growth of protected areas network, 1875–2005

Sinharaja Forest Reserve established in 1875, while parts of the Bangladesh and Indian Sundarbans were designated as forest reserves in 1878. The first of the modern conservation-oriented protected areas in the region were established in India and Sri Lanka from the 1930s, including Corbett National Park in India, established in 1936. During the 1960s–1970s, there was a rapid expansion in both the number and size of protected areas: Bangladesh established the Sunderbans South Wildlife Reserve in 1960; Pakistan, the Ras Koh Wildlife Sanctuary in 1962; Bhutan, the Manas Wildlife Sanctuary (now a national park) in 1966; and Nepal, the Royal Chitwan National Park in 1973 (part of the area had been included in a royal hunting reserve since 1846). By contrast, the Maldives and British Indian Ocean Territory did not establish any protected areas until the late 1990s.

Although a number of sites extend to the coast, the protection of open marine waters has been very slow to come to the region. India has some large sites, notably three marine national

South Asia: Growth in the number of protected areas, 1875–2005

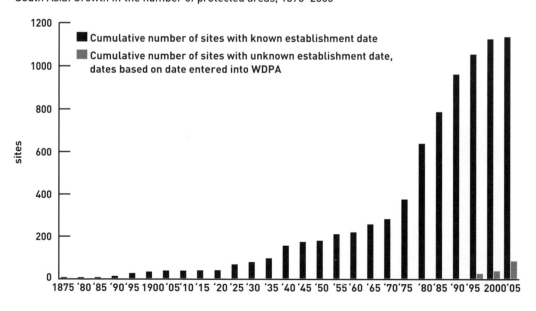

M Gilles/Bios/Still Pictures

Indian rhinoceros (*Rhinoceros unicornis*) in Royal Chitwan National Park, Nepal, a World Heritage site.

Areas of South Asia protected (by country), 2005

Country/territories	Land area (km²)	Total protected area (km²)	Total number of sites
Bangladesh	144 000	2 409	21
Bhutan	47 000	12 408	9
British Indian Ocean Territory	60	1 374	6
India	3 287 260	178 282	662
Maldives	300	<1-	25
Nepal	147 180	25 621	22
Pakistan	796 100	75 311	208
Sri Lanka	65 610	14 877	264

parks, and there are small sites scattered across the region. Even among the existing sites there are problems associated with weak legal regimes or poor enforcement. The 'dive sites' in the Maldives have few regulations, and the large marine protected areas in the British Indian Ocean Territory, although closed to fishing, have exempted the only commercial fishing that takes place in the territory.

THE PROTECTED AREA NETWORK

The World Database on Protected Areas (WDPA) records 1 217 protected areas covering 310 282 km². Most of this is terrestrial and 6.9 percent of the region's land surface is protected. This is the lowest proportion of any inhabited WCPA region.

There are 184 marine protected areas recorded for the region, but the total area of these is the smallest of any WCPA region and also occupies the smallest proportion of any region's maritime boundaries, only 0.11 percent.

The majority of the protected areas in the region are designated in Category IV, representing just half of the total area protected. Category II sites are also numerous, covering 22 percent of the total protected area. Although there is a large number of sites with no known IUCN category, they are typically smaller.

Despite the low regional average protected area coverage, several countries in the region have quite extensive protected area networks, notably Sri Lanka, Nepal, and Pakistan, and these incorporate most major habitat types. Bhutan has the largest coverage in the region: more than 25 percent of the land area is protected, with corridors linking all protected areas, and modest use by local people within the protected areas. The protected areas of Sri Lanka are also extensive: about 23 percent of the total area is protected for biodiversity conservation, with further large areas of natural forest reserved

for production purposes. Pakistan's protected areas network, although extensive, fails to cover some critically threatened ecosystems.

Nepal's protected areas cover 17 percent of its total land area, with sites protecting historic, natural, and cultural values. Recent developments have included the introduction of Buffer Zone Management Regulations (1996), allowing for the designation of buffer zones around settlements, agricultural lands, village open spaces, and other land uses, intended to help communities adjacent to protected areas (Sharma and Shaw, 1996). A new category of protected area – conservation area – has enabled communities and non-governmental organizations to become more involved in collaborative management with the government in protected areas such as Annapurna Conservation Area and the Makalu-Barun National Park and Conservation Area. Makalu-Barun was officially established in 1992 to implement an innovative conservation model integrating protected area management and community development. The 2 330 km² area ranges from tropical forests to ice-bound mountain summits, and is the only protected area on Earth with an elevation range of 8 000 meters (The Mountain Institute, 2004).

India has significantly expanded its protected area network, although it still covers only about 5 percent of national territory. National reviews have suggested that the network is not yet representative of the biogeographic regions of the country, and needs further expansion. In 2002, India added two new categories of protected area: community reserves and conservation reserves, both of them allowing for much greater participation by local people than the existing national parks and sanctuaries.

Establishment and management of marine protected areas tends to be weak in the region, owing to insufficient attention from governments, and deficient funding and capacity building for conservation. This is particularly notable in those coastal areas where marine resources play a critical role in human activities, through tourism or fisheries, and where more sustainable manage-ment, including protected areas if managed in participation with local people, could greatly improve the livelihoods.

Other forms of protection

There are a large number of formal and informal arrangements for protecting biodiversity in South Asia. Many community forests, forest reserves, private forests, buffer zones, jungle corridors, and others are included in the WDPA, but it is likely that some may have been missed. There are also thousands of community conserved areas, either traditional ones continuing into the present, or new initiatives. These include sacred groves and wetlands, catchment forests, village wetlands, coastal and freshwater river stretches, and bird and turtle nesting sites. Most of these are not yet incorporated into PA systems or into the WDPA.

International sites

There is involvement in international agreements on protected areas across the region. By 2005, 54 sites were designated under the Ramsar Convention, including a number of very large sites such as the 5 663 km² Rann of Kutch and the 4 728 km² Indus Delta Ramsar Sites in Pakistan.

Biosphere reserves have not been widely adopted across the region, despite the fact that many nationally designated sites include settlements and human activities, and there is growing recognition of the use of buffers and corridors, all principles widely used in biosphere reserves. The largest site in the region is the 10 500 km² Gulf of Mannar Biosphere Reserve in India, an important coastal site incorporating fishing villages, mangrove forests, coral reefs, and seagrass beds.

One site, the Sundarbans mangrove forests between India and Bangladesh, is covered under a complex array of protection, including national protection in a range of protected areas in both countries, a biosphere reserve in India, a Ramsar site in Bangladesh, and World Heritage sites in both countries. Although the existing natural World Heritage sites in the region include some of the most spectacular and ecologically important features in the region, from Sagarmatha to

South Asia: Protected areas network by IUCN category, 2005

IUCN category	Total sites	Total area (km²)
Ia	19	2 490
Ib	2	825
II	133	67 341
III	–	–
IV	661	160 877
V	11	1 394
VI	12	26 126
No category	379	51 228
Total	1 217	310 281

South Asia: Protected areas network by IUCN category (percentage of total area), 2005

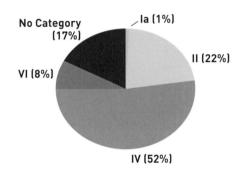

South Asia: Number of protected areas by IUCN category, 2005

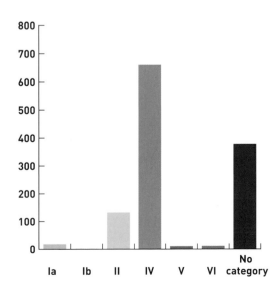

South Asia: Internationally protected areas, 2005

Country.territories	No. of sites	Protected area (km²)
Biosphere reserves		
India	4	31 511
Pakistan	1	658
Sri Lanka	4	630
TOTAL	9	32 799
Ramsar sites		
Bangladesh	2	6 112
British Indian Ocean Territory	1	354
India	25	6 771
Nepal	4	235
Pakistan	19	13 436
Sri Lanka	3	85
TOTAL	54	26 993
World Heritage sites		
Bangladesh	1	1 397
India	5	3 001
Nepal	2	2 080
Sri Lanka	1	113
TOTAL	9	6 591

the Sundarbans, there are relatively few sites considering the vast size of South Asia.

FUTURE DIRECTIONS

The national biodiversity strategies and action plans of various South Asian countries have stressed the need to strengthen their protected area networks, notably addressing neglected biomes such as marine and freshwater systems. Most also stress the need to move into more participatory forms of management. These, as well as a number of other measures, are considered necessary to strengthen and improve the protected area network and to safeguard the region's biodiversity. They include the following items.

❏ Protected areas must be linked into the larger landscape and seascape, built into a broader

system of management for land and water in which the various departments and sectors are coordinated, and conservation and sustainable use are achieved. One ongoing attempt at this, which is providing valuable lessons, is the Terai Arc Landscape program in Nepal and India.

❏ Collaborative management of protected areas and buffer zones must be encouraged and improved, in which local communities are involved in decision making from the stage of conceptualization through to their management and monitoring. These same local communities must also become substantial beneficiaries of conservation.

❏ Recognition and support must be given to community conserved areas, in ways that the relevant communities find appropriate.

❏ Policies and programs for the sustainable use of genetic/biological resources must be established, incorporating systems for the fair and equitable sharing of the benefits accrued from such use.

❏ Indigenous knowledge and innovations should be acknowledged and protected, and, where relevant, incorporated in the conservation and management system.

❏ Development-related policies and programs need to be reoriented to make them more sensitive to conservation issues.

❏ Management capacity for all staff, local communities, and NGOs involved in protected areas needs to be improved.

❏ The public must be made more aware of the benefits of conservation.

❏ Research into the threats facing biodiversity, including inappropriate development, invasive alien species, climate change, and over-exploitation, and into possible measures to address these threats, must be strengthened.

A stronger engagement with the international site-based conventions would also be desirable in the region.

East Asia

CHINA, DEMOCRATIC PEOPLE'S REPUBLIC OF KOREA, JAPAN, MONGOLIA, REPUBLIC OF KOREA, TAIWAN POC

Contributors: Shin Wang, J. Jamsramjav

REGIONAL DESCRIPTION

This region covers a large part of the Asian continent, from the Altai Mountains and the Mongolian Plateau in the north, to the Tibetan Plateau in the south. The coastline borders the Japanese, Yellow, and East China seas in the east, and the South China Sea in the southeast.

The continental land masses lie on the Eurasian Tectonic Plate. Japan is located on the margins between this plate and the Pacific and Philippine plates, and is a land of considerable tectonic activity, with more than 60 active volcanoes and numerous earthquakes every year. The collision of the Eurasian and Philippine Plates is also responsible for the mountainous landscape on the islands of Taiwan POC.

The north and northwestern part of the region is arid, dominated by grassland, and by the Gobi Desert (1.3 million km^2) and the Taklimakan Desert (325 000 km^2) in Mongolia and China. To the south the Qinghai-Tibet Plateau extends to the Himalayas, including part of Qomolangma (Mount Everest) in China. By contrast, the eastern part of the region experiences a monsoon climate, due to the proximity of the Pacific Ocean. Tropical evergreen rainforest occurs in the lowlands of southeastern China, including the eastern sides of Hainan Island and Taiwan Island. Subtropical forest is found in southern Japan, southeastern China between the Yangtze and Hongshui river basins, in Taiwan POC, and along the southern coast of the Republic of Korea. Mangrove forests fringe parts of the southern Chinese coast and the southern Japanese islands. Temperate deciduous broadleaf forests are found in the northeastern and northern part of the region. Various types of sub-Arctic coniferous taiga forests and cold temperate mixed forests are found in the northern part of the region in northern Mongolia, northeastern China, and the northern parts of the Democratic People's Republic of Korea.

The region is of great biological richness. China alone is one of the five richest countries in the world in terms of species number. Several biological hotspots are recognized, including the eastern Himalayas, Hengduan Mountains, and southwest Yunnan. As well as biologically rich tropical and subtropical areas, the region also contains by far the richest temperate ecosystems of the planet. The rich mesophyll forests of temperate central China are amazingly abundant in tree and other plant species, including several relict species. The Qionglai Mountains have more than 10 000 plant species – approximately the same as the whole of Germany. Both Japan and Taiwan POC have high levels of species endemism.

The eastern part of the region contains a diverse range of islands. Japan consists of more than 3 800 islands, although 97 percent of the total land area is clustered in four main islands. These are dominated by sub-Arctic coniferous forest, deciduous broadleaved forests, and broadleaved evergreen forest. The Republic of Korea also has numerous small islands. Most of these are uninhabited and they support a variety of indigenous species rarely found on the mainland (Dong-Gon Hong, 2002).

There are extensive coral reefs around the small Japanese islands of the Nansei Shoto Chain, including the Yaeyama and Ryukyu islands. Scattered coral reefs are also found in the South China Sea, including offshore atolls, but also fringing reefs in Taiwan POC and Hainan.

Population densities vary considerably, from very low levels in northwest and western China and

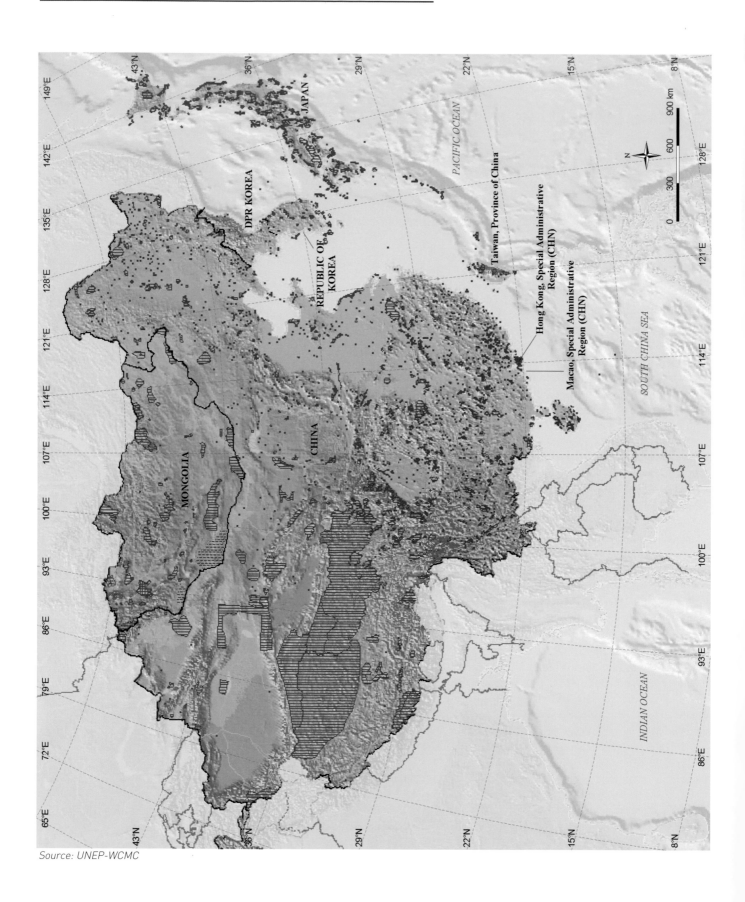

Source: UNEP-WCMC

Mongolia (1.5 people per km² in 2000), to the most densely populated places, including Taiwan POC (622 per km², 2002) and the urban region of southeastern China, Hong Kong (6 148.8 per km², 2001), and Macao. There is also a diverse range of land-use practices. There is little or no agriculture in the deserts. Grasslands in the semi-arid parts of Mongolia and northwestern China support large numbers of free-ranging wild ungulates and livestock. By contrast, the eastern part of the region has largely been converted to agricultural use, including arable and irrigated land for rice, cotton, tea, soybeans, and corn. Coastal waters throughout the region have been transformed by some of the most intensive industrial and artisanal fisheries in the world. Many of the major urban areas, and big cities such as Hong Kong and Tokyo, are also located in the coastal zone.

HISTORICAL PERSPECTIVE

Throughout the history of the region, religion (including animism, shamanism, Confucianism, Taoism, and Buddhism) has played an important role in the protection of the natural environment. The first protected areas in this region included sacred forests, holy mountains, and magnificent scenery. One of the first reserves was declared in 1778 in Mongolia: Bogdo-uul, a mountain taiga forest ecosystem that is still protected as a holy mountain today.

The modern creation of protected areas largely dates from the second half of the last century. However, 12 sites were designated as protected areas in Japan between 1934 and 1936. Protected area development in the other countries of the region began later. In 1946, the government of the Democratic People's Republic of Korea passed the necessary legislation to create natural monuments and designated the first sites. China established its first nature reserve in 1956 (Dinghushan). In Taiwan POC the first wildlife protected area was established in 1974. Mongolia declared its first nature reserve in 1957 (Batkhan), and the Republic of Korea in 1965 (Soraksan). Since the 1970s, there have been rapid increases in the number of protected areas established in most countries across East Asia, from less than 500 sites in 1973 to more than 3 000 by 2003.

Land ownership varies considerably from country to country. For instance, Mongolia developed under the Soviet system for more than 70 years, during which all land, forest, and water were

Eiichi Ito/UNEP

the property of the state. As a result, all protected areas in Mongolia are state owned. Protected areas in the Democratic People's Republic of Korea and in China are also owned by the state. In contrast, private land can be designated as a national park in Japan, and some of the forest reserves in the Republic of Korea belong to private cooperatives.

THE PROTECTED AREAS NETWORK

There are 3 267 protected areas listed for the East Asia region in the World Database on Protected Areas (WDPA). Most are terrestrial, and represent 15 percent of the region's land surface. The statistics are dominated by a number of very large sites: the Qiangtang Nature Reserve (298 000 km²) in the Taklimakan Desert and the Sanjiangyuan Nature Reserve (152 300 km²) on the Tibetan Plateau, both in China, are two of the ten largest protected areas in the world. Another important site is the 53 000 km² Great Gobi Strict Protected Area in Mongolia, the largest Category Ia protected area in the world.

The degree of protection differs in each country, with the lowest proportion of land surface protected being in the People's Democratic Republic of Korea. Limited funding in most of the protected areas in Mongolia and China restricts conservation activities, research, and training of protected area staff.

Until recently, the need to protect marine biodiversity, including coral reefs, coastal mudflats,

Protected areas in Mongolia date back to the late 18th century.

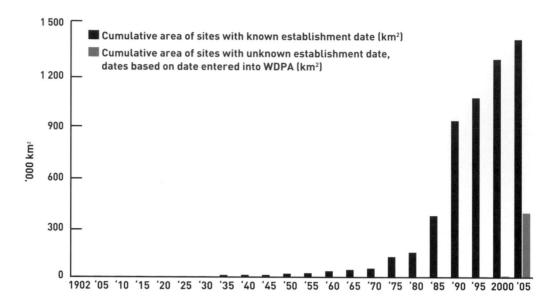

East Asia: Growth of protected areas network, 1902–2005

and estuarine areas, was not well recognized. At present, there are 285 marine protected areas in the region, covering an estimated 26 309 km². However, this figure represents less than 0.5 percent of the total marine waters of the region (to 200 nautical miles). Hong Kong enacted the Marine Parks Ordinance in 1995. Taiwan POC is planning marine protected areas, and a draft Marine Law was prepared in 2002 to direct reasonable development of coastal areas, to prevent coastal pollution, and to reach the goal of national land security (Shin Wang,

2002). In the last few years, China has designated several coral reef and coral ecosystem nature reserves, which aim to protect and restore coral ecosystems in the South China Sea. China is also designating reserves with the aim of protecting coastal mudflats and estuarine marshes. Xie Yan and Lishu Li (2004) recently mapped 80 marine protected areas in China.

Other forms of protection
Temple gardens, restricted hunting areas,

East Asia: Growth in the number of protected areas, 1902–2005

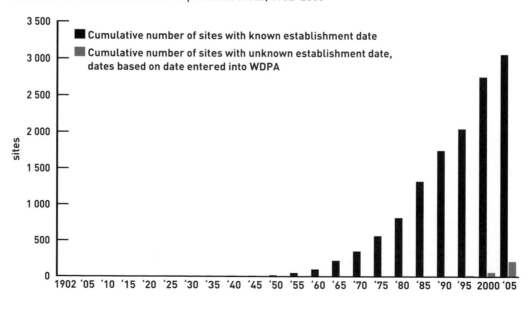

J Thorsell

Jinsha River, one of the Three Parallel Rivers of Yunnan Protected Areas World Heritage Site, China.

East Asia: Protected areas network by IUCN category, 2005

IUCN category	Total sites	Total area (km²)
Ia	43	62 843
Ib	34	43 399
II	78	98 820
III	34	19 507
IV	121	6 111
V	2 144	1 444 754
VI	78	59 339
No category	734	29 869
Total	3 266	1 764 642

East Asia: Protected areas network by IUCN category (percentage of total area), 2005

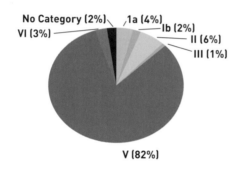

East Asia: Number of protected areas by IUCN category, 2005

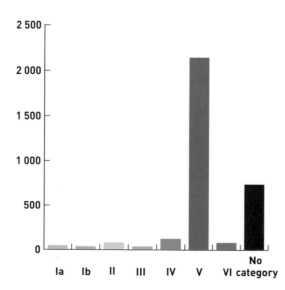

landscape forests, and privately owned forests play an important role for species protection alongside state-protected areas in this region. There are also some large private forest reserves. At the present time, it is not certain what proportion of these are represented in the WDPA.

International sites

Participation in the three major international protected area conventions is generally good, and currently there are 77 Ramsar sites, 39 biosphere reserves, and 12 natural and mixed World Heritage sites.

Mongolia's 11 Ramsar sites include five large lake sites designated in 2004; Mongolia's first natural World Heritage site is also recent, having been designated as a transboundary site in 2003. China's eight World Heritage sites include four sites of mixed cultural and natural importance, incorporating monasteries and temples, and landscapes that lie at the center of thousands of years of art and culture, showing the close links between people and the natural landscape in this region. The Three Parallel Rivers of Yunnan Protected Areas World Heritage Site, designated in 2003, is the largest World Heritage site in the region, and is spread across multiple locations, lying in what is probably the most biodiverse temperate region of the world, straddling the boundaries of the Tibetan Plateau, East Asia, and Southeast Asia.

FUTURE DIRECTIONS

There is a need to further improve the regional protected area system, including greater effort to achieve full representation of richer and lower altitude habitats, many of which are already highly threatened and reduced by human development. Ecosystem restoration should be considered in many cases. Designation of protected areas within comprehensive regional development planning and zoning is needed. Selection of protected areas on the basis of species needs or habitat cover often fails to win essential alliances with other strong agencies that can help support protected area establishment. Planners therefore need to pay much more attention to promoting the ecological services, and economic and social benefits that habitat protection or restoration can achieve in the local development context.

Many protected areas are too small to retain

Areas of East Asia protected (by country)

Country.territories	Land area (km²)	Total protected area (km²)	Total number of sites
China	9 562 070*	1 467 363	2 027
Hong Kong	1 062	551	103
Japan	377 800	64 312	962
Korea, Democratic People's Republic	120 540	3 159	31
Korea, Republic	99 260	7 004	44
Macao	20	–	–
Mongolia	1 566 500	217 912	51
Taiwan, Province of China	35 980	4 340	49

*This figure excludes land area for Taiwan POC, Hong Kong, and Macao for the purposes of this analysis.

their original complement of species. They will lose species as a result of island biogeographic principles (the number of species that can be supported is proportional to the area occupied). But this process can be minimized if connectivity can be maintained or re-created, if distances to other similar habitats are not too great, or habitat islands are available to act as stepping stones to provide links. Corridors may need to be established between protected areas to allow migration and genetic exchange between otherwise isolated and inbred populations – building ecological networks.

Thirty three of Japan's wetlands are protected under the Ramsar Convention.

UNEP

East Asia: Internationally protected areas, 2005

Country	No. of sites	Protected area (km²)
Biosphere reserves		
China	26	45 540
Japan	4	1 158
Korea, Democratic People's Republic	2	1 320
Korea, Republic of	2	1 225
Mongolia	5	74 900
TOTAL	39	124 143
Ramsar sites		
China	30	29 375
Japan	33	1 299
Korea, Republic of	3	10
Mongolia	11	14 395
TOTAL	77	45 079
World Heritage sites		
China	8	20 226
Japan	3	838
Mongolia[1]	1	9 467
TOTAL	12	30 531

1 The Uvs Nuur Basin World Heritage Site is a transboundary site between Mongolia and Russia.

Protected area effectiveness can be greatly enhanced if some level of connectivity can be established between them, or artificial movement of organisms is employed to maintain breeding between otherwise isolated populations. In some cases where *in-situ* conservation alone seems doomed to fail, higher levels of management intervention or *ex-situ* conservation actions may also be required.

While management capacity varies across the region, generally there is a need to raise management standards, which will require:
- ❑ fundraising;
- ❑ establishment of monitoring systems;
- ❑ strengthening legal systems and law enforcement;
- ❑ training of staff and capacity building;
- ❑ increasing international cooperation;
- ❑ improving public awareness and involving local people.

Much of the regional conservation estate is state owned and governments need to pay greater attention to the involvement of local communities in the establishment and management of protected areas. Whether a protected area succeeds or fails will depend on whether it is accepted and actively supported by local communities.

More attention must be paid to the development of marine protected areas or marine protection measures (quotas, agreements on fishing areas, agreements on equipment allowed). In this regard it is important to reach international agreement about resource use within disputed waters. Countries may not agree on who owns an area of sea, but, if all agree that in any case it should be protected, there can be a basis for cooperative research and protection activities.

New threats such as invasive alien species are becoming more important issues. These must be tackled at frontiers and by other agencies rather than by the management staff of protected areas when species have already arrived there.

Southeast Asia

Brunei Darussalam, Cambodia, Indonesia, Lao PDR, Malaysia, Myanmar, Philippines, Singapore, Timor-Leste, Thailand, Viet Nam

Contributors: Effendy A. Sumardja, J. MacKinnon, S. Chape

REGIONAL DESCRIPTION

The Southeast Asian region comprises the territories of the 10 Association of Southeast Asian Nations (ASEAN) countries, and the newly independent Timor-Leste. Biogeographically, apart from artificially dividing the island of New Guinea into two regions, these countries closely correspond with the Indochinese, Sundaic, Philippine, and Wallacean subregions of the Indo-Malayan Realm (MacKinnon and MacKinnon 1986), and part of the Papuan subregion in the Oceanian Realm.

The total land area is almost 4.5 million km² and contains a population of almost half a billion people. In addition there is a considerable sea area. Most of this region is tropical and moist, but some parts have a pronounced dry season, resulting in monsoon forests such as those of central Myanmar, central Indochina, parts of the Philippines, and north Sumatra, east Java, the Lesser Sundas, and southeast Irian Jaya (West Papua) in Indonesia. Several major river deltas and large lakes occur in the region and many mountain ranges provide distinct habitat types. In both northern Myanmar and central West Papua, peaks rise above the snow line and permanent glaciers are found. Other peaks provide cloud forest habitat. Some mountain ranges are volcanic and there are many active volcanoes throughout the region. Other distinctive habitat types include extensive karst limestone formations and some ultrabasic hills. The marine areas include shallow seas over the Sunda and Sahul continental shelves, with deeper seas elsewhere, and very deep sea trenches to the east of the Philippines, north of Tanimbar, and south of Java.

The entire region is regarded as unusually rich in biodiversity. The coral reefs, mangroves, and seagrass beds of the region are the richest in the world. The Indonesian and Philippine archipelagos are both rich in terrestrial species and contain very high levels of insular endemism. The Indochinese subregion, Sundaic subregion, and Papuan subregion contain some of the richest rainforests in the world. In total the region contains about 30 percent of all known species on the planet. This biodiversity importance has been recognized in all global biodiversity assessments – there are 37 endemic bird areas, and most of the land and sea area of the region falls within one or more of 21 terrestrial, 10 freshwater, and four marine important ecoregions (WWF Global 200).

The human population is generally dense but some areas such as Java and the major river deltas (Red River, Mekong, Chao Phraya, and Irrawaddy) support some of the highest human densities in the world, and this places a great pressure on the biological resources of the region. The ten ASEAN countries contain a diverse collection of different races, cultures, religions, political systems, and stages in economic development, but have joined together in a single association since they share similar conditions and aspirations. The region is largely a producer of raw materials (timber, economic crops, fish, and oil) which are traded mostly with China, the Republic of Korea, and Japan. Light industries such as processing of economic crops, garments, and production of shoes, microchips, and other end-products are increasing, whilst tourism remains an important growth industry.

Source: UNEP-WCMC

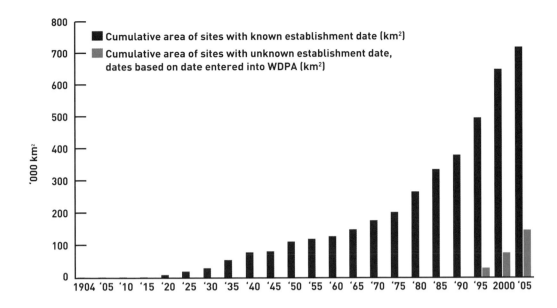

Southeast Asia: Growth of protected areas network, 1904-2005

HISTORICAL PERSPECTIVE

Apart from Brunei and Thailand, the other territories have all experienced a period of European colonization. The earliest establishment of protected areas dates from this colonial period. In 1840, for instance, the Governor of Singapore "prohibited the further destruction of forests on the summit of hills." By 1882 a system of forest reserves was established, although this was revoked and reorganized in 1939. Nature reserves were not legislated in Singapore until 1951. By independence in the mid-20th century, Malaysia, the Philippines, and Indonesia had already established basic protected area systems, but virtually no sites – with the exception of hunting reserves – were established in the Indochina countries while they were under French influence. In Myanmar, only wildlife sanctuaries were declared, in which wildlife but not habitat was protected.

Lao PDR and Cambodia have been the latest

Southeast Asia: Growth in the number of protected areas, 1904-2005

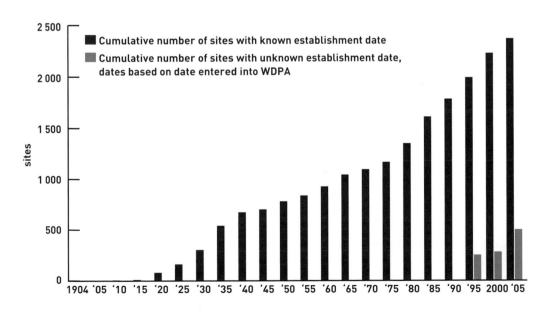

Areas of Southeast Asia protected (by country), 2005

Country	Land area (km²)	Total protected area (km²)	Total number of sites
Brunei Darussalam	5 770	3 421	47
Cambodia	181 040	43 465	30
Indonesia	1 904 570	462 646	1 162
Lao PDR	236 800	37 904	27
Malaysia	329 750	87 922	767
Myanmar	676 580	35 443	55
Philippines	300 000	56 493	379
Singapore	620	40	7
Thailand	513 120	111 762	290
Timor-Leste	153 870	1 876	15
Viet Nam	331 690	20 742	116

countries in Southeast Asia to embark on establishing major protected area systems. Viet Nam astonishingly found time to open its first national park in the middle of the Viet Nam War in 1962. Cambodia had made its first protected area as early as 1925, but this was replaced by a system of large reserves covering 5 percent of the country starting in 1960. This was again replaced after the Khmer Rouge period by a new system of 23 areas protected under royal decree in 1993. Lao PDR's extensive system of national conservation areas also dates from 1993.

THE PROTECTED AREAS NETWORK

The growth of protected area systems in the region over the last 25 years has been remarkable. There are now 2 895 protected areas recorded in the World Database on Protected Areas, and the terrestrial coverage of these represents almost 19 percent of the total land surface.

The dominant IUCN protected area management categories in terms of area coverage are II and VI, the latter including large numbers of forest reserves. Sites that have not been assigned a category are also widespread across the region, and these also include a number of forest reserve sites.

Although there are 390 marine protected areas across the region, representing all the coastal countries, the total area covered is still quite small – 76 463 km² – which represents only about 0.9 percent of the marine waters claimed by the countries of the region (to 200 nautical miles).

Although the protected area system continues to grow, gap analyses continually point out new needs. Current protected area systems are biased towards montane areas and weak in protection of lowland moist forests, karst limestone, and wetlands. Some regions are also poorly covered, such as the Mollucas and Lesser Sundas of Indonesia, and the Visayas of Philippines. Lao PDR has an extensive system, developed through IUCN technical assistance in the 1980s-1990s, with most areas having high biodiversity value. The protected areas along the Annamite Range bordering Viet Nam are particularly important for regional conservation. Since the early 1990s this area has been the focus of attention because of the discovery of at least one new mammal genus and several new species (Duckworth, Salter & Khounboline 1999). Despite their high biodiversity values, all Lao national protected areas have been assigned IUCN Category VI and there is a major emphasis, which is yet to be effectively realized, on sustainable use of natural resources within the protected areas by local communities.

Analysis of the important bird areas identified by BirdLife International indicate that only half of the important sites are within protected areas. For the Philippines, according to a recently completed multi-taxa review of critical areas for conservation, only half of the priority areas identified already fall within protected areas. It is recommended that each country undertakes its own systems review, tries to fill identified gaps, and may need to drop some degraded sites.

Many protected areas contain extensive areas of degraded or even converted habitats so the total area of "natural" protected area is considerably less than official figures. Also, levels of protective management may be poor, and some countries have limited capacity for effective management. As a result, many sites are only protected on paper.

S Chape

Nakai-Nam Theun National Protected Area, Lao PDR bordering Viet Nam.

Southeast Asia: Protected areas network by IUCN category, 2005

IUCN category	Total sites	Total area (km²)
Ia	292	22 527
Ib	12	111 398
II	329	254 656
III	83	24 849
IV	206	142 526
V	129	20 837
VI	985	200 833
No category	859	184 087
Total	2 895	861 714

Southeast Asia: Protected areas network by IUCN category (percentage of total area), 2005

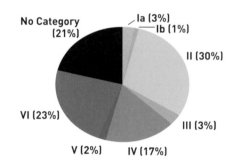

Southeast Asia: Number of protected areas by IUCN category, 2005

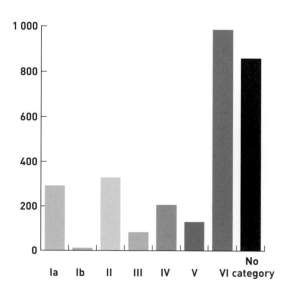

Other forms of protection

There are few private reserves in the region and they are very small. However, the Danum Valley Conservation area in Sabah, Malaysia, is an interesting case. This area of 43 800 hectares of lowland and hill dipterocarp forest, surrounded by much larger areas of selectively logged timber concessions, is part of the forest holding of Yayasan Sabah, a state-wide foundation mostly concerned with forestry and logging. The Danum Valley site has been set aside, placed under a management board, and has prepared management plans for protection, use as a tourist area, and site of research. An excellent research camp, laboratories, and tourist lodge are available and a long-term relationship with the Royal Society of the UK has ensured a record of high-quality research into forest ecology, dynamics, and succession, taxonomic interests, and low-impact logging. This important site has now been officially recognized and given nature reserve status.

Other important examples of local reserves can be found among coastal fishing communities. Following initial studies and a model established at Apo Reef in the Philippines, some 400 locally managed no-fishing areas are now established in the Philippines, the majority of which are not held in the World Database on Protected Areas. Data show that within a few years of the establishment of no-fishing areas, representing about 20 percent of the total fishing area, the local fishermen had already realized an increase in total catch and catch per unit effort as a result of adult fish emigrating out of the protected areas into nearby waters. At Apo, after 20 years, the graph of increasing catch continues to rise. Interestingly, those reserves that were taken over by local government appear to be less effective than those protected and managed by the local fishermen themselves.

International sites

The region shows considerable variation in the level of participation in international conventions. Brunei, Lao PDR, Myanmar, Singapore and Timor-Leste, have no sites. The first biosphere reserves in the region were declared in 1976 (Thailand) and 1977 (Indonesia and Philippines), and the current array of sites includes important marine and coastal areas, including Can Gio Mangrove Biosphere Reserve in Viet Nam, Ranong Biosphere Reserve in Thailand, Puerto Galera in the Philippines, and Komodo National Park in Indonesia. The largest single site is

Tonle Sap in Cambodia, covering 14 813 km² of the largest freshwater lake in Southeast Asia and its floodplain, with three distinct zones: an open lake at its center, a freshwater swamp forest surrounding it, and seasonally flooded grasslands at the margins, mainly in the eastern shore. The adjacent Boeng Chmar Lake, a Ramsar site, merges with Tonle Sap Lake in the wet season.

World Heritage sites in the region cover a broad range of natural habitats and landforms, including the spectacular Puerto-Princesa Subterranean River National Park in the Philippines, and the karst landforms and surrounding seascape of Ha Long Bay in Viet Nam. Important forest sites include the 6 222 km² Thung Yai-Huai Kha Khaeng in Thailand and the 26 000 km² complex of protected areas in Sumatra, inscribed in 2004. The Lorentz National Park in West Papua covers more than 25 000 km² and spans the ecological gradient from the coast to the highest peak of the country at 4 884 meters, with permanent ice caps.

In addition to these global agreements, the member countries have established another regional class of protected area, ASEAN Heritage Parks, established under the 1984 ASEAN Declaration on Heritage Parks and Reserves and selected to be typical of the major habitats of the region. Currently, 35 sites have been designated (see table), 13 of which are also World Heritage sites.

FUTURE DIRECTIONS

There is still an urgent need to secure new areas for conservation; in the coming decades this will become increasingly difficult as remaining natural areas are diminished and land ownership changes. However most countries are already struggling in their capacity to manage their existing protected areas. In addition, protected area management authorities have failed to convince governments and planners of the economic value of protected areas in national economies. Interest in new proposals for protected areas is thus diminishing.

Efforts to improve capacity include many international aid projects; the development of ASEAN-endorsed protected area occupational standards by the ASEAN Centre for Biodiversity (previously the ASEAN Regional Centre for Biodiversity Conservation); and regional training program. However, more effort is clearly needed to address this critical issue since it is fundamental to achieving management effectiveness across the region.

Southeast Asia: Internationally protected areas, 2005

Country	No. of sites	Protected area (km²)
Biosphere reserves		
Cambodia	1	14 813
Indonesia	6	20 616
Philippines	2	11 740
Thailand	4	845
Viet Nam	4	3 593
TOTAL	17	51 607
Ramsar sites		
Cambodia	3	546
Indonesia	2	2 427
Malaysia	5	554
Mayanmar	1	3
Philippines	4	684
Thailand	10	3 706
Viet Nam	2	258
TOTAL	27	8 177
World Heritage sites		
Indonesia	4	51 924
Malaysia	2	1 282
Philippines	2	534
Thailand	2	11 930
Viet Nam	2	1 500
TOTAL	12	61 170

Many of the existing, long-term threats to natural ecosystems, such as logging and forest clearance for agriculture, need addressing. With continuing depletion of natural resources outside of protected areas, more pressure will be placed on existing conservation areas – rather than provide scope for needed additions to existing networks. The impact of disastrous flooding in upland areas of Thailand and China in the past 20 years has led to logging bans and limits in those countries, which have then procured timber from neighboring countries, especially Laos and Cambodia. At the same time there are growing numbers of new threats including invasive alien species, climate change (including impacts of sea-level rise, changes in temperature regimes, and forest fires). In the marine environment, blasting of reefs and catching fish with cyanide poison continue to be serious threats, with anchor damage and bleaching of corals in El Niño periods, and marine pollution also serious problems. Some marine areas are

ASEAN Heritage Parks, 2003

Country	Site	Size (km²)	Features/Habitat
Brunei	Tasek Marimbun	78	Freshwater swamps
Cambodia	Virachey National Park	3 325	Montane evergreen and deciduous forest
	Preah Monivong (Phnom Bokor) National Park	1 400	Mixed deciduous forest and moist evergreen forest
Indonesia	Barisan Selatan National Park	3,650	Lowland rainforest and wetlands
	Leuser National Park	10 947	Lowland and montane rainforests
	Kerinci-Seblat National Park	13 750	Lowland and montane rainforests
	Komodo National Park	2193	Grass-woodland savannah habitat of Komodo Dragon
	Lorenz National Park	25 056	Glaciers, montane and lowland rainforests
	Ujung-Kulon National Park	800	Lowland evergreen forest habitat of Javan rhino
Lao PDR	Nam Ha National Protected Area	2 224	Evergreen forest and grassland
Malaysia	Kinabalu Park	754	Geological and montane rainforest
	Gunung Mulu National Park	554	Karst landscape and montane rainforest
	Taman Negara National Park	4 525	Lowland and hills rainforest
Myanmar	Alaungdaw Katthapa National Park	1 607	Moist mixed deciduous forest, pine and evergreen forests
	Meinmahla Kyun Wildlife Sanctuary	137	Mangrove forest
	Indawgyi Lake Wildlife Sanctuary	775	Semi-evergreen forest and moist deciduous forest
	Inlay Lake Wildlife Sanctuary	642	Swamp forest, evergreen and deciduous forests, grassland and pine forest, wetland
	Khakaborazi National Park	3 812	Conifer forest and evergreen forest
	Lampi Marine National Park	205	Mangrove forest, evergreen forest, and marine
Philippines	Mt Apo National Park	632	Montane and lowland rainforest
	Iglit-Baco National Park	970	Grassland and forest ecosystem
	Puerto Princesa Subterranean River National Park	202	Limestone karst landscape
	Tubbataha Reef Marine Park	332	Reef ecosystems
Singapore:	Sungei Buloh Wetland Reserve	1.3	Mangrove swamp
Thailand	Ao Phang-nga Marine National Park	400	Coastal forest, karst formations and marine ecosystems
	Khao Yai National Park	2 168	Lowland and hill rainforest
	Tarutao National Park	1 490	Marine ecosystem and islands
	Mu Ko Surin National Park	158	Coral reefs, mangrove forest, and tropical evergreen forest
	Kaeng Krachan National Park	3 027	Mixed deciduous and evergreen forests
	Thung Yai-Huay Kha Khaeng National Park	2,575	Semi-evergreen lowland forest, deciduous dipterocarp forest and mixed forest
Viet Nam	Hoang Lien Sa Pa Nature Reserve	247	Savanna, sub-montane dry evergreen forest, montane deciduous forest, and subalpine forests
	Ba Be National Park	76	Limestone karst forest and lowland evergreen forest
	Kon Ka Kinh Nature Reserve	417	Mixed coniferous and broadleaf forests
	Ha Long Bay	1,500	Limestone islands and karst forest
	Phong Nha-Ke Bang National Park	2,746	Tropical moist evergreen forest on limest

Source: ASEAN Centre for Biodiversity

further compromised by complex overlapping territorial claims which prevent important areas such as the Spratly Islands being protected.

The emergence of China as a rich neighbor with an insatiable demand for timber, marine products, and many types of wildlife as foods or for medicines puts a severe strain on protecting resources in Southeast Asia. Both legal and illegal trade routes drain important species (primates, reptiles, pangolins, birds) from natural habitats and protected areas of the region. Growing populations and higher disposable incomes are also increasingly damaging fisheries, with both general overfishing and the widescale commercial extinction of key target species such as sharks and other predatory fish.

The region is experimenting with various models of involvement of local people in planning and co-managing protected areas. For example, progressive laws in the Philippines ensure that protected area management boards with local representation direct the program of management, but there are concerns that this may lead to a dilution of conservation objectives and degradation of some important sites. A number of countries have put major international assistance resources into developing integrated approaches to conservation and development in protected areas, with mixed results (MacKinnon & Wardojo 2001, Chape 2001). Nonetheless, given the pressures and expectations placed on protected areas in the region, effective mechanisms for integrating conservation and development objectives need to be pursued.

Regional cooperation on protected areas, within a much-needed cooperative conservation and development framework, must continue to be developed. There is considerable scope for strengthening not only cooperation on transborder protected areas (for example, the existing initiatives to establish transborder reserves between Malaysia and Indonesia on Borneo, and between the Philippines and Malaysia on the Turtle Islands) but also broader environmental cooperation that has a direct impact on the viability of protected areas. Regional development cooperation mechanisms, in particular ASEAN, the Mekong River

S Chape

Commission, and the Asian Development Bank Greater Mekong Subregion (GMS) program, need to be harnessed to strengthen regional conservation. This must include, as it already does for the GMS, the involvement of China if regional issues are to be effectively addressed. A recent study (ICEM 2003) concluded that "a regional conservation agreement and special institutional arrangements are becoming essential to long-term regional development" and proposed establishment of a regional conservation fund.

**Lowe's Gully,
Mt. Kinabalu Park
World Heritage Site,
Malaysia.**

Australia

and

New Zealand

Contributors: A.Bignell, L. Molloy

REGIONAL DESCRIPTION

New Zealand and Australia span five time zones, with the main land masses stretching from 113° to 179°E and from 10° to 47°S. Beyond these land masses there are also several remote island groups in the Indian Ocean (Australia's Cocos (Keeling) and Christmas Islands) and the Pacific (Lord Howe and Norfolk Islands of Australia, Kermadec and Chatham Islands of New Zealand). Both countries also manage a number of sub-Antarctic islands.

Australia is the most low-lying continent, and is dominated by low-relief landscapes, with mountain ranges mainly restricted to the eastern continental edge. By contrast, large areas of New Zealand are mountainous, including the 750 km chain of the Southern Alps which runs along the western margin of the South Island, rising to 3 754 meters (Aoraki/Mount Cook) and carrying hundreds of glaciers. These contrasting structures are related to their tectonic settings. Australia lies on the Indian/Australian Plate, while New Zealand sits astride the boundary between this plate and the Pacific Plate. Rhyolitic and andesitic volcanoes of the central North Island have a long history of extremely violent eruptions, and lava and tephra mantle shape much of the landscape.

Tectonic history has also greatly influenced the ecology of this region, with Australia and New Zealand becoming separated from most other continental land masses during the early to mid Cretaceous, and remaining isolated through most recent evolutionary history.

The combined maritime areas of the two countries (not including offshore territories) is 11 500 000 km². Australia has a considerable marine area including large tracts of the Indian and Pacific Oceans. Along its northern shore the shallow waters of the Timor and Arafura Seas separate Australia from Indonesia. To the northeast lies the Coral Sea, with a number of remote shallow banks and reefs, and to the southeast the Tasman Sea. For the most part, Australia's continental shelf is broad; however, to the southwest and southeast the oceanic waters come close to the coast and are affected by the south-flowing Leeuwin Current and East Australia Current respectively.

New Zealand's major maritime feature is the Subtropical Convergence, where the warm waters (of subtropical origin) of the West Wind Drift come into contact with the cooler, less saline waters of sub-Antarctic origin. This convergence, coupled with an extensive continental shelf and very long coastline, results in a wide variety of marine habitats.

Australia's vast land mass is dominated by drylands but some lush tropical, subtropical, and temperate areas exist with a considerable diversity of ecosystems. Snow is common in the Australian Alps where minimum recorded temperatures have dropped to –23ºC. In the arid northwest summer temperatures often exceed 50ºC (the maximum recorded is 53.1ºC). The Australian continent under the Interim Biogeographic Regionalisation for Australia (IBRA) has been stratified into 85 biogeographic regions, while the Interim Marine and Coastal Regionalisation of Australia (IMCRA) has recognized 60 marine biogeographic regions.

New Zealand has a temperate maritime climate, with vegetation strongly influenced by the topography. The Southern Alps are a barrier to the wet westerly winds, causing sharp landscape contrasts – rainforests in the west but semi-arid tussock grasslands in the east where the rain-

S. Chape

Kalbarri National Park, Western Australia.

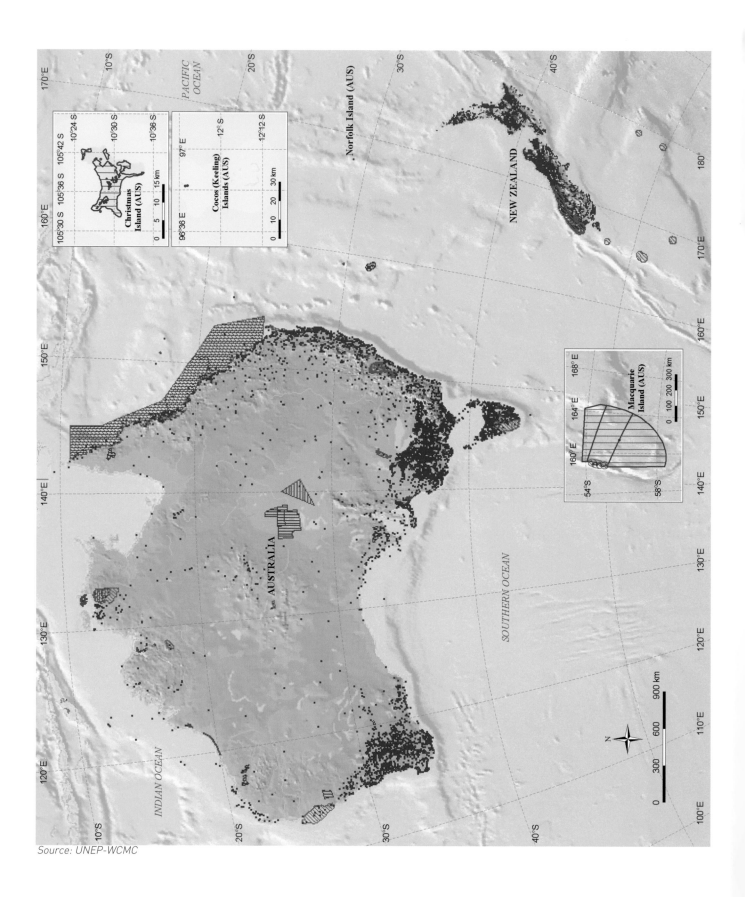

Source: UNEP-WCMC

shadow covers the intermontane basins of Canterbury and Otago.

Evolutionary isolation led to the survival of ancient species lost on other parts of the planet, and to the evolution of many others found nowhere else in the world. Australia has been identified as one of 17 "megadiversity" countries (Mittermeier et al. 1997): 92 percent of Australia's vascular plants are endemic and 85 percent of flowering plants (angiosperms) are also endemic (Commonwealth of Australia (CoA) 1996a); 74 percent of Australia's non-fish vertebrates are endemic, ranking them first in the world (Groombridge 1992); about 83 percent of mammals also occur nowhere else, as well as 45 percent of birds, 89 percent of reptiles, and 93 percent of frogs (CoA 1996a, CoA 1996b).

Although not possessing the same number of species, New Zealand is rich in endemics. The islands of New Zealand are among the most isolated on Earth. They were separated from the continental land mass of Gondwana more than 80 million years ago, before the ascendancy of mammals, and much of the biota has evolved in considerable isolation. Endemic species include four primitive frogs and all 60 reptiles (including the ancient relict reptile order, Sphenodontia - the tuatara). Endemism runs to 90 percent of insects and marine molluscs, 80 percent of higher plants, and 55 percent of indigenous birds. An interesting feature is the high proportion of birds that became large and flight-less, largely due to the absence of mammalian predators. Alpine flora is particularly rich, with more than 25 percent of New Zealand's higher plants found above the treeline.

Some 18 priority ecoregions have been identified in the WWF Global 200 framework, which cover almost all of the freshwater, and a large proportion of the terrestrial ecosystems and surrounding marine areas. BirdLife International has identified 14 endemic bird areas, including most of New Zealand and many of the coastal areas of Australia, as well as the oceanic islands.

New Zealand was probably the last major habitable land mass to be settled, probably about 1 000 years ago. Today the population is only 4 million, mostly located in cities around the country's extensive coastline. Humans probably first reached Australia some 40 000 years ago. However, population densities remained low and their impacts on the natural environment, although significant, were far less than in many other continents. The present population of Australia is estimated to be more than 21 million, with approximately 460 000 identified as being of Aboriginal or Torres Strait descent. The majority of the population is concentrated in urban areas in the east and southeast of eastern Australia with a smaller concentration in the southwest of Western Australia. About 84 percent of Australia's population live in only 1 percent of its land area.

HISTORICAL PERSPECTIVE

Australia and New Zealand were among the first nations to dedicate land as national parks, leading the way in protected area systems establishment. The first parks in Australia were not the traditional protective institutions they are today. In 1879 the National Park, later renamed Royal National Park, was established principally as a recreational area for Sydney inhabitants. New Zealand's first national park was initiated when the paramount chief of the Ngati Tuwharetoa tribe presented the summits of the sacred Tongariro volcanoes to the nation as a gift in 1887. These volcanoes became the nucleus of Tongariro National Park, established in 1894. Both Tongariro and Royal National Park were primary steps in the development of comprehensive national park and reserve networks.

In New Zealand national parks management was consolidated under the National Parks Act of 1952, and a parallel system of forest reserves and forest parks was also set up by the Forest Service. A major protected areas controversy arose in the 1960s around plans to raise water levels in lakes of the Fiordland National Park for hydroelectricity generation. This debate lasted ten years, but also served to raise the issue of natural heritage loss within the minds of urban populations and highlighted a skew in the protected area system towards mountain and montane forest. The Reserves Act 1977 and a new National Parks Act in 1980, gave impetus to protecting more representative ecosystems, such as coastal, wetland, marine, lowland forest, and tussock grassland ecosystems. Between 1975 and 1985 a series of conflicts occurred as conservation non-governmental organizations (NGOs) sought to achieve protection of New Zealand's remaining lowland forests and wild rivers.

A major advance in protected area administration occurred in 1987 when the government consolidated all its natural and historic resource conservation agencies into the single Department of Conservation (DOC) (subsequently assisted by

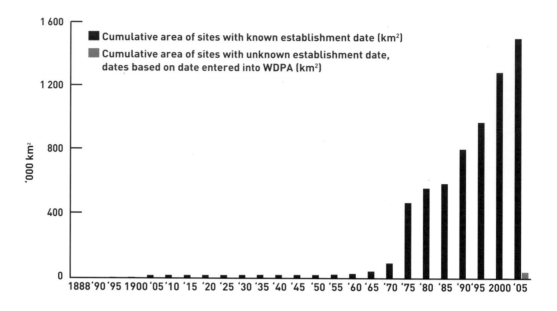

Australia and New Zealand: Growth of protected areas network, 1888-2005

regional citizen Conservation Boards). Since then, DOC has provided leadership in the management of the protected area system and the restoration of New Zealand's indigenous biodiversity – often in partnership with local *iwi* (Maori tribes). The New Zealand Biodiversity Strategy was accepted enthusiastically in 2000 by the government and its conservation partners, leading to major improvements in the management of what is now an impressive public land protected area system

extending across nearly 32 percent of New Zealand's terrestrial ecosystems.

In Australia most state and territory park agencies grew from beginnings in State Forest Services or similar agencies. It was not until the 1960s and 1970s that separate national park services were established. A growing community awareness through improved mobility and access to natural areas and through the activities of the voluntary conservation movement in the 1960s,

Australia and New Zealsnd: Growth in the number of protected areas, 1888-2005

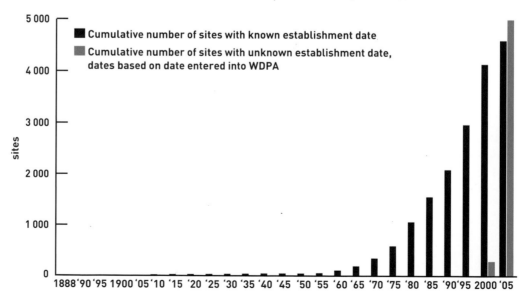

1970s, and 1980s led to substantial increases in protected areas. Key additions were often related to important locations and issues: the Great Barrier Reef, coastal sand masses such as Fraser Island, Cooloola and Myall Lakes, old-growth wet eucalypt forests, tropical rainforests, wilderness in Southwest Tasmania, and the wetlands of Kakadu. Through the Commonwealth/State Government Regional Forest Agreement process approximately 2 million hectares of dedicated reserves were added to the protected area estate. Between 1968 and 2004, the total area protected increased from 9.4 million hectares to 80.89 million hectares, or 10.5 percent of the land area of Australia.

THE PROTECTED AREA NETWORKS

The World Database on Protected Areas (WDPA)lists a total of 9 595 protected areas in Australia and New Zealand, although it does not include 1 244 Category Ia Heritage Agreement Areas in Australia as data were incomplete for these. However, these sites cover only 6 000 km² and so do not greatly alter the overall statistics.

Largely as a result of action taken in Australia, this region has the most comprehensive marine protection in the world. The WDPA lists 422 marine protected areas, covering a total of 568 872 km². This represents 4.6 percent of the total marine area claimed by these states and, while some 60 percent of the total is protected within the single site of the Great Barrier Reef Marine Park, this still leaves a very large area protected in the remaining sites.

The Australian states and territories operate their own systems of terrestrial and marine protected areas under their own legislation. The Federal Government also manages a small number of reserves originally established on Commonwealth Crown land or in the Australian External Territories, as well as marine reserves established in Commonwealth waters. The nine separate terrestrial protected area systems are collectively known as the National Reserve System (NRS), while the eight separate marine protected area systems are collectively known as the National Representative System of Marine Protected Areas (NRSMPA). These arrangements have resulted in a system with more than 40 categories of protected area nationally. However, in 1994 the jurisdictions agreed to adopt the IUCN 1994 classification of protected areas and to use the IUCN system of management categories for documenting and reporting on their protected

Australia and New Zealand: Protected areas network by IUCN category, 2005

IUCN category	Total sites	Total area (km²)
Ia	2 136	217 035
Ib	38	41 898
II	701	347 408
III	3 946	33 806
IV	1 657	269 247
V	217	22 502
VI	489	596 246
No category	411	9 702
Total	9 595	1 537 845

Australia and New Zealand: Protected areas network by IUCN category (percentage of total area), 2005

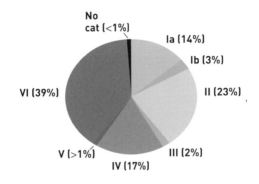

Australia and New Zealand: Number of protected areas by IUCN category, 2005

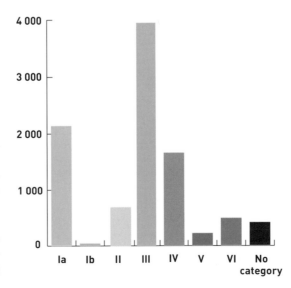

Areas of Australia and New Zealand protected (by country, 2005)

Country/territories	Land area (km²)	Total protected area (km²)	Total number of sites
Australia	7 741 220	1 445 200	5688
Christmas Island	140	87	1
Cocos (Keeling) Islands	14	1	1
New Zealand	270 530	92 550	3 904
Norfolk Island	30	7	1

area estates. Data on Australia's protected areas are collated into the Collaborative Australian Protected Area Database (CAPAD), which is maintained and updated biannually by the Department of Environment and Water Resources for national and international reporting purposes.

In 1993, the Federal Government, in cooperation with the states and territories, initiated the National Reserves System Program, designed to further develop the protected area estate and to ensure that the different administrative systems are working within a common framework in collaboration with other stakeholders. The program provided funds for land acquisitions and protected areas assessment work, and was given a major funding boost with the commencement of the Natural Heritage Trust in 1996.

Australia, along with New Zealand, is considered a world leader in joint management of protected areas with the land's indigenous traditional owners. In 1978, the first joint management arrangement was made with the traditional owners of Kakadu National Park. Under the Kakadu arrangement, traditional owners lease the land to the (federal government) Director of National Parks in return for an annual lease fee plus a proportion of revenue earned from park user fees. A Board of Management made up of a majority of representatives of traditional owners is responsible for the preparation of a management plan for the reserve, monitoring the implementation of the plan, and making decisions on management of the reserve consistent with the plan. Currently nine reserves in Australia operate under joint management arrangements.

With a large marine jurisdiction, the Commonwealth Government is implementing the Australia Oceans Policy (1998), which outlines commitments and actions to the ongoing establishment of the NRSMPA for conservation purposes and to give regional security for industry access to ocean resources and their sustainable use. The Commonwealth Government has pro-

vided extensive funding over the past decade to progress establishment of the NRSMPA, including funding for work to map habitats, develop planning approaches, and declare new marine protected areas.

In New Zealand, as already mentioned, the majority of protected areas are managed and administered by the Department of Conservation (DOC). DOC now oversees about 86 000 km² (excluding marine reserves), or nearly 32 percent of New Zealand's land area. Even more striking is the achievement of conserving this huge land area under unified management and policies (the DOC and general policies under the Conservation Act and the National Parks Act).

The terrestrial strict nature reserves (Category Ia) include many of the most important remnants of New Zealand's biodiversity, including:

❑ offshore and outlying island nature reserves and scientific reserves, such as Codfish Island (Whenua Hou) the most important habitat for the flightless night parrot, the kakapo;
❑ the ecological areas and sanctuary areas which primarily protect representative forests, shrublands, and wetlands ecosystems;
❑ a number of special areas in national parks, including the 518 km² Murchison Mountains in Fiordland National Park, protecting the takahe (an endangered flightless rail).

The 28 existing marine reserves cover around 7.6 percent of New Zealand's territorial sea (but more than 99 percent of this total consists of the two very large marine reserves around outlying island groups - the 7 480 km² Kermadec Marine Reserve and the 4840 km² Auckland Islands Marine Reserve).

New Zealand now has 14 national parks, with a total area of 30 858 km² (or 11.5 percent of the country's land area). Other important categories for wild land protection include extensive wilderness areas and conservation parks. Efforts are underway

S. Chape

to secure large areas of the eastern South Island high country tussock lands for conservation (through a process of 'tenure review' of long-standing pastoral leases on public lands). The transfer of 1 300 km² of West Coast indigenous forest, formerly managed for timber production, to the Department of Conservation was completed in April 2002. These forests were the largest single addition to public conservation land since 1989, and around 180 km² have since been added to Kahurangi, Paparoa, and Westland/Tai Poutini National Parks.

Other forms of protection

Both Australia and New Zealand have actively tried to encourage indigenous people to conserve their lands. Australia has the Indigenous Protected Areas program that provides incentives for indigenous people to participate in the National Reserve System by voluntarily declaring protected areas and becoming involved in the management of existing statutory protected areas. So far, 19 Indigenous Protected Areas covering 137 900 km² have been added to the National Reserve System. New Zealand's DOC has sought to implement the spirit of the Treaty of Waitangi by trying to actively engage *iwi* in partnerships of conservation. "Cultural redress" under the Ngai Tahu Treaty settlement in

1998 had a number of very significant implications for the management of South Island's protected areas, and a wide range of conservation issues are currently being negotiated as part of settlements for several North Island *iwi*. Additionally the Nga Whenua Rahui fund was established in 1990 to facilitate the voluntary protection by Maori of indigenous ecosystems on Maori-owned land. It has proved a very appropriate approach to landscape and biodiversity protection, particularly through protecting and enhancing the cultural and spiritual values that *tangata whenua* associate with their natural heritage.

The Nature Heritage Fund (established in 1990) has been a key factor in protecting nature on private land in New Zealand,. To date more than 700 projects have protected 2 560 km² of indigenous ecosystems, through direct purchase or covenanting, at an average cost to the New Zealand taxpayer of only around NZ$388 per hectare. The fund ranks the importance of potential acquisitions and has thus focused on ecosystems that are underrepresented in the DOC-managed protected areas system.

As 60 percent of Australia's land surface is privately owned (either as freehold land, approximately 20 percent, or as Crown leasehold, approximately 40 percent), the covenanting of private lands

Tussock Grasslands, South Island, New Zealand

Australia and New Zealand: Internationally protected areas, 2005

Country/territories	No. of sites	Protected area (km²)
Biosphere reserves		
Australia	13	50 063
TOTAL	13	50 063
Ramsar sites		
Australia	63	73 719
Christmas Island	1	>0
New Zealand	6	391
TOTAL	70	74 110
World Heritage sites		
Australia[2]	15	426 202
New Zealand[3]	3	40 664
TOTAL	19	466 860

1 Includes Macquarie Island.
2 Includes Heard and McDonald Islands and Macquarie Island.
3 Includes the Sub-Antarctic Islands World Heritage Site .

is very important. Recently there has been rapid growth in conservation covenants, e.g. National Trust of Australia and Bushcare covenants, placed on the title of freehold lands, and special conditions on leasehold lands, to enable their management as private protected areas.

Another Australian initiative is the Register of the National Estate that contains about 13 000 heritage places, including more than 2 000 natural areas. Entry places obligations on Federal Government agencies to avoid damaging listed places and requires them to consult the Australian Heritage Council and comply with the Environment Protection and Biodiversity Conservation Act 1999 about any action that might significantly affect a registered place.

International sites

Both countries are actively involved in international agreements to establish protected areas. Australia has 15 natural World Heritage sites, including Heard and McDonald Islands, the largest number of any country. These sites span a considerable range of the country's diversity, including temperate and tropical rainforests, marine areas (including the world's largest World Heritage site, the Great Barrier Reef, at 349 000 km²), mountains, and off-shore islands. New Zealand itself has one natural World Heritage site, the very large 260,000 km² Te Wahipounamu (South West New Zraland) site which is 10% of New Zealand's land area;, one mixed site,

Tongatito National Park, and the New Zealand Sub-Antarctic Islands World Heritage Site,consisting of five island groups in the Southern Ocean south-east of New Zealand.

Ramsar sites are also well represented, and Australia has some very large sites, including the Coral Sea Reserves (Coringa-Herald and Lihou Reefs and Cays), which are predominantly marine sites covering highly remote reefs in the Coral Sea. Only Australia has designated biosphere reserves.

FUTURE DIRECTIONS

From a terrestrial perspective, the Australian National Land and Water Resources Audit Report, Australian Terrestrial Biodiversity Assessment 2002, concluded that some 46 bioregions (out of 85) had less than 10 percent of their area in reserves, 16 bioregions had less than 2 percent, and two had no protected areas. The report also concluded that only 67 percent of Australia's ecosystems are sampled within national parks and formal reserves. There thus remains a considerable need for establishing more protected areas, and to this end the Federal Government has extended the successful NRS program under the Natural Heritage Trust initiative and will continue to fund acquisition/covenanting of land and reserve assessment studies that meet the criteria under the Australian Guidelines for Establishing the National Reserve System. By 2006 the program had provided financial assistance of nearly A$105m for the acquisition or covenanting of more than 26.5 million hectares of protected areas estate.

The Australian Federal and State Governments have developed the paper *Directions for the National Reserve System – A Partnership Approach*, to assist government agencies, NGOs, and the community in the ongoing development and management of a comprehensive, adequate, and representative protected area system. The paper, which was available for public comment until 2004, recognizes that NGOs, indigenous landholders, and individual property owners can contribute to achieving the goals of the NRS through the inclusion of private protected areas and Indigenous Protected Areas (IPAs) (that meet the NRS standards) into the NRS. Both private land and IPAs will increase in the future.

The development of jurisdictional marine planning initiatives has seen acceleration in the number of areas identified for possible protection. This is particularly true for the Commonwealth

Government, with the first Regional Marine Plan identifying 11 broad areas of interest off south-eastern Australia for further assessment. The Victorian State Government has established an system of marine protected areas representative of the bioregions within its marine jurisdiction.

For heavily used marine protected areas, establishing detailed zoning schemes that adequately protect biodiversity while allowing ecologically sustainable activities, including fishing, is likely to be a priority. Another emerging priority is the need to coordinate research efforts to report on the performance of the NRSMPA in protecting Australia's marine ecosystems.

Future directions for New Zealand's protected areas are largely guided by the NZ Biodiversity Strategy 2000. Although a large proportion of the land is already protected, there is no room for complacency for two main reasons: (a) there are still major gaps in the range of ecosystems represented; and (b) despite the legal protection there remain very significant threats, notably from invasive alien species.

Lowland and coastal forest remnants, dune-lands, indigenous shrublands, wetlands, and lowland tussocklands are the terrestrial under-represented in New Zealand's protected area network. Many of these habitats are now scarce and often located on private (or Crown leasehold) land. Improvements in biodiversity mapping and evaluation will further help to identify the gaps to be brought into the protected area network. Increasing use of the Nature Heritage and Nga Whenua Rahui funds, coupled with the continued use of con-servation covenants administered by the Queen Elizabeth II Trust, is expected to accelerate the rate of protection of these habitats on private land.

The difficulty of getting fishing industry and community support for the protection of marine ecosystems continues to be one of the greatest challenges facing conservation in New Zealand. The national Biodiversity Strategy has set marine bio-diversity as a high conservation priority. To address the unsatisfactory marine environment protection situation, the New Zealand government has carried out wide consultation with all marine stakeholder groups and, in January 2006, released a policy and implementation plan for developing a network of marine protected areas. Proposed new legislation will place greater emphasis on the role of marine reserves in conserving biodiversity. The policy stresses a science-based approach to marine habitat and ecosystem classification, and the involvement of regional councils, tangata whenua, commercial and recreational fishers, and con-servation groups in achieving the Biodiversity Strategy goal of protecting 10 percent of New Zealand's marine environment (under some type of protected area) by 2010.

Prior to the implementation of the NZ Biodiversity Strategy 2000, weed and pest control efforts throughout the protected area network were insufficient to maintain biodiversity values. The government has since provided for a marked escalation in control measures including emphasis upon species recovery programs for the most threatened species (such as the kiwi, kokako, mohua, and kakapo – the latter benefiting from a remarkably successful breeding season in 2002, which increased the number of birds by 39 percent, to 86 in total). The reputation of DOC as an international leader in eradication of animal pests has been demonstrated in the successful restor-ation of a number of island habitats over the past 20 years. An ambitious programme to eliminate cats, rats, stoats and mice and other mammalian pests has seen more than 80 offshore and outlying islands secured as biodiversity havens. In 2001, DOC began the most ambitious rodent eradication attempt on a large oceanic island anywhere in the world and successfully removed Norway rats from the rugged 11,268 ha Campbell Island in the difficult subantarctic environment. It is intended to pro-gressively apply these pest elimination techniques to even larger islands and 'mainland islands' on the North and South Islands.

Pacific Islands

AMERICAN SAMOA (USA), COOK ISLANDS, FEDERATED STATES OF MICRONESIA, FIJI, FRENCH POLYNESIA (FRANCE), GUAM (USA), HAWAII (USA), KIRIBATI, MARSHALL ISLANDS, NAURU, NEW CALEDONIA (FRANCE), NIUE, NORTHERN MARIANA ISLANDS, PALAU, PAPUA NEW GUINEA, PITCAIRN (UK), SAMOA, SOLOMON ISLANDS, TOKELAU, TONGA, TUVALU, UNITED STATES MINOR OUTLYING ISLANDS, VANUATU, WALLIS AND FUTUNA (FRANCE)

Contributors: S. Sesega, M. Spalding

REGIONAL DESCRIPTION

The nations and territories of the Pacific Ocean, often collectively referred to as Oceania, extend over most of the world's largest ocean, from the shores of Asia and Australia towards the Americas. The WCPA region comprises 24 countries and territories, including the US state of Hawaii. The region includes seven overseas territories of France, the UK, and the USA, as well as the United States Minor Outlying Islands of Howland and Baker, Palmyra and Jarvis. The islands cover about 570 000 km² of land area, a total that is dominated by one nation, Papua New Guinea (470 000 km²). The vast majority of countries have very small land surfaces, but are surrounded by extensive marine resources, and the combined exclusive economic zones (EEZs) of this region total some 32 million km², over twice that of any other WCPA region.

The region is underlain by complex patterns of tectonic plates. Most of the islands are linked either to plate margin volcanism and mountain building, or to mid-plate hotspots. The western margin of the Pacific Plate with a number of smaller plates has given rise to island chains ranging from the Northern Mariana Islands, Guam, and Palau, to Papua New Guinea, the Solomon Islands, Vanuatu, and out to Tonga. Hotspots beneath the Earth's crust have formed other island groups such as Hawaii, Samoa, and French Polynesia. Such islands begin as volcanic formations over a mid-plate hotspot, but as the hotspot diminishes or changes position the islands have been maintained, in many areas, by the prolific growth of corals which have formed barrier reefs, atolls, and platforms. In a few places subsequent uplift has raised these coral formations out of the ocean again to build uplifted limestone islands (*makatea*) such as Niue, Nauru, and the southern Cook Islands. New Caledonia is one of the few fragments of continental rock, which broke away from Australia 65 million years ago.

The terrestrial biodiversity of this region is exceptional, especially in view of the relatively small land area. Tropical forests are the predominant vegetation, but there are also dry forests, shrubland, savannas, and even small areas of montane forests and cloud forests. The underlying geology further influences the habitats, with volcanic and limestone soils predominating. In Micronesia and

S Chape

Marovo Lagoon, Solomon Islands

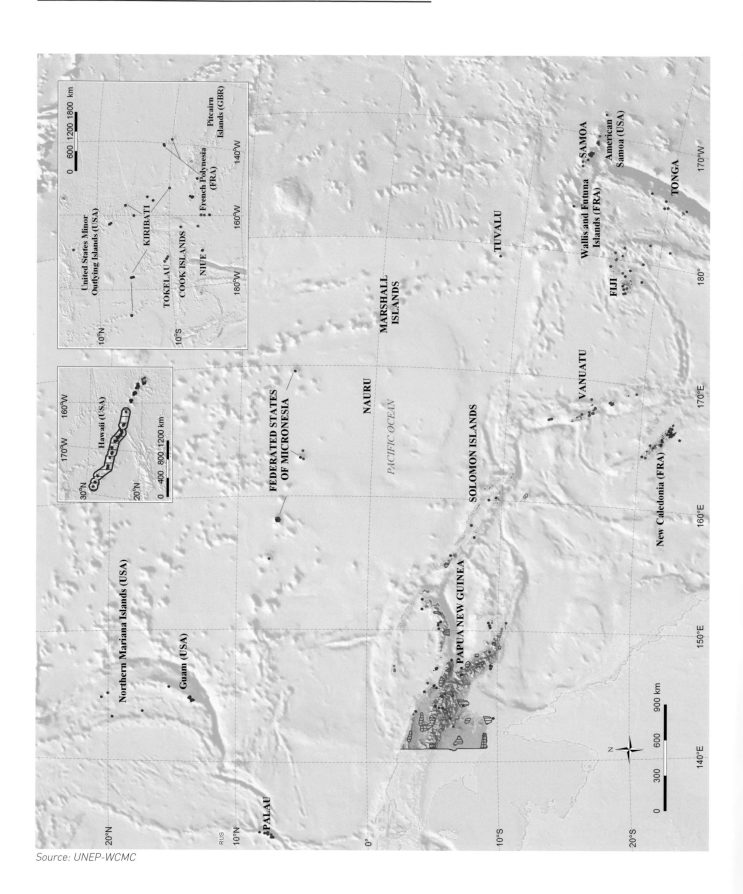

Source: UNEP-WCMC

Polynesia combined, some 6 500 plant species have been described, over half of them endemic. Melanesia, which runs from Papua New Guinea to Fiji, has considerably higher levels of biodiversity, with many of the larger islands still densely covered in tropical moist and tropical dry forests, with some areas of savanna. New Caledonia is another biodiversity hotspot; of its 3 300 plant species some 2 500 are endemic. The island of New Guinea, which includes Papua New Guinea, is the most species-rich island on the planet with an estimated 17 000 plant species and 10 200 endemics.

Birdlife International lists 24 endemic bird areas (EBAs) across the Pacific (excluding New Zealand and Australia) and a further six in mainland Papua New Guinea. Those around Papua New Guinea and the Solomon Islands have the highest levels of endemism of any EBAs, with 79 restricted-range species recorded from the Solomon group.

The surrounding marine waters are also home to exceptional biodiversity. Coral reefs are the dominant nearshore habitat, but there are also wide areas of mangrove and seagrasses. There is a clear pattern to this marine biodiversity which is highest in the west, and diminishes towards the east. The coral reefs of Papua New Guinea, although not well studied, may have levels of diversity equal to the global hotspot of coral reef diversity which encompasses the Philippines and central and eastern Indonesia. Although less diverse, levels of endemism remain high in the marine fauna, particularly in more isolated islands such as Hawaii.

This was one of the last regions of the planet to be settled by humans. The first arrivals to New Guinea have been traced back some 30–40 000 years, but most of the smaller islands were settled by a range of ethnic groups from about 3 500 years ago to about 1 000 years ago. These patterns of settlement by different groups have led to one of the major recognized subdivisions of the region into Melanesia: Papua New Guinea southeast to Fiji; Polynesia: Tonga to Hawaii in the north, and French Polynesia in the southeast; and Micronesia: the northern islands from Palau to Kiribati.

In many countries, traditional lifestyles have been maintained, with a heavy dependence on fishing and agriculture. Western-style development, however, is growing. Mining is a major industry in Papua New Guinea and New Caledonia, while tourism is an important sector on many islands. Humans have had an impact on the natural environment ever since the first arrivals, bringing invasive alien species, clearing natural vegetation, and causing the extinction of many endemic species. In the modern context, population growth, development, and the breakdown of traditional management systems, have added to these threats. Over wide areas, less than 25 percent of the original primary vegetation cover remains intact.

HISTORICAL PERSPECTIVE

Traditional methods of natural resource management in many parts of the Pacific include regulations covering seasons, methods of capture or harvest of natural resources, and restrictions on who can utilize particular resources. In quite a number of cases these regulations include the closure of certain areas to activities such as fishing or hunting. Such regulations, developed over many centuries, thus include the first protected areas of the region. In some traditional societies such sites are still maintained, although they are not always documented. There have been some recent efforts to include such protection in new legislation.

The same traditional systems of tenure (including land and sea areas) inhibited many early efforts to establish centrally planned protected areas systems – local peoples were unwilling to relinquish control of lands and waters that were traditionally theirs and which, in many cases, they were managing perfectly well. The Hawaiian Islands National Wildlife Refuge, a bird reservation established in 1909, was the first modern protected area in the Pacific Islands, followed in 1916 by the Hawaii National Park (now Hawaii Volcanoes and Haleakala National Parks). Following this, sanctuaries, botanical gardens, and other species-based reserves were established in relatively small areas in New Caledonia, Fiji, and the Solomon Islands. Between 1950 and 1960, additional protected areas were established in Guam, Kiribati, Palau, and Samoa. Widespread development of new protected areas took place between 1971 and 1990, when 215 – more than 50 percent of all protected areas set aside to date – were established in all categories.

The mid-1990s and early 2000s saw another development in area-based conservation. The emphasis on parks and strict reserves gave way to the concept of "conservation areas," in which sustainable harvest, direct involvement of local resource owners and users, and the development of compatible income-generating activities were central to protected area design. This continues, with a wide cross-section of stakeholders including

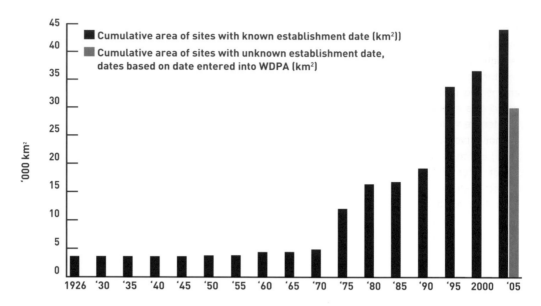

Pacific Islands: Growth of protected areas network, 1926-2005

indigenous non-governmental organizations and local communities becoming engaged in protected areas selection and management. Areas hitherto inaccessible for conservation purposes due to property rights disputes with traditional owners can now be brought under conservation management without removing traditional rights.

THE PROTECTED AREA NETWORK

Information on the extent of the Pacific Islands protected area network is somewhat incomplete.

The total number of protected areas in all categories (including uncategorized ones) varies among different sources. The WDPA listing of just more than 400 sites is probably very conservative, and does not include all of the large number of community conserved areas. One exception is Fiji, where a number of such areas are recorded. The vast surface area occupied by these sites is to a great extent inflated by the single 341 362 km² marine area of Hawaiian Papahānaumokuākea Marine National Monument (excluded from the

Pacific Islands: Growth in the number of protected areas, 1926-2005

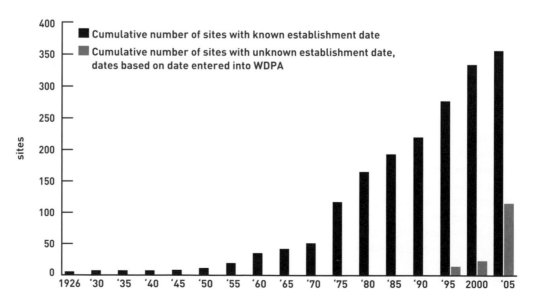

diagrams). The total land area protected is some 55 000 km², which is only some 9.6 percent of the land area of the region.

The high number of uncategorized sites is at least in part indicative of the various innovations in management and protection approaches that are emerging in this region. Many areas are under customary tenure which often means legal boundaries are not surveyed and exact areas not known.

There is considerable variation in the numbers of sites listed for each country or territory, with statistics dominated by Hawaii and Papua New Guinea. About 240 sites (47 percent of the total) include marine and coastal areas, and the protected marine surface covers some 364 000 km² – just over 1 percent of the total maritime area of the region. If Papahānaumokuākea is excluded the proportion protected becomes a very small fraction indeed.

Other forms of protection

Reserves of varying sizes set up under the authority of traditional leaders are increasingly being used throughout the Pacific Islands to regulate resource use. In many cases these follow traditional forms of resource protection that can be traced back well before modern concepts of conservation were introduced to the islands. Such reserves can check resource overexploitation and protect particular species under the threat of overharvesting. In Samoa, for instance, 70 coastal villages have established fisheries reserves where fishing is banned for extended periods, with populations of specific species of shellfish directly replenished. In the Cook Islands, 16 similar areas, locally called *raui*, protect 1 270 hectares of marine areas in Rarotonga, Aitutaki, and Pukapuka. Other locally managed marine and terrestrial areas are reported in Fiji, Tonga, Tokelau, and Tuvalu.

In addition to area-specific protection, traditionally imposed resource bans (*tapu*, *tabu*, or *raui*) are also used to manage and regulate the harvesting of specific species. In many Pacific Islands, birds, flying foxes, dugongs, clams, trochus, and turtles are protected in this way, as are tree species such as *Intsia bijuga* and *Pterocarpus indicus* in parts of Samoa and Vanuatu respectively.

On an altogether different scale, there are growing regional efforts to protect cetaceans. To date, nine countries and territories (American Samoa, Baker Island, Cook Islands, Fiji, French Polynesia, Jarvis Island, Niue, Tonga, and

Pacific Islands: Protected areas network by IUCN category, 2005

IUCN category	Total sites	Total area (km²)
Ia	31	3 6269
Ib	2	576
II	42	9 195
III	24	523
IV	106	4 515
V	24	10 611
VI	59	11 696
No category	183	33 390
Total	471	74 133

Pacific Islands: Protected areas network by IUCN category (percentage of total area), 2005

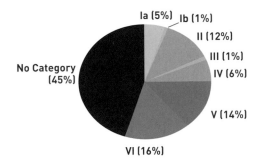

Pacific Islands: Number of protected areas by IUCN category, 2005

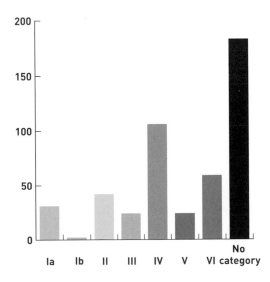

Areas of the Pacific Islands protected (by country), 2005

Country/territories	Land area (km²)	Total protected area (km²)	Total number of sites
American Samoa	200	210	13
Cook Islands	230	22	12
Fiji	18 270	488	47
French Polynesia	4 000	237	11
Guam	550	158	16
Hawaii	16 637	8 006	60
Kiribati	730	379	12
Marshall Islands	180	701	6
Micronesia (Federated States of)	700	95	20
New Caledonia	18 580	1 857	72
Niue	260	54	5
Northern Mariana Islands	480	34	12
Palau	460	1 348	23
Papua New Guinea	462 840	43 826	75
Pitcairn	62	37	1
Samoa	2 840	149	12
Solomon Islands	28 900	412	6
Tokelau	10	10	3
Tonga	750	10 105	14
Tuvalu	30	36	1
United States Minor Outlying Islands	658	5 801	7
Vanuatu	12 190	194	42
Wallis and Futuna Islands	270	1	2

Vanuatu) have declared their exclusive economic zones (EEZs), a total of 10.9 million km², as whale sanctuary areas. In 2002 Samoa and Papua New Guinea made known their intentions to follow suit, which would increase the total area of EEZs dedicated to whale protection to 13.8 million km².

International sites

Involvement in major international protected areas agreements is extremely poor across this region, and is disproportionately represented by the islands which are linked to the larger and wealthier nations of France, the UK, and the USA. This lack of involvement is almost certainly associated with the economic and social challenges for small, remote nations, often with low incomes, to interact and partake in costly and time-consuming global activities. The current international protected areas, either alone or combined, provide sufficient representative coverage of the biodiversity found across the region.

Despite the lack of involvement in global activities, the sovereign states and territories of the region (together with Australia and New Zealand) collaborate and work together closely through a range of bilateral and multilateral arrangements. A distinctive feature are the eight regional intergovernmental organizations and institutions created specifically to counteract the challenges resulting from the islands' smallness and geographical isolation, and to assist on issues where regional approaches are necessary and cost effective. One of these mechanisms is the Secretariat of the Pacific Regional Environment Programme (SPREP), the regional organization mandated with promoting sound environmental management and the conservation of the region's rich biodiversity. A key role for SPREP is support for implementation of the Convention on Conservation of Nature in the South Pacific. Article 2 of the Convention calls on Parties to create protected areas to "safeguard representative samples of natural ecosystems, superlative scenery, striking geological formations and regions and objects of aesthetic, historic, cultural or scientific value."

FUTURE DIRECTIONS

There is increasing interest and commitment amongst Pacific Island communities in the sustainable management and conservation of key areas, species, and resource systems. This has arisen out of a complex interplay of factors, including many years of advocacy and public environmental education; concerns over the repeated devastation caused by frequent cyclones; the growing impacts of climate change; and the reality of rapidly diminishing resources following years of overharvesting and poorly planned development. External conservation and development organizations have also helped in raising interest and awareness.

The main ongoing and likely ongoing trends in protected areas in the region are as follows.

❑ The use of community-based conservation areas in different forms as the main tool for protecting biodiversity and achieving sustainable resource management.

❑ The increasing involvement of local communities and civil society in general in nature conservation.

❑ Interest in placing on the World Heritage List sites of outstanding universal significance, notably for their marine biodiversity.

❑ Obligations under other international conventions including the Convention on Biological Diversity and the Ramsar Convention.

❑ The development of a *de facto* South Pacific Whale Sanctuary as more Pacific Island countries declare their EEZs as whale sanctuary areas, with or without International Whaling Commission endorsement.

The direct benefits already reaped by local communities from marine and fisheries reserves is promoting increased protection of marine ecosystems and setting a basis for permanent, strictly protected marine areas. This is the biggest growth area for protected area development in the immediate future. At the same time, inroads into previously inaccessible customary-owned terrestrial areas of high biodiversity value have been made using community-based approaches, and it is likely that more terrestrial areas will be brought under conservation management in the coming

Pacific Islands: Internationally protected areas, 2005

Country	No. of sites	Protected area (km²)
Biosphere reserves		
French Polynesia	1	9
Hawaii	1	995
Micronesia (Fed. States)	1	<1
Palau	1	130
TOTAL	4	1133.8
Ramsar sites		
Fiji	1	5
Hawaii	1	4
Marshall Islands	1	690
Palau	1	5
Papua New Guinea	2	5 949
Samoa	1	0
TOTAL	7	6 654
World Heritage sites		
Hawaii	1	929
Pitcairn	1	37
Solomon Islands	1	370
TOTAL	3	1 336

years. The lack of good data on the region's biodiversity is a major constraint and a priority area that must be addressed.

Regional initiatives are also being developed to strengthen national capacity to combat invasive alien species, which is second only to ecosystem/habitat loss and fragmentation as a key threat to the region's biodiversity. Improved access to Global Environment Facility funds for the 13 Pacific nations that are party to the Convention on Biological Diversity is enabling the implementation of national biodiversity strategies that are targeting the protection of biodiversity of global significance. Similar funding initiatives include the Critical Ecosystem Partnership Fund (CEPF), which is targeting the protection of key threatened species and ecosystems.

Bibliography

Abramovitz, J.N. (1996) *Imperilled Waters, Impoverished Future: The Decline of Freshwater Ecosystems*. Worldwatch Paper 128. Worldwatch Institute, Washington D.C.

ACIUCN (Australian Committee for the International Union for the Conservation of Nature) (2002) *Australian Natural Heritage Charter*. [2nd edn.] Australian Heritage Commission, Canberra.

Ahmad Khan, A. (1997) *Support Strategy for Protected Areas Network of Pakistan*. WWF Pakistan, Peshawar.

Amend, S. and Amend, T. (eds) (1992) *National Parks Without People? The South American Experience*. IUCN, Gland, Switzerland.

ANAM (2003) Informe Nacional Sobre la Gestión Técnica y Administrativa del Sistema Nacional de Areas Protegidas. Panamá.

Anon (2003) Special Feature: Innovation and MPAs in the Mediterranean Sea. *MPA News* 5(3). Washington, D.C.

Appeldoorn, R.S. and Lindeman, K.C. (2003) *A Caribbean-Wide Survey of Marine Reserves: Spatial Coverage and Attributes of Effectiveness*. Gulf and Caribbean Research.

Areas Protegidas (Protected Areas) http://www.areasprotegidas.org (December, 2007).

Australian Antarctic Division (2005) http://www.antdiv.gov.au/default.asp?casid=1295 (June, 2005)

Bailey, R.G. (1998) *Ecoregions: The Ecosystem Geography of Oceans and Continents*. Springer, New York.

Bakarr, M., Bailey, B., Byler, D., Ham, R., Olivieri, S. and Omland, M. (eds) (2001) *From the Forest to the Sea: Biodiversity Connections from Guinea to Togo*. Conservation International, Washington, D.C.

Balmford, A. and T. Whitten. 2003. Who should pay for tropical conservation, and how could the costs be met? *Oryx* 37: 238-250. Fauna & Flora International, Cambridge, UK.

Balmford, A., Bruner, A., Cooper, P., Costanza, R., Farber, S., Green, R.E., Jenkins, M., Jefferiss, P., Jessamy, V., Madden, J., Munro, K., Myers, N., Naeem, S., Paavola, J., Rayment, M., Rosendo, S., Roughgarden, J., Trumper, K. and Turner, R.K. (2002). Economic Reasons for Conserving Wild Nature. *Science*, Vol. 297. AAAS, Washington, D.C.

Barber, C.V., Miller, K.R. and Boness, M. (ed.) (2004). *Securing Protected Areas in the Face of Global Change: Issues and Strategies*. IUCN, Gland, Switzerland.

Barnes, B.V. 1991. Deciduous forests of North America. In *Ecosystems of the World 7: temperate deciduous forests*, Röhrig, E. and Ulrich, B. (eds), 219-344. Elsevier, Amsterdam.

Bartol, K., Martin, D., Tein, M. and Matthews, G. (1998) *Management: A Pacific Rim Focus*. [2nd edn.] McGraw-Hill, Sydney.

Beavers, R L (2001). USGS science for coastal national parks. In *Natural Resource Year in Review 2001*. National Park Service, US Department of Interior, Washington, D.C.

Bennett, A.F. (2003) *Linkages in the Landscape: The Role of Corridors and Connectivity in Wildlife Conservation*. [2nd edn.] IUCN, Gland, Switzerland.

Bennett, G. and Wit, P. (2001) *The Development and Application of Ecological Networks: A Review of Proposals, Plans and Programmes*. IUCN – The World Conservation Union, Gland, Switzerland, and AIDEnvironment, Amsterdam, Netherlands.

Benzing, D.H. 1989. Vascular epiphytism in America. In *Ecosystems of the World 14B: tropical rain forest ecosystems: biogeographical and ecological studies*, H. Lieth and M.J.A Werger. (eds), 133-154. Elsevier, Amsterdam.

Bernstein J. and Mitchell B.A. 2005. Land trusts, private reserves and conservation easements in the United States. *Parks* 15: 48-60. IUCN, Gland, Switzerland.

Besançon, C. and Savy, C. E. (in press). Global list of internationally adjoining protected areas and other transboundary conservation initiatives. In *Transboundary Conservation: A new vision for protected areas* (working title). Mittermeier, R., Mittermeier, C.G., Kormos, C., Sandwith, T. and Besançon, C. (eds). CEMEX/Conservation International.

Bezaury-Creel J. (2003) Las Areas Naturales Protegidas Costeras y Marinas de México. In: Rivera-Arriaga E., Villalobos-Zapata, G., Rosado-May, F., and Azuz-Adeath, I. (eds) (2003) *El Manejo Costero en México, Parte III Protección de la Zona Costera*. UAC-UQROO-CETYS- SEMARNAT.

Bezaury-Creel, J., Waller, R., Sotomayor, L., Li, X., Anderson, S., Sayre, R. and Houseal, B. (2000) *Conservation of Biodiversity in Mexico: Ecoregions, Sites and Conservation Targets – Synthesis of Identification and Priority Setting Exercises*. The Nature Conservancy, Arlington, VA, USA.

Birckhead, J., Collins, J., Sakulas, H. and Bauer, J. (2000) Caring for country today? Towards an ecopolitics of sustainable indigenous land management regimes. In: Saunders, D., Craig, J. and Mitchell, N. (eds) *Nature Conservation in Production Environments: Managing the Matrix*. Surrey Beatty and Sons, Sydney.

Bird, C. (1991) Medicines from the rainforest. *New Scientist*, 17 August: 34-39. London.

BirdLife International (2000) *Threatened Birds of the World*. Lynx Edicions and BirdLife International, Barcelona and Cambridge.

Birdsey, R., Weaver, P. and Nicholls, C. (1986) The *Forest Resources of St. Vincent, West Indies*. Research Paper SO-229. US Department of Agriculture, Forest Service, Southern Forest Experiment Station, New Orleans, LA.

Bodmer, RE. and Puertas, P.E. (2000). Community-based co-management of wildlife in the Peruvian Amazon. In *Hunting for Sustainability in Tropical Forests*, Robinson, J.G. and Bennett, E.L. (eds), 395-409. Columbia University Press, New York

Boitani, L., Corsi, F., De Biase, A., Carranza, I.D.I., Ravagli, M., Reggiani, G., Sinibaldi, I. and Trapanese, P. (1999) *A Databank for the Conservation and Management of the African Mammals*. Istituto di Ecologia Applicata, Rome.

BP (2003). Defining our Path: Sustainability Report 2003. London.

Brandon, K., Redford, K.H. and Sanderson, S.E. (1998) *Parks in Peril: People, Politics and Protected Areas*. The Nature Conservancy, Island Press, Washington, D.C.

Brar, A.S. (1996) Case Study 4: India - Keoladeo National Park. In: Hails, A.J. (ed.) *Wetlands, Biodiversity and the Ramsar Convention*. Ramsar, Gland, Switzerland.

Brazil MMA (1999) *First National Report for the Convention on Biological Diversity Brazil*. Secretaria de Biodiversidade e Florestas (SBF), Ministério do Meio Ambiente (MMA), Brasília.

Brazil MMA (2002) *Biodiversidade Brasileira: Avaliação e Identificação de Áreas e Ações Prioritárias para Conservação, Utilização Sustentável e Repartição de Benefícios da Biodiversidade Brasileira*. Secretaria de Biodiversidade e Florestas (SBF), Ministério do Meio Ambiente (MMA), Brasília.

Briassoulis, H. (1989) Theoretical orientations in environmental planning: an inquiry into alternative approaches. *Environmental Management* 13:381–92. Springer, New York.

Brockman, C.F. and Curry-Lindahl, K. (1964). Problems of nomenclature: the need for definitions. In: *Proceedings of the First World Conference on National Parks*. National Park Service, US Department of Interior, Washington D.C.

Brugiere, D. (1999) Analysis of the protected area network in Gabon. *Nature et Faune/Wildlife and Nature*. FAO Regional Office for Africa, Accra.

Brunner, R. D. and Clark T. W. (1997). A practice-based approach to ecosystem management. *Conservation Biology* 11: 48-58. Arlington, VA, USA.

Buckley, R. and Pannell, J. (1990) Environmental impacts of tourism and recreation in national parks and conservation reserves. *Journal of Tourism Studies* 1(1). Townsville, QLD, Australia.

Buckley, R., Pickering, C.M. and Weaver, D.B. (eds) (2003) *Nature-based Tourism, Environment and Land Management*. CABI Publishing, New York.

Burger, J. (1990) *The Gaia Atlas of First Peoples: A Future for the Indigenous World*. Penguin, London.

Burgess, N.D., D'Amico-Hales, J.A., Underwood, E., Dinerstein, E., Olson, D., Schipper, J., Ricketts, T., Itoua, I. and Newman, K. (2004) *The Terrestrial Ecoregions of Africa and Madagascar: A Conservation Assessment*. WWF-USA and Island Press, Washington, D.C.

Burgess, N.D., Fjeldså, J. and Botterweg, R. (1998)

The faunal importance of the Eastern Arc Mountains. Special Issue of the *Journal of the East African Natural History Society* 87:37-58. Nairobi, Kenya.

Burke, L., Selig, L. and Spalding, M. (2002) *Reefs at Risk in Southeast Asia*. World Resources Institute, Washington, D.C

CAFF (Conservation of Arctic Flora and Fauna) (2001) *Arctic Flora and Fauna: Status and Conservation*. CAFF (Arctic Council Working Group), Helsinki.

CAFF (Conservation of Arctic Flora and Fauna) (2000) *A Summary of Legal Instruments and National Frameworks for Arctic Marine Conservation* (text: J. Pagnan). CAFF, Reykjavik.

CAFF (Conservation of Arctic Flora and Fauna) (1996) *Circumpolar Protected Area Network Strategy and Action Plan*. CAFF, Trondheim.

CAFF (Conservation of Arctic Flora and Fauna) (1994) *The State of Protected Areas in the Circumpolar Arctic 1994*. Habitat Conservation Report No. 1. CAFF, Trondheim.

Camrath, R., R. K. Loh, and J. T. Tunison. 1997, unpublished. The distribution of faya tree, 1992. In *Management and ecology of faya tree, Hawaii Volcanoes National Park*, Tunison, J. T. (ed). Cooperative National Park Resources Studies Unit Technical Report Un-numbered. University of Hawaii at Manoa, Department of Botany, Honolulu, HI, USA.

Carey, C., Dudley, N. and Stolton, S. (2000) *Squandering Paradise*. WWF, Gland, Switzerland.

Carter, E., Adams, W.M. and Hutton, J. (in press). Private Protected Areas: Management regimes, tenure arrangements and protected area categorization in East Africa. Submitted to *Oryx*. Fauna & Flora International, Cambridge, UK.

Carlton, J. T. (1999). *The global consequences of not managing ballast water*. Presented at workshop: Our Voyage Towards Better Ballast Water Management, IMO, MEPC-43 meeting, London.

Castaño Uribe, C. (1992) Human occupancy of Colombia's national parks: policies and prospects. In: Amend, S. and Amend, T. (eds) *National Parks Without People? The South American Experience*. IUCN, Gland. Switzerland. 191-206.

Castro Parga, I., Moreno Saiz, J.C., Humphries, C.J.and Williams, P.H. (1996) Strengthening the natural and national park system of Iberia to conserve vascular plants. *Botanical Journal of the Linnean Society* 121: 189-205. Blackwell, Oxford, UK.

Castro, F. and De Leon, F. (2003) Informe Nacional de Areas Protegidas de Guatemala. CONAP, Guatemala.

CCAD (1992) *Convenio para la Conservación de la Biodiversidad y Protección de Areas Silvestres Prioritarias de América Central*. UICN-CCAD, Costa Rica.

CCAD (2002) *Plan de Negocios 2003-2007; Naturaleza, gente y bienestar: Articulando el desarrollo sostenible en Mesoamerica*. Edit. Inbio. Costa Rica.

CCEA (Canadian Council on Ecological Areas) (2002) *Eco* No. 14, December 2002. Official Newsletter of CCEA. Woodlawn, ON, Canada

Ceballos, G. (1995). Vertebrate diversity, ecology and conservation in neotropical dry forests. In *Seasonally Dry Tropical Forests*, S.H. Bullock, H.A. Mooney and E. Medina. (eds), 195-220. Cambridge University Press, Cambridge, UK.

Ceballos-Lascurain, H. (1996) *Tourism, Ecotourism and Protected Areas*. IUCN, Gland, Switzerland.

CEC (Commission for Environmental Cooperation) (1997) *Ecological Regions of North America: Toward a Common Perspective*. CEC, Montreal, Canada.

CEC (Commission for Environmental Cooperation) (2003) *Securing the Continent's Biological Wealth: Towards Effective Biodiversity Conservation in North America*. Section 2.5 – Protected Areas. Prepared by Agardy, T., Hanson, A.J. and Gil Salcido, R.P. for the CEC. CEC, Montreal, Canada.

Cesar, H.S.J. (ed.) (2000) *Collected Essays on the Economics of Coral Reefs*. CORDIO, Kalmar University, Kalmar, Sweden.

Chape, S. (2001). An Overview of Integrated Approaches to Conservation and Community Development in the Lao People's Democratic Republic. In *Parks* Vol 11/2, 24-32. IUCN, Gland, Switzerland.

Chape, S., Blyth, S., Fish, L., Fox, P. and Spalding, M. (compilers) (2003) *2003 United Nations List of Protected Areas*. UNEP-World Conservation Monitoring Centre, Cambridge, UK and IUCN – The World Conservation Union, Gland, Switzerland.

Chape, S., Harrison, J., Spalding M. and Lysenko, I. (2005). Measuring the extent and effectiveness of protected areas as an indicator for meeting global biodiversity targets. *Phil. Trans. R. Soc. B* 360, 443-455. The Royal Society, London.

Chen, K. and Yan, C. (1996) Case Study 2: P.R. China - Dongdongtinghu (East Dongting Lake). In: Hails, A.J. (ed.) *Wetlands, Biodiversity and the Ramsar Convention*. Ramsar, Gland, Switzerland.

Ching, K.K. 1991. Temperate deciduous forests in East Asia. In *Ecosystems of the World 7: temperate deciduous forests*, Röhrig, E. and Ulrich, B. (eds), 539-556. Elsevier, Amsterdam.

Christ, C., Hillel, O., Matus, S. and Sweeting, J. (2003) *Tourism and Biodiversity: Mapping Tourism's Global Footprint*. Conservation International, Washington, D.C.

Christiansen, J., Hall, R., Chandler, H., Torfs, M., Zogbi, M., Lovera, S. and Liebman, D. (2005) *Nature for Sale: the impacts of privatizing water and diversity*. Friends of the Earth International, Amsterdam.

Civeyrel, L. and Simberloff, D. (1996) A tale of two snails: Is the cure worse than the disease? *Biodiversity and Conservation*, **5**, 1231-1252. Springer, Netherlands.

Clarke, R.N. andStankey, G.H. (1979) *The Recreation Opportunity Spectrum: A Framework for Planning, Management and Research*. General Technical Report PNW-98. USDA Forest Service, Fort Collins, CO, USA.

CNAP (Centro Nacional de Áreas Protegidas) (1998) Expedientes de los Sitios de Patrimonio *Mundial Parques Nacionales Alejandro de Humboldt y Desembarco del Granma*. Cuba.

CNAP (Centro Nacional de Áreas Protegidas) (2002) Sistema Nacional de Áreas Protegidas. Cuba. Plan 2003-2008.

Cochrane, M. A. 2001. Synergistic Interactions Between Habitat Fragmentation and Fire in Evergreen Tropical Forests. *Conservation Biology* 15: 1515-1521. Arlington, VA, USA.

Cochrane, M.A., Skole, D.L., Matricardi, E.A.T., Barber, C. and Chomentowski, W. (2002). *Interaction and Synergy between Selective Logging, Forest Fragmentation and Fire Disturbance in Tropical Forests: Case Study Mato Grosso, Brazil* . CGCEO/RA03-02/w. Michigan State University, East Lansing, MI, USA.

Coles, R. and Fortes, M. (2001) Protecting seagrasses – approaches and methods. In *Global Seagrass Research Method*, F.T. Short and R.G. Coles (eds). Elsevier Science, Amsterdam.

Comité Nacional Pro Defensa de Fauna y Flora (National Committee for the Defense of Fauna and Flora) http://www.codeff.cl/ (December, 2006).

Commonwealth of Australia (2003) *Tourism White Paper: A Medium to Long Term Strategy for Tourism*. Commonwealth of Australia, Canberra.

Commonwealth of Australia (2004). *Directions for the National Reserve System – A Partnership Approach*. Prepared by the National Reserve System Taskforce of the NRM Ministerial Council's Land, Water and Biodiversity Committee.

Commonwealth of Australia 1996a. *The National Strategy for the Conservation of Australia's Biological Diversity*. DEST, Canberra.

Commonwealth of Australia 1996b. *Australia: State of the Environment 1996*. CSIRO Publishing, Melbourne.

CONANP (Comisión Nacional de Areas Naturales Protegidas) (2003) CONANP Secretaría de Medió Ambiente y Recursos Naturales. http://conanp.gob.mx (January 2008)

CONANP (Comisión Nacional de Areas Naturales Protegidas) (2003) Protected Areas Data Base. CONANP Secretaría de Medió Ambiente y Recursos Naturales (systematically updated).

Cordell, J. (1993) Who owns the land? Indigenous involvement in protected areas. In: Kempf, E. (ed.) *Indigenous Peoples and Protected Areas: The Law of the Mother*. Earthscan, London.

Costanza, R., d'Arge, R., de Groot, R., Farber, S., Grasso, M., Hannon, B., Limburg, K., Naeem, S., O'Neill, R.V., Paruelo, J., Raskin, R.G., Sutton, P. and van den Belt, M. (1997) The value of the world's ecosystem service and natural capital. *Nature* 387:253-260. London.

Côté, I.M., Mosqueira, I. and Reynolds, J.D. (2001) Effects of marine reserve characteristics on the protection of fish populations: a meta-analysis. *J. Fish Biol.* 59:178-189. Blackwell, Oxford, UK.

Cowardin, L.M., Carter, V., Golet, F.C. and LaRoe, E.T. (1979) *Classification of Wetlands and Deepwater Habitats of the United States*. United States Fish and Wildlife Service, Washington, D,C.

Cowardin, L.M. and Golet, F.C. (1995) US Fish and

Wildlife Service 1979 wetland classification: a review. *Vegetatio* 118:139-152. Springer, Netherlands.

Cowling, R.M. and Pressey, R.L. (2003) Introduction to systematic conservation planning in the Cape Floristic Region. *Biological Conservation* 112: 1-13. Elsevier, Amsterdon, London, New York.

Cowling, R.M., Pressey, R.L., Rouget, M. and Lombard, A. (2003) A conservation plan for a global biodiversity hotspot – the Cape Floristic Region, South Africa. *Biological Conservation* 112: 191-216. Elsevier, Amsterdon, London, New York.

Cross, R. (1991) 35th Working Section IUCN Commission on National Parks and Protected Areas, Santo Domingo, 29 April - 3 May. [Pers. comm.]

Davey, A.G. (1998) *National System Planning for Protected Areas*. Best Practice Protected Area Guidelines Series No. 1, ed. Phillips, A. IUCN World Commission on Protected Areas, Gland, Switzerland.

Desanker, P. and Madadza, C. (eds) (2001). Africa. In *Climate change 2001: Impacts, adaptation and vulnerability*. McCarthy, J.J., Canziani, O.F., Leary, N.A., Dokken, D.J. and White, K.S. (eds), 487-531. Intergovernmental Panel on Climate Change and Cambridge University Press, UK.

DGMA (2000) Plan Ambiental de la Región Centroamericana; PARCA. DGMA-SICA. San José, Costa Rica.

Dhammika, S. (1993) *The Edicts of King Asoka*. The Wheel Publication No. 386/387. Buddhist Publication Society, Kandy, Sri Lanka.

Dick, G., Dvorak, M., Grüll, A., Kohler, B. and Rauer, G. (1994) *Vogelparadies mit Zukunft? Ramsar-Bericht 3, Neusiedler See-Seewinkel*. Umweltbundesamt Wien. Vienna, Austria.

Dong-Gon Hong (2002). Protected Area Conservation Policies of the Republic of Korea. In *Proceedings of IUCN/WCPA East Asia Taipei Conference* 57-63. Taipei, Taiwan POC.

Du Toit, J.T., Rogers, K.H. and Biggs, H.C. (2003) *The Kruger Experience: Ecology and Management of Savanna Heterogeneity*. Island Press, Washington, D.C.

Duckworth, J.W, Salter R.E. and Khounboline, K. (1999). *Wildlife in Lao PDR: 1999 Status Report*. IUCN-The World Conservation Union, The Wildlife Conservation Society and Center for Protected Areas and Watershed Management, Vientiane, Lao PDR.

Dudley, N. (1997) *The Year the World Caught Fire*. WWF International, Gland, Switzerland.

Dudley, N. and Stolton, S. (2003). Ecological and socio-economic benefits of protected areas in dealing with climate change. In *Buying time: A user's manual for building resistance and resilience to climate change in natural systems*, 217–233. Hansen, L.J., Biringer, J.L. and Hoffman, J.R. (eds). World Wildlife Fund for Nature, Gland, Switzerland.

Dudley, N., Hockings, M. and Stolton, S. (1999) Measuring the effectiveness of protected areas management. In: Stolton, S. and Dudley, N. (eds) *Partnerships for Protection – New Strategies for Planning and Management for Protected Areas*. Earthscan, London.

Dudley, N. and Stolton, S. (2002) *To Dig or Not to Dig?* WWF International, Gland, Switzerland.

Du Toit, J.T., Rogers, K.H. and Biggs, H.C. (2003) *The Kruger Experience: Ecology And Management Of Savanna Heterogeneity*. Island Press, Washington D.C.

Eagles, P.F.J. and McCool, S.F. (2002) *Tourism in National Parks and Protected Areas, Planning and Management*. CABI Publishing, New York.

Eagles, P.F.J., McCool, S.F. and Haynes, C. (2002) *Sustainable Tourism in Protected Areas: Guidelines for Planning and Management*. Best Practice Protected Area Guidelines Series No. 8, ed. Phillips, A. IUCN World Commission on Protected Areas, Gland, Switzerland.

Eaton, D. and Sarch, M. (1997) *The Economic Importance of Wild Resources in the Hadejia-Nguru Wetlands, Nigeria*. Working Paper No. 13, Collaborative Research in the Economics of Environment and Development. International Institute for Environment and Development, London.

Elkan, P. (2000). Managing hunting in a logging concession in Northern Congo. In *Hunting of wildlife in tropical forests: implications for biodiversity and forest peoples*, Bennett, E. L. and Robinson, J. G. 28-29. The World Bank, Washington, D.C.

Emerton, L., Iyango, L., Luwum, P. and Malinga, A. (1999) *The Economic Value of Nakivubo Urban Wetland, Uganda*. Uganda National Wetlands Programme, Kampala and IUCN – The World Conservation Union, Eastern Africa Regional Office, Nairobi, Kenya.

Emerton, L. and Kekulandala, B. (2002) *Assessment of the Economic Value of Muthurajawela Wetland*. IUCN – The World Conservation Union, Sri Lanka Country Office and Regional Environmental Economics Programme Asia, Colombo, Sri Lanka.

Enemark, J., Wesemüller, H. and Gerdiken, A. (1998) The Wadden Sea: an international perspective on managing marine resources. *Parks* **8**(2):36-40. IUCN, Gland, Switzerland.

Ervin, J. (2003) *WWF: Rapid Assessment and Prioritization of Protected Area Management (RAPPAM) Methodology*. WWF, Gland, Switzerland.

FAO(1996). Malawi Fishery Country Profile.

FAO Fisheries Department website available online at: http://www.fao.org/fi/fcp/malawie.htm. (December, 2007)

FAO (2000). Land Cover Classification System. Food and Agriculture Organisation, Rome.

FAO (2001). *Global Forest Resouces Assessment 2000*. Food and Agriculture Organisation, Rome.

FAO (2002) *The State of World Fisheries and Aquaculture 2002*. FAO Fisheries Department, Rome.

FAO (2003) *State of the World's Forests 2003*. Food and Agriculture Organisation, Rome.

FAO (2004). *The State of the World's Fisheries and Aquaculture 2004*. Food and Agriculture Organization of the United Nations, Rome.

FAO (2006). *The State of the World's Fisheries and Aquaculture 2006*. Food and Agriculture Organization of the United Nations, Rome.

Farjon, Aljos and Christopher N. Page (compilers). (1999). *Conifers: Status survey and conservation action plan*. IUCN/SSC Conifer Specialist Group. IUCN, Gland, Switzerland.

Finger, A. (1999) *Metals from the Forest*, Arborvitae special. IUCN and WWF, Gland, Switzerland.

Finlayson, C.M., Howes, J., Begg, G. and Tagi, K. (2002a) A strategic approach for characterising wetlands – the Asian Wetland Inventory. *Proceedings of Asian Wetland Symposium*, Penang, Malaysia, 27-30 August, 2001.

Finlayson, C.M., Howes, R., van Dam, R.A., Begg, G. and Tagi, K. (2002b) The Asian Wetland Inventory as a tool for providing information on the effect of climate change on wetlands in Asia.

Fitzgibbon, C.D., Mogaka, H. and Fanshawe, J.H. (2000). Threatened mammals, subsistent harvesting, and high human population densities: a recipe for disaster? In *Hunting for Sustainability in Tropical Forests*, J.G. Robinson and E.L. Bennett, (eds), 154-167. Columbia University Press, New York.

Foro Sudamericano de Areas Protegidas (Protected Areas South American Forum) http://www.sur.iucn.org/cmp/foro_sudamericano.htm (August, 2005).

Furze, B., De Lacy, T. and Birckhead, J. (1996) *Culture, Conservation and Biodiversity: The Social Dimension of Linking Local Development and Conservation through Protected Areas*. John Wiley & Sons, London.

Galapagos Conservation Trust (2005) http://www.gct.org/issues.html (January 2008).

Gee, C.Y., Makens, J.C. and Choy, D.J.L. (1997) *The Travel Industry. [3rd edn.]* Van Nostrand Reinhold, New York.

Gell, F.R. and Roberts, C.M. (2003) Benefits beyond boundaries: the fishery effects of marine reserves and fishery closures. *Trends in Ecology and Evolution* 18: 448-455. Elsevier, Amsterdam, London, New York.

Gell, F.R. and Roberts, C.M. (2002) *The Fishery Effects of Marine Reserves and Fishery Closures*. WWF-US, Washington D.C.

Gentry, A.H. (1988a). Changes in plant community diversity and floristic composition on environmental and geographical gradients. *Annals of the Missouri Botanical Garden* 75: 1-34.

Gentry, A.H. (1988b). Tree species richness of upper Amazonian forests. *Proceedings of the National Academy of Sciences of the USA* 85:156-159. Washington, D.C.

Gentry, A.H. (1995). Diversity and floristic composition of neotropical dry forests. In: *Seasonally Dry Tropical Forests*, Bullock, S.H., Mooney, H.A., and Medina, E. (eds), 146-194. Cambridge University Press, Cambridge, UK.

Ghimire, K.B. and Pimbert, M.P. (1997) Social change and conservation: an overview of issues and concepts. In: Ghimire, K.B., Pimbert, M.P. (eds) *Social Change and Conservation: Environmental Politics and Impacts of National Parks and Protected Areas*. Earthscan Publications, London.

Girot, P. (2000) *Raíz y Vuelo: El Uso de los Recursos Naturales en Mesoamerica. UICN-SUI*. San José, Costa Rica.

Global Ballast Water Management Programme (2005) http://globallast.imo.org/index.asp (January 2008)

Global Witness (1995) *Forests, Famine and War: The Key to Cambodia's Future.* Global Witness Briefing Document. London.

Global Witness (1996) *Corruption, War and Forest Policy: The Unsustainable Exploitation of Cambodia's Forests.* London.

Global Witness (1998) Press release, February 1998. London

Gobierno de Chile Comisión Nacional del Medio Ambiente (Chilean Government National Commission for the Environment) http://www.conama.cl/portal/1255/channel.html (December, 2007).

Godoy, J.C. (1997) *Hacia el Consenso del Sistema Centroamericano de Areas Prioritarias. Proarca-Capas.* CCAD-IRG-TNC-USAID, Guatemala.

Graham, J., Amos, B. and Plumptre, T. (2003) *Governance Principles for Protected Areas in the 21st Century.* Prepared for the Vth World Parks Congress, Durban, South Africa.

Green, M.J.B. and Paine, J. (1997) State of the World's Protected Areas at the End of the Twentieth Century. Paper presented at IUCN World Commission on Protected Areas Symposium *Protected Areas in the 21st Century: From Islands to Networks.* Albany, Australia.

Green, R. and Higginbottom, K. (2001) *Negative Effects of Wildlife Tourism on Wildlife.* Wildlife Tourism Research Report No 5. CRC for Sustainable Tourism, Gold Coast.

Groombridge, B. (ed.) (1992). *Global Diversity - Status of the Earth's Living Resources.* Compiled by the World Conservation Monitoring Centre. Chapman & Hall, London, UK.

Groombridge, B. and Jenkins, M.D. (1998) *Freshwater Biodiversity: A Preliminary Global Assessment.* WCMC-World Conservation Press, Cambridge UK.

Groombridge, B. and Jenkins, M.D. (2000) *Global Biodiversity: Earth's Living Resources in the 21st Century.* WCMC-World Conservation Press, Cambridge, UK.

Grove, R.H. (1995) *Green Imperialism: Colonial Expansion, Tropical Island Edens and the Origins of Environmentalism, 1600-1860.* Cambridge University Press, UK.

Groves, C., Valutis, L., Vosick, D., Neely, B.,

Wheaton, K., Touval, J. and Runnels, B. (2000) *Designing a Geography of Hope: A Practitioner's Handbook for Ecoregional Conservation Planning.* The Nature Conservancy, Arlington VA, USA.

GRoWI (1999) www.wetlands.agro.nl/Wetland_Inventory/GroWi_2nd_edn/welcome.html (2004).

Gujja, B. and Perrin, M. (1999) *A Place for Dams in the 21st Century?* WWF International, Gland, Switzerland.

Gujja, B. and Perrin, M. (1999) *A Place for Dams in the 21st Century?* WWF International, Gland, Switzerland.

Halpern, B.S. (2003) The impact of Marine Reserves: Do Reserves Work and Does Size Matter? *Ecological Applications* 13, No. sp1, 117–137. Ithaca, NY, USA.

Harcourt, C.S. and Sayer, J.A. (eds) (1996). *The conservation atlas of tropical forests: the Americas.* Simon and Schuster, New York.

Hardin, G. (1968) The tragedy of the commons. *Science.* Vol 162, Issue 3859, 1243-1248. AAAS, Washington, D.C.

Harmon, D. and Putney, A.D., eds. 2003. *The Full Value of Parks: From Economics to the Intangible.* Rowman & Littlefield, Lanham, MD, USA.

Haroon, A.I. (2002) Ecotourism in Pakistan: a myth? *Mountain Research and Development* 22(2):110–12. Berne, Switzerland.

Harrison, I.J., Stiassny, M.J. (1999) The quiet crisis: a preliminary listing of the freshwater fishes of the world that are extinct or "missing in action". In: MacPhee, R.D.E. (ed.) *Extinctions in Near Time.* Kluwer Academic/Plenum Publishers, New York, NY. 271-331.

Hart, J.A. (2000). Impact and sustainability of indigenous hunting in the Ituri Forest, Congo-Zaire: a comparison of unhunted and hunted duiker populations. In *Hunting for Sustainability in Tropical Forests*, Robinson, J.G., and Bennett, E.L. (eds), 106-153. Columbia University Press, New York.

Hart, T. (2002). Conservation in anarchy: key conditions for successful conservation of the Okapi Faunal Reserve. In *Making Parks Work: Strategies for Preserving Tropical Nature*, J. Terborgh, J., van Schaik, C., Davenport, L. and Rao, M. 86-96. Island Press, Washington D.C.

Hedgpeth, J. W. (1957). Marine biogeography. In *Treatise on marine ecology and paleoecology*, Hedgpeth, J.W. (ed.), 359-382. *Geol. Soc. Am.*

Mem. 67 (1). Boulder, Colorado.

Heylings, P. and Bravo, M. (2001). Survival of the fittest? Challenges facing the co-management model for the Galapagos Marine Reserve. *CM News* 5: 10–13. Rio de Janeiro, Brazil.

Hilton-Taylor, C. (compiler)(2000). *2000 IUCN Red List of Threatened Species*, IUCN, Gland, Switzerland.

Hoang Ho-Dzung (1987). The moss flora of the Baektu mountain area. 9-31. In *The TemperateForest Ecosystem*, Yang, H., Z. Wang, Z., Jeffers, J.N.R. and Ward, P.A. (eds). Institute of Terrestrial Ecology Symposium 20, NERC, UK.

Hockings, M (2003) Systems for assessing the effectiveness of management in protected areas. *BioScience* 53 (9):823-832. Washington, D.C.

Hockings, M., Stolton, S., Dudley N. (2000) *Evaluating Effectiveness: A Framework for Assessing the Management of Protected Areas.* IUCN World Commission on Protected Areas, Gland, Switzerland.

Hockings, M., Stolton, S., Leverington, F., Dudley, N. and Courrau, J. (2006) *Evaluating Effectiveness: A framework for assessing management effectiveness of protected areas. 2nd Ed.* IUCN Gland, Switzerland.

Holdsworth, A.R and Uhl, C. (1997). Fire in Amazonian selectively logged rain forest and the potential for fire reduction. *Ecological Applications* 7: 713-725. Ithaca, NY, USA.

Honey, M. (1999) *Ecotourism and Sustainable Development: Who Owns Paradise?* Island Press, Washington, D.C.

Howard, G.W. (2003) *Invasive Alien Species in Africa's Wetlands.* IUCN East Africa Office, Nairobi, Kenya.

http://www.enjoyperu.com/naturaleza/reservas-%20nacion/paracas/index2.htm (June, 2006).

http://www.inparques.gov.ve/parques_nac/parques_nac.html (July, 2005).

http://www.parquesnacionales.gov.co (December, 2007).

http://www.sernap.gov.bo/ (December, 2007).

http://www.unesco.org.uy/mab/reser.html (December, 2007).

Hutton, J.M. and N. Leader-Williams (2003). Sustainable use and incentive-driven conservation: realigning human and conservation interests. *Oryx* 37 (2), 215-226. Fauna & Flora International, Cambridge, UK.

ICEM (2003). *Regional Report on Protected Areas and Development: Lower Mekong River Region.* International Centre for Environmental Management, Indooroopilly, Queensland, Australia.

ICEM 2003. *Cambodia National Report on Protected Areas and Development.* Review of Protected Areas and Development in the Lower Mekong River Region. Indooroopilly, Queensland, Australia.

IJHD (International Journal of Hydropower and Dams) (1998) *1998 World Atlas and Industry Guide.* Aqua-Media International, Surrey, UK.

Instituto Nacional de Parques de Venezuela (INPARQUES) (Venezuelan National Parks Institute) http://www.inparques.gov.ve/parques_nac/parques_nac.htm (December, 2007)

IPCC/Intergovernmenal Panel on Climate Change (2001). Climate Change 2001: Synthesis Report. IPCC, Geneva.

Issa Sylla, S. (2002) *Fadama: Special Issue on the Niger Basin Initiative 5.* Senegal, Wetlands International, West Africa Programme.

IUCN – The World Conservation Union (2002) *2002 IUCN Red List of Threatened Species.* IUCN, Gland, Switzerland. Available on-line at http://www.redlist.org (December, 2007).

IUCN – The World Conservation Union (2003) *100 of the World's Worst Invasive Alien species. A selection from the global invasive species database.* IUCN Invasive Species Specialist Group. IUCN, Gland, Switzerland.

IUCN (1991) *Strategy for Antarctic Conservation.* IUCN, Gland, Switzerland. Vii + 85.

IUCN (1992) *Protected Area of the World, Vol 3. Africa.* IUCN, Gland, Switzerland..

IUCN (1994) *Guidelines for Protected Area Management Categories.* CNPPA with the assistance of WCMC. IUCN, Gland, Switzerland.

IUCN (1998) *Economic Values of Protected Areas: Guidelines for Protected Area Managers.* Produced by the Task Force on Economic Benefits of Protected Areas of the World Commission on Protected Areas (WCPA) of IUCN in collaboration with the Economics Services Unit of IUCN. IUCN, Gland, Switzerland.

IUCN (1998) *Economic Values of Protected Areas: Guidelines for Protected Area Managers.* IUCN, Gland, Switzerland.

IUCN (2000) *Financing Protected Areas*. IUCN World Commission on Protected Areas, Gland, Switzerland.

IUCN-SSC, CI-CABS (2003) *Global Amphibian Assessment*. IUCN, Gland, Switzerland and Conservation International, Washington D.C.

James, A.N., M.J.B. Green and J.R. Paine (1999). *A Global Review of Protected Areas Budgets and Staff*. UNEP-WCMC, Cambridge, UK.

Jameson, S.C., Tupper, M.H., Ridley, J.M. (2002) The three screen doors: can marine "protected" areas be effective? *Mar. Poll. Bul.* 44:1177-1183. Elsevier, Amsterdam, London, New York.

Janzen, D.H. (1988). Tropical dry forests, the most endangered tropical ecosystem. In *Biodiversity*, E.O.Wilson. (ed), 13-137. National Academy Press, Washington, D.C.

Jenkins, M. 1992. Biological diversity. In *The conservation atlas of tropical forests: Africa*, Sayer, J.A., Harcourt, C.S. and Collins, N.M.H. 26-32. Macmillan Publishers Ltd., London.

Jenkins, M. (2003). Prospects for Biodiversity. *Science* vol 302:1175-1177. AAAS, Washington, D.C.

Johnson, K.N., Swanson, F.J., Herring, M., and Greene, S. (eds) (1999) *Bioregional Assessments: Science at the Crossroads of Management and Policy*. Island Press, Washington D.C.

Johnston, P. and McRea, I. (eds) (1992) *Death in Small Doses: The Effects of Organochlorines on Aquatic Systems*. Greenpeace, London.

Jones, M.E. (2000). Road upgrade, road mortality and remedial measures: impacts on a population of eastern quolls and Tasmanian devils. *Wildlife Research*, 27 (3) 289-296. Collingwood, Australia.

Kamdem-Toham, A., D'Amico, J., Olson, D., Blom, A., Trowbridge, L., Burgess, N., Thieme, M., Abell, R., Carroll, R.W., Gartlan, S., Langrand, O., Mikala Mussavu, R., O'Hara, D. and Strand, H. (eds) (2003) *Biological Priorities for Conservation in the Guinean-Congolian Forest and Freshwater Region*. WWF- CARPO, Libreville, Gabon.

Kanyamibwa, S. (1998) Impacts of war on conservation: Rwanda environment and wildlife in agony. *Biodiversity and Conservation* 7:1399-1406. Springer, Netherlands.

Kanyamibwa, S. (1998) Impacts of war on conservation: Rwanda environment and wildlife in agony. *Biodiversity and Conservation* 7:1399-1406. Springer, Netherlands.

Kapos, V., I. Lysenko and R. Lesslie. (2000). *Assessing Forest Integrity and Naturalness in Relation to Biodiversity*. UNEP-WCMC, Cambridge, UK.

Karanth, K.U. (2002). Nagarahole: limits and opportunities in wildlife conservation. In *Making Parks Work: Strategies for Preserving Tropical Nature*, J. Terborgh, C. van Schaik, L. Davenport and M. Rao. 189-202. Island Press, Washington D.C.

Kay, E.A. (ed.) (1995) *The Conservation Biology of Molluscs*. Proceedings of a symposium held at the 9th International Malacological Congress, Edinburgh, Scotland, 1986 including a status report on molluscan diversity. IUCN – The World Conservation Union, Gland, Switzerland.

Kelleher, G. (1999) *Guidelines for Marine Protected Areas*. Best Practice Protected Area Guidelines No. 3. IUCN – The World Conservation Union, Gland, Switzerland.

Kelleher, G., Bleakley, C. and Wells, S. (eds) (1995) *A Global Representative System of Marine Protected Areas*. 4 Volumes. Great Barrier Reef Marine Park Authority, World Bank and IUCN – The World Conservation Union, Washington, D.C.

Kempf, E. (ed.) (1993) *Indigenous Peoples and Protected Areas: The Law of the Mother*. Earthscan, London.

Kröncke, I. (1998) Macrofauna communities in the Amundsen Basin, at the Morris Jesu Rise and at the Yermak Plateau (Eurasian Arctic Ocean). *Polar Biology*. 19:383-392. Springer, Germany.

Krug, W. (2001) *Private Supply of Protected Land in Southern Africa: A Review of Markets, Approaches, Barriers and Issues*. Workshop Paper, World Bank/OECD International Workshop on Market Creation for Biodiversity Products and Services, Paris, 25 and 26 January 2001.

Lal, M., Harasawa, H. and Murdiyarso, D. (eds) (2001). Asia. In *Climate change 2001: Impacts, adaptation and vulnerability*. McCarthy, J.J., Canziani, O.F., Leary, N.A., Dokken, D.J. and White, K.S. (eds), 532–590. Intergovernmental Panel on Climate Change and Cambridge University Press.

Langholz, J. (1996) Economics, objectives, and success of private nature reserves in sub-Saharan Africa and Latin America.

Conservation Biology 10(1):271-280. Arlington, VA, USA.

Las Reservas Nacionales, Naturaleza, Ecología y Biodiversidad en el Peru (National Reserves, Nature, Ecology and Biodiversity in Peru) http://www.enjoyperu.com/naturaleza/reservas-nacion/paracas/index2.htm (March, 2006)

Laurance, W.F. and Bierregaard, R.O. (eds) (1997). *Tropical forest remnants: ecology, management and conservation of fragmented communities.* University of Chicago Press, Chicago, USA.

Lean, J., Bunton, C.B., Nobre, C.A. and Rowntree, P.R (1996). The simulated impact of Amazonian deforestation on climate using measured ABRACOS vegetation characteristics. in *Amazonian Deforestation and Climate.* Gash, J.H.C., Nobre, C.A., Roberts, J.M. and Victoria, R.L. (eds), 549–576. John Wiley & Sons, Chichester, UK.

Leverington, F., and M. Hockings. 2004 Evaluating the Effectiveness of Protected Area Management:the Challenge of Change. in *Securing Protected Areas in the Face of Global Change: Issues and Strategies.* Barber, C.V., Miller, K.R. and Boness, M. (eds). 169-214. IUCN, Gland, Switzerland.

Lindberg, K. (1998) Economic aspects of ecotourism. In: Lindberg, K., Epler-Wood, M. and Engeldrum, D. (eds) *Ecotourism: A Guide for Planners and Managers, Vol. 2.* Ecotourism Society, North Bennington, VT, USA..

Lista de Reservas de Biósfera en América Latina y El Caribe (Biosphere Reserves in Latin America and the Caribbean). *http://www.unesco.org. uy/mab/reser.html* (December, 2007)

Longhurst, A. (1998) *Ecological Geography of the Sea.* Academic Press, San Diego, London and Boston.

Loomis, J.B. and Walsh, R.G. (1997) *Recreation Economic Decisions: Comparing Benefits and Costs.* (2nd edn.) Venture Publishing, Inc., State College, PA, USA.

Loveland, T.R., Reed, B.C., Brown, J.F., Ohlen, D.O., Zhu, J, Yang, L. and Merchant, J.W. (2000). Development of a Global Land Cover Characteristics Database and IGBP DISCover from 1-km AVHRR data. *International Journal of Remote Sensing* 21(6/7):1303-1330. Taylor & Francis, London.

Lubchenco, J., Palumbi, S., Gaines, S. and Andelman, S. 2003. Plugging a hole in the ocean: the emerging science of marine reserves. *Ecological Applications* 13, S3-S7. Ithaca, NY, USA.

Lutchman, I., Hoggarth, D. (1999) *Net Losses: Untying the Gordian Knot of Fishing Overcapacity.* IUCN – The World Conservation Union, Gland, Switzerland.

Lysenko, I., and Zöckler, C. (2001) *The 25 largest unfragmented areas in the Arctic.* Unpublished report for the WWF Arctic Programme.

MA/Millennium Ecosystem Assessment (2005a). *Ecosystems and Human Well-being: Synthesis.* Island Press, Washington D.C.

MA/Millennium Ecosystem Assessment (2005b). *Ecosystems and Human Well-being: Biodiversity Synthesis.* Island Press, Washington D.C.

Machlis, G.E. and Field, D.R. (eds) (2000a) *National Parks and Rural Development: Practice and Policy in the United States.* Island Press, Washington, D.C.

Machlis, G.E. and Field, D.R. (2000b) Conclusion. In: Machlis, G.E. and Field, D.R. (eds) *National Parks and Rural Development: Practice and Policy in the United States.* Island Press, Washington, D.C.

MacKinnon, J. and MacKinnon, K. (1986). *Review of the Protected Areas in the Indo-Malayan Realm.* IUCN - The World Conservation Union, Gland, Switzerland and United Nations Environment Programme, Nairobi, Kenya.

MacKinnon, J., MacKinnon, K., Child, G. and Thorsell, J. (1986) *Managing Protected Areas in the Tropics.* IUCN World Commission on Protected Areas, Gland, Switzerland

MacKinnon, K. (ed.) (2002). *Parks* - ICDPs Vol. 11 No. 2. IUCN Protected Areas Programme.

MacKinnon, K. and Wardojo, W. (2001). ICDPs - Imperfect Solutions for Imperilled Forests in South-East Asia. In *Parks* Vol 11/2, 50-59. IUCN, Gland, Switzerland.

Magin, C. and Chape, S. (2004). *Review of the World Heritage Network: Biogeography, Habitats and Biodiversity.* UNEP-World Conservation Monitoring Centre, Cambridge, UK and IUCN-The World Conservation Union, Gland, Switzerland.

Maisels, F., Keming, E., Kemei, M. and Toh, C. (2002). The extirpation of large mammalsand implications for montane forest conservation: the case of the Kilum-Ijum Forest, Northwest Province, Cameroon. *Oryx*, 29: 115-122. Fauna

& Flora International, Cambridge, UK.

Margules, C. (1989) Introduction to some Australian developments in conservation evaluation. *Biological Conservation* 50:1–11. Elsevier, Amsterdon, London, New York.

Margules, C.R. and Pressey, R.L. (2000) Systematic conservation planning. *Nature* 405:243–253. London.

Marín, M. (1999) Creación de Reservas Naturales Privadas en Centroamérica. PROARCA/CAPAS/USAID. Red Costarricense de Reservas Naturales Privadas, Costa Rica.

MARN.(2003) Informe Nacional del Estado Actual de las Areas Naturales Protegidas. San Salvador, El Salvador.

Mascia, M.B. (2003) The human dimension of coral reef marine protected areas: recent social science research and its policy implications. *Conservation Biology* 17(2):630-632. Arlington, VA, USA.

Mason, C. (2003) *The 2030 Spike: Countdown to Global Catastrophe*. Earthscan, London.

Mason, C.F. (1996) *Biology of Freshwater Pollution*. (3rd edn.) Longman Group, Harlow, UK.

Matveyeva, N. and Chernov, Y. (2000) Biodiversity of terrestrial ecosystems. In: Nuttall, N., and Callaghan, T.V. (eds) *The Arctic. Environment, People, Policy*. Harwood Academic Publishers: 233-273.

Mauchamp, A. 1997. Threats from alien plants species in the Galápagos Islands. *Conservation Biology* 11(1): 260-263. Arlington, VA, USA.

McAllister, D.E., Hamilton, A.L. and Harvey, B. (1997) Global freshwater biodiversity: striving for the integrity of freshwater ecosystems. *Sea Wind—Bulletin of Ocean Voice International* 11(3):1-140. Ontario, Canada.

McCarthy, R. Salas, A., Godoy, J.C., Corrales, L. and Cardenal, L. (2003) *Estado del Sistema Centroamericano de Areas Protegidas: Síntesis Regional*. CCAP, Managua, Nicaragua.

McCarthy, R., Godoy, J. C., Salas, A. Cruz and Carlos, J. (1997) *Buscando Respuestas: Nuevos Arreglos para la Gestión de Areas Protegidas y del Corredor Biológico en Centroamérica*. CCAD-UICN-WCPA-PFA.

McClanahan, T.R. 2004. The Limits to Beyond Boundaries. *Aquatic Conservation: Marine and Freshwater Ecosystems* 14(1): 1-4. John Wiley and Sons, Chichester, UK

McNeely, J.A. (1995) *Expanding Partnerships in Conservation*. IUCN and Island Press, Washington, D.C.

McNeely, J.A. (1998) How protected areas can respond to the changing nature of society. In: *Protected Areas in the 21st Century: From Islands to Networks*. IUCN, Gland, Switzerland.

McNeely, J.A. (ed.) (2003) *Protected Areas in 2023: Scenarios for an Uncertain Future*. IUCN, Gland, Switzerland.

McShane, T.O. (2003). The Devil in the Detail of Biodiversity Conservation. *Conservation Biology* Volume 17 Issue 1, 1-3. Arlington, VA, USA.

Menaut, J.C., Lepage, M. and Abbadie, L. 1995. Savannas, woodlands and dry forests in Africa. In *Seasonally Dry Tropical Forests*, Bullock, S.H., Mooney, H.A., and Medina,E. (eds), 64-92. Cambridge University Press, Cambridge, UK.

Miller, K. Chang, E. and Johnson, N. (2001) *En busca de un enfoque común para el Corredor Biológico Mesoamericano*. WRI-WWF-CATIE,Washington, D.C.

Mittermeier, R.A., Fonseca, G.A.B. da, Rylands, A.B. and Mittermeier, C.G. (1997) Brazil. In: Mittermeier, R.A., Robles Gil, P. and Mittermeier, C.G. (eds) *Megadiversity: Earth's Biologically Wealthiest Nations*. CEMEX, S.A., Mexico: 38-73.

Mittermeier, R.A., Mittermeier, C.G., Robles Gil, P., Pilgrim, J., Fonseca, G.A.B. da., Brooks, T. and Konstant, W.R. (eds.) (2002) *Wilderness: Earth's Last Wild Places* CEMEX, S.A., Mexico.

Mittermeier, R.A., Myers, N., Mittermeier, C.G. and Robles Gil, P. (eds) (1999) *Hotspots: Earth's Biologically Richest and Most Endangered Terrestrial Ecoregions*. CEMEX SA, Mexico DF.

Mittermeier, R.A., Robles-Gil, P. and Mittermeier, C.G. (Eds.). 1997. *Megadiversity. Earth's Biologically Wealthiest Nations*. Mexico City: CEMEX/Agrupación Sierra Madre.

Morales, R. and Cifuentes, M. (1989) Sistema Regional de Areas Silvestres Protegidas en América Central; Plan de Acción 1989-2000. CATIE-UICN-WWF, Turrialba, Costa Rica.

Munasinghe, M. and McNeely, J. (eds) (1994) *Protected Area Economics and Policy: Linking Conservation and Sustainable Development*. World Bank and IUCN, Washington D.C.

Murray, J., Murray, E., Johnson, M. S. and Clarke, B. (1988). The extinction of *Partula* on Moorea. *Pacific Science* 42:150-153. Honolulu, HI, USA.

Murray, S. N., Ambrose, R. F., Bohnsack, J. A.,

Botsford, L. W., Carr, M. H., Davis, G. E., Dayton, P. K., Gotshall, D., Gunderson, D. R., Hixon, M. A., Lubchenco, J., Mangel, M., MacCall, A., McArdle, D. A., *et al*. (1999). No-take Reserve Networks: Sustaining Fishery Populations and Marine Ecosystems. *Fisheries* 24:11-25.

Myers, J. H., Simberloff, D., Kuris, A.M. and Carey, J. R. 2000. Eradication revisited: dealing with exotic species. *Trends in Ecology and Evolution 15*: 316-320. Elsevier, Amsterdaom, London, New York.

Myers, N. (1997) The rich diversity of biodiversity issues. In: Reaka-Kudla, M.L., Wilson, D.E. and Wilson, E.O. (eds) *Biodiversity II: Understanding and Protecting Our Biological Resources.* Joseph Henry Press, Washington, D.C. 125-138.

Myers, N., Mittermeier, R.A., Mittermeier C.G., Fonseca, G.A.B. da and Kent, J. (2000) Biodiversity hotspots for conservation priorities. *Nature* 403: 853-858. London.

Zabelina, N.M., Isaeva-Petrova, L.S. and Karaseva, S.E. (1989). The Condition of the Protected Area Network of the USSR. In *Organisation of Protection Forms of Objects of the Nature-Zapovednik Fund.* Moscow. 3-24.

Nantel, P., Bouchard, A., Brouillet, L. and Hay, S. (1998) Selection of areas for protecting rare plants with integration of land use conflicts: a case study for the west coast of Newfoundland, Canada. *Biological Conservation* 84:223-234. Elsevier, Amsterdam, London, New York.

Neumann, R.P. (1998) *Imposing Wilderness: Struggles over Livelihood and Nature Preservation in Africa.* University of California Press, Berkeley.

Newsome, D., Moore, S.A. and Dowling, R.K. (2002) *Natural Area Tourism: Ecology, Impacts and Management.* Channel View Publications, Sydney.

Noss, R. (1992) The Wildlands Project land conservation strategy. *Wild Earth.* Special Issue:10-25. Richmond, VT, USA.

Noss, R.F., Strittholt, J.R., Vance-Borland, K., Carroll, C. and Frost, P. (1999) A conservation plan for the Klamath-Siskiyou ecoregion. *Natural Areas Journal* 19:392–411. Bend, OR, USA.

Núñez Jiménez, A. (1982) *Cuba: La Naturaleza y el Hombre. El Archipiélago.* Editorial Letras Cubanas, La Habana.

Nuñez, O. (2000) *El Comanejo y la participación de la sociedad civil en las Areas Protegidas de Centroamérica.* Guatemala. Defensores-Proarca-TNC.

Nybakken JW, 1993. *Marine Biology – an ecological approach.* Third edition, Harper Collins College Publishers, New York.

Oates , J.F. (1995). The dangers of conservation by rural development: a case study from the forests of Nigeria. *Oryx*, 29:115-122. Fauna & Flora International, Cambridge, UK.

Oates, J.F. (1999). *Myth and Reality in the Rain Forest: How Conservation Strategies are Failing in West Africa.* University of California Press, Berkeley, California.

Oates, J.F., Abedi-Lartey, M., McGraw, W.S., Struhsaker, T.T. and Whitesides, G.H. (2000). Extinction of a West African colobus monkey. *Conservation Biology*, 14:1526. Arlington, VA, USA.

Oehme, M., Schlabach, M., Kallenborn, R. and Haugen, J.E. (1996) Sources and pathways of persistent pollutants to remote areas of the North Atlantic and levels in the marine food chain: a research update. *The Science of the Total Environment* 186:13-24.

OGP (International Association for Oil and Gas Producers) (2002) *Oil and Gas Exploration and Production in Arctic Offshore Regions – Guidelines for Environmental Protection.* OGP, London.

Ohba, H. 1996. A brief overview of the woody vegetation of Japan and its conservation status. 81-88. In, Hunt, D. (ed). *Temperate trees under threat.* International Dendrology Society, UK.

Olson, D.M. and Dinerstein, E. (1998) The Global 200: a representation approach to conserving the Earth's most biologically valuable ecoregions. *Conservation Biology* 12:502-515. Arlington, VA, USA.

Olson, D.M., Dinerstein, E., Wikramanayake, E.D., Burgess, N.D., Powell, G.V.N, Underwood, E.C., D'Amico, J.A., Strand, H.E., Morrison, J.C., Loucks, C.J., Allnutt, T.F., Lamoreux, J.F., Ricketts, T.H., Itoua, I., Wettengel, W.W. and Kura, Y. (2001) A new map of life on earth. *BioScience* 15:933-938. Washington, D.C.

Omernik, J.M. (1995) Level III Ecoregions of the Continental US. Map 1:7,500,000 Scale. National Health and Environment Effects Research Laboratory, US Environmental Protection Agency, Washington D.C.

Orians, G.H. (1993) Endangered at what level? *Ecological Applications* 3:206–208. Ithaca, NY, USA.

Ostrom, E. (1990) *Governing the Commons: The Evolution of Institutions for Collective Action.* Cambridge University Press, Cambridge.

Pagnan, J. and Legare, G. (2002) *Protected Areas of the Arctic – Conserving a Full Range of Values.* Conservation of Arctic Flora and Fauna (CAFF), Ottawa.

Parks Canada (1998) *State of the Parks 1997 Report.* Minister of Public Works and Public Services Canada, Ottawa.

Parques Nacionales de Colombia (Colombian National Parks). http://www.parquesnacionales.gov.co//areas.htm (January, 2008).

Patterson, B.D., Ceballos, G., Sechrest, W., Tognelli, M.F., Brooks, T., Luna, L., Ortega, P., Salazar, I. and Young, B.E. (2003) Digital Distribution Maps of the Mammals of the Western Hemisphere – Version 1.0. NatureServe, Arlington VA.

Pauly, D. and Christensen, V. (1995) Primary production required to sustain global fisheries. *Nature* 374:255–257. London.

Peres, C.A. (2000). Evaluating the impact and sustainability of subsistence hunting at multiple Amazonian forest sites. In *Hunting for Sustainability in Tropical Forests*, J.G. Robinson and E.L. Bennett, (eds), 31-56. Columbia University Press, New York.

Petersen, Æ., Þorvarðardóttir, G., Pagnan, J. and Einarsson, S. (1998) Breiðafjörður, West-Iceland: an Arctic marine protected area. *Parks* 8(2):23-28. IUCN, Gland, Switzerland.

Phillips, A. (2000). Mining and protected areas: an IUCN viewpoint. In *Industry and Environment* Volume 23 Special Issue 2000, 88-89. UNEP DTIE, Paris.

Phillips, A. (2001). *Mining and Protected Areas.* Report commissioned by the Mining, Minerals and Sustainable Development project of IIED. International Institute for Environment and Development (IIED) and World Business Council for Sustainable Development.

Phillips, A. (2002) *Management Guidelines for IUCN Category V Protected Areas: Protected Landscapes/Seascapes.* Best Practice Protected Area Guidelines Series No. 9, ed. Phillips, A. IUCN World Comission on Protected Areas, Gland, Switzerland.

Phillips, A. (2003) Turning ideas on their head: the new paradigm for protected areas. In: Jaireth,

H. and Smyth, D. (eds) *Innovative Governance: Indigenous Peoples, Local Communities and Protected Areas.* Ane Books, New Delhi.

Phillips, A. (2003). A new paradigm for protected areas. In *World Conservation*, 2/2003 6-7. IUCN-The World Conservation Union, Gland, Switzerland.

Pigram, J.J. and Jenkins, J.M. (1999) *Outdoor Recreation Management.* Routledge, London.

Pires, J.M. 1957. Noçoes sobre ecologia e fitogeografia da Amazônia. *Norte Agronômico* 3:37-53.

Pisanty-Baruch, I., Barr, J., Wiken, E.B. and Gauthier, D. (1999) Reporting on North America. Continental Connections. in *The George Wright Forum* 16:2.

PNUMA (2000) Las Áreas y Flora y Fauna Silvestres Especialmente. Protegidas en la Región del Gran Caribe. Un Protocolo regional sobre biodiversidad. http://www.cep.unep.org/pubs/legislation/SPAWfactsheetSpanish.doc (March, 2005). UNEP, Nairobi, Kenya.

PNUMA (2002) Perspectivas del Medio Ambiente Mundial 2002. GEO 3. UNEP, Nairobi, Kenya.

Poffenberger, M. (ed.) (1998) *Stewards of Vietnam's Upland Forests.* Asia Forest Network, Research Network Report No. 10. Berkeley, California.

Postel, S. and Carpenter, S. (1997) Freshwater ecosystem services. In: Daily, G.C. (ed.) *Nature's Services: Societal Dependence on Natural Ecosystems* 195–214. Island Press, Washington D.C.

Postell, S.L., Daily, G.C. and Ehrlich, P.R. (1996) Human appropriation of renewable freshwater. *Science* 271:785–788. AAAS, Washington, D.C.

Pounds, J.A., Fogden M.P.L., and Campbell, J.H. (1999). Biological response to climate change on a tropical mountain. *Nature* Vol 398 611-615. April 1999. London.

Prance, G.T. 1989. American tropical forests. 99-132. In, Lieth, H. and Werger, M.J.A. (eds). *Ecosystems of the World 14B: tropical rain forest ecosystems: biogeographical and ecological studies.* Elsevier, Amsterdam.

Pressey, R.L. (1994) Ad hoc reservations – forward or backward steps in developing representative reserve systems. *Conservation Biology* 8: 662-668. Arlington, VA, USA.

Pressey, R.L. (1998) Systematic conservation planning for the real world. *Parks* 9(1):1-6. IUCN, Gland, Switzerland.

Pressey, R.L., Bedward, M. and Keith, D.A. (1994)

New procedures for reserve selection in New South Wales: maximising the chances of achieving a representative network. In: Forey, P.L., Humphries, C.J. and Vane-Wright, R.L. (eds) *Systematics and Conservation Evaluation.* Oxford University Press, Oxford.

Pressey, R.L., Ferrier, S., Hager, T.C., Woods, C.A., Tully, S.L. and Weinman, K.M. (1996) How well protected are the forests of northeastern New South Wales? Analyses of forest environments in relation to formal protection measures, land tenure, and vulnerability to clearing. *Forest Ecology and Management* 85:311-333. Elsevier, Amsterdam, London, New York.

Pressey, R.L., Johnson, I.R. and Wilson, P.D. (1994) Shades of irreplaceability – towards a measure of the contribution of sites to a reservation goal. *Biodiversity and Conservation* 3:242-262. Springer, Netherlands.

Pressey, R.L. and Taffs, K.H. (2001) Scheduling conservation action in production landscapes: priority areas in western New South Wales defined by irreplaceability and vulnerability to vegetation loss. *Biological Conservation* 100:355-376. Elsevier, Amsterdon, London, New York.

Putney, A. (ed.) (2000) Parks: non-material values of protected areas. Special edition of *Parks* Vol 10(2). IUCN, Gland, Switzerland.

QPWS (Queensland Parks and Wildlife Service) (2000)(2000) *User-pays Revenue.* Benchmarking and Best Practice Program. ANZECC, Canberra.

Radu, S. (1995) The actual state, problems and trends in the conservation of forests in Romania. In: Paulenka, J. and Paule, L. (eds) *Conservation of Forests in Central Europe.* Arbora Publications, Zvolen, Slovakia.

Ramsar Sites Database (2003) Unpublished data provided by Wetlands International, July 2003.

Rashid, H.E. and Kabir, B. (1998) Case study: Bangladesh – Water resources and population pressures in the Ganges River Basin. In: de Sherbinin, A. and Dompka, V. (eds) *Water and Population Dynamics: Case Studies and Policy Implications.* American Association for the Advancement of Science and others, Washington D.C. 171-194.

Redford, K.H. (1992). The empty forest. *Bioscience* 42, 412-422. Washington, D.C.

Reeve, I., Marshall, G. and Musgrave, W. (2004) *Resource Governance and Integrated Catchment Management.* Institute for Rural Futures. University of New England, Armidale, NSW, Australia.

Resolution 1831 (XVII) (1962) Economic development and the conservation of nature, 18 December, 1962.

Resolution No. 713 of the 27th Session of the UN Economic and Social Council.

Revenga, C., Brunner, J., Henninger, N., Kassem, K. and Payne, R. (2000) *Pilot Analysis of Global Ecosystems: Freshwater Systems.* World Resources Institute, Washington D.C. Online at: http://www.wri.org/wr2000/freshwater_ page.html (March 2006).

Revenga, C. and Kura, Y. (2003). *Status and Trends of Biodiversity of Inland Water Ecosystems.* CBD Technical Series. Secretariat of the Convention on Biological Diversity, Montreal.

Revenga, C., Murray, S., Abramovitz, J. and Hammond, A. (1998) *Watersheds of the World: Ecological Value and Vulnerability.* World Resources Institute and Worldwatch Institute, Washington D.C.

Ricciardi, A. and Rasmussen, J.B. (1999) Extinction rates of North American freshwater fauna. *Conservation Biology* 13(5):1220–1222. Arlington, VA, USA.

Rice, T. and Counsell, S. (1998) *Out of Commission: The Environmental and Social Impacts of European Union Development Funding in Tropical Forest Areas.* The Rainforest Foundation, London.

Ricketts, T. H., Dinerstein, E., Olson, D. M., Loucks, C.J., Eichbaum, W., DellaSala, D., Kavanagh, K., Hedao, P., Hurley, P. T., Carney, K. M., Abell, R. and Walters, S. (1999). *Terrestrial Ecoregions of North America: a conservation assessment.* Island Press, Washington, D.C.

Robbins, S.P., Bergman, R., Stagg, I. and Coulter, M. (2003) *Foundations of Management.* Prentice Hall Australia, Sydney.

Roberts, C.M. (1997) Connectivity and management of Caribbean coral reefs. *Science* 278:1454-1457. AAAS, Washington, D.C.

Roberts, C.M. (2002) Deep impacts: the rising toll of fishing in the deep sea. *Trends in Ecology and Evolution* 17(5):242-245. Elsevier, Amsterdaom, London, New York.

Roberts, C.M., Bohnsack, J.A., Gell, F., Hawkins, J.P. and Goodridge, R. (2001) Effects of marine reserves on adjacent fisheries. *Science* 294:1920-1923. AAAS, Washington, D.C.

Roberts, C.M., Bohnsack, J.S., Gell, F., Hawkins, J.P. and Goodridge, R. (2001) Effects of marine reserves on adjacent fisheries. *Science* 294:1920-1923. AAAS, Washington, D.C.

Roberts, C.M. and Hawkins, J.P. (2000) *Fully-protected Marine Reserves: A Guide*. WWF Endangered Seas Campaign and Environment Department, University of York, Washington, D.C. and York, UK.

Roberts, M.C., McClean, C.J., Veron, J.E.N., Hawkins, J.P., Allen, G.R., McAllister, D.E., Mittermeier, C.G., Schueler, F.W., Spalding, M., Wells, F., Vynne, C. and Werner, T.B. (2002) Marine biodiversity hotspots and conservation priorities for tropical reefs. *Science* 295:1280-1284. AAAS, Washington, D.C.

Robinson, J.G. and Bennett, E.L. (eds) (2000a). *Hunting for Sustainability in Tropical Forests*. Columbia University Press, New York.

Robinson, J.G. and Bennett, E.L. (2000b). Carrying Capacity Limits to sustainable hunting in tropical forests. In *Hunting for Sustainability in Tropical Forests*, Robinson, J.G. and Bennett, E.L. (eds), 13-30. Columbia University Press, New York.

Robinson, J.G. and Bennett, E.L. (2002). Will alleviating poverty solve the bushmeat crisis? *Oryx* 36:332. Fauna & Flora International, Cambridge, UK.

Rodgers, W.A. (1993) The conservation of the forest resources of eastern Africa: past influences, present practices and future needs. In: Lovett, J.C., Wasser, S. (eds) *Biogeography and Ecology of the Rain Forests of Eastern Africa*. 283-331. Cambridge University Press, Cambridge.

Rodríguez, J. (compiler) (1998) *Estado del Ambiente y los Recursos Naturales en Centroamérica*. CCAD, San José, Costa Rica.

Rodrigues, A., Andelman, S.J., Bakarr, M.I., Boitani, L., Brooks, T.M., Cowling, R.M., Fishpool, L.D.C., Fonseca, G.A.B. da, Gaston, K.J., Hoffmann, M., Long, J., Marquet, P.A., Pilgrim, J.D., Pressey, R.L., Schipper, J., Sechrest, W., Stuart, S.N., Underhill, L.G., Waller, R.W., Watts, M.E.J. and Yan, X. (2003) Global Gap Analysis: towards a representative network of protected areas. *Advances in Applied Biodiversity Science* No.5. Conservation International, Washington, D.C.

Rojas, Z., Cruz, J.C. (eds) (1998) *State of Environment and Natural Resources in Central America 1998*. Central American Commission for Environment and Development, San José, Costa Rica.

Rojstaczer, S., Sterling, S.M. and Moore, N.J. (2001) Human appropriation of photosynthesis products. *Science* 294:2549–2552. AAAS, Washington, D.C.

Rosado, N. (2003) MofNR, Belmopan, Belize.

Rössler, M. (2000). Mining and World Heritage considerations. In *Industry and Environment* Volume 23 Special Issue 2000, 88-89. UNEP DTIE, Paris.

Russ, G.R. and Alcala, A.C. (1996) Do marine reserves export adult fish biomass? Evidence from Apo Island, central Philippines. *Mar. Ecol. Prog. Ser.* 132:1-9. Oldendorf/Luhe, Germany

Rylands, A.B. and Pinto, L.P. de S. (1998) Conservação da biodiversidade na Amazônia brasileira: Uma análise do sistema de unidades de conservação. *Cadernos FBDS*, No. 1. Fundação Brasileira para o Desenvolvimento Sustentável (FBDS), Rio de Janeiro.

Salm, R.V., Clark, J.R. and Siirlila, E. (2000b) *Marine and Coastal Protected Areas: A Guide for Planners and Managers*. IUCN – The World Conservation Union, Washington D.C.

Sanderson, E.W., Jaiteh, M., Levy, M.A., Redford, K.H., Wannebo, A.V. and Woolmer, G. (2002) The human footprint and the last of the wild. *Bioscience* 52(10):891-904. Washington, D.C.

Sandwith, T., Shine, C., Hamilton, L. and Sheppard D. (2001) *Transboundary Protected Areas for Peace and Co-operation*. IUCN – The World Conservation Union, Gland, Switzerland.

Sayer, J.A., Harcourt, C.S. and Collins, N.M. (eds) (1992) *The Conservation Atlas of Tropical Forests: Africa*. IUCN, Gland, Switzerland.

SCBD/Secretariat of the Convention on Biological Diversity (2004a) Decisions adopted by the Conference of the Parties to the Convention on Biological Diversity at its Seventh Meeting. UNEP/CBD/COP/7/21, SCBD Montreal.

SCBD/Secretariat of the Convention on Biological Diversity (2004b). *Programme of Work on Protected Areas*. Montreal.

Schmitt, K. and Sallee, K. (2002) *Information and Knowledge Management in Nature Conservation*. http://www.uwa.or.ug/Mist.pdf (December, 2007).

Schofield, E. K. 1989. Effects of introduced plants

and animals on island vegetation: Examples from the Galapagos archipelago. *Conservation Biology* 3(3):227-238. Arlington, VA, USA.

Scott, J.M., Davis, F.W., McGhie, R.G., Wright, R.G., Groves, C. and Estes, C. (2001b) Nature reserves: do they capture the full range of America's biological diversity? *Ecological Applications* 11:999-1007. Ithaca, NY, USA.

Scott, M.J., Abbitt, R.J.F. and Groves, C.R. (2001a) What are we protecting? The United States conservation portfolio. *Conservation Biology in Practice* 2:18-19. Blackwell, Maiden, MA, USA.

Sermeño, A. (2002) *Datos actualizados del Sistema Salvadoreño de Areas Protegidas.* MARN, San Salvador, El Salvador.

Servicio Nacional de Areas Protegidas de Bolivia (Bolivian Protected Areas National Service). http://www.sernap.gov.bo/ (December, 2007)

Sharma, S. R and Shaw, W. W. (1996). Nepal: impact zones and conservation – an innovative approach to securing the boundaries of the Royal Chitwan National Park. In *The Rural Extension Bulletin,* 9 33-37.

Shin Wang (2002). The Development and Management of Taiwan's Protected Areas. In *Proceedings of IUCN/WCPA East Asia Taipei Conference* 133-143. Taipei, Taiwan POC.

Shtilmark, F. (2003). *History of the Russian Zapovedniks 1895-1995.* Russian Nature Press, Edinburgh.

Sigurdsson, H. and Sparks, R.S.J. (1979) An active submarine volcano [Kick-'em-Jenny]. *Natural History* 88:38-43.SINAC-MINAE (2003) Informe Nacional sobre el Sistema de Areas Silvestres Protegidas, San José, Costa Rica.

Singh, S. (1999) *Assessing Management Effectiveness of Wildlife Protected Areas in India.* Paper presented to the Workshop on Management Effectiveness of Protected Areas, Turialba, Costa Rica, June 1999.

Singh, S. (2000) Assessing management effectiveness of national parks in India. *Parks* 9 (2):34-49. IUCN, Gland, Switzerland.

SINAC-MINAE (2003) *Informe Nacional sobre el Sistema de Areas Silvestres Protegidas.* San José, Costa Rica.

Slack, N., Chambers, S. and Johnston, R. (2001) *Operations Management. [3rd edn.]* Prentice Hall, London. Canadian Museum of Nature, Ottowa.

Sobel, J. (1996) Marine reserves: necessary tools for biodiversity conservation? *Global Biodiversity* 6:8-18.

Soulé, M.E. and Terborgh, J. (1999) Conserving nature at regional and continental scales – a scientific program for North America. *BioScience* 49:809–817. Washington, D.C.

Sournia, G. (1998) *Les Aires Protégées d'Afrique Francophone.* Éditions Jean-Pierre de Monza, Paris.

Sournia, G. (1998) *Les Aires Protégées d'Afrique Francophone.* Éditions Jean-Pierre de Monza, Paris.

Spalding, M.D., Ravilious, C. and Green, E.P. (2001) *World Atlas of Coral Reefs.* University of California Press, Berkeley, CA, USA.

Stevens, S. (1997) *Conservation Through Cultural Survival: Indigenous Peoples and Protected Areas.* Island Press, Washington, D.C.

Stolton, S., Dudley, N. and Rowell, A. (compilers) (1997) *Spotlight on Solutions: A Handbook of Case Studies on Local Implementation of Agenda 21.* WWF International, Gland, Switzerland.

Stolton, S., Geier, B. and McNeely, J.A. (2000) *The Relationship between Nature Conservation, Biodiversity and Organic Agriculture.* IFOAM, IUCN and WWF.

Stolton, S., Geier, B. and McNeely, J.A. (2000) *The Relationship between Nature Conservation, Biodiversity and Organic Agriculture.* IFOAM, IUCN and WWF.

Sullivan, S. (2005) Backgrounder 13.1 Cultural heritage in protected areas. In: Worboys, G., Lockwood, M. and De Lacy, T. (eds) *Protected Area Management: Principles and Practice.* [2nd edn.] Oxford University Press, Melbourne.

Sullivan, S. and Lennon, J. (2003) Cultural values. In: *An Assessment of the Values of Kosciuszko National Park.* Independent Scientific Committee Report. NSW Naational Parks and Wildlife Service, Queanbeyan. Australia.

Tai, H.S. (2002) On Sustainable Use of Renewable Resources in Protected Areas as an Instrument of Biodiversity Conservation: A Bioeconomic Analysis. PhD dissertation, Ruprecht-Karls-Universität Heidelberg, Germany.

The Mountain Institute (2004). *Makalu-Barun Conservation Program.* Synopsis available at www.mountain.org/work/himalayas/makalu-barun.cfm. (January, 2008).

Thieme, M.L., Abell, R.A., Lehner, B., Dinerstein, E., Stiassny, M.L.J., Skelton, P.H., Teugels, G.G., Kamdem-Toham, A. and Olson, D.M. (2005)

Freshwater Ecoregions of Africa: A Conservation Assessment. WWF-US, Washington, D.C.

Thompson, L. G., Mosley-Thompson, E., Davis, M. E., Henderson, K. A., Brecher, H. H., Zagorodnov, V.S., Mashiotta, T. A., Lin, P-N., Mikhalenko, V. N., Hardy, D. R. and Beer, J. (2002). Kilimanjaro ice core records: evidence of Holocene change in tropical Africa. *Science* 298:589-593. AAAS, Washington, D.C.

Tickle, A., with Fergusson, M. and Drucker, G. (1996) *Acid Rain and Nature Conservation in Europe: A Preliminary Study of Areas at Risk from Acidification.* WWF International, Gland, Switzerland.

Tickle, A., with Fergusson, M. and Drucker, G. (1996) *Acid Rain and Nature Conservation in Europe: A Preliminary Study of Areas at Risk from Acidification.* WWF International, Gland, Switzerland.

Tukhanen, S. 1999. The northern timberline in relation to climate. 29-62. In, Kankaapää, Tasanen, Sutinen, S.T. and M.-L. (eds). *Sustainable development in northern timberline forests.* Finnish Forest Research Institute Research papers 734.

Turner, G.F., Seehausen, O., Knight, M.E., Allender, C.J. and Robinson, R.L. (2001) How many species of cichlid fishes are there in African lakes? *Molecular Ecology* 10:793-806. Blackwell, Oxford, UK.

Udall, S.L. (1964) Nature islands for the world. In: Adams, A.B. (ed.) *Proceedings of the First World Conference on National Parks.* National Parks Service, US Department of the Interior, Washington D.C.

Udvardy, M.D.F. (1975) *A Classification of the Biogeographical Provinces of the World.* IUCN Occasional Paper No. 18. IUCN, Gland, Switzerland.

UNEP (2002) *Global Environmental Outlook 3: Past, Present and Future Perspectives.* Earthscan, London.

UNEP (2003) Atlas of International Freshwater Agreements. UNEP/DEWA/DPDL/RS.02-4. UNEP, Nairobi, Kenya.

UNEP-WCMC (2002) Biodiversity Map Library. Cambridge, UK.

UNEP-WCMC (2005) UN List of National Parks and Protected Areas. http://www.unep-wcmc.org/protected_areas/data/cnppa.html (December, 2007).

UNEP-WCMC (Custodian) (2003) World Database on Protected Areas.

UNESCO (1973). International classification and mapping of vegetation. United Nations Educational, Scientific and Cultural Organization, Paris.

Väisänen, R., Biström, O. and Heliövaara, K. 1993. Sub-cortical Coleoptera in dead pines and spruces: is primeval species composition maintained in managed forests? *Biodiversity and Conservation* 2(2): 95-113. Springer, Netherlands.

Van der Linde, H., Oglethorpe, J., Sandwith, T., Snelson, D. and Tessema, Y. (with contributions from Anada Tiéga and Thomas Price) (2001) *Beyond Boundaries: Transboundary Natural Resource Management in Sub-Saharan Africa.* Biodiversity Support Program, Washington D.C.

Van Schaik, C., Terborgh, J., Davenport, L. and Rao, M. (2002) Making parks work: past, present, and future. In: Terbough, J., Van Schaik, C., Davenport, L., Rao, M. (eds) *Making Parks Work: Strategies for Preserving Tropical Nature*, 468-481. Island Press, Washington, D.C.

Vega, A. (ed.) (1994) *Corredores Conservacionistas en la Región Centroamericana.* TR&D-Paseo Pantera-WCS, Gainesville, USA.

Ward, T. and Hegerl, E. (2003). *Marine Protected Areas in Ecosystem-based Management of Fisheries.* Report for the Department of the Environment and Heritage, Canberra, Australia.

Watkins, G. and Cruz, F. (2007). *Galapagos at Risk: A Socioeconomic Analysis of the Situation in the Archipelago. Puerto Ayora, Province of Galapagos, Ecuador.* Charles Darwin Foundation, Glapagos, Ecuador.

Watkins, C. W. and Green, M.J.B. (1996) The Contribution of Private Initiatives in Conserving Biological Diversity: A Pilot Study. Paper presented at Workshop on Stewardship – Promoting Conservation and Sustainable Use on Private Lands, World Conservation Congress, Montreal, Canada, October 1996.

WCPA (IUCN World Commission on Protected Areas) (2000) Internal Report. Unpublished report. IUCN World Commission on Protected Areas, Task Force on the Non-Material Values of Protected Areas.

WCPA (World Commission on Protected Areas) (2003) Caribbean. http://www.iucn.org/themes/wcpa/region/caribbean/

caribbean.html. (January, 2008)

WCPA (World Commission on Protected Areas) Arctic Task Force (2000) Report of Arctic Planning Session.

Weaver, D., Opperman, M. (2000) *Tourism Management*. John Wiley and Sons, Sydney.

Weber, W., White, L.T.J., Vedder, A., and Naughton-Treves, L. (2000) *African Rain Forest Ecology and Conservation*. Yale University Press, New Haven, CT, USA.

Wells, M., McShane, T.O., Dublin, H.T., O'Connor, S. and Redford, K.H. (2004). The future of integrated conservation and development projects: building on what works. In Wells, M., and McShane, T. (eds) *Getting Biodiversity Projects to Work: Towards More Effective Conservation and Development*. Columbia University Press, New York.

White, F. (1983) The vegetation of Africa, a descriptive memoir to accompany the UNESCO/AETFAT/UNSO Vegetation Map of Africa (3 Plates, Northwestern Africa, Northeastern Africa, and Southern Africa, 1:5 000 000. UNESCO, Paris.

White, F. (1983) *The Vegetation of Africa*: A descriptive memoir to accompany the UNESCO/AETFAT/UNSO vegetation map of Africa. UNESCO, Paris.

White L.J. T. (2001). The African Rainforest: climate and vegetation. In *African Rain Forest Ecology and Conservation*, Weber, W., White, L.J.T., Vedder, A. and Naughton-Treves, L. (eds), 3-29. Yale University Press, New Haven, CT, USA..

Wiken, E.B., Gauthier, D. (1996) Conservation and ecology in North America. In: *Reflections of Home Place*. Caring for Home Place: Protected Areas and Landscape Ecology Conference, 1996. Canadian Plains Research Center and University Extension Press, Regina, Canada.

Wildlife Conservation Society, Sarawak Forest Department (1996). *A Master Plan for Wildlife in Sarawak*. Wildlife Conservation Society and Sarawak Forest Department, Kuching, Sarawak.

Wilkinson, C., Green, A., Almany, J. and Dionne, S. (2003) *Monitoring Coral Reef Marine Protected Areas: A Practical Guide on how Monitoring can Support Effective Management of MPAs*. Australian Institute of Marine Science and IUCN Global Marine Program, Townsville, Australia and Gland, Switzerland.

Wilkinson, T., Bezaury-Creel, J., Gutierrez, F.,

Hourigan, T., Janishevski, L., Madden, C., Padilla, M. and Wiken, E. (2003) *Marine and Estuarine Ecological Regions of North America*. Commission for Environmental Cooperation.

Williams, P., Gibbons, D., Margules, C., Rebelo, A., Humphries, C. and Pressey, R. (1996) A comparison of richness hotspots, rarity hotspots, and complementary areas for conserving diversity of British birds. *Conservation Biology* 10:155-174. Arlington, VA, USA.

Williams J. A. and West C. J. (2000). Environmental weeds in Australia and New Zealand: issues and approaches to management. *Austral Ecol.* 25, 42544. Blackwell, Richmond, Vic., Australia.

Wilson, D.E. and Reeder, D.M. (1993) *Mammal Species of the World*. [2nd edn.]. Smithsonian Institution Press, Washington and London.

Wilson, E.O. (2000) A personal brief for the wildlands project. *Wild Earth* 10,1. Richmond, VT, USA.

Windevoxhel, N. (1997) *Situación del Manejo Integrado de Zonas Marino Costeras de Centroamérica; sus perspectivas para el manejo de áreas protegidas marino costeras*. IUCN, Gland, Switzerland.

Witte, F., Goldschmidt, T., Wanink, J.H., van Oijen, M., Goudswaard, P.C., Witte-Maas, E. and Bouton, N. (1992) The destruction of an endemic species flock: quantitative data on the decline of the haplochromine cichlids of Lake Victoria. *Environmental Biology of Fishes* 34:1-28. Springer, Netherlands.

Worboys, G., Lockwood, M. and De Lacy, T. (2005) *Protected Area Management: Principles and Practice* [2nd edn.] Oxford University Press, Melbourne.

Worboys, G.L. (2004) *Protected Area Management Effectiveness Evaluation Requirements*. PhD Confirmation Report, Canberra, Australia.

World Commission on Dams (2000) *Dams and Development: A New Framework for Decision Making*. Earthscan, London.

World Commission on Dams (2000) *Dams and Development: A New Framework for Decision Making*. Earthscan, London.

WRI, IUCN, IWMI, Ramsar (2003) Watersheds of the World_CD. Water Resources eAtlas. World Resources Institute, Washington D.C.

WTTC (World Travel and Tourism Council) (2003) *BluePrint for New Tourism*. http://www.wttc.org (December, 2007).

WWF (World Wide Fund for Nature) (2006) *Living Planet Report 2006*. WWF International, Gland, Switzerland.

WWF (World Wide Fund for Nature) (2004) *Living Planet Report 2004*. WWF International, Gland, Switzerland.

WWF (2003) Global 200: Blueprint for a living planet. Biogeographic realm, Neotropical. http://www.panda.org/about_wwf/where_we _work/ecoregions/global200/pages/neotropical. htm (December, 2007).

WWF (World Wide Fund for Nature) (2003). *No Place to Hide: Effects of Climate Change on Protected Areas*. WWF International, Gland, Switzerland.

WWF (World Wide Fund for Nature) (2000) *Living Planet Report 2000*. WWF International, Gland, Switzerland.

WWF, IUCN and IUCN WCPA (2001) *The Status of Natural Resources of the High Seas*. WWF/IUCN/IUCN World Commission on Protected Areas, Gland, Switzerland.

Xie Yan and Lishu Li (2004). Gap Analysis of Nature Reserve System, In Xie Yan, Wang Su and Schei, P. (eds), *China's Protected Areas* 203-208. Tsinghua University Press, Beijing, China.

Yoshi, I. (2003) Traditional Marine Resource Management and Traditional Ecological Knowledge: An Anthropological Approach. PhD thesis. *Zapovednik Fund* 3-24. Moscow

Zöckler, C. (1998) Patterns in Biodiversity in Arctic Birds. WCMC. *Biodiversity Bull.* 3:1- 15. Cambridge, UK.

Zoltai, S.C., Vitt, D.H. (1995) Canadian wetlands: environmental gradients and classification. *Vegetatio* 118:131-137. Springer, Netherlands.

Index

(1980) 5, *8*
World Conservation Union, *see* IUCN
World Database on Protected Areas 4–5, 9, 11, 48, 177
World Heritage Convention (1972) 5, *8*, *23*, 25–6
World Heritage sites 25–6
 affected by mining 85
 Australia and New Zealand 310, *310*
 Brazil 215, *215*
 Caribbean region *198*
 cave/karst features 63–4
 Central America 204, *205*
 East Asia 290, *292*
 Europe *235*
 List of Sites in Danger 54, *86–7*, *116*
 nomination and listing 25–6
 North America 186, *186*
 Northern Africa/Middle East 266, *266*
 Northern Eurasia 274–5, *275*
 Pacific Islands *319*
 relationship to other protected areas 26, *26*
 South America 223, *224*
 South Asia 283, *284*

Southeast Asia 299, *299*
West and Central Africa 245, *246*
World Parks Congresses 5, *8*
 IIIrd (Bali) *8*, 140
 IVth (Caracas) *8*, 140–1
 Vth (Durban) 2, *8*, 39, 40, 98, 110, 115, 162, 164–7, 169
World Summit on Sustainable Development 162
World Tourism Organization (WTO) 134–5, 267
World Travel and Tourism Council (WTTC) 133–6
World Wide Fund for Nature (WWF) *6*, 230
 climate change impact categories 93–7
 conservation of Fiji's crested iguana *110–11*
 Ecoregion Conservation *45*, *46*
 Global 200 analysis *45*
 RAPPAM methodology *144–5*
Wrangel Island Nature Reserve and World Heritage Site 61

Y

Yadua Taba island, Fiji *110–11*
Yaeyama islands 285

Yanomami Indigenous Park, Brazil *19*
Yarlung Zambo arid steppe *65*
Yayasan Sabah 298
Yellowstone National Park 4, *38*, *86–7*, 181
Yellowstone to Yukon Conservation Initiative 188
Yemen 261, 264, *264*
Yosemite National Park and World Heritage Site 4, *5*, *6*, 181, 182
Yucatán 179, 203
Yukon Delta wildlife refuge, USA *19*

Z

Zagros Mountains 258
zakaznik 272
Zambezian biome 248
Zambia 254, *255*
zapovednik system 38, 272, 273, 274, 275
Zimbabwe 254, *255*, 257
zoning, marine protected areas 151, 155